Lecture Notes in Computer Science 11567

Commenced Publication in 1973
Founding and Former Series Editors:
Gerhard Goos, Juris Hartmanis, and Jan van Leeuwen

More information about this series at http://www.springer.com/series/7409

Masaaki Kurosu (Ed.)

Human-Computer Interaction

Recognition and Interaction Technologies

Thematic Area, HCI 2019
Held as Part of the 21st HCI International Conference, HCII 2019
Orlando, FL, USA, July 26–31, 2019
Proceedings, Part II

Springer

Editor
Masaaki Kurosu
The Open University of Japan
Chiba, Japan

ISSN 0302-9743 ISSN 1611-3349 (electronic)
Lecture Notes in Computer Science
ISBN 978-3-030-22642-8 ISBN 978-3-030-22643-5 (eBook)
https://doi.org/10.1007/978-3-030-22643-5

LNCS Sublibrary: SL3 – Information Systems and Applications, incl. Internet/Web, and HCI

This Springer imprint is published by the registered company Springer Nature Switzerland AG
The registered company address is: Gewerbestrasse 11, 6330 Cham, Switzerland

Foreword

The 21st International Conference on Human-Computer Interaction, HCI International 2019, was held in Orlando, FL, USA, during July 26–31, 2019. The event incorporated the 18 thematic areas and affiliated conferences listed on the following page.

A total of 5,029 individuals from academia, research institutes, industry, and governmental agencies from 73 countries submitted contributions, and 1,274 papers and 209 posters were included in the pre-conference proceedings. These contributions address the latest research and development efforts and highlight the human aspects of design and use of computing systems. The contributions thoroughly cover the entire field of human-computer interaction, addressing major advances in knowledge and effective use of computers in a variety of application areas. The volumes constituting the full set of the pre-conference proceedings are listed in the following pages.

This year the HCI International (HCII) conference introduced the new option of "late-breaking work." This applies both for papers and posters and the corresponding volume(s) of the proceedings will be published just after the conference. Full papers will be included in the *HCII 2019 Late-Breaking Work Papers Proceedings* volume of the proceedings to be published in the Springer LNCS series, while poster extended abstracts will be included as short papers in the HCII 2019 *Late-Breaking Work Poster Extended Abstracts* volume to be published in the Springer CCIS series.

I would like to thank the program board chairs and the members of the program boards of all thematic areas and affiliated conferences for their contribution to the highest scientific quality and the overall success of the HCI International 2019 conference.

This conference would not have been possible without the continuous and unwavering support and advice of the founder, Conference General Chair Emeritus and Conference Scientific Advisor Prof. Gavriel Salvendy. For his outstanding efforts, I would like to express my appreciation to the communications chair and editor of *HCI International News,* Dr. Abbas Moallem.

July 2019 Constantine Stephanidis

HCI International 2019 Thematic Areas and Affiliated Conferences

Thematic areas:

- HCI 2019: Human-Computer Interaction
- HIMI 2019: Human Interface and the Management of Information

Affiliated conferences:

- EPCE 2019: 16th International Conference on Engineering Psychology and Cognitive Ergonomics
- UAHCI 2019: 13th International Conference on Universal Access in Human-Computer Interaction
- VAMR 2019: 11th International Conference on Virtual, Augmented and Mixed Reality
- CCD 2019: 11th International Conference on Cross-Cultural Design
- SCSM 2019: 11th International Conference on Social Computing and Social Media
- AC 2019: 13th International Conference on Augmented Cognition
- DHM 2019: 10th International Conference on Digital Human Modeling and Applications in Health, Safety, Ergonomics and Risk Management
- DUXU 2019: 8th International Conference on Design, User Experience, and Usability
- DAPI 2019: 7th International Conference on Distributed, Ambient and Pervasive Interactions
- HCIBGO 2019: 6th International Conference on HCI in Business, Government and Organizations
- LCT 2019: 6th International Conference on Learning and Collaboration Technologies
- ITAP 2019: 5th International Conference on Human Aspects of IT for the Aged Population
- HCI-CPT 2019: First International Conference on HCI for Cybersecurity, Privacy and Trust
- HCI-Games 2019: First International Conference on HCI in Games
- MobiTAS 2019: First International Conference on HCI in Mobility, Transport, and Automotive Systems
- AIS 2019: First International Conference on Adaptive Instructional Systems

Pre-conference Proceedings Volumes Full List

1. LNCS 11566, Human-Computer Interaction: Perspectives on Design (Part I), edited by Masaaki Kurosu
2. LNCS 11567, Human-Computer Interaction: Recognition and Interaction Technologies (Part II), edited by Masaaki Kurosu
3. LNCS 11568, Human-Computer Interaction: Design Practice in Contemporary Societies (Part III), edited by Masaaki Kurosu
4. LNCS 11569, Human Interface and the Management of Information: Visual Information and Knowledge Management (Part I), edited by Sakae Yamamoto and Hirohiko Mori
5. LNCS 11570, Human Interface and the Management of Information: Information in Intelligent Systems (Part II), edited by Sakae Yamamoto and Hirohiko Mori
6. LNAI 11571, Engineering Psychology and Cognitive Ergonomics, edited by Don Harris
7. LNCS 11572, Universal Access in Human-Computer Interaction: Theory, Methods and Tools (Part I), edited by Margherita Antona and Constantine Stephanidis
8. LNCS 11573, Universal Access in Human-Computer Interaction: Multimodality and Assistive Environments (Part II), edited by Margherita Antona and Constantine Stephanidis
9. LNCS 11574, Virtual, Augmented and Mixed Reality: Multimodal Interaction (Part I), edited by Jessie Y. C. Chen and Gino Fragomeni
10. LNCS 11575, Virtual, Augmented and Mixed Reality: Applications and Case Studies (Part II), edited by Jessie Y. C. Chen and Gino Fragomeni
11. LNCS 11576, Cross-Cultural Design: Methods, Tools and User Experience (Part I), edited by P. L. Patrick Rau
12. LNCS 11577, Cross-Cultural Design: Culture and Society (Part II), edited by P. L. Patrick Rau
13. LNCS 11578, Social Computing and Social Media: Design, Human Behavior and Analytics (Part I), edited by Gabriele Meiselwitz
14. LNCS 11579, Social Computing and Social Media: Communication and Social Communities (Part II), edited by Gabriele Meiselwitz
15. LNAI 11580, Augmented Cognition, edited by Dylan D. Schmorrow and Cali M. Fidopiastis
16. LNCS 11581, Digital Human Modeling and Applications in Health, Safety, Ergonomics and Risk Management: Human Body and Motion (Part I), edited by Vincent G. Duffy

17. LNCS 11582, Digital Human Modeling and Applications in Health, Safety, Ergonomics and Risk Management: Healthcare Applications (Part II), edited by Vincent G. Duffy
18. LNCS 11583, Design, User Experience, and Usability: Design Philosophy and Theory (Part I), edited by Aaron Marcus and Wentao Wang
19. LNCS 11584, Design, User Experience, and Usability: User Experience in Advanced Technological Environments (Part II), edited by Aaron Marcus and Wentao Wang
20. LNCS 11585, Design, User Experience, and Usability: Application Domains (Part III), edited by Aaron Marcus and Wentao Wang
21. LNCS 11586, Design, User Experience, and Usability: Practice and Case Studies (Part IV), edited by Aaron Marcus and Wentao Wang
22. LNCS 11587, Distributed, Ambient and Pervasive Interactions, edited by Norbert Streitz and Shin'ichi Konomi
23. LNCS 11588, HCI in Business, Government and Organizations: eCommerce and Consumer Behavior (Part I), edited by Fiona Fui-Hoon Nah and Keng Siau
24. LNCS 11589, HCI in Business, Government and Organizations: Information Systems and Analytics (Part II), edited by Fiona Fui-Hoon Nah and Keng Siau
25. LNCS 11590, Learning and Collaboration Technologies: Designing Learning Experiences (Part I), edited by Panayiotis Zaphiris and Andri Ioannou
26. LNCS 11591, Learning and Collaboration Technologies: Ubiquitous and Virtual Environments for Learning and Collaboration (Part II), edited by Panayiotis Zaphiris and Andri Ioannou
27. LNCS 11592, Human Aspects of IT for the Aged Population: Design for the Elderly and Technology Acceptance (Part I), edited by Jia Zhou and Gavriel Salvendy
28. LNCS 11593, Human Aspects of IT for the Aged Population: Social Media, Games and Assistive Environments (Part II), edited by Jia Zhou and Gavriel Salvendy
29. LNCS 11594, HCI for Cybersecurity, Privacy and Trust, edited by Abbas Moallem
30. LNCS 11595, HCI in Games, edited by Xiaowen Fang
31. LNCS 11596, HCI in Mobility, Transport, and Automotive Systems, edited by Heidi Krömker
32. LNCS 11597, Adaptive Instructional Systems, edited by Robert Sottilare and Jessica Schwarz
33. CCIS 1032, HCI International 2019 - Posters (Part I), edited by Constantine Stephanidis

34. CCIS 1033, HCI International 2019 - Posters (Part II), edited by Constantine Stephanidis
35. CCIS 1034, HCI International 2019 - Posters (Part III), edited by Constantine Stephanidis

http://2019.hci.international/proceedings

Human-Computer Interaction Thematic Area (HCI 2019)

Program Board Chair(s): **Masaaki Kurosu, *Japan***

- Jose Abdelnour-Nocera, UK
- Mark Apperley, New Zealand
- Kaveh Bazargan, France
- Simone Borsci, The Netherlands
- Kuohsiang Chen, P.R. China
- Stefano Federici, Italy
- Isabela Gasparini, Brazil
- Ayako Hashizume, Japan
- Wonil Hwang, Korea
- Mitsuhiko Karashima, Japan
- Shinichi Koyama, Japan
- Naoko Okuizumi, Japan
- Takanobu Omata, Japan
- Katsuhiko Onishi, Japan
- Philippe Palanque, France
- Alberto Raposo, Brazil
- Guangfeng Song, USA
- Hiroshi Ujita, Japan

The full list with the Program Board Chairs and the members of the Program Boards of all thematic areas and affiliated conferences is available online at:

http://www.hci.international/board-members-2019.php

HCI International 2020

The 22nd International Conference on Human-Computer Interaction, HCI International 2020, will be held jointly with the affiliated conferences in Copenhagen, Denmark, at the Bella Center Copenhagen, July 19–24, 2020. It will cover a broad spectrum of themes related to HCI, including theoretical issues, methods, tools, processes, and case studies in HCI design, as well as novel interaction techniques, interfaces, and applications. The proceedings will be published by Springer. More information will be available on the conference website: http://2020.hci.international/.

General Chair
Prof. Constantine Stephanidis
University of Crete and ICS-FORTH
Heraklion, Crete, Greece
E-mail: general_chair@hcii2020.org

http://2020.hci.international/

Contents – Part II

Mobile Interaction

Facial Expressions and Emotions Recognition

Eye-Gaze, Gesture and Motion-Based Interaction

Interaction in Virtual and Augmented Reality

Mobile Interaction

Investigation of the Effect of Letter Labeling Positions on Consecutive Typing on Mobile Devices

Hsi-Jen Chen(✉) and Chia-Ming Kuo

Department of Industrial Design, National Cheng Kung University, No. 1, University Road, Tainan City 701, Taiwan
Hsijen_chen@mail.ncku.edu.tw

Abstract. Using soft keyboard is the main text entry method on mobile devices. However, texting on small mobile devices, such as smartphones remains challenging and inconvenient. It's because of the small size of keys, the difference between view angle and touch point, the tilt of the device etc. When entering text, the human eye conducted visual search for the target key, then casted their attention on the symbol on the button. In this research we would like to understand how the touch points would be affected by the symbol positions on the button. A click-based App has been designed to observe, record, and analyze the data and behaviors of the subjects when they clicked on the keypad buttons. In the experiments the subjects have been asked to perform a series of clicking on the target points under five conditions that the symbols appeared at the center of the buttons, the upper right portions, the lower right portions, the upper left portions and the lower left portions. According to analyses we fund that under the circumstances of different symbol positions, the subjects tended to click on the positions where the symbols appeared instead of the centers of the buttons.

Keywords: User interfaces · Interaction styles · Mobile device · Text entry · Touchscreen · Symbol position

1 Introduction

Small mobile devices have been integrated into most people's lives already. According to the surveys, the penetration rate of global smart phones has exceeded 62% in 2017. The most commonly used functions for surfing the Internet with a smartphone are "visiting the social network" (71%), "using a search engine" (64%), and "consulting a map" (60%) [1]. All of the above-mentioned functions require text input that apparently "text input" plays an important role in the use of mobile devices. Even though using large-screen mobile devices is becoming a trend, the virtual keyboard button sizes of iPhone 6s Plus's 5.5-in. screens are only about 5.8 × 7.5 mm. Such figures are still lower than the recommendations of the iOS Human Interface Guidelines [2]. Therefore, understanding the keyboard usage habits and improving the entry efficiency of using the virtual keyboard remains a topic worth exploring.

M. Kurosu (Ed.): HCII 2019, LNCS 11567, pp. 3–16, 2019.
https://doi.org/10.1007/978-3-030-22643-5_1

The virtual keyboard entry on the mobile device is not as efficient as the traditional physical keyboard [3], and the screen space's limitation which results in the keys' being too small is one of the important reasons to reduce data entry efficiency [4]. When text inputs are performed on a mobile device, there exists offsets from the touch points perceived by the user and the actual touch points [5, 6]. It is also a reason for what affects data entry accuracy when the targeted keys are blocked by the finger, and even the directions, distances, and speeds of finger movements can affect data entry accuracy too [7].

When a user performs continuous inputs on the mobile device, it is impossible to tap blindly. It is still necessary to focus on finding the targeting keys, and definitely people would feel curious about whether the user's attention is focusing on the "button center" or "symbol". On the keypad of a common mobile device, the symbol position locates at the center of the key. If both positions are different, how will the user react? Therefore, this study wants to know whether the "symbol positions" on the keys affect the touch points when continuous data entry is made on the keypad of a mobile device, and whether the touch points would change when the symbol positions on the keys have changed.

2 Related Work

2.1 Target Size

There have been a variety of discussions on the sizes of touch targets, and the levels of input error rates are absolutely related to the targets' being too small [4]. The keys' being too small increases input time and input error rate [8]. Different scholars have different opinions on the sizes of the touch screen buttons. Traditionally, the button size is 22 mm [9], but other studies have argued for smaller sizes, for instance, 11.5 mm [10] and 10.5 mm [5]. The iOS Human Interface Guidelines 2010 [2] suggests that the button or target sizes should be no smaller than 6.74 × 6.74 mm when designing an app, while the sizes of the buttons on smart watches still have the potential to be smaller [11].

2.2 Offsets for Touch Points

Henze et al. found that when a user selects a target on a mobile device, the wrong clicks are affected by the positions and the sizes of the buttons, and the drop points are biased with inclined concentration. Usually the point touched which user consider to be the touch point will be offset from the actual touch contact [5]. The offset can be due to the fact that the target is covered by the finger, and which portion of the finger to touch the screen is very vague and difficult to control [5]. Holz and Baudish [12] further explore how fingers touch the screens, and pointed out that different users, the tilt angles of the fingers, and the angles of rotations of the fingers will cause certain offsets between the gaze points and the touch contacts, and emphasized that such offsets are the main causes for the touch input method's being not accurate enough. Furthermore, when using a thumb for input under a one-hand operation circumstance, the offset issue will be even more severe when you click on the left and right buttons [13, 14].

2.3 Text Entry Performance

Both data entry speed and error rate are two frequently-used indicators for evaluating an input device [15]. The measurement of data entry speed can be expressed by "characters per second" (CPS) or "words per minute" (WPM). Among them, WPM is used more often. In WPM's calculation rules, a "word" is defined as "five keystrokes". These five strokes can contain all letters, numbers, blank key, punctuation, back key, etc. [15, 16]. However, Arif and Stuerzlinger [17] further argued that the calculation rule of WPM should be slightly adjusted. They think that the correct total number of keystrokes needs to be reduced by one, because the timing usually starts after the first key is tapped. Current data entry speeds on small mobile devices range from 35 to 50 WPM depending on the modes of operation [6, 18].

Compared with measuring data entry speeds, the error ratio calculations while making entry measurements are relatively more complicated, and the causes of the errors and the ways of calculations are very diverse. The nature of data entry errors can be divided into four categories: wrong entry (substitution), missing characters (omission), over entry (insertion) and transpositions with neighboring characters (transposition). The number of corrective actions varies according to different circumstances [19]. A more widely known and simple way to measure error ratio is to calculate the ratio of keystrokes to characters (Key Strokes per Character, KSPC), which is the actual number of keystrokes/number of due keystrokes [17, 20].

2.4 View Point from Cognitive Psychology

First of all, gestalt psychology advocates that the best way to understand human psychology is to regard it as a complete and structured whole, rather than a fragmented part, thus the idea that "the sum of parts is not equal to the whole" has been submitted [21]. In gestalt psychology, it has been further studied based on human visual perception and recognized that humans perceive it as the simplest or most regular form according to the visual array they see, called law of Pragnanz [22, 23]. Therefore, when we receive visual information, we will not only receive sensory elements that are messy and cannot be processed. For example, a keypad which is covered by a finger will not be considered as a notched keypad.

Secondly, visual attention factors may also have influences on the target selection. When the human brain processes visual information, it filters out unnecessary information and focuses on specific and meaningful visual information, and such process is called "selective attention" [24]. The factors which affect such visual attention can be divided into two types:

(a) Bottom-up Activation:
The inputs are made through sensory stimulations, triggering a series of internal recognitions, and quickly and involuntarily shifting attention to distinctive visual features. Such process relies on visual cortical function [25]. For example, we will pay attention to a white point in a black curtain [26–28].

(b) Top-down Activation:
Based on long-term cognitive experiences, the situation will arise attention, and it relies on the neural network of the frontal and parietal lobe [25]. This is a spontaneous visual search that varies according to one's own experiences and contexts of the time [26, 28].

All in all, the bottom-up vision leads people's attention to objects or images on the projections in the field of view which are prominent or special. As to the top-down vision, the visual attention will spontaneously be shifted based on people's experiences and visual context.

We may know from the above literature that there are many factors which affect whether the targets can be clicked precisely, and symbol position is likely to be one of them. Especially from the selective attention point of view, when the button is clicked, if the attention of the user is placed on the symbol and the position of the symbol changes, the click point should change accordingly. On the contrary, if attention is concentrated on the center of the button, the change in symbol position will not affect the clicking point. Therefore, this study will explore based on the "correlation between symbol positions and touch points".

3 Method

3.1 App Design for Usability Test

In this study a click-based App has been designed to observe, record, and analyze the data and behaviors of the subjects when they clicked on the keypad buttons. From the literature we learned that the general experimental method for testing text entry efficiency is to make the subject to input a series of sentences, and then calculate entry speeds and error rates. Under this experimental method the subject must first look at the topic article, then look at the keypad to find the correct button positions, and finally watch the input fields to confirm whether the data entry is correct. Thus the subjects must constantly switch the viewpoints among the titles, entry fields and keypad fields. In the case of general text entry, the users know which keys to enter, no need to do too much gaze conversions between the entry fields, title fields and the keypads, but focus on the keypads to search for the target buttons. The purpose of this experiment is to investigate whether the symbol positions on the buttons would affect touch points. For this purpose, there is no need to test with meaningful words or sentences, so the keypads used in the experiment will rid off the letter symbols and only leave the buttons for the input tests.

The way of App operation is that the buttons on the keypads will be randomly lit, and the subjects must click in order. However, in the real text entry scenarios the users know the positions of the next button in advance, therefore three buttons are randomly lit on the screen, and the number letters "1", "2", "3" are displayed in red respectively. The testee would click according to the numerical order. When a second button is clicked, the other three buttons are randomly lit to display the English letters "A", "B" and "C" in blue. The subjects must click on the numbers in order, then click on the English letters in order, and repeat in this way until the end of the experiment. In this way, the subjects can see through the colors of their eyes or scan the screens to know what the next buttons should be clicked and where the positions are, and that would make the tests proceed smoother and even more similar to the text entry actions (Fig. 1) In the App used for this experiment, symbols can appear in the center of the button and in the upper left, upper right, lower left, and lower right corners, a total of five positions, and random position mode (Fig. 2).

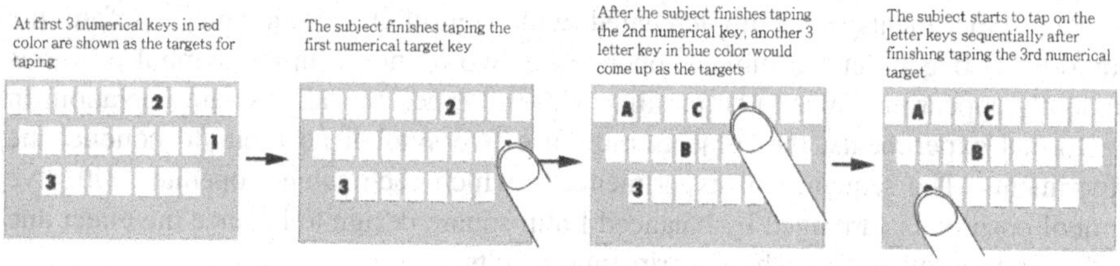

Fig. 1. Process of entry task

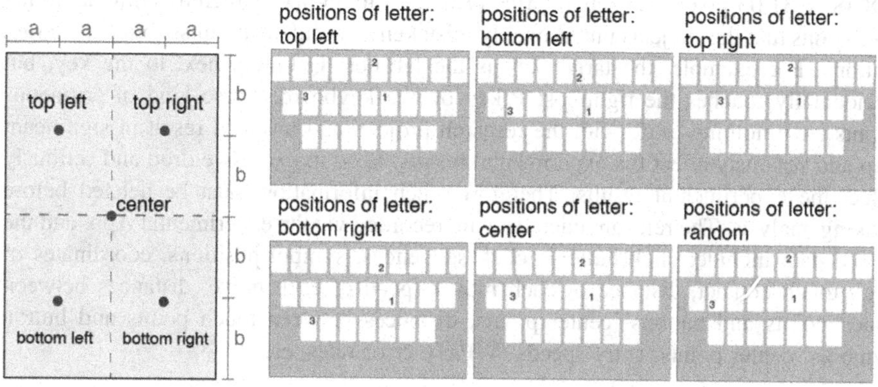

Fig. 2. Positions of symbols

3.2 Participants

According to the surveys, in Taiwan, the penetration rate of smart phones between 25–30 years old is as high as 96%, and is also as high as 95% for those under 25 years old. [1] Therefore 20–30 years old smartphone users have been selected as the subjects for this experiment. In order to avoid impact due to unfamiliarity with the touch screen operation, the testes must have more than six months of experiences in using smart phones. In addition, this study will focus on right-handed users, and they must be able to use their right thumbs for text entry. This experiment has invited a total of 30 subjects, half male and half female, to conduct the experiments.

3.3 Experiment

This study will use Usability Test as the main research method. During the experiments, the subjects have been arranged to conduct the experiments in a quiet laboratory, and the whole process was recorded. The experimental devices were of iPhone 6S with screen resolution of 1334 × 750 pixels, 326 ppi, while the experimental App's screen coordinate settings were set to horizontal length of 375 pixels, vertical length of 667 pixels, and the upper left corner of the screen as the origin.

The Experiments were implemented with right-thumb data entry. Before the experiments began, let the subjects operate for two rounds with the symbol positions randomly appearing, so as to be familiar with the experimental software operation. In the formal experiments, the subjects must use five symbol positions to conduct the experiments. The sequence of experiments in which each subject operates with five symbol positions is arranged by balanced Latin square design to balance the effect due to the learning effect from the experimental results.

3.4 Collecting Data

The button design of this experiment's App has included both visual target (48.48 × 31.03 pixel) and actual target (72.72 × 46.55 pixel), thereby eliminating the conditions that the subjects unreasonably mistaken or accidentally miss-touch the target buttons. For example, the target key is the leftmost Q button next to the key, but accidentally touches the rightmost P key on the keyboard. These kind of erroneous inputs have nothing to do with the research project, and that will result in significant gap and seriously affect the experimental results. Lead to excessive drop and seriously affect the experimental results. Therefore, such information must be deleted before making analysis. The relevant click data are recorded via the experimental App, and the stored data include: click buttons, click sequences, symbol positions, coordinates of each touch contact, distance of each move, speed of each move, distances between touch points and buttons' center points, distances between touch points and button symbols' center points, entry speeds (WPM), error rates, etc.

4 Results

As shown in Table 1, 12 subjects have participated in the study, and a total of 6511 valid click data have been collected with an average input speed (WPM) of 23.13 and an error rate of 90.64%. The data in Table 1 were analyzed by descriptive statistics and analysis of variance. In the analyses the X-axis and Y-axis conditions have been analyzed separately to explore on how may symbol positions affect the touch points.

4.1 Effect of Symbol Positions on Touch Points

The first analysis item was to verify whether the touch points of the clicking vary differently if the positions of the symbols were different. The distance differences between all touch points and the center points of the buttons were variables, and One-

Table 1. Overall number and proportion of the symbol positions

Letter labeling position	Frequency	Percent	Error rate	WPM
top right (tr)	1298	19.9	12.68%	22.7475
top left (tl)	1314	20.2	8.1%	23.3445
bottom right (br)	1266	19.4	11.51%	22.8654
bottom left (bl)	1268	19.5	7.52%	22.8717
center (c)	1365	21	6.98%	23.8225
Total	6511	100	9.36%	23.1303

way ANOVA analysis was performed with the symbol positions as the factors. The results on the X-axis have shown significant ($F(4, 6506) = 206.587$, $p <. 001$), and when we further checked the differences between the five symbol positions with Post Hoc Tests, it indicated that only what between the symbol positions "top right" & "bottom right" and "top left" & "bottom left" were not significant. As to the Y-axis, due to the fact that the Test of Homogeneity of Variances indicated different values, while the results of the Brown-Forsythe test were significant, ANOVA was thus proceeded and significant results were obtained ($F(4, 6506) = 343.355$, $p <. 001$). When we took a closer look at the differences between the five symbol positions by using Post Hoc Tests, we have obtained the results through Games-Howell test, showing that the symbol positions "top right" & "top left" and "bottom right" & "bottom left" were not significant. Table 2 presents the average distance differences between the touch point positions and the centers of the buttons in the X and Y axis. The above analysis shows that the symbol positions would affect touch points.

Table 2. Average distance differences between touch point positions and centers of the buttons

Avg. distance differences between touch points and centers of the button		N	Mean	Std. deviation	Minimum	Maximum
On X-axis	tr	1298	3.7261	7.83268	−35.13	28.59
	tl	1314	−1.8550	7.47139	−33.78	31.50
	br	1266	4.2188	7.97130	−30.77	35.41
	bl	1268	−2.3022	7.36184	−25.69	22.88
	center	1365	1.5821	7.35893	−32.77	30.05
	Total	6511	1.0721	8.06567	−35.13	35.41
On Y-axis	tr	1298	8.4983	8.89207	−29.59	32.87
	tl	1314	9.1621	8.96325	−41.13	40.32
	br	1266	0.0024	8.29644	−46.59	31.41
	bl	1268	0.1512	8.26440	−28.68	47.32
	center	1365	3.9576	8.05331	−46.13	30.41
	Total	6511	4.4028	9.35188	−46.59	47.32

4.2 Distances Between Touch Points and Centers of the Symbol

The second analysis item examined whether there existed any differences between the touch points v.s. the absolute distances of the corresponding symbol centers, despite the directions of the corresponding symbol centers. The individual distances between the touch points and the center points of the symbol were the variables, and the symbol positions were used as factors. For example, when performing an experiment on the "top left" portion, One-way ANOVA analysis was made with all the distances between touch points and the centers of the "top left" symbol. In the X-axis, as the Test of Homogeneity of Variances have shown results of different Mean values, but the Brown-Forsythe test results were significant, thus ANOVA could be proceeded to obtain significant results ($F(4, 6506) = 24.291$, $p <. 001$). The Games-Howell based Post Hoc Tests have shown that only "top right & bottom right" and "top left & bottom left" had the results with no significant difference. We also obtained significant results ($F(4, 6506) = 265.401$, $p <. 001$) when we analyzed in the same way on Y-axis upwards. Post Hoc Tests showed non-significant results between "top right & top left", "top right & center", "top left & center" and "bottom right & bottom left". We obtained significant results ($F(4, 6506) = 189.647$, $p <. 001$) too when we analyzed the touch points regarding the overall distance of symbol center points in the same way. The Post Hoc Tests showed that non-significant results only existed between "top right & center" and "bottom right & bottom left". Table 3 has shown the average distances between the touch points and the centers of the corresponding symbols. According to the above analysis, it indicates that the distances between the touch points and the centers of their corresponding symbols are different.

Table 3. Distances between touch points and the corresponding centers of the symbols

		N	Mean	Std. deviation	Minimum	Maximum
Avg. distance between touch points and center of symbols on X-axis	tr	1298	6.7241	5.79284	−13.26	42.88
	tl	1314	7.7707	5.53440	0.01	39.26
	br	1266	6.5787	5.72385	0.01	38.52
	bl	1268	7.3965	5.40614	0.01	30.63
	center	1365	5.8874	4.68744	0.05	32.77
	Total	6511	6.8626	5.47378	−13.26	42.88
Avg. distance between touch points and center of symbols on Y-axis	tr	1298	7.2027	6.31672	−18.25	41.71
	tl	1314	7.3489	5.93450	0.20	53.25
	br	1266	12.6674	7.43877	0.01	43.54
	bl	1268	12.7099	7.57360	0.01	59.44
	center	1365	7.2587	5.27273	0.13	46.13
	Total	6511	9.3790	7.05526	−18.25	59.44
Avg. distance between touch points and center of symbols	tr	1298	10.7011	7.03675	−15.43	44.88
	tl	1314	11.8911	6.23048	0.29	53.43
	br	1266	15.4314	7.32709	0.35	46.32
	bl	1268	15.6894	7.52706	0.12	62.09
	center	1365	10.3048	5.56062	0.43	46.55
	Total	6511	12.7494	7.13810	−15.43	62.09

4.3 Touch Points' Distribution Differences on X and Y Axes

The purpose of this analysis was to see if there existed differences in the distribution of touch points in the two axial directions. The five symbol positions were discussed separately and analyzed by Paired Sample t test to compare the differences between the touch points and the centers of the corresponding symbols in the X and Y axis. The results showed that when the symbol positions were "top right", the t value was −2.14, the two-tailed significance $p = 0.033 < 0.05$; while the symbol positions were "top left", the t value was 1.872, and the two-tailed significance $p = 0.061 > 0.05$. When the symbol positions were "bottom right", the t value was −22.865, the two-tailed significance was $p < 0.001$. When the symbol positions were "bottom left", the t statistic value was −21.681 with the two-tailed significance $p < 0.001$. When the symbol positions were "center", the statistical t value was −7.005 with two-tailed significance $p < 0.001$. All in all, the distances of the touch points from the centers of the symbols on the Y-axis were more significant than what on the X-axis. Non-significant results were only seen on those symbol positions of "top left" (Table 4).

Table 4. Result of Paired Sample t test for touch points' distribution differences

Avg. distance between the touch point and the symbol center		Mean	N	Std. deviation	Sig.
tr	on the X axis	6.7241	1298	0.16079	0.033
	on the Y axis	7.2027	1298	0.17533	
tl	on the X axis	7.7707	1314	0.15268	0.061
	on the Y axis	7.3489	1314	0.16371	
br	on the X axis	6.5787	1266	0.16087	0.000
	on the Y axis	12.6674	1266	0.20907	
bl	on the X axis	7.3965	1268	0.15182	0.000
	on the Y axis	12.7099	1268	0.21269	
center	on the X axis	5.8874	1365	0.12687	0.000
	on the Y axis	7.2587	1365	0.14271	

5 Results

The first analysis could confirm that the changes of the symbol positions significantly affected the touch points when the buttons were tapped. Figure 3 showed the relative-position correlations between buttons' center positions and both the symbol positions and touch points. First of all, according to the results of ANOVA, when the symbol positions appeared in the center positions, there existed significant differences between the corresponding touch points and the touch points of other four symbol positions. Interestingly, if we only observed the conditions on the X-axis, when the symbols appeared at center positions the touch points were at 1.58 pixel on the right side of the button center. When the symbols appeared on the right side, there was no significant difference in the corresponding touch points found between "top right" and "bottom right". In this case, the touch points were about 4 pixels to the right of the centers of the buttons. On the contrary, when the symbols were on the left side, there was no significant difference in the corresponding touch points found between "top left" and "bottom left", and the touch points were about 2 pixels to the left of the centers of the buttons. Such phenomenon also occurred on the Y axis. When the symbols appeared at the center, the touch points were 3.96 pixels above the centers of the buttons. When the symbols appeared at upper portions, the touch points were about 9 pixels above the centers of the buttons. When the symbols appeared at lower portion, the touch points were about at the centers of the buttons. Generally, the changes of the symbol positions affected the touch points when the buttons were tapped. The subjects would tend to click on the positions where the symbols appeared, and the coordinate position differences of the touch points were smaller when the symbols appeared on the right and the bottom sides.

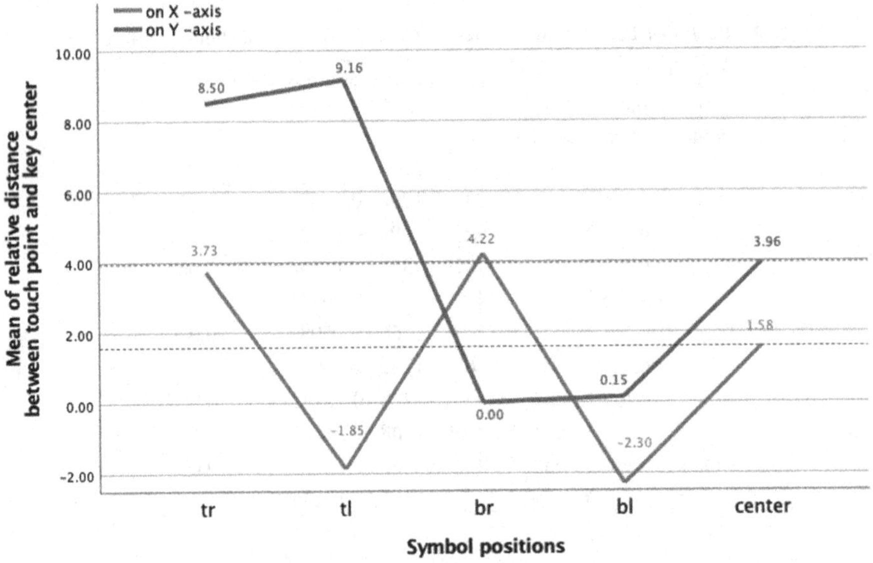

Fig. 3. Relative positions of the touch points to the centers of the buttons

It could be seen from the second analysis that when the symbols appeared on the lower and left portions the absolute distances of the touch points to the positions of symbols were farther away, and such phenomenon was especially noticeable on the Y-axis. When the symbols appeared in the "lower right" and "lower left" portions, the average distances of touch points from the positions of the symbols were 12.67 pixels and 12.71 pixels respectively, which were higher than the 7.2 pixels and 7.35 pixels of what for the "upper right" and "upper left". The result in Fig. 4 shows that the influence upon the subjects' tapping habits would be relatively not as significant if the symbols

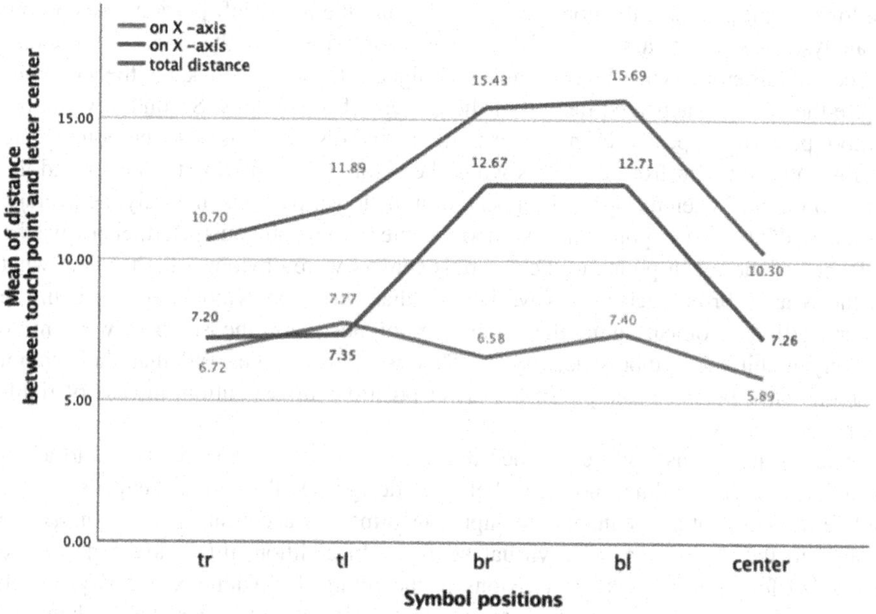

Fig. 4. Dispersion level of distances from the touch point to the positions of the symbols

appeared on the lower portion. The reason might be that the subjects could not hit the symbol accurately when the symbols appeared on the lower portion, and thus consequently resulted bigger distances between the touch points and the symbol centers.

It could be found from the third analysis that the distances between the touch points and the centers of the symbols in the Y-axis were significantly larger than what in the X-axis, except for the condition in which the symbols appeared in the upper left corner. Especially when the symbols appeared in the lower portions, the differences of the touch points could be up to 6 pixels or so on the Y-axis and the X-axis. We could also tell from Fig. 4 that the distances between the touch points and the centers of the symbols on the Y-axis significantly affected the total distance. The reason has been speculated that because the shapes of the buttons were rectangle, the differences in the longitudinal direction were larger than the lateral direction. According to these two analyses, it could be found that the circumstances would be obviously different when the symbols appeared in the lower right and the lower left v.s. the cases when the symbols appeared in the upper right, upper left and central positions.

6 Conclusion

This study explored the correlations between the mobile devices' symbol positions of the virtual buttons and their corresponding touch points. In the experiments the subjects have been asked to perform a series of clicking on the target points under five conditions that the symbols appeared at the center of the buttons, the upper right portions, the lower right portions, the upper left portions and the lower left portions. According to analyses two important results have been summarized. Firstly, under the circumstances of different symbol positions, the subjects tended to click on the positions where the symbols appeared instead of the centers of the buttons. Secondly, when the symbol positions appeared in the lower portions, the distributions of touch points were significantly different from the cases when the symbols appeared at the upper and the center portions. When the symbols appeared in the lower portions, not only the average distances of the touch points and symbols centers were obviously farther away, the distances of the touch points to the symbols centers were obviously higher than what on the X-axis. From such results we believe that when the symbols appeared in the lower portions, comparing to the other symbol positions, the subjects were more unlikely to hit the symbols accurately. Therefore, we recommend that the symbol positions have better not be put in the lower positions of the button, in case of right-thumb operations.

The results of this study confirmed that the positions of the symbols would affect touch points. The findings not only help the designs of the virtual keypads on the mobile devices, but also enhance the input performances accordingly, and can also be applied to the designs of other virtual keypads. In addition, this study can also be proceeded for more in-depth discussions in the future, for example, to analyze each button according to each individual status, and to research on the correlations between button sizes and symbol positions, etc.

References

1. Consumer Barometer with Google. https://www.consumerbarometer.com
2. Themes - iOS - Human Interface Guidelines - Apple Developer. https://developer.apple.com/design/human-interface-guidelines/ios/overview/themes/
3. Hoggan, E., Brewster, S.A., Johnston, J.: Investigating the effectiveness of tactile feedback for mobile touchscreens. In: Proceedings of the SIGCHI Conference on Human Factors in Computing Systems, pp. 1573–1582. ACM, New York (2008)
4. Henze, N., Rukzio, E., Boll, S.: 100,000,000 taps: analysis and improvement of touch performance in the large. In: Proceedings of the 13th International Conference on Human Computer Interaction with Mobile Devices and Services, pp. 133–142. ACM, New York (2011)
5. Vogel, D., Baudisch, P.: Shift: a technique for operating pen-based interfaces using touch. In: Proceedings of the SIGCHI Conference on Human Factors in Computing Systems, pp. 657–666. ACM, New York (2007)
6. Azenkot, S., Zhai, S.: Touch behavior with different postures on soft smartphone keyboards. In: Proceedings of the 14th international Conference on Human-Computer Interaction with Mobile Devices and Services, pp. 251–260. ACM, New York (2012)
7. Chen, H.-J., Kuo, C.-M., Cheng, Y.-C.: Investigating the behavior of sequence typing on the mobile devices. In: Kurosu, M. (ed.) HCI 2018. LNCS, vol. 10902, pp. 526–541. Springer, Cham (2018). https://doi.org/10.1007/978-3-319-91244-8_41

8. Colle, H.A., Hiszem, K.J.: Standing at a kiosk: effects of key size and spacing on touch screen numeric keypad performance and user preference. Ergonomics **47**, 1406–1423 (2004). https://doi.org/10.1080/00140130410001724228
9. Lee, S., Zhai, S.: The performance of touch screen soft buttons. In: Proceedings of the SIGCHI Conference on Human Factors in Computing Systems, pp. 309–318. ACM, New York (2009)
10. Wang, F., Ren, X.: Empirical evaluation for finger input properties in multi-touch interaction. In: Proceedings of the SIGCHI Conference on Human Factors in Computing Systems, pp. 1063–1072. ACM, New York (2009)
11. Cha, J.-M., Choi, E., Lim, J.: Virtual sliding QWERTY: a new text entry method for smartwatches using Tap-N-Drag. Appl. Ergon. **51**, 263–272 (2015). https://doi.org/10.1016/j.apergo.2015.05.008
12. Holz, C., Baudisch, P.: The generalized perceived input point model and how to double touch accuracy by extracting fingerprints. In: Proceedings of the SIGCHI Conference on Human Factors in Computing Systems, pp. 581–590. ACM, New York (2010)
13. Park, Y.S., Han, S.H.: Touch key design for one-handed thumb interaction with a mobile phone: effects of touch key size and touch key location. Int. J. Ind. Ergon. **40**, 68–76 (2010). https://doi.org/10.1016/j.ergon.2009.08.002
14. Park, Y.S., Han, S.H.: One-handed thumb interaction of mobile devices from the input accuracy perspective. Int. J. Ind. Ergon. **40**, 746–756 (2010). https://doi.org/10.1016/j.ergon.2010.08.001
15. MacKenzie, I.S., Soukoreff, R.W.: Text entry for mobile computing: models and methods, theory and practice. Hum.-Comput. Interact. **17**, 147–198 (2002). https://doi.org/10.1080/07370024.2002.9667313
16. Gentner, D.R., Grudin, J.T., Larochelle, S., Norman, D.A., Rumelhart, D.E.: A glossary of terms including a classification of typing errors. In: Cooper, W.E. (ed.) Cognitive Aspects of Skilled Typewriting, pp. 39–43. Springer, New York (1983). https://doi.org/10.1007/978-1-4612-5470-6_2
17. Arif, A.S., Stuerzlinger, W.: Analysis of text entry performance metrics. In: Proceedings IEEE TIC-STH 2009, pp. 100–105. IEEE (2009)
18. Rudchenko, D., Paek, T., Badger, E.: Text text revolution: a game that improves text entry on mobile touchscreen keyboards. In: Lyons, K., Hightower, J., Huang, E.M. (eds.) Pervasive 2011. LNCS, vol. 6696, pp. 206–213. Springer, Heidelberg (2011). https://doi.org/10.1007/978-3-642-21726-5_13
19. Suhm, B., Myers, B., Waibel, A.: Model-based and empirical evaluation of multimodal interactive error correction. In: Proceedings of the SIGCHI Conference on Human Factors in Computing Systems, pp. 584–591. ACM, New York (1999)
20. Soukoreff, R.W., MacKenzie, I.S.: Metrics for text entry research: an evaluation of MSD and KSPC, and a new unified error metric. In: Proceedings of the SIGCHI Conference on Human Factors in Computing Systems, pp. 113–120. ACM, New York (2003)
21. Koffka, K.: Principles of Gestalt Psychology. Routledge (2013)
22. Sternberg, R.J., Sternberg, K.: Cognitive Psychology. Wadsworth/Cengage Learning (2011)
23. Spelke, E.S.: Principles of object perception. Cogn. Sci. **14**, 29–56 (1990). https://doi.org/10.1207/s15516709cog1401_3
24. Moran, J., Desimone, R.: Selective attention gates visual processing in the extrastriate cortex. Science **229**, 782–784 (1985)

25. Corbetta, M., Shulman, G.L.: Control of goal-directed and stimulus-driven attention in the brain. Nat. Rev. Neurosci. **3**, 201–215 (2002). https://doi.org/10.1038/nrn755
26. Wolfe, J.M.: Guided search 2.0 a revised model of visual search. Psychon. Bull. Rev. **1**, 202–238 (1994). https://doi.org/10.3758/bf03200774
27. Itti, L., Koch, C., Niebur, E.: A model of saliency-based visual attention for rapid scene analysis. IEEE Trans. Pattern Anal. Mach. Intell. **20**, 1254–1259 (1998). https://doi.org/10.1109/34.730558
28. Connor, C.E., Egeth, H.E., Yantis, S.: Visual attention: bottom-up versus top-down. Curr. Biol. **14**, R850–R852 (2004). https://doi.org/10.1016/j.cub.2004.09.041

Study on Size Design of Touch-Sensitive Button

Xiaoli Fan[1,2,3], Huimin Hu[1,2,3(✉)], Chaoyi Zhao[1,2,3], and Wei Zhang[1,2,3]

[1] SAMR Key Laboratory of Human Factors and Ergonomics, Beijing 100191, China
{fanxl,huhm}@cnis.gov.cn
[2] China National Institute of Standardization, Beijing 100191, China
[3] Tsinghua University, Beijing 100084, China

Abstract. To examine the effects of button size with different shape on the usability of touch screen devices. Considering the forefinger operation, the subjective and objective evaluation were combined to assess the ergonomics of the touch-sensitive button size, so as to obtain the recommended range of button size. With the size of touch-sensitive buttons specified setting from 3 mm to 25 mm respectively, where the step size was 2 mm, thirsty subjects participated in the test. One-way ANOVA was used to analyze the operational performance (reaction time and error rate) at different key sizes, and then the S-N-K-hoc multiple pairwise comparison test was used for pairwise comparison. The results demonstrated that the recommended range for rounded corner touch button is from 11 mm to 19 mm, round touch button in the recommended range is from 13 to 19 mm. It is also confirmed that the rounded corner touch buttons are superior to round touch buttons in the same size. This research can provide a basis for the design of button size of enterprise electronic products, and has important guiding significance.

Keywords: Touch-sensitive button · Size · Human-computer interaction

1 Introduction

With the development of science and technology and economy, people's standard of living has been improved continuously, and the requirement of comfort has also been raised. At present, all kinds of electronic products sold in the market, such as home appliances, mobile phones and so on, are gradually using touch screen technology to replace the traditional mechanical button technology. The so-called touch screen is a transparent panel that forms input instructions directly by touching [1]. Compared with traditional input tools such as mechanical buttons, it has a more direct human-computer interaction experience, easy to manipulate and use. There are now 16 kinds of touch screen technologies on the market, 8 of which have become common technologies [2]. It has been widely used in actual products, such as Apple's iPad and other products, most of which are multi-touch technology. So far, the new touch screen technology, which has the function of "dynamics feedback", has also been marketed [1]. With the rapid development of technology, people pay more attention to the fluency of human-computer interaction on touch screen. Having good usability and ease of use to meet

M. Kurosu (Ed.): HCII 2019, LNCS 11567, pp. 17–27, 2019.
https://doi.org/10.1007/978-3-030-22643-5_2

the needs and satisfaction of consumers is the development trend of touch screen in the future. However, the common problem is that the touch screen displays a lot of information, but the interaction space is relatively limited. If the relationship between the two is not handled properly, it is likely to lead to poor user experience. Therefore, it is necessary to study the layout of touch screen buttons in order to realize the clear display of many kinds of information and the effective operation of interactive control in a limited plane.

In recent years, there have been a lot of button characteristics at home and abroad on the impact of operational performance, such as button size, button spacing and input situation, and achieved a series of results. In their study, Park and Han [3] discussed the influence of the three button sizes of 4 mm, 7 mm, 10 mm on the performance of the operation. The results showed that the button size of 7 mm, 10 mm could provide the best performance. By studying the button size of smart phone interface, Jung and Im [4] pointed out that the hit ratio of the button mainly depended on the touchable area of the button, that was, the size of the button. The results of Colle and Hiszem [5] showed that the 20 mm buttons could provide the optimal operation performance, but the different button spacing (1 and 3 mm) has little effect on the user's performance. In addition, some scholars had studied the effect of these button feature factors on the performance of the operation in different situations and groups. Conradi et al. [6] had shown that the 8 mm button size was suitable for static standing. But this size increased input errors, and the 14 mm button size caused a lower error rate when used while walking. Hwangbo et al. [7] studied the operation of the touch screen of the old people. The results showed that the greater the size and spacing of the buttons, the better the operation performance, the higher the subjective evaluation, and when the size of the button was large, the button spacing did not have a significant effect on the performance of the click operation. The results of Jin [8] et al. showed that the elderly can get the highest correct operation rate at the button size of 19.05 mm and the button spacing of 6.35 mm, but the larger button spacing increased the response time for the elderly. At present, most of the related research on touch screen buttons are from western countries. Due to the large differences in human morphological parameters between China and the West, their research results are not suitable for Chinese, only for reference. Some scholars had made some researches on the touch-screen button-related problem interiorly. The experimental results of Zhang Wenlin [9] showed that the button size had a significant effect on the landing point, offset and error rate of the click-through operation, while the effect of button spacing on the operation performance was affected by the button size. When the single button is less than 6 cm in width, it is recommended that the smaller the spacing design of the button, the better the operation accuracy; If the width of the button is more than 6 cm, the distance can be widened, but it is recommended to keep the width of the single button above 6 cm to avoid reducing the accuracy of the operation. At present, the factors such as the relevant size and layout of the touch screen at home and abroad have not yet formed a unified standard. The ANSI/HFES 100-2007 standard [10] recommends that the button size be at least 9.5 mm, and the button spacing be 3.2 mm. The ISO 9241-9 standard suggests that the button size should be the same as the width of the distal knuckles of the 95th percentile male (about 22–23 mm). Other standards [11] suggested that the button size should be 19.05 mm, and the button spacing should be matched with 6 mm.

In previous studies, there has been no mention of the effect of button shape on touch button operation. At the same time, the objective evaluation method is used in the study to analyze the influence of various factors on the operation performance, and the subjective feelings of the users are not considered. Based on the above factors, this paper mainly aimed at the ergonomics evaluation of touch button size with different shapes by combining subjective evaluation with objective evaluation under the condition of standing touch screen in order to obtain the recommended range of button size under different touch button shape, providing data support and scientific basis for ergonomic design of touch screen button on enterprise, so as to improve the layout of touch screen and enhance user satisfaction.

2 Method

2.1 Subjects

The subjects were required to meet the following conditions: normal vision or correction above 1.0, no cognitive impairment, between 22 and 50 years old, having experience in the use of touch-screen electronics. In order to ensure the reliability and effectiveness of the results, the subjects were evenly distributed in different age groups. The total number of samples was 30, among which, 15 males and 15 females. The subjects volunteered to participate in the experiment, and filled out a written consent form. After the completion of the experiment, they were paid a certain amount of money. Before the experiment, none of the subjects had been exposed to the task.

2.2 Experiment Design and Variables

2 × 12 within-group design was used in the study, in which variables were: button shape (round and rounded corner) and button size (3 mm, 5 mm, 7 mm, 9 mm, 11 mm, 13 mm, 15 mm, 17 mm, 19 mm, 21 mm, 23 mm, 25 mm). Through the actual investigation of the touch button spacing of the related electronic products in the market, combining with the existing literature theories, the reasonable horizontal and vertical spacing were selected, which were set as 8 mm and 12 mm respectively. It had been verified through pre-experiment that the selected button spacings were within reasonable ranges, which would not affect the final results of the experiment. On the basis of this, the experiment task of touch button operation was designed to explore the effect of button size on operation performance and user satisfaction under the shape of two kinds of buttons. Among them, the operation performance was evaluated by two indictors, reaction time and error rate. The user satisfaction was measured by a subjective evaluation scale with five levels as shown in Fig. 1.

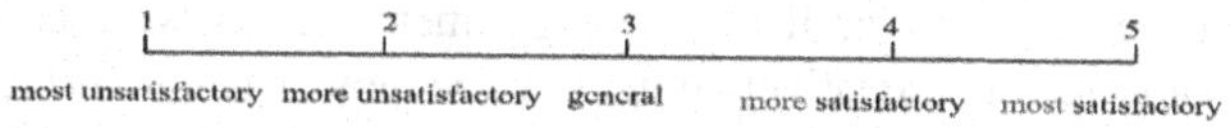

Fig. 1. Subjective evaluation scale

2.3 Experimental Software

The touch button operation task software was programmed in C# on NET Framework platform. The shape of the button and the size of the button could be set according to the experimental design. Button styles including font type, size, font color and background color could also be set according to the actual situation. Figure 2 showed the main interface of the task. It mainly included the task displaying area and the button operation area. The displaying area would generate N numbers randomly, and the operation area was consisted of 9 numeric buttons from 1 to 9. The sizes of buttons were fixed according to the parameters that had been set, and they would not change along with the size of the touch screen. When the stimulus displayed in the displaying area, subjects were required to enter the corresponding digitals as quickly and accurately as possible by using the digital buttons in the operation area, and then began the next trial until the end of the task. After the experiment, the software records the results of this operation automatically.

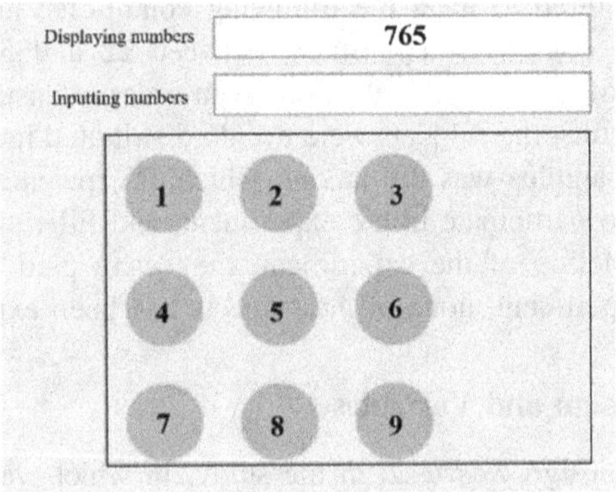

Fig. 2. The main interface of task presentation

2.4 Experimental Process

Based on the above software, the ergonomics recommendation range of the size of the touch buttons was determined by conducting button-press operation tasks, combined with the users' experience and evaluation. During the test, each subject was required to perform 2 × 12 tasks. Each task was consisted of 20 trials, and each trial randomly displayed 3 numbers. The subjects were asked to enter the corresponding numbers as quickly and accurately as possible using the touch buttons in the operation. After each task, the subject needed to rate the satisfactory scores of the button sizes combining with their own feeling. Meanwhile they were required to rest for 5 min after each test task avoiding the fatigue effect on result which was caused by long-time experiment, and then began the next task until all the experimental tasks were completed. The experiment was arranged in a relatively quiet environment. The touch-screen notebook with touch button operation task software was put on a lifting table before the experiment. The subjects adjusted the height of the table according to their comfort. Then formal experiment was conducted.

2.5 Statistical Analysis

The behavioral performance data and the satisfaction rating data during the experiment was collected, and SPSS 19.0 was used to analyze the data. One-way ANOVA was used to analyze the performance data (reaction time and error rate) of touch-sensitive buttons with different shapes under different button sizes [12]. Then S-N-K post hoc test was used to carry on the pairwise comparison [13]. At the same time, the subjective satisfaction rating was used to demined the optimal recommendation range of button size. All significant levels were $\alpha = 0.05$.

3 Result and Discussion

3.1 Analysis of the Results of Rounded Corner Touch Button

Figure 3 showed the changing trend of task performance with button size for a rounded corner touch button. It could be seen that the average reaction time and error rate decreased gradually along with the increase of button size. One-way ANOVA was used to analyze the reaction time of the rounded corner button with different sizes, as shown in Table 1. Combined with Fig. 3(a) and Table 1, the result was obtained that the reaction time was significantly reduced ($F = 11.560$, $P < 0.05$) as the button size increased. Further pairwise comparison by S-N-K-hoc test found there was no significant difference in the reaction times of buttons with sizes ≥ 7 mm, that was, the button size needed to be ≥ 7 mm to ensure the high efficiency of operation. Similarly, One-way ANOVA was used to analyze the error rate of the rounded corner button in different sizes. The results were shown in Table 2. Combined with Fig. 3(b) and Table 2, the result was obtained that the error rate was reduced significantly ($F = 18.269$, $P < 0.05$) with the increase of button size. Further pairwise comparison by S-N-K-hoc test found that the error rates of button sizes ≥ 7 mm had no significant difference, that was, the button size needed to be ≥ 7 mm, in order to ensure the high accuracy of touch button operation.

Table 3 showed the statistical results of subjective satisfaction scores with different sizes of rounded touch buttons (mean + standard deviation). Figure 4 showed the curve of the subjective satisfaction scores varying with the button sizes of the rounded corner buttons. It could be seen from the diagram that the subjective satisfaction increased firstly and then decreased with the button size.

In summary, the operation task performance of the rounded corner touch button was analyzed and the results showed that the size of the rounded corner square button should be at least >=7 mm in order to satisfy the efficiency and accuracy of the operation. At the same time, considering the subjective satisfaction evaluation, satisfaction score >=4 was chose, then the recommended range of the final rounded corner button was obtained: $11 \sim 19$ mm.

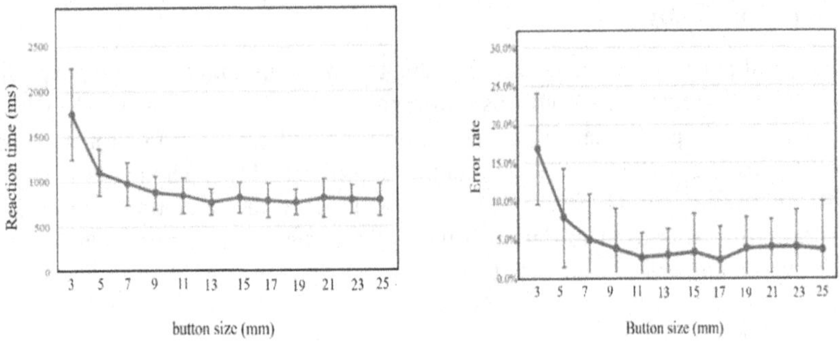

(a) Reaction time (b) Error rate

Fig. 3. Behavior performance with different button sizes

Table 1. One-way ANOVA results of reaction time with different button sizes

	Sum of squares	df	Mean square	F	Sig.
Between group	5058214.067	11	459837.642	11.560	.000
Within group	13842577.533	348	39777.522		
Total	18900791.600	359			

Table 2. One-way ANOVA results of error rate with different button sizes

	Sum of squares	df	Mean square	F	Sig.
Between group	.522	11	.047	18.269	.000
Within group	.903	348	.003		
Total	1.425	359			

Table 3. Subjective satisfaction score under different sizes of rounded touch buttons

Button size	Mean	S.D.
3	1.50	0.82
5	2.57	0.90
7	3.07	0.94
9	3.57	0.77
11	4.13	0.82
13	4.27	0.69
15	4.33	0.66
17	4.33	0.80
19	4.20	0.92
21	3.87	1.04
23	3.50	1.14
25	3.33	1.27

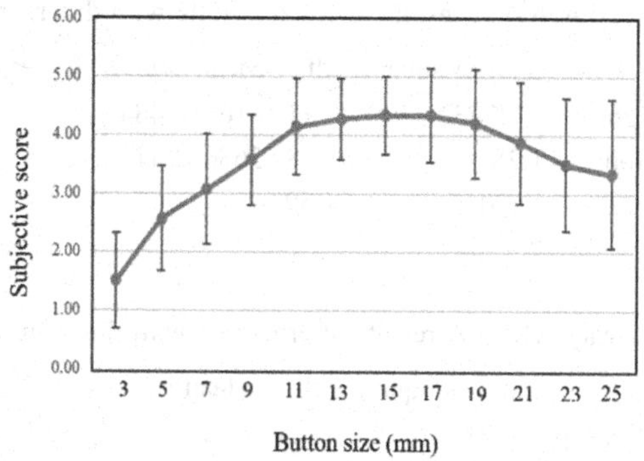

Fig. 4. Subjective satisfaction scores with different button sizes

3.2 Analysis of the Results of Round Touch Button

Figure 5 showed the changing trend of task performance with button size for round touch buttons. It could be seen that reaction time and error rate decreased with the increase of button size. The reaction times of round touch buttons at different sizes were analyzed using One-way ANOVA. The results were shown in Table 4. Combined with Fig. 5(a) and Table 4, the result was obtained: the reaction time decreased significantly with the increase of button size ($F = 16.715$, $P < 0.05$). Further pairwise comparison by S-N-K-hoc test found there was no significant difference in the reaction times of buttons with sizes >=9 mm ($P > 0.05$). Therefore, the button size should be >9 mm to ensure the high efficiency of touch button operation. Similarly, the error rate of round touch buttons at different sizes was analyzed using One-way ANOVA. The results were shown in Table 5. Combined with Fig. 5(b) and Table 5, the result was obtained: the error rate decreased significantly with the increase of button size ($F = 8.093$, $P < 0.05$). Further pairwise comparison by S-N-K-hoc test found there was no significant difference in the error rates of buttons with sizes >=9 mm ($P > 0.05$). Therefore, the button size should be >9 mm to ensure the high efficiency of touch button operation.

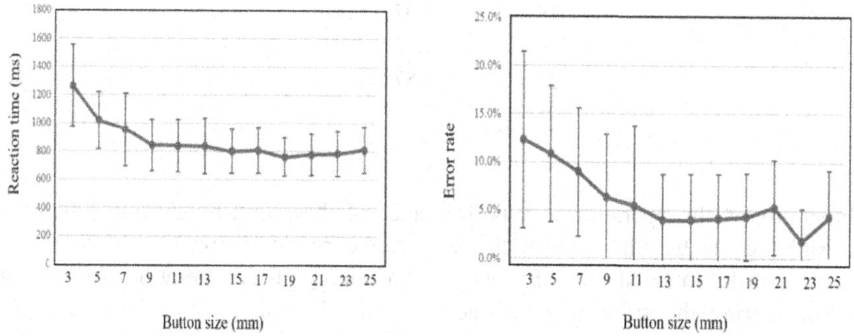

(a) Reaction time (b) Error rate

Fig. 5. Behavior performance with different button sizes

Table 4. One-way ANOVA results of reaction time with different button sizes

	Sum of squares	df	Mean square	F	Sig.
Between group	6777732.322	11	616157.484	16.715	.000
Within group	$1.283E^7$	348	36862.747		
Total	$1.961E^7$	359			

Table 5. One-way ANOVA results of error rate with different button sizes

	Sum of squares	df	Mean square	F	Sig.
Between group	.323	11	.029	8.093	.000
Within group	1.261	348	.004		
Total	1.584	359			

Table 6 showed the statistical results of subjective satisfaction scores with different sizes of rounded touch buttons (mean + standard deviation). Figure 6 showed the curve of the subjective satisfaction score varying with the size of the round touch button. It could be seen from the diagram that the subjective satisfaction score increased firstly and then decreased with the increase of button size.

Table 6. Subjective satisfaction score under different sizes of rounded touch buttons

Button size	Mean	S.D.
3	1.33	0.48
5	1.83	0.75
7	2.47	0.68
9	2.97	0.72
11	3.50	0.86
13	4.00	0.64
15	4.17	0.70
17	4.17	0.87
19	4.07	0.94
21	3.83	1.09
23	3.57	1.19
25	3.13	1.28

In summary, the operation task performance of the round touch button was analyzed and the results showed that the size of the round button should be at least >=9 mm in order to satisfy the efficiency and accuracy of the operation. At the same time, considering the subjective satisfaction evaluation, satisfaction score >=4 was chose, then the recommended range of the final round button was obtained: 13 ~ 19 mm.

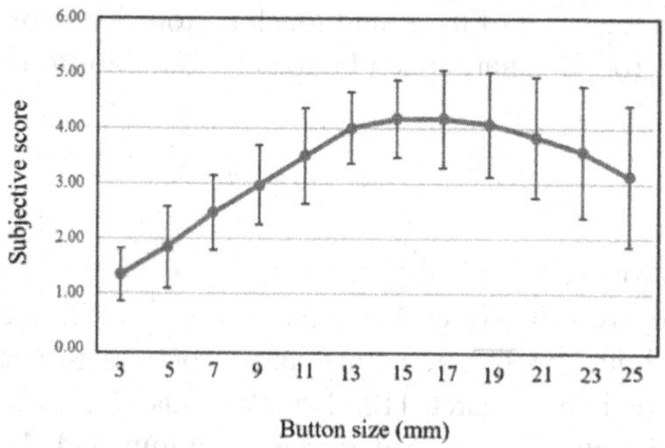

Fig. 6. Subjective satisfaction scores with different button sizes

3.3 Comparison of Operation Results Between Rounded Corner and Round Buttons

The behavior performance and subjective satisfaction results between the operations with rounded corner and round touch buttons were compared. Figure 7 showed their comparative curves. It can be seen from the figure that the reaction time of using round square touch button and round touch button operation is basically the same, but the error rate of round square touch button operation is obviously lower than that of round touch button. At the same time, the user's subjective satisfaction of the round square

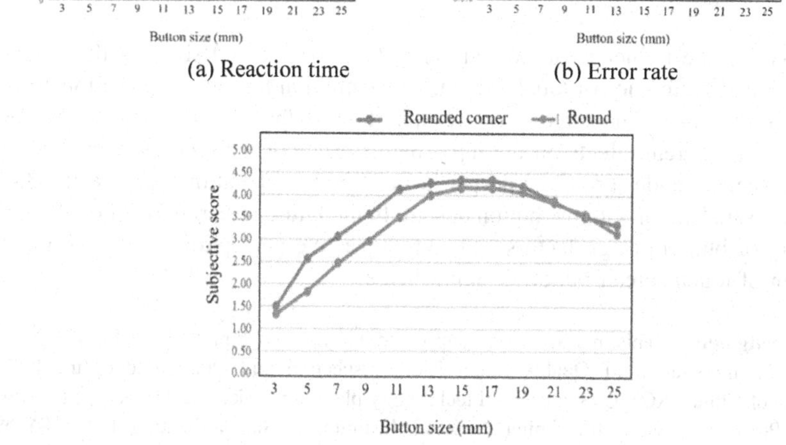

(a) Reaction time

(b) Error rate

(c) subjective score

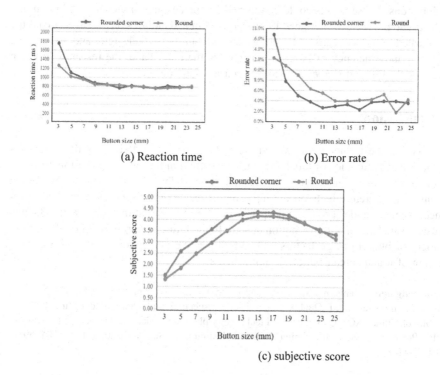

Fig. 7. Comparison of operation results between round corner and round buttons

touch button is higher than that of the round touch button. Therefore, it can be inferred that, at the same size, round square touch buttons are superior to round touch buttons.

4 Discussion

The influence of button size with different shapes on touch screen operation was discussed in the paper. Results showed that there was a negative correlation between the button size and both the reaction time and error rate respectively, which was consistent with the previous research [12, 15]. Previous studies had showed that the input performance of buttons with size between 19 mm and 22 mm was optimal. Furthermore, the button size ranges for different button shapes were given in the study respectively. The button sizes were at least 7 mm and 9 mm for round corner touch buttons and round touch buttons respectively, which could ensure the efficiency and effectiveness of the operation. However, the increase of button size on this basis had no significant effect on the improvement of input performance. Clearly, the satisfaction of the users' experience had become a major factor. That was, on the basis of ensuring the input performance, the subjective satisfaction of the user should be considered. The subjective and objective evaluation methods were combined to obtain the final results: the recommended size range of round corner touch button was 11 ~ 19 mm and that of round touch buttons was 13 ~ 19 mm. At the same time, the input performance and user experience satisfaction of round corner touch buttons were higher than round touch buttons. These results could be referred for the design of touch screen button size of electronic products which need to be operated in a standing state, so as to avoid the complicated interface caused by unreasonable button size design, and ensure the simplicity and efficiency of interface design. On the other hand, the research on touch buttons with different shapes was more accurate and comprehensive.

5 Conclusion

By exploring the influence of two button features (shape and size) on the input performance and preference of touch screen, a new opinion for the design of touch screen button is provided. The experiment results showed that the size and shape of the buttons had different effects on the input performance of the touch screen. User preference affected the design of the deeper layer of button operation and directly affected the user's satisfaction with the button design. In the future research, we should consider a variety of button design factors and user subjective perception to explore the optimization of touch screen button design scheme.

Acknowledgments. This research was supported by 2017NQI project (2017YFF0206603), General Administration of Quality Supervision, Inspection and Quarantine of the People's Republic of China (AQSIQ) science and technology planning project (2016QK177) and Project of the President's Fund for China National Institute of Standardization (522018Y-5984; 522016Y-4488).

References

1. Park, Y., Han, S.: Touch key design for one-handed thumb interaction with a mobile phone: effects of touch key size and touch key location. Int. J. Ind. Ergon. **40**(1), 68–76 (2010)
2. Jung, E., Im, Y.: Touchable area: an empirical study on design approach considering perception size and touch input behavior. Int. J. Ind. Ergon. **49**(1), 21–30 (2015)
3. Colle, H.A., Hiszem, K.J.: Standing at a kiosk: effects of key size and spacing on touch screen numeric keypad performance and user preference. Ergonomics **47**(13), 1406–1423 (2004)
4. Conradi, J., Busch, O., Alexander, T.: Optimal touch button size for the use of mobile devices while walking. Procedia Manufact. **3**(1), 387–394 (2015)
5. Hwangbo, H., Yoon, S.H., Jin, B.S.: A study of pointing performance of elderly users on smartphones. Int. J. Hum.-Comput. Interact. **29**(9), 604–618 (2013)
6. Jin, Z., Plocher, T., Kiff, L.: Touch screen user interfaces for older adults: button size and spacing. In: Conference on Universal Access in Human-Computer Interaction, pp. 933–941. Springer, Heidelberg (2004)
7. Wenlin, Z.: Effects of button and gap sizes on task accuracy for keyboard of touch sensitive mobile phone. Institute of Design, National Taiwan University of Science and Technology, Taiwan (2011)
8. Greiner, T.: Hand Anthropometry of U.S. Army Personnel. U. S. Army Report NATICK/TR-92 011. U. S. Army Natick, Research, Development and Engineering Center, Natick, Massachusetts (1991)
9. Telecommunications Industry Association. Resource Guide for Accessible Design of Consumer Electronics. Electronic Industries Association and the Electronic Industries Foundation, Washington D.C. (1996)
10. Bing, H.: Touch screen technology and its application. Chem. Ind. **32**(5), 175–176 (2008)
11. S3C2440A Chinese Handbook (Ma Zhijing's translation) (2007)
12. Chen, K., Savage, A., Chourasia, A.: Touch screen performance by individuals with and without motor control disabilities. Appl. Ergon. **44**(2), 297–302 (2013)
13. Chourasia, A., Wiegmann, D., Chen, K.: Effect of sitting or standing on touch screen performance and touch characteristics. Hum. Factors **55**(4), 789–802 (2013)
14. Jin, Z.X., Plocher, T., Kiff, L.: Touch screen user interfaces for older adults: button size and spacing. In: Stephanidis, C. (ed.) UAHCI 2007. LNCS, vol. 4554, pp. 933–941. Springer, Heidelberg (2007). https://doi.org/10.1007/978-3-540-73279-2_104
15. Kim, H., Kwon, S., Heo, J.: The effect of touch-key size on the usability of in-vehicle information systems and driving safety during simulated driving. Appl. Erogon. **45**(3), 379–388 (2014)

The Effect of Progress Indicator Speeds on Users' Time Perceptions and Experience of a Smartphone User Interface

Shasha Li(✉) and Chien-Hsiung Chen

Department of Design, National Taiwan University of Science and Technology, Taipei, Taiwan
shashali479@gmail.com, cchen@mail.ntust.edu.tw

Abstract. The primary goal of this study focused on manipulating the speed of the progress indicator to decrease users' time perception and improve satisfaction with and personal preference for a smartphone user interface. The experiment of this study adopted a 3×2 mixed factorial design using ANOVA to examine the three progress indicator speeds, i.e., normal, slow to fast and fast to slow, and two wait durations, 5 s and 15 s, using different progress indicators. The results show that speed has no significant effect on time perception. However, a more complex feedback type may increase participants' time perception, especially for a long wait duration (i.e., 15 s). The speed of "fast to slow" can make participants more satisfied than the speed "slow to fast," just in the case of the bar indicator. Participants were more satisfied with 5 s than 15 s. Finally, there was a positive impact on the participants' preferences when they perceived a shorter wait duration.

Keywords: Progress indicator speed · Time perception · Smartphone application · User interface · User experience

1 Introduction

In recent years, the habit of watching videos on a smartphone has become a popular activity in peoples' daily life. This means that the interface needs to be further improved in terms of user experience for better usage. However, the wait state on smartphone interfaces is unavoidable, especially when using interactive applications to access media videos. Numerous researchers have found that users' experience may be negative when facing the interface wait.

Facing the waiting problem, the original solution was to keep the user informed of the application wait state to alleviate the user's negative experiences. However, modern users require a more intelligent and interesting way to deal with their experience. Hornik (1984) indicated that individuals have a tendency to overestimate wait duration. Therefore, waiting is a problem that is difficult to solve on the user interface. Although some studies have investigated the function of different progress behaviors on website user interfaces, the specific visual progress indicator applied to the smartphone interface needs further study.

M. Kurosu (Ed.): HCII 2019, LNCS 11567, pp. 28–36, 2019.
https://doi.org/10.1007/978-3-030-22643-5_3

Nielsen (2010) indicated that even a few seconds' waits is enough to create an unpleasant user experience. Thus, it is especially important to design appropriate indicators to deliver the negative influence for smartphone applications. A good indicator behavior should relieve the users' negativity experience of the user-smartphone interaction (i.e., reduce time perception and improve satisfaction). The relationship between the speed of the visual progress indicator and time perception has been found. Some studies have revealed that different progress bar behaviors appear to have a significant effect on users' perception of wait duration for website interfaces (Enomoto et al. 2006; Harrison et al. 2007; Branaghan and Sanchez 2009; Harrison et al. 2010). Kum et al.'s (2008) results showed that the duration estimates were influenced by the user's time paradigm and the variable speed with which time passage is perceived. However, there are still uncertain results in the early literature on the speed of progress indicators. Conrad et al. (2010) indicated that if the early feedback indicated slow progress, the user's subjective experience would be more negative than if the early feedback indicated faster progress. The "fast-to-slow" indicators reduced drop-off rates because they provide the encouragement users need (Villar et al. 2013; Kim et al. 2017). In contrast, Harrison et al. (2007) suggested that users are most willing to tolerate negative progress behavior, i.e., stalls and inconsistent progress, at the beginning of an operation. Participants prefer a linear moving progress bar and will judge that the process duration is shorter (Branaghan and Sanchez 2009; Amer and Johnson 2016). Therefore, this study aimed to investigate how the speed of visual progress indicators and wait durations affected users' wait time perceptions and user experience focusing on smartphone interface design.

2 Method

2.1 Participants

The purposive sampling procedure was used in this study. A total of 96 participants were invited to participate in our study (69 females, 27 males). They ranged in age from 16–39 years. The majority of participants were students (72%) and the others were office workers (28%). Almost all of the participants had experience of using smartphones to watch videos, with 41% watching for less than 30 min every day, 27% spending an average of 31–60 min, and 31% more than 1 h.

2.2 Apparatus and Prototype

The experimental design in this study adopted the "Illustrator" software for graphic design, then used the "Flash" software to produce the "progress indicator" gif animation, and finally used "Proto.io" to make the application (app) prototype. The progress indicators are shown in Fig. 1. The prototype is a smartphone app developed to simulate an online video. The target users are young people. We used IOS (Ipone7 plus) version 1.3.3 installed on a smartphone with a 5.5-in. screen. In all, 24 versions of the app prototype were created for the experiment. The progress indicator speeds were normal, slow to fast, and fast to slow.

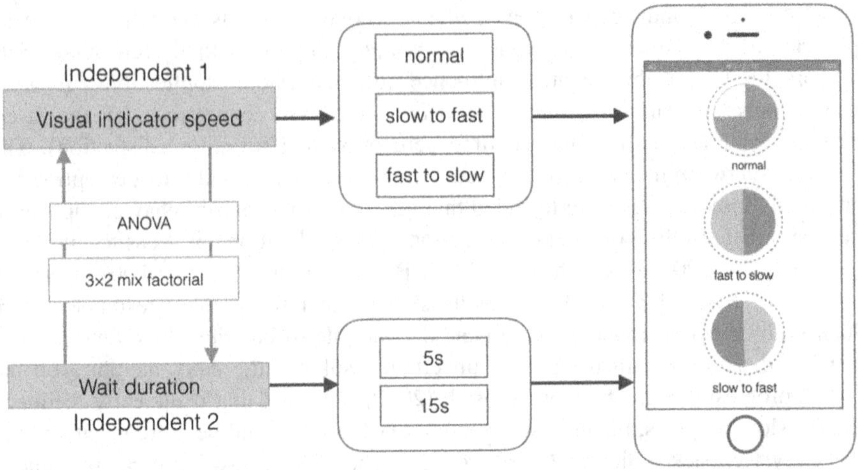

Fig. 1. The progress indicator speeds (normal, slow to fast, and fast to slow). The variable speed of visual types starts from the middle (e.g., Round-cake, 5 s wait duration). The wait durations (5 s and 15 s).

2.3 Design

The research approach included the gathering of quantitative and qualitative data from the experiment. A total of 96 (69 females, 27 males) participants were invited to participate in this study. The study employed a mixed factorial design (3×2), whereby each participant experienced three visual indicator speeds, i.e., normal speed, fast to slow ("fast-first-then-slow"), and slow to fast ("slow-first-then-fast"), and two wait durations, i.e., 5 s and 15 s. A total of six experiments were conducted. In the normal speed design, the progress shown is constant to the wait durations. In the "fast to slow" case, the speed of the progress goes from fast to slow across the screen, moving fast during the first half of the progress and slowing down in the second half. The "slow to fast" indicator is just the opposite: the progress is slow during the first half of the progress and speeds up in the second half. Presentation order was randomized for each participant on the smartphone screen. In this study, we used verbal estimation to judge the perceived wait duration. The research model is shown in Fig. 2.

2.4 Procedure

The research approach combined the gathering of quantitative and qualitative data. Participants were tested individually in an area free from auditory and visual distractions. At the start of the exercise, participants were provided with a smartphone, and were informed that the purpose of the study was to focus on the "progress indicators." The task operations were "search for a film," "play the film," and "download the film." Then, the participants were asked to give their personal details, including name, age, profession, and experience of using video apps. After the task was completed, the participants had to estimate the wait duration using a scale ranging from 1 s to 60 s,

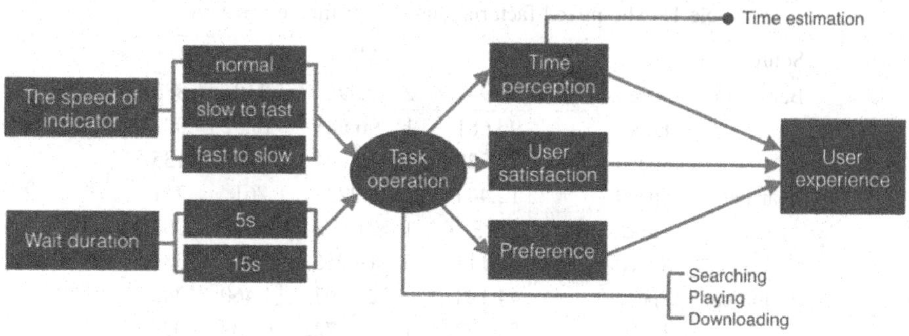

Fig. 2. An Integrative Model of this research.

and rate their satisfaction on a 7-point Likert scale (from 1 "less satisfied" to 7 "greatly satisfied"). When the participants experienced the different progress indicators, they were forced to choose which speed of the progress indicator they liked the most. Finally, we conducted a simple interview with the subjects regarding their experience. Each participant took about 20 min to conduct the face-to-face experiment.

3 Results and Discussion

In this study we conducted a mixed factorial analysis of variance (ANOVA). The wait duration was the between-participants factor, and progress indicator speed was the within-participants factor to test the different feedback types. In the analyses, we estimated the effects of the speed of the indicator on the users' perceptions, experience, and preferences, and the interaction effects between the wait duration and progress indicator speed.

3.1 The Mixed Factorial Analysis of "Time × Speed"

The results were generated from the mixed factorial ANOVA, which is related to the comparison of the two wait durations, and the comparison of the three indicator speeds.

3.2 Time Perception

Based on the results illustrated in Table 1, the main effects of the progress indicator speed showed no significant difference for all the feedback types. However, the main effects of "Wait duration" were a significant difference regarding the participant's time perception. The "bar" type was ($F_{1,22}$ = 13.323, P = .001 < .01), the "bear-bar" was ($F_{1,22}$ = 8.695, P = .007 < .01), the "round-cake" was ($F_{1,22}$ = 6.267, P = .020 < .05), and the "bear-cup" was ($F_{1,22}$ = 1.187, P = .004 < .01). The pairwise comparisons of the Wait durations for all of the feedback types showed that the participants estimated the time of 15 s as always greater than 5 s, which seems to be a common sense result.

Table 1. The mixed factorial analysis of time estimation.

Source		SS	df	MS	F	P
Bar	Speed	2.194	2	1.097	.119	.888
	Time	96.681	1	96.681	13.323	.001**
	Speed * Time	38.528	2	19.264	2.095	.135
Bear bar	Speed	12.444	2	6.222	.261	.771
	Time	2123.347	1	2123.347	8.695	.007**
	Speed * Time	38.111	2	19.056	.800	.381
Round-cake	Speed	44.194	2	22.097	1.460	.243
	Time	734.722	1	734.722	6.267	.020*
	Speed * Time	2.028	2	1.014	.985	.381
Cartoon	Speed	4.694	2	2.347	.220	.803
	Time	968.000	1	968.000	1.187	.004*
	Speed * Time	2.583	2	1.292	.121	.886

*P < .05 **P < .01

Through a more detailed discussion, the "bar" and "round-cake" types were overestimated at 5 s and underestimated at 15 s. However, the "bear-bar" and "bear-cup" types were overestimated at both 5 s and 15 s. This is an interesting result, and a possible reason is that the "bear-bar" and "bear-cup" are more complex visual presentations. The overestimation of the long Wait duration can be explained by Vierordt (1968) who stated that in unusual or stressful situations, longer durations are usually overestimated. Brown (1995) suggested that greater numbers of moving stimuli would lead to a further lengthening of perceived time if the stimuli were highly distinctive. The estimation of duration involves memory when the time duration is over 5 s (Fraisse 1984). The processing of long durations requires sustained attention and memory processes (Droit-Volet et al. 2016). Lallemand and Gronier (2012) indicated that users tend to focus on temporal signals in relatively detailed feedback, opening the attentional gate and leaving free passage to many pulses, thus lengthening the time. Therefore, the results can be explained by some theories, and it is easy to increase the time perception of the participants when presenting a more complex visual presentation, especially for shorter wait times (i.e., 5 s).

3.3 The Degree of Satisfaction

Based on the mixed ANOVA results shown in Table 2, for the "bar" type, the main effect of the progress indicator speed showed a significant difference ($F_{2,44} = 3.348$, $P = .044 < .01$). The Post Hoc test showed that the progress indicator speeds of "fast to slow" ($M = 4.04$, $SD = 1.23$) and "slow to fast" ($M = 3.37$, $SD = 1.31$) showed a significant difference ($P = .026 < .05$). Obviously, the participants were satisfied with "fast to slow" and were not satisfied with "slow to fast."

For the "Bear bar" type, the main effect of wait duration showed a significant difference ($F_{1,22} = 7.579$, $P = .012 < .05$). It demonstrated that participants were more satisfied with 5 s ($M = 5.22$), and slightly satisfied with 15 s ($M = 4.19$).

Table 2. The two factors ANOVA factorial analysis of satisfaction.

Source		SS	df	MS	F	P	POST-HOC(LSD)
Bar	Speed	5.444	2	2.722	3.348	.044*	Fast to slow > slow to fast
	Time	8.681	1	8.681	2.492	.129	
	Speed * Time	1.444	2	.722	.888	.419	
	Speed	1.083	2	.542	.378	.687	
Bear bar	Time	8.681	1	19.014	7.579	.012*	5 s > 15 s
	Speed * Time	2.528	2	1.264	.882	.421	
	Speed	.083	2	.042	.064	.938	
Round-cake	Time	33.347	1	33.347	7.497	.012*	5 s > 15 s
	Speed * Time	1.861	2	.931	1.426	.251	
	Speed	.657	2	.328	.749	.487	
Bear-cup	Time	2.731	1	2.731	1.585	.240	
	Speed * Time	3.687	2	1.843	4.206	.032*	

*P < .05 **P < .01

For the "round-cake" type, the main effect of wait duration showed a significant difference ($F_{1,22} = 7.497$, $P = .012 < .05$). It demonstrated that the participants were more satisfied with 5 s (M = 5.22), and not satisfied with 15 s (M = 3.86).

For the "bear-cup" type, the interaction effect between the progress indicator speed and Wait duration showed a significant difference ($F = 4.206$, $P = .032 < .05$).

As described in the caption in Fig. 3, the analysis shows that the participants were more satisfied with 15 s and less satisfied with 5 s for "slow to fast." In contrast, the participants were more satisfied with 5 s and less satisfied with 15 s for "normal" and "fast to slow."

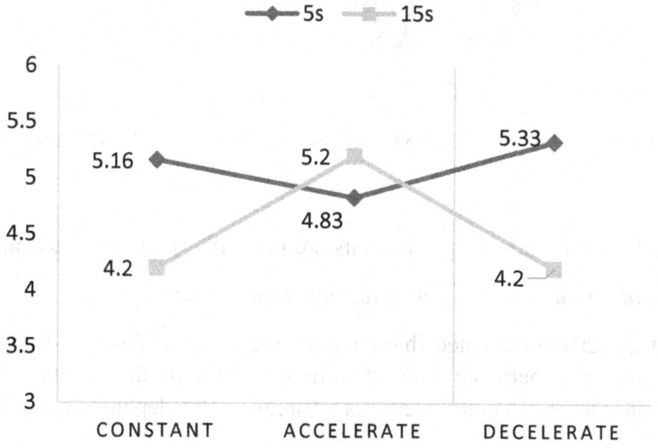

Fig. 3. Interaction effects of Speed × Time for the "bear-cup" type. Note: The vertical axis reflects the score, where higher scores on this measure indicate that time was more "satisfactory." The horizontal axis represents the progress indicator speed.

The data above reveal that no matter for which feedback type, the participants were satisfied with "fast to slow" and were not satisfied with "normal" or "slow to fast." In addition, they were more satisfied with the wait duration of 5 s and less satisfied with the wait duration of 15 s. This is consistent with Hoxmeier and DiCesare (2000), who indicated that satisfaction decreases as response time increases, and there appears to be a level of intolerance in the 12 s response range.

3.4 Individual Preference

The mean average of preference is shown in Fig. 4. Overall, 29% of the participants preferred "normal," 28% preferred "slow to fast," and 39% preferred "fast to slow." The results indicated that the participants preferred the Speed of "fast to slow" compared to "slow to fast" and "normal." An explanation for this result from the analysis of the qualitative interview data is that: (1) progressing fast at first gives a better first impression and anticipation that the loading will finish soon, and (2) becoming slow at the end is acceptable because loading is almost finished. These results were consistent with the work by Kim et al. (Kim et al. 2017).

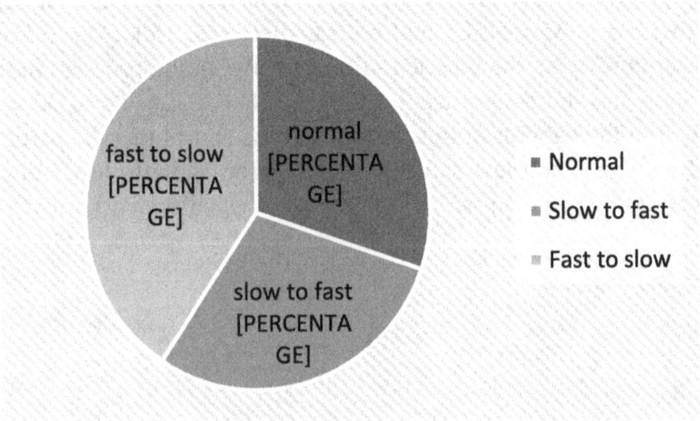

Fig. 4. The preference of feedback types (The fraction represents the percentage and the range is 0–60).

Additionally, we found that participants are more likely to fast speed at beginning:

'if the initial speed was slow, they did not want to wait'.

Conrad et al. (2010) indicated that encouraging early feedback led respondents to perceive the whole experience more favorably. Through the results of the mean analysis and interviews, we concluded that preference also depends on the individual's characteristics.

4 Conclusions

In this paper, we have several implications about the visual speeds indicator and wait duration impacts for several indicator types on the smartphone user interface. The present research concludes with several design guides which can be applied to smartphone applications that employ visual indicators to contribute to a faster perception, greater satisfaction, and user preference. The results of our study are summarized as follows:

1. The different speeds of the visual indicator did not significantly reduce the participants' perceived time for any of the wait durations. Thus, smartphone application designers should not consider that the visual indicator speed will reduce perceived time.
2. It should be noted that the wait duration of 15 s was not always underestimated. More complex visual patterns may increase participants' time perception for relatively long wait durations.
3. The visual indicator speed of "fast to slow" can help participants perceive a shorter wait duration than "slow to fast."
4. The participant's satisfaction could be possibly improved as the wait duration decreases. Participants were more satisfied with 5 s than with 15 s.
5. Most of the participants preferred the speed of "fast to slow" to "normal" and "slow to fast." From the interviews, we noted that user's preference was also dependent on the individual's characteristics.

The speed of visual feedback experienced on a smartphone wait interface can have interesting theoretical implications and important commercial consequences. Designers can contribute to progress indicators to either reduce users' wait duration or improve the user experience.

5 Limitation and Future Work

The factors that may influence the perception of Wait duration deserve mention: the block area size of the progress indicator, the participant's level of interest in the video contents, the screen background color, and the gender difference, with women providing longer duration estimates than men (Block et al. 2000; Yarmey 1993). In our study, the number of women are more than that of men. Users may have different levels of perception and cognition. Finally, our study focuses on a no percent-done progress indicator design.

The future research might expand the feedback types and speed behaviors, the amount of feedback information, and at least several levels of duration in an attempt to manipulate the users' time perception, experience, and preference.

References

Amer, T.S., Johnson, T.L.: Information technology progress indicators: temporal expectancy, user preference, and the perception of process duration. Int. J. Technol. Human Interact. **12** (4), 1–14 (2016)

Brown, S.W.: Time, change, and motion: the effects of stimulus movement on temporal perception. Percept. Psychophys. **57**(1), 105–116 (1995)

Branaghan, R.J., Sanchez, C.A.: Feedback preferences and impressions of wait. Int. J. Hum Comput Stud. **67**, 475–481 (2009)

Conrad, F.G., Couper, M.P., Tourangeau, R., Peytchev, A.: The impact of progress indicators on task completion. Interact. Comput. **22**(5), 417–427 (2010)

Droit-Volet, S., Trahanias, P., Maniadakis, M.: Passage of time judgments in everyday life are not related to duration. Acta Physiol. (Oxf) **173**, 116–121 (2016)

Enomoto, T., Ohnishi, K., Yoshida, K.: A study on the relationship between progress bar movement and subjective speed impression. In: Proceedings of the 8th Annual Conference of Japan Society for Fuzzy Theory and Intelligent Informatics, Kyushu Chapter, pp. 37–40 (2006)

Fraisse, P.: Perception and estimation of time. Annu. Rev. Psychol. **35**(1), 1–37 (1984)

Harrison, C., Yeo, Z., Hudson, S.E.: Faster progress bars: manipulating perceived duration with visual augmentations. In: Proceedings of the SIGCHI Conference on Human Factors in Computing Systems, Paris, pp. 1545–1548 (2010)

Harrison, C., Amento, B., Kuznetsov, S., Bell, R.: Rethinking the progress bar. In: Proceedings of the 20th Annual ACM Symposium on User Interface Software and Technology, Newport, RI, pp. 115–118 (2007)

Hornik, J.: Subjective vs. objective time measures: a note on the perception of time in consumer behavior. J. Consum. Res. **11**(1), 615–618 (1984)

Hoxmeier, J.A., DiCesare, C.: System response time and user satisfaction: an experimental study of browser-based applications. In: AMCIS 2000 Proceedings, p. 347 (2000)

Kum, D., Lee, Y.H., Yeung, C.: The speed of time: primacy and recency effects on time perception. The speed of time: primacy and recency effects on time perception. In: Angela, Y. L., Soman, D., Duluth, M.N. (eds.) NA - Advances in Consumer Research, vol. 35, p. 943. Association for Consumer Research (2008)

Kim, W., Xiong, S., Liang, Z.: Effect of loading symbol of online video on perception of waiting time. Int. J. Hum.-Comput. Interact. **12**(33), 1001–1009 (2017)

Lallemand, C., Gronier, G.: Enhancing user experience during waiting time in HCI: contributions of cognitive psychology. In: Proceedings of the Designing Interactive Systems Conference, pp. 751–760. ACM, June 2012

Nielsen, J.: Website response times. Nielsen Norman Group, 21(06) (2010)

Ornstein, R.E.: On the Experience of Time. Penguin, Hammandsworth (1969)

Villar, A., Callegaro, M., Yang, Y.: Where am I? A meta-analysis of experiments on the effects of progress indicators for web surveys. Soc. Sci. Comput. Rev. **31**(6), 744–762 (2013)

Vierordt, K.: Der zeitsinn nach versuchen. Laupp, Tübingen (1868)

Mobile Phone-Based Device for Personalised Tutorials of 3D Printer Assembly

Xiangdong Li[1(✉)], Wenqian Chen[1], Yunzhan Zhou[1], Surabhi Athalye[2], Wai Kit Daniel Chin[2], Russell Goh Wei Kit[2], Vincent Setiawan[2], and Preben Hansen[3]

[1] Department of Design, Zhejiang University, Hangzhou 310027, People's Republic of China
{axli, 21821005, billyzyz}@zju.edu.cn

[2] Singapore University of Technology and Design, 8 Somapha Road, Singapore 487372, Singapore
{surabhi_athalye, daniel_chin, russell_goh, setiawan_vincent}@mymail.sutd.edu.sg

[3] Department of Computer System and Science, Stockholm University, Kista, Sweden
preben@dsv.su.se

Abstract. There are a number of studies exploring materials and mechanisms of 3D printers that can help product designers develop and evaluate interactive systems efficiently. As 3D printers are increasingly adopted, designers are more likely to encounter difficulties in assembling 3D printers on their own, as the assembly process involves specialised skills and knowledge of fitting components in right positions. Conventional solutions use text and video manuals but still requires high understandings of the assembly. We designed and evaluated the mobile phone-based device for personalised tutorials of 3D printer assembly. The device consists of a modified dongle and mobile phone application. The former detects electromagnetic signals upon physical contacts with the components and the latter displays tutorials accordingly. The contributions include the device design with electromagnetic signal-based object detection and importantly, the approach to integrating component touching with component detection for personalised interactions. Generalising implications for the approach are discussed.

Keywords: Mobile phone · 3D printer assembly · Personalised tutorial · Electromagnetic object detect

1 Introduction

Desktop 3D printers have been widely adopted in design studios, research laboratories, and teaching classes. With different printer mechanisms e.g., jet printing and laser sintering, and materials e.g., plastic and metal, 3D printers can accelerate conventional prototype process and support iterative design and evaluation. Importantly, 3D printers provide amateur designers easy access to making and testing ideas in a flexible and low-cost manner [1]. Occupational product designers and engineers are familiar with

M. Kurosu (Ed.): HCII 2019, LNCS 11567, pp. 37–48, 2019.
https://doi.org/10.1007/978-3-030-22643-5_4

3D printing functions, as the concept is basically derived from the conventional ink-based printing. When 3D printers are increasingly emerging, designers are having increasing opportunities of assembling 3D printers on their own, which are more likely to cause difficulties to most product designers, especially to the amateur. Designers will have to deal with numerous components with insufficient instructions. As such, the assembly becomes a process that can only be well handled with good knowledge of mechanisms and engineering, which are essential to identify components and fit each piece into right positions in specific sequences [2].

To enhance the use of assembly for both professional and amateur product designers, conventional approaches use paper and electronic manuals that explain the key assembly steps. Other approaches include short videos and virtual reality (and augmented reality) demonstration. Especially, mobile phones are frequently used as a general-purpose platform of assembly tutorials e.g., mobile phone-based tutorials for complicated energy management system configurations [2] and mobile phone camera scanning QR codes to track components to assembly [3]. As so, designers can learn how to assemble a 3D printer at any time and from anywhere [4, 5]. In addition, mobile phones can integrate attachments such as external sensors and widgets to augment functions and interaction experience [6]. Despite known benefits, mobile phone camera scanning is an interruptive approach, as which must stop ongoing tasks to proceed with the scanning and assembly tutorials [7].

Given the inevitable physical contact with the target components in assembly, we are inspired to implement a mobile phone-based device. The device integrates electromagnetic signal-based object detection technique to detect foreign objects upon physical contact with the 3D printer components and there is a dedicated mobile phone application accordingly displays text and animation tutorials of current component. The device and application together underwent usability evaluation. The paper's main contributions include: (a) the design of the mobile phone-based device that can detect components upon physical touch; (b) the approach that integrates the object recognition process into essential assembling operations. Taking together, we propose the system for personalised tutorials of 3D printer assembly for both professional and amateur designers.

2 Related Work

2.1 Personalised Tutorials for 3D Printer Assembly

3D printers have the potential to enable iterative prototyping and evaluation on an individual basis [8] and are easy to use with no need of extra training. However, it is a contrast that most designers, including the experienced and amateur ones, are likely to encounter technical and cognitive difficulties when assembling a 3D printer. Due to the growing numbers and types of 3D printers, the conventional paper and electronic instructions appear to be insufficient in catering individual designers' needs for assembly.

Recently, researchers have developed more accessible manuals by taking advantage of mobile phone and related sensors e.g. integrated camera. Users can scan QR codes that are enclosed in the components to gain relevant instructions, or they can take a picture of target components and search for related information. RFID is adopted to mark up and recognise components [9]. These approaches help designers understand (and manage) the components but may disrupt the current assembly process [10]. Take mobile phone camera scanning for example, user will have to stop current assembling activities, start the camera for related tutorials, and resume the previous task. The disruption impairs the overall naturalness of assembly procedures and results in unnecessary distractions and inefficiency. Furthermore, it raises a higher bar for personalised learning due to the requirements for user's experience beforehand [11]. Handheld objects recognition such as [12] provide a useful example of integrating object detection with user's objects seeing, which achieved greater naturalness.

The technical development and applications of 3D printers are spread in diverse domains, and technology-enhanced learning [13] and personalisation optimisation [14] are involved in the context of online education and distance learning. But in overall, little is concerned about how to design and deliver personalised tutorials to support 3D printer assembly and more assembly-specialised results are expected.

2.2 Electromagnetic Signal-Based Object Detection

To achieve natural object detection, researchers have presented many techniques and one of recent works is electromagnetic signal-based object detection, which utilises electromagnetic (EM) signals to detect the target object upon physical contact [15, 16]. EM detection has advantages over other object detection techniques, as it is markerless, mobile phone inhabitable, and spontaneously integrated with object touch [17].

Electronic devices produces significant levels of electromagnetic (EM) emissions due to circuitry operations [15]. Given the governmental regulations e.g. FCC' mandatory standards at the devices' electromagnetic noises, these unintentional emissions can be received and transformed into electromagnetic signals, albeit the initial signals are interweaved with background noises. A few categories of non-electronic objects such as metallic objects also have unique electromagnetic signatures [18]. This shows possibility of detecting mundane objects by simple touching.

To read the EM emissions and extract particular patterns out of the signals, device-mediated sensing and body-communication are used [19]. The former instruments devices such as electronic wires and the latter instruments the user through conductive body which acts as an antenna. For example, the device-mediated sensing used to be designed in an instrument that requires direct touch with the target object, as in [17]. In contrast, the body-communication sensing reads EM signals through human body upon physical contact with the object, as in [15, 18]. Clearly, the body-communication sensing has advantages in dual-hand interaction tasks, but it also influences the detected EM signals. Figure 1 shows the respective EM signal spectrums of objects being scanned with different methods.

Extracting unique EM signal patterns out of the noises includes several steps. Firstly, building an EM signal scanner hardware. Basic RFID reader and low cost open-source software defined radio (SDR) modules with minor circuitry modifications were adopted to read low frequency EM signals [18]. Secondly, visualising the EM signal spectrum, as shown in Fig. 1. Thirdly, extracting EM signal patterns. This consists of

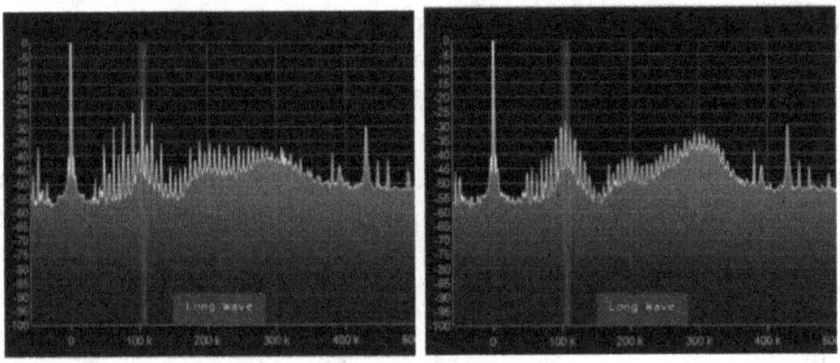

Fig. 1. Electromagnetic spectrums of two electromagnetic signal detection methods with the same object (left: device-mediated sensing, right: body-communication sensing)

two processes: setup a baseline threshold to filter off the unwanted signals, and then employing statistical analysis of the EM signal profiles. Similar details of this process can refer to [18]. Finally, categorising EM patterns according to object types. The extracted patterns are used as input for object classification. That is, each unique pattern is assigned to a specific object. Once the above processes are completed, the objects' EM patterns are parsed and preserved in a database, which can be used for later object detection. The hardware and process algorithms, which were partially implemented and tested in our previous works in [20], were evaluated in multiple studies with reliable and robust performance [17].

2.3 Mobile Phones for Personalised Tutorials

Mobile phones are an ideal platform for personalised tutorials, as mobile phones are a ubiquitous personal device and compatible with external devices such as the electromagnetic sensors. There are a huge number of mobile phones in the use and a large portion of these are for personal learning, including for language learning tutorials [21] and distant courses [22]. Due to the mobility and other features accumulated through successive generations of development e.g. camera and gyroscope, mobile phones have promoted designers and researchers to take a pedagogical view towards supporting tutorial applications in versatile scenarios such as 3D printer assembly and system setup [1]. The existing studies put a strong emphasis on mobile phone-based system design as well as system effectiveness [22].

Mobile phones have become an effective tutorial tool and are increasingly incorporating object recognition capabilities, e.g. EM signal detection, to build tangible systems [23]. Mobile phone-inhabited object recognition systems open a wide range of applications and novel interaction forms, despite the forms of mundane objects. For example, mobile phones support augmented virtual assembly of architectures [24].

Object recognition and other mobile phone sensing e.g. location-aware allow non-language learning and enhance user's perception of the relationships between the physical objects and spaces [25]. Especially, optical scanning attachments can be coupled with the mobile phones and provide intuitive and efficient interaction. In this regard, previous studies successfully designed electromagnetic interference systems, Emi-spy, to support proxemic interaction [16].

3 Method

The preceding reviews raise two main requirements for personalised tutorials for a 3D printer assembling, including (a) accurate object detection that needs to be naturally and seamlessly integrated in essential assembling operations, and (b) natural interaction that needs to support user's personalised access to the components without early experience requirements. To meet these requirements, we prototyped a mobile phone-inhabited two-part system. This section describes the details.

3.1 System Design

The device consists of two main parts, the hardware dongle that connects to the hosting mobile phone for electromagnetic signal capture (Fig. 2) and the software application that detects incoming signals and displays corresponding tutorials of component. The dongle only harvests electromagnetic signals, as the application subsequently interprets components with different signal patterns and displays component tutorials that are prepared beforehand.

Fig. 2. The original receiver and inner circuit board (left), the modified receiver embedded in the case (mid), and the final attachment coupled with a mobile phone (right)

Hardware Dongle

As a device for personal use, it needs to be compact and low energy consuming. We chose a low-cost RTL2832U USB software defined radio receiver as the detector of electromagnetic signals (Fig. 2, top). Two capacitors on the circuit board were removed and replaced with a wideband transformer in the original receiver, so to be able to detect low band electromagnetic signals. The modification re-adjusted the receiver's signal detecting range to 1 Hz to the in-board oscillator's highest frequencies of 28.8 MHz. Technical details of the modification can refer to previous studies e.g. [15, 18].

We removed the original receiver's outer case and embedded the inter circuit board in a 3D printed dongle (Fig. 2, mid). The receiver's full-sized USB interface was modified to a smaller USB-C interface, so it can directly connect to the mobile phone. To support electromagnetic signal conduction, the receiver's antenna was welded to a large piece of copper foil (Fig. 2, bottom). As such, the dongle can detect signals upon direct physical contact with the objects, alternatively it can capture signals when a user holds the antenna in one hand and touches target objects with the other, which supports the signals to travel through conductive human body.

Object Signal Process

The signals captured by the dongle were processed as follows. The signals were trimmed to 0 Hz–1 MHz by shifting the symmetric bypass window. Then, the signals went through a fast Fourier Transform for frequency domain values. In this step, the background noises that were sampled from the last 5 s were subtracted from the raw signals. In Fig. 3, we show an example of two signal spectrums of 3D printer components, indicating that the results are replicated and reliable in different environments.

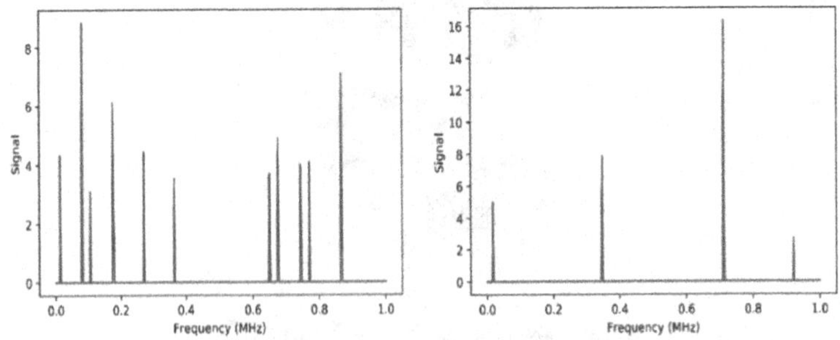

Fig. 3. The shifted signals of two different components

The signal patterns consist of two main features, the amplitudes (as the peaks in Fig. 3) and frequencies (as the positions of the frequency in Fig. 3). The patterns are stored in a local relational database. Before inserting a new signal pattern into the database, we compared the detected signal patterns with the existing ones by using rudimentary mathematical techniques, one of them being the least squares method. Unknown signal patterns were passed through various levels before the outcome was given. The sum of the square of errors between unknown signal peaks and the catalogued ones were computed and the entries that provided errors larger than an acceptable error limit (which was set and calibrated beforehand) were directly rejected. Another level with the algorithm checked if the error between majority of the peak values was within a limit (which was more fine-tuned than the earlier mentioned one). All the elementary signal processing and identification were implemented using Python.

Signal Pattern Sampling

We took samples of electromagnetic signal patterns from 16 different components of a 3D printer (model: MakerBot Replicator 2) and recorded these samples in the local database. In addition, we extracted electromagnetic signal patterns from another 12 components of laptops and desktop monitors and saved the results in the database.

The signal patterns in the database were assessed in three different environments (3D printing laboratory, meeting room, and office), so to ensure the reliability and validity of these patterns. We tested all signal patterns in another locations (corridor hall, coffee bar, and modelling laboratory) and achieved 97.6% (82 out of 84) detection accuracy.

Application and User Interfaces

We designed an Android mobile phone application to process signals and display text and amination tutorials (Fig. 4a). In addition to the tutorials for the overall 3D printer (Fig. 4b), each component in the database also had a dedicated tutorial page (Fig. 4c). In addition, the application included a search page that provided extensive learning contents of 3D printing (Fig. 4d).

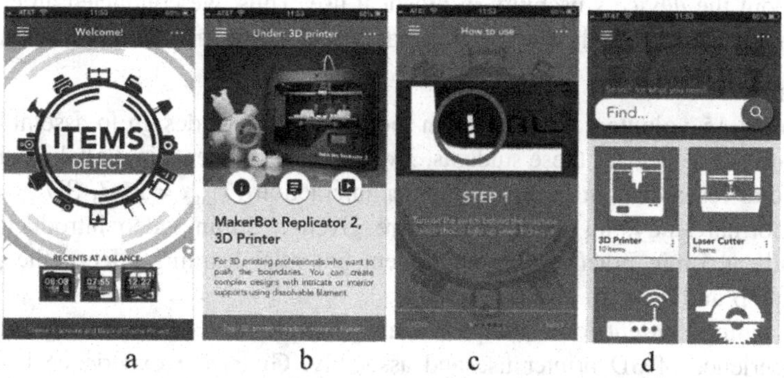

Fig. 4. Mobile phone application tutorial pages (a: splash page with recent detected tutorials on the bottom, b: overall 3D printer tutorial page, c: detailed tutorial page of a component, d: search page for extensive learning)

The application included two parallelly running threads. The detection thread monitored any incoming electromagnetic signal streams and detected the components. In the case of no matching results, the application displayed the search page, otherwise displaying tutorials of the component.

We illustrate a scenario of procedural device use in Fig. 5. Firstly, the user attached the dongle to mobile phone and launched the application that automatically initialised the electromagnetic signal receiver and the local database. Secondly, the user touched the copper foil antenna of the dongle while holding the mobile phone and device in the one hand. This ensures quality transmission of electromagnetic signals when the other hand had physical contact with components (see Fig. 5 the blue dashed line that indicates signal flows).

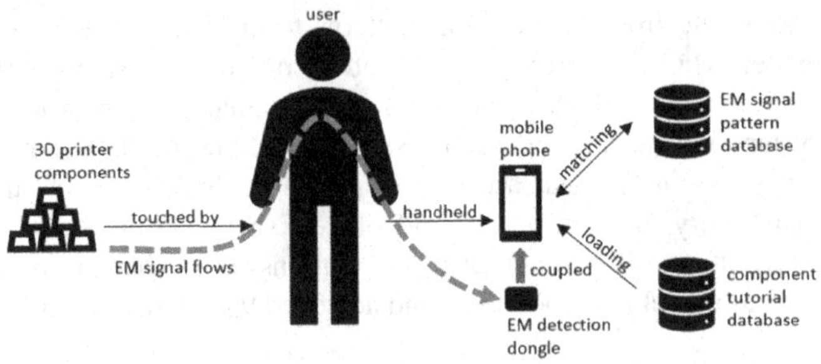

Fig. 5. Procedural flows of electromagnetic signal detection and processing in personalised tutorial delivery process (Color figure online)

3.2 System Evaluation

The device, both the dongle and application, was strictly engineered and tested in multiple locations and scenarios. Despite high accuracy in signal sampling, little is known about the device's usability in practical use. Thus, we conducted an empirical study to understand how the device affected student designers' 3D printer assembly.

Participants
We recruited 15 volunteer students from the department of design to assembly a 3D printer with the device. Of these students, 3 were Master students in digital media and 1 was doctoral researcher in human-computer interaction ($M_{age} = 21.7$, $SD_{age} = 0.61$). Prior to formal study, all participants were given a 2 min video introduction and sequentially a 5 min practice. To circumvent potential learning effects, the practice used a laptop and a 24 in. desktop monitor.

After signing consent form, the participants completed a self-report regarding previous experience of 3D printer use and assembly. Given the experience levels, the participants were divided into two groups. 11 participants with little experience were in group A and the other 4 participants were in group B. Group A used system usability scales as it was an intuitive approach to quantitatively measuring usability [26]. In contrast, group B adopted heuristic evaluation by following Neilson's heuristic process because it allowed the participants to flexibly explore the usability [27].

Procedures
For group A. The task was to use the device to assemble the 3D printer that was previously used for signal sampling. There were 20 components in total to assemble, 16 of these were prepared in the database and the other 4 were not. The task lasted 30 min,

regardless of completeness. After the task, the participants were required to fulfil the 5-Likert usability questionnaires.

For group B. The experimental settings and task procedures were the same as group A's. After the task, the participants needed to rate the device against a sheet of heuristics.

Results
The results of the device's usability were quantitative and qualitative. Despite relatively small sample sizes, the SUS evaluation results indicated greater overall usability than average levels (standard average score is 68 and the study results were 80). In addition, the mean score of all questions was 3.8 (SD = 0.69), indicating extraordinarily positive feedbacks on the usability of the device in supporting 3D printer assemble (Fig. 6).

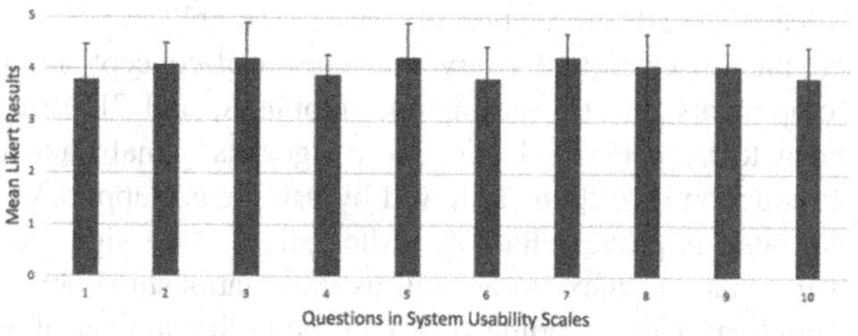

Fig. 6. Results of the ten questions in system usability scales evaluation

In group B, the participants' heuristics evaluation revealed two important factors that attributed to good usability. The compact hardware design and intuitive dongle coupling with mobile phone were useful to users and importantly, the approach to detect target components through physical contacts was of great novelty to the participants. In overall, participants in group B reported no severe usability issues but commented on a number of user interface designs e.g. font sizes.

In addition, the participants' overall efficiency was qualitatively examined. Based on the experimenter's observations on the participants' device use, the participants assembled the components quickly once they gained corresponding tutorials. Otherwise, the participants took longer time to think about which positions the current component fitted into.

4 Discussion

The novelty of the device design is the approach that integrates the process of component detection into the essential operations of 3D printer assembling. It is different from conventional personalised design methods in several perspectives.

Firstly, existing object detection systems e.g. barcode and QR code scanners may disrupt ongoing operations, which leads to a consequence of task interventions and low engagement level. Our approach takes advantage of the inevitable activities – user's hands will have to touch the components during assembling, and as a reaction, the approach implements a detection technique – electromagnetic signal detection – to merge the detection process into the core operations. It is a more natural way than the conventional ones with respect to task flows.

Secondly, the approach, as well as its implementation of the prototype system, not only has greater naturalness but also has potential benefits of higher productivity. The task performance results indicate that the participants' interactions were relatively high, as that they saved the object scanning time by following an intuitive process that was very similar to the natural 'seeing-doing' loops.

Thirdly, the approach is generalising to multiple mobile device-based applications. For example, the object detection process can be integrated with user's eye-seeing activities for those working in a parcel picking production line. Finally, on the ground of mobile learning – especially its mobility and ubiquity, the approach is also supportive to personalised tutorial delivery, as that the users can touch any interested components and learn related information of device assembly.

As mentioned, the device currently serves as a proof-of-concept and works reliably with a set of components, mostly the laptops, monitors, and 3D printers. Possible improvements need to be performed with more rigorous signal data processing by improving noise reduction algorithms followed by using e.g. Support Vector Machine (SVM). This may also improve reliability. Alternatively, the signal can be further analysed to find minima and maxima as well as the relationships between these key features such as gradient between points, etc. Increasing the number of attributes used to classify an object can only lead to greater accuracy although that may come at the expense of processing speed, since each additionally processing step would incur additional time in the overall process.

5 Conclusion

The paper presents the design of a mobile phone-inhabited system that is served to supply personalised tutorials for a 3D printer assembly. The detailed procedures, as well as the specifications of the system design, are provided. Furthermore, the study adds an empirical evaluation of the system with respect to usability which reveals potential influence on user's learning of device assembling. The results show that the system design, which integrate object detection within essential assembling operations, is very effective. Moreover, generalising implications for personalised system design for learning purposes are discussed.

Acknowledgements. The authors thank the reviewers' comments. This research was supported by the funding from Cloud-based natural interaction devices and tools (2016YFB1001304) and NSFC project (61802341).

References

1. Conner, B.P., et al.: Making sense of 3-D printing: creating a map of additive manufacturing products and services. Addit. Manuf. **1**, 64–76 (2014)

2. Vallina-Rodriguez, N., Crowcroft, J.: Energy management techniques in modern mobile handsets. IEEE Commun. Surv. Tutor. **15**(1), 179–198 (2013)
3. Liu, Y., Yang, J., Liu, M.: Recognition of QR code with mobile phones. In: Control and Decision Conference, CCDC 2008, Chinese. IEEE (2008)
4. Motiwalla, L.F.: Mobile learning: a framework and evaluation. Comput. Educ. **49**(3), 581–596 (2007)
5. Henkemans, O.A.B., et al.: Design and evaluation of a personal robot playing a self-management education game with children with diabetes type 1. Int. J. Hum Comput Stud. **106**, 63–76 (2017)
6. Le, H.V., et al.: A smartphone prototype for touch interaction on the whole device surface, pp. 1–8 (2017)
7. Jacob, S.M., Issac, B.: The mobile devices and its mobile learning usage analysis. arXiv preprint arXiv:1410.4375 (2014)
8. Ludwig, T., Boden, A., Pipek, V.: 3D printers as sociable technologies: taking appropriation infrastructures to the internet of things. ACM Trans. Comput.-Hum. Interact. **24**(2), 17 (2017)
9. Kesler, M.P., et al.: RFID tag and transponder detection in wireless energy transfer systems. Google Patents (2017)
10. Lane, N.D., et al.: A survey of mobile phone sensing. IEEE Commun. Mag. **48**(9), 140–150 (2010)
11. Norman, D.A.: The Design of Everyday Things. Basic Books, New York (2002)
12. Ren, X., Philipose, M.: Egocentric recognition of handled objects: benchmark and analysis. In IEEE Computer Society Conference on Computer Vision and Pattern Recognition Workshops, pp. 2160–7508 (2009)
13. Brinkman, W.-P., et al.: HCI for technology enhanced learning. In: Proceedings of the 22nd British HCI Group Annual Conference on People and Computers: Culture, Creativity, Interaction, vol. 2. BCS Learning & Development Ltd. (2008)
14. Jeske, D., Bagher, M., Pantidi, N.: HCI expertise needed!: personalisation and feedback optimisation in online education. In: Proceedings of the 31st British Computer Society Human Computer Interaction Conference. BCS Learning & Development Ltd. (2017)
15. Yang, C.J., Sample, A.P.: EM-comm: touch-based communication via modulated electromagnetic emissions. Proc. ACM Interact. Mob. Wearable Ubiquit. Technol. **1**(3), 118 (2017)
16. Zhao, N., et al.: EMI spy: harnessing electromagnetic interference for low-cost, rapid prototyping of proxemic interaction, pp. 1–6 (2015)
17. Yang, C., Sample, A.P.: EM-ID: tag-less identification of electrical devices via electromagnetic emissions. In: 2016 IEEE International Conference on RFID (RFID). IEEE (2016)
18. Laput, G., et al.: Em-sense: touch recognition of uninstrumented, electrical and electromechanical objects. In: Proceedings of the 28th Annual ACM Symposium on User Interface Software and Technology. ACM (2015)
19. Lam, Y., et al.: TouchCom-creating real excalibur experience with body touch communication. In: Proceedings of the 13th Annual International Conference on Mobile Systems, Applications, and Services. ACM (2015)
20. Li, X.A., Hansen, P., Lou, X., Geng, W., Peng, R.: Design and evaluation of cross-objects user interface for whiteboard interaction. In: Streitz, N., Markopoulos, P. (eds.) DAPI 2017. LNCS, vol. 10291, pp. 180–191. Springer, Cham (2017). https://doi.org/10.1007/978-3-319-58697-7_13
21. Burston, J.: Realizing the potential of mobile phone technology for language learning. IALLT J. Lang. Learn. Technol. **41**(2), 56–71 (2016)
22. Wu, W.-H., et al.: Review of trends from mobile learning studies: a meta-analysis. Comput. Educ. **59**(2), 817–827 (2012)

23. Yeo, H.-S., et al.: Workshop on object recognition for input and mobile interaction, pp. 1–5 (2017)
24. Brohm, D., et al.: Future trends of augmented reality. In: Augmented Reality for Food Marketers and Consumers, pp. 1681–1685. Wageningen Academic Publishers (2017)
25. Cates, S., Barron, D., Ruddiman, P.: MobiLearn go: mobile microlearning as an active, location-aware game. In: MobileHCI 2017, pp. 1–7. ACM, Veinnna (2017)
26. Peruri, A., Borchert, O., Cox, K., Hokanson, G., Slator, Brian M.: Using the system usability scale in a classification learning environment. In: Auer, M.E., Guralnick, D., Uhomoibhi, J. (eds.) ICL 2016. AISC, vol. 544, pp. 167–176. Springer, Cham (2017). https://doi.org/10.1007/978-3-319-50337-0_14
27. Inostroza, R., et al.: Developing SMASH: a set of SMArtphone's uSability Heuristics. Comput. Stand. Interfaces **43**, 40–52 (2016)

Micro Touch Board Specially Designed for SliT that Is the Japanese Character Input Method for Smartwatches

Toshimitsu Tanaka(✉), Koutaro Saka, Kohei Akita, and Yuji Sagawa

Department of Information Engineering, Faculty of Science and Technology, Meijo University, Shiogamaguchi 1-501, Tenpaku-ku, Nagoya 468-8502, Japan
toshitnk@meijo-u.ac.jp

Abstract. We developed a touch board to solve the problem of smartwatches that screen is hidden by the finger during character input. It is used attached to the watchband under the screen. The board is optimized for the character input method named SliT (*Slide-in and Tap method*). Advantage of SliT is that the input speed of the novice is fast and the screen occupancy rate is low. Specifically, the speed is 28.7 [CPM (Characters Per Minute)] and the rate is 26.4%.

In SliT, Japanese hiragana characters are input by combining 12 kinds of strokes and 8 tapping points. The board is designed to detect only those strokes and the taps. Eight touch sensors are arranged so as to surround the circular area placed at the center of the touch board. Between the sensors, numbers from 1 to 8 are allocated clockwise. Only when two adjacent sensors are touched at the same time, the number assigned to their boundary is entered. In stroke input, a fingertip is slid until passing through three boundaries, and three continuous numbers are entered. However, in rare cases, the last number may be lost. So, the stroke is judged from the first two numbers. The stroke recognition rate by this method is 98.7%. In tap input, users touch only one boundary. However, in a very few cases, an unnecessary number is added. In this case, the tap is judged from the first number. The tap recognition rate by this method is 99.4%.

Keywords: Micro touch board · Touch sensor · Smartwatch · Character input device · Japanese language

1 Introduction

The flick keyboard and the software QWERTY keyboard are standard methods for entering characters to smartphones. However, the smartwatch screen is too small to display the QWERTY keyboard. Although it is possible to display the flick keyboard, it occupies most of the screen, so the area for displaying entered characters is very small. In addition, the flick keyboard places more than 20 keys on a small screen. Therefore, each key is too small compared to the fingertip. As a result, the key adjacent to the target key is often unintentionally entered. This is called fat finger error [1].

In order to solve these problems, the character input method SliT (*Slide-in and Tap method*) [2] was developed. The main purpose of SliT is to reduce screen occupancy in input wait state. Its screen occupancy rate is only 26.4%, which is the lowest among

M. Kurosu (Ed.): HCII 2019, LNCS 11567, pp. 49–61, 2019.
https://doi.org/10.1007/978-3-030-22643-5_5

competitive methods. However, since it is a method of inputting characters by touching the screen, it is inevitable that the finger hides the screen during the operation. To solve this problem completely, an input device independent of the screen is necessary. Therefore, we developed a micro touch board specially designed for SliT. This board is attached to the watchband under the screen. Its touch sensors detect the strokes and taps necessary for SliT operation. This paper introduces the design and performance of the touch board.

2 Related Researches

Many devices have been developed for entering characters under mobile environment.

By using the glove type device [3] developed by Fujitsu Ltd. or the ring type device [4] such as Ring ZERO [5], it is possible to enter characters by drawing them in the air. However, since it is difficult to draw complicated characters like kanji correctly in 3D space, the input error rate is high. In addition, as the arm must be moved widely, the input speed is slow.

There is a method of using the user's hands and arms as a touch pad or a virtual keyboard. In one such method, SkinTrack [6], it is necessary to touch the naked skin with a finger wearing a ring-shaped transmitter. This is because to detect the position of the finger with high frequency current flowing on the surface of the skin. ARmKeypad [7] projects the keyboard onto user's arm using AR technology. Therefore, it is necessary to wear a see-through type HMD. In FingersT9 [8] and DigiTouch [9], it is necessary to attach one touch sensor to each node of the fingers in order to use the user's fingers as a keyboard. Finger tactile [10] also uses a finger as a keyboard, but this projects the virtual keyboard from the device attached to the user's wrist onto the hand. Haier's Asu Smartwatch [12] builds a projector in to project a virtual keyboard onto the back of the hand. With these two methods, if the angle of the wrist is not properly maintained, the shape of the projected keyboard will be distorted.

TAP [11] is a plate-shaped device to be used with five fingers. A character is selected by a combination of fingers to be tapped. Therefore, it is necessary to learn patterns assigned to each character. In Float [13], one character is selected by combination of wrist angle measured with acceleration sensor built in smart watch. In WristWhirl [14], one letter is selected by the movement of the wrist. In WrisText [15], the key of the One Line keyboard [16] is selected by the angle of the wrist measured by the sensor attached to the watch band. In every method, it is necessary to learn the wrist angle and/or the wrist motion assigned to each character.

Speech recognition technology allows the user to enter sentences by speaking them to a smartwatch. However, it is difficult to correct wrong input by voice only. In addition, there are disadvantages that the people around can listen to the utterance.

3 Character Input Method SliT

The touch board proposed in this research is optimized to the character input method SliT. The first feature of SliT is that the screen occupancy rate is low. To leave a large area for displaying sentences, the keys of the SliT are allocated on narrow area on the surrounding the screen. The second feature is that beginners will be able to enter characters in a short time. A smartwatch is usually linked to a smartphone or a tablet. In this circumstance, the smartwatch will be assumed to use to enter a few short messages, because the large screen of the smartphone or the tablet is convenient for entering long sentences. Therefore, it is designed to be able to enter characters quickly even if there are few opportunities to use. A summary of SliT is shown below.

In SliT, one Japanese hiragana character is entered by choosing a Gyou (the rows of the table of Japanese syllabary), then choosing a Dan (the columns of the table). Figure 1(a) shows the initial display of the user interface. Each of the left edge, the upper edge, and the right edge of the screen is divided into two segments, and two Gyous are assigned to each segment.

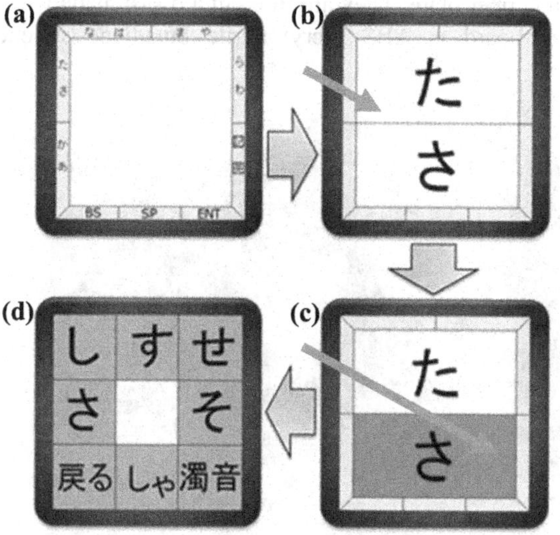

(a) This is the initial display. The yellow narrow area is the keyboard. One segment is selected with slide-in.

(b) When the finger crosses the keyboard, the screen is split and the names of Gyou assigned to the intersected segment are displayed one by one.

(c) When the finger enters either area, its background turns green. The Gyou written in the area is selected by releasing the finger.

(d) The characters belonging to the selected Gyou is displayed. One is selected by tapping.

Fig. 1. Changes in screen display of SliT during entering a hiragana character. (Color figure online)

One Gyou is selected with one slide-in. Slide-in is an operation of sliding a finger touched outside the screen toward the inside. When the slide-in passes through a segment, the screen is split into two areas as shown in Fig. 1(b). Two Gyous assigned to the intersected segment are indicated one for each area. When the finger moves into one of the areas, its background turns green as shown in Fig. 1(c). By leaving the finger from the screen, the Gyou written in the area is selected. Subsequently, as shown in

Fig. 1(d), five hiragana characters belonging to the Gyou are displayed, so one is select by tapping. It is possible to select voiced, semi-voiced, and lowercase characters by tapping the bottom right button and changing the display.

The screen share of the keyboard in Fig. 1(a) is 26.4%. It is lower than the competitive software keyboards for smartwatches such as 5-TILES [17], TouchOne Keyboard [18], and ZoomBoard [19]. In the experiment, the speed after inputting 125 characters from the beginning of use was 28.7 [CPM (Characters Per Minute)]. Since this speed is reached in 320-s usage on average, it can be said that inputs at practical speeds are possible even for short-time use. The rate of erroneous input was 4.7%.

4 Design of the Touch Board

Figure 2(a) is a design drawing of the touch board. Eight brown trapezoids from "a" to "h" are touch sensors. They are equally spaced around the circular area placed at the center of the touch board. When two adjacent sensors are touched at the same time, the number assigned between them is output. So that, it is possible to judge the finger position from the output value. Figure 2(b) is a photo of the touch board. Eight touch sensors are made by cutting a thin copper plate. They are fitted in a board made with a 3D printer. The material of the board is ABS (acrylonitrile butadiene styrene) copolymer.

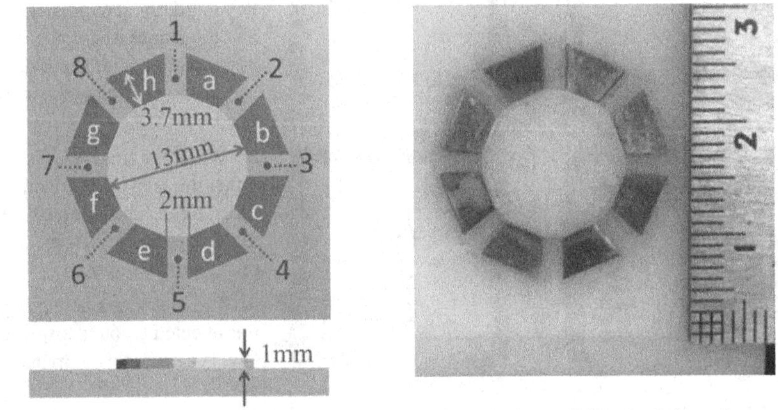

(a) Sensor layout and number assignment (b) Prototype of the touch board

Fig. 2. Design of the touch board.

In Gyou selection of SliT, 12 kinds of slide-in (2 directions from each of 6 segments) are used. Each is specified by a sequence of three positions where the fingertip passes. For example, "た" Gyou is selected with a stroke from upper left to upper right, which is the motion from the sensor "g" to "b" passing "h" and "a". When a finger passes the border of two sensors, the number assigned between them is output, because the finger contacts with both sensors at the same time. Using such numbers, the stroke of "た" Gyou is defined as sequence 8, 1, 2. Other strokes are defined as the sequences shown in Table 1. In Dan selection of SliT, the eight keys displayed in light blue in Fig. 1(d) are used. Those keys are replaced by the positions 1 to 8 shown in Fig. 2(a). Each of which is selected by tapping.

Table 1. Definition of the order of three positions for selecting each Gyou.

Gyou	あ	か	さ	た	な	Symbol
Sequence	6, 5, 4	7, 8, 1	7, 6, 5	8, 1, 2	8, 7, 6	3, 2, 1
Gyou	は	ま	や	ら	わ	Mode change
Sequence	1, 2, 3	1, 8, 7	2, 3, 4	2, 1, 8	3, 4, 5	4, 5, 6

The circular area at the center of the board in Fig. 2 is intended to avoid touching extra sensors. This area is elevated 1 [mm] from the sensors. As shown in Fig. 3(a), if the angle of the finger to the touch board is small, the fingertip can not reach the sensor. However, as shown in Fig. 3(b), by placing the finger at an angle close to the vertical to the board, the fingertip touches the board. This angle reduces the contact area of the fingertip, so reducing input errors due to touching surrounding sensors.

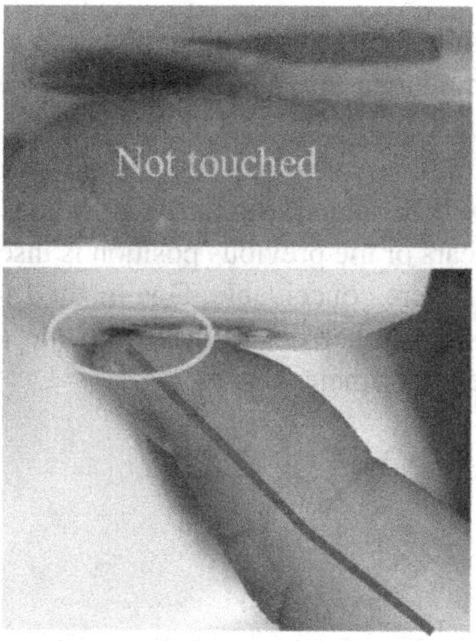

(a) The case that the angle of the finger to the touch board is small.

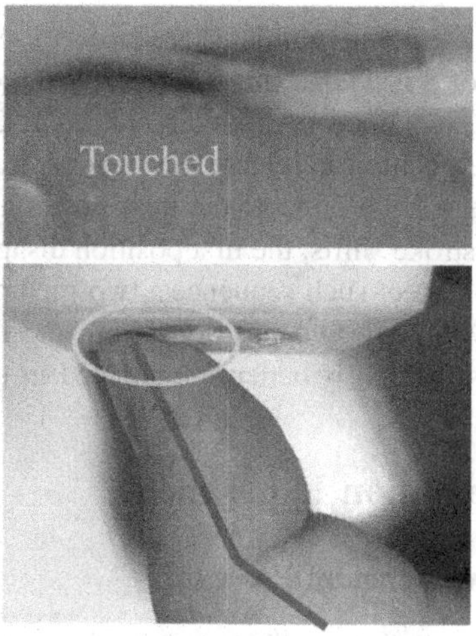

(b) The case that the finger close to the vertical to the board.

Fig. 3. The angle of the finger to the touch board.

The state of each sensor is detected using Arduino Uno, and transmitted to the host every millisecond. When the finger touches two adjacent sensors, Arduino outputs numbers from 1 to 8. Otherwise, it outputs 0. While the finger is moving, it may float from the board momentarily and/or touch only one sensor for a short time. Thus, zeros inserted in the numbers to be send. For example, in the stroke of "た" Gyou, zeros are inserted between the series of 8, 1 and 2, as shown in Fig. 4(a). So that, short zero sections are deleted. In practice, consecutive zeros less than 100 in length are deleted. This processing removes the red zero in Fig. 4(b) and corrects the output to Fig. 4(c). After that, by consolidating consecutive same numbers into one, the output will be the sequence of 0, 8, 1, 2, 0. The first and last zeros indicate that the finger is away the touch board.

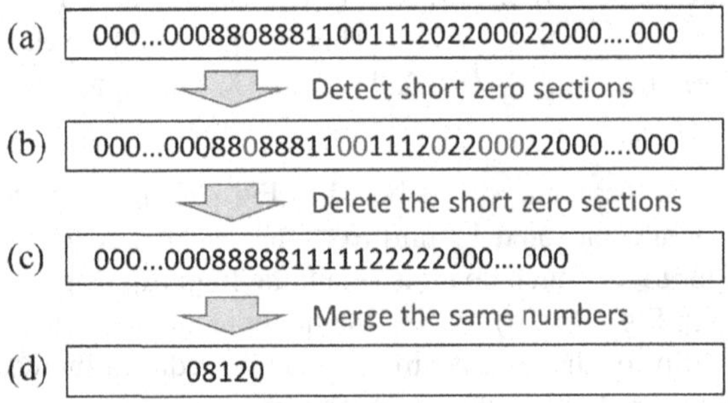

Fig. 4. Signal processing of the touch board. (Color figure online)

If the entered numbers are not consecutive (under the definition that the next number of 8 is 1) and the difference is 2, complement the numbers between them. For example, sequence 1, 3 is corrected to 1, 2, 3.

If the position to release the finger shifts in the stroke input, the last position of the sequence will be gone or the next position will be added. Similarly, if the position to start the stroke shifts, the first position disappears or the previous position is inserted. In order to correct such sequences, two methods were conceivable. One method judges a stroke with only two positions from the first. Another determines from the last two positions. Which is better is evaluated in the experiment.

5 Evaluation Experiment

5.1 Experimental Procedure

For this experiment, the smartwatch shown in Fig. 5 was used. The band of it was created with a 3D printer, and our touch board and SONY Smartwatch 3 is embedded. The subject wears it on the wrist and operates it with the thumb of the dominant hand. The position of the fingers and hands other than the thumb was free as long as they did not touch the board.

Prior to the experiment, how to use the touch board and the experiment procedure are explained in about 5 min in total. Next, the subject experiences to enter the strokes and learns the angle needed to touch the thumb to sensors. Here, one task of the experiment is executed as practice. When all stokes of the task are correctly entered, the experiment is started. If incorrect input occurs, after briefly teaching about the angle of

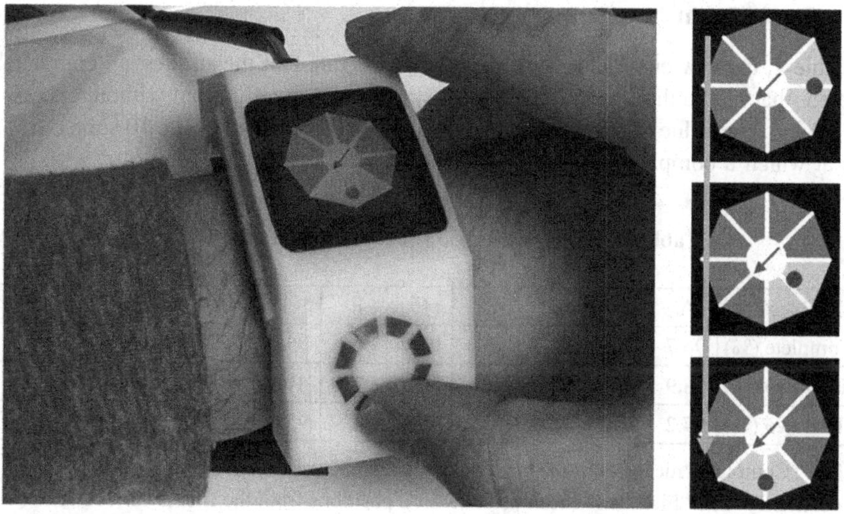

Fig. 5. Equipment used for the experiments (the left) and a sample of animation displayed to control stroke input speed (the right).

the thumb necessary to touch the sensors, an additional task is executed and this verification process is repeated. However, five minutes after the start of the practice, the experiment is started regardless of the status. For the experiment entering taps, "stroke" in this procedure is changed to "tap".

In the stroke experiment, the subject enters the 12 kind strokes, which were shown in Table 1. Each stroke is a movement through three consecutive positions. In one task, each of 12 kinds is entered once in random order. This task is repeated 15 times with a 10 [s] break.

According to the research by Akita et al. [2], a person skilled in SliT can enter one character at about 1 [s]. Since one character is specified by a pair of one stroke and one tap, the time spent for the stroke is considered to be about 0.5 [s].

Therefore, we induced the subjects to execute strokes at this speed using animation. As shown in Fig. 5, a blue dot is displayed on the screen. The dot moves from the start position of the stroke to the end at 0.5 [s] in constant velocity. We asked the subjects to track the dot with their thumbs. However, even if the speed of the fingertip differs from the speed of the dot, input is accepted.

In the tap experiment, each of the eight positions is entered once per each task. This task is repeated 15 time with a 10 [s] break. The order of the touch positions is randomly changed each task. In this experiment, the subjects tap the blue dot immediately after it is displayed. The position of the fingertip is judged by output from the board up to 0.5 [s] after the dot is displayed.

We conducted this experiment with 10 subjects. Their age is 20 to 24 years old. All subjects are right-handed. They have never used our touch board before this experiment. In all tasks, subjects are not notified whether the input is correct or not.

5.2 Stroke Input

In Table 2, the row entitled "Complete" shows the rate that the strokes are completely entered, that is, the three positions of each stroke are correctly input without excess or deficiency. The value at the right end of the table is the average of the 10 subjects. The rate at which a complete stroke is input is 94.7%.

Table 2. Percentage of the strokes recognized correctly.

Subject	A	B	C	D	E	F	G	H	I	J	av.
Complete (%)	96.7	97.8	91.1	98.3	93.9	86.1	95.0	96.1	94.4	97.2	94.7
First two (%)	**98.9**	**99.9**	**97.8**	**100**	**96.1**	**97.8**	**100**	**98.9**	**97.8**	**100**	**98.7**
Last two (%)	97.2	98.3	92.8	98.3	**96.1**	87.8	95.0	97.2	95.6	97.2	95.6

* The "Complete" means all three positions of the stroke ware entered without excess or deficiency. The "First two" mean that at least 2 positions from the first is correct. The "Last two" means that at least 2 positions from the last is correct. Therefore, they include the complete strokes.

The row of "First two" shows the rate that both the first and the second positions of each stroke were correctly entered. This includes the case where the third position is lost or where the fourth position is added, in addition the complete strokes. In opposition, the "Last two" row shows the rate that two or more positions from the last are correct. About all subjects in Table 2, the value of the "First two" row is higher than or equal to that of "Last two". By the calculation of the t-test using the values of those two rows, t = 2.18 and P = 0.013. This P value ensures with a significance level of 5% that stroke judgement with the first two positions is more reliable than that with the last two. It is the same judgment result in Mann-Whitney U test. By judging from the first two positions, the average input rate rises to 98.7%. This rate is sufficiently high.

Of the total 1,800 trials, 96 incomplete inputs occurred. Table 3 shows the five strokes with many incomplete inputs. Since inputs lost the first position of the stroke are fewer than the input lost the last position, it is more reliable to judge using the first positions in the input sequence.

Table 3. Number of incomplete strokes.

Sequence	1,8,7	1,2,3	3,4,5	2,1,8	8,1,2	Others	Total
Lost the first position	0	1	**8**	0	**7**	0	16
Lost the last position	**15**	**18**	**8**	**11**	0	**9**	**61**
Others	9	1	0	1	4	4	19
Total	24	20	16	12	11	13	96

Almost half of the incorrect inputs occurred on two strokes starting at position 1. In these strokes, the thumb moves from the center top of the board to the middle of the right end or left end. In our touch board, it is necessary to move the thumb along the curved edge of the center raised area. Because the speed increases in the movement from top to bottom, it is expected that the thumb may be off from the sensor at the last position.

The stroke 3, 4, 5 is performed at the lower right part of the board. Since the sensors must be touched by bending the thumb, position control may be difficult. The last position of the stroke 2, 1, 8 is 8 and the first position of 8, 1, 2 is also 8. That is, mistakes occurred at the position 8. To touch that position, the thumb must be extended. The angle of the thumb to the board decreases. The belly of the thumb contacts the lifted area. As the result, the contact point shifts out of the sensors.

5.3 Tap Input

Table 4 shows the percentage of taps. The "Complete tap" means that only the correct position is entered. The average is 97% that is higher than that of strokes shown in Table 2. The "First is correct" row indicates the percentage of the case at least the first position is correct. This case includes both when only the correct position is entered and when a position is added after the correct position. The "Last is correct" shows the percentage at least the last position is correct. In the calculation of the t-test with these rows, $t = 2.11$ and $P = 0.001$. This shows that the first position is more reliable than the last when the significance level is 5%. Therefore, we judge the position that was input first as the position of the fingertip. As the result, the input rate of taps becomes 99.4%.

Table 4. Percentage of the taps recognized correctly.

Subject	A	B	C	D	E	F	G	H	I	J	av.
Complete tap (%)	97.8	97.8	97.8	98.9	95.6	93.9	97.8	95.6	98.9	96.1	97.0
First is correct (%)	**100**	**100**	**98.9**	**100**	**98.3**	**97.8**	**100**	**100**	**100**	**98.9**	**99.4**
Last is correct (%)	97.8	97.8	98.9	98.9	97.2	96.1	97.8	95.6	98.9	97.2	97.6

* The "Complete tap" means that only the correct positions were entered. The "First is correct" and the "Last is correct" mean that even if the extra position is added the first and the last position is the correct position, respectively.

Table 5 shows the number of erroneous inputs for each position in 1200 taps in total. No errors occur except for the four positions shown in the table. The row titled "Add after" indicates the number of errors that occurred because an unnecessary position was added after the correct position. The row "Add before" indicates the error caused by having been added before. Since the former is more than the latter, judging with the first position increases the recognition rate of the tap.

Table 5. Incorrect input patterns of taps and the number of them.

Position	8	6	4	1	total
Add after: [sequence] times	[8,**1**] 23	[6,**5**] 18	[4,**5**] 2		**43**
Add before: [sequence] times			[**5**,4] 7	[2,1] 4	11
Total of errors	23	18	9	4	54

* "Add after" is a case where an unnecessary position was added after the target position. "Add before" is the case before the target. Numbers in brackets indicate the entered sequence of positions.

In both the error patterns at positions 8 and 6, the position to the right is entered after the target position. It necessary to stretch the thumb for touching to position 6 or 8, so the thumb is close to parallel to the board. For this reason, the accidentally touching to the next position increases during subjects return their thumbs. Position 4 is touched by bending the thumb. Position 5 is inserted before the position 4 when the thumb contacts the board before it is completely bent.

6 Character Input Using the Touch Board

The created touch board is connected to the smartwatch with Bluetooth. On/off of the eight sensors of the touch board are combined into one byte data with Arduino every millisecond. Here, 'on' means that the sensor is touched. Its value is 1. That data is send to the smartwatch with Bluetooth. The program running on the smartwatch judges the type of stroke and the position of the tap.

If the judgment is made after checking the fingertip has left the board, an input delay that the user can definitely feel is generated. This markedly deteriorates the usability of the input device. Therefore, the stroke judgement algorithm has been modified. The computer experiment in Sect. 5 showed that the first two positions of each stroke are reliable. Accordingly, we judge the stroke from only the first two positions. Since the stroke is decided during the fingertip moving, the delay is solved. In addition, the threshold of consecutive zeros to be deleted has been reduced to 5 in order to detect early that the thumb left the board. This is necessary to shorten tap judgment.

Table 6 shows the definition of the strokes and taps in Dan selection after the modification. Here, the first digit pair in each cell is a standard decision rule used primarily. Pairs of italic digits are prepared to repair the error where the middle position is not entered. Pairs of bold digits are to correct the tapping when the fingertip moves after touching the board.

We measured input speed of one subject who is skilled in the operation of both touch board and touch screen of SliT method. In this experiment, the subject inputs 5 hiragana words in each task. The task is repeated 5 times with 3-min break between. The length of the words is 4, 5, or 6 characters. For each word length, 50 words were selected in the most frequently used order [20]. After sorting 150 words in total at

Table 6. Sequences of positions determining the strokes and the taps after the modification.

Sequence	Input	Sequence	Input	Sequence	Input
6,5 *6,4*	あ	7,8 *7,1*	か	7,6 *7,5*	さ
8,1 *8,2*	た	8,7 *8,6*	な	1,2 *1,3*	は
1,8 *1,7*	ま	2,3 *2,4*	や	2,1 *2,8*	ら
3,4 *3,5*	わ	3,2 *3,1*	Symbol	4,5 *4,6*	Mode
6,0 **6,7**	BS	5,0 **5,4 5,6**	Space	4,0 **4,3**	Enter

random, 10 sets of 5 words from the top of the word list were cut out. Thus the same word never appears twice in the tasks. On the first day, the input speed was measured with the touch screen, on the second day with a touch board.

Table 7 shows the result. The standard deviation of each experiment is small. That means that the person is mastering how to operate. The input speed on the touch board is about 80% of that on the screen. This is because there were relatively many input errors. In particular, many errors occurred in the tap operation for replacing to voiced or semi-voiced sounds. In this operation, the right low position of the board is tapped. Although when input with the touch board, both of the fingertip and the screen must be watched, that position is far from the screen. In addition, since the board is at an angle to the screen, the touch position may be hidden by the finger used for operation. It is considered that the error occurred due to these reasons.

Table 7. Input speed of a person skilled in SliT.

Task	1	2	3	4	5	Avg.	SD
touch board [CPM]	54.4	50.8	54.0	54.6	52.4	53.2	1.61
touch screen [CPM]	67.7	68.0	65.1	70.3	67.3	67.7	1.85

Avg. = average input speed of the 5 tasks, SD = standard deviation

In order to reduce that tap mistake, we plan to make the sensors protrude a little from the surface of the touch board. This makes it possible to find the sensor gap by the feel of the fingertip, so the user can notice the tap mistake. In order to make the user aware of the character replacement, we will paint different colors on the background of voiced, semi-voiced, and unvoiced characters. Adding touch buttons to the upper band of the screen is another solution. In this case these buttons are tapped by the forefinger.

7 Conclusion

We developed a touch board dedicated to SliT which is the character input method for smartwatch. On the board, eight sensors are equally spaced around the center circle. When two adjacent sensors are touched at the same time, the position number assigned between them are output.

In SliT, specify one character by one stroke and one tap. By judging the stroke from the first two positions through which the finger passes, 98.7% of the 1800 strokes were correctly recognized. Even if an additional position was entered, 99.4% of 1200 taps were correctly recognized by judging the first position as the tap position. Therefore, it is considered that the touch board achieves sufficiently high accuracy as an input device of SliT.

The character input speed with the touch board was about 80% of that with the touch screen. This decrease in input speed is mainly caused by that voiced or semi-voiced characters were entered as unvoiced characters due to tap failure. However, this experiment has done only one person. We will do the same experiment for many persons and investigate the cause of the difference of input speed. After that, we will improve the touch board in order to improve input speed.

Acknowledgement. This work was supported by JSPS KAKENHI Grant Number JP16K00286.

References

1. Siek, K.A., Rogers, Y., Connelly, K.H.: Fat finger worries: how older and younger users physically interact with PDAs. In: Costabile, M.F., Paternò, F. (eds.) INTERACT 2005. LNCS, vol. 3585, pp. 267–280. Springer, Heidelberg (2005). https://doi.org/10.1007/11555261_24
2. Akita, K., Tanaka, T., Sagawa, Y.: SliT: character input system using slide-in and tap for smartwatches. In: Kurosu, M. (ed.) HCI 2018. LNCS, vol. 10903, pp. 3–16. Springer, Cham (2018). https://doi.org/10.1007/978-3-319-91250-9_1
3. Fujitsu Develops Glove-Style Wearable Device. http://www.fujitsu.com/global/about/resources/news/press-releases/2014/0218-01.html. Accessed 20 Dec 2018
4. Ring-Type Wearable Device Enables Users to Write in the Air with Finger. https://journal.jp.fujitsu.com/en/2015/02/10/01/. Accessed 20 Dec 2018
5. Ring Zero. https://logbar.jp/en/index.html. Accessed 25 Dec 2018
6. Zhang, Y., Zhou, J., Laput, G., Harrison, C.: SkinTrack: using the body as an electrical waveguide for continuous finger tracking on the skin. http://www.gierad.com/assets/skintrack/skintrack.pdf. Accessed 25 Dec 2018
7. NEC develops ARmKeypad air, a contact-free virtual keyboard for a user's arm. https://www.nec.com/en/press/201607/global_20160713_01.html. Accessed 25 Dec 2018
8. Wong, P., Zhu, K., Fu, H.: FingerT9: leveraging thumb-to-finger interaction for same-side-hand text entry on smartwatches. In: Proceedings of CHI 2018, Paper no. 178 (2017)
9. Whitmier, E., et al.: DigiTouch: reconfigurable thumb-to-finger input and text entry on head-mounted displays. In: Proceedings ACM IMWUT 2017, vol. 1, no. 3, Article 133 (2017)
10. Finger Touching. http://www.yankodesign.com/2007/10/02/wearable-mobile-device-for-enhanced-chatting/. Accessed 25 Dec 2018
11. Tap. http://www.tapwithus.com. Accessed 25 Dec 2018
12. Haier Asu Smartwatch. https://www.digitaltrends.com/smartwatch-reviews/haier-asu-review/. Accessed 25 Dec 2018
13. Sun, K., Wang, Y., Yu, C., Yan, Y., Wen, H., Shi, Y.: Float: one-handed and touch-free target selection on smartwatches. In: Proceedings of CHI 2017, pp. 692–704 (2017)
14. Gong, J., Yang, X., Irani, P.: WristWhirl: one-handed continuous smartwatch input using wrist gesture. In: Proceedings of UIST 2016, pp. 861–872 (2016)

15. Gong, J., et al.: WrisText: one-handed text entry on smartwatch using wrist gestures. In: Proceedings of CHI 2018, Paper no. 181 (2018)
16. Li, F., Guy, R., Yatani, K., Truong, K.: The 1line keyboard: a QWERTY layout in a single line. In: Proceedings of UIST 2011, pp. 461–470 (2011)
17. 5-TILES. https://en.wikipedia.org/wiki/5-Tiles, https://9to5google.com/2015/07/07/wear-5-tiles-is-a-text-messaging-app-with-a-keyboard-for-your-wear-watch/, https://techcrunch.com/2014/05/24/5-tiles-keyboard/. Accessed 25 Dec 2018
18. TouchOne Keyboard. http://www.touchone.net. Accessed 25 Dec 2018
19. Oney, S., Harrison, C., Ogan, A., Wiese, J.: ZoomBoard: a diminutive QWERTY soft keyboard using iterative zooming for ultra-small devices. In: ACM CHI 2013, pp. 2799–2802 (2013)
20. The word list of the Balanced Corpus of Contemporary Written Japanese of the National Institute for Japanese Language and Linguistics. http://pj.ninjal.ac.jp/corpus_center/bccwj/en/freq-list.html. Accessed 23 Jan 2019

Emotion and Movement with AppIHC: Promoting Interaction and Socialization Among Participants of Scientific Events via Mobile Application

Aline Tramontin[1], Ricardo Sohn[1], Bruna de Oliveira[1], Roberto Pereira[2], and Isabela Gasparini[1](✉)

[1] Graduate Program in Applied Computing (PPGCA), Department of Computer Science, Santa Catarina State University (UDESC), Joinville, SC, Brazil
aline.tramontin@gmail.com, ricardosohn@gmail.com, oliver.brunaa@gmail.com, isabela.gasparini@udesc.br
[2] Department of Computer Science, Federal University of Paraná (UFPR), Curitiba, PR, Brazil
rpereira@inf.ufpr.br

Abstract. Scientific events bring together a large number of researchers and are composed of different types of sessions, consisting of workshops, mini-courses, full papers, etc., with different topics. The high content diversity may cause an overload of information to attendees, making it difficult to choose between all sessions. This paper describes a mobile application called AppIHC to help attendees access event's schedule and promote users' engagement. Developed for the Android platform, the application has a Recommender System that uses information from the users' profile and their interests to generate recommendation by content, and also produces social recommendations from a pre-existent database of co-authoring from previous event editions. A gamification process was applied to promote engagement between the attendees. The application was used during the event XVI Brazilian Symposium on Human Factors in Computing Systems (IHC 2017) and had 108 registered users, being evaluated through a satisfaction questionnaire and through analysis of activity records. The results indicate the goal of facilitating access to information and improving user participation in the event has been achieved.

Keywords: Application · Scientific event · Recommendation · Social · Gamification

1 Introduction

Scientific/Academic events can be defined as a gathering of people interested in a particular area of knowledge or culture whose propose is to present and discuss ideas on specific topics over a period of time. Event activities (e.g., workshops, lectures, posters, technical sessions) are defined based on the objectives of each event [1] and usually involve the dissemination of research results. Papers may be grouped into

M. Kurosu (Ed.): HCII 2019, LNCS 11567, pp. 62–75, 2019.
https://doi.org/10.1007/978-3-030-22643-5_6

sessions that will be part of the event schedule. In order to help participants with easy access to this schedule, several scientific events have already made or use mobile applications, such as [2–4].

Existing applications typically offer functionalities such as calendar management, keynote speakers, sessions information, etc. However, the personalization of these applications is still a gap [5]. In many scientific events the schedule allows sessions to occur in parallel [6], which can give the attendee difficulty in choosing which sessions to participate in. Recommender Systems (RS) can help attendees find the sessions best suited to their particular interests because these systems provide personalized recommendations that best fit the tastes and preferences of the attendees [7].

RS are a set of techniques that select items for users of a particular system based on the interaction data and interests of those users. RS may be used in different applications and for different recommendations, such as movies, music, products in virtual stores. The use of RS to recommending sessions in scientific event applications can help attendees in the decision process by which session to participate based on their interests. This paper presents a solution to help participants in scientific events to obtain information about the event's schedule as well as to promote their engagement. This solution was designed through a Mobile Application called AppIHC and applied in the XVI Brazilian Symposium on Human Factors in Computing Systems (IHC 2017). This paper presents its conception, functionalities, experiment and achieved results.

The paper is organized as follows: Sect. 1 presents the Introduction. Section 2 describes the AppIHC, its design, functionalities and architecture. Section 3 details the Recommender System Module. Section 4 presents the evaluation of the AppIHC, how participants interacted with the app, the evaluation process and the achieved results. Section 7 presents the conclusion and future works.

2 AppIHC

The Mobile Application for Scientific Events called AppIHC was developed aiming to facilitate attendees' access to event's information. AppIHC helps participants find information about sessions, through schedule, recommendations, favorite items, and a gamified environment. The application was designed in a generally way, in a manner that it could be used in any scientific event.

The application was developed for the Android OS, for devices with OS version 4.4 (Android Kit-kat) or higher. The choice of this version was motivated by the number of users that the application would achieve, about 95% of Android devices [8]. The target audience of the application is composed of the participants of the event (e.g., lecturers, researchers, students, organizers). The technologies used for development were Java, Android Studio, Firebase and the principles of Material Design.

To represent the target audience, we used the Personas technique. Figure 1 presents a Persona created, named Junior da Silva, his profile, occupation, wishes and needs regarding the use of the application (*in Portuguese*).

As an example for the use of a mobile application in scientific events, a scenario was created with the persona Junior presented in Fig. 1:

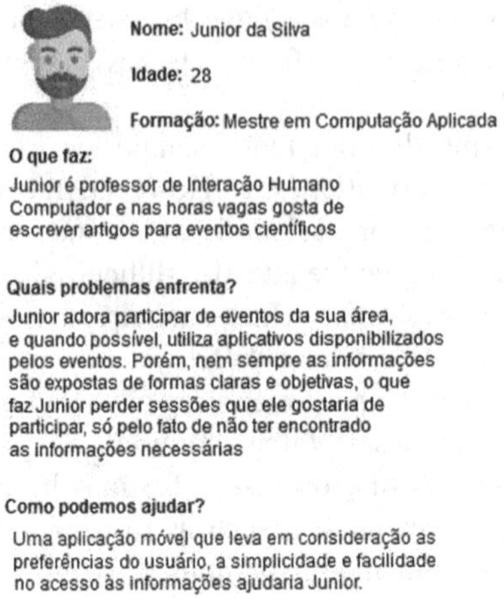

Nome: Junior da Silva
Idade: 28
Formação: Mestre em Computação Aplicada
O que faz:
Junior é professor de Interação Humano Computador e nas horas vagas gosta de escrever artigos para eventos científicos
Quais problemas enfrenta?
Junior adora participar de eventos da sua área, e quando possível, utiliza aplicativos disponibilizados pelos eventos. Porém, nem sempre as informações são expostas de formas claras e objetivas, o que faz Junior perder sessões que ele gostaria de participar, só pelo fato de não ter encontrado as informações necessárias
Como podemos ajudar?
Uma aplicação móvel que leva em consideração as preferências do usuário, a simplicidade e facilidade no acesso às informações ajudaria Junior.

Fig. 1. Junior's Persona

"Junior saw a post about the IHC Symposium on a social network page, stating that registration for the event was open, and as soon as he could, he made his application. On the same page, Junior received information about the AppIHC application for the event, and decided to use it to check some details of the event's schedule. To use the application, Junior registers with his personal information. In the application, Junior can quickly view the information of all sessions, and decides to look for a technical session about accessibility that he knew would occur on the first day and, through the search, Junior finds the desired information about the technical session. To make it even quicker, he adds it to his favorite sessions list. On the second day of the event, Junior has already added several sessions to his favorites list and received his daily recommendations, based on his interests. Arriving at event, he does not remember exactly in which room the session will take place, and to avoid delays he quickly opens the app and checks in his favorites that the session will take place in room "A". Throughout the day of the event, Junior continues to use the application to view information about event programming quickly and easily. He checks the app and prepares to attend the sessions according to his preferences."

To identify the main functionalities that the application needed, brainstorming sessions and workshops with user groups were conducted. At the same time, other event-oriented systems were investigated to observe essential functionalities. The following functionalities were specified after development team meetings:

User Registration: Each user has unique information, such as his/her profile, topics of interest, favorite sessions, recommended items, ranking position of users and responses to the satisfaction questionnaire. During the registration, the user's co-authors are also verified, if they exist. If the user has co-authors in previous event's editions, the schedule shows some implicit co-authoring recommendation.

Profile: It should be possible to change data such as: name, surname, institution, topics of interest.

Schedule: The schedule is divided in tabs, one tab for each day, and each tab is divided into sessions, which usually has different works/papers. Each tab shows a list of event sessions with information such as: session type (e.g., Technical Session, Panels, Posters), session name, time, location. It should be possible to add sessions to the favorites list for easy access. It should be possible to locate information in the schedule list quickly and efficiently by means of a search, which takes into account all the information previously mentioned, allowing the creation of filters according to the desired information. If the user has co-authors in a session, a co-authoring icon is displayed in this session in question and a text field informing the co-authorship. If there are no items to display, a screen should report this.

Favorites: Favorite items in the schedule should be separated into another screen that is similar to the schedule but that only shows the sessions selected by the user. The user can add or remove each item in an easy way.

Recommendations: Based on the user profile, recommendations are generated by an external module, which is also included in the database. Recommendations are daily and for each recommendation users can give their feedback by selecting one of the two feedback buttons ("like" and "dislike"). If there are no items to display, a screen should inform the user.

Login: Authentication is performed via email and password provided by Firebase Authentication. The user must be able to recover the password if needed.

About: Information about the application and of support.

The following shows the application architecture, the gamification system, as well as the content-based and social recommendation modules.

The general architecture is illustrated in Fig. 2. The **user interface** is the communication module with users, in which the users inform their data and topics of interest in the register process. Once the registration is done, interface helps users interact and browse through the system, access to information about event programming, favorite items, select sessions as favorites, receive recommendations and provide explicit feedback to be used to generate the new recommendations, respond to the satisfaction questionnaire, etc.

Figure 2 also shows **the recommender module** (implemented on the server), which uses the content-based approach and generates daily recommendations when the user interacts with the recommended items screen. The "G" that appears next to the database represents the **gamification module**. The "RC" that also appears next to the database represents the **co-authorship recommendation data and the content recommendation data**, stored in the same database.

The gamification is implemented by "Easter Eggs" technique. Through hidden "hashtags" in the event's physical environment, including moving elements like hashtags stuck in people, different keywords were created with topics related to the event. These topics became available in the environment, in different limited time period. Each new word could be inserted into the app through a specific code screen, and so the participants could increase their number of points. Figure 3 shows an example of moving code placed on the back of an event participant.

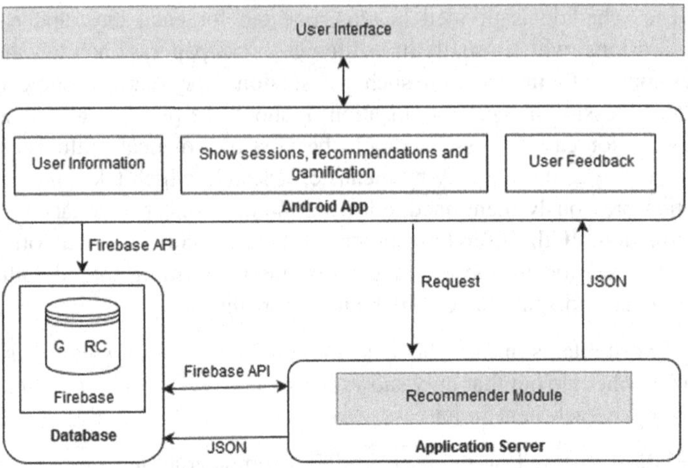

Fig. 2. AppIHC architecture

Fig. 3. A hashtag on the back of an event participant

The final ranking of the event had top five places awarded with prizes. This ranking was visible and public to the users of the application in real time. Gamification was an important part of the participants' engagement. The evaluation section will detail the results achieved.

3 Recommender Module

The recommender module is composed of content and social recommendations.

3.1 Content-Based Recommendation

In the content-based recommendation there are gathered data from users' registration (name, email, topics of interest and institution) and data from explicit feedbacks through the interaction with the system. Topics of interest are presented at the time of registration by means of a list of topics, in which the user can select the ones that correspond to their interests. This list represents the topics of the event IHC 2017, with a total of 42 topics. The selection of topics at the time of registration is not mandatory. In this way, the user who wants to make changes in topics of interest has the option to access his profile and edit it, being able to remove, change or insert topics.

Using the application when the event was occurring, explicit user feedbacks were collected to improve the recommendations. In addition, this feedback helped to generate recommendations for users who did not select topics of interest to complete their profile. Explicit feedback is collected in two ways, analyzing the sessions users put on their favorites list and through positive or negative user feedback for each session that is already recommended. This choice is represented by the "Positive feedback" and "Negative feedback" buttons. Figure 4 shows the Recommendations of one screen. In this screen, user can check the recommended items as well as select the feedback regarding the recommendation received.

Fig. 4. Recommendations screen for an event participant IHC 2017

The recommendations are pre-generated daily, based on the sessions that occur on the day and recalculated each time the user accesses the "Recommended of the Day" menu item, that is, in real time. So, each time user interacts with the system and accesses the "Recommended of the Day" the recommender module will improve the recommendations.

The programming language used for content-based RS development was Python. Profile data and topics of interest are stored in Firebase. All explicit feedback provided by the user while using the system is also stored in Firebase. In addition, information related to the Symposium sessions is also stored. This way, when users access the

"Recommended of the Day" (in Portuguese "Recomendados do Dia") in the AppIHC menu, the Recommender Module requests the user's data and the previously registered sessions and calculates the similarity of each session of the day with the user profile by calculating the Cosseno [10].

To facilitate the understanding of how the user profile is represented, an example is illustrated in Fig. 5, with a limited number of topics. The vectors have size 5 and each letter (A, B, C, D and E) represents a topic of interest addressed. Thus, when the user inserts the topics of interest A and B in his/her profile, the vector of topics of interest receives 1 in the positions referring to topics A and B, remaining 0 in the other positions. When the user favors the X session, the topics covered in that session (A, B, and E) receive 1 in the positions related to them in the subject session vector of favored sessions. For positive feedbacks, when the user positively evaluates the recommended Y session, session related topics (B and E) receive 1 in the positions related to them in the vector with the topics of the positive sessions. In Fig. 5 it is possible to see that when the user provides negative feedback for session Z that addresses topics A, C, and E; topics A and E are not inserted as 1 in the vector with negative session topics. This is because topic A is in the topic vector of user interest, and topic E is in the vector with topics from the favored sessions. Thus, topic C is the only one inserted in the negative topic vector, since it is the only one that is not either in the vector of topics of interest nor in the vector with the topics of the favorite sessions.

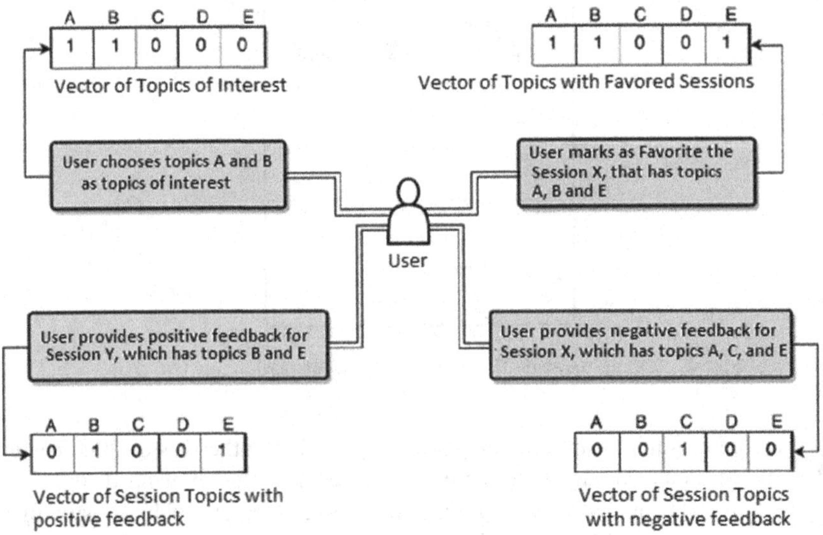

Fig. 5. Representation of user profile vectors

In order to calculate the similarity between the sessions and the user profile, the following formula was used:

$$sim(di, dj) = \frac{\sum_{i=1}^{k} w_{i,c} w_{i,s}}{\sqrt{\sum_{i=1}^{k} w_{i,c}^2} \sqrt{\sum_{i=1}^{k} w_{i,s}^2}} \qquad (1)$$

The term $w_{i,c}$ represents the profile of a user as a vector. A user's profile, containing his/her preferences, can be represented as a weight vector (***wc1 ... wck***), in which each weight ***wc1*** illustrates the importance of a word (term) ***ki*** for the user ***c*** and can be calculated from individually categorized content vectors using a variety of techniques. The term $w_{i,s}$ represents the contents of a document as a vector. The contents of a document can be represented as a TF-IDF vector of word weights. Finally, k is the total number of terms present in the vectors [11].

The complement of the result is used to calculate the Cosine between the sessions of a certain time and the vector with the topics of the sessions that received negative feedback. This is because the calculation of the Cosine indicates how similar a given session is to a user's profile, where 1 indicates total similarity and 0 indicates dissimilarity. Thus, the greater the similarity between the user vector that contains the threads of the sessions that received negative feedback and a particular session, the lower it indicates to be the user's interest in the session. For the other vectors of the user profile, the calculation of the Cosine is also performed, not undergoing changes. At the end of all calculations, a weighted average is performed with all resulting values. The similarity value between the session and the vector of the topic of interest has the greatest weight, being 40%. The remaining values remain equal weight of 20%. Thus, the similarity value between a session and the user profile remains between 0 and 1. The higher weight is set to vector of topics of interest because the topics of interest are the items provided directly by the user. Therefore, in order to determine which of the sessions is most related to the user profile, the calculation of the Cosine between the sessions and the vectors are performed. Sessions most similar to users' profile are recommended to them.

3.2 Social Recommendation

Interpersonal influence is an important contextual factor, and it follows the idea that a person tends to attend events accompanied by his/her friends. The similarity between friends is also an aspect that contributes to the recommendation process, as well as the frequency of interactions and participation in events, important social characteristics and that contribute greatly to the improvement of the recommendation process. Different approaches can be used to recommend events. One of the most used is the Collaborative Filtering approach. Recently the contextual dimensions is being add in social recommender systems.

Choosing the most relevant lectures/sessions and meeting potential collaborators with similar interests may be a difficult task at large events, especially because parallel sessions occur. Scientific/academic conferences are dynamic, the participants are moving, participating in different presentations in different environments and

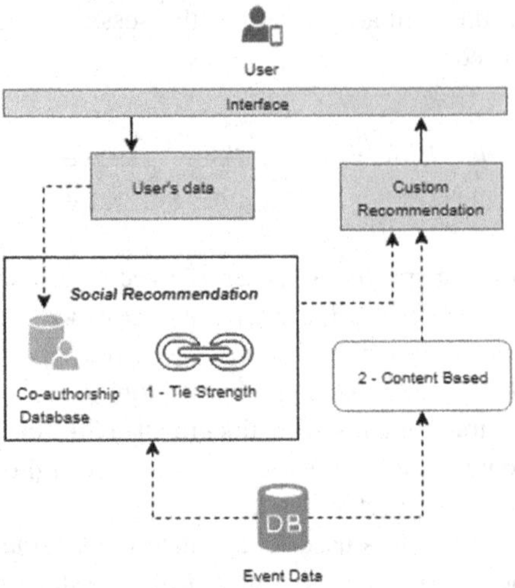

Fig. 6. Social recommendation process

schedules. Considering the mentioned aspects, a social recommender model was developed that considers social relations as co-author relations. Figure 6 shows the basic recommendation procedure.

A social network is created from the co-authorship researcher's history, based on who have already published in the event. Then, the first step is to calculate the tie strength among authors within the network. The calculation is made through the frequency of publications between two authors, inferring that, the greater the number of publications in co-authorship, the stronger the tie between the authors. Thus, the recommendation to the target user is generated based on the interests of the co-author with strong ties, and in publications which the target user is not a co-author. The tiebreaker is held by the most recent co-authorship.

The co-authorship network can be represented as a non-directed graph, with the following representation: the authors are the vertices and the publications are the edges. The objective is to quantify the number of co-authored publications, that is, how many edges each pair has in the network. Thus, according to Fig. 7, the co-authorship relationship between two authors, vertices *u2* and *u3*, is represented by a prominent link, since they have more than one work together.

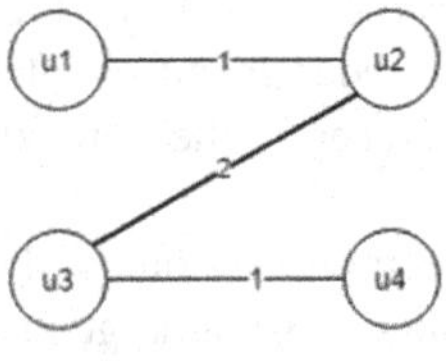

Fig. 7. Representation of the tie strength in the co-authorship network

4 Evaluation

The AppIHC application, its recommendation and gamification systems were evaluated in the IHC 2017 event. The app was available on Google Play and was made available to event participants.

4.1 AppIHC General Usage Data at IHC 2017

The IHC 2017 had a total of 250 participants enrolled and of these, 108 registered in the AppIHC during the event. Application usage data was obtained through Firebase Analytics.

According to Fig. 8, it is possible to verify the engagement of the users with the application, in minutes. Users used the application from October 22 to October 27 (event period). By calculating the average daily engagement, it was found that users spent about 13 min and 45 s using the application every day.

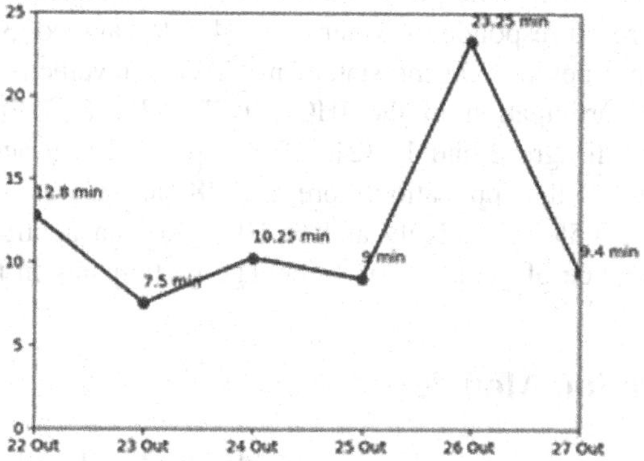

Fig. 8. User engagement

User Registration and Topic of Interest activities had the longest average interaction time (42 s), meaning that users' longest interactions with the application occurred during the registration and insertion of topics of interest. Following this order, the main activity of the application appears in the next position, with an average interaction time of 32 s. The average duration of the interactions of the other activities was 18 s, much smaller than those previously mentioned.

Using the event database in the Firebase Realtime Database, it was found that of the 108 users of the application, 74 users (68%) obtained some content-based recommendation, 66 users (61%) used the feature of adding a session to the favorites list, 47 users (43%) used and evaluated the recommendation system, 56 users (51%) used some printed code to score in the gamification and 55 users (51%) answered the satisfaction questionnaire.

The questionnaire was created based on the Likert scale with three response options, represented by emoticons: I do not agree, neutral and agree. The neutral was created to allow the user not to be forced to make a choice between extremes (no and yes) or if he/she does not want or has no opinion on the issue. The questionnaire was added to AppIHC itself and it was used to get answers about application usage and the content-based recommendation system.

Of the 55 users who answered the questionnaire, 46 users (83.6%) answered that they were assisted in obtaining information faster and 9 users (16.4%) responded in a neutral way. About the functionalities of the application being useful, the data collected showed that 44 of the 55 users (80%) agreed with the statement, 10 users (20%) answered in a neutral way and no users disagreed. Regarding the content displayed on the screens were clear and organized, 43 users (78.2%) agreed with the statement, 8 users (14.5%) answered in a neutral way and 4 users (7.3%) disagreed.

On gamification, Fig. 8 also highlights the increase in user engagement on October 26, the day that hashtags were most heavily included in the event, and users knew that it would be the last day to improve their rankings by entering the codes in the application. A gamification award was given at the end of the day. In addition, the satisfaction questionnaire presented two issues related to gamification.

Regarding the statement "The proposed challenges stimulated my participation in the event", there were 56 respondents, where 36 (64.28%) agreed, 3 (5.3%) disagreed and 17 (30.35%) were neutral. On the statement "My achievements at the end of the event reflected my participation in the IHC 2017", 37 (66.97%) agreed with the statement, 7 (12.5%) disagreed and 12 (21.42%) responded in a neutral way. On the statement "Playing made the application more fun" 48 participants (85.71%) answered in the affirmative, 2 (3.5%) negatively and 6 (10.71%) in a neutral way. This issue highlights the importance of gamification to engage participants in the IHC 2017.

5 Recommendation Module

The content-based recommendation was explicitly displayed and the social recommendation was presented implicitly, so the evaluations of the recommendations were performed separately.

The evaluation of the content-based recommendation in AppIHC was performed in two ways: (1) quantitative analysis and (2) satisfaction questionnaire. The first was based on the positive and negative feedbacks given by users with the likes and dislikes buttons to know how many users who received the recommendations considered these recommendations positive or negative. The second was through a questionnaire that allowed to acquire a greater amount of feedback on the recommendations generated, since the questions contained in it were more specific about each detail of the recommendations.

For the users who used the recommendations, of 108 AppIHC users, 73 (around 67.6%) used the recommendations at least one day during the IHC 2017. In order to know who used the recommendations, it was verified within the profile of each user in the database, since this field is only created if the user has accessed the "Recommended of the Day" at least once during the event week.

For the 73 users who used the AppIHC recommendations, a total of 537 sessions were recommended during the event IHC 2017. Of this total of recommended sessions,

180 (33.5%) received evaluations of 47 users. The users provided positive feedbacks for the total of 156 recommended sessions (86.66% of the evaluations) and negative feedback for 24 sessions (13.33% of the evaluations). It was possible to notice that most of the recommended sessions that received evaluations were evaluated positively, indicating that the recommendations were satisfactory for the majority of users.

The social recommendation by co-authoring was added implicitly in order to not conflict with the content recommendation. When using AppIHC, the user receives recommendations through text and icon in the event schedule, presented per day according to Fig. 9.

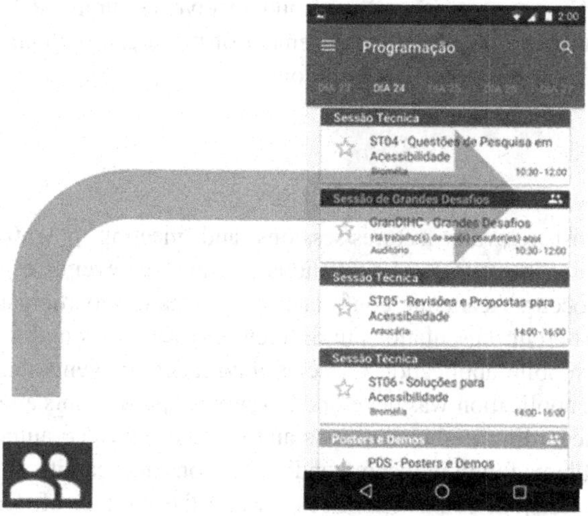

Fig. 9. Social icon and social recommendation.

From the 108 users enrolled in the application, the social recommender system identified 35 event participants who are co-authors, but only 14 of them used the AppIHC application. A questionnaire was sent after the event to these 14 participants, but only 8 users answered the following questions on Table 1:

Table 1. Closed questions about social recommendation

Questions	Yes	No answer	No
Q1. Did you notice the indication that your co-author(s) are in a given session?	5	2	1
Q2. This information influenced your decision-making about which sessions to attend?	1	2	5
Q3. Do you find useful indicate co-authoring to recommend sessions?	5	2	1

Although the participants affirmed that they were not influenced by the coauthoring recommendation, we could see in the database that they mark some of the sessions recommended as favorite. This could indicate that although the user considers not to have been influenced, he/she liked the recommended session.

The other questions were open and aimed to identify suggestions for improvements to the recommendation process, with and without the use of social elements. These suggestions made it possible to obtain requirements for the improvement of the recommendation module and the application.

In terms of social issues, users suggested: allowing the selection and visualization of co-authors' interests; create a network of friends by adding people from the academic community, not necessarily co-authors; share preferences, interests and works to be presented, with due consent; recommend and receive recommendations from other users. The evaluation provided the improvement of the social recommendation model that were applied it in the event 2018 edition.

6 Discussion

Choosing the most relevant lectures/sessions and meeting potential contributors/partners with similar interests can be a tedious task at large events, especially because parallel sessions occur. Academic conferences are dynamic, participants are moving, participating in different presentations in different environments and at different times.

AppIHC is a mobile application for scientific/academic events that helps users to find sessions. The application was developed to support participants attending the event to find sessions according to their interests and collaborations/co-authors/partners.

The main problems found in recommending sessions are scarcity of evaluations and cold start. The scarcity of evaluations occurs when the number of items evaluated is much smaller than that of items available in the system, making it difficult to obtain similarities between people. The cold start problem occurs when a new user or item is entered into the system because there are no evaluations of the item or no items evaluated by the user, so it is not possible to recommend items or find similar users. In the case of the recommender systems for events, the above problems are aggravated due to the short period of time that an event exists and the lack of history of participations and evaluations.

To make recommendations through the use of the content-based approach, it is necessary to know only the target user of the recommendation and to compare the content similarity of the works to be presented with the user's tastes. A good point that helps to solve the mentioned problems, since evaluations are not necessary to initiate the recommendations by content, in this case they are used to improve the recommendations every user interaction with the AppIHC.

However, interpersonal influence is an important contextual factor. The similarity between friends can be an aspect that contributes to the recommendation process, as well as the frequency of interactions and participation in events, important social characteristics that contribute greatly to the improvement of the recommendation process. For this reason, the social recommendation by co-authoring has the objective of helping the participants to find their coauthors in the sessions of the scientific event.

This way, the recommender system present in AppIHC reduces the users' attention overload when navigating the event schedule by searching for sessions of their interest.

7 Considerations

This applied research aimed to describe, discuss and evaluate a mobile application to facilitate the participants' access to the event's programming and to promote their engagement. This application was used and evaluated during and after the IHC 2017 event. AppIHC includes a recommender system that uses information from the user profile and his/her interest to generate recommendation by content, and generates social recommendation through the co-authoring IHC network.

As future work new social elements, in addition to co-authorship relationships, are being added to the social recommendation model. In addition, the application is also being improved and developed for other platforms and is being used in different scientific events.

References

1. Schmidt, L., Ohira, M.L.B.: Bibliotecas Virtuais e Digitais: Análise das Comunicações em Eventos Científicos (1995/2000). Revista ACB **7**(1), 73–97 (2002). (in Portuguese)
2. App of CBIE e LACLO (2015). https://play.google.com/store/apps/details?id=net.moblee.cbieelaclo&hl=pt
3. App of SBSC e IHC (2015). https://play.google.com/store/apps/details?id=br.unifacs.ihc2015
4. App of SIGGRAPH: Special interest group on graphics and interactive techniques (2016). https://play.google.com/store/apps/details?id=me.doubledutch.siggraph2015&hl=pt
5. Arens-Volland, A., Naudet, Y.: Personalized recommender system for event attendees. In: 11th International Workshop on Semantic and Social Media Adaptation and Personalization (SMAP). IEEE (2016)
6. Asabere, N.Y., et al.: Improving smart conference participation through socially aware recommendation. IEEE Trans. Hum. Mach. Syst. **44**(5), 689–700 (2014)
7. Gedikli, F.: Recommender Systems and the Social Web: Leveraging Tagging Data for Recommender Systems. Springer Vieweg, Wiesbaden (2013). https://doi.org/10.1007/978-3-658-01948-8
8. Google inc.: Meet android studio android studio (2017). https://developer.android.com/studio/intro/index.html. Accessed 11 Aug 2018
9. Draw.io: Online diagrams (2017). https://www.draw.io/. Accessed 11 Aug 2018
10. Ricci, F., Rokach, L., Shapira, B.: Introduction to recommender systems handbook. In: Ricci, F., Rokach, L., Shapira, B., Kantor, P.B. (eds.) Recommender Systems Handbook, pp. 1–35. Springer, Boston (2011). https://doi.org/10.1007/978-0-387-85820-3_1
11. Gediminas, A., Tuzhilin, A.: Toward the next generation of recommender systems: a survey of the state-of-the-art and possible extensions. IEEE Trans. Knowl. Data Eng. **17**(6), 734–749 (2015)

Heterogeneous Device Arrangements Affect Both Partners' Experiences in Collaborative Media Spaces

Baris Unver[1,2](✉), Jasmine Jones[1], Alexander Thayer[2], and Svetlana Yarosh[1]

[1] University of Minnesota, Minneapolis, MN 55455, USA
{verxx003, jazzij, lana}@umn.edu
[2] HP Labs, Palo Alto, CA 94304, USA
huevos@alumni.washington.edu

Abstract. HCI has a history of developing rich media spaces to support collaboration between remote parties and testing such systems in investigations where each partner uses the same device setup (i.e., homogeneous device arrangements). In this work, we contribute an infrastructure that supports connection between a projector-camera media space and commodity mobile devices (i.e., tablets, smartphones). Deploying three device arrangements using this infrastructure, we conducted a mixed-methods investigation of device heterogeneity in media space collaboration. We found that the commodity devices provided a worse user experience, though this effect was moderated in some collaboration tasks. Collaborating with a partner who was using a commodity device also negatively affected the experience of the other user. We report specific collaboration concerns introduced by device heterogeneity. Based on these findings, we offer implications for the design of media spaces that use heterogeneous devices.

Keywords: Media spaces · Computer-mediated communication · Distributed collaboration · Projector-camera systems · Mobile devices · Asymmetry

1 Introduction

The proliferation of smart mobile devices [1] has led to a significant expansion in the availability of synchronous communication tools and diversity of device platforms. Each device used in collaboration may have significantly different capabilities and may provide different affordances for interaction and representations of the same information. For example, an online whiteboard drawing application may be simultaneously used by someone using a finger to draw on a 4-in. Android phone screen, someone using a stylus on a 13-in. iPad Pro, and someone using a mouse on a Windows laptop computer. Cross-platform compatibility and development to enable this kind of interaction are a major push in the industry development [2]. The impact of devices on the remote collaboration experience remains an open question and recent studies have shown that even minor differences in the presentation of digital content can lead to a

M. Kurosu (Ed.): HCII 2019, LNCS 11567, pp. 76–98, 2019.
https://doi.org/10.1007/978-3-030-22643-5_7

significant amount of miscommunication (e.g., [3]). The first contribution of this work is an empirical investigation examining the effect of device type on media space collaboration experiences of both partners.

In contrast to the cross-platform push in the industry, research investigations have almost exclusively focused on the interaction across homogeneous system setups. For example, a significant suite of studies has explored the role of the duplex pro-cam systems for communication and collaboration [4–6]. These systems typically provide a rich face-to-face media space and a shared tabletop or wall-wide projection surface for supporting collaboration on tasks, typically through the substantial use of custom hardware. In all the previous investigations, these novel systems were tested in a setup where each participant had identical access to the rich features of each system. As pro-cam communication systems become available on commodity hardware and show the potential for expansion into the real-world use (e.g., [7]), we need to consider how others may connect to and interact with such systems using a diverse suite of devices and how such an interaction may affect the collaboration experience. The second contribution of this work is the development of an infrastructure and system to support the collaboration between video-based media spaces running on heterogeneous device arrangements. We implemented three specific examples of how this infrastructure may be adapted to support collaboration between a projector-camera media space and commodity devices like tablets and smartphones.

In this paper, we describe the development of the ShareSuite infrastructure which addresses the research gap in understanding media spaces which use heterogeneous device arrangements. Through a mixed-methods investigation of three device arrangements and an analysis of qualitative feedback following the experiment, our work addresses three research questions:

- RQ1: How does the device (pro-cam vs. tablet vs. tablet & smartphone) used in a media space collaboration affect a one's experience?
- RQ2: How does the device used by one's communication partner in a media space collaboration affect one's experience?
- RQ3: What specific concerns and challenges are introduced with the use of heterogeneous device arrangements in remote collaboration?

We begin with a discussion of related work, describing previous investigations of novel media space collaboration systems and previous work on cross-device interaction. We describe the ShareSuite infrastructure. We report the methods and results of a 48-participant mixed-methods study where we compare collaboration experiences between multiple device arrangements. Our results demonstrate that using a commodity device negatively impacts the experience of the user and (to a lesser extent) their communication partner and introduces a new set of concerns and collaboration challenges. Finally, we offer future research and design directions based on our findings.

2 Related Work

We review relevant research and related fields that influenced both the system design and the research questions of this work.

2.1 Media Spaces for Remote Collaboration: Homogeneous Arrangements

Media spaces are collaboration technologies that combine video, audio, and other potential forms of synchronous media. This class of technologies was originally developed for an office context in the early 1990s, but has since become a common technological trope in home settings as well [1]. Media spaces may aim to increase general awareness of remote partners (e.g., [8]), enhance social contact and communication (e.g., [9]), or serve as a shared workspace where tasks may be synchronously accomplished (e.g., [10]). The latter is most relevant to this work. While a media space may consist of exclusively one type of media (e.g., just video [11]), media spaces for accomplishing synchronous tasks typically combine a "person-space" and a "task-space."

Previous work has pointed out that "media spaces are an inherently asymmetrical technology" with regard to several socio-technical dimensions, such as different levels of participation in, engagement with, and benefit from the collaboration [12]. These asymmetries have been investigated as side effects in previous collaboration studies. For example, in a study of a community awareness system, the users who chose not to share the video were neglected by others and felt like "2nd class citizens" [13]. In other investigations, asymmetries of participation arose from the specifics of a collaboration task (e.g., an expert instructing a worker [14]). Asymmetries of benefit have been discussed in media spaces aimed at connecting the parents and children in divorced [6] and/or work-separated families [15], where the child, the remote parent, and the co-present parent may all have different motivations, benefits, and costs. However, while these asymmetries have been acknowledged and briefly discussed, media spaces are typically deployed and evaluated in ways that artificially create homogeneity and symmetry. Our investigation addresses this gap by developing an infrastructure for heterogeneous media spaces and examining the role heterogeneous device arrangements on collaboration.

2.2 Device Ecosystems: Rise of Heterogeneous Arrangements

Research focus on homogeneous arrangements in media space development and testing is in stark contrast to other areas of HCI, which have sought to leverage the pervasiveness and diversity of available mobile devices by focusing on the cross-device interaction and diverse device ecosystems. Cross-device interaction allows multiple mobile devices to support different parts of a given task, leveraging the multi-device ecosystem available to most of the users [1]. Such cross-device interactions have been termed Distributed User Interfaces (DUIs) [16] and they may include interfaces distributed across multiple devices, multiple displays, etc. [17]. As an example of this work, Hamilton et al., investigated how to use multiple devices adjunct to each other for creating larger displays by developing a framework conductor which supports cross-device application interaction [18].

In comparison to these endeavors outside of a collaboration context, the role of mobile device ecosystems and the effects of heterogeneous device arrangements in media spaces has not been adequately investigated. Even as mobile devices become increasingly important to how people seek to share their experiences [19–24], video sharing applications are frequently poorly adapted for mobile platforms [25]. Our work contributes an infrastructure for and an empirical investigation of heterogeneous device arrangements (including DUIs) in dual-space media spaces.

2.3 Dual Space Media Spaces: Prototypes vs. Infrastructure

This investigation focuses on dual-space media spaces, which combine a person-space and a task-space. A person-space provides audio and video of a remote collaborator to increase workspace awareness and allow verbal conversations and expressions to be exchanged remotely [26]. Previous work has shown that such a "face-to-face" view is necessary and helpful in collaborative tasks like remote assistance [27]. A task-space provides a view of the artifacts in the workspace and ideally allows for some manipulation of these artifacts and some gestures over the shared task-space. The availability of such a shared space has been shown to provide necessary conversational grounding in remote tasks [28], resulting in better task performance [29].

HCI researchers have developed many dual space media spaces. One of the earliest such systems (VideoDraw [30]), allowed people to draw directly on a digital display and captured this activity with a top-down camera to transmit to a remote display. Many more recent systems use top-down projector-camera (pro-cam) setups to create a shared tabletop task-space [5, 6, 31, 32]. Other systems use horizontally-mounted (e.g., ClearBoard [33], C-Slate [34]) or vertically-mounted (e.g., ImmerseBoard [35]) displays that combine cameras, multi-touch, and styluses to support remote collaboration. The person-space in these systems is typically either shown on a separate vertical display (e.g., [6]), superimposed on the task space (e.g., [33]), or shown in a separate window on the same display as the task-space (e.g., [36]). Each approach to dual-space media spaces has different benefits for users and introduces a different set of technical challenges to resolve.

Fig. 1. Three device set used implemented to demonstrate the ShareSuite media space infrastructure: an HP Sprout duplex pro-cam system, a commodity tablet device, and a distributed user interface that combines a tablet and a smartphone.

These previous investigations share many common features. First, they all require custom hardware modifications and each system is developed only for the specific hardware that is utilized in the prototype deployment. In contrast, in this work, we offer an infrastructure that abstracts the idea of "task-space" and "person-space" and intelligently designates these to appropriate devices (or areas of devices) based on device availability. Second, the media spaces above have been tested exclusively in homogenous device arrangements. The present work leverages our infrastructure to offer an empirical investigation of collaboration in heterogeneous dual-space media space arrangements.

3 ShareSuite Infrastructure

The ShareSuite infrastructure supports collaboration across dual-space media spaces on a variety of devices. We designed this infrastructure to support the following motivating example of a heterogeneous device media space collaboration:

> *Simon wants some feedback from Zahra on a design sketch. His office is equipped with a projector-camera media space, and he logs into the ShareSuite, initiates a connection, and places some of his paper sketches on the table. Zahra is traveling and receives the contact request on her iPad Pro. As she answers the contact, her device splits the available screen real estate so that the Simon's person-space video appears next to the camera feed from his tabletop display. Zahra sketches on her iPad with a stylus and her contribution is projected directly onto Simon's table; conversely, Zahra can see Simon's sketches and gestures over the tabletop displayed as a video on her tablet. Wanting to have a bigger workspace while still seeing Simon's face, Zahra also logs into the ShareSuite on her Android smartphone. The ShareSuite readjust the workspaces so that the phone becomes the new person-space and the tablet becomes entirely task-space, allowing her to work with Simon more efficiently.*

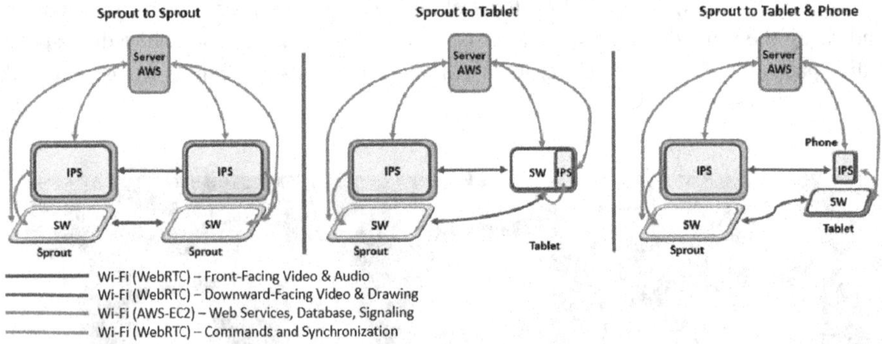

Fig. 2. Three collaboration arrangements supported by our system infrastructure shows Shared Workspace (SW) and Interpersonal Space (IPS) representation on each device; data transmission between devices and Amazon Web Services (AWS).

Below, we describe the device-side and server-side infrastructure of the ShareSuite, as well as three different device arrangements implemented over the ShareSuite infrastructure for the purpose of this investigation (see Figs. 1 and 2).

3.1 Device-Side Infrastructure and Functionalities

The ShareSuite infrastructure was designed to be adapted to multiple device types. Each device must have at least one screen, at least one camera, and the ability for manipulating the task-space (e.g., touch screen so that the user can draw on the screen). The device communicates the screen area available for the task-space and resolution of the screen to the server (see Sect. 3.2) allowing to send the appropriate video channel to the screen. To support a common task-space, we implemented a draw-over-video environment with standard digital tools (e.g., similar to Ou's et al. [37]). To support heterogeneous device arrangements, we implemented coordinate transformation to allow devices with different screen resolutions and dimensions. Each device receives a video stream of the task-space from the server along with the coordinate system describing the capture characteristics of the origin device. The device than converts the video to the local coordinate system (preserving the aspect ratio). In cases where a single screen must support both a task-space and a person-space, the device receives multiple video streams from the server. In the current implementation, the device splits screen area between task and person-space in a way that best preserves the aspect ratio while maximizing the task area, however the infrastructure supports dynamic adjustment in future instantiations.

3.2 Server-Side Infrastructure

ShareSuite's seamless connection between devices and its adaptive display reconfiguration is handled by a cloud-based server. The server infrastructure is hardware agnostic to ensure compatibility across commodity devices.

The ShareSuite clients and cloud server exchange audiovisual information using three simultaneous data channels, implemented as WebRTC-enabled web pages (see Fig. 2). The person-space channel carries the front-facing video, audio, and data for call initiation. The task-space channel can transmit an additional camera channel or a stream of digital drawing data from the shared workspace. The support channel provides synchronization, information, and command transfer between the audiovisual channels.

The ShareSuite provides a common authorization infrastructure across clients. Signing in on multiple devices (e.g., a phone and a tablet) intelligently divides the task- and person-spaces. Each instance connects to the AWS-EC2 web server to load the browser-based interface and video content. After loading the content, ICE/STUN server accessed over web socket to assign a unique Peer ID for the WebRTC connections to overcome cross-networking connections issues. All data and connections are requested, stored, processed, and delivered via a RESTful API from an Amazon Web Services Elastic Compute Cloud (AWS-EC2) server, running Apache, MySQL, and PHP.

3.3 Devices Implemented for Investigation

We implemented the ShareSuite to support three example device sets (see Figs. 1 and 2). In Sect. 4.2, we describe how these device sets are combined into heterogeneous arrangements order to investigate how collaboration may be affect.

Duplexed Projector-Camera Tabletop as Task Space, Vertical Display as Person Space. We implemented a full-duplex projector-camera system, over an off-the-shelf HP Sprout personal computer. We implemented the task-space on the Sprout's horizontal multi-touch mat with a top-down pro-cam display (HP DLP 1024 × 768 projection, 14.6 MP downward-facing camera, 20-point multitouch). Participants could draw directly on the multitouch mat using their finger. The person-space was placed on the Sprout's large vertical monitor (23″ 1920 × 1080 display, 1 MP front-facing camera), showing the face-to-face video of the collaborator. To enable access the Sprout's built-in hardware, we deployed our WebRTC ShareSuite solution in a Chromium CefSharp instance (rather than in a browser). We refer to this device as "Sprout" or "S" throughout this paper.

Commodity Tablet Split for Task and Person Spaces. The second device we implemented to connect with the ShareSuite infrastructure was a conventional tablet. We used a Nexus 7 tablet (7″ 1280 × 800 display, 1.2 MP camera) with a split screen to display the task- and person-spaces. We deployed the ShareSuite in a browser-instance as described above. We refer to this device as "Tablet" or "T".

Commodity Tablet Split for Task and Person Spaces. Finally, to demonstrate the DUI capabilities of the ShareSuite infrastructure, we implemented a dual-device set that combines a tablet and a smartphone. We deployed the ShareSuite in a browser-instance on both devices as described above. The tablet was a Nexus 7 (7″ 1280 × 800 display, 1.2 MP camera) and was fully dedicated to the task-space. The LG G2 Android smartphone (5.2″ 1920 × 1080 display, 2.1 MP camera) was fully dedicated to the person-space. We refer to this arrangement as "Tablet&Phone" or "TP".

4 Methods

To investigate our research questions regarding collaboration across heterogeneous device arrangements, we conducted a mixed-design lab experiment. Participants (N = 48) completed a collaborative task in pairs, with each pair completing one of two collaborative tasks using each of the three different device arrangements: Sprout-to-Sprout (S-S), Sprout-to-Tablet (S-T), and Sprout-to-Tablet&Phone (S-TP). In this section, we describe the study design, participant recruitment, data collection, and data analysis methods.

4.1 Participants

We recruited 48 participants internally in a large U.S. technology company through word-of-mouth and email solicitations and grouped them into 24 pairs for our study. Fifteen of the participants were female (33 male), and they ranged in age from 18 to 57 (M = 28.8, SD = 9.9). None of the pairs knew each other prior to the start of the study. Each participant received a $25 gift card.

4.2 Study Design

The study took place in a research lab with multiple separate partitioned spaces. Participants were randomly assigned into pairs upon recruitment and were given an overview of their roles on the tasks. We demonstrated all three device sets to each participant, ensuring that they were familiar with their functionality. At least one member of the research team was available in the room to answer questions and help resolve technical difficulties.

We chose to test two tasks in our experiment to observe the use of heterogeneous device arrangements in tasks that are typically carried out in a mutual way verses tasks that typically require an asymmetric collaboration. In the mutual collaboration task, the participant pairs were asked to work together to create a logo for a fictional company. A short, written scenario describing the company was provided to both the participants. Each of the three times they repeated the task, it had a similar goal, but the specific details of the fictional company differed. In the helper-worker task, participants were assigned to either a worker or a helper role. The helper was asked to instruct the worker to construct a specific Lego Duplo structure consisting of 13 bricks (based on a step-by-step manual provided to the helper). All tasks were piloted by confederates to insure consistent complexity and that each task took about 10 min to complete. Throughout the paper, we refer to these two tasks as "Logo" and "Lego" tasks respectively.

To address RQ1 (effect of the device on the user's experience), one partner was assigned to switch technologies (Sprout, Tablet, and Tablet&Phone) for each of the three tasks. The specific order of the three technologies was counterbalanced to avoid order effects. To address RQ2 (effect of the partner's device on the user's experience), the other partner was assigned to use the Sprout device throughout the three tasks. In other words, the first participant experienced switching devices with all other aspects held stable (task, partner, partner's device), while the second participant experienced their partner switching devices with all other aspects held stable (task, partner, their device). We refer to these two types of participant roles as "Switching" and "Non-Switching" throughout the paper.

Thus, this study constitutes a mixed-design: Lego/Logo and Switching/Non-Switching assignment was between-subjects, while the specific type of the technology arrangement was varied within-subjects. Upon completion of each round, the participants completed several short post-task questionnaires (see Sect. 4.3). After the participants had completed all three tasks, one researcher interviewed each participant about their overall experience.

4.3 Metrics and Analysis

We employed several complementary empirical strategies to understand our participants' experiences:

- **Video and Audio Recordings:** We collected video and audio recordings of the sessions as the basis for verbatim transcription and post-hoc coding. The lead author reviewed all the recordings and coded examples of miscommunications, struggles, and challenges.

- **Satisfaction and Preference Questionnaire:** To complement this qualitative understanding we deployed a questionnaire investigating users' holistic satisfaction, condition preference, and comparison to an unmediated interaction:
  - Comparison to Unmediated Interaction/Satisfaction with Collaboration: a single Likert-type item where a higher score indicates a higher level of similarity/ satisfaction, answered for each condition and analyzed with a repeated-measure ANOVA.
  - Condition Preference: after completing all three conditions, we asked participants to specify a preferred device arrangement (or "None" if they had a similar experience with all three). These were analyzed using categorical comparison tests (Chi-Square, Fisher Exact) as appropriate.
- **Perceived Message Understanding (PMU):** We used the 6-question Perceived Message Understanding scale [38] to help address RQ1 and RQ2. The scale is scored by averaging the six Likert-type items within the scale—a higher score corresponds to a greater perception of understanding and being understood by the partner. We compared conditions using a repeated-measures ANOVA.
- **Open-Ended Debriefing Interview:** After the completion of the experiment, we interviewed each participant individually. The semi-structured interview contained five open-ended questions about the collaboration and lasted approximately 15 min. We asked participants to reflect and provide feedback about their experience using the ShareSuite, including their opinions of each device arrangement, how the devices compared, and any recommendations they might have for future collaborative systems. Interviews were audio recorded and transcribed. We followed a data-driven inductive process of analysis where we first open-coded the transcripts for individual units of meaning, clustered these codes using an affinity map, and iterated on the clusters to arrive at emergent themes. We are confident that we reached data saturation, as major themes began repeating and no new themes emerged after interview 19 for either task.

All sources are used for all three research questions. We focus primarily on qualitative data. Quantitative comparisons and descriptive statistics are used when appropriate as an additional source of evidence.

4.4 Method Limitations

We conducted a lab study with short, constrained tasks. There may be more emergent effects that could arise in a longer-term, less-controlled study. Nevertheless, similar previous studies showed that the task duration (10-min) is adequate to obtain reliable results [14, 29, 39]. We limited our study to two possible examples of heterogeneous device arrangements (Sprout-to-Tablet and Sprout-to-Tablet&Phone). Of course, the possible number of device arrangements grows exponentially with the number of supported devices and it is not feasible to test a complete crossing of all possible device arrangements (in this case, a full-crossing would have required us to test six different arrangements, which would have been impractical in a within-subjects study). Thus, we focused on three arrangements. The Sprout-to-Sprout arrangement provides an example of a homogenous pro-cam arrangement similar to those tested in previous work, serving as a point of comparison. We chose to explore connections to Tablet and Tablet&Phone as particular heterogeneous device arrangements because they represent the connection of a rich media space to two more limited (yet commonly available) devices (Table 1).

Table 1. Means and variance of the Satisfaction, Perceived Message Understanding (PMU), and Similarity to Unmediated measures for participants across the within-subjects (tech) and between-subjects (role, task) factors.

Role (each, N = 24)	Tech (each, N = 24)	Task (each, N = 12)	Satisfaction (out of 7)	PMU (out of 7)	Unmediated (out of 7)
Switching partner	S-S	Lego	5.67, *SD* = 1.23	4.83, *SD* = 1.03	5.83, *SD* = 1.33
		Logo	6.04. *SD* = 0.75	4.67, *SD* = 0.89	5.67, *SD* = 1.37
	S-TP	Lego	5.71, *SD* = 1.07	4.33, *SD* = 0.99	5.58, *SD* = 1.51
		Logo	5.13, *SD* = 1.33	4.25, *SD* = 1.29	5.08, *SD* = 1.38
	S-T	Lego	6.03, *SD* = 0.62	4.50, *SD* = 0.67	5.67, *SD* = 1.07
		Logo	4.92, *SD* = 1.21	4.08, *SD* = 0.90	5.17, *SD* = 1.70
Non-switching partner	S-S	Lego	5.97, *SD* = 0.88	4.67, *SD* = 0.49	6.08, SD = 0.67
		Logo	5.68, *SD* = 1.09	5.25, *SD* = 0.87	5.50, *SD* = 0.67
	S-TP	Lego	5.48, *SD* = 1.06	4.33, *SD* = 0.65	5.33, *SD* = 1.50
		Logo	5.61, *SD* = 1.00	5.33, *SD* = 1.16	5.42, *SD* = 1.38
	S-T	Lego	5.45, *SD* = 1.06	4.42, *SD* = 0.79	5.25, *SD* = 1.14
		Logo	5.53, *SD* = 1.64	5.00, *SD* = 1.21	5.25, *SD* = 1.22

5 Results

In the following sections, we present both qualitative and quantitative evidence regarding the effect of the device arrangement on satisfaction & preference, perceived similarity to unmediated collaboration, perceived message understanding, and asymmetries in participation.

Table 2. Stated preference between the three conditions and a Chi-Square Goodness of Fit comparison to an equal distribution. "None" specifies that the participant said that all conditions were equivalent for them (and was excluded from the Chi-Square).

Tech	Task	S-to-S	S-to-T&P	S-to-T	None	Chi-Square GoF
Switching partner	Logo task	12	0	0	0	$X^2 = 24.244$, $p < 0.001$***
	Lego task	9	1	2	0	$X^2 = 9.597$, $p = 0.008$**
Non-switching partner	Logo task	8	0	1	3	$X^2 = 12.796$, $p = 0.002$**
	Lego task	7	2	1	2	$X^2 = 6.264$, $p = 0.044$*

5.1 Satisfaction and Preference

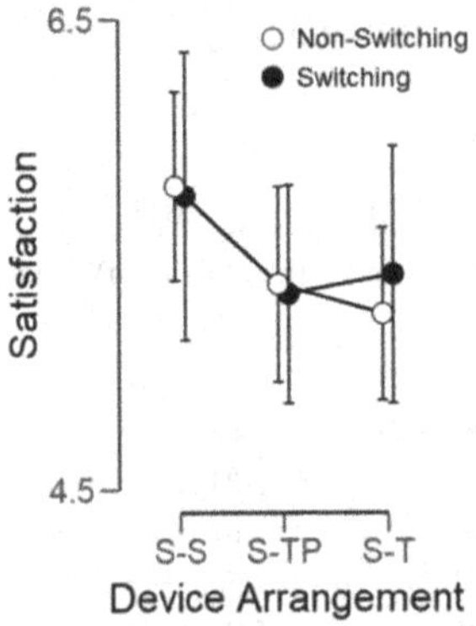

Fig. 3. Satisfaction ratings across device arrangements by participants in switching and non-switching roles. Error bars represent 95% confidence interval.

Given that we were interested in the holistic evaluation of the experience in each condition, we focused on qualitative feedback, self-reported satisfaction, and an explicit statement of preference between conditions to understand how the specific devices affected the experience of both participants.

The ShareSuite was overall well-received by participants, with the average satisfaction rating across devices at 5.49 (out of 7, $SD = 1.26$). Participants who switched devices mentioned that they appreciated the seamless transition between the three device arrangements afforded by the ShareSuite infrastructure: *"the app is really good because it worked fine also with the mobile devices."* Other participants who switched devices also note that the experiences across all three devices were comparable in that they and their partner *"were able to achieve the outcome desired in reasonable amount of time."*

While participants recognized that connection with mobile devices enabled previously-impossible contexts of collaboration, they also noted that it was not as rich as the connection afforded by the Sprout device. Participants indicated in the interviews that Sprout was the richer method of interaction due to screen size and ability to communicate gestures, e.g., *"Sprout was probably the best one because the screen was bigger"* and *"he pointed sometimes at the bricks that I've used, and this was very helpful."* When comparing across conditions, the Sprout-to-Sprout arrangement was the clear preference among all participants (see Table 2). It is not surprising the participants in the "switching" role would strongly prefer the Sprout condition, as it was the richest of three and provides the larger task- and person-spaces. It is perhaps more surprising that the non-switching partners (who always used the Sprout) had a similar preference towards the symmetric Sprout-to-Sprout condition, as nominally their experience with each condition featured the same partner, task, and device.

Descriptively, it may appear that S-S may have been particularly preferred by those doing the Logo task. While the difference in distributions is not statistically significant (Fisher Exact Test, $p = 0.157$), qualitative data points at a possible effect of the task factor. Namely, many participants found the low contrast lighting of the projector on the Sprout problematic in the Lego task, especially when the projection was onto a physical object rather than on the mat: *"I couldn't actually see the image of his hands out in the Legos."* This may have been exacerbated by the fact that this particular pro-cam solution used ambient light to address video echo that arises in full-duplex pro-cam systems [7], which washed out colors and reduced contrast. This was particularly problematic for depth perception in the Lego tasks:

> *I kept getting the feedback from my partner that the depth perception and other things were much better viewed [S-T] as compared to the first two and he was able to describe to me exactly what I needed to do.*

Overall, participants saw some positives and negatives in each device arrangement, though there was a marked preference towards the Sprout-to-Sprout setup. However, the satisfaction rating responses were less clearly divided, perhaps due to a ceiling effect (see Fig. 3). While descriptively, the S-S condition had greater satisfaction ratings and the device arrangement accounted for greatest variance in satisfaction ratings ($\eta 2 = 0.05$), the difference was not statistically significant ($p = 0.112$).

Table 3. Statistical significance and effect sizes for repeated-measure ANOVAs for PMU and "Similarity to Unmediated" measures. No values reported for any cases where p > 0.1

Factor	PMU	Similarity to Unmediated
Tech (S-S vs. S-TP vs. S-T)	$p = 0.074$ ($\eta^2 = 0.06$)	**$p = 0.036^{*1}$ ($\eta^2 = 0.08$)**
Role (Switch vs. Non-Switch)	n.s.	$p = 0.080$ ($\eta^2 = 0.07$)
Tech * Role * Task	**$p = 0.031^{*}$ ($\eta^2 = 0.08$)**	n.s.

Post-Hoc Paired t-Test w/ Bonferroni Correction	
S-S vs. S-T	**$p = 0.047^{*}$ ($d = 0.362$)**
S-S vs. S-TP	n.s.
S-T vs. S-TP	n.s.

[1] After applying Greenhouse-Geisser Sphericity Correction to correct for violation of Sphericity assumption

5.2 Similarity to Unmediated Interaction

While replicating unmediated face-to-face interaction is not always the "holy grail" of collaboration [40], it remains a reasonable comparison and baseline for synchronous collaboration technologies. We asked participants to compare their experience in each of the three device arrangements with that of collaborating in the same room. Qualitatively, participants described the ShareSuite as a *"a viable substitute"* for face-to-face collaboration. However, at least one participant reported that all three devices had low similarity to unmediated interaction due to the specifics of the dual-space media space setup:

> *Across all three, one thing I noticed is that me and my partner were both looking at the top of each other's heads a lot [as we bent our heads to draw on the surface] ... so to communicate with her I'd have to go through the canvas and not through the face.*

Aside from this participant, most others felt that different arrangements had different effects on comparison with unmediated interaction. Some participants made strong claims about the S-S arrangement being "just the way" in-person collaboration works:

When we are trying to collaborate across different offices, then this system is very useful, especially considering that we are not face to face but we are still able to see each other, and we are still able to communicate and collaborate just the way you would when you're sitting face to face with someone.

One aspect of this comparison related to the specific orientation of the person and task spaces. Particularly, the fact that the Sprout-to-Sprout condition separated the two workspaces into the horizontal and vertical screens was viewed as particularly *"natural"* and *"helpful"* e.g.:

It felt like he is sitting in front of me, and also with his hands, he pointed sometimes at the bricks that I've used, and this was very helpful.

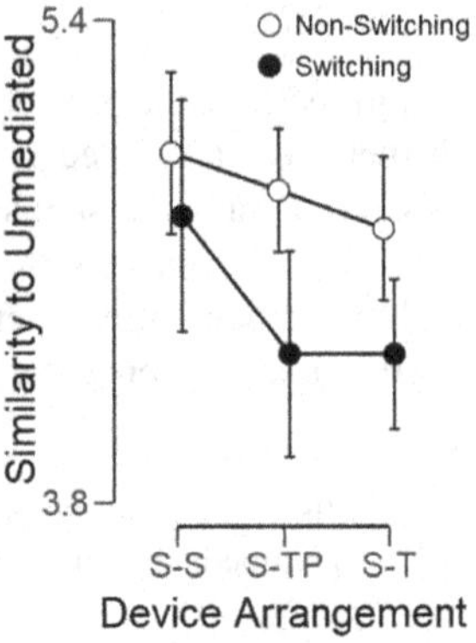

Fig. 4. Ratings of similarity to unmediated collaboration across device arrangements by participants in switching and non-switching roles. Error bars represent 95% confidence interval.

One switching participants expressed that the S-TP condition provided some similar affordances because of a similar division of spaces, stating that it helped to distinguish when she was focused on her drawing task and when she was talking to her partner: *"I wasn't drawing, I was looking at a person. It felt more natural."* In contrast, when using the Tablet, interaction could feel less natural. Non-switching participants using the Sprout explained that it was not clear whether a person was concentrating on the task or looking at them for more direction: *"It seemed that he wasn't looking at me, just looking on the surface of the tablet."*

Beyond the orientation of the two spaces, participants noted rating the Sprout-to-Sprout condition higher because it provided a natural size correspondence in the task-space, rather than scaling the task-space space to a smaller screen:

I loved the space availability that I had. I could draw on the Legos in 1:1 size analogy and my partner could easily follow my hints. I could use various ways of communication with my partner.

The quantitative analysis of participant responses rating each condition based on its similarity to unmediated interaction corroborate these qualitative comparisons (see Fig. 4 and Table 3). There was a statistically-significant main effect of the device condition ($p = 0.036$) with a medium effect size ($\eta 2 = 0.08$). A pairwise comparison within device arrangement conditions revealed that the difference between S-S and S-T was statistically significant ($p = 0.047$), though descriptively the S-S condition was also rated as more similar to unmediated interaction than the S-T&P condition.

5.3 Perceived Message Understanding

Perceived Message Understanding (PMU) refers to each participant's perceived ability to understand their partner during the task and their estimation of how well their partner understood them, measured using the 6-item PMU scale from the Networked Mind Social Presence Measure [38]. Quantitatively, their responses had a statistically-significant ($p = 0.031$, $\eta 2 = 0.08$) three-way interaction between the device arrangement, task type, and participant role (see Table 3 and Fig. 5). The non-switching partners' PMU measures remain more-or-less consistent across conditions. However, the PMU of the partner who is switching devices seems to be affected by the task, with the S-S condition supporting PMU better than S-T on the Logo task. Given the complexity of this three-way interaction, we turn to the factors participants mentioned in the interviews to understand how PMU was affected by device type and participant role.

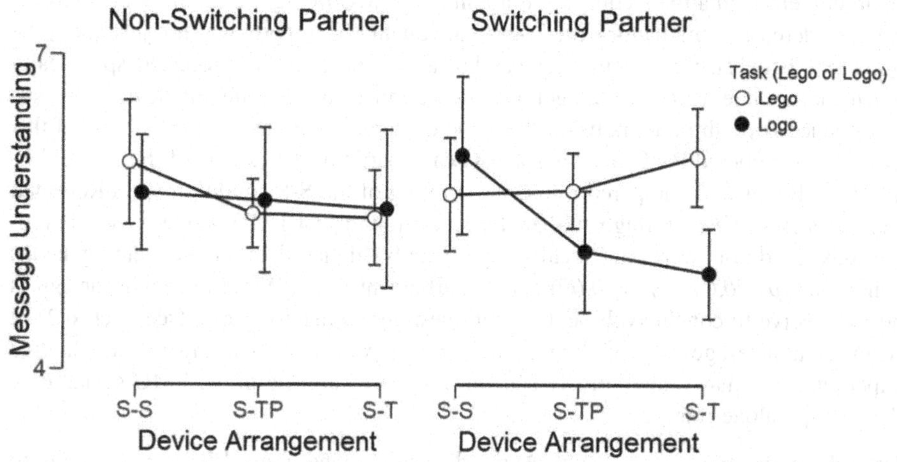

Fig. 5. Perceived message understanding ratings across participant roles (switching and non-switching), tasks (Lego and Logo), and device arrangements (S-S, S-TP, and S-T). Error bars represent 95% confidence interval.

Establishing Common Ground. Collaborators using the same device (S-S condition) reported little difficulty understanding their partner. As one non-switching participant remarked: *"You wouldn't have to worry about if they are seeing the same thing, because you know it's the same setup."*

However, in the heterogenous device arrangements, participants had to work to establish a shared reference and accurate understanding of what the other person was seeing. The differences across each device arrangement was especially salient to the Sprout user as their partner switched from device to device: *"the visual representation between our screens was not consistent and I had no idea what my collaborator could see."* The smaller-display commodity devices also conveyed less information about their users' actions, which sometimes left the non-switching user guessing about what their partner was doing and left the switching user having to find new ways of establishing common ground. One participant explained that when he switched to the Tablet and Tablet&Phone during a Logo task, his partner on the Sprout could no longer see the natural gestures he was making: *"My partner couldn't see my hands ... she wasn't exactly able to anticipate what I was going to do and so there was sort of a gap in communication."*

Participants reported that it was difficult to establish common ground during the Lego task, which was particularly sensitive to the orientation and description of the pieces. One participant said she had a hard time interpreting the instructions that her partner was giving her about how to build their assigned structure, because she could not interpret the perspective he was communicating from: *"I didn't really understand what he was seeing on the other side"* and *"I don't know if she's seeing what I'm seeing."*

These qualitative reports conflict with the quantitative PMU score on one major aspect: the non-switching partners reported being affected by the heterogeneous device setup in their qualitative feedback but not in their PMU rating. As a follow-up analysis, we considered that the factor called out in the qualitative reports was not just about the difference between the specific devices but about the trouble introduced specifically when the arrangement is heterogenous (two partners using different devices) versus homogeneous (both partners using the same device). To do an exploratory test of this assertion, we pooled PMU averages across each participant's ratings of the S-T and S-T&P conditions and compared to the PMU rating of the S-S condition via a Repeated Measures ANOVA. Through this analysis, we found that PMU scores in the homogeneous condition were statistically significantly higher than in the heterogeneous conditions ($p = 0.041$, $\eta 2 = 0.09$) across participant roles. While our study design is not conducive to conclusively addressing questions of heterogeneity (see Sect. 6.2), it seems that heterogeneity of devices may better reflect the participant's qualitative experience and may quantitatively account for more variance in the PMU scores than device type alone role.

Verbal Interaction as a Work-Around. Across-condition PMU scores seem to suggest that device arrangement only mattered in the Logo task, even though participants mentioned several common ground issues in the Lego task condition. We observed that participants may have been able to overcome message understanding issues in the Lego task through verbal work-arounds, which may have smoothed PMU differences across Lego device arrangement conditions.

For example, we saw in our video observations that several of the participant pairs in the Lego task developed verbal practices (e.g., *"take the red 2 × 4 brick"*) that leveraged the simple physical characteristics of the Lego bricks to communicate in a detailed and specific manner:

> *It felt like when I had the mat to work with I started drawing on it, but it ended up not being very effective [in other conditions] ... I think [I liked] being more specific with the dimensions verbally.*

However, though this collaboration style was effective in completing the Lego task, it could have limited applicability to other types of tasks where the there are fewer verbal shortcuts. This may explain the significant interaction with task and why the Lego task PMU appeared more resistant to condition affects.

Difficulty of Switching Between Displays. When discussing the merits of each device, participants pointed out several PMU issues that were particular to the Sprout and the Tablet & Phone devices. A key challenge was maintaining awareness of their partner's actions and attention across multiple displays, as they switched between talking, gesturing, and drawing.

One participant commented that she found herself ignoring all visual cues from her partner as she focused only on her drawing: *"What I noticed is you're just focusing down here, so you're not really focusing on the other person, even if it's up there."* Another participant reported that he missed when his partner was attempting to switch contexts between talking or drawing:

> *I didn't see when he was looking at the front camera or if he was drawing on this thing [the mat] ... when I was watching at this part of the Sprout, I couldn't see that he was doing something on the screen because it was out of my [peripheral vision] and until I figured out that he was doing something on this screen, it was already like 4 or 5 seconds.*

Participants felt that missing these attention cues and other non-verbal gestures would impact their ability to understand be understood:

> *It is sometimes important to see the other person, focus on the other person and see how he's reacting or how he's feeling, that might come out of the gestures he's making.*

In light of this, some participants reported that the side-by-side person- and task-space on the tablet provided the best awareness of their partners: *"it would have been much nicer if I could see the video ... on the mat."*

It seems that each device type introduced a different set of potential limitations to Perceived Message Understanding, leading complex interaction that a single PMU score may have failed to capture with appropriate nuance.

5.4 Asymmetries of Participation

Working on different devices introduced significant challenges for participants in both non-switching and switching roles. Participant interviews revealed equality of participation as another important aspect of collaboration across devices.

We observed that having less drawing space in the Tablet and Tablet & Phone conditions than on the Sprout had a negative effect on the participation level of the user in the switching role. When using different devices to collaborate, switching participants' activity shifted to make the non-switching Sprout user the primary driver of the task, or *"the main person drawing,"* and the switching user became *"more of a facilitator."* One reason for switching into this facilitator role was inability to precisely draw on the small screen:

> *Drawing on the tablet this time was very difficult because of small screen size. Several times, I had to tell my partner what to draw and she would draw it for me.*

While these issues were particularly pernicious in the Logo task, we saw aspects of participation affected by device used the Lego task as well. We noticed in our video observations that switching participants in the Lego task exhibited a similar trend of decreasing hands-on participation as they moved to the smaller devices. Participants used sketches and gestures more to direct their partner when they were using the Sprout, but relied more on verbal instructions and feedback when using a different device. This may have been one aspect that may have negatively influenced the non-switching participants experience with the collaboration even when they themselves continued using the richer Sprout media space.

All in all, participants seemed to strongly prefer an arrangement that would let both people see and experience the same thing, as that would best support and equality of participation and experience:

> *Sprout-to-Sprout, worked better just because they're the same technology in front of us. So, it was equal communication.*

While media space asymmetries of participation have been considered in previous investigations [12], our work suggests device heterogeneity may be an important factor amplifying such asymmetries.

6 Discussion

We enumerate our contributions and discuss opportunities for future research and design.

6.1 Contributions

Previous work has focused almost exclusively on homogeneous device arrangements in such systems. Our work addresses this gap by contributing a technical infrastructure for heterogeneous device media spaces and an empirical investigation that uses this infrastructure to answer three research questions regarding device heterogeneity in media space collaboration.

Empirical Contribution. We were motivated by three research questions. First, we asked how the device (Sprout vs. tablet vs. phone and tablet DUI) used in a media space collaboration affects the participants' experience. To answer this, we asked half of our participants to try three different devices to collaborate with their partner on three similar tasks (i.e., "switching" role). We found that switching participants were strongly affected by the device type, generally preferring the Sprout, expressing highest levels of satisfaction with the Sprout, finding the Sprout to be most similar to unmediated collaboration, identifying the Sprout as the condition with the highest level of perceived message understanding for drawing tasks, and participating more equally when using the Sprout. This is not particularly surprising, but is nonetheless important to consider and quantify as more collaboration moves to commodity mobile devices [1], as it may make the commodity device user into a second-class citizen when collaborating with a partner who uses a richer device.

Second, we asked the converse question: how does the device used by one's communication partner in a media space collaboration affect one's experience?

To answer this, we asked half of our participants to do the same task, with the same partner, and the same device three times (i.e., "non-switching" role), while their partner switched between a Sprout, table, and tablet & phone. We found that the partner's device affected the non-switching participants' experience in similar though more muted ways. For example, non-switching participants expressed a strong preference for the condition where their partner used the Sprout as well and exhibited similar metrics on measures of satisfaction to their partner in each of the three conditions. The non-switching partner was also affected by the asymmetry of participation in the commodity mobile device conditions, receiving less active help and participation from their collaboration partner. The effect of device choice on the collaborative partner is important to consider since many may think of one's device choice as an individual matter, without reflecting on how it may affect the collaboration as a whole.

Finally, we sought to uncover specific concerns and challenges introduced with the use of heterogeneous device arrangements in remote collaboration. We uncovered four specific concerns that are amplified by heterogenous device arrangements:

- As scaling and perspective across devices differ, collaboration feels less natural and more mediated
- Establishing common ground may require additional effort when working on different devices
- Adding multiple screens or displays (i.e., DUIs) may make it difficult to attend to the right signals
- Equality of participation may be affected by partners having devices with different affordances

These aspects are critical to consider when designing collaboration systems and infrastructures that may connect people via diverse devices or systems of devices.

System Contribution. Our second contribution is in the design and implementation of the ShareSuite infrastructure. The ShareSuite allows for device-agnostic implementation of media spaces that combine synchronous real-time video-based task- and person-spaces. The implementation consists of a backend signaling server and device-side WebRTC components that can be easily implemented on many commodity devices. To demonstrate this infrastructure's ability to support collaboration across multiple devices, we implemented three example device sets: a fully duplexed pro-com HP Sprout device, a commodity tablet, and a distributed user interface (DUI) that uses a commodity tablet and a commodity smartphone in concert.

6.2 Implications for Research

Almost all the previous studies of synchronous collaboration have focused on the deployment and evaluation of the user experience in homogeneous device arrangements (e.g., [5, 6, 14, 29, 41]). As remote collaboration systems and ideas move beyond research prototypes and onto commodity devices (e.g., as the HP Sprout has enabled a duplex pro-cam system to be instantiated on an off-the-shelf device), it is critical to consider the role of device heterogeneity. There is no way to ensure that all communication partners will be using devices with equal screen sizes, equal precision pointers, and similar hardware capabilities. This paper is a first step in this direction and we suggest two critical future research directions.

First, our findings on establishing common ground suggest that a salient feature of heterogeneous device systems may be not just in the specifics of the device, but in the factor of heterogeneity itself—collaboration may be affected by using different devices regardless of the specific features of the device. This effect is confounded in our study since the only homogeneous condition is also the richest media space. A future investigation may set up a 2 × 2 design where two interfaces are each investigated in heterogeneous and homogeneous arrangements. Based on our effect sizes, a comparison between a pro-cam and a tablet-based interface may yield most substantial results.

Second, we investigated device heterogeneity in a lab setting to be able to quantify the effects of the factors and gather recorded observational data. However, this controlled setup inherently advantages the richest condition since the main benefits of commodity mobile devices (e.g., portability, quick setup) are irrelevant in the controlled setting. Field studies of device heterogeneity in collaboration may reveal a different set of trade-offs and long-term effects. For example, the inequality of participation (see Sect. 5.4) observed in our study may be ameliorated by being able to contribute in previously unsupported contexts (i.e., contributing at 75% capacity but doubling the number of sessions where one is able to contribute would still be a net positive). We contribute the robust ShareSuite infrastructure for future field investigations.

6.3 Implications for Design

As media space systems move onto commodity devices and out of the lab, it is increasingly important to consider implications for design to help manage some of the challenges that arise from heterogeneous device use in collaboration.

Reveal the Constraints of the Partner's Device. The partner's device affects the collaboration experience. Aspects like screen size, available pointing precision, and camera perspective may all influence how the remote partner can collaborate. Once both participants are aware of each other's constraints, they may adapt their approach to avoid some of the challenges. Currently, most media space systems leave the participants guessing about the constraints of their partner's device on the unspoken assumption that everybody is connecting via an equivalent device setup. At the very least, systems should reveal the remote device display size(s), pointing precision, and other key capabilities to all collaboration parties.

Provide a Task-Space Feedback Window. Understanding exactly what one's partner is seeing was an important challenge that was amplified by the use of heterogeneous devices. Standard video chat typically provides a "feedback" window showing how the front-facing camera feed appears to the partner. Though the practice is not entirely uncontroversial [42], it nonetheless has been shown to be an important tool in managing one's actions towards the partner (e.g., [43]). It may be beneficial to provide a similar feature for the task-space in dual-space media spaces, particularly when it is possible to represent both the remote size and any degradation, latency, etc. due the transmission to help the partner on the richer interface be more aware of the others' experience.

Manage Attention Switching Between Multiple Displays. Our study, like previous work in other collaborative contexts [43], has revealed some challenges with managing attention between multiple displays, whether in pro-cam media spaces or in multi-device distributed user interface systems. One solution may be abandoning the idea of multiple displays and placing both the person-space and the task-space on the same display. However, this solution would reduce the screen real estate available for the task-space and undermine the natural division in orientation that people appreciated and rated as more similar to unmediated collaboration. An alternative solution may be to increase awareness of which display is currently attended by the partner. As webcam-based eye-tracking systems become more robust, one can provide a visual indication of the partner's gaze to help inform joint attention across multiple displays.

7 Conclusion

The assumption that each partner is using an identical device to connect in a media space collaboration may impact HCI's ability to transition research prototypes to commodity systems and into wide adoption. We contribute the ShareSuite infrastructure which supports implementation of device-agnostic dual-space media spaces. We demonstrate this infrastructure by instantiating it on three diverse devices sets. We conducted a mixed-methods investigation of device heterogeneity in media space collaboration, examining the effect of device on its user and the user's communication partner. We identify four core challenges introduced by heterogeneous device arrangements. First, scale and display arrangement may vary across device sets, which may make the interaction feel more mediated and less natural. Second, the two partners may now have different visibility and perspective of the task space, requiring additional effort to establish common ground. Third, diverse number and arrangement of displays and spaces may make it more difficult to achieve joint attention. Finally, asymmetries in the capabilities of each device (e.g., precision in pointing) may lead to asymmetries of participation, affecting the collaboration. We provide implications for future research and design to further investigate these issues.

Acknowledgements. We would like to thank to Mirjana Spasojevic, Mia Minhyang Suh, Mithra Vankipuram, Sabirat Rubya, Aysegul Kuzulu for their support and all the participants for their contributions. This work is supported by NSF grants #1526085, #1651575.

References

1. Anderson, M.: Technology device ownership: 2015 (2015). http://www.pewinternet.org/2015/10/29/technology-device-ownership-2015/
2. Xanthopoulos, S., Xinogalos, S.: A comparative analysis of cross-platform development approaches for mobile applications. In: Proceedings of the 6th Balkan Conference in Informatics, pp. 213–220. ACM, New York (2013)
3. Miller, H., Thebault-Spieker, J., Chang, S., Johnson, I., Terveen, L., Hecht, B.: "Blissfully happy" or "ready to fight": varying interpretations of emoji. In: ICWSM 2016 (2016)

4. Yarosh, S., Cuzzort, S., Müller, H., Abowd, G.D.: Developing a media space for remote synchronous parent-child interaction. In: Proceedings of the 8th International Conference on Interaction Design and Children, pp. 97–105. ACM, New York (2009)
5. Junuzovic, S., Inkpen, K., Blank, T., Gupta, A.: IllumiShare: sharing any surface. In: Proceedings of the SIGCHI Conference on Human Factors in Computing Systems, pp. 1919–1928. ACM, New York (2012)
6. Yarosh, S., Tang, A., Mokashi, S., Abowd, G.D.: "Almost Touching": parent-child remote communication using the sharetable system. In: Proceedings of the 2013 Conference on Computer Supported Cooperative Work, pp. 181–192. ACM, New York (2013)
7. Unver, B., McRoberts, S.A., Rubya, S., Ma, H., Zhang, Z., Yarosh, S.: ShareTable application for HP sprout. In: Proceedings of the 2016 CHI Conference Extended Abstracts on Human Factors in Computing Systems, pp. 3784–3787. ACM, New York (2016)
8. Greenberg, S., Rounding, M.: The notification collage: posting information to public and personal displays. Presented at the proceedings of the SIGCHI conference on human factors in computing systems, 1 March 2001
9. Saslis-Lagoudakis, G., Cheverst, K., Dix, A., Fitton, D., Rouncefield, M.: Hermes@Home: supporting awareness and intimacy between distant family members. In: Proceedings of the 18th Australia Conference on Computer-Human Interaction: Design: Activities, Artefacts and Environments, pp. 23–30. ACM, New York (2006)
10. Ishii, H.: TeamWorkStation: towards a seamless shared workspace. In: Proceedings of the 1990 ACM Conference on Computer-Supported Cooperative Work, pp. 13–26. ACM, New York (1990)
11. Judge, T.K., Neustaedter, C., Kurtz, A.F.: The family window: the design and evaluation of a domestic media space. In: Proceedings of the SIGCHI Conference on Human Factors in Computing Systems, pp. 2361–2370. ACM, New York (2010)
12. Voida, A., Voida, S., Greenberg, S., He, H.A.: Asymmetry in media spaces. In: Proceedings of the 2008 ACM Conference on Computer Supported Cooperative Work, pp. 313–322. ACM, New York (2008)
13. Romero, N., McEwan, G., Greenberg, S.: A field study of community bar: (mis)-matches between theory and practice. In: Proceedings of the 2007 International ACM Conference on Supporting Group Work, pp. 89–98. ACM, New York (2007)
14. Kirk, D., Stanton Fraser, D.: Comparing remote gesture technologies for supporting collaborative physical tasks. In: Proceedings of the SIGCHI Conference on Human Factors in Computing Systems, pp. 1191–1200. ACM, New York (2006)
15. Yarosh, S., Abowd, G.D.: Mediated parent-child contact in work-separated families. In: Proceedings of the SIGCHI Conference on Human Factors in Computing Systems, pp. 1185–1194. ACM, New York (2011)
16. Gallud, J.A., Tesoriero, R., Vanderdonckt, J., Lozano, M., Penichet, V., Botella, F.: Distributed user interfaces. In: CHI 2011 Extended Abstracts on Human Factors in Computing Systems, pp. 2429–2432. ACM, New York (2011)
17. Vanderdonckt, J.: Distributed user interfaces: how to distribute user interface elements across users, platforms, and environments. In: Proceedings of XIth Congreso Internacional de Interacción Persona-Ordenador Interacción 2010, Valencia (2010)
18. Hamilton, P., Wigdor, D.J.: Conductor: enabling and understanding cross-device interaction. In: Proceedings of the SIGCHI Conference on Human Factors in Computing Systems, pp. 2773–2782. ACM, New York (2014)
19. O'Hara, K., Black, A., Lipson, M.: Everyday practices with mobile video telephony. In: Proceedings of the SIGCHI Conference on Human Factors in Computing Systems, pp. 871–880. ACM, New York (2006)

20. Inkpen, K., Taylor, B., Junuzovic, S., Tang, J., Venolia, G.: Experiences2Go: sharing kids' activities outside the home with remote family members. In: Proceedings of the 2013 Conference on Computer Supported Cooperative Work, pp. 1329–1340. ACM, New York (2013)
21. Kim, S., Junuzovic, S., Inkpen, K.: The nomad and the couch potato: enriching mobile shared experiences with contextual information. In: Proceedings of the 18th International Conference on Supporting Group Work, pp. 167–177. ACM, New York (2014)
22. Oduor, E., et al.: The frustrations and benefits of mobile device usage in the home when co-present with family members. In: Proceedings of the 2016 ACM Conference on Designing Interactive Systems, pp. 1315–1327. ACM, New York (2016)
23. Unver, B., D'Angelo, S., Miller, M., Tang, J.C., Venolia, G., Inkpen, K.: Hands-free remote collaboration over video: exploring viewer and streamer reactions. In: Proceedings of the 2018 ACM International Conference on Interactive Surfaces and Spaces, pp. 85–95. ACM, New York (2018)
24. Venolia, G., Tang, J.C., Inkpen, K., Unver, B.: Wish you were here: being together through composite video and digital keepsakes. In: Proceedings of the 20th International Conference on Human-Computer Interaction with Mobile Devices and Services, pp. 17:1–17:11. ACM, New York (2018)
25. Jones, B., Witcraft, A., Bateman, S., Neustaedter, C., Tang, A.: Mechanics of camera work in mobile video collaboration. In: Proceedings of the 33rd Annual ACM Conference on Human Factors in Computing Systems, pp. 957–966. ACM, New York (2015)
26. Gutwin, C., Greenberg, S.: The importance of awareness for team cognition in distributed collaboration (2001)
27. Watts, L., Monk, A.F.: Remote assistance: a view of the work and a view of the face? In: Conference Companion on Human Factors in Computing Systems, pp. 101–102. ACM, New York (1996)
28. Fussell, S.R., Kraut, R.E., Siegel, J.: Coordination of communication: effects of shared visual context on collaborative work. In: Proceedings of the 2000 ACM Conference on Computer Supported Cooperative Work, pp. 21–30. ACM, New York (2000)
29. Kraut, R.E., Gergle, D., Fussell, S.R.: The use of visual information in shared visual spaces: informing the development of virtual co-presence. In: Proceedings of the 2002 ACM Conference on Computer Supported Cooperative Work, pp. 31–40. ACM, New York (2002)
30. Tang, J.C., Minneman, S.L.: VideoDraw: a video interface for collaborative drawing. In: Proceedings of the SIGCHI Conference on Human Factors in Computing Systems, pp. 313–320. ACM, New York (1990)
31. Wellner, P.: Interacting with paper on the DigitalDesk. Commun. ACM **36**, 87–96 (1993). https://doi.org/10.1145/159544.159630
32. Tang, A., Neustaedter, C., Greenberg, S.: VideoArms: embodiments for mixed presence groupware. In: Bryan-Kinns, N., Blanford, A., Curzon, P., Nigay, L. (eds.) People and Computers XX — Engage, pp. 85–102. Springer, London (2007). https://doi.org/10.1007/978-1-84628-664-3_8
33. Ishii, H., Kobayashi, M.: ClearBoard: a seamless medium for shared drawing and conversation with eye contact. In: Proceedings of the SIGCHI Conference on Human Factors in Computing Systems, pp. 525–532. ACM, New York (1992)
34. Izadi, S., Agarwal, A., Criminisi, A., Winn, J., Blake, A.: C-slate: a multi-touch and object recognition system for remote collaboration using horizontal surfaces. In: Proceedings of the Second Annual IEEE International Workshop on Horizontal Interactive Human-Computer Systems (Tabletop 2007). IEEE (2007)

35. Higuchi, K., Chen, Y., Chou, P.A., Zhang, Z., Liu, Z.: ImmerseBoard: immersive telepresence experience using a digital whiteboard. In: Proceedings of the 33rd Annual ACM Conference on Human Factors in Computing Systems, pp. 2383–2392. ACM, New York (2015)
36. Weibel, N., Signer, B., Norrie, M.C., Hofstetter, H., Jetter, H.-C., Reiterer, H.: PaperSketch: a paper-digital collaborative remote sketching tool. In: Proceedings of the 16th International Conference on Intelligent User Interfaces, pp. 155–164. ACM, New York (2011)
37. Ou, J., Chen, X., Fussell, S.R., Yang, J.: DOVE: drawing over video environment. In: Proceedings of the Eleventh ACM International Conference on Multimedia, pp. 100–101. ACM, New York (2003)
38. Harms, P.C., Biocca, P.F.: Internal consistency and reliability of the networked minds measure of social presence. Presented at the international workshop on presence (2004)
39. Fussell, S.R., Setlock, L.D., Kraut, R.E.: Effects of head-mounted and scene-oriented video systems on remote collaboration on physical tasks. In: Proceedings of the SIGCHI Conference on Human Factors in Computing Systems, pp. 513–520. ACM, New York (2003)
40. Hollan, J., Stornetta, S.: Beyond being there. In: Proceedings of the SIGCHI Conference on Human Factors in Computing Systems, pp. 119–125. ACM, New York (1992)
41. Fussell, S.R., Setlock, L.D., Yang, J., Ou, J., Mauer, E., Kramer, A.D.I.: Gestures over video streams to support remote collaboration on physical tasks. Hum. Comput Interact. **19**, 273–309 (2004). https://doi.org/10.1207/s15327051hci1903_3
42. Miller, M.K., Mandryk, R.L., Birk, M.V., Depping, A.E., Patel, T.: Through the looking glass: the effects of feedback on self-awareness and conversational behaviour during video chat. In: Proceedings of the 2017 CHI Conference on Human Factors in Computing Systems, pp. 5271–5283. ACM, New York (2017)
43. Yarosh, S., Inkpen, K.M., Brush, A.J.B.: Video playdate: toward free play across distance. In: Proceedings of the SIGCHI Conference on Human Factors in Computing Systems, pp. 1251–1260. ACM, New York (2010)

G-Menu: A Keyword-by-Gesture Based Dynamic Menu Interface for Smartphones

Jean Vanderdonckt[1](✉) and Éric Petit[2]

[1] Université catholique de Louvain, 1348 Louvain-la-Neuve, Belgium
jean.vanderdonckt@uclouvain.be

[2] Orange Labs, 28 chemin du Vieux Chêne, 38240 Meylan, France
eric.petit@orange.com

Abstract. Instead of relying on graphical or vocal modalities for searching an item by keyword (called K-Menu), this paper presents the G-Menu exploiting gesture interaction and gesture recognition: when a user sketches a keyword by gesturing the first letters of its label, a menu with items related to the recognized letters is constructed dynamically and presented to the user for selection and auto-completion. The selection can be completed either gesturally by an appropriate gesture (called the G-Menu) or by touch only (called the T-Menu). This paper compares the three types of menu, i.e., by keyword, by gesture, and by touching, in a user study with twenty participants on their item selection time (for measuring task efficiency), their error rate (for measuring task effectiveness), and their subjective satisfaction (for measuring user satisfaction).

Keywords: Gesture interaction · Menu selection · Search by keyword

1 Introduction

As a mobile devices, such as smartphones and tablets, continue to embark more off-line functions and on-line services, their menu structure largely increases in terms of amount of menu items (e.g., labels in a list or icons in a palette), menu depth, and hierarchy. This menu immediately becomes constrained by the screen resolution of the target device, which is capable of only displaying a limited amount of items and a single menu level at a time. This forces the end user to scroll vertically to browse all items in a menu and to swipe left or right to navigate across menu levels. Therefore, instead of navigating through the menu structure, end users tend to search for an item by keyword, for example by typing progressively "Weather" to reach any application of weather forecasts. This technique, called a "K-Menu" [15], is a keyword text-entry menu (Fig. 1a). Existing operating systems usually offer the K-Menu for searching for a menu item by keyword: when a user enters a keyword, a menu with items related to the keyword is constructed dynamically by inspecting a table of menu items and presented to the user. The end user then selects an item in this list or exploits auto-completion to select the complete item when no ambiguity persists.

M. Kurosu (Ed.): HCII 2019, LNCS 11567, pp. 99–114, 2019.
https://doi.org/10.1007/978-3-030-22643-5_8

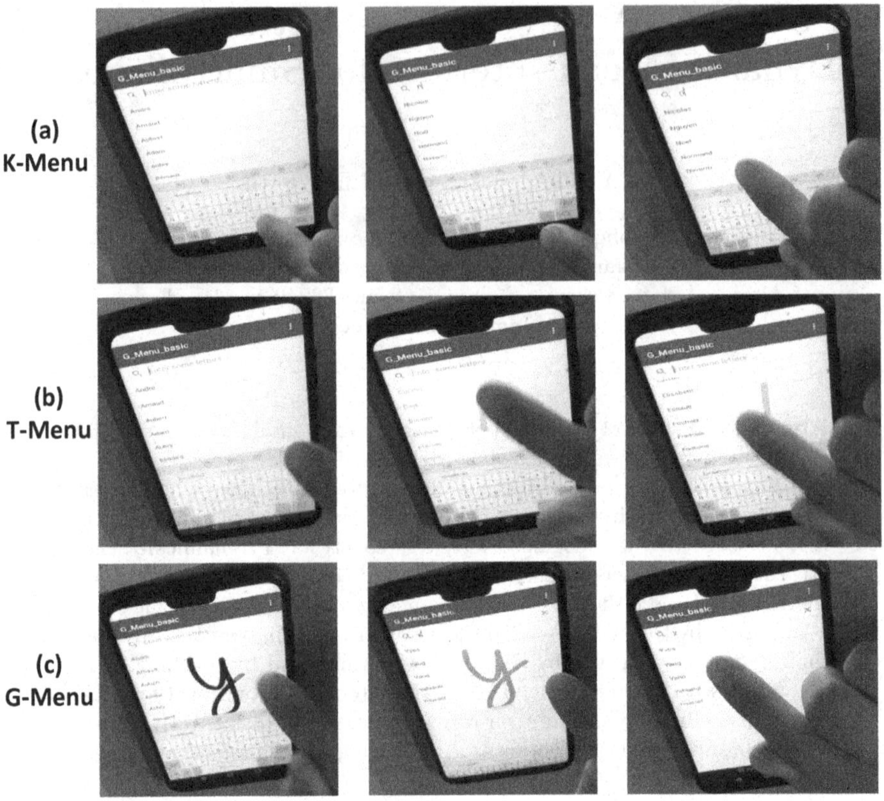

Fig. 1. The three menu conditions: (a) K-Menu for selecting the item "Navarro", (b) T-Menu for selecting the item "Fournier", and (c) G-Menu for selecting the item "Yang".

Operating systems also sometimes offer a similar capability supported by voice recognition: a pronounced word is captured vocally, then submitted to speech recognition, and transformed into a searchable keyword (keyword voice-entry menu). Often, no distinction is made between menu items and other labels used in settings of applications. The end user is still invited to select the desired items by touch, which comes back to the initial item selection mechanism.

Instead of relying on graphical or vocal modalities, this paper presents the *G-Menu* exploiting gestural interaction and recognition for keyword gesture-entry menu [26]: when a user sketches a keyword by gesturing the first letters of its label, a menu with items related to the recognized letters is constructed dynamically and presented to the user for further selection. The selection can be completed either gesturally by an appropriate gesture (called the *G-Menu*: Fig. 1c) or by touching (called the *T-Menu*: Fig. 1b). While the *K-menu* certainly remains the most frequently used and popular menu, the *G-Menu* and the *T-Menu* may offer new affordance that we did not thought of before. To better understand these differences, this paper compares the three types of menu, i.e., by keyword (*K-Menu*), by gesture (*G-Menu*), and by touching (*T-Menu*) in a user study with twenty participants on their item selection time (for measuring task efficiency), their error rate (for measuring task effectiveness), and their subjective satisfaction (for measuring user satisfaction).

The remainder of this paper is structured as follows: Sect. 2 discusses work related to the problem of selecting menu items on a smartphone by keyword and alternate approaches. Section 3 explains our implementation of the G-Menu and T-menu in the context of MenuDFa [20], an initiative to provide end users of mobile phones with an adaptive interface depending on their profile [6] as a Graphical Adaptive Menu (GAM) [25]. Section 4 defines three hypotheses to be investigated in an experiment to determine the potential advantages and shortcomings of a T-Menu and a G-Menu over the well-known K-Menu.

2 Related Work

This section is divided into two parts: prior work related to graphical adaptive menu (GAM) and selected work in this area to support menu adaptivity.

2.1 Graphical Adaptive Menus

Visual Menu techniques are not only very numerous, but also very diversified in terms of capabilities and implementations [2]. Graphical Adaptive Menus (GAMs) are a particular class of graphical menus where their menu items are subject to some adaptivity [11,25], i.e. some adaptation of the menu initiated by the system based on internal data of the end user, such as the navigation history [10]. Contrarily to menu recommendation which adapts the menu based on data external to the user (e.g., recommendations from a cluster of users, from the crowd), menu adaptivity only takes into account data internal to the user (e.g., navigation history, recency or frequency of usage [12]). Many forms of adaptivity may be considered [4], ranging from shorten the label of menu items [8] and changing the form of selection zone [1] to changing the input/output modality [27], such as in *polymodal menus* [5]. Menu adaptation, whether it is initiated and controlled by the system in adaptivity or by the end user in adaptability, could lead to different appreciations by end users [7], which in turn depend on individual traits of the end user [11]. Between full adaptability and adaptivity resides a wide range of mixed-initiative possibilities [16], which may be subject to optimization of menu selection [2]. To characterize this range more precisely, we revisit the Automation Level Description (ALD) [19], which defines ten levels of automation for any system where automation in general is defined as

> "the execution by a machine agent (usually a computer) of a function that was previously carried out by a human. What is considered automation will therefore change with time. When the reallocation of a function from human to machine is complete and permanent, then the function will tend to be seen simply as a machine operation, not as automation."

Based on this definition, we hereby define the Adaptation Automation as any component of the interactive application, primarily its Graphical User Interface (GUI), which achieves the GUI adaptation as a function that was previously ensured by the end user. Table 1 defines ten levels of Adaptation Automation, ranging from full adaptability (level = 1) to full adaptivity (level = 10). While this scale is useful for characterizing the Adaptation Automation Level (AAL), it requires further investigation on how to specify, design, and implement the functions involved in mixed-initiative as some of them are cumulative or exclusive.

Table 1. Adaptation Automation Level (AAL), revisited from [19].

Level	Description
1	The GUI offers no assistance: the end user must take all decision and actions
2	The GUI offers a complete set of decision/action alternatives, or
3	Narrows the selection down to a few, or
4	Suggests one alternative, and
5	Executes that suggestion if the end user approves, or
6	Allows the end user a restricted time to veto before automatic execution, or
7	Executes automatically, then necessarily informs the end user, and
8	Informs the end user only if asked, or
9	Informs the end user only if the GUI decides to
10	The GUI decides everything and acts autonomously, ignoring the end user

2.2 Interaction Techniques for Menu Adaptivity

FaThumb [14] is aimed at overcoming the limitations induced by keyword text-entry menu. Instead of typing a keyword, facet navigation across a hierarchy of metadata is promoted to differentiate items proposed: either a menu item is not relevant and it is de-emphasized, or it is relevant and it is highlighted based on iterative data filtering. Keyword text-entry menu is more powerful when the label of the target menu item is known, while facet navigation is more effective and preferred, especially when the label of the menu item researched in not known, but its characteristics revealed by facets are. TapGlance [21] uses a zooming metaphor to unify navigation within and across applications based on faceted search. Its spatial metaphor could therefore be considered as an alternative menu search for smartphones. Substituting the item selection based on graphical point-and-click paradigm by another modality, such as vocal or gestural, may present some interesting opportunities to investigate. Menu selection by gesture has already been investigated, mainly by directional gestures (i.e., a particular item is associated to the direction of a marking menu, which is easy to produce but not very meaningful), by pointing gestures (i.e., a particular item is contained in a dedicated region) or by combining directional gestures and letters (i.e., a particular item or set of items is assigned to a letter gesture followed by a marking menu in AugmentedLetters [22]). But these different gesture types may be subject to different recall rates or not [9]. For example,

M3 GESTURE MENU displays menu items on a grid of a smartphone, prefers gestural shapes rather than directional marks, and has constant and stationary space use.

3 Context of the G-Menu

3.1 Context and Motivations of the Study

Smartphones are probably the devices that are today used by the widest possible population when considering profiles, preferences, habits, and abilities of their impediment thereof. Towards this goal, Orange Lab releases and continually maintains *MenuDFa* [20], an Android OS-based package supporting user interface adaptation up to $AAL = 5$. Since several adaptation techniques could be considered to adapt the smartphone user interface to the end user, it is vital to retain only those techniques that have been empirically validated. Therefore, observing visually disabled and able-bodied users together through user studies allows to pinpoint several user interfaces elements important when building interfaces for sight-impaired people as well as visually-disabled ones.

3.2 Implementation

The *G-Menu* and *T-Menu* were developed in Java in Android Software Development Toolkit (SDK) based on the following modules:

- A stroke gesture recognizer captures and recognizes over 100 allographs, both unistroke and multistroke, covering the ten digits and twenty-six letters of the Latin alphabet both in lowercase and uppercase. For some cases, several variants of a same digit or figure are provided to support Anglo-Saxon style, such as for the 'seven' or the 'four' digits.
- A gesture recognition engine embedding the stroke gesture recognizer to avoid mismatching between menu-oriented gestures issued by the keyword and non-oriented gestures (e.g., navigation gestures such as swipes, flicks, and drags). This engine exploits dynamic attributes such as gesture velocity and execution time to distinguish direct pointing gestures (i.e., related to direct manipulation) from operative gestures (i.e., related to gesture command).
- A module constructing a dynamic menu based on the gesture recognition by keyword text-entry menu matching and menu ranking scheme.
- An interaction technique offering both gesturally and graphically-oriented menu selection with a log file storing item selection time and error rate.

The *G-Menu* relies on both the gesture recognition engine and the dynamic menu filtering with two gestural commands: the last letter input could be erased by a left flick and the complete entry could be erase by a left-right flick (round-trip). The G-Menu and the T-Menu are delivered in a package called "Tactile Facile"[1] with five predefined interaction profiles: `Easy+` mode which is the by

[1] https://boutique.orange.fr/informations/accessibilite-autonomie/tactile-facile.php.

default mode, `Vision+` mode for people having light visual disabilities, `Vision++` mode for people having important visual deficiencies, `Motor+` for motor-impaired users, and `MicroGesture` for exploiting micro-gestures.

3.3 Hypotheses

Since we are confronted with three types of menu, i.e., the *K-Menu*, the *G-Menu*, and the *T-Menu*, the main research question arises: which menu type is the best and under which conditions? Three variables are usually manipulated in an experiment to differentiate menus of these types: item selection time for measuring task efficiency, error rate for measuring task effectiveness, and subjective satisfaction for measuring user satisfaction. We therefore formulate three hypotheses:

H_{11} = *The users select items in the K-Menu faster than in the G-Menu and the T-Menu.* The goal of this first hypothesis is to verify that the K-Menu still remains the fastest menu for search by keyword. The keyword text-entry method has always been revealed the fastest one [14] since people are used to efficiently rely on a keyword.

H_{21} = *The users select items in a T-menu faster than the other menus if the target menu item is close to the location where users initiate the search.* Indeed, if the user has to find an item that is close to the current position, the selection will be faster by slightly scrolling up and down than by searching it with a keyword. The hierarchical structure of the application will make it faster for users to find words that are near to their position.

H_{31} = *The users produce more errors with a G-menu than with the K-Menu and the T-Menu.* The G-Menu is a new sort of menu in which drawing a letter is probably more difficult than just tapping a keyword on the screen or to scroll to a word. Therefore, we believe that the G-menu will produce more selection errors than the others.

4 Method

Procedure. Each participant performed the task in a controlled environment. Prior to the task each participant was welcomed, had the process explained to them, signed a consent form, and filled in a questionnaire on their background. After the questionnaire was completed, the experimenter demonstrated the three types of menu with one example of item selection each. The participants were given 5 min to familiarize themselves with the menus and ask any question. The participants could finish this part early, then received a list of items to select from (Fig. 2). They had to cover the whole list with a paper, then they had to find the first item with the corresponding menu category. Once they found the item using the specific menu, they were asked to select it to confirm, then they could move the paper to the second item, and so on until the list is completed. They were given 15 min to complete the task, which was assessed as much more than needed. At the end, participants received a questionnaire and were interviewed to determine what they liked and what they did not like about each menu and about the experiment overall, in order to have a subjective feedback. Our study was within-subjects with one independent variable: the Menu Type, a nominal variable with three conditions, one representing the baseline (*K-Menu*) and two for testing (*T-Menu* and *G-Menu*).

Fig. 2. Setup of the experiment with the list of 18 random items.

Stimuli. Thirty different lists of 18 items each (6 items for *K-Menu* + 6 items for the *T-Menu* + 6 items for the *G-Menu*) were randomly generated by using dCode (https://www.dcode.fr/tirage-au-sort-nombre-aleatoire) from a pool of 50 items extracted from the 130 menu items delivered in the MenuDfa application. All items were individually randomly presented and associated to one of the three conditions. The design was therefore as follows: 30 participants × 18 items = 540 samples. Each session was also video-recorded.

Apparatus. Android-based Google Nexus smartphones were used, with 2 Gb LPDDR3 RAM, 16 Gb of storage and a 1920 × 1080 pixel resolution (423 ppi).

Quantitative and Qualitative Measures. The dependent variables were:

1. The menu item selection time (in sec), which was measured as the time taken from identifying the next requested target item in the list until its final selection.
2. The error rate (in percentage %), which was measured as the ratio of successfully achieved selections by the total amount of selections. Every time an item was not selected correctly, or every time the user had to go back in order to find the item, or every time a letter was drew wrong (for *G-Menu*), we counted it as one error with a maximum of 5.

3. The values filled in by each participant for a post-test questionnaire, which enables participants to express their level of satisfaction regarding five statements about the ease, the task completion, the speed, the learning and the productivity of each menu. Each statement is captured using a 3-point rating scale (1st = best, 2 = average, 3 = worst).

Analysis. After each participant completed the procedure, the measures, questionnaire, and ranking data was entered into a spreadsheet in an anonymous format so the participants could not be identified and be GDPR compliant.

5 Experiment

5.1 Participants

The sample included thirty participants (13 female and 17 male) recruited through mailing and contact lists, from different ages (min: 19, max: 70, $M = 25.73$, $SD = 10.05$), with diverse education degrees (i.e., secondary school, higher education, bachelor, master ...). Although most of the participants were students in these different domains, there were also some other participants with various occupations (e.g., workers, unemployed, retired). In average, the participants were all well acquainted with the device (smartphone) and use it frequently (80%). However, older people were not necessarily as familiar with smartphones, which made them less comfortable with the device used, which influenced their data for the time and error rate. 40% of them never use a tablet, or almost never. On a frequency scale from 1 to 7, the rest of them vary between 5 and 2. No compensation was offered. Overall, the experiment lasted between 2 and 3 min per participant.

5.2 Results and Discussion

Out of the initial 540 trials, 33 outliers were removed for various reasons: they did not complete the full list (e.g., one item was skipped inadvertently), they selected an item for a wrong condition (e.g., G-Menu instead of K-Menu), the video record was interrupted, etc. The final breakdown was therefore: 170 *K-Menu* trials + 174 *T-Menu* trials + 170 *G-Menu* trials = 517 trials.

First Hypothesis: Selection Time. Figure 3 reproduces the item selection time aggregated for all participants, then for each participant. Not surprisingly, the K-Menu ($M = 4.09$, $SD = 2.32$) benefit from the fastest item selection time, followed by the T-Menu ($M = 8.07$, $SD = 5.30$), and the G-Menu ($M = 8.43$, $SD = 7.30$). All menus received a wide interval between the minimum and the maximum values: *K-Menu* ($min = 2, max = 18$), *T-Menu* ($min = 1, max = 35$), *G-Menu* ($min = 2$, $max = 50$). This is reflected that there is an important standard deviation between participants, the widest being for the *G-Menu*.

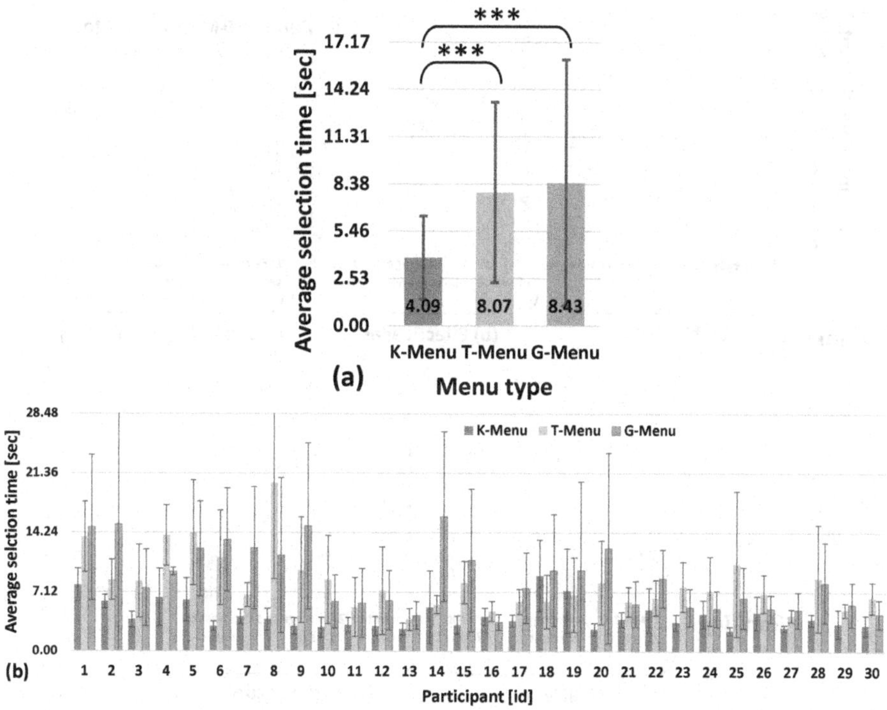

Fig. 3. Item selection time aggregated for all participants (a), then per participant (b). Error bars show the standard deviation.

We computed a series of Student's t-tests with two paired samples to determine whether there was any significant difference between the menu types. There was a very highly significant difference in the selection time for *K-Menu* and *T-Menu* conditions; $df = 342$, $t = 1.64$ for one-tail, $t = 1.96$ for two-tail, $p^{***} < .001$, Cohen's $d = .92$. There was also a very highly significant difference in the selection time for *K-Menu* and *G-Menu* conditions but with a smaller magnitude; $df = 341$, $t = 1.65$ for one-tail, $t = 1.97$ for two-tail $p^{***} < .001$, Cohen's $d = .81$. There was no significance between the *T-Menu* and *G-Menu* ($df = 345$, $t = 1.65$ for one-tail, $t = 1.97$ for two-tail, $n.s. = p > .05$). There is some concordance between those results and the statements assessed in the post-test questionnaire. Indeed, when asked to rank the three menu types regarding their speed, 20 participants out of 30 thought that the *K-menu* was the fastest to perform the task. Half of the participants thought the *G-menu* was the slowest, the other half thinking it was the *T-Menu* (Fig. 4-Speed). In conclusion, H_{11} is supported.

Second Hypothesis: Selection Time for *T-Menu* When Item is Close. To test this hypothesis, we decided to work with two groups of items. First, it is the group of items whose location is close to the place where the participant initiates the search (relative displacement ≤ 41 [17]). When the participant is searching for keyword, she begins in general at the top of the menu. But when

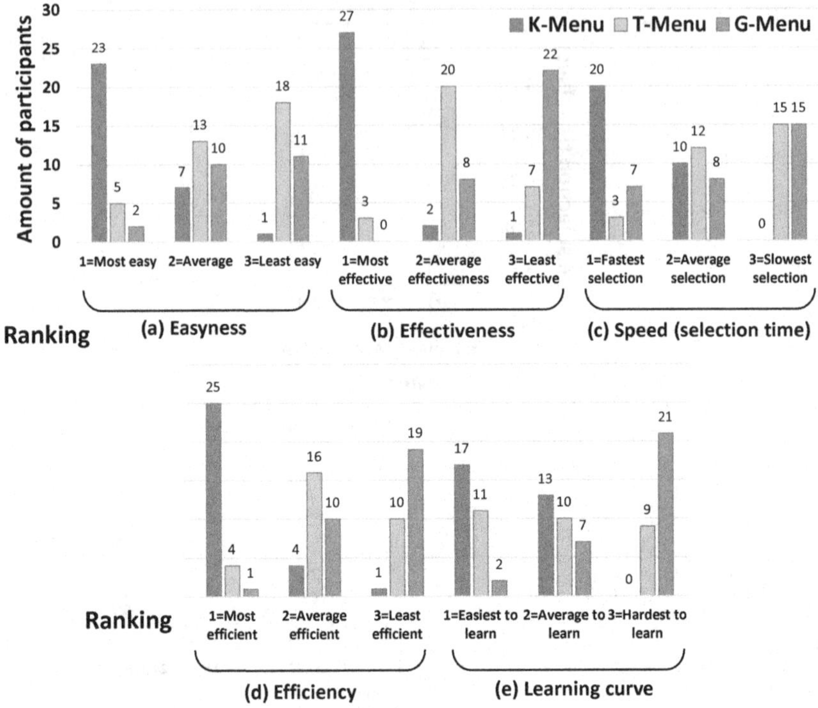

Fig. 4. Ranking of menu types per statement.

the participant utilizes T-Menu (mainly for scrolling) and that she selects the searched item, she stays at the same positions of this item in the menu. Therefore, we used the relative position instead of the normal position in the menu. This relative position, or relative displacement, gives us some information about how far the target item is from the participant's current locus of control. For an item with a relative position less or equal than 41, the *T-Menu* condition is expected be faster. The *T-Menu* condition has a highly significant smaller selection time ($t = 2.86$, $p^{**} = .004$) than the *G-Menu* but not lower than the *K-Menu* condition ($t = 4.80$, $p^{***} = .00003$). The *T-Menu* condition is significantly faster than the *G-Menu* condition if the relative position of the item is under 41. If we take all items (under and above 41), this conclusion cannot be deduced. The *K-Menu* condition stays faster than the *T-Menu*, even with items with a relative position under 41. Therefore, H_{21} is not fully supported. When such an item becomes visible on the main screen, it is not always obvious that the participant will switch to pointing instead of keyword or gesture because this requires some mode switching, which induces some additional work load.

Third Hypothesis: Error Rate. Figure 5 reproduces the error rate aggregated for all participants, then for each participant. We observe that the *K-Menu*

($M = .26$, $SD = .12$) benefits again from the lowest error rate, followed by the *T-Menu* ($M = .36$, $SD = .24$), and the *G-Menu* ($M = 1.04$, $SD = 0.83$). All menus received this a more concentrated interval between the minimum and the maximum values: *K-Menu* ($min = 0$ which means that no errors were produced, $max = .50$), *T-Menu* ($min = 0$, $max = .83$), *G-Menu* ($min = 0$, $max = 3.17$). We can observe that some participants were quite efficient in Fig. 5 when they did not generate any error, which is reflected by a null error rate. Some other participants were on the contrary much more error prone. We have not been able to identify the reasons why some participants remain error-prone vs error-resistant as this behaviour seems to propagate for all menu types, and not for a certain menu in particular. But it is sure that the *K-Menu* has the lowest error rate in all cases. Similarly, we computed three Student's t-tests with two paired samples to determine whether there was any significant difference between the menu types in terms of error rate. There was a highly significant difference in the error rate for *K-Menu* and *T-Menu* conditions ($df = 30$, $t = 2.78$, $p^{**} = .0047$), for the *K-Menu* and the *G-Menu* conditions ($df = 30$, $t = 3.98$, $p^{***} = .0002$), and for the *T-Menu* and *G-Menu* conditions ($df = 30$, $t = 3.65$, $p^{***} = .0005$). Once again, there is a concordance between these results and the questionnaire results. When asked to rank the three menus regarding their easiness (Fig. 4a), 25 participants out of 30 expressed that the *K-menu* is the easiest one to perform the task, which makes sense with the small amount of errors. 19 out of 30 participants thought the *G-Menu* is the least easy menu since it has the highest amount of errors. One potential observation is that participants experienced some trouble to recognize the letters drawn (in particular the letters "g", "q" or "f"), which is mainly due to the gesture recognizer. We gave them an alphabet to show how to write these letters but this did not helped them a lot, they still had difficulties to draw these letters by gesture. The stroke gesture recognition could be trained to learn new end-user defined gestures, which is particularly useful in case of disambiguation. For example, if there is some confusion between the "u" and the "v" letters, which can be detected after issuing correction gesture, the underlying model of the recognition engine implicitly considers that the new alternative may be the correct one and automatically adapts the likelihood accordingly. This feature is considered particularly useful on the long-term, but it was not exploited during the experiment. In conclusion, H_{31} is supported.

5.3 Further Discussion

Although some participants experienced some trouble in producing the gestures, not because they could not, but simply because they did not remember the shape of the stroke, we observed that some women had less trouble in producing the difficult letters because they draw "complexifier" letters like in Fig. 6a, b. Another common error comes with the scrolling: some participants scrolled up and down in the menu and then clicked to quickly on the item, which resulted into the letter "i" being produced Fig. 6c. This could explain why the *T-menu* has significantly more errors than the *K-Menu*. There were also errors made by the condition of the application. Some people saw the letter "G" expressing the

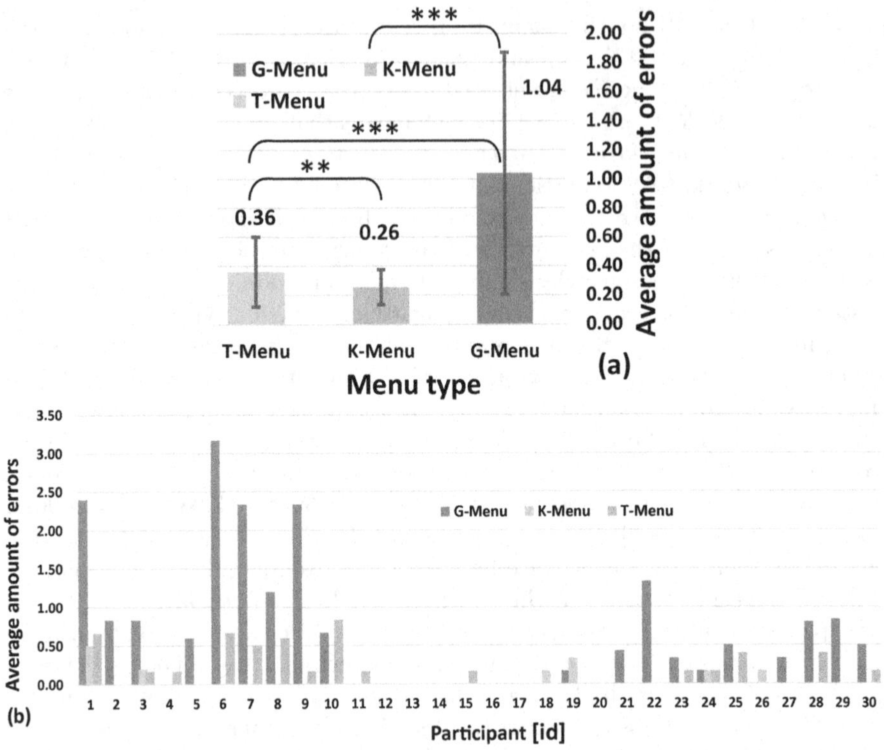

Fig. 5. Average error rate for all participants (a), then per participant (b).

G-Menu on the screen and then began drawing the letter "g" in place of the first letter of the keyword searched. We can call these three types of errors "system" errors. Regarding the five statements reported in Fig. 4, we can see that the general trend is to prefer *K-Menu* to the other menus. People find it more easy, more useful for a task achievement, faster, they felt more productive and it was revealed easier to learn if you work with a *K-Menu* than with the other menus. This goes in the same way that our hypotheses.

So, if the *T-Menu* and *G-Menu* were suggested to be slower and more error-prone than the *K-Menu*, what are its advantages over them? Based on the interviews, we collected some positive user feedback as follows:

- The *G-Menu* always remains at immediate availability and use since the gesture can be issued on any screen, and not just on a particular area as the *K-Menu*. When participants go deeper in the menu structure, coming back to the first or dedicated screen where the keywords can be types requires some swiping time that was not taken into account in the experiment. There was only one screen. This suggest to replicate the experiment with various menu structures.

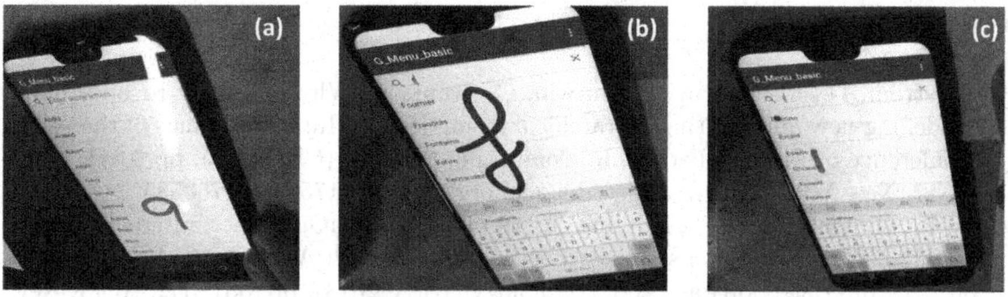

Fig. 6. Cases for gesture recognition.

- The *G-Menu* is always very natural since it is based on stroke gesture recognition of "naturally" produced gestures. The recognition accuracy of recognizers is therefore important in both user-dependent and user-independent scenarios [24].
- The *G-Menu* may be experienced as an enjoyable menu considered as an alternative to the most powerful *K-Menu* when conditions imposed by the context of use are more demanding. Indeed, the *K-Menu* requires reaching a small zone for entering the keyword by tapping, which may cause some trouble for people having some disabilities, like vision or motor impairments. We did not test participant belonging to this population, but we know that gestures need to be adapted to them in terms of articulation. The five statements (Fig. 4) did not cover playfulness or enjoyability, which might be another criteria to consider for the next experiment.

The limitations of the *G-Menu* over the *T-Menu* and *K-Menu* will never be compensated, but could be tackled by offering more significant gestures that are easier to produce, to remember, and to recognize, which is a common problem in gesture recognition.

6 Conclusion and Future Work

This paper presented and compared the G-Menu with respect to the T-Menu and the popular K-Menu against the usual variables of usability: it is slower and more error prone than the others. On the other hand, the experiment did not investigate other variables that go beyond the mere usability and which enters the user experience, such as intuitiveness, playfulness, and immediate usage. These advantages are elsewhere than in the variables controlled in the experiment. The key aspect concerns the stroke recognition: we could also try to find why the G-Menu recognizes some letters with more accuracy than other letters and then exploiting the automatic learning facility of the stroke recognition engine. Another option is to study a composition of these menus: a *GK-menu* which combines gesture and keyword text-entry menus.

Acknowledgments. The authors would like to thank Lucas Hodeige, Alexandre Noel and Pieter-Paul Van Laere for conducting the user study.

References

1. Ahlström, D., Cockburn, A., Gutwin, C., Irani, P.: Why it's quick to be square: modelling new and existing hierarchical menu designs. In: Proceedings of the ACM Conference on Human Factors in Computing Systems (CHI 2010), pp. 1371–1380. ACM, New York (2010). http://doi.acm.org/10.1145/1753326.1753534
2. Bailly, G., Oulasvirta, A., Kötzing, T., Hoppe, S.: MenuOptimizer: interactive optimization of menu systems. In: Proceedings of the 26th Annual ACM Symposium on User Interface Software and Technology (UIST 2013), pp. 331–342. ACM, New York (2013). http://doi.acm.org/10.1145/2501988.2502024
3. Bailly, G., Lecolinet, E., Nigay, L.: Visual menu techniques. ACM Comput. Surv. **49**(4), 60:1–60:41 (2017). http://doi.acm.org/10.1145/3002171
4. Bezold, M., Minker, W.: A framework for adapting interactive systems to user behavior. J. Ambient Intell. Smart Environ. **2**(4), 1364–1876 (2010). http://dl.acm.org/citation.cfm?id=2021081.2021084
5. Bouzit, S., Calvary, G., Chêne, D., Vanderdonckt, J.: Polymodal menus: a model-based approach for designing multimodal adaptive menus for small screens. In: Proceedings of ACM Human-Computer Interaction. EICS, vol. 1, pp. 15:1–15:19 (2017). http://doi.acm.org/10.1145/3099585
6. Chêne, D., Petit, É., Zijp-Rouzier, S.: How to achieve design for all: "List", "Focus" and "Multimodality" as minimal requirements. In: Antona, M., Stephanidis, C. (eds.) UAHCI 2016. LNCS, vol. 9738, pp. 117–128. Springer, Cham (2016). https://doi.org/10.1007/978-3-319-40244-4_12
7. Findlater, L., McGrenere, J.: A comparison of static, adaptive, and adaptable menus. In: Proceedings of the ACM International Conference on Human Factors in Computing Systems (CHI 2004), pp. 89–96. ACM, New York (2004). http://doi.acm.org/10.1145/985692.985704
8. Fischer, S., Schwan, S.: Adaptively shortened pull down menus: location knowledge and selection efficiency. Behav. Inf. Technol. **27**(5), 439–444 (2008). https://doi.org/10.1080/01449290701497095
9. Fruchard, B., Lecolinet, E., Chapuis, O.: How memorizing positions or directions affects gesture learning? In: Proceedings of the ACM International Conference on Interactive Surfaces and Spaces (ISS 2018), pp. 107–114. ACM, New York (2018). https://doi.org/10.1145/3279778.3279787
10. Fukazawa, Y., Hara, M., Onogi, M., Ueno, H.: Automatic mobile menu customization based on user operation history. In: Proceedings of the 11th International Conference on Human-Computer Interaction with Mobile Devices and Services (MobileHCI 2009), pp. 50:1–50:4. ACM, New York (2009). http://doi.acm.org/10.1145/1613858.1613921
11. Gajos, K.Z., Chauncey, K.: The influence of personality traits and cognitive load on the use of adaptive user interfaces. In: Proceedings of the 22nd International Conference on Intelligent User Interfaces (IUI 2017), pp. 301–306. ACM, New York (2017). http://doi.acm.org/10.1145/3025171.3025192
12. Gobert, C., Todi, K., Bailly, G., Oulasvirta, A.: SAM: a modular framework for self-adapting web menus. In: Proceedings of ACM International Conference on Intelligent User Interfaces (IUI 2019). ACM, New York (2019)

13. Huang, S.-C., Chou, I.-F., Bias, R.G.: Empirical evaluation of a popular cellular phone's menu system: theory meets practice. J. Usability Stud. **1**(2), 91–108 (2006). http://dl.acm.org/citation.cfm?id=2835658.2835662
14. Karlson, A.K., Robertson, G.G., Robbins, D.C., Czerwinski, M.P., Smith, G.R.: FaThumb: a facet-based interface for mobile search. In: Proceedings of ACM Conference on Human Factors in Computing Systems (CHI 2006), pp. 711–720. ACM, New York (2006). http://dx.doi.org/10.1145/1124772.1124878
15. Lee, S.E., Lee, G.: K-menu: a keyword-based dynamic menu interface for small computers. In: Proceedings of Extended Abstracts on Human Factors in Computing Systems (CHI EA 2007), pp. 2543–2548. ACM, New York (2007). https://doi.org/10.1145/1240866.1241038
16. López-Jaquero, V., Vanderdonckt, J., Montero, F., González, P.: Towards an extended model of user interface adaptation: the ISATINE framework. In: Gulliksen, J., Harning, M.B., Palanque, P., van der Veer, G.C., Wesson, J. (eds.) DSV-IS/EHCI/HCSE -2007. LNCS, vol. 4940, pp. 374–392. Springer, Heidelberg (2008). https://doi.org/10.1007/978-3-540-92698-6_23
17. Norrie, L., Murray-Smith, R.: Investigating UI displacements in an adaptive mobile homescreen. Int. J. Mob. Hum. Comput. Interact. **8**(3), 1–17 (2016). http://dx.doi.org/10.4018/IJMHCI.2016070101.oa
18. Peillon, A., Chêne, D., Chaumon, M.-E.B.: HMI and visually-disabled user: the emergence of specific issues. In: Proceedings of 28ème conference francophone sur l'Interaction Homme-Machine (IHM 2016), pp. 259–263. ACM, New York (2016). https://doi.org/10.1145/3004107.3004136
19. Parasuraman, R., Riley, V.: Humans and automation: use, misuse, disuse, abuse. Hum. Factors **39**(2), 230–253 (1997). https://doi.org/10.1518/001872097778543886
20. Petit, E., Chêne, D.: MenuDfA : un composant de navigation gestuelle tactile conçu pour tous. In: Proceedings of 27eme Conf. francophone sur l'Interaction Homme-Machine (IHM 2015). ACM International Series, New York, Article d03 (2015). https://hal.archives-ouvertes.fr/hal-01219909/file/d03-petit.pdf
21. Robbins, D.C., Lee, B., Fernandez, R.: TapGlance: designing a unified smartphone interface. In: Proceedings of the 7th ACM Conference on Designing interactive systems (DIS 2008), pp. 386–394. ACM, New York (2008). http://dx.doi.org/10.1145/1394445.1394487
22. Roy, Q., Malacria, S., Guiard, Y., Lecolinet, E., Eagan, J.: Augmented letters: mnemonic gesture-based shortcuts. In: Proceedings of the ACM Conference on Human Factors in Computing Systems (CHI 2013), pp. 2325–2328. ACM, New York (2013). https://doi.org/10.1145/2470654.2481321
23. Vanderdonckt, J.: A MDA-compliant environment for developing user interfaces of information systems. In: Pastor, O., Falcão e Cunha, J. (eds.) CAiSE 2005. LNCS, vol. 3520, pp. 16–31. Springer, Heidelberg (2005). https://doi.org/10.1007/11431855_2
24. Vanderdonckt, J., Roselli, P., Pérez-Medina, J.L.: !FTL, an articulation-invariant stroke gesture recognizer with controllable position, scale, and rotation invariances. In: Proceedings of the ACM International Conference on Multimodal Interaction (ICMI 2018), pp. 125–134. ACM, New York (2018). http://doi.acm.org/10.1145/3242969.3243032
25. Vanderdonckt, J., Bouzit, S., Calvary, G., Chêne, D.: Exploring a design space of graphical adaptive menus: normal vs small screens. ACM Trans. Intell. Interact. Syst. (TiiS) **9**, 4 (2019)

26. Zhai, S., Kristensson, P.O.: The word-gesture keyboard: reimagining keyboard interaction. Commun. ACM **55**(9), 91–101 (2012). https://doi.org/10.1145/2330667.2330689
27. Zheng, J., Bi, X., Li, K., Li, Y., Zhai, S.: M3 gesture menu: design and experimental analyses of marking menus for touchscreen mobile interaction. In: Proceedings of the ACM Conference on Human Factors in Computing Systems (CHI 2018). ACM, New York, Paper 249 (2018). https://doi.org/10.1145/3173574.3173823

Facial Expressions and Emotions Recognition

Deep Convolutional Neural Networks for Feature Extraction in Speech Emotion Recognition

Panikos Heracleous[1(✉)], Yasser Mohammad[2], and Akio Yoneyama[1]

[1] KDDI Research, Inc., 2-1-15 Ohara, Fujimino-shi, Saitama 356-8502, Japan
{pa-heracleous,yoneyama}@kddi-research.jp
[2] Artificial Intelligence Research Center, AIST,
2-4-7 Aomi, Koto-ku, Tokyo 135-0064, Japan
yasserm@aun.edu.eg

Abstract. Speech emotion recognition is a task designed to automatically identify human emotions in spoken utterances. The current study focuses on speech emotion recognition based on deep convolutional neural networks (DCNNs) and extremely randomized trees. Specifically, we propose a method based on DCNN, which extracts informative features from the speech signal, and those features are then used by an extremely randomized trees classifier for emotion recognition. The CNNs are a special variant of conventional feed-forward deep neural networks (DNNs), and have been used in many speech applications. Another method is also proposed which integrates DCNN with i-vectors for emotion recognition. The proposed methods were evaluated using the state-of-the-art English IEMOCAP and FAU Aibo German emotional corpora for the recognition of four and five emotions, respectively. When using the IEMOCAP English corpus and DCNN with extremely randomized trees, a 63.9% unweighted average recall (UAR) was obtained. In the case of using the German children's Aibo corpus, a 61.8% UAR was achieved. These results are very promising showing the effectiveness of the proposed methods in speech emotion recognition. The proposed methods were compared with a baseline approach based on support vector machines (SVM), and they showed superior performance.

Keywords: Speech emotion recognition · Deep convolutional neural networks · Informative features · i-vectors · Extremely randomized trees

1 Introduction

Emotion recognition plays an important role in human-computer interaction and is attracting a high level of attention because of its real world applications [1]. Emotion recognition can be applied in human-robot interaction to detect the user's emotions, or in call-centers to identify the caller's emotional state.

M. Kurosu (Ed.): HCII 2019, LNCS 11567, pp. 117–132, 2019.
https://doi.org/10.1007/978-3-030-22643-5_9

In particular, in cases of emergency, emotion recognition can provide feedback to the operator so that he or she can respond in an appropriate way. Furthermore, the emotional state of the caller may be very informative concerning the level of customer satisfaction.

The current study focuses on emotion recognition based on the speech modality. A method is proposed which uses DCNN to extract informative features from each layer of the network, and the extracted features are then flattened and used by extremely randomized trees [2] for emotion recognition. Extremely randomized trees are similar to random forest [3], but with random tree splitting. The motivation for using extremely randomized trees is due to the lower computational cost, and additionally the method shows a high level of performance in the case of a small number of features.

A CNN [4,5] is a special variant of conventional neural networks consisting of convolution and pooling layers. Many studies have reported results for speech emotion recognition [6], image classification [7], and sentence classification [8] based on CNNs. In particular, CNNs are very popular in image classification and most of the recent related studies are based on CNNs. In the current study, CNNs are used because of their simplicity compared to a conventional feed-forward DNN. Due to parameter sharing, computational and memory costs are lower.

In addition to DCNN with extremely randomized trees, another method based on conventional CNNs is also experimentally investigated. In this case, instead of using extremely randomized trees for classification, a fully connected layer is added on the top of convolutional layers of the DCNN, and emotion recognition is performed using the features of the last layer. When using the two methods, the neural networks are fed with frame-level spectral features. Furthermore, for more comprehensive investigations, DCNNs fed with i-vectors [9] are also applied in speech emotion recognition. In the i-vector paradigm, the spoken utterance is represented by a small number of factors, which comprise the variability of speaker, channel, emotion, or language. Although i-vectors have been successfully used in speech emotion recognition [10–12], the integration of deep learning (DL) and i-vectors has not been investigated comprehensively so far, and only very few studies addressed this issue [13]. As a result, DL and i-vectors for speech emotion recognition are still an open research area and further investigations are necessary.

In a previous study [14], the authors demonstrated experimental results on far-field speech emotion recognition using a DCNN for feature extraction and extremely randomized trees for classification. In the current study, the DCNN architecture is simplified by excluding network pre-training, and, also, by using the features of all convolutional layers to select the learned features used in classification. The motivation for using the features from all layers lies in the fact that lower-level features may be also very informative resulting in higher classification rates when included. Furthermore, in the proposed methods are evaluated using also the English IEMOCAP corpus [15] for classification of four emotions.

Regarding the emotional data used, the proposed methods are evaluated using the state-of-the-art English IEMOCAP and German FAU Aibo [16] corpora for the classification of four and five emotions, respectively. For comparison purposes, a baseline speech emotion recognition experiment using the popular SVM classifier [17] with i-vectors was also conducted.

2 Related Work

Previously, several studies addressed the problem of emotion recognition using different modalities, classifiers, and feature extraction methods. Emotion recognition can be performed using speech signal [18], visual/facial information [19], electroencephalography (EEG) signals [20], and also using physiological signals such as, blood volume pulse (BVP), electromyography (EMG), skin conductance (SC), skin temperature (SKT) and respiration (RESP) [21].

Speech emotion recognition using Gaussian mixture models (GMMs) was reported in [22,23]. In [24], hidden Markov model- (HMM) based speech emotion recognition was presented. SVM is among the most popular classifier used in speech emotion recognition [25,26]. More recent studies are based on neural networks (NN) [27,28]. Currently, speech emotion recognition using deep neural networks is being investigated [29,30].

Mel-frequency cepstral coefficients (MFCC) [31] are very commonly and widely used features in speech emotion recognition. In addition to MFCC features, shifted delta-cepstral (SDC) coefficients [32,33] can also be applied. Originally, SDC coefficients were used in spoken language identification showing superior performance compared with the sole use of MFCC features. In the current study, SDC coefficients are concatenated with MFCC features to form the basic feature vectors. In many recent studies, low-level descriptors (LLD) and functionals [34] are used as features. Considering the success of i-vectors in speaker recognition and spoken language identification [35], however, studies on speech emotion recognition using i-vectors and neural networks have also been presented in a small number of studies. In the current study, the i-vectors used by conventional CNN architecture are extracted from concatenated MFCC features and SDC coefficients.

3 Methods

3.1 Emotional Corpora

In the current study, the FAU Aibo and the IEMOCAP data are used. The FAU Aibo German corpus consists of 9 h of speech uttered by 51 children while interacting with Sony's Aibo robot. The spontaneous Aibo speech was recorded using a close-talking microphone, and was annotated into 11 categories by five human annotators. However, in the current study, the 5-class task is considered, and data for the emotions angry, emphatic, joyful, neutral, and rest were used for the classification. For training, 590 utterances for each emotion were used, and

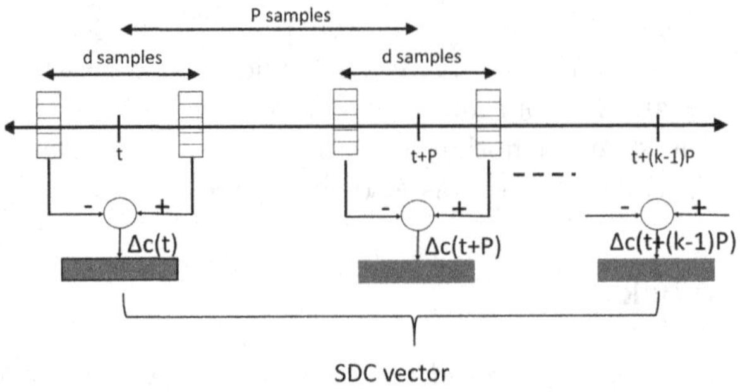

Fig. 1. Computation of shifted delta cepstral (SDC) coefficients.

for testing, 299 utterances for each emotion were used. The data were randomly selected from the entire data set.

The IEMOCAP database was collected at the SAIL lab of the University of Southern California. It contains 12 h of audiovisual data produced by 10 actors. The data were annotated into categorical labels as well as dimensional labels. In the current study, categorical labels were used to classify the emotional states of neutral, happy, angry, and sad. To avoid unbalanced data, 250 utterances for training and 70 utterances for testing randomly selected from each emotion were used.

3.2 Feature Extraction

Cepstral Features. MFCCs are the basic features used in the current study. The MFCC features are extracted every 10 ms using a window-length of 20 ms.

In addition to MFCC features, SDC coefficients are also used. The SDC feature vectors are obtained by concatenating delta cepstra across multiple, and they are described by the N number of cepstral coefficients, d time advance and delay, k number of blocks concatenated for the feature vector, and P time shift between consecutive blocks. For each SDC final feature vector, kN parameters are used. In contrast, in the case of conventional cepstra and delta cepstra feature vectors, $2N$ parameters are used. The SDC is calculated as follows:

$$\Delta c(t + iP) = c(t + iP + d) - c(t + iP - d) \tag{1}$$

The final vector at time t is given by the concatenation of all $\Delta c(t + iP)$ for all $0 \leq i < k$, where $c(t)$ is the original feature value at time t. Figure 1 shows the computation procedure for the SDC coefficients. Therefore, in modeling the emotions being classified, this study also used MFCC features, concatenated with SDC coefficients to form feature vectors of length 112. In the case of using CNN and i-vectors, the concatenated MFCC/SDC features were used to extract the i-vectors used by the classifier. In the other two cases, neural networks fed by blocks of MFCC/SDC (center frame ± 10 frames) features were applied.

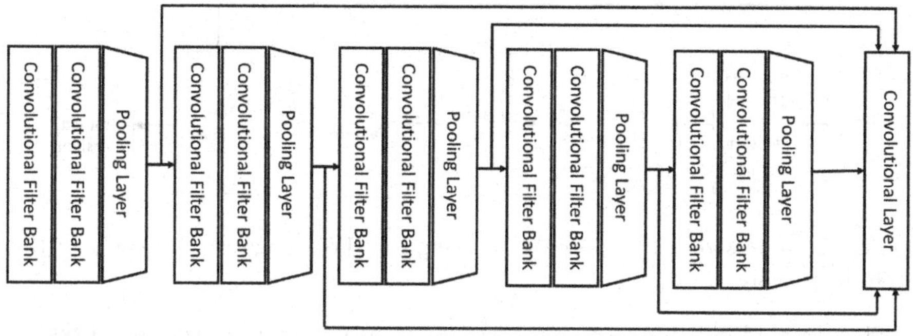

Fig. 2. The architecture of the deep feature extractor along with the classifier used during feature learning.

I-Vector Features. A widely used classification approach in speaker recognition is based on GMMs with universal background models (UBM). In this approach, each speaker model is created by adapting the UBM using maximum a posteriori (MAP) adaptation. A GMM supervector is constructed by concatenating the means of the adapted models. As in speaker recognition, GMM supervectors can also be used for emotion classification.

To overcome the limitations of the high dimensionality of GMM supervectors, the i-vectors model the variability contained in the supervectors with a small set of factors. In this case, an input utterance can be modeled as:

$$\mathbf{M} = \mathbf{m} + \mathbf{T}\mathbf{w} \tag{2}$$

where $\mathbf{M}$ is the emotion-dependent supervector, $\mathbf{m}$ is the emotion-independent supervector, $\mathbf{T}$ is the total variability matrix, and $\mathbf{w}$ is the i-vector. Both the total variability matrix and emotion-independent supervector are estimated from the complete set of training data.

Proposed Feature Extraction and Selection Approach. In this paper, DCNN for learning informative features from the speech signal that is then used for emotion classification is investigated. The MFCC and SDC features are calculated using overlapping windows with a length of 20 ms. This generates a multidimensional time-series that represent the data for each session. The proposed method is a simplified version of the method recently proposed in [36] for activity recognition using mobile sensors.

The proposed classifier consists of a DCNN followed by extremely randomized trees instead of the standard fully connected classifier. The motivation for using extremely randomized trees lies in previous observations showing their effectiveness in the case of a small number of features. The network architecture is shown in Fig. 2, and consists of a series of five blocks, each of which consists of two convolutional layers (64 5×5) followed by a max-pooling layer (2×2). Outputs from each block are then combined and flattened to represent the learned features.

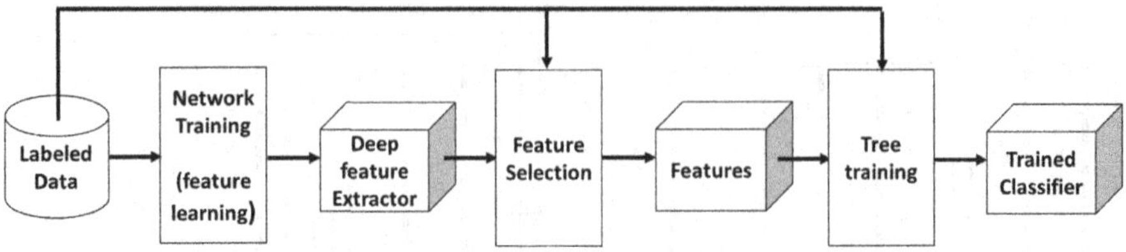

Fig. 3. The proposed training process showing the three stages of training and the output of each stage.

The main idea behind the proposed approach is to use deep networks as feature learners only, but not classifiers, and then utilize feature selection to determine a small set of neurons that provide maximal information for an efficient activity recognizer. This approach combines elements from standard deep learning methodology. However, the approach treats the problem of generating an efficient feature extractor given an accurate, yet inefficient deep neural network, as a feature selection problem instead of using standard neural network compression techniques like optimal brain damage [37].

The training process is shown in Fig. 3, and consists of two main stages: feature learning and feature selection. In the feature learning stage, labeled data are used to train a deep neural architecture as a feature extractor. The goal of this step is to produce a large set of features that are as informative about the emotion recognition problem as possible. To achieve that, no attempt is made at this stage to optimize the computational cost, resulting thus in a slow feature extractor. Feature selection is then used to keep a small fraction of the learned features in the fast feature extractor upon which a classifier can be trained to solve emotion recognition problem. During recognition, only the fast feature extractor and final classifier are kept.

During training, a classifier consisting of a fully connected network (two layers with 16 and 16 *ReLU* neurons) followed by a sigmoid layer with the number of target emotions takes the output of all layers in the architecture through bypass connections. These bypass connections allow the fully connected network to utilize low level features extracted in early convolution filters instead of having to rely on the higher level features learned by the capping CNN. The obvious problem with this design is that the number of inputs to the classifier increases dramatically. For this reason, we employ L_1 regularization during the training process to generate a sparse representation in the classifier by setting most of the weights in its earlier layers to zero. This reduces the effective input size. Other forms of pruning can be used at this stage to reduce the computational cost of the classifier [38].

Furthermore, during training, neurons in early stages are subjected to multiple updates at every gradient-based weight update due to the use of bypassing connections. For this reason, the learning rate used for a neuron in layer i (η_i) is calculated from the base learning rate (η) as:

$$\eta_i = \frac{\eta}{n - i}, \tag{3}$$

where n is the total number of layers.

Although, it is possible to just use the described classifier for emotion recognition (i.e., conventional DCNN), in the proposed approach, the final shallow classifier, after this training is completed, is removed and replaced with an extremely randomized trees classifier trained on a subset of the neurons that is selected.

The feature extractor learned through the proposed method will be impractical for a real applications (e.g., applications on a mobile devices) due to its large size resulting from using bypassing connections from all neurons to the output. This problem can be alleviated while improving the generalization capacity of the system using feature selection.

Selecting appropriate bypass connections from the slow feature selector can be thought of as a standard feature selection problem which is solved in this paper using a multi-criteria wrapper method. Each feature (neuronal output i) is assigned a total *quality* ($Q(i)$) according to Eq. 4 where $\bar{I}_j(i)$ is z-score normalized feature *importance* ($I_j(i)$) according to a base feature selection method.

$$Q(i) = \sum_{j=0}^{n_f} w_j \bar{I}_j(i), \tag{4}$$

The raw *importance* measure is calculated as a weighted summation of multiple base feature selector importance measures after z-score normalization. In this work, we utilize two base selectors: randomized logistic regression [39], and extremely randomized trees. Random linear regression (RLR) estimates feature importance by randomly selecting subsets of training samples and fitting them using a L_1 sparsity inducing penalty that is scaled for a random set of coefficients. The features that appear repeatedly in such selections (i.e., features with high coefficients) are assumed to be more important and are given higher scores. The second feature selector employs extremely randomized trees. During fitting decision trees, features that appear at lower depths are generally more important. By fitting several such trees, feature importances can be estimated as the average depth of each feature in the trees.

Feature selection uses n-fold cross validation to select an appropriate number of neurons to keep in the final (i.e., fast) feature extractor. For each fold, the quality of each neuron is calculated using Eq. 4 employing its training set and then an extremely randomized tree classifier is fitted to the training set and evaluated on the validation set. The process is repeated recursively on the top-half of the neurons until a single neuron is kept in the feature set. The number of features/neurons that maximizes the F_1-measure on the validations sets is finally kept.

Table 1. Recalls for individual emotions when using MFCC features with/without SDC coefficients [%] (FAU Aibo).

Feature for i-vector extraction	Emotion					
	Angry	Emphatic	Joyful	Neutral	Rest	UAR
MFCC	46.5	35.1	53.5	33.8	28.8	39.5
MFCC+SDC	55.5	62.9	71.2	68.2	41.1	59.8

Table 2. EERs for individual emotions when using MFCC features with/without SDC coefficients [%] (FAU Aibo).

Feature for i-vector extraction	Emotion					
	Angry	Emphatic	Joyful	Neutral	Rest	Average
MFCC	32.8	35.0	26.8	35.4	41.8	34.4
MFCC+SDC	20.1	19.7	16.1	19.7	29.8	21.8

4 Results

This section presents the results obtained using the FAU Aibo and IEMOCAP corpora. The proposed method based on DCNN and extremely randomized trees is compared with three other classifiers namely, DCNN with a fully-connected layer on top fed with MFCC/SDC features, DCNN fed with i-vectors, and SVM fed also with i-vectors. In this section, the improvements when using SDC coefficients along with MFCC features compared to the sole use of MFCC are also described.

For evaluation, the equal error rate (EER) and the UAR are used. The UAR is defined as the mean of the recalls of the individual classes.

4.1 Emotion Recognition Using the German FAU Aibo Corpus

Table 1 shows the recalls and the UAR when using DCNN with/without SDC coefficients in the i-vector extraction. The results show that when using MFCC only in the i-vector extraction, the UAR was as low as 39.5%. When MFCC features were concatenated with SDC coefficients, the UAR improved to 59.8% showing a 20.3% absolute improvement. As show, the emotion *joyful* shows superior performance, and the emotion *rest* shows the lowest recall. A possible reason might be the fact that the class *rest* consists of several emotions not belonging to other classes. The results obtained when using also SDC are very promising and superior to the results obtained in similar studies [40]. The results also show the effectiveness of integrating i-vectors and CNN for speech emotion recognition using only 590 training i-vectors for each emotion.

Table 2 shows the EERs of the five emotions when using the FAU Aibo corpus. When using MFCC features only in the i-vectors extraction, the average EER was 34.4%. When SDC coefficients were also concatenated, the EER improved to

Table 3. Recalls for individual emotions when using three different classifiers [%] (FAU Aibo).

Classifier	Emotion					
	Angry	Emphatic	Joyful	Neutral	Rest	UAR
Deep convolutional neural networks + Extremely randomized trees	62.9	63.5	61.9	60.2	60.5	**61.8**
Deep convolutional neural networks + Fully connected layer	51.5	53.8	51.8	52.5	52.5	52.4
Support vector machine	55.2	44.5	62.2	35.5	46.5	48.8

21.8% showing an absolute reduction of 13.4%. The lowest EER was obtained in the case of the emotion *joyful*, and the highest EER was achieved in the case of the emotion *rest*. Tables 1 and 2 show the effectiveness of using SDC coefficients in speech emotion recognition. Therefore, in the following experiments, MFCC features concatenated with SDC coefficients will be used.

Table 3 shows the recalls of the individual classes, and also the UAR obtained. As shown, using DCNN for feature extraction and extremely randomized trees for classification, a 61.8% UAR was obtained. This is the highest UAR among the four classifiers. In the case of using conventional DCNN with a fully connected layer on top, the UAR was 51.4%. Finally, when using SVM, a 48.8% UAR was achieved. The results show, that in the two cases of using DCNN with extremely randomized trees and with a fully-connected layer, similar recalls were obtained across the five emotions. In the case of using SVM with i-vector features, the emotion *joyful* was classified with the highest recall, and the emotions *neutral* and *rest* showed the lowest recalls. This is similar to the case when DCNN with i-vectors was used. Previous studies reported that when short utterances were used for speaker recognition, the extracted i-vectors become unreliable [41]. Also, in the case of using i-vectors, the optimal case is when long training and long test utterances are used. It may happen, therefore, that in the current study training and test utterances of different lengths were randomly selected resulting in a higher recall variability. Note, however, that when using DCNN with i-vectors, the second highest UAR was obtained, and i-vectors can still be considered to be a very effective feature extraction method in speech emotion recognition.

Tables 4, 5, 6, and 7 show the confusion matrices when using the four classifiers. As shown, a higher variability in misclassification is obtained when i-vectors were used.

4.2 Emotion Recognition Using the English IEMOCAP Corpus

Table 8 shows the recalls of the four emotions in the case of using the IEMOCAP corpus. In this case, DCNN fed with i-vectors were used. For i-vector extraction MFCC features alone and also MFCC features concatenated with SDC coefficients were used. As shown, when using MFCC features only, an UAR of 55.5%

Table 4. Confusion matrix [%] of five emotions recognition when using DCNN with i-vectors (FAU Aibo).

	Angry	Emphatic	Joyful	Neutral	Rest
Angry	55.5	18.1	7.0	6.4	13.0
Emphatic	11.4	62.9	0.3	18.4	7.0
Joyful	2.7	2.7	71.2	5.7	17.7
Neutral	1.0	13.0	4.1	68.2	13.7
Rest	11.4	10.0	20.1	17.4	41.1

Table 5. Confusion matrix [%] of five emotions recognition when using DCNN and extremely randomized trees (FAU Aibo).

	Angry	Emphatic	Joyful	Neutral	Rest
Angry	62.9	13.0	9.0	6.7	8.4
Emphatic	8.7	63.5	11.7	10.0	6.1
Joyful	11.4	9.0	61.9	9.7	8.0
Neutral	9.0	11.1	11.0	60.2	8.7
Rest	12.4	6.4	12.7	8.0	60.5

Table 6. Confusion matrix [%] of five emotions recognition when using DCNN with a fully connected layer (FAU Aibo).

	Angry	Emphatic	Joyful	Neutral	Rest
Angry	51.5	15.1	11.4	10.0	12.0
Emphatic	10.8	53.8	14.7	12.7	8.0
Joyful	13.4	12.0	51.8	12.1	10.7
Neutral	11.7	13.4	12.4	52.5	10.0
Rest	13.7	8.0	16.4	9.4	52.5

Table 7. Confusion matrix [%] of five emotions recognition when using SVM with i-vectors (FAU Aibo).

	Angry	Emphatic	Joyful	Neutral	Rest
Angry	55.2	15.7	6.0	7.0	16.1
Emphatic	16.7	44.5	3.3	17.1	18.4
Joyful	3.3	2.7	62.2	4.7	27.1
Neutral	7.7	12.4	13.6	35.5	30.8
Rest	11.4	9.4	18.7	14.0	46.5

was obtained. When SDC coefficients were also concatenated, the UAR improved to 62.0%. The results also show that in most of cases (three out of four) the SDC coefficients resulted in higher recalls. The highest rates of recognition were for the *angry* and *sad* emotions. In contrast, the lowest recall was achieved in the case of the emotion *happy*.

Table 8. Recalls for individual emotions when using MFCC features with/without SDC coefficients [%] (IEMOCAP).

Feature for i-vector extraction	Emotion				
	Neutral	Happy	Angry	Sad	UAR
MFCC	46.0	40.0	66.0	70.0	55.5
MFCC+SDC	48.0	36.0	88.0	76.0	62.0

Table 9 shows the EERs when using DCNN fed with i-vectors. In the case of using MFCC features only, the average EER was 26.5%. When SDC coefficients were also used, a 22.2% EER was obtained. The results show that when also using SDC coefficients, significant improvements were obtained. Therefore, in the following experiments, MFCC features concatenated with SDC coefficients will be considered.

Table 9. EER for individual emotions when using MFCC features with/without SDC coefficients [%] (IEMOCAP).

Feature for i-vector extraction	Emotion				
	Neutral	Happy	Angry	Sad	Average
MFCC	30.0	36.0	18.0	22.0	26.5
MFCC+SDC	32.0	26.7	12.0	18.0	22.2

Table 10 shows the recalls and the UARs in the case of the IEMOCAP corpus and when using three different classifiers. As shown, when using DCNN for feature extraction and extremely randomized trees for classification, a 63.9% UAR was obtained, which is the highest among the four classifiers. This result is very promising and superior to the results obtained in similar studies [42, 43]. The results also show the effectiveness of the proposed method when DCNN is used for informative feature extraction. When using DCNN with a fully connected layer on top, a 59.3% UAR was achieved. Finally, the UAR in the case of SVM with i-vectors was as low as 36.8%. Tables 11, 12, 13, and 14 show the confusion matrices in the case of the IEMOCAP corpus and when using the four classifiers described previously. As shown, the emotion *neutral* is classified with the lowest recall in all cases.

Table 10. Recalls for individual emotions when using three different classifiers [%] (IEMOCAP).

Classifier	Emotion				
	Neutral	Happy	Angry	Sad	UAR
Deep convolutional neural networks + Extremely randomized trees	55.7	68.6	67.1	64.3	**63.9**
Deep convolutional neural networks + Fully connected layer	48.6	64.3	61.4	62.9	59.3
Support vector machine	26.0	39.0	45.0	37.0	36.8

Table 11. Confusion matrix [%] of four emotions recognition when using DCNN with i-vectors (IEMOCAP).

	Neutral	Happy	Angry	Sad
Neutral	48.0	18.0	14.0	20.0
Happy	34.0	36.0	14.0	16.0
Angry	4.0	4.0	88.0	4.0
Sad	12.0	8.0	4.0	76.0

Table 12. Confusion matrix [%] of four emotions recognition when using DCNN with extremely randomized trees (IEMOCAP).

	Neutral	Happy	Angry	Sad
Neutral	55.7	15.7	20.0	8.6
Happy	14.3	68.6	10.0	7.1
Angry	8.6	14.3	67.1	10.0
Sad	12.9	11.4	11.4	64.3

Table 13. Confusion matrix [%] of four emotions recognition when using DCNN with a fully-connected layer (IEMOCAP).

	Neutral	Happy	Angry	Sad
Neutral	48.6	12.8	24.3	14.3
Happy	15.7	64.3	11.4	8.6
Angry	14.3	12.9	61.4	11.4
Sad	15.7	12.9	8.6	62.8

Table 14. Confusion matrix [%] of four emotions recognition when using SVM with i-vectors (IEMOCAP).

	Neutral	Happy	Angry	Sad
Neutral	37.1	32.9	14.3	15.7
Happy	8.6	55.7	17.1	18.6
Angry	10.0	15.7	64.3	10.0
Sad	8.5	24.3	14.3	52.9

5 Discussion

A limitation of the current study is the small volume of training data used in the classification experiments. Specifically, in the case of using the FAU Aibo corpus, 590 training utterances for each emotion were used, and in the case of using the IEMOCAP corpus, 250 training utterances were used, respectively. Considering that DL based methods require a large amount of training data for accurate parameter estimation, further improvements may be possible by increasing the amount of data. The features used in the current study were based on MFCC and SDC coefficients, and also on the i-vectors. Although, several alternatives were considered (e.g., bottleneck features, LLD, etc.), well-known and very effective features were selected. Also, in particular the authors were interested in investigating the use of i-vectors with CNN due to the very small number of studies that have addressed this issue.

6 Conclusions

The current study focused on speech emotion recognition based on deep learning. We proposed a method based on DCNN, which extracts informative features used by extremely randomized trees for emotion recognition. When using the German FAU Aibo corpus for the recognition of five emotions, the proposed method achieved a 61.8% UAR. In the case of the IEMOCAP corpus, a 63.9% UAR was obtained. These results are very promising and show the effectiveness of the proposed method in speech emotion recognition. Additionally, several other classification and features extraction methods were experimentally investigated. The proposed method, however, showed superior performance. Currently, speech emotion recognition in adverse environments is being investigated.

References

1. Busso, C., Bulut, M., Narayanan, S.: Toward effective automatic recognition systems of emotion in speech. In: Gratch, J., Marsella, S. (eds.) Social Emotions in Nature and Artifact: Emotions in Human and Human-Computer Interaction, pp. 110–127. Oxford University Press, New York, November 2013

2. Geurts, P., Ernst, D., Wehenkel, L.: Extremely randomized trees. Mach. Learn. **63**(1), 3–42 (2006)
3. Ho, T.K.: Random decision forests. In: Proceedings of the 3rd International Conference on Document Analysis and Recognition, pp. 278–282 (1995)
4. Krizhevsky, A., Sutskever, I., Hinton, G.E.: Imagenet classification with deep convolutional neural networks. In: Pereira, F., Burges, C.J.C., Bottou, L., Weinberger, K.Q. (eds.) Advances in Neural Information Processing Systems, vol. 25, pp. 1097–1105. Curran Associates, Inc. (2012)
5. Abdel-Hamid, O., Mohamed, A.R., Jiang, H., Deng, L., Penn, G., Yu, D.: Convolutional neural networks for speech recognition. IEEE/ACM Trans. Audio, Speech Lang. Process. **22**, 1533–1545 (2014)
6. Lim, W., Jang, D., Lee, T.: Speech emotion recognition using convolutional and recurrent neural networks. In: Proceedings of Signal and Information Processing Association Annual Summit and Conference (APSIPA) (2016)
7. Rawat, W., Wang, Z.: Deep convolutional neural networks for image classification: a comprehensive review. Neural Commun. **29**, 2352–2449 (2017)
8. Kim, Y.: Convolutional neural networks for sentence classification. In: Proceedings of the 2014 Conference on Empirical Methods in Natural Language Processing (EMNLP), pp. 1746–1751 (2014)
9. Dehak, N., Kenny, P.J., Dehak, R., Dumouchel, P., Ouellet, P.: Front-end factor analysis for speaker verification. IEEE Trans. Audio, Speech Lang. Process. **19**(4), 788–798 (2011)
10. Gomes, J., El-Sharkawy, M.: i-vector algorithm with gaussian mixture model for efficient speech emotion recognition. In: Proceedings of International Conference on Computational Science and Computational Intelligence (CSCI), pp. 476–480 (2015)
11. Liu, R.X.Y.: Using i-vector space model for emotion recognition. In: Proceedings of Interspeech, pp. 2227–2230 (2012)
12. Gamage, K.W., Sethu, V., Le, P.N., Ambikairajah, E.: An i-vector GPLDA system for speech based emotion recognition. In: Proceedings of APSIPA Annual Summit and Conference, pp. 289–292 (2015)
13. Zhang, T., Wu, J.: Speech emotion recognition with i-vector feature and RNN model. In: Proceedings of ChinaSIP, pp. 524–528 (2015)
14. Heracleous, P., Mohammad, Y., Takai, K., Yasuda, K., Yoneyama, A., Sugaya, F.: A study on far-field emotion recognition based on deep convolutional neural networks. In: Proceedings of International Conference on Computational Linguistics and Intelligent Text Processing (2018)
15. Busso, C., et al.: IEMOCAP: interactive emotional dyadic motion capture database. J. Lang. Resour. Eval. **42**, 335–359 (2008)
16. Steidl, S.: Automatic Classification of Emotion-Related User States in Spontaneous Children's Speech. Logos Verlag, Berlin (2009)
17. Cristianini, N., Shawe-Taylor, J.: Support Vector Machines. Cambridge University Press, Cambridge (2000)
18. Basu, S., Chakraborty, J., Bag, A., Aftabuddin, M.: A review on emotion recognition using speech. In: International Conference on Inventive Communication and Computational Technologies (ICICCT), pp. 109–114 (2017)
19. Metallinou, A., Busso, C., Lee, S., Narayanan, S.: Visual emotion recognition using compact facial representations and viseme information. In: Proceedings of ICASSP, pp. 2474–2477 (2010)
20. Alarcao, S.M., Fonseca, M.J.: Emotions recognition using EEG signals: a survey. IEEE Trans. Affect. Comput. (2017)

21. Maaoui, C., Pruski, A.: A comparative study of SVM kernel applied to emotion recognition from physiological signals. In: Proceedings of 5th International Multi-Conference on Systems, Signals and Devices (2008)
22. Tang, H., Chu, S., Johnson, M.H.: Emotion recognition from speech via boosted gaussian mixture models. In: Proceedings of ICME, pp. 294–297 (2009)
23. Xu, S., Liu, Y., Liu, X.: Speaker recognition and speech emotion recognition based on GMM. In: 3rd International Conference on Electric and Electronics (EEIC 2013), pp. 434–436 (2013)
24. Schuller, B., Rigoll, G., Lang, M.: Hidden markov model-based speech emotion recognition. In: Proceedings of the IEEE ICASSP, vol. I, pp. 401–404 (2003)
25. Pan, Y., Shen, P., Shen, L.: Speech emotion recognition using support vector machine. Int. J. Smart Home **6**(2), 101–108 (2012)
26. Chavhan, Y., Dhore, M.L., Yesaware, P.: Speech emotion recognition using support vector machine. Int. J. Comput. Appl. **1**(20), 6–9 (2010). (0975–8887)
27. Nicholson, J., Takahashi, K., Nakatsu, R.: Emotion recognition in speech using neural networks. Neural Comput. Appl. **9**(4), 290–296 (2000)
28. Shaw, A., Vardhan, R.K., Saxena, S.: Emotion recognition and classification in speech using artificial neural networks. Int. J. Comput. Appl. **145**(8), 5–9 (2016). (0975–8887)
29. Stuhlsatz, A., Meyer, C., Eyben, F., Zielke1, T., Meier, G., Schuller, B.: Deep neural networks for acoustic emotion recognition: raising the benchmarks. In: Proceedings of ICASSP, pp. 5688–5691 (2011)
30. Han, K., Yu, D., Tashev, I.: Speech emotion recognition using deep neural network and extreme learning machine. In: Proceedings of Interspeech, pp. 2023–2027 (2014)
31. Sahidullah, M., Saha, G.: Design, analysis and experimental evaluation of block based transformation in MFCC computation for speaker recognition. Speech Commun. **54**(4), 543–565 (2012)
32. Bielefeld, B.: Language identification using shifted delta cepstrum. In: Fourteenth Annual Speech Research Symposium (1994)
33. Torres-Carrasquillo, P.A., Singer, E., Kohler, M.A., Greene, R.J., Reynolds, D.A., Deller, Jr., J.R.: Approaches to language identification using gaussian mixture models and shifted delta cepstral features. In: Proceedings of ICSLP2002-INTERSPEECH 2002, pp. 16–20 (2002)
34. Schuller, B., et al.: The relevance of feature type for the automatic classification of emotional user states: low level descriptors and functionals. In: Proceedings of Interspeech, pp. 2253–2256 (2007)
35. Ranjan, S., Yu, C., Zhang, C., Kelly, F., Hansen, J.H.L.: Language recognition using deep neural networks with very limited training data. In: Proceedings of ICASSP, pp. 5830–5834 (2016)
36. Mohammad, Y., Matsumoto, K., Hoashi, K.: Deep feature learning and selection for activity recognition. In: Proceedings of the 33rd ACM/SIGAPP Symposium on Applied Computing, pp. 926–935. ACM SAC (2018)
37. LeCun, Y., Denker, J.S., Solla, S.A.: Optimal brain damage. In: Advances in Neural Information Processing Systems, vol. 2, pp. 598–605 (1990)
38. Yu, J., Lukefahr, A., Palframan, D., Dasika, G., Das, R., Mahlke, S.: Scalpel: customizing DNN pruning to the underlying hardware parallelism. In: Proceedings of the 44th Annual International Symposium on Computer Architecture, pp. 548–560. ACM (2017)

39. Friedman, J., Hastie, T., et al.: Additive logistic regression: a statistical view of boosting (with discussion and a rejoinder by the authors). Ann. Stat. **28**(2), 337–407 (2000)
40. Attabi, Y., Alam, J., Dumouchel, P., Kenny, P., Shaughnessy, D.O.: Multiple windowed spectral features for emotion recognition. In: Proceedings of ICASSP, pp. 7527–7531 (2013)
41. Zhang, J., Inoue, N., Shinoda, K.: I-vector transformation using conditional generative adversarial networks for short utterance speaker verification. In: Proceedings of Interspeech, pp. 3613–3617 (2018)
42. Tzinis, E., Potamianos, A.: Segment-based emotion recognition using recurrent neural networks. In: Proceedings of ACI, vol. I, pp. 190–195 (2017)
43. Huang, C.W., Narayanan, S.: Attention assisted discover of sub-utterance in speech emotion recognition. In: Proceedings of Interspeech, pp. 1387–1391 (2016)

A Preliminary Experiment on the Estimation of Emotion Using Facial Expression and Biological Signals

Yuya Kurono, Peeraya Sripian(✉), Feng Chen, and Midori Sugaya

Shibaura Institute of Technology, 3-7-5,
Toyosu, Koto-ku, Tokyo 135-8548, Japan
peeraya@shibaura-it.ac.jp, doly@shibara-it.ac.jp

Abstract. Imagine the day that a robot would comfort you when you feel sad. In the field of artificial intelligence and robot engineering, there are many research regarding automatic classification of human emotion to enhance human-robot communication, especially for therapy. Generally, estimating emotions of people is based on information such as facial expression, eye-gazing direction, and behaviors that are expressed externally and the robot can observe through a camera and so on. However, there is some invisible information that cannot be expressed, or control not to express. In this case, it is difficult to estimate the emotion even if the analysis technologies are sophisticated. The main idea of this research is to compare the classified emotion based on two different sources: controllable and uncontrollable expression. The preliminary experiments show that our proposed method suggested that the classification of emotion from biological signals outperform the classification from facial expression.

Keywords: Emotion classification · Robotics · Biological signals · Facial expression · Sympathy · Feeling

1 Introduction

Nowadays, communication robots (social robots) are widely used at various sites such as commercial facilities and medical/nursing care facilities. According to the Ministry of Internal Affairs and Communications of Japan, the survey about communication robot usage shows that around 50% are actively willing to use the communication robot [1]. Breazeal et al. [2] proposed a robot with expressive acts to interact socially with humans. In their proposed system, the robot's gaze is changed according to the expression of human to maintain a regular social interaction. Also, many robots are build to have body elements which are similar to human and utilize those elements for their interaction [3, 4]. On the other hand, Hirth et al. [5] developed a robot, "ROMAN" that can express six emotions consisting of anger, disgust, fear, happiness, and sadness. However, there is little discussion on the emotion expression of the robot itself in correspondence to various context.

We focused on the feeling of "empathy", which is considered important in human-to-human communication, to enhance mutual reliability and relationship building [6].

M. Kurosu (Ed.): HCII 2019, LNCS 11567, pp. 133–142, 2019.
https://doi.org/10.1007/978-3-030-22643-5_10

Here, "empathy" is defined as synchronizing with the feelings of the opponent. It could be possible that the robot would mutually understand human emotion and empathize, similar to the communication between human. It was found that when a robot expresses emotion that is close to what human feels, an affinity relationship can be made from the empathy feeling. Misaki et al. [7] build a robot that its facial expression is synchronized with human emotion estimated from speech recognition. They used the SD method to evaluate and found that the positive items were significantly selected, hence, the participants had a positive impression on the robot because of empathy [7]. Haneda and Takeuchi [8] investigated how empathy between people and CG character could affect people. They found that when the participant's mental state is "angry" and the CG character is also "angry," the more helping behavior is observed as a result of emotion synchronization. Therefore, a friendly relationship could be established when the other person expresses emotions close to our own, even though he/she is a CG character [8]. However, there is not sufficient study regarding the accurate measurement of human emotions.

There is many studies that proposes the estimation of human emotion based on voice and facial expression. Ikeda et al. [9] classified emotion with facial expression and biological signals. Facial expression was derived through a computer vision method, and face recognition technique. They found that biological signals performed better in the estimation of genuine emotion. The emotion expressed through facial expression or voice tone is carried by the somatic nervous system which is a voluntary nervous system, could be controlled by the sender. On the other hand, biological signals such as heart rate and brain waves could not be controlled by the sender because it is driven by the autonomic nervous system, which is an involuntary nervous system, or the unconscious mind.

However, Ikeda et al.'s work did not describe whether the participant favor "controllable" emotion or "uncontrollable" emotion.

In this work, we propose a system for classifying emotions from controllable expression and uncontrollable expression and compared the classified emotions with the subjectively evaluated emotion in the experiment.

2 Literature Review

Various studies have performed human emotion estimation using biological signals based on Russell's Circumplex Model of Affection [10]. The model, known as a structure to classify emotion, suggests that emotions are distributed into two dimensional circular space, arousal and valence dimensions. The vertical axis is represented by Arousal, and Valence represents the horizontal axis. The neutral valence and medium level of arousal are indicated with the center location of the circle.

Ikeda et al. [9] proposed a method of estimating emotion using involuntary biological signals. The proposed method uses brain waves and heart rate for estimating the actual emotion of the participant, which is the result of the unconscious mind. From their series of experiments, they found that more accuracy could be derived by including biological signals in the emotion estimation other than using the observable emotion alone. Also, they found that there was a correlation between parts of the personality and the accuracy of the estimated results. To estimate emotion, they use the pNN50 method for pulse analysis [11], combining with Y-axis of Russel's Circumplex Model. pNN50 measurement is a time domain method for Heart Rate Variability (HRV), which analyzes the physiological phenomenon of the oscillation in the interval between consecutive heartbeats. From the combination of the pNN50 pulse interval and the awakening degree, the "joy" emotion can be defined when the awakening degree is 0 or more, and pNN50 is 0.3 or more.

The International Affective Picture System (IAPS) [12] has been widely used to study emotion and attention in psychological research. IAPS is an international image database developed by the Center for the Study of Emotion and Attention: CSEA, University of Florida. IAPS is a large set of standardized, emotionally-evocative, internationally-accessible, color photographs that includes contents across a wide range of semantic categories. The images set is accompanied by a detailed list of the average rating of the emotions elicited by each picture. Such an average rating procedure for the IAPS is based on the assumption that emotional assessments are identifiable by the three dimensions: valence, arousal, and dominance [13]. Each image is registered with discrete values of 1 to 9 for Arousal dimension (**Sleepiness-Arousal**) and the Valence dimension (**Misery-Pleasure**) dimension which corresponds to both dimensions in the Russell's Circumplex Model of Affection.

The rating procedure for IAPS is done through many subjective evaluation experiments. The participants are asked to rate how pleasant/unpleasant, how calm/excited and how controlled/in-control they felt when looking at each picture. The Self-Assessment Manikin (SAM) [14] is used for this rating procedure. The SAM is a non-verbal pictorial assessment technique that directly measures the feeling of pleasure, arousal, and dominance that are associated with a person's affective reaction to a variety of stimuli. This type of non-verbal assessment, although easy to administer and quick, it is highly correlated with ratings obtained using the verbal or lengthier semantic differential scale.

3 Proposed Method

Figure 1 shows the proposed system. Two types of input data will be retrieved from the participant; the **controllable** expression and the **uncontrollable** expression. The system will estimate emotion based on these input data, and send the estimated emotion to the robot to be displayed. Here, we use facial expression as the controllable expression and biological signals: heart rate and brain wave, are used as the uncontrollable expression. Since biological signals are controlled by autonomic nerves which are involuntary nervous systems, it is considered difficult to change them arbitrarily. In this paper, we focus on the measurement and comparison of biological signals and the facial expression to subjective evaluation of emotion (See Fig. 1 left square).

3.1 Emotion Estimation Using the Biological Signals

We use the method for the estimation of emotion from the biological signals proposed by Ikeda et al. [9]. This method estimates eight types of emotion from the data

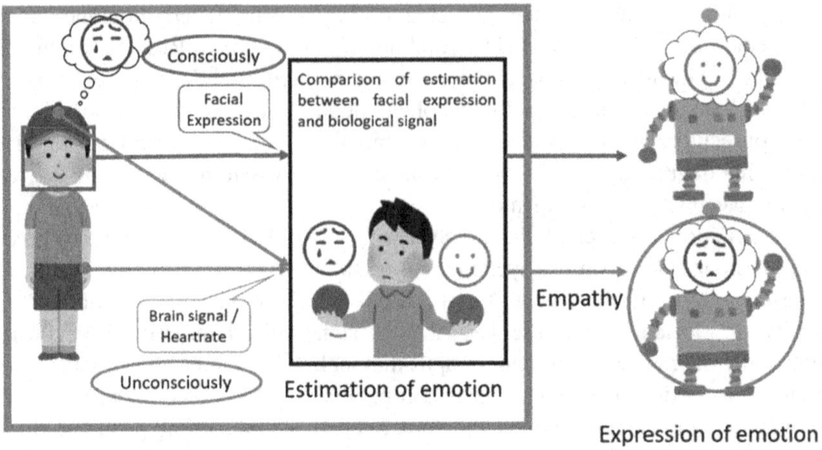

Fig. 1. Overview of the system

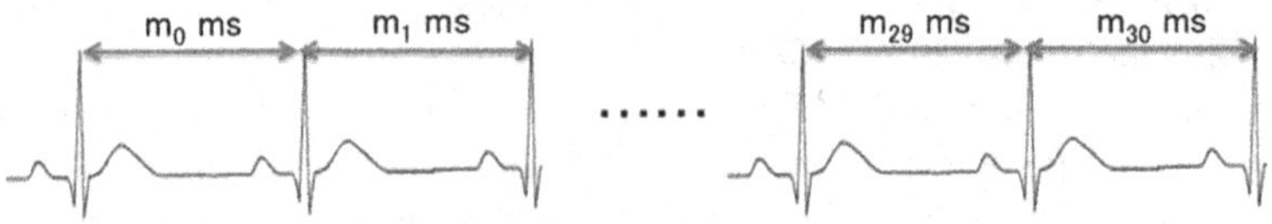

Fig. 2. pNN50, Pulse interval

calculated from brain waves and heart rate. A heart-shaped pulse sensor [15] by World Famous Electronics llc. is used to measure a heart rate in this work. The value at the pulse over a one-minute interval, or pNN50, is used to estimate emotion. The pNN50 is defined using time domain measurement of HRV measures.

Figure 2 shows the R-R Interval. RR_i denotes the time from the ith to the $i + 1^{st}$ R peak. $\overline{RR}$ is the average interval, giving n intervals in total. pNN50 can be obtained using the following equation;

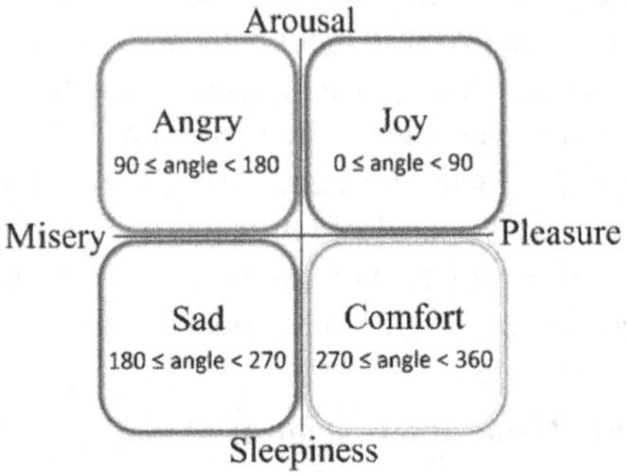

Fig. 3. Emotion estimation model

$$\text{pNN50:} = \mathrm{P}(|RR_{i+1} - RR_i| > 50\ \text{ms}) \tag{1}$$

Generally, since RR_i is presumed to have a certain fluctuation due to the influence of respiration and blood pressure, pNN50 is set to a pleasant state [16] when it is 0.3 or more. Therefore, we associate pNN50 with the horizontal axis or the **Pleasure dimension** in Russell's Circumplex Model of Affection by setting pNN50 at 0.3 as an origin point.

For brain wave measurement, we use NeuroSky™ MindWave Mobile. The sensor from this electroencephalograph measures EEG/ECG signal and calculates the level of the attention and meditation and return the value from 0 to 100. In this work, the output value is positioned on the vertical axis or the **Arousal dimension** on Russell's Circumplex Model of Affection (Fig. 3). Therefore, the Arousal dimension at the origin or zero means that the value of attention is equal to meditation from the brain wave measurement.

Hence, the combination of pNN50 and the brain wave measurement can be set to (x, y) coordinate on Russell's Circumplex Model of Affection to estimate emotion. In summary, the **joy** emotion can be estimated when the arousal value is a positive value and pNN50 is 0.3 or more.

4 Experiment

Before proceeding to the comparison with robot expression, we conduct a preliminary experiment for validation of the estimated emotion. The objective of this experiment is to find out that the estimated emotion from a different source (controllable expression/uncontrollable expression), which matches more with the participant's emotion (answered by the questionnaire).

During the whole experiment, the participant is asked to wear an electroencephalograph and a pulse sensor. In each trial, the participant is shown an image that will induce one of the four basic emotions; **Joy, Angry, Sad, Comfort**. The participant will fill in the questionnaire regarding his/her emotion toward the shown image. After the experiment, we calculated emotions derived from two sources; biological sensors and the facial expression and analyzed the concordance rate between estimated emotion and subjective evaluation (Fig. 1).

4.1 Subjects

Two male students (20–25 years old) voluntarily participated in the experiment with consent.

4.2 Stimuli

Ten color pictures were taken from the International Affective Picture System [14]. The pictures ranged from somewhat negative (low valence and medium arousal) to neutral (medium valence and low arousal) to somewhat positive (high valence and medium arousal). The pictures represented various content. The order of presentation is random.

4.3 Devices

- Pulse sensor from World Famous Electronics llc. and NeuroSky™ MindWave Mobile are used for biological signals measurement.
- Omron's OKAO™ Vision facial image analysis software is used for the measurement of facial expression.

4.4 Procedure

Figure 4 shows overview of the evaluation procedure. The participant is asked to wear a brain wave sensor and a pulse sensor during the whole experiment. OMRON's OKAO™ Vision is set on a table in front of the participant to detect the participant's facial expression. After begin retrieving all input data from all sensors, the experimental procedure is as follows.

1. The participant stays still (Rest) for 30 s.
2. A standby image (Symbol) is presented on the screen for 10 s.
3. The stimulus image is presented for 15 s.
4. The participant evaluates the stimulus image using SAM [14] on a paper questionnaire.

The above procedure is repeated until all ten stimulus images were evaluated.

4.5 Emotion Classification

We divide the input data into two types; the controllable expression and the uncontrollable expression. The controllable expression is the expression that human has control over, for example, facial expression. Meanwhile, the uncontrollable expression is origin from the unconscious mind, such as heart rate and brain waves.

Emotion Classification From the Uncontrollable Expression
The input data from a brain wave sensor and a pulse sensor is positioned on x,y coordinate of Russell's Circumplex Model of Affection. The classification method is adapted from Ikeda et al. [9], which the emotions are classified into eight types. In order to correlate the estimated emotion with OMRON's OKAO™ Vision output, we classify the emotion into four types. The figure shows the proposed adapted model for emotion classification. As mentioned in Sect. 3.1, the vertical axis is represented by the value from the brain wave sensor, and the horizontal axis is represented by the value calculates from a pulse sensor.

Emotion Classification From the Controllable Expression
In our work, we classify controllable emotion from the participant's facial expression. The device's output is classified into five kinds of emotion: Neutral, Happy, Sorrow, Furious, Surprise at the intervals of 0.2 to 0.3 s. For the comparison in our work, we regroup the emotions classified by the device into four types of emotion using the proposed classification table in Table 1.

Table 1. The emotion classification table

Classified emotion	Joy	Angry	Sad	Comfort
Output emotion from OKAO™ Vision	Happiness Surprise	Furious	Sorrow 1/3 Neutral	2/3 Neutral

Emotion Evaluation Method

Given X as a type of emotion (joy, angry, sad and comfort) occurring at each second i, we can obtain the total presented emotion during the stimulus exposure time EM_X as follows.

$$EM_X \sum\nolimits_{i=0}^{i=N} X_i \qquad (2)$$

Here, the stimulus exposure time is 15 ms, therefore N = 15. We take the largest value of *EM* from the four types of emotion as the presented emotion for further evaluation.

4.6 Subjective Evaluation of Emotion Using SAM

Subjective evaluation for emotion is performed using SAM (Self-Assessment Manikin) [14], a non-verbal pictorial assessment technique used to measure pleasure, arousal, and dominance. After finishing each stimulus exposure, the participant is asked to rate how he/she felt for the stimulus in terms of pleasure and arousal, using nine levels of facial expression of the manikin illustration. The pleasure dimension has the leftmost picture indicating lowest pleasure (unhappy) and the rightmost illustration indicated the highest pleasure (happy). Accordingly, the leftmost illustration in the arousal dimension indicates the lowest arousal (calm) and the rightmost illustration indicates the highest arousal (excitement). With values on each dimension, we can position the pleasure rating onto X-axis and the arousal rating onto Y-axis in Russell's Circumplex Model of Affection to derive subjectively evaluated emotion toward a stimulus.

5 The Analysis of the Result

To analysis the result, we calculate the concordance rate (%), C, as follows;

$$C = \frac{N_{Match}}{10} \cdot 100 \qquad (3)$$

Here, N_{Match} is the number of images (out of ten) where the classified emotion is the same as the subjective emotion. The concordance rates for each participant are described in Table 2.

From Table 2, the concordance rate of participant 1 is rank higher for facial expression and vice versa for participant #2. Although the result does not agree, we can imply that the biological signals gave a rather high (around 50%) concordance rate in both participants, whereas the facial expression resulted in as low as 20% concordance rate for participant 2.

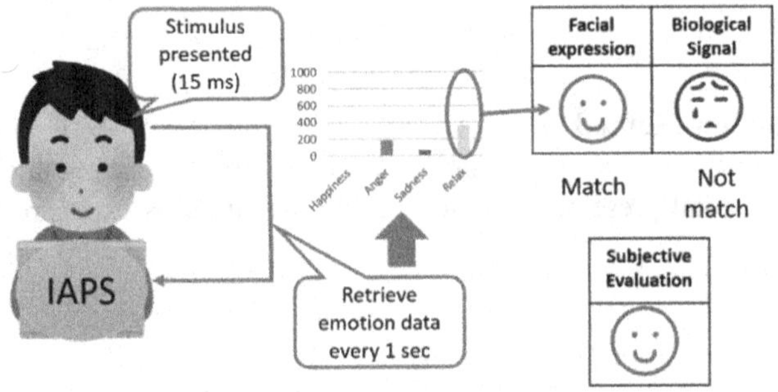

Fig. 4. Overview of the evaluation procedure

Figure 5 shows the transition of each type of emotion from the biological signals and facial expression of participant 2 from the presentation of stimulus 10. The strength of each emotion is a normalized value of 0 to 100. Using facial expression in the classification, we can observe that the classified emotion of "sad" stays higher than other types of emotion throughout 15 ms exposure time.

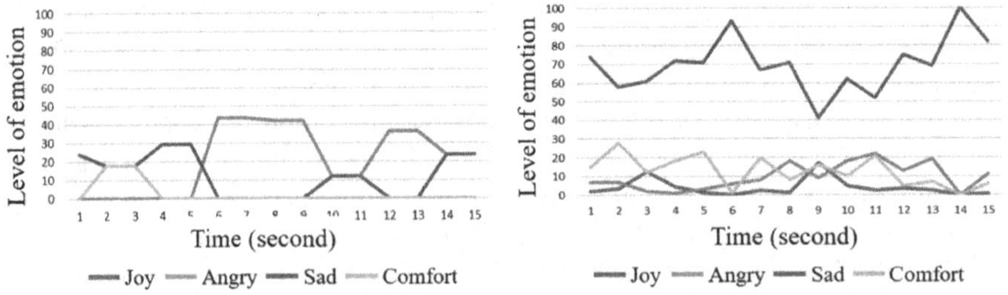

Fig. 5. Left: Classified emotions from the biological signals of trial #10 for participant #2. **Right**: Classified emotions from facial expression of trial #10 for participant #2.

6 Discussion

The images used as stimuli in this experiment was selected with arousal normative values were in the medium range. We assumed that there is a possibility that images presented did not induce strong emotion, therefore, there is no significant change in emotional value observed with the biological signals. When further analysis is performed, we found that most of the facial expression is classified as "sad." In our work, we include "neutral" expression when weight for the "sad" classification, therefore, it may affect the result.

In the experiment, there are possibly other uncontrollable factors that could affect the expressed emotion of the participant. For example, boredom from the experiment could result in many "neutral" or "sad" facial expression. Hence, the extremely high classification for "sad" is observed in Fig. 5 Right. We assumed from the experiment result that the biological signals could provide a more genuine emotion classification. Hence, a better impression may be achieved when further applied the classified emotion on the robot expression.

In the future, more participants are necessary for more reliability of the data analysis. Experiment procedure could be improved such as selection of stimuli, presented time, record time and so on. Stimuli that could induce more explicit emotion could be used for more distinct facial expression.

Table 2. The concordance rates of participant 1 and 2, comparison between emotion classified by facial expression and emotion classified by biological signals.

	Participant 1	Participant 2
Facial expression	60%	20%
Biological signals	40%	50%

7 Conclusion

We proposed the emotion classification method from biological signals and facial expression and compared with subjectively evaluated emotion in this research. For classification procedures, biological signals and facial expression are separately calculated to be positioned in the coordinate of Russell's Circumplex Model of Affection. Similarly, we positioned the participant rating of arousal and pleasant level in the same model of affection for comparison. The concordance value for emotion classified from biological signal and emotion classified from facial expression are compared. Although there is no significant difference observed because of the limited number of participants, it can be implied that emotion classified with biological signals resulted in high concordance for all participants. The finding from this work will lead to the development of the system for the next experiment, to finally compare with the emotion expressed in the robot.

References

1. Ministry of Internal Affairs and Communication. http://www.soumu.go.jp/johotsusintokei/whitepaper/ja/h27/html/nc241350.html. Accessed 15 Feb 2019
2. Breazeal, C., Scassellati, B.: A context-dependent attention system for a social robot. rn **255**, 3 (1999)
3. Komatsu, T., Kuki, N.: Investigating the contributing factors to make users react toward an on-screen agent as if they are reacting toward a robotic agent. In: RO-MAN 2009 - The 18th IEEE International Symposium on Robot and Human Interactive Communication, pp. 651–656. IEEE (2009)

4. Mutlu, B., Osman, S., Forlizzi, J., Hodgins, J., Kiesler, S.: Perceptions of ASIMO: an exploration on co-operation and competition with humans and humanoid robots. In: Proceedings of the 1st ACM SIGCHI/SIGART Conference on Human-Robot Interaction, pp. 351–352. ACM (2006)
5. Hirth, J., Schmitz, N., Berns, K.: Emotional architecture for the humanoid robot head ROMAN. In: 2007 IEEE International Conference on Robotics and Automation, pp. 2150–2155. IEEE (2007)
6. Satoshi, U., et al.: Cognitive Science in Communication 2: Empathy (Iwanami lecture). Iwanami Shoten (2014). in Japanese
7. Misaki, Y., Ito, T., Hashimoto, M.: Proposal of human-robot interaction method based on emotional entrainment. In: HAI Symposium (2008). in Japanese
8. Haneda, T., Takeuchi, Y.: Study of empathy feeling of CG facial expression (2003)
9. Ikeda, Y., Horie, R., Sugaya, M.: Estimate emotion with biological information for robot interaction. In: 21st International Conference on Knowledge-Based and Intelligent Information & Engineering Systems (KES-2017), Marseille, France, pp. 6–8 (2017)
10. Russell, J.A.: A circumplex model of affect. J. Pers. Soc. Psychol. **39**, 1161 (1980)
11. Ewing, D.J., Neilson, J., Travis, P.: New method for assessing cardiac parasympathetic activity using 24 hour electrocardiograms. Heart **52**, 396–402 (1984)
12. Lang, P.J., Bradley, M.M., Cuthbert, B.N.: International affective picture system (IAPS): technical manual and affective ratings. In: NIMH Center for the Study of Emotion and Attention, pp. 39–58 (1997)
13. Osgood, C.E.: The nature and measurement of meaning. Psychol. Bull. **49**, 197 (1952)
14. Bradley, M.M., Lang, P.J.: Measuring emotion: the self-assessment manikin and the semantic differential. J. Behav. Ther. Exp. Psychiatry **25**, 49–59 (1994)
15. World Famous Electronics llc. https://pulsesensor.com/pages/code-and-guide. Accessed 15 Feb 2019
16. de Carvalho Abreu, E.M., de Souza Alves, R., Borges, A.C.L., Lima, F.P.S., de Paula Júnior, A.R., Lima, M.O.: Autonomic cardiovascular control recovery in quadriplegics after handcycle training. J. Phys. Therapy Sci. **28**, 2063–2068 (2016)

Application of Classification Method of Emotional Expression Type Based on Laban Movement Analysis to Design Creation

Yuki Ono[1(✉)], Saizo Aoyagi[2], Masashi Sugimoto[1], Yoichi Yamazaki[1], Michiya Yamamoto[1], and Noriko Nagata[1]

[1] School of Science and Technology, Kwansei Gakuin University, Sanda, Hyogo, Japan
{y.o,michiya.yamamoto}@kwansei.ac.jp
[2] Faculty of Information Networking for Innovation and Design, Toyo University, Kita-ku, Tokyo, Japan

Abstract. Emotion estimation is one of the most essential research areas along with the progress of human sensing and AI technologies. We have already proposed a classification method of emotional expression type based on Laban movement analysis, which is a typical theory for dancers. In this study, we applied the classification method to design creation, which is typically performed in digital fabrication. First, we made clear what kinds of emotions are evoked in digital fabrication tasks by using the evaluation grid method, and we analyzed the emotions by constructing a core affect model for the task. Next, we performed an experiment to measure the dataset of body motions and emotions by performing an experiment using SONY FES Watch U. By using the dataset, we classified users by body motions, estimated the evoked emotions by using the classified dataset, and realized emotion estimation at about 80%. We could estimate emotions even when the body motions were not so large or activated compared with the fabrication task. The results showed the general effectiveness of the classification method.

Keywords: Design creation · Laban movement analysis · Emotion extraction

1 Introduction

Along with the improvements of human sensing and AI technology, various studies of emotion recognition are performed more than ever. A study by Ekman proposing recognition of six basic emotions by using facial expressions is one of the most typical in this research field. In this case, feature values of facial expressions are calculated from images or videos shot by cameras to recognize emotion.

Body movements are another key to estimating or recognizing emotions, and there are many studies on this. However, in contrast to recognition by facial expressions, the targeted emotions change in each study [1]. Here, variations of sensing methods and target situations make these studies more difficult to conclude in general findings [2]. The feature values, which depend on sensors and situations, also change in each study. The numbers of open datasets show this difficulty.

M. Kurosu (Ed.): HCII 2019, LNCS 11567, pp. 143–154, 2019.
https://doi.org/10.1007/978-3-030-22643-5_11

We have focused on Laban movement analysis (LMA) to recognize emotions in a more general way [3]. LMA was proposed originally as a general method to interpreting human movements and has been used by dancers, actors, etc. [4]. LMA is composed of several characteristic elements, such as space (direct/indirect), weight (light/strong), and time (sudden/sustained). Space means direction bias of body movements, weight means strength of motions, and time means haste of change of body movements. Nevertheless, they are not defined numerically.

In our previous study, we defined our original feature values based on LMA and enabled the estimation of eight emotions with 60% or more accuracy [5, 6]. However, we needed to capture all motions during the task and then ask that participants answer the emotions during the task. We also proposed a classification method of emotional expression by body movements [7]. Here, we made clear that we could classify and define types of motional expression by body movements, and it became possible to realize semi-supervised learning for emotion estimation. For example, when we classified into three types, the estimation accuracy was about 68%. For both studies, we selected personal fabrication as the target situation, in which various motions and actions occurred.

In this study, we apply our LMA values and the classification method of emotional expression by body movements into a design creation task, one of a new digital fabrication task when using 3D printers, laser cutters, etc. [8]. So, we first reveal what kinds of emotions are evoked and what kinds of characteristics are observed during the design creation task. Next, we preform measurement of the body movements and the emotion interview during the design creation task. Then, we perform evaluation and clarify that our proposed method is applicable to the design creation task.

2 Classification Method of Emotional Expression Type

2.1 The Feature Values Based on Laban Movement Analysis

To estimate emotions from body movements, we focused on Laban theory [4], which is known as the mainstream method worldwide for interpreting human movements such as dance. We proposed an original method for a classification method of emotional expression type on LMA, which applied the theory to action analysis and emotion recognition. Laban suggested a notation method of "Effort-shape description" concerning body movements [5]. In this notation method, we focused on Effort, which expresses movements with respect to inner intention and is deeply related to emotion. Effort has four factors: Space, Weight, Time, and Flow. Among these factors, we selected three factors and defined our original feature values, as shown in Fig. 1. Space refers to biases of directions (Direct/Indirect) of body parts in LMA and is defined as the area of the triangle formed by the head position and the positions of the wrists. Weight refers to strength of motions (Strong/Light) in LMA and is defined as the vertical position of the head. Time refers to the haste of change (Sudden/Sustained) in body movements in LMA and is defined as the maximum value of moving averages of the speed of the head and the wrists across 60 s.

Fig. 1. The feature values based on Laban Movement Analysis.

2.2 Emotion Interview

We also needed to decide target emotions to measure emotions. So, we focused on the core affect model [9]. In this model, various emotions are arranged on a circle that is composed of the horizontal axis representing the pleasant/unpleasant and the vertical axis representing arousal/calm. According to this model, we chose eight target emotions, as shown in Fig. 2. Next, emotions in fabrication are measured by an emotion interview. The emotion interview looks back on the video after fabrication and makes the fabricator select suitable emotions and intensity (5 grades).

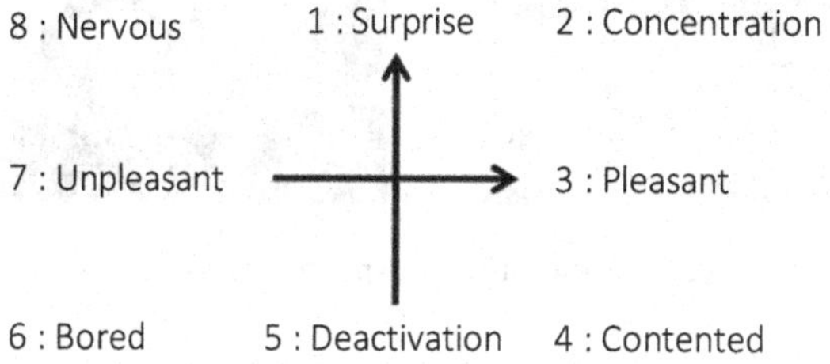

Fig. 2. Emotions used in the emotion interview.

2.3 Classification Method of Emotional Expression

We assumed that emotions are expressed via body movements. This was partially clarified by our previous study [5, 6] because we could estimate emotions by using LMA feature values and simple decision trees. However, there is a question of whether the expressed movements have some typical types just like facial expressions. If there are such types, it becomes possible to estimate emotions by using semi-supervised learning.

For this purpose, we first proposed a method to classify expression types only by movements. Here, we focused on sensitivity analysis, which can analyze complex systems by observing inputs and outputs [10]. Based on this, we defined the parameter called expression sensitivity (ES) for each LMA value of Space, Weight, and Time. After this, we introduced Ward's method for hierarchical by using the normalized ES parameters [7].

Then, as the next step, we analyzed each type of movement. If there were differences in feature values of movements, we concluded how internal emotions are expressed as external movements.

After these steps, we evaluated estimation rate to evaluate the method. If there were some types, emotions could be estimated at a high rate.

2.4 Evaluation Experiment

To verify the effectiveness of our method, we performed an experiment that included measurement of body movements and emotion interview in a fabrication task. The participants were twelve male and eight female Japanese students.

First, we asked participants to make their original synthesizer in pairs by using the electronic building blocks (KORG, littleBits). During fabrication, participants' body motions were shot using a motion capture system (Vicon, Bonita 10) and video cameras, as shown in Fig. 3. We calculated LMA values from these data. Next, we made participants perform an emotion interview, and we extracted emotions during fabrication.

Fig. 3. LittleBits and experimental scene.

We applied our proposed method to measured datasets and extracted three emotional expression types, as shown in Fig. 4. In the figure, ** means $p < 0.01$, and * means $p < 0.05$. Here, we calculated the accuracy of estimations for each type of dataset and randomly chosen dataset by tenfold cross-validations using a discriminator, which we constructed in a support vector machine (SVM). As a result, we were able to estimate the average of each dataset as 67.97% and each randomly chosen dataset as 51.02%. Therefore, our proposed method showed the validity in fabrication.

3 Design Creation Task for FES Watch U

In this study, we selected a design creation task for digital fabrication by using a display watch (SONY, FES Watch U) with which we could design the face and the belt parts. We prepared tools for the design creation using Microsoft Surface Pro 4, the Surface Pen, and a mouse. In the experiment, participants designed a template image of the FES Watch U using Adobe's Illustrator or Photoshop, as shown in Fig. 5. Then, participants transferred the design image to Apple iPad Pro and Fes Watch U using an

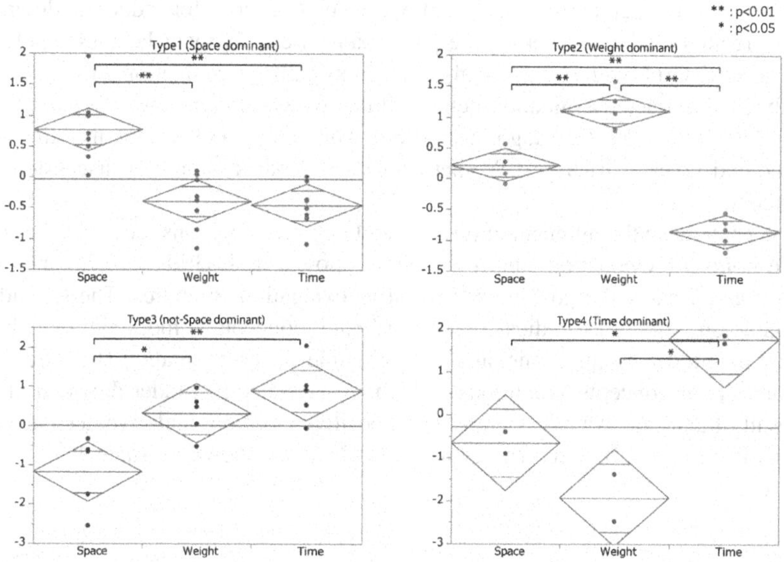

Fig. 4. Distribution of the classification features.

application termed FES Closet. It was possible to design in full color, but the design was displayed in monochrome on FES Watch U because its face was made by electronic paper.

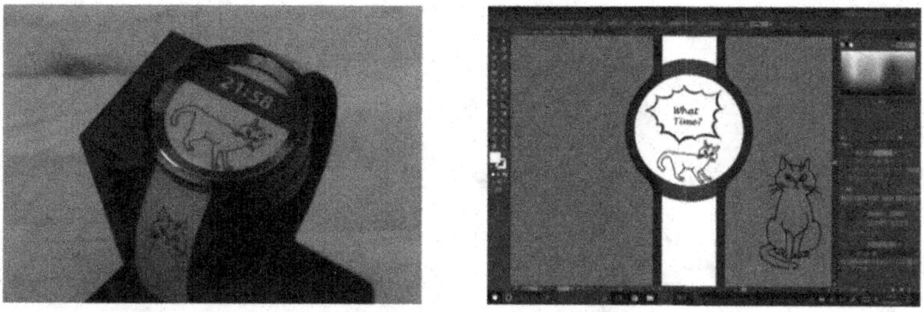

Fig. 5. FES Watch U and example of a design.

4 Analysis of Evoked Emotions in Design Creation

4.1 Interview for Extraction of Evoked Emotions

We performed an experiment in which participants performed design creation tasks as described in Sect. 3. After that, we performed an interview for extraction of evoked emotions based on the evaluation grid method [11]. In the interview, we instructed participants to comment positive and negative points in design creation as much as possible. Then, for each commented point, we asked questions for rudder up/down and extracted related evaluation items. The participants were six male Japanese students.

We used E-Grid, which is a visual analytics system for evaluation structures [12], for analysis of extracted evaluation items. All the evaluation items were inputted to E-Grid, and we integrated the categories into one when they had the same meanings. We also modified inverse structures. We performed the modification after discussion with two authors.

In order to make the numbers of positive and negative emotions the same, we set up the thresholds of evaluation items, which is shown in E-Grid as 0.75 and 0.64. Figures 6 and 7 show the positive and negative evaluation structures. The left side of the evaluation structures indicates superordinate concepts (emotions), which are extracted by rudder-up questions, and the right side of the evaluation structures indicates subordinate concepts (conditions), which are extracted by rudder-down questions. As a result of analysis, we extracted fourteen positive emotions and seventeen negative emotions from each structure. The evoked emotions are shown in Table 1.

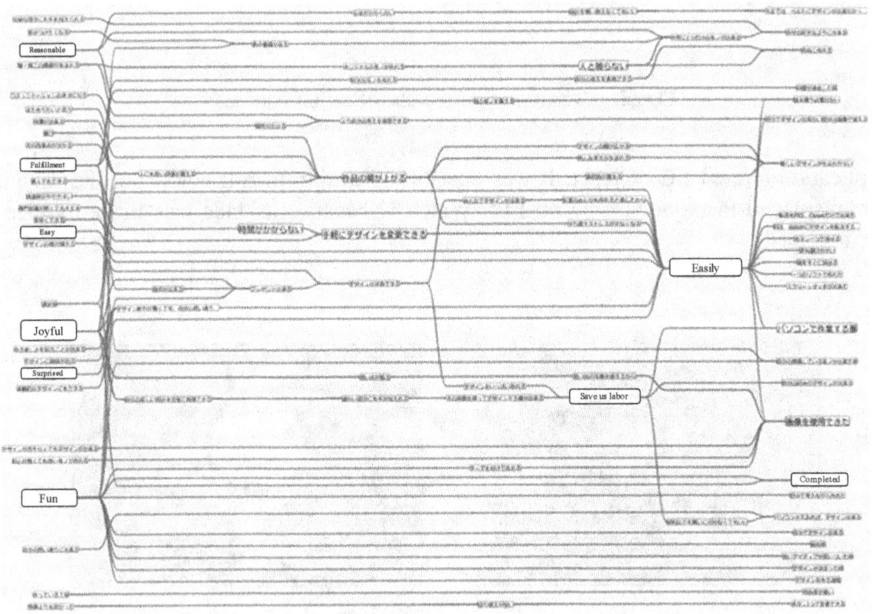

Fig. 6. Positive evaluation structure in design creation.

4.2 Construction of Core Affect Model

In our evaluation experiment, we analyzed the characteristics of thirty-one extracted emotions by using a two-dimensional plane that consisted of the pleasant/unpleasant axis and the arousal/calm axis, termed the core affect model by Russel [9]. First, we asked participants to evaluate one of the emotions according to the five-point Likert scale.

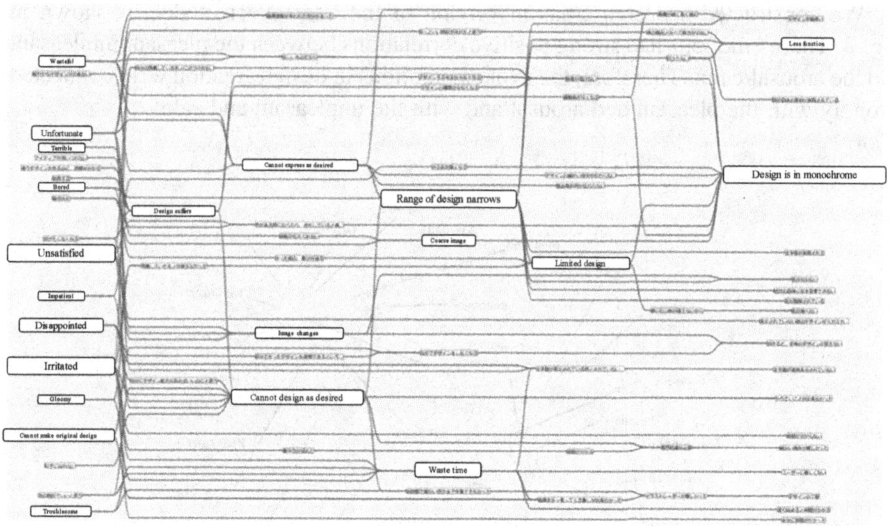

Fig. 7. Negative evaluation structure in design creation.

Table 1. Evoked emotions by Evaluation Grid Method in design creation.

Positive emotion	Negative emotion
Fulfilled	Bored
Fun	Irritated
Excited	Impatient
Proud	Unsatisfied
Joyful	Disappointed
Satisfied	Tired
Reasonable	Wasteful
Motivated	Unfortunate
Surprised	Terrible
Easy	Confused
Happy	Sorrowful
Inspired	Shameful
Pleasure	Regretful
Interested	Fatigued
	Troublesome
	Disgusted
	Gloomy

Next, we converted the evaluated data to be within a minimum value of –2 and a maximum value +2 and then calculated the average of each emotion. We arranged each emotion on the core affect model based on the data. The participants were six male and three female Japanese students using the FES Watch U.

We constructed a design creation version of the core affect model, as shown in Fig. 8. These emotions had strong positive correlations between the pleasant/unpleasant and the arousal/calm. Therefore, the evoked emotions in design creation were connected strongly with the pleasant and arousal and with the unpleasant and calm.

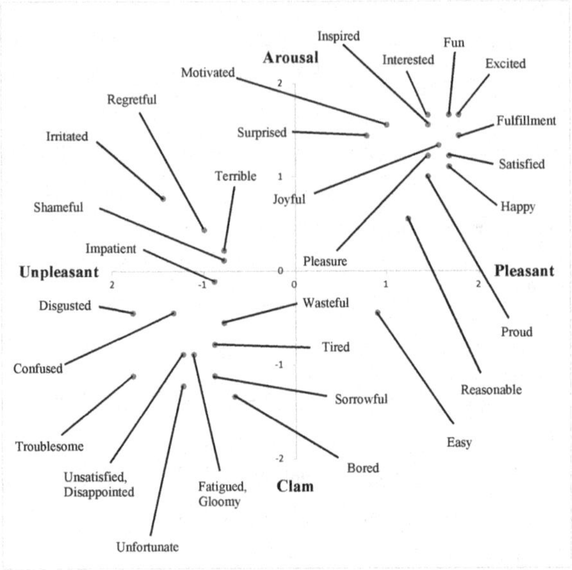

Fig. 8. Core affect model of design creation version (in Japanese).

5 Application of Proposed Method to Design Creation

5.1 Experiment

We performed an experiment for measuring body movements and emotion interviews in design creation, as shown in Sect. 3. Experimental scenery and its setup are shown in Fig. 9. During the experiment, we attached plates of motion capture markers on participants' head, back, arms, and wrists. We shot their body movements using a motion capture system and video cameras. When participants answered the emotion interview, they used the core affect model, which is shown in Fig. 10. This is the emotional model based on Fig. 2, but we added words to describe details based on the results of Sect. 4. The participants were eight male and fifteen female Japanese students.

5.2 Application of Classification Method of Emotional Expression Type

We applied our proposed method in Sect. 2 to design creation. The same analysis procedure in Sect. 2 was performed using SAS JMP 13. First, we quantified measured data in 5.1 into LMA values and calculated ES values from them. Afterward, we classified the emotional expression type by introducing Ward's method for hierarchical clustering analysis. As a result of clustering, we extracted four types (Fig. 11).

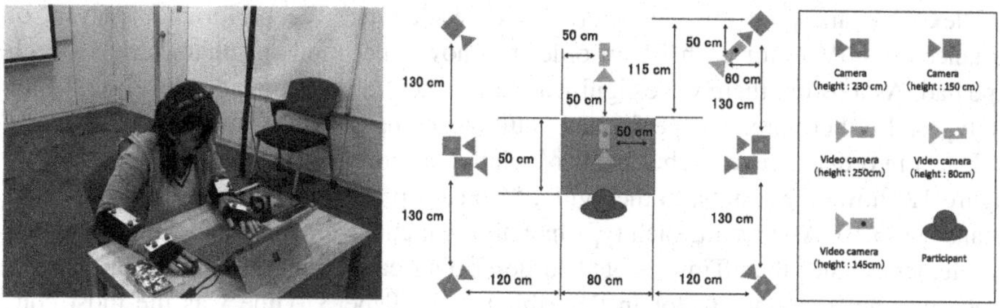

Fig. 9. Experimental scene and environment.

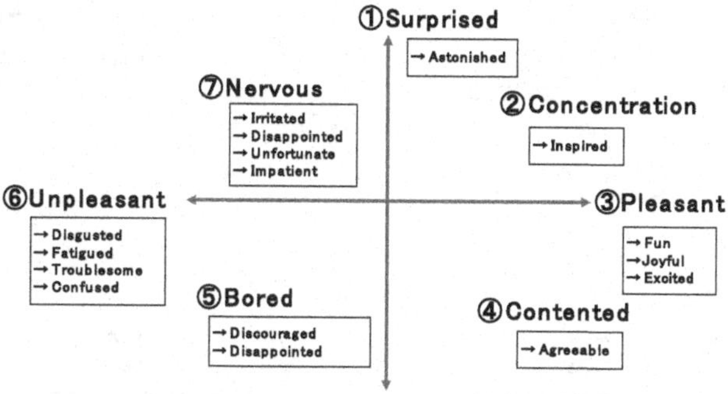

Fig. 10. Emotions used in the emotion interview of design creation.

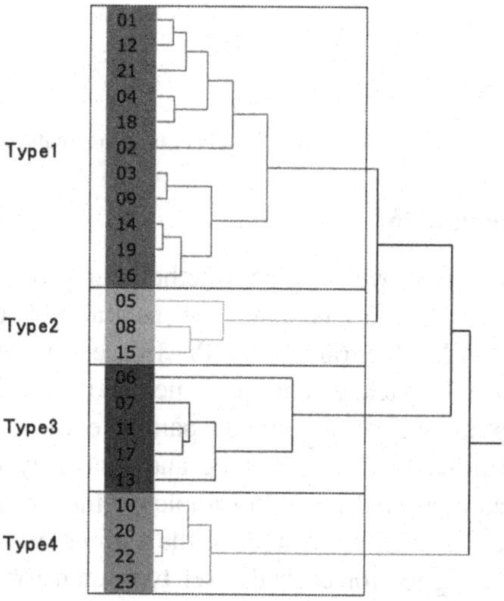

Fig. 11. Results of hierarchical clustering

Next, we analyzed the characteristics of each type. We performed analysis of variance (ANOVA) for each ES in order to know what kinds of characteristics each type had. As a result, there were significant differences at a significance level of 5% for all types. Furthermore, we performed multiple comparisons using Tukey-Kramer's HSD test in order to reveal what kinds of relations were between each ES in each type. Figure 12 shows the results. In the figure, ** means $p < 0.01$, * means $p < 0.05$, and † means $p < 0.10$. As a result, each type had different characteristics. In detail, in Type 1, the elements other than Time related to describing emotional expression. In Type 2, Space was an important factor in describing it. In Type 3, Time was the most contributing value. On the other hand, in Type 4, Weight contributed to describing emotional expression.

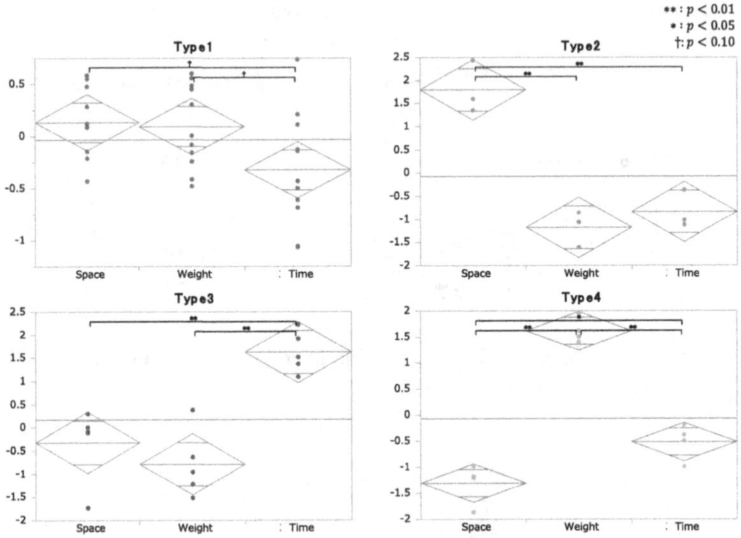

Fig. 12. Distribution of the classification features.

5.3 Evaluation by Using SVM

Regarding estimation accuracy, we verified whether our proposed method could be applied to design creation. So, we calculated the accuracy by using a discriminator, which was a constructed SVM. We trained the SVM-based discriminator with a radical basis function using the e1071 package and implemented it in R. We performed tenfold cross-validations and optimized the adjustment parameters (gamma and C). We separately trained the discriminators for each type and randomly chosen dataset. Here, randomly chosen datasets consisted of 5076 samples, which were the chosen datasets of all participants. Table 2 shows the results of the estimation. As shown, estimation accuracy was about 20% higher for each dataset type than for the randomly chosen datasets, and our proposed method was valid in design creation. Also, we compared the accuracy of each task and obtained equivalent results. Therefore, our proposed method was applicable to design creation.

Table 2. Result of estimation.

Emotional expression type	C	γ	Accuracy [%]	N
Type 1 (not-Time dominant)	25.10	25.10	76.33	11230
Type 2 (Space dominant)	25.10	15.80	86.53	2734
Type 3 (Time dominant)	100.00	15.80	83.37	2930
Type 4 (Weight dominant)	39.80	10.00	82.59	3412
Randomly chosen dataset	10.00	39.80	61.95	5076
Average of individual	–	–	88.00	882
Whole dataset	25.10	39.80	75.11	20306

6 Discussion

In this study, we made clear that the classification method of emotional expression type proposed in our previous study was applicable for a different task with different body motions. This means that the classification method is effective in various fabrication tasks. Also, we concluded that this method can be potentially applicable to extracting emotions in various scenes of using PCs, such as during work, school, and private space via body movements.

In this study, our method realized estimation accuracy for each type at an average of 80%. In order to perform higher estimation accuracy, it will be necessary to precisely analyze body movements and include it as a parameter. For example, detection of the particular body movements for each task, especially the timing of changing emotion, would be effective.

We proposed an emotion extraction method via body movements using a motion capture system, but the scenarios in which this equipment can be used are limited. A novel parameter that replaces our LMA values is needed in order to use our method in various situations. So, we plan to use some particular values that can be measured from general PC devices, such as mouse movements and head movements that can be measured using a PC camera.

7 Summary

In this study, we clarified that the classification method of emotional expression type is applicable to design creation by evaluating an accuracy of estimations. First, we extracted the evoked emotions in a design creation task and revealed the characteristics by introducing the evaluation grid method. Next, we performed an experiment to measure body movements and emotions in design creation using FES Watch U. Then, we applied the method to measured datasets. As a result, we extracted four types with different characteristics. Also, we compared estimation accuracy for a fabrication task and a design task, and the results showed that our proposed method can be applicable to design creation as well.

Acknowledgement. This research was partially supported by JST COI Program "Center of Kansei-oriented Digital Fabrication" and JSPS KAKENHI 16H03225 etc.

References

1. Kleinsmith, A., Bianchi-Berthouze, N.: Affective body expression perception and recognition: a survey. IEEE Trans. Affect. Comput. **4**(1), 15–34 (2013)
2. Karg, M., Samadani, A., Gorbet, R., Kuhnlenz, K., Hoey, J., Kulic, D.: Body movements for affective expression: a survey of automatic recognition and generation. IEEE Trans. Affect. Comput. **4**(4), 341–359 (2013)
3. Bartenieff, I., Lewis, D.: Body Movement: Coping with the Environment. Gordon & Breach Science Publishers, New York (1980)
4. Laban, R.: The Mastery of Movement, 2nd edn. McDonald and Evans, London (1960)
5. Tanaka, K., Yamamoto, M., Aoyagi, S., Nagata, N.: An affect extraction method in personal fabrication based on Laban movement analysis. In: HCI 2016: HCI International 2016 – Posters' Extended Abstracts, pp. 188–193 (2016)
6. Yamazaki, Y., Yamamoto, M., Nagata, N.: Estimation of emotional state in personal fabrication: analysis of emotional motion based on Laban movement analysis. In: 2017 International Conference on Culture and Computing, pp. 71–74 (2016)
7. Ono, Y., Aoyagi, S., Yamazaki, Y., Yamamoto, M., Nagata, N.: A classification method of emotional expression by body movements based on Laban movement analysis and sensitivity analysis. In: 2019 8th International Conference on Informatics, Electronics & Vision (ICIEV) (2019, Accepted)
8. Anderson, C.: Makers: The New Industrial Revolution. Crown Business, New York (2012)
9. Russell, J.A.: A circumplex model of affect. J. Pers. Soc. Psychol. **39**, 1161–1178 (1980)
10. Saltelli, A.: Sensitivity analysis for importance assessment. Risk Anal. **22**(3), 579–590 (2002)
11. Sanui, J.: Interview research for product planning: oresent status and issues to be solved. Jpn. Soc. Qual. Control **33**(3), 13–20 (2013)
12. Onoue, Y., Kukimoto, N., Sakamoto, N., Koyamada, K.: E-Grid: a visual analytics sys-tem for evaluation structures. J. Vis. **19**(4), 753–768 (2016)

How to Compare and Exchange Facial Expression Perceptions Between Different Individuals with Riemann Geometry

Masashi Shinto(✉) and Jinhui Chao

Department of Information and System Engineering, Chuo University, 1-13-27 Kasuga, Bunkyo-ku, Tokyo 112-8551, Japan
a14.n6na@g.chuo-u.ac.jp, jchao@ise.chuo-u.ac.jp

Abstract. Facial expression recognition has been a major theme in researches of human-centric science and technology. An open question remained is that it is difficult to find an objective representation for facial expressions so that one can compare perceptions between different individuals. It is partially due to that psychological spaces of facial expressions until now were built from subjective evaluations such as SD score or Affective grid, in which it is difficult to find correspondence between physical stimuli and psychological responses. Recently, Sumiya et al. built a psychophysical facial expression space by measuring JND thresholds in the facial image space, which define the space as a Riemann manifold [7]. In this paper, we present algorithms to compare and exchange facial expression perceptions between individuals using isometry or a distance-preserving map between the Riemann spaces.

Keywords: Facial expression · Emotion · Categorical theory · Dimensional theory · JND thresholds · Riemannian geometry

1 Introduction

The action of changing facial expression is one of major means for communicating what one is feeling and thinking to others. Understanding and recognition of facial expressions therefore have been an important subject in researches both scientific and engineering and found many important applications in communication and medical areas.

Among theoretical models supporting current engineering approaches on facial expression recognition, the categorical theory by Ekman claims universal existence of basic facial expressions (Anger, Disgust, Fear, Surprise, Happiness, Sadness) which are independent of culture and race or individual experience [1,2]. The 7 expressions with the Neutral added to basic facial expressions are still used for labeling expression images in many facial expression databases. This discrete theory certainly provides a convenient way for classification and symbolic processing and also a common basis for comparison and mutual understanding of facial expressions and emotions among individuals in the linguistic

M. Kurosu (Ed.): HCII 2019, LNCS 11567, pp. 155–167, 2019.
https://doi.org/10.1007/978-3-030-22643-5_12

level. On the other hand, it is difficult to deal with ambiguous and subtle expressions. Besides, there is no place to take into account of individual variations.

As to the first problem, the dimension theory to describe expressions with a small number of dimensions provided a partial answer. In fact, this model represents expressions on a 2D or 3D space with continuous coordinates and seek for inter-relationship among the basic expressions described by their positions in the space, such as the circular model proposed by Russell et al. [3]. One of the problems with these approaches is that the psychological expression space has no direct correspondence with physical stimuli or the facial images.

There is another problem seemed still remained open, which is also related with the difficulty to describe individual characteristics in expression perception, is that it is difficult to find an objective representation for facial expressions so that one can compare perceptions between different individuals.

Recently, Sumiya et al. reported construction of a psychophysical space of the facial expressions in which one can find direct correspondence between psychological responses and physical stimuli [7]. The new facial expression space was obtained by measurement of JND (just noticeable difference) thresholds of facial expressions in the image space or its PCA subspaces. It is also revealed that the facial expression space is not a Euclidean space but a Riemann space, of which the Riemann metric tensor is defined by the JND thresholds.

In this research, we try to model personal characteristics in expression perception using geometry of the expression space as a Riemann space, and propose a method to compare facial expression perceptions between different individuals then furthermore to exchange or share their impressions with each other. In particular, we shown algorithms to build an isometric or a distance-preserving mapping which transform JND threshold ellipsoids between individuals.

2 Space of Facial Expressions

The first representation of facial expressions in a spacial form was the dimensional theory which places the expressions in a space of small dimension obtained from MDS or PCA and called it a facial expression space. A well know circular model of expressions by Russell et al. [3] showed that basic facial expressions have a circular like distribution in the space of two dimensions: "Pleasure-Displeasure" and "Arousal-Sleep".

These facial expression spaces in the dimensional theory are actually psychological spaces since they are obtained from evaluation scores of psychological experiments such as SD tests and Affect Grid, these high dimensional data are then mapped to low dimensional subspaces by dimension reduction using MDS or PCA. Hence it is difficult to find direct correspondence with physical stimuli. In fact, the coordinates of points in the space become continuous only after projections by MDS or PCA, before that they are discrete levels of relative rather than abstract evaluations. Therefore, such a spacial coordinates seemed not an ideal option as a continuous and quantitative representation for facial expressions.

Recently a facial expression space in which one can track correspondence between physical stimuli and psychological response was proposed by Sumiya et al. [7]. The psychophysical space is obtained by measurements of the facial expression JND thresholds in the image space or PCA subspaces. In addition, it is discovered that the facial expression space is not a Euclidean space but a complicatedly curved space or a Riemannian manifold.

To be specific, recall that a Riemannian space S is a space in which a Riemann metric tensor $G(\boldsymbol{x}) = (g_{ij})$ is smoothly defined on a point $\boldsymbol{x}$ in the space. The inner product between two infinitesimal vectors $\boldsymbol{a}, \boldsymbol{b}$ centered as the point $\boldsymbol{x}$ or two tangent vectors in the tangent space $T_{\boldsymbol{x}}S$ at $\boldsymbol{x}$ is defined as

$$(\boldsymbol{a}, \boldsymbol{b}) := \boldsymbol{a}^T G(\boldsymbol{x}) \boldsymbol{b} = \sum_{ij} g_{ij} a^i b^j, \quad \forall \boldsymbol{a} = (a^i), \boldsymbol{b} = (b^j) \in T_{\boldsymbol{x}}S$$

Therefore the local distance from the point $\boldsymbol{x}$ to $\boldsymbol{x} + \boldsymbol{a}$, and the "unit circle" centered at $\boldsymbol{x}$ is defined as

$$\|\boldsymbol{a}\|^2 = (\boldsymbol{a}, \boldsymbol{a}) := \boldsymbol{a}^T G(\boldsymbol{x}) \boldsymbol{a} = \sum_{ij} g_{ij} a^i a^j = 1 \quad \forall \boldsymbol{a} = (a^i) \in T_{\boldsymbol{x}}S$$

The matrix $G(\boldsymbol{x})$ is called the Riemann metric tensor which determines geometry of the space [10].

In fact, the Riemann metric tensor in the facial expression space in [7] is defined by the JND thresholds known as subjective unit circles in the image space or its PCA subspaces. The measurements of JND thresholds showed a stable common pattern among different observers, meanwhile individual variations were also observed. Therefore, this approach actually also suggested possibility to model personal characteristics in facial expression perception through Riemann metric tensors in the facial expression space of each observer.

3 Compare and Exchange Facial Expression Perceptions

It seemed that among numerous researches of facial expressions, there are few ones focusing on the individual difference in facial expression recognition and cross examination of the perceptions between different observers.

Here, we propose to use the Riemann metric tensor in the facial expression space as characteristic in perception per individual and show algorithms of comparison and exchange or sharing subjective facial expressions between different individuals. In particular we consider hereafter two observers names Alice and Bob.

The proposed method consists of the following five steps, and Sects. 3.1, 3.2 and 3.3 were based on procedures by Sumiya et al. [4].

3.1 Build PCA Subspaces of the Image Space and Morphing

First we prepare the image space of facial expressions and morphing sequences required in the experiments which are then projected to a low dimensional subspace by dimension reduction. In this paper, we applied principal component analysis to obtain these PCA subspaces. Figure 1 shows an example of a two-dimensional subspace of the image space of facial expressions by PCA. The morphing sequences between Neutral and basic expressions in the image space are also shown.

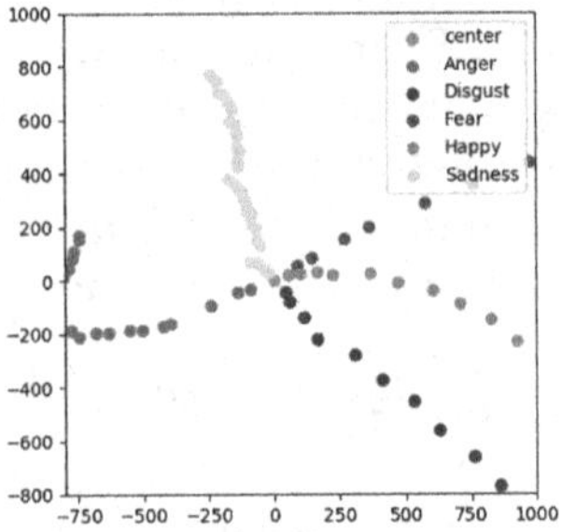

Fig. 1. Image subspace obtained by PCA and morphing sequences

3.2 Measure JND Thresholds for Alice and Bob

The next, is to measure the facial expression JND thresholds of Alice and Bob. In particular, a continuous sequence of images from one expression to another is shown to the observer and the point where the facial expression is judged as changed is recorded as the expression JND threshold.

3.3 Estimate the JND Ellipsoids

We then calculate the equation of the ellipsoids of JND thresholds of Alice and Bob obtained in the previous experiments. We used the Fundamental Numerical Scheme (FNS) [5] to fit the points in the PCA subspace with an ellipse, which has the equation as

$$Ax^2 + Bxy + Cy^2 = 1.$$

Define the variable vector as

$$\theta \equiv (A, B, C, D)^T \qquad D = -1$$

and the data vector as

$$\xi_\alpha \equiv (x_\alpha, 2x_\alpha y_\alpha, y_\alpha, 1)^T.$$

Then the covariance matrix of the data vectors is defined as

$$V[\xi_\alpha] = \begin{pmatrix} \overline{x}_\alpha^2 & \overline{x}_\alpha \overline{y}_\alpha & 0 & 0 \\ \overline{x}_\alpha \overline{y}_\alpha & \overline{x}_\alpha^2 + \overline{y}_\alpha^2 & \overline{x}_\alpha \overline{y}_\alpha & 0 \\ 0 & \overline{x}_\alpha \overline{y}_\alpha & \overline{y}_\alpha^2 & 0 \\ 0 & 0 & 0 & 0 \end{pmatrix}.$$

Here the Sampson error J is defined as

$$J = \frac{1}{N}\Sigma_{\alpha=1}^{N}\frac{(\xi_\alpha, \theta)^2}{(\theta, V[\xi_\alpha]\theta)}.$$

The value of θ which minimizes the Sampson error therefore provides estimate of A, B, C.

3.4 Find Riemann Metric and the Isometry or Metric Preserving Map

Here we shown how to obtain the Riemann metric matrix G and the isometry or the map preserving distance.

The Riemann metric matrix G can be found from the ellipses of Alice and Bob at different expressions obtained in Sect. 3.2 as follows. Denote for the ellipses at a point $\boldsymbol{x}$, the long axis of the ellipses as a, the short axis as b, rotation angle of the axis as θ, then G can be calculated as

$$G = \begin{pmatrix} g_{11} & g_{12} \\ g_{21} & g_{22} \end{pmatrix}$$

$$g_{11} = \frac{a^2 \sin^2\theta + b^2\cos^2\theta}{a^2b^2}$$

$$g_{12} = g_{21} = \frac{\sin\theta\cos\theta(b^2 - a^2)}{a^2b^2}$$

$$g_{22} = \frac{a^2\cos^2\theta + b^2\sin^2\theta}{a^2b^2}.$$

Now denote the JND threshold ellipses of Alice and Bob as follows

$$X^TG_1X = 1, \qquad Y^TG_2Y = 1 \tag{1}$$

where the Riemann metric matrices of Alice and Bob are

$$G_1 = \begin{pmatrix} g_{11}^{(1)} & g_{12}^{(1)} \\ g_{21}^{(1)} & g_{22}^{(1)} \end{pmatrix}, \qquad G_2 = \begin{pmatrix} g_{11}^{(2)} & g_{12}^{(2)} \\ g_{21}^{(2)} & g_{22}^{(2)} \end{pmatrix}$$

Now we wish to find a map from the space of Alice to the space of Bob while preserving the Riemann metric therefore the distance and geometry in the space. Such a map is called an isometry in Riemannian geometry. Since the Riemann metric G_1 and G_2 at every points of the facial expression space characterize the subjective perceptions on facial expressions for Alice and Bob respectively, an isometry between expression spaces of Alice and Bob will preserve such perceptional properties.

In particular, we show how to find a local linearization of the nonlinear map, or a local isometry as a matrix M, which by definition actually maps the JND threshold ellipses of Alice exactly onto the JND ellipses of Bob. This JND ellipses matching between Alice and Bob is shown in Fig. 2. Indeed, denote the local linear map by M as

$$Y = MX \tag{2}$$

By (1), (2), the matrix M should meet the following condition in order to be an isometry:

$$G_1 = M^T G_2 M \tag{3}$$

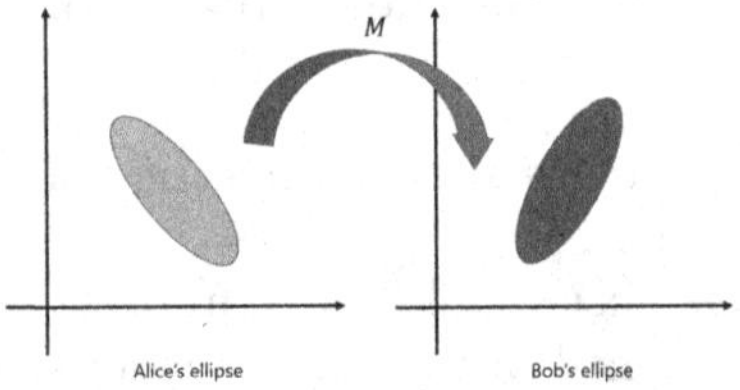

Fig. 2. An isometry matches ellipses in both spaces

In fact, such a matrix is not unique since M has 4 entries but (3) only has 3 independent equations. So we here assume M has the following form

$$M = \begin{pmatrix} M_1 & M_2 \\ M_3 & M_4 \end{pmatrix} := \begin{pmatrix} \cos\theta & -\sin\theta \\ \sin\theta & \cos\theta \end{pmatrix} \begin{pmatrix} a & 0 \\ 0 & b \end{pmatrix} \tag{4}$$

In general, we can use an n by n matrix $M \in GL(n)$ as an isometry in nD space to be the product of $R \in O(n)$ or an orthogonal matrix (or $SO(n)$ instead) and A an n by n diagonal matrix. The condition (3) gives $n(n+1)/2$ equations and since dim$O(n)$=dim $SO(n)$ $= n(n-1)/2$, so the number of variables is $n(n-1)/2 + n = n(n+1)/2$ and the solution is unique.

The M can be found from solutions of the following quadratic equations according to (3), (4), (see also [9]).

$$\begin{aligned} g_{11}^{(1)} &= g_{11}^{(2)} M_1^2 + 2g_{12}^{(2)} M_1 M_3 + g_{22}^{(2)} M_3^2 \\ g_{12}^{(1)} &= g_{11}^{(2)} M_1 M_2 + g_{12}^{(2)} (M_1 M_4 + M_2 M_3) + g_{22}^{(2)} M_3 M_4 \\ g_{22}^{(1)} &= g_{11}^{(2)} M_2^2 + 2g_{12}^{(2)} M_2 M_4 + g_{22}^{(2)} M_4^2 \\ 0 &= M_1 M_2 + M_3 M_4 \end{aligned}$$

3.5 Comparison of Expression Perceptions

Now we can use the isometry M to match between the JND threshold ellipses of Alice and Bob as in Sect. 3.4 therefore to compare and exchange facial expression perceptions between them. To map by M the image in the Alice's space $P_1 = (x_1, y_1)$ to the space of Bob as a new image $P_2 = (x_2, y_2)$, which preserves Alice's perceptional properties therefore shows to Bob what Alice feels. The isometry from Bob's space to Alice's space is defined by M^{-1}.

4 Experiments

The above procedures were implemented using the database "A database of facial expressions in younger, middle-aged, and older women and men" [6]. An experimental image was created by dividing the morphing movie for each frame, reducing the size of the images and the number of pixels, then transform to grayscale. Figure 3 shows an example of the created facial expression image sequence.

Fig. 3. An example used in the experiment

4.1 Estimate of JND Thresholds

For the two subjects as Alice and Bob, we measured facial expression JND thresholds of facial expression images that change from the Neutral to five basic expressions, and estimated JND thresholds ellipse at the Neutral. Five facial expression JND thresholds were determined by the adjustment method. We measured the discrimination threshold 4 times in total, twice from the Neutral towards another expression, twice from another expression to the Neutral, and taking the average. Figure 4 shows the facial expression JND thresholds and JND ellipses of two subjects. Individual differences can be observed easily.

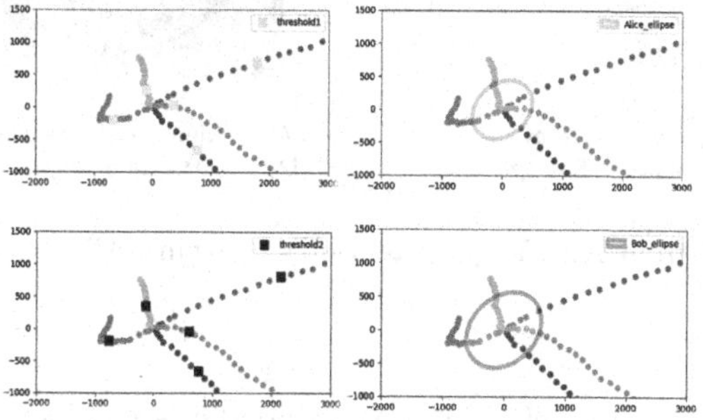

Fig. 4. Facial expression JND thresholds and JND threshold ellipses of Alice and Bob

4.2 Comparison and Exchange Experiments

Here, a comparison experiment of expression sensation is performed using JND ellipses of Alice and Bob, which are as shown in Fig. 5 by the experiment in the last section. By applying the method in Sects. 3.4 and 3.5 to these ellipses, it

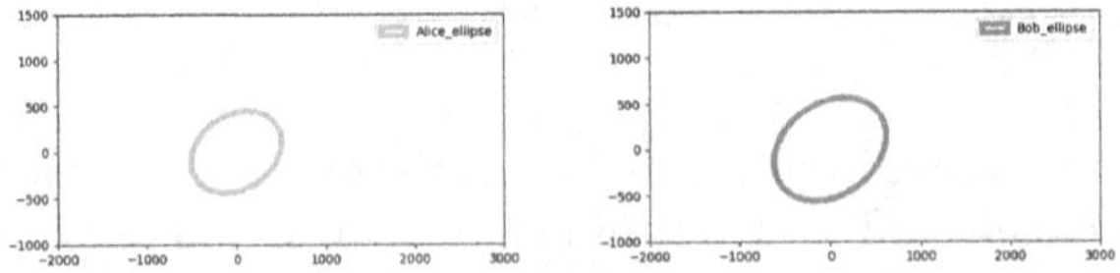

Fig. 5. Facial expression JND threshold ellipses of Alice and Bob

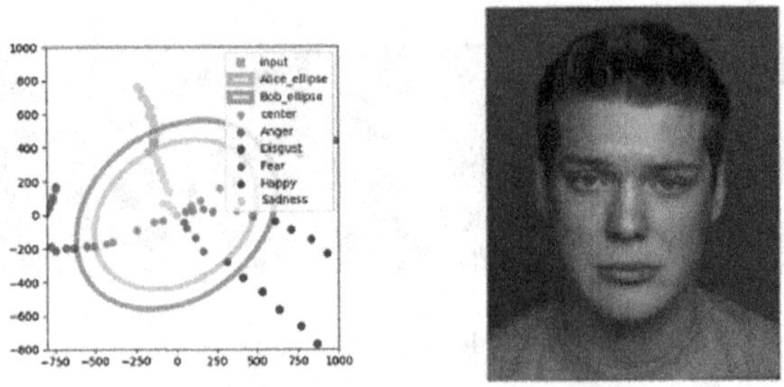

Alice and Bob's ellipse and Input Image as the orange square

Input image to Alice and Bob

Fig. 6. Input image to Alice and Bob (Sadness version)

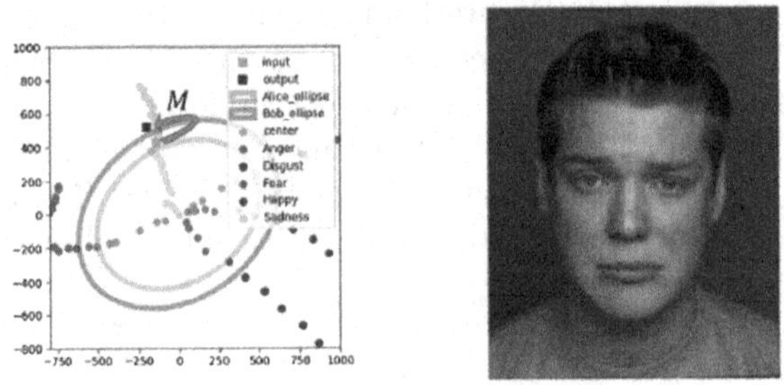

Isometry M from Alice's Space to Bob space

Alice's view transformed by M to Bob's expression space

Fig. 7. Isometry M from Alice's space to Bob's, showing Alice's view to Bob space (sadness version)

is possible to define an isometry map M from Alice's facial expression space to Bob's space. This makes it possible for Bob to compare Alice's facial expression perception with his own and also to share Alice's perception.

For example, suppose that the expression image shown to both Alice and Bob is Fig. 6 as a common input. This image was selected from the morphing sequence of images changing from the Neutral to the Sadness. By multiplying the isometry matrix M to the vector of the input, the image is mapped from Alice's space to Bob's space, the result is Fig. 7 which now shows to Bob the expression perception of Alice on the input Fig. 6. Therefore, Bob can compare the original

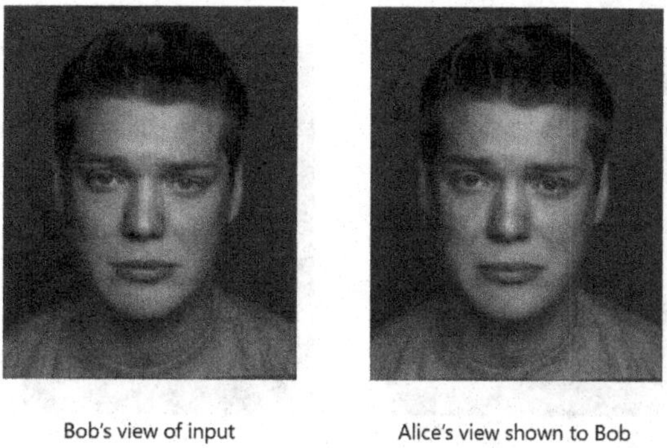

Fig. 8. Bob compares Alice's view with his own one (sadness version)

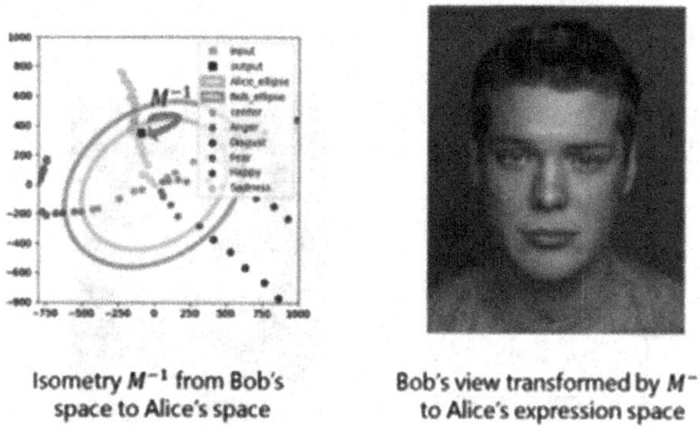

Isometry M^{-1} from Bob's space to Alice's space
Bob's view transformed by M^{-1} to Alice's expression space

Fig. 9. Isogemy M^{-1} from Bob's space to Alices's, showing Bob's view to Alice (sadness version)

input he saw and Fig. 7 by Alice, as shown in Fig. 8. It is also possible now for him to share perception the same as Alice by looking at Fig. 7 instead of the original input. On the other direction, by applying the inverse map M^{-1} of the isometry M to the input in Fig. 6, it is transformed from Bob's space to Alice' space, the result is Fig. 9. Now Alice can compare her own view on the input image and Bob's view in Fig. 9 and understand the difference, as shown in Fig. 10. By looking at Fig. 9 instead of the original input, Alice is possible to obtain the same facial expression perception as Bob. Next, we try different groups of expression images using the same isometry M obtained earlier. The input image shown to Alice and Bob is Fig. 11, which is selected from the morphing sequence changing from the Neutral to the Anger. The isometry M maps the input image Fig. 11 from Alice's space to Bob's space, the resulting image in Bob's space is Fig. 12 which shows to Bob the expression perception of Alice. Comparing it with Bob's own view on the same input, he could realized the different between him and her as shown in Fig. 13. He can also obtain the same perception as Alice by looking at Fig. 12 instead of the original input. Again, by applying the inverse map M^{-1}

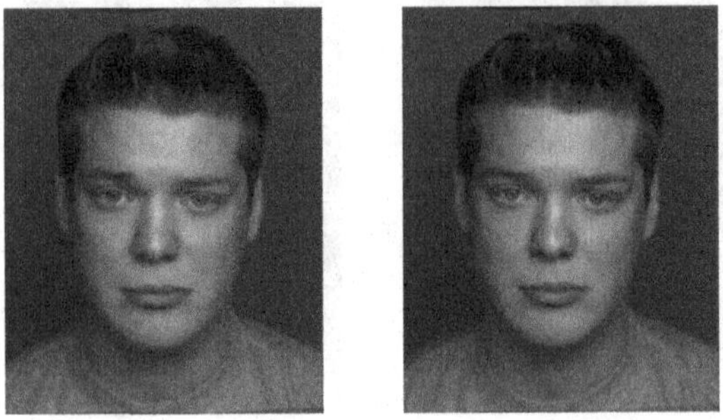

Alice's view of input

Bob's view shown to Alice

Fig. 10. Alice compare Bob's view with her own one (sadness version)

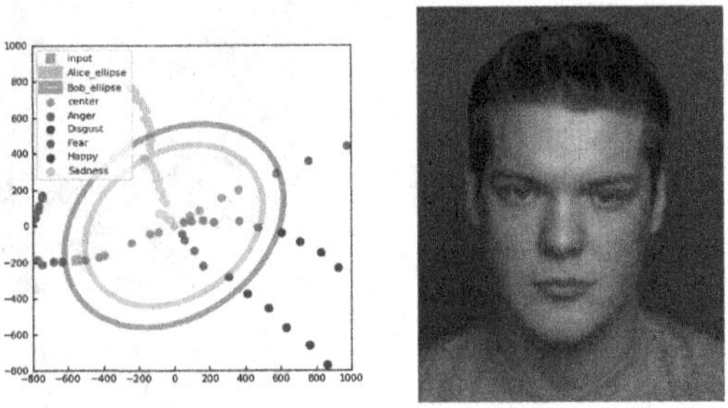

Alice and Bob's ellipse and input image as the orange square

Input image to Alice and Bob

Fig. 11. Input image to Alice and Bob (anger version)

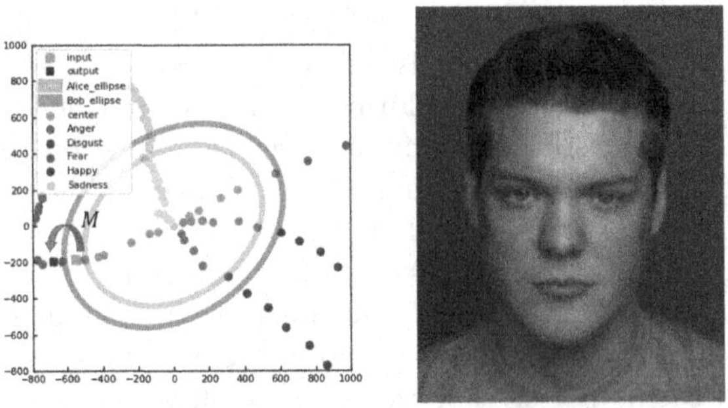

Isometry M from Alice's space to Bob's space

Alice's view transformed by *M* to Bob's expression space

Fig. 12. Isometry M from Alice's space to Bobs, showing Alice's view to Bob (anger version)

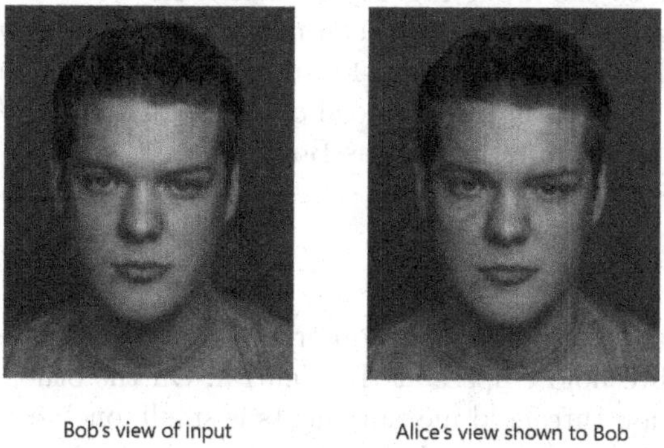

Fig. 13. Bob compares Alice's view with his own one (Anger version)

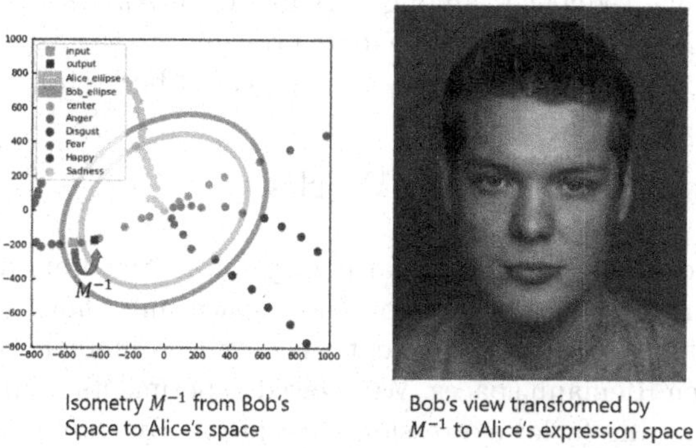

Fig. 14. Isogemy M^{-1} from Bob's space to Alice's, showing Bob's view to Alice (anger version)

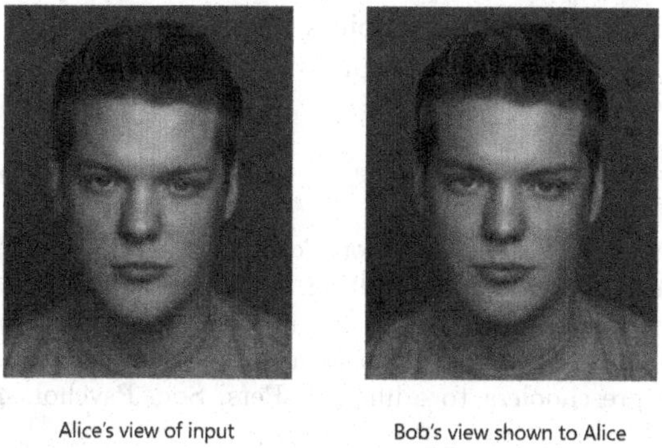

Fig. 15. Alice compare Bob's view with her own one (anger version)

of the isometry M to the input Fig. 11 so maps it from Bob's space to Alice's, the result is in Fig. 14. Similarly Alice can now compare her view looking at the original input with Bob's view in Fig. 14 and find the discrepancy between her and him. By looking at this image instead of the original input Alice can obtain the same facial expression perception as Bob (Fig. 15).

5 Discussions

In the experiments in Sect. 4.1, we observed individual differences in facial expression JND threshold ellipses at the Neutral. On the other hand, since the number of expression threshold measurements is small, one need to improve the accuracy of ellipse estimation and the expression discrimination thresholds as well by increasing the number of morphing sequences. A problem is that most of facial expression images in the published database are of Ekman's basic 6 facial expressions therefore do not provide enough variations. One possibility is to produce image sequences among various facial expressions using tools in CG etc. Also, PCA is used here to create expression image space, but nonlinear dimension reduction such as manifold learning could be useful.

6 Conclusions and Future Works

We proposed to characterize individual perception in facial expressions by Riemann metric tensor in the facial expression space and showed algorithms to compare and exchange subjective perceptions between different individuals using isometries between Riemann spaces. We showed experiments to model individual differences and sharing facial expression perception. By transforming the input with isometry, it became possible subjectively to compare impressions between individuals and also to share the way the other person feels about the same facial expression image.

The future works include to extend the isometry to other expressions in order to build a global isometry for the space. It is known that it is possible to smoothly paste up local isometry at different points [10]. Another way is to build global isometry directly. See [8] for related works.

References

1. Ekman, P., Friesen, W.V.: Facial Action Coding System: A Technique for the Measurement of Facial Movement. Consulting Psychologists Press, Palo Alto (1978)
2. Ekman, P.: An argument for basic emotions. Cogn. Emot. **6**(3–4), 169–200 (1992)
3. Russell, J.A., Bullock, M.: Multidimensional scaling of emotional facial expressions: similarity from preschoolers to adults. J. Pers. Soc. Psychol. **48**(5), 1290–1298 (1985)
4. Sumiya, R., Lenz, R., Chao, J.: Measurement of discrimination thresholds in facial expression recognition and investigation on expression space. In: HCG symposium 2017, pp. 25–28 (2017)

5. Chojnacki, W., Brooks, M.J., van den Hengel, A., Gawley, D.: On the fitting of surfaces to data with covariances. IEEE Trans. Patt. Anal. Mach. Intell. **22**(11), 1294–1303 (2000)
6. Ebner, N.C., Riediger, M., Lindenberger, U.: FACES-a database of facial expressions in young, middle-aged, and older women and men: development and validation. Behav. Res. Methods **42**, 351–362 (2010)
7. Sumiya, R., Lenz, R., Chao, J.: Measurement of JND thresholds and Riemannian geometry in facial expression space. In: Kurosu, M. (ed.) HCI 2018. LNCS, vol. 10901, pp. 453–464. Springer, Cham (2018). https://doi.org/10.1007/978-3-319-91238-7_37
8. Sumiya, R., Chao, J.: Transform facial expression space to euclidean space using Riemann normal coordinates and its applications. In: Kurosu, M. (ed.) HCII 2019, LNCS 11567, pp. 168–178. Springer, Heidelberg (2019)
9. Mochizuki, R., Kojima, T., Lenz, R., Chao, J.: Color-weak compensation using local affine isometry based on discrimination threshold matching. J. Opt. Soc. Am. A, Optica, Image Sci. Vis. **32**(11), 2093–2103 (2015)
10. Petersen, P.: Riemannian Geometry. GTM, 3rd edn. Springer, Heidelberg (2006). https://doi.org/10.1007/978-3-319-26654-1

Transform Facial Expression Space to Euclidean Space Using Riemann Normal Coordinates and Its Applications

Runa Sumiya(✉) and Jinhui Chao

Department of Information and System Engineering,
Chuo University, 1-13-27, Kasuga, Bunkyo, Tokyo, Japan
rsumiya603@gmail.com, jchao@ise.chuo-u.ac.jp

Abstract. It is reported recently in [1] on construction of the psychophysical space of facial expressions through measurement of JND thresholds in the space. It is shown that the facial expression space is, in fact, not a Euclidean space but a Riemann space of which the Riemann metric is defined by the JND thresholds. In this paper, we shown how to transform the facial expression space to Euclidean space in a way to preserve geometry such as distances and angles in the Riemannian space. We build the Riemann normal coordinate system in the facial expression space, which can be regarded as a generalized polar coordinate system consisted of geodesics emanating from the origin and concentric circles with the radius measured by geodesic distances. Results by applying the above method to the JND data in [1] are shown together with application to expression recognition.

Keywords: Facial expressions · Emotions · Categorical theory · Dimensional theory · JND thresholds · Riemannian geometry

1 Introduction

There are several models and theories for facial expressions presently [2–4,13,22]. The famous categorical theory by pioneering works of [5] is lucid and powerful, matched well with early engineering applications. One of the reasons is that the classification to basic expressions is easy to understand to human being. On the other hand, recent facial expression analysis has reached a dimension which demands higher sophistication and accuracy, e.g. to capture and understand ambiguous and even obscure expressions. In this sense, the dimensional theory e.g. [9] represented in a spacial form of the basic and other expressions, which paid the way to a quantitative representation of the facial expressions. Unfortunately the psychological spaces used in the dimensional theory were built from psychological evaluations by PCA or MDS which are difficult to find direct correspondence with physical stimuli.

Recently [1] shown construction a psychophysical facial expression space by measurements of the JND thresholds in the facial expression image space or the

M. Kurosu (Ed.): HCII 2019, LNCS 11567, pp. 168–178, 2019.
https://doi.org/10.1007/978-3-030-22643-5_13

PCA subspaces. It turned out the facial expression space is not a Euclidean space but a distorted or curved space which can be represented as a Riemann space. It is theoretically interesting to find nontrivial properties on expression perception in terms of geometry of the space. This fact is also particularly meaningful in practice since major facial expression recognition algorithms including various neural networks compute measure of similarity by straight-line distance between input and templates in a feature space such as PCA, AU or certain layers of neural networks, under tacit assumption that the space is Euclidean. In fact, it is known that in a Riemann space the straight lines are curves called geodesics, just like light traces curves around sun, due to the spatial curvature in gravitational field. This means in the facial expression space, the straight-lines are curved and distance should be measured along geodesics, the currently algorithms are incorrect therefore could lead to mis-recognition.

In this paper we show how to transform this Riemann space into a Euclidean space while preserving the distances between any two stimuli, which means to preserve subjective difference in facial expression perception. The approach we used is to construct an isometry or a distance-preserving map from the Riemann space to a Euclidean space. In particular to build this isometry map, we use tools in Riemann geometry called Riemann normal coordinates, which can be regarded as a generalized polar coordinate system.

We applied this approach to the JND data obtained in [1] to build Riemann coordinate system in the facial expression space. The isometry or the distance preserving map is readily to obtain from the system and polar coordinate system in Euclidean space. In order to verify the truth of the isometry we also calculated the JND thresholds mapped into the Euclidean space which are close to unit circles. As an application, we also shown results in facial expression recognition to differentiate subtle differences between facial expressions which are difficult using the traditional methods.

2 Spacial Representations of Facial Expressions

To represent an object in a spacial form such as points or vectors in a space is very useful and powerful as well. e.g. inter-relationships and structures between different objects and their groups can be formalized and analyzed in terms of geometric properties of the space. Novel insights and approaches could also be obtained from mathematical tools for the space with a particular geometry.

The facial expressions have a natural form of representation as vectors in the image space. In fact, in most the facial expression recognition including neural networks, the differences between facial images are evaluated by the Euclidean distance between the two image vectors. One of the problems with such an approach is that the dimension of the space is very high. An approximative solution to it is to use the principal subspaces obtained using e.g. PCA or MDS [12]. Another problem is that facial images are not facial expressions and contains much information irrelevant to expressions. So the image space serves only the space of physical stimuli for the subjective perception.

On the other hand, facial expressions have two major psychological representations: the categorical model and the dimensional model. The former by Ekman et al. [5] is a discrete and linguistic representation, convenient to symbolic processing but without geometric or spacial attributes. The original dimensional theory was intended to find order or geometric structure between these basic categories such as Woodworth and Schlosberg [6–8] then generalized to two and three dimension models [9–11]. A major problem for the psychological space of facial expressions in the dimensional theory is that the spaces are obtained from psychological evaluations in SD tests or Affect grid in which direct correspondence with physical stimuli were missing. Besides, the analog-looking coordinates obtained from discrete levels of relative evaluations by PCA or MDS do not provide a meaningful and reliable quantitative representation.

Therefore, a continuous and quantitative representation of facial expressions in a space form which has direct correspondence with physical stimuli or facial images is desirable.

3 Facial Expression Space as a Riemannian Space

It is shown in [1] that a psycho-physical space of facial expressions was built from the facial image space through measurement of JND thresholds [14–18] for the expressions.

The JND discrimination thresholds in the facial expression space obtained in [1] are shown here again in Figs. 1, 2 and 3.

In particular, the JND ellipsoids are measured for 7 basic expression and 21 AU images from the Bosphorus database [19–21] to produce from 616 Morphing sequences, 57844 images and 2233 threshold points were used to fit 23 ellipsoids from a single observer. The results of 3D, 1st-2nd and 1st-3rd PCA projections are shown in Figs. 1, 2 and 3 respectively.

An obvious observation is that since the JND thresholds from every expressions in the space are supposed to be subjective unit spheres centered at these expressions, these variations of shapes and sizes of the JND ellipsoids at different expressions suggest that the facial expression space is not Euclidean but a distorted or curved space, in fact, a Riemannian space.

Recall that a Riemannian space S is a space in which a metric tensor $G(\boldsymbol{x}) = (g_{ij})$ is smoothly defined at every point $\boldsymbol{x} \in S$ such that the inner product between two infinitesimal shifts $d\boldsymbol{x}_1, d\boldsymbol{x}_2$ from $\boldsymbol{x}$, or two vectors in the tangent space $T_{\boldsymbol{x}}S$, at $\boldsymbol{x}$ equals

$$(d\boldsymbol{x}_1, d\boldsymbol{x}_2) = d\boldsymbol{x}_1^T G(\boldsymbol{x}) d\boldsymbol{x}_2 = g_{ij} dx_1^i dx_2^j, \quad \forall d\boldsymbol{x}_1, d\boldsymbol{x}_2 \in T_{\boldsymbol{x}}S$$

(Here and after the Einstein summation convention is used.) The unit sphere centered at $\boldsymbol{x}$ is defined as

$$ds^2 = \|d\boldsymbol{x}\|^2 = (d\boldsymbol{x}, d\boldsymbol{x}) = d\boldsymbol{x}^T G(\boldsymbol{x}) d\boldsymbol{x} = 1, \quad \forall d\boldsymbol{x} \in T_{\boldsymbol{x}}S$$

which e.g. in 3D space are actually ellipsoids of which the size and shape are determined by the Riemann metric $G(\boldsymbol{x})$.

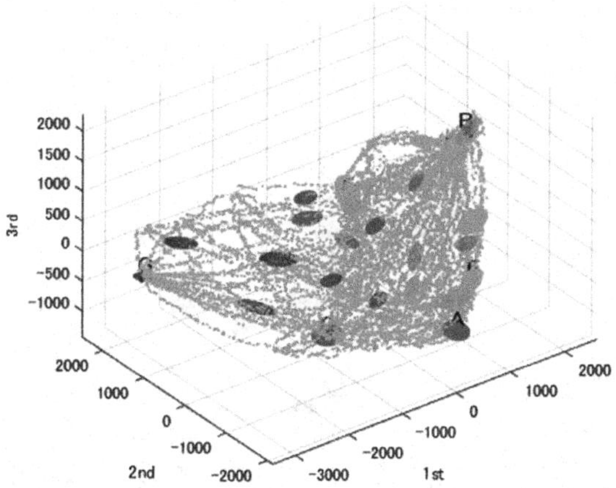

Fig. 1. 23 Ellipsoids in the 3D, PCA space [1]

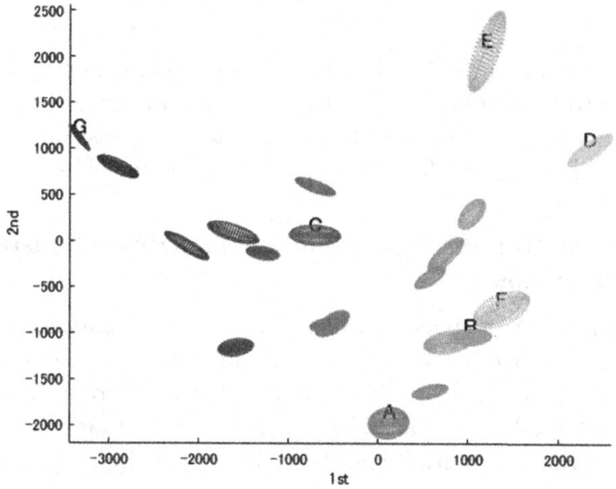

Fig. 2. 23 Ellipses in 1st-2nd PCA space [1]

Therefore the facial expression space obtained in [1] is a Riemann space. The JND thresholds then define the Riemann metric for the facial expression space.

4 Riemann Spaces and Isometry Between Them

The first implication that the facial expression space is a non-Euclid space is that the inter-relationship between different expressions for us could be much more complicated than expected and against intuitions. The second is that all expression recognition algorithms trying to reduce the relative errors between an input image and a template expression could be misleading. Besides, it is hopeful to discover intrigue properties using Riemannian geometry and novel

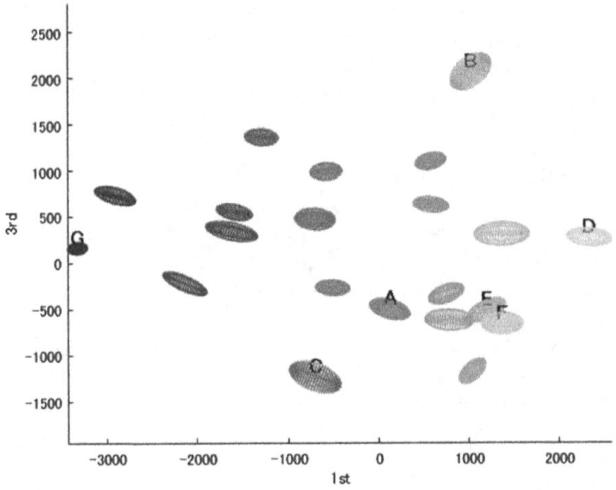

Fig. 3. 23 Ellipses in 1st-3rd PCA space [1]

models to analyze and understand our facial expression perception. Potential new applications to facial expression recognition are also expected.

In order to achieve this understanding of facial expression space, here we discuss the possibility to transform the space to a Euclidean space.

4.1 Distances in Rieman Spaces and Isometries or Distance Preserving Maps

Different from a Euclidean space in which the distance is measured by straight-line distance, the distance between two points in a Riemannian space is defined as the length of the geodesic connecting the two points. Here, as a generalization of straight-line in a Euclidean space, a geodesic u in a Riemann space is obtained by the solution of the differential equations (in the local coordinates u^i)

$$\frac{d^2u^i}{ds} + \Gamma^i_{jk}\frac{du^j}{ds}\frac{du^k}{ds} = 0, \tag{1}$$

where Γ^i_{jk} is the Christoffel symbol defined as:

$$\Gamma^i_{jk} = \frac{1}{2}g^{i\alpha}\left(\frac{\partial g_{\alpha j}}{\partial u^k} + \frac{\partial g_{\alpha k}}{\partial u^j} - \frac{g_{jk}}{\partial u^\alpha}\right). \tag{2}$$

Here the metric tensor and its inverse are denoted by $G = (g_{ij}), G^{-1} = (g^{ij})$.

Among two Riemannian spaces S_1 and S_2, an isometry or a distance-preserving map $f : S_1 \longrightarrow S_2 : \boldsymbol{y} = f(\boldsymbol{x})$ between them is defined as such that

$$\forall \boldsymbol{x}_1, \boldsymbol{x}_2 \in S_1, d(\boldsymbol{x}_1, \boldsymbol{x}_2) = d(\boldsymbol{y}_1, \boldsymbol{y}_2), \qquad \boldsymbol{y}_i = f(\boldsymbol{x}_i) \in S_2$$

here $d(\boldsymbol{p}, \boldsymbol{q})$ denotes the distance between $\boldsymbol{p}$ and $\boldsymbol{q}$. It is known that such a map will preserve the Riemann metric at every point therefore the geometry of the spaces [27,28].

4.2 Riemann Normal Coordinates

Here we show a way to build an isometry between the facial expression space to a Euclidean space using Riemann normal coordinates.

A Riemann normal coordinates can be regarded as a generalization of the polar coordinates system in a Euclidean space. In fact, choose a point $\boldsymbol{x}_0 \in S$ as the center or the origin, the Riemann normal coordinates of a point $\boldsymbol{x} \in S$ is provided by the geodesic connecting $\boldsymbol{x}$ and $\boldsymbol{x}_0$. The direction of this geodesic starting from the center $\boldsymbol{x}_0$ or its tangent vector at $\boldsymbol{x}_0$ has a spacial angle $\boldsymbol{\theta}$. The length of this geodesic between two points is the distance $l = d(\boldsymbol{x}_0, \boldsymbol{x})$. The Riemann normal coordinates of $\boldsymbol{x}$ is defined as $(l, \boldsymbol{\theta})$, which provide a map from the Riemann space S to a Euclidean space of the same dimension. Indeed, if one chooses the origin of a Euclidean space as the image of the above map, and the image of $\boldsymbol{x}$ as the point $\boldsymbol{y}$ in the Euclidean space with the same polar coordinates as $(l, \boldsymbol{\theta})$, then the map is obviously an isometry.

5 Construction of Riemann Normal Coordinates

To calculate a Riemann normal coordinates system could be difficult, especially it is costly to find the geodesics connecting two particular points.

We here use an efficient strategy to construct a Riemann normal coordinates. (For details see [25]).

After appropriate choice of the origin $\boldsymbol{x}_0 \in S$, we calculate all geodesics emanating from the origin $\boldsymbol{x}_0$, which are uniformly separated from each other with the constant spacial angular increment $\boldsymbol{\theta}$ (measured with the Riemann metric). In fact, the geodesics from a point with specified direction is easy to find using an ODE solver. Then we find the concentric circles, which are not geodesics, but can be easily obtained by connecting all points along the adjacent geodesics which have the same distance r from the center point $\boldsymbol{x}_0$. Then we have a pre-calculated coordinates grids consisting of geodesics of angle $\boldsymbol{\theta}$ and concentric circles of radius r.

For a point $\boldsymbol{x} \in S$, the two parameters $(r, \boldsymbol{\theta})$, the angle and the distance, will provide $\boldsymbol{x}$ a unique coordinates in the space which corresponding also to the angle and distance in a polar coordinates system in a Euclidean space. If $\boldsymbol{x}$ is not lie exactly on a geodesic but in between two adjacent geodesics with angles as $\boldsymbol{\theta}$ and $\boldsymbol{\theta} + \boldsymbol{\delta}$, one can choose the angle closest to $\boldsymbol{x}$, otherwise one can calculate a new geodesics with angle $\boldsymbol{\theta} + \boldsymbol{\delta}/2$ starting from the origin $\boldsymbol{x}_0$. In fact, the spacial resolution $\boldsymbol{\delta}$ can be predetermined according to required accuracy and computational cost in trade-off.

Therefore we obtain an isometry between the neighborhood of $\boldsymbol{x}_0$ in the Riemann space and the Euclidean space. In particular, the point $\boldsymbol{x}$ in the Riemann space $\boldsymbol{x} \in S$ has an coordinates consists of an angle $\boldsymbol{\theta}$ and the distance r from $\boldsymbol{x}_0$, the values of coordinates can read out readily from the corresponding grid of the polar coordinates in the Euclidean space as shown in Fig. 4. As a result the ellipsoids in Riemann space are transformed to unit circles in Euclidean space as shown in Fig. 5.

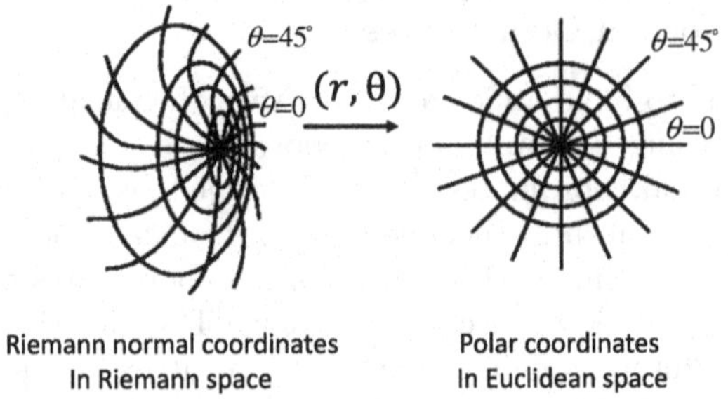

Fig. 4. Transform Riemann to Euclidean space and Riemann normal coordinates

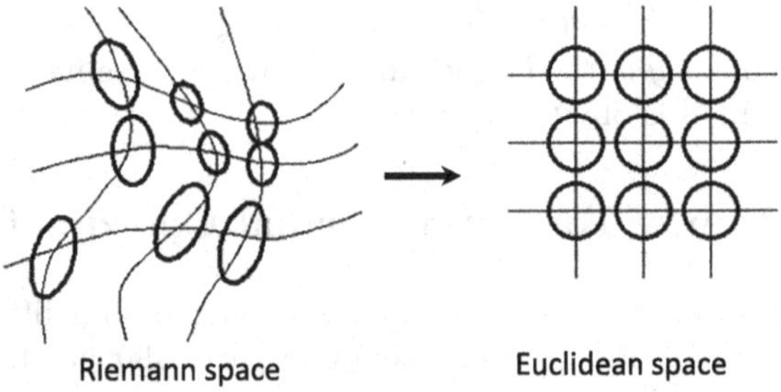

Fig. 5. Locally the elliptic "unit circles" become real unit circles

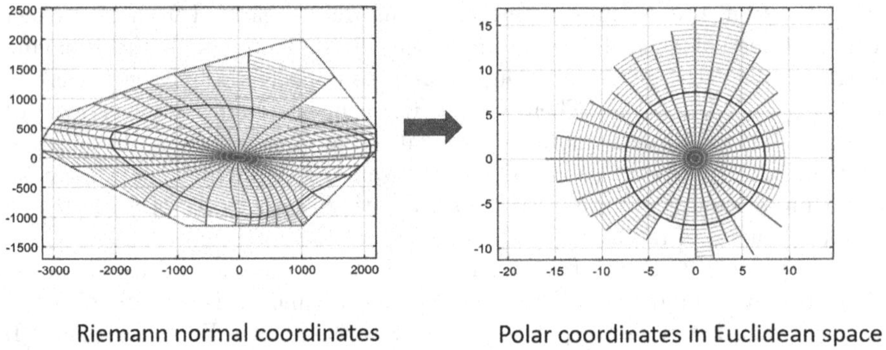

Fig. 6. Facial expression space transformed to Euclidean space

6 Results and Applications

The above algorithms are applied to the JND threshold data in [1] to transform the facial expression space to Euclidean space with Riemann normal coordinates.

The results, in particular a projection to the 1st-3rd PCA subspace is shown in Fig. 6.

The effect and accuracy of this transformation from the Riemann space to Euclidean space can be evaluated by the closeness of the images of the local JND

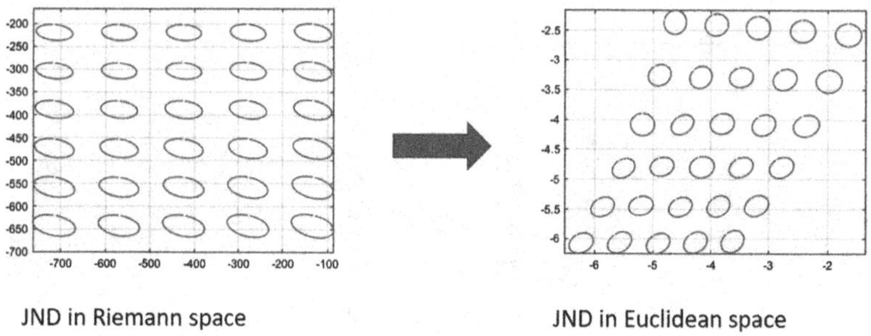

Fig. 7. JND ellipses mapped to unit circles in Euclidean space

ellipses to unit circles in Euclidean space. It is shown in Fig. 7 that the images of JND ellipses are very closed to unit circles in Euclidean space, which shows that the transformation is successful since that a global isometry is also a local isometry and vice versa [27,28].

We then applied the above method to facial expression recognition. Instead of measuring differences between input images and template images along straight-lines or with Euclidean distances as in current recognition methods, we measure the subjective differences in the facial expression space by geodesic distances.

The two inputs A and B in Fig. 8 are quite similar as images but very different as expressions. As shown in Fig. 9, they are close to each other in the image space by the straight-line distance showing on the left hand side, but actually separated by the geodesic distance in the Riemann space, which can be read out from the polar coordinate system in the Euclidean space on the right hand side.

The two inputs C and D in Fig. 10 are quite different as images but similar as expressions. As shown in Fig. 11, they are separated in the image space by the straight-line distance showing on the left hand side, but actually close to each other by the geodesic distance in Riemann space, which can be read out from the polar coordinate system in the Euclidean space on the right hand side.

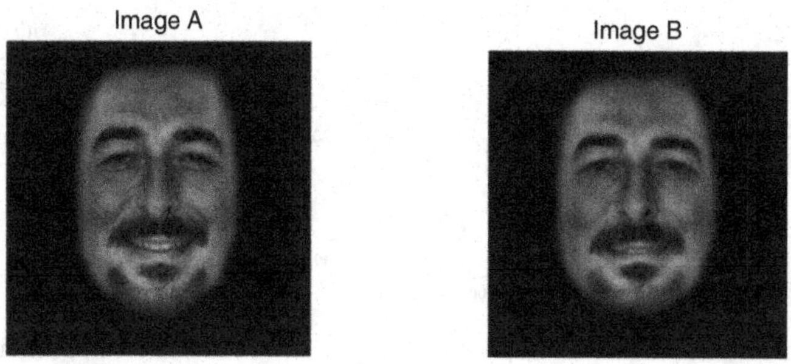

Fig. 8. Two inputs separate in image space but close by geodesic distance

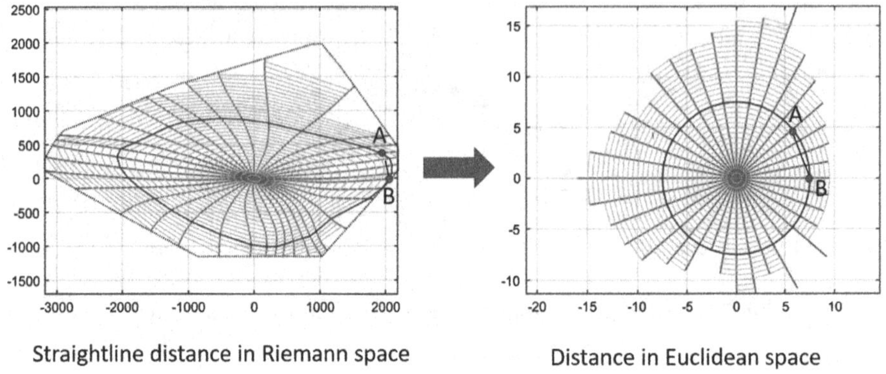

Fig. 9. Discrepancy between image A and B in image distance and geodesic distance

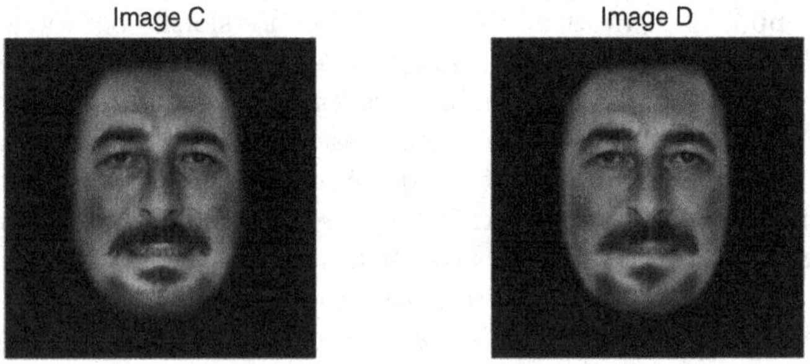

Fig. 10. Two inputs close in image space but separate by geodesic distance

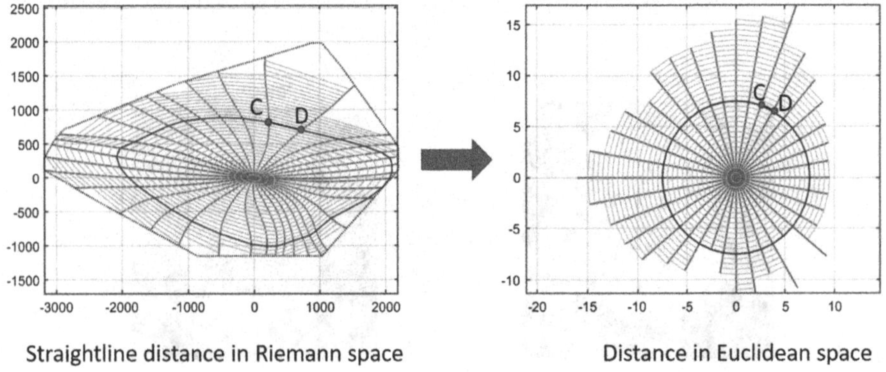

Fig. 11. Discrepancy between image C and D in image distance and geodesic distance

7 Discussion, Conclusions and Future Work

We showed how to transform the facial expression space to a Euclidean space by Riemann normal coordinates which is expected to bring forth various applications in both theoretical modeling and practical recognition of facial expressions.

Another application is to compare the facial expression perceptions between different observers and furthermore to exchange their impressions. For a recent different approach of this problem see [23].

To estimate the Riemannian metric in a d-dimensional space is to measure the JND thresholds or the $d \times d$ symmetric matrices $G(\boldsymbol{x}) = (g_{ij})$ which contains $d(d+1)/2$ entries. When the dimension d increased, the number of the variables therefore the number of measurement data in order to determine these variables increases rapidly. Therefore it is important to determine the effective dimension of the facial expression space. The same time, one needs a fast and accurate procedure to measure JND threshold hyper-ellipsoids in a high dimensional space. As shown above, however, applications of the above algorithms to subspaces which are meaningful in certain applications are also useful.

Another implement issue is that theoretically it may not be able to transform the facial expression space into a single Euclidean space but a multi-patch approach is needed. It is related with the topology and curvature of the Riemann space and the so-called injectivity radius, which should be investigated in the future. For further information see [25,26].

Acknowledgment. The authors wish to thank Prof. Miyuki Kamachi for suggestions and discussions in this research.

References

1. Sumiya, R., Lenz, R., Chao, J.: Measurement of JND thresholds and riemannian geometry in facial expression space. In: Kurosu, M. (ed.) HCI 2018. LNCS, vol. 10901, pp. 453–464. Springer, Cham (2018). https://doi.org/10.1007/978-3-319-91238-7_37
2. Jain, A.K., Li, S.Z.: Handbook of Face Recognition. Springer, New York (2011). https://doi.org/10.1007/978-0-85729-932-1
3. Benitez-Quiroz, C.F., Srinivasan, R., Martinez, A.M.: EmotioNet: an accurate, real-time algorithm for the automatic annotation of a million facial expressions in the wild. In: Proceedings of the IEEE Conference on Computer Vision and Pattern Recognition (2016)
4. Du, S., Tao, Y., Martinez, A.M.: Compound facial expressions of emotion. Proc. Natl. Acad. Sci. **111**(15), E1454–E1462 (2014)
5. Ekman, P., Friesen, W.V.: Facial Action Coding System: A Technique for the Measurement of Facial Movement. Consulting Psychologists Press, Palo Alto (1978)
6. Woorworth, R.S.: Experimental Psychology. Henry Holt, New York (1938)
7. Schlosberg, H.: A scale for the judgement of facial expressions. J. Exp. Psychol. **29**, 229–237 (1941)
8. Schlosberg, H.: The description of facial expression in terms of two dimensions. J. Exp. Psychol. **44**(4), 229 (1952)

9. Russell, J.A., Bullock, M.: Multidimensional scaling of emotional facial expressions: similarity from preschoolers to adults. J. Pers. Soc. Psychol. **48**(5), 1290 (1985)
10. Russell, J.A., Weiss, A., Mendelsohn, G.A.: Affect grid: a single-item scale of pleasure and arousal. J. Pers. Soc. Psychol. **57**, 493–502 (1989)
11. Russell, J.A.: A circumplex model of affect. J. Pers. Soc. Psychol. **39**, 1161–1178 (1980)
12. Richardson, M.W.: Multidimensional psychophysics. Psychol. Bull. **35**(9), 659–660 (1938)
13. Calder, A.J., Young, A.W., Perrett, D.I., Rowland, D.: Categorical perception of morphed facial expressions. Vis. Cogn. **3**, 81–117 (1996)
14. Gescheider, G.A.: Psychophysics, The Fundamentals. 3rd edn. Psychology Press (1997)
15. Wyszecki, G., Stiles, W.S.: Color Science: Concepts and Methods, Quantitative Data and Formulae, 2nd edn. Wiley, New York (1982)
16. Wright, W.D., Pitt, F.H.G.: Hue-discrimination in normal color-vision. Proc. Phys. Soc. **46**(3), 459–473 (1942)
17. MacAdam, D.L.: Visual sensitivities to color differences in daylight. J. Opt. Soc. Am. **32**(5), 247–274 (1942)
18. Brown, W.R.J., MacAdam, D.L.: Visual sensitivities to combined chromaticity and luminance differences. J. Opt. Soc. Am. **39**(10), 808–834 (1949)
19. Savran, A., et al.: Bosphorus database for 3D face analysis. In: The First COST 2101 Workshop on Biometrics and Identity Management (BIOID 2008), Roskilde University, Denmark, 7–9 May 2008
20. Savran, A., Sankur, B.L., Bilge, M.T.: Comparative evaluation of 3D versus 2D modality for automatic detection of facial action units. Pattern Recogn. **45**(2), 767–782 (2012)
21. Savran, A., Sankur, B.L., Bilge, M.T.: Regression-based intensity estimation of facial action units. Image Vis. Comput. **30**(10), 774–784 (2012)
22. Young, A.W., Rowland, D., Calder, A.J., Etcoff, N.L., Seth, A., Perrett, D.I.: Facial expression megamix: test of dimensional and category accounts of emotion recognition. Cognition **63**(3), 271–313 (1997)
23. Shinto, M., Chao, J.: How to compare and exchange facial expression perceptions between different individuals with Riemann geometry. In: Kurosu, M. (ed.) HCII 2019, LNCS 11567, pp. 155–167 (2019)
24. Mochizuki, R., Kojima, T., Lenz, R., Chao, J.: Color-weak compensation using local affine isometry based on discrimination threshold matching. J. Opt. Soc. Am. A Opt. Image Sci. Vis. **32**(11), 2093–2103 (2015)
25. Oshima, S., Mochizuki, R., Lenz, R., Chao, J.: Modeling, measuring, and compensating color weak vision. IEEE Trans. Image Process. **25**(6), 2587–2600 (2016)
26. Toko, K., Chao, J., Lenz, R.: On curvature of color spaces and its implication. In: Proceedings of 5th European Conference on Colours in Graphics, Imaging, and Vision, CGIV 2010, Jeonsuu, Finland, pp. 393–398, 14–17 June 2010
27. Do Carmo, M.P.: Riemannianian Geometry. Birkhäuser, Boston (2013)
28. Petersen, P.: Riemannian Geometry. Springer, New York (2006). https://doi.org/10.1007/978-0-387-29403-2

Affective Monitor: A Process of Data Collection and Data Preprocessing for Building a Model to Classify the Affective State of a Computer User

Sudarat Tangnimitchok(✉), Nonnarit O-larnnithipong, Neeranut Ratchatanantakit, and Armando Barreto

Florida International University, Miami, FL 33174, USA
{stang018,nolar002,nratc001,barretoa}@fiu.edu

Abstract. This paper outlines the first phase of our implementation of a system for non-intrusive estimation of a computer user's affective state based on the Circumplex Model of Affect [1], from monitoring the user's pupil diameter and facial expression [2]. The details of the original design plan for this system have been described previously [2]. The outline describes each part of data collecting process including: Obtaining 3D facial coordinates by Kinect, recording the pupil diameter signal, embedding the facial expression to Facial Animation Parameter indices, and the description of how the experiment will be setup.

Keywords: Affective computing · Facial expression recognition · Eye-gaze tracking · AffectiveMonitor

1 Introduction

As we have described in our proposal [2] for a non-intrusive estimation of a computer user's affective state based on the Circumplex Model of Affect [1], our goal is to build a supervised machine learning system to classify the user's state of affect. Thus, the design of the data collecting process plays an extremely important role to achieve the right result. To collect the data, we set up the experiment in a scenario where human subjects will be presented with images from the International Affective Picture System (IAPS) [3] to elicit from them affective reactions that will be manifested through their involuntary changes in pupil diameter and in their facial expressions, while also reporting the subjective assessment of their reactions through the Self-Assessment Manikin (SAM) [4]. During the recording sessions a Kinect sensor will be used to collect the 3D facial coordinates and the Facial Animation Parameter Units (FAPUs) [5] from the subject's face, as well as an estimate of the illumination level in the area around the eyes of the subject. Simultaneously, an Eye Gaze Tracking (EGT) system will be used to record the pupil diameter in the eyes of the subject.

M. Kurosu (Ed.): HCII 2019, LNCS 11567, pp. 179–190, 2019.
https://doi.org/10.1007/978-3-030-22643-5_14

The self reports of arousal and valence marked by the subject in SAM for each IAPS image will also be recorded into the dataset for later use. The last part of this section will contain some brief explanation of terms used throughout this article. Then, in the following section, we will discuss in detail the experiment procedure, and the process of data acquisition as previously described in the early part of the section.

Circumplex Model of Affect: The Circumplex model of affect was introduced by Russell [1] as a proposal to model the affective state of a human. Russell proposed that an affective state consists of two parameters: arousal and valence. Their relationship can be visualized as a four-quadrant graph where valence is the horizontal axis and arousal is the vertical axis. Other studies have shown a similar trend where models have two parameters that are referred using different words [6,7].

The International Affective Picture System: The International Affective Picture System (IAPS) is a large set of color photographs that elicit shifts in the subject's arousal and valence. IAPS contains a wide variety of stimulus types for more than 1,000 exemplars of human experience such as joyful, sad, fearful, attractive, angry, simple objects, scenery, etc. The idea is to present the subject with visual stimuli to modify his/her affective state while recording his/her reaction. The IAPS has been used across various fields of study to investigate emotion and attention worldwide and it is well-known for its replication and robustness. Pictures from IAPS are rated with arousal, pleasure, and dominance mean values, based on reactions from men and women, which make them suitable to be used as stimuli in this study. More in-depth information about IAPS can be found in [3].

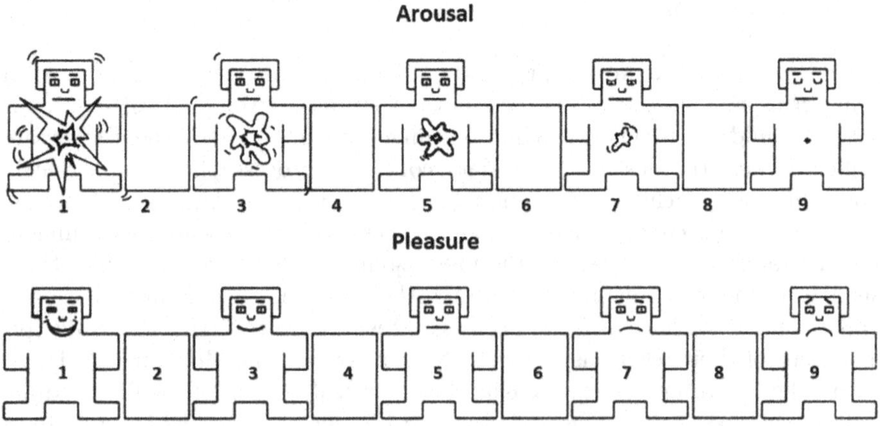

Fig. 1. Self-Assessment Manikin (SAM) (from [3])

Self-Assessment Manikin: The Self-Assessment Manikin (SAM) [4] is a tool for a non-verbal, pictorial assessment reporting technique that directly expresses the pleasure, arousal, and dominance associated with the affective state of the subject while being exposed to a stimulus. We mainly focus on the 2-dimensional Circumplex Model of Affect; therefore, dominance reactions are not considered. As demonstrated in Fig. 1, the SAM figure varies along each scale. In the arousal scale, the left-most figure corresponds to the most extremely stimulated, excited, frenzied, jittery, wide-awake, or aroused state. While the other end of the scale represent a completely relaxed, calm, sluggish, dull, sleepy, or unaroused state. The scale ranges from 1 to 9 for the purpose of intermediate fine-grained rating. For the pleasure (valence) assessment, the scale works the same way as in arousal except, in this case, the left-most figure represents a highly happy, pleased, satisfied, contended, hopeful state; while the opposite end represents a very unhappy, annoyed, unsatisfied,melancholic, despaired, bored state.

2 Experiment Setup

The entire data collection process is depicted in the diagram shown in Fig. 2. The diagram describes the process handled by the AffectiveMonitor application [2] and indicates the list of output files for post-data analysis. Kinect, running on the primary machine is responsible to obtain 3D facial coordinates while the TM3 Eye-Gaze Tracker device running on a secondary machine records the pupil diameter signals and sends them over to the primary machine. Desired data are then recorded during the experiment session and are written out in a timely manner, for each frame, to output files. We show how the experiment has been set up and its environment in Fig. 3a.

2.1 Experiment Procedure

AffectiveMonitor has a separate "Experiment" interface tab section (Fig. 3b) to conduct the experiment from the start to the end. The experiment takes about 35 min and before the experiment session begins, the subject will go through the calibration process consisting of adjusting the shape of a 3D facial model, and adjusting the subject's position for pupil diameter recording. 70 pictures selected from IAPS will be shown to the subject, one after another, until all samples are presented. For each sample, the subject is asked to look at the picture for 6 s, then immediately after, rate their affective state assessment via SAM (5 s). In between samples, a gray screen is shown during the resting period. The subject is urged to stay still during the first 6 seconds, when he/she is first presented with the stimulus in order to reduce the measurement interference that could occur during the recording process.

2.2 Sample Selection

For the experiment, we selected IAPS pictures on the basis of the mean and variance of arousal and valence that come with each picture from the IAPS

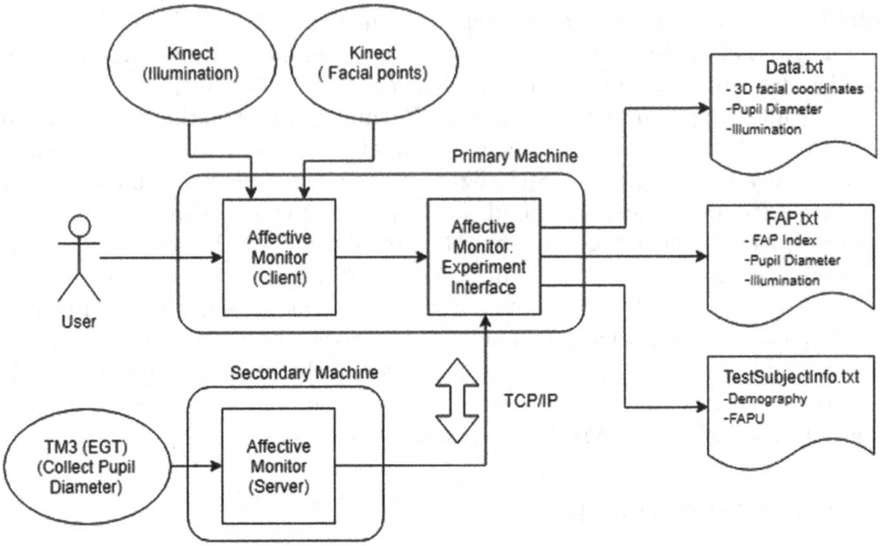

Fig. 2. Bird's eye view of the system (data collection process)

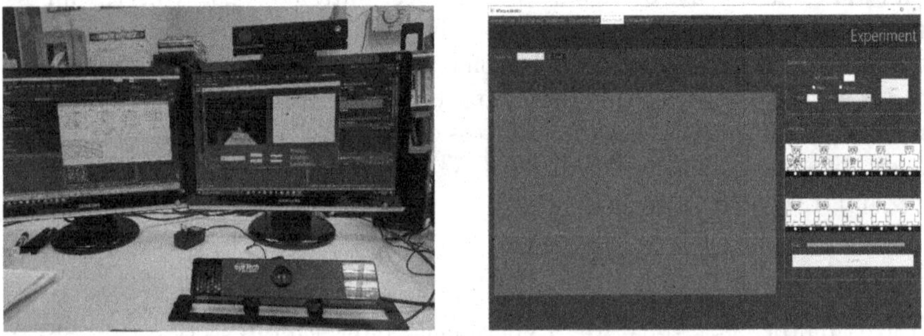

(a) System's environment (b) AffectiveMonitor: Experiment Interface

Fig. 3. An entire system including Kinect V2 (on top of the screen) and TM3 (in front of the computer) is shown in (a). (b) shows an experiment interface of the Affective-Monitor application

repository. Our criterion on selecting the samples is based on the study of a 12-Point Affect Circumplex (12-PAC) model of Core Affect [8] which is also based on the Circumplex Model of Affect. The study introduces the modification of hypothetically dividing the Circumplex model into twelve segments called the 12-Point Affect Circumplex (12-PAC) structure. By finding the correlation between many previous studies and their own, the authors report their analysis, and their placement of moods on a 12-PAC structure as shown in Fig. 4b. Based on this study, we selected the IAPS samples that are located around desired angles of those core affects that have more than 60% likelihood to appear in the

Circumplex Model. Accordingly, we selected 70 samples as shown in Fig. 4a and we also list the samples in Table 1 by the picture ID from IAPS, categorized by core affect description.

Table 1. Selected samples listed by picture ID from IAPS

	Pleasure	Joviality	Attentiveness	Disgust	Fear	Negative	Sadness	Tiredness	Calmness
1	1440	8499	4664	9301	9252	9007	2456	2399	5811
2	2550	8501	4604	7359	9413	9320	2095	2039	5870
3	2260	8080	4689		9940	9342	2301	2752	1604
4	2070	7600	8179		6550	9295	2141	9390	5875
5	5831	7451	8490		2981		2799	9913	1419
6	7200	2092	4574		9491		4598	9395	2000
7	2154	8300	4232		9042			9190	5410
8	2151	8200	5950		6250			2400	7325
9	5910	4626	1050		9325			2695	5725

3 Data Acquisition

In this section, we explain the method of obtaining each parameter including 3D facial coordinates, pupil diameter, Facial Animation Parameter (FAP), and illumination around the facial area. All of them are recorded with the same timestamp by the AffectiveMonitor application.

3.1 3D Facial Coordinates

Kinect has provided the basic framework software called HD face [9]. The framework can detect the face of the closest person in front of the Kinect sensor and generate the person's 3D facial mesh model in real-time. Another interesting prospect of this framework is an ability to reconstruct the person's face shape by 3D scanning to acquire a very accurate characterization of the person's face. Given all that, we have integrated this framework into our AffectiveMonitor application to benefit from all the functionality that Kinect has to offer. The mesh model can also be represented by 3D coordinates and can be thought of as markers attached on the subject's face so whenever the subject's facial expression changes, the markers also move according to the corresponding facial muscle movement. By recording frame by frame, we can observe the changes of 3D facial coordinates that occurs because of the subject's facial expression.

One problem that arises during the design of the experiment is the impossibility to restrain the movement of the subjects during the experiment. Body shifts can alter the position and orientation of the subject's face, which may complicate their processing. To circumvent the issue, we have built a feature in AffectiveMonitor to artificially re-position and re-orient the subject's face before recording the values. Fortunately, Kinect also provides the pivot point as well as the orientation (in quaternion) of the face. Thus, we can reverse the rotation and transform the point cloud to neutral position at the origin by applying a change of coordinate frame as described in [10].

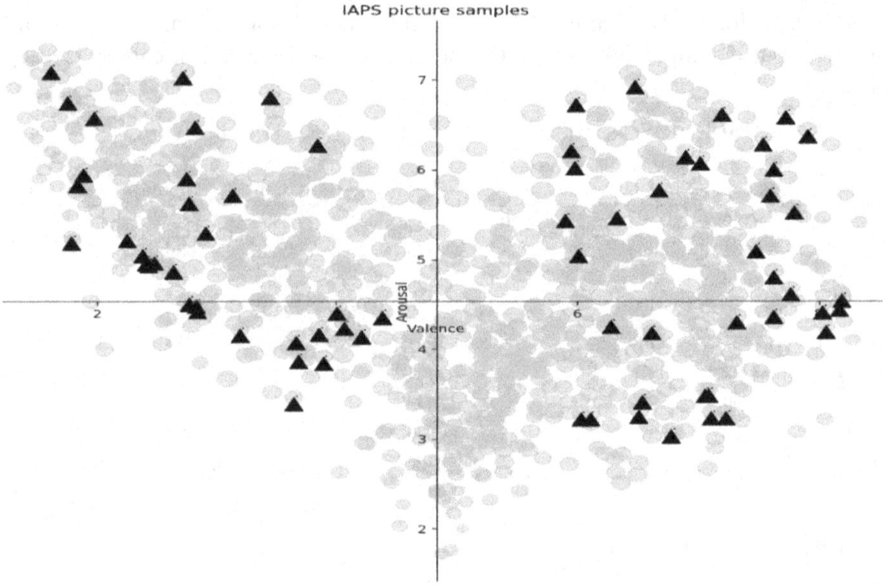

(a) IAPS pictures selected for our study (▲)

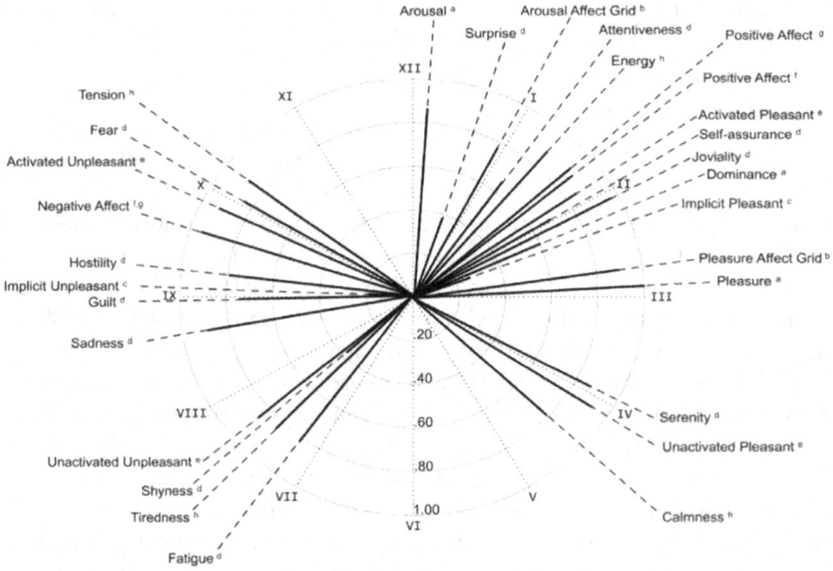

(b) Core Affects on 12-PAC structure (from[8])

Fig. 4. (a) shows a plot of means of arousal and valence for images in the IAPS repository on top of the Circumplex Model of Affect. Notice that the radius of each plotted circle varies according to its variance. The triangular labels indicate the images chosen for use samples in this experiment. (b) demonstrates thirty mood scales which are placed within the 12-PAC structure with CIRCUM-extension method [8]. The length of the solid line from the center can be roughly described as the maximum likelihood of placing a mood on the designated angle

3.2 Pupil Diameter and Illumination

To acquire pupil diameter signals, we utilize the TM3 Eye-Gaze Tracker (EGT), which has a capability to measure the pupil diameter using the dark-pupil method. We set the sampling interval at 0.33 s and average samples in an average window of 30-samplewidth. The pupil diameter signals are then transferred to the primary machine via TCP/IP, over ethernet cable. AffectMonitor has a feature to plot the average of the pupil diameter dynamically as shown in Fig. 6a.

Many studies have shown that the pupil diameter is under the influence of the Autonomous Nervous System (ANS) and can be used as a marker for arousal level [11]. Unfortunately, pupil diameter is also susceptible to the amount of light on the retina. To bypass this issue, we plan to perform a post-processing step to eliminate the effect of the pupillary light reflex using an adaptive signal processing technique. In order to attain that goal, illumination around the eyes must also be recorded as one of the output parameters. We obtain the illuminance utilizing Kinect's RGB camera by cropping the video around the eye area (Fig. 6b) and calculating the illumination based on the cropped video. A more detailed explanation on this subject will be reported in a separate article, under preparation (Fig. 5).

Table 2. Facial Animation Parameter Unit (FAPU)

Description		FAPU Value
IRISD0 = 3.1.y 3.3.y = 3.2.y − 3.4.y	Iris diameter (by definition it is equal to the distance between upper ad lower eyelid) in neutral face	IRISD = IRISD0/1024
ES0 = 3.5.x − 3.6.x	Eye separation	ES = ES0/1024
ENS0 = 3.5.y − 9.15.y	Eye - nose separation	ENS = ENS0/1024
MNS0 = 9.15.y − 2.2.y	Mouth - nose separation	MNS = MNS0/1024
MW0 = 8.3.x − 8.4.x	Mouth width	MW = MW0/1024

3.3 Facial Animation Parameter

The Facial Animation Parameter (FAP) is one concept of the components in MPEG-4 Face and Body Animation (FBA) International Standard (ISO/IEC 14496 -1 & -2) [13]. It describes a standard protocol to encode the virtual representation of human and humanoid movement, specifically around the facial region of a body. FAP is commonly used to describe basic actions of facial expression for a synthetic face; for instance, in the CANDIDE model [5]. The ability of FAP to encode the primitive expression information with small memory usage makes it interesting as an alternative method to preserve the subject's facial expression.

The Facial Animation Parameters (FAP) are defined by the displacement between facial feature points defined by FBA (See Fig. 7) which are measured

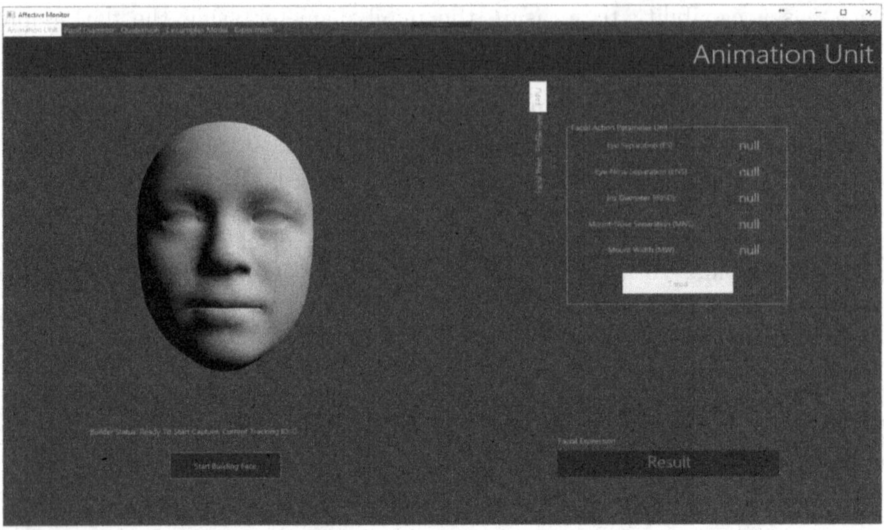

(a) Facial mesh construction

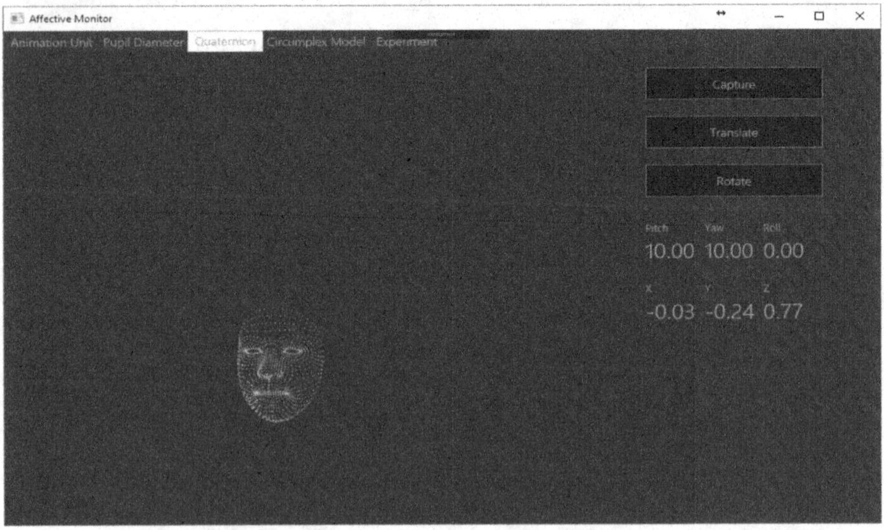

(b) Re-positioning and re-orienting facial points

Fig. 5. (a) shows the interface of AffectiveMonitor for mesh construction. (b) displays the interface of AffectiveMonitor used for resetting the facial point cloud to its neutral position. The interface shows the shift in position and orientation in the Euclidean domain.

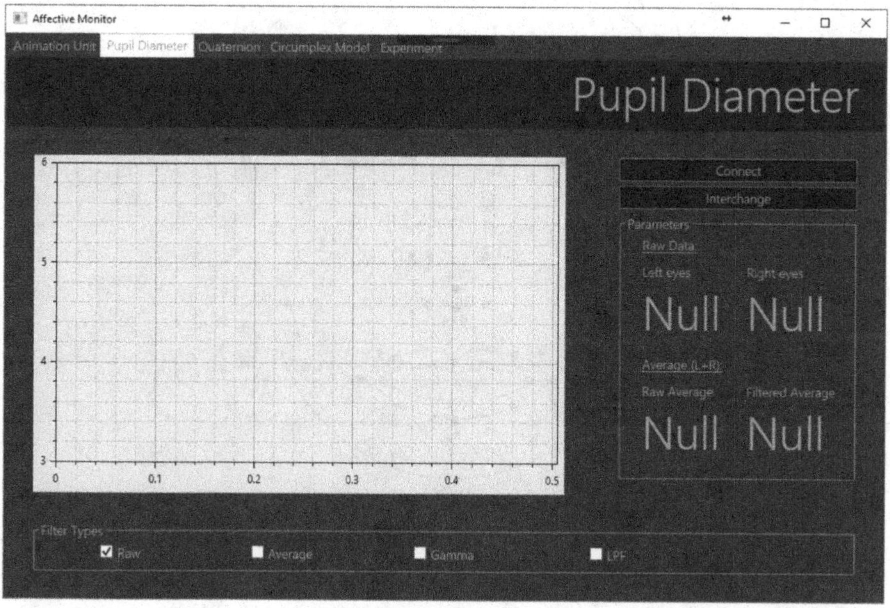

(a) Pupil Diameter interface

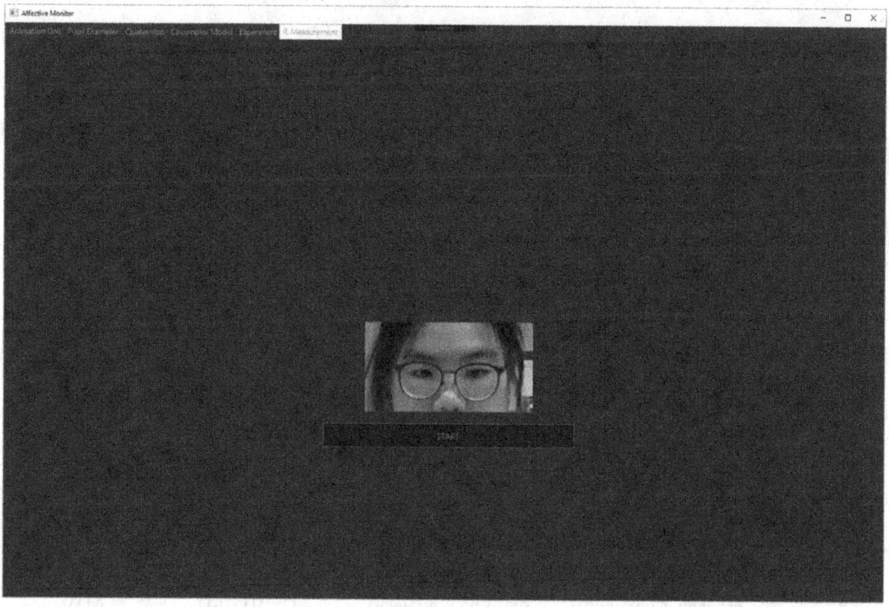

(b) Cropped video

Fig. 6. (a) shows the interface of AffectiveMonitor for dynamic plotting of pupil diameter. (b) shows the cropped video used for illumination measurement around the eyes.

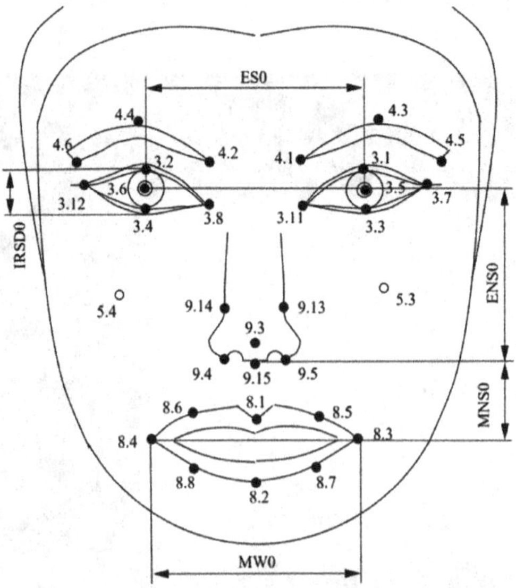

Fig. 7. Facial feature points and Facial Animation Parameter (FAPU) (from [12])

Table 3. FAP measurement with facial feature points (FBA & Kinect)

FAP index	FAP Name	Distance of two feature points (FBA)	Distance of two feature points (Kinect)	FAPU
31	raise_l_i_eyebrow	Dy(4.2, 3.8)	Dy(346, 210)	ENS
32	raise_r_i_eyebrow	Dy(4.1, 3.11)	Dy(803, 843)	ENS
35	raise_l_o_eyebrow	Dy(4.6, 3.12)	Dy(140, 469)	ENS
36	raise_r_o_eyebrow	Dy(4.5, 3.7)	Dy(758, 1117)	ENS
37	squeeze_l_eyebrow	Dx(4.4, 3.8)	Dx(222, 210)	ES
38	squeeze_r_eyebrow	Dx(4.3, 3.11)	Dx(849, 843)	ES
19	close/open_t_l_eyelid	Dy(3.6, 3.2)	Dy(241, 1104)	IRSD
20	close/open_t_r_eyelid	Dy(3.5, 3.1)	Dy(731, 1090)	IRSD
41	lift_l_cheek	Dy(5.4, 3.12)	Dy(458, 469)	ENS
42	lift_r_cheek	Dy(5.3, 3.11)	Dy(674, 117)	ENS
61	stretch_l_nose	Dy(9.14, 3.8)	Dy(210, 1170)	ENS
62	stretch_r_nose	Dy(9.13, 3.11)	Dy(843, 1162)	ENS
59	raise/lower_l_cornerlip_o	Dy(8.4, 3.12)	Dy(91, 469)	MNS
60	raise/lower_r_cornerlip_o	Dy(8.3, 3.11)	Dy(687, 117)	MNS
53	stretch_l_cornerlip	Dx(8.4, 9.15)	Dx(91, 14)	MW
54	stretch_r_cornerlip	Dx(8.3, 9.15)	Dx(687 14)	MW
5	raise/lower_b_midlip	Dy(8.2, 9.15)	Dy(8, 14)	MNS
4	lower_t_midlip	Dy(8.1, 9.15)	Dy(19, 14)	MNS
3	open_jaw	Dy(8.2, 8.1)	Dy(19, 8)	MNS

by Facial Animation Parameter Units (FAPUs). FAPUs are normally calculated from a neutral face and divided by 1024 so that the unit is small enough to enable FAPs to be represented in integer numbers. The purpose of FAPUs is to allow a consistent way to interpret FAPs indices for any facial model regardless of their shape and dimension. The description of the FAPUs and how to calculate them are listed in Table 2. We decide to output 19 FAPs listed in Table 3 which are actively related to basic facial expressions as desired output from the total of 68 FAPs [12]. Note that in Fig. 7, the numbering of the facial feature points is according to FBA; while, the index coordination system from Kinect is in different listing. See Table 3 for the correspondence between Kinect's index coordination system and FBA's coordination system.

4 Discussion and Conclusion

Given all the previous explanations, we would like to reemphasize that the purpose of this work is to collect the data suitable to train a supervised machine learning model, to classify the affective state of the subject in a Circumplex Model of Affect. In order to achieve that, we have to estimate two parameters, arousal and valence, our model. In case of arousal, we have found strong evidence supporting the notion that pupil diameter is influenced by the Autonomous Nervous System, which is responsible for the state of arousal. While, in the case of valence, we decided to estimate this parameter on the basis of the subject's facial expression since pleasure and displeasure are directly expressed naturally by activity of the facial muscles. Two data formats representing facial expression are recorded, 3D facial coordinates and Facial Animation Parameter index and each has pros and cons. 3D coordinates are practical because they preserve the whole information recorded in the facial expression without losing any; while, FAP is better in the aspect of memory management. Other data that are collected along during the experiment, such as illuminance around the eye area, distance between the subject's face and the Kinect sensor, and FAPU, are necessary for scaling adjustment and calibration. Data are obtained in a time-stamped manner where pupil diameter, FAP, 3D facial coordinates, and others are captured simultaneously and recorded together. Additionally, they are recorded in a customized output file for facilitating the transfer of the data to the analysis phase.

Acknowledgement. This research was supported by National Sciences Foundation grants HRD- 0833093 and CNS-1532061 and the FIU Graduate School Dissertation Year Fellowship awarded to Ms. Sudarat Tangnimitchok.

References

1. Russell, J.A.: A circumplex model of affect. J. Pers. Soc. Psychol. **39**(6), 1161–1178 (1980)
2. Tangnimitchok, S., O-larnnithipong, N., Ratchatanantakit, N., Barreto, A., Ortega, F.R., Rishe, N.D.: A system for non-intrusive affective assessment in the circumplex model from pupil diameter and facial expression monitoring. In: Kurosu, M. (ed.) HCI 2018. LNCS, vol. 10901, pp. 465–477. Springer, Cham (2018). https://doi.org/10.1007/978-3-319-91238-7_38
3. Lang, P.J.: International affective picture system (IAPS): affective ratings of pictures and instruction manual. Technical report (2005)
4. Bradley, M.M., Lang, P.J.: Measuring emotion: the self-assessment manikin and the semantic differential. J. Behav. Ther. Exp. Psychiatry **25**(1), 49–59 (1994)
5. Ahlberg, J., Ahlberg, J.: CANDIDE-3 - an updated parameterised face (2001)
6. Lang, P.J.: The emotion probe studies of motivation and attention. Technical report (1995)
7. Barrett, L.F., Bliss-Moreau, E.: Chapter 4 affect as a psychological primitive (2009)
8. Yik, M., Russell, J.A., Steiger, J.H.: A 12-point circumplex structure of core affect. Emotion **11**(4), 705–731 (2011)
9. Rahman, M.: Understanding how the kinect works. In: Beginning Microsoft Kinect for Windows SDK 2.0, pp. 21–40. Apress, Berkeley(2017)
10. Kuipers, J.: Quaternions and Rotation Sequences: A Primer With Applications To Orbits, Aerospace and Virtual Reality. Princeton University Press, Princeton (1999). kuipers jb, 41 william street, Princeton, NJ 08540, USA. 1999. 372pp. Aeronaut. J. (1999)
11. Gao, Y., Barreto, A., Adjouadi, M.: Detection of sympathetic activation through measurement and adaptive processing of the pupil diameter for affective assessment of computer users. Am. J. Biomed. Sci **1**(4), 283–294 (2009)
12. Zhang, Y., Ji, Q., Zhu, Z., Yi, B.: Dynamic facial expression analysis and synthesis with mpeg-4 facial animation parameters. IEEE Trans. Circ. Syst. Video Technol. **18**(10), 1383–1396 (2008)
13. Pandzic, I.S., Forchheimer, R.: MPEG-4 fAcial Animation: The Standard, Implementation and Applications. Wiley, Hoboken (2003)

Influence of EQ on the Difference of Biometric Emotion and Self-evaluated Emotion

Reiji Yoshida and Midori Sugaya(✉)

Shibaura Institute of Technology, 3-7-5 Toyosu,
Koto-Ku, Tokyo 1358548, Japan
doly@shibaura-it.ac.jp

Abstract. There are many methods to estimating human emotions based on data obtained by sensors. The well-known examples are emotion recognition by analyzing image data of the facial expression and speech emotion recognition analyzing voice data. However, since facial expressions and speech can be arbitrarily changed, they can be said to lack objectivity, which is necessary for emotion estimation. Therefore, emotional analysis using biological signal such as heartbeat and brain waves has been studied. Biological signal cannot be changed arbitrarily, therefore can be said to suit the necessity of being objective, meaning more suitable for emotion estimation. To measure the accuracy of the emotion estimation method using biological signal, it is common to obtain the degree of error between the estimation method and subjective evaluation of one's emotion. However, the problem with this method is that there is no guarantee that the subjective evaluation is equal to the actual "real feeling" that one's embracing. Therefore, in this study, we evaluated the emotion estimation method using biological signal using Emotional Intelligence Quotient (EQ). We examined whether the degree of error between the emotion estimation by biological signal and subjective evaluation of one's emotion can be explained by the level of EQ. In this study, emotions were estimated using biometric data calculated by brainwaves and heartbeat obtained from sensors. As a result, we were able to show the effectiveness of EQ as the indicator of how close bio-estimated emotion is to the subjective emotion evaluation.

Keywords: Emotions in HCI · Emotional intelligence quotient · Emotion estimation

1 Introduction

In recent years, healthcare has been performed to record the daily exercise amount and travel distance based on physical sensor data such as six axis sensors and GPS on mobile terminals such as smartphones [1]. In addition to this, life logs have been performed to record daily health by recording not only data from physiological sensor, but also data from physiological sensors such as skin temperature sensors and pulse sensors of wearable terminals such as smart watch [2]. Based on the time-series data of these sensors, context-aware computing [3] that provides optimal content in consideration of not only the current state of the user, but also the previous and next states have been proposed. Also, emotion-aware computing [4] that provides contents

M. Kurosu (Ed.): HCII 2019, LNCS 11567, pp. 191–200, 2019.
https://doi.org/10.1007/978-3-030-22643-5_15

suitable for the estimation result of the user's emotions based on these sensor data has been proposed.

Numerous methods for estimating human emotions based on physical sensor data have been studied, such as image analysis [5] and speech recognition [6]. Emotion estimation using image analysis shows more than 90% accuracy by using machine learning [5], emotion estimation using speech recognition is necessary for realizing natural dialogue between people and things [6]. However, in the emotion estimation by image analysis, the cultures that are hard to express emotion by facial expression [7], the complexity of the processing the background of the subject [8], etc. are problems, and in emotion estimation by voice recognition, the environment and personality of the subject that cannot be obtained by sensor data is necessary to take in account [6].

Methods for estimating emotions using physiological sensor data have already been proposed [9–11]. Nasoz et al. and Kim et al. estimated the emotion from biological signal such as perspiration, pulse, skin temperature, etc. using a noninvasive simple sensor [9, 11]. In the existing study of Sakamatsu et al. [12] it has been shown that emotion estimation using biological signal such as pulse is effective for prevention and improvement of deterioration of mental health condition. In addition, Ikeda et al., Hiramatsu et al., Koelstra et al. showed that the emotion estimation result by biological signal can fully explain subjective emotional evaluation [10, 13, 14]. On the other hand, in these studies, each indicator of biological signal is analyzed as an independent or integrated indicator, and interaction between indicators and subjective evaluation are not fully taken into consideration.

In this research, in order to solve the above problem, an evaluation was done against an emotion estimation method using biometric emotion as the answer to know to what extent people can understand and express their emotions. In evaluating multiple biometric signal, emotions were defined by the emotional model by Mehrabian et al. and the authenticity of the subjective evaluation was evaluated by the EQ in order to know how well the subjective evaluation can expresses the evaluator. For emotion estimation, a general stimulus was used to avoid limiting the application environment of the emotion estimation method. In addition, emotion estimation was performed using two biological signals, which were brain wave and of pulse.

In emotion estimation experiments using biological signal conducted by Sakamatsu, Ikeda, Hiramatsu et al., it was found that self-evaluated emotion and biometric emotion against a given stimuli were correlated. However, in the experiments that they performed, the stimulus for evoking emotions was limited, the lag before biological signal shows reaction was not considered, and there is not enough discussion about the validity of the subjective evaluation in the first place. In solving these problems, we describe the details of the emotion estimation method, evaluation method and its index used in our research, and the stimulus used to evoke emotion.

2 Emotion Estimation by Biological Signal

2.1 Biological Signals Used

Means of estimating emotions based on biometric signal have been actively studied in recent years. In particular, the PAD model by Mehrabian et al. evaluate emotion by Pleasure (degree of comfortableness to a certain event), Arousal (how active and bored one feels), and Dominance (how much control you have or how obedient you are) [15]. In addition, Russell et al. proposed a circular model of emotion by Valence and Arousal (Circumplex Model of Affect) [16] using Pleasure and Arousal, which relates to the PAD model of Mehrabian.

This model suggests that emotions are plotted on a circle on a two-dimensional coordinate axis. Many methods of classifying emotions using this circular model have been proposed, and Tanaka et al. plotted the position of emotion using EEG and nose thermal image processing on the circumplex model and visualized them [17]. Here, Tanaka et al. proposed a method to associate brain waves to Arousal and nasal skin temperature to Valence, and estimated emotion using these indices [17]. In addition, Ikeda et al. proposed a method to estimate emotion by correlating the value obtained by pulse measurement rather than nose thermal image processing with Arousal [13]. In this proposal, Ikeda et al. showed that there is little error between self-evaluated emotion estimation biometric emotion. Therefore, in this study like Ikeda et al., we used brain waves and pulse to estimate emotion.

2.2 The Biometric Emotion

In this study, the values obtained from the brain waves and pulses were calculated so as to correspond to the Arousal axis and the Valence axis of Russell's circumplex model, and the values of Arousal and Valence were plotted on the two-dimensional coordinate.

The brain wave value associated with the Arousal axis was measured using an electroencephalograph called NeuroSky's MindWave Mobile [18]. We used the value Attention and Meditation calculated by this electroencephalograph. Attention and Meditation are each a value indicating the degree of concentration and the resting degree of the person, and are calculated at the level of 0 to 100. From this, in this study, we assumed that the difference between the value of Attention and Meditation was appropriate to express the degree of arousal of a person and corresponded to the value of Arousal axis of Russell's circular model.

The value of the Valence axis was correlated with the pulse rate earned by the Sparkfun's Pulse Sensor [19]. This sensor measures pulse rate by photoelectric volumetric pulse wave recording method, and pNN50 was used as a pulse value corresponding to the Valence axis. The pNN50 shows the rate at which the difference between the 30 adjacent RR intervals exceeds 50 ms. Generally, pNN50 is said to indicate the degree of tension of the vagus nerve, and the smaller the value, the more tense/uncomfortable a person is. Therefore, it can be said that when someone is normal/pleasant, the RR interval exceeds 50 ms for a fair amount. From this, pNN50 was calculated at a rate of 0 to 1.0, and the value was correlated with the Valence axis.

3 Emotion Estimation by Self-evaluation

3.1 Self-evaluated Emotion

In a study of emotion estimation using biometric signal, a comparison between the proposed method and subjective evaluation is generally done. Here, the subjective evaluation is a subjective judgment of what kind of emotion was evoked for the presented stimulus. For example, evaluating a horror image as "scary" when viewing it is a subjective evaluation for that image.

3.2 Evaluation Method

There is SAM (Self-assessment Mannequin) used by Lang et al. [20] as a method for quantitatively measuring subjective evaluation for presented stimuli. SAM is a system that evaluates continuously varying scales for three indicators of PAD model by Mehrabian et al. using images imitating human beings. Regarding the Pleasure index, it is treated as a Valence index like Russell et al. It is displayed in the range of the image from an image of a person frowning to an image of a person smiling, and the Arousal index displayed in the range of an image of a person whose eyes are opened largely with a big impulse, to a person whose eyes are closed shut. For the Dominance index, it is displayed from the image of a person in a small corner to a person who protrudes the frame and is folding the arm. Each index is scaled in 9 stages, where 9 is the highest rating (high Valence, high Arousal, high Dominance), 1 is the lowest rating (low Valence, low Arousal, low Dominance).

In this research, only Valence and Arousal were evaluated according to the biological signal used (Fig. 1).

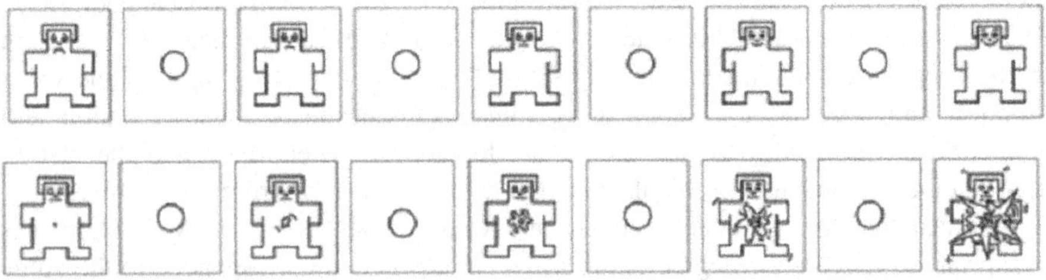

Fig. 1. SAM used in the experiment.

4 Evaluation of Emotion Estimation by EQ

4.1 The Emotional Intelligence Quotient

There are many studies showing the usefulness of biometric signal to estimate a person's emotion by showing that there is only a small difference between the biometric emotion and the self-evaluated emotion, but the correctness of the self-evaluation has not been discussed enough in the first place. Therefore, in this study, an index called

EQ (Emotional Intelligence Quotient) was used to evaluate the correctness of subjective evaluation.

The EQ index is a numerical value of the intelligence of the mind (EI, Emotional Intelligence), which is an ability to perceive the feelings of self and other people in general and to control their own emotions. In this research, we used a method [21] to evaluate each ability by dividing EQ proposed by Goleman et al. into four fields.

The four areas are "Self-Awareness", "Self-Management", "Social Awareness" (understanding of emotions) and "Relationship Management" (emotional adjustment). To quantitatively evaluate these, we used the questionnaire created by Takayama et al. [22].

4.2 Experiment Conducted

The purpose of the experiment was to estimate the emotion based on the brain waves and pulses, to clarify the difference from the subjective evaluation, and to clarify what effect the EQ has on it, when a generalized stimulus is presented. In an environment at room temperature of 26° and humidity of 58%, experiments were conducted with 20 subjects (10 males, 10 females, average age 22 years) according to the following procedure.

1. Answer to questionnaire about EQ
2. Attach EEG, pulse sensor and rest for 30 s
3. Present standby image for 5 s
4. Present images that evoke emotion for 6 s
5. Perform a subjective evaluation on the presented image for 15 s
6. Repeat steps 3 to 5 for each image corresponding to the four quadrants of Russell's circular model (a total of 4 times).

Subjective evaluation needs to be done immediately after the stimulus is presented to obtain a fresh subjective assessment of the stimulus. In order to realize this, we developed a subjective evaluation system using a web browser. In addition, images registered in IAPS (International Affective Picture System) [20] were used as stimuli (Fig. 2).

4.3 Experiment Results

Figure 3 shows the pNN50 and the degree of arousal of two subjects. For the subject A, there is a tendency to decrease after an increases for both pNN50 and degree of arousal after stimulus presentation. On the other hand, for subject B, while pNN50 continues to decrease, it can be confirmed that the degree of arousal has increased after the initial decrease. While subject A had a high EQ score, subject B didn't have such a high score. Therefore, it can be said that people with high EQ score have a tendency to self-evaluate accordingly to biometric signals, whereas people with low EQ score do not.

We also conducted a t-test on the average of the differences between biometric signal and subjective evaluation for the presented images of the group with low EQ ability and the average of the difference between the biometric signal and the subjective evaluation for the presented images of the group with high EQ ability. To this end, the

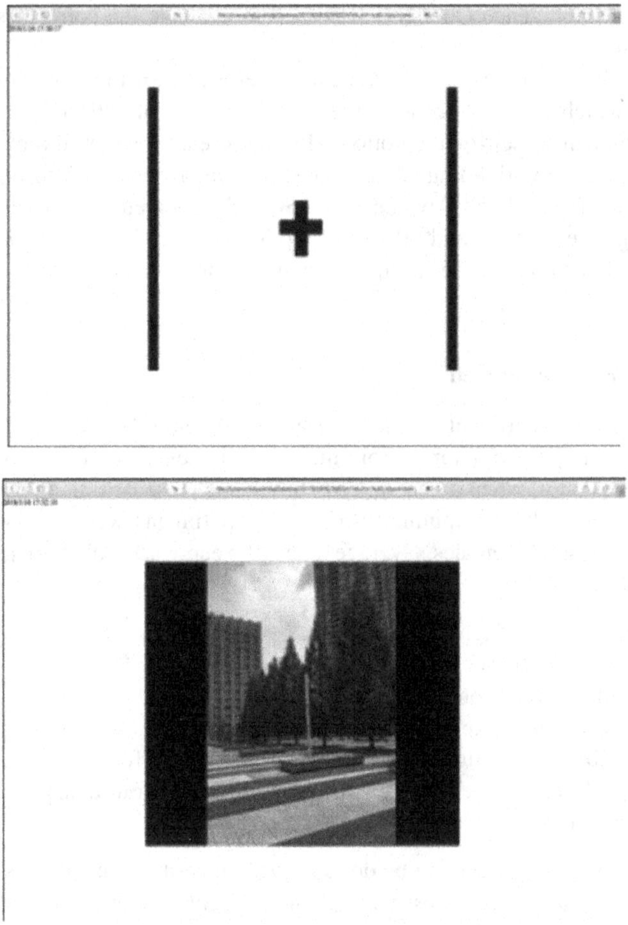

Fig. 2. System used to present stimulus.

difference between each biometric signal and subjective evaluation was obtained by the following formula. In applying this formula, each biological signal was similarly scaled in 9 steps in order to be comparable with SAM which is a subjective evaluation.

$$\text{Valence Difference} = |\text{Biometric Valence Evaluation(pNN50)} - \text{SelfValence Evaluation(Valence SAM)}| \quad (1)$$

$$\text{Arousal Difference} = |\text{Biometric Arousal Evaluation(Degree of Arousal)} - \text{Self Arousal Evaluation(Arousal SAM)}| \quad (2)$$

For all four EQ abilities, there was no decisive significant difference in the Valence evaluation in the classification based on the high and low of its abilities. However, a

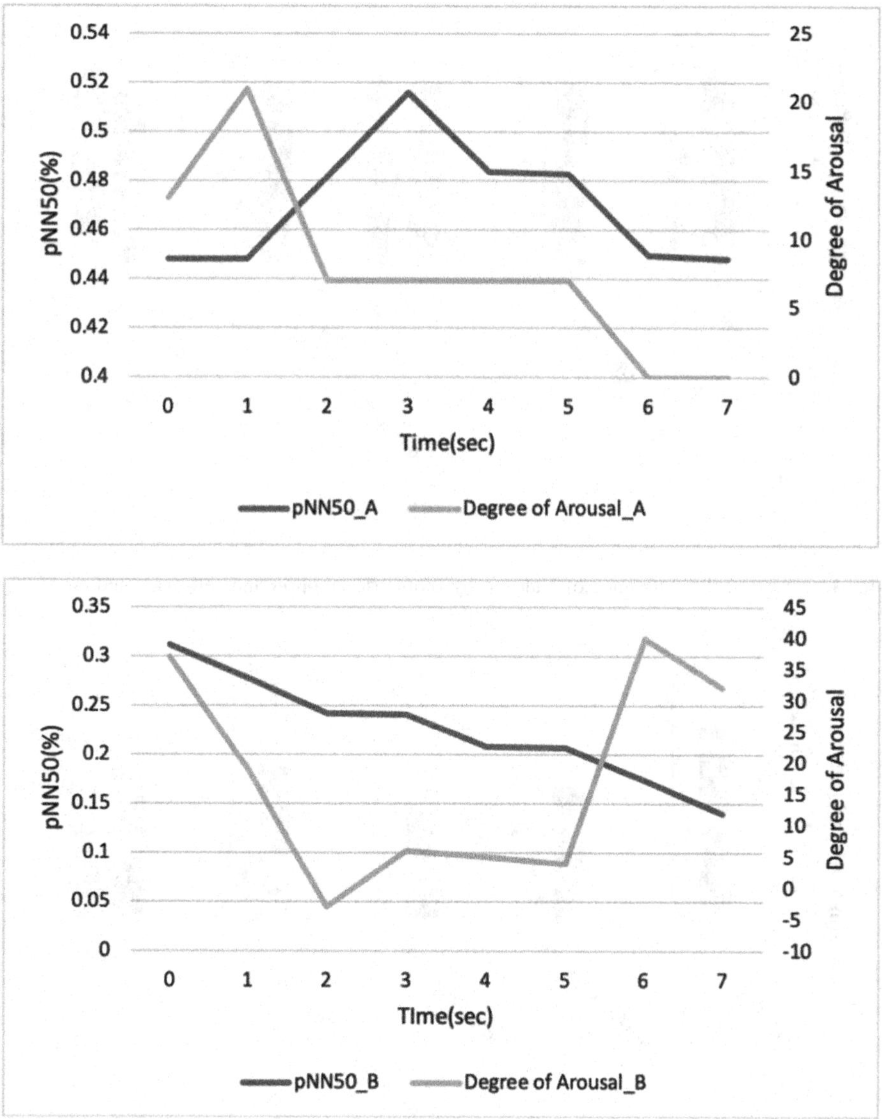

Fig. 3. Time-lapse data of Pleasure and Attention of 2 subjects.

significant tendency ($p < .15$) was observed for classification by "Self-Awareness" (Fig. 4).

Also, there was no significant difference in Arousal evaluation between classification by "Self-Management" and classification by "Social Awareness". However, from Fig. 5, a significant difference was found at $p < .05$ in the classification based on the ability to "Self-Awareness" and classification by "Relationship Management".

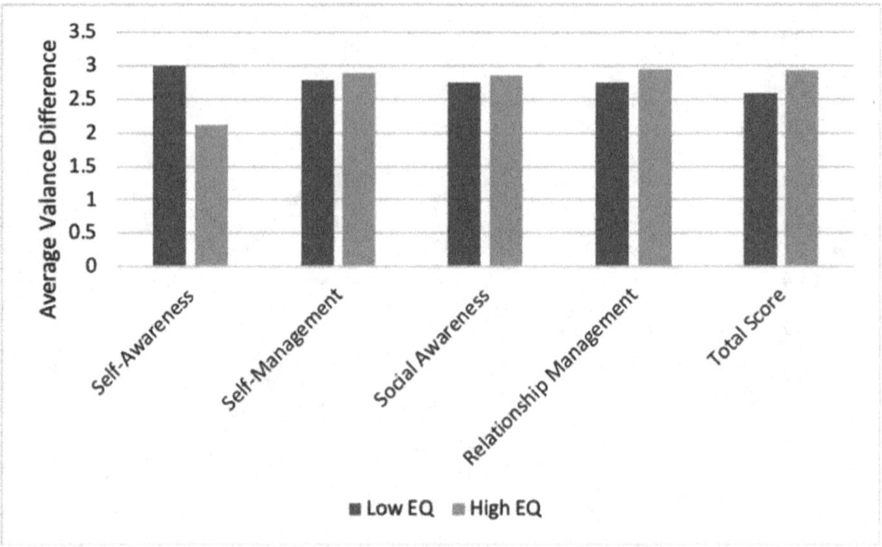

Fig. 4. T-test on the difference of Valence by biometric emotion and self-evaluated emotion.

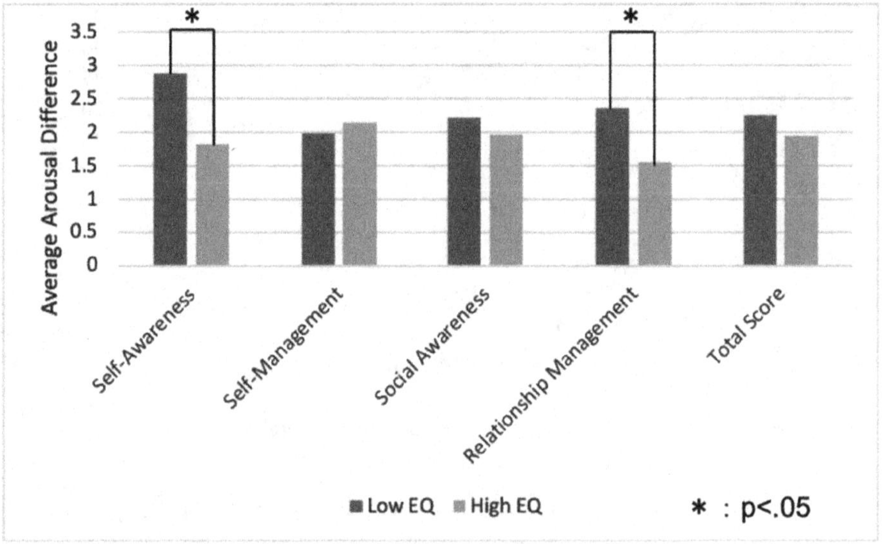

Fig. 5. T-test on the difference of Arousal by biometric emotion and self-evaluated emotion.

4.4 Consideration and Discussion

Based on the experiment results, the difference in valence depends on the subjects' "Self-Awareness", while the difference in arousal depends on the subjects' "Self-Awareness" and "Relationship Management".

1. "Self-Awareness"
   "Self-Awareness" shows how well you can understand and accurately assess your own emotional state. "Self-Awareness" is the ability to perceive emotion, so it can be comprehended as the ability to correctly recognize the response to a stimulus as an emotion.
2. "Relationship Management"
   "Relationship Management" expands your awareness to others, showing how well you can emphasize to others' emotions. It can be comprehended as the ability to manipulate one's own emotions accordingly to the given stimuli.

From these facts, when a person has high "Self-Awareness", it is possible to accurately ascertain the biological signal as a subjective evaluation, and when a person has high "Relationship Management", he/she can change subjective evaluation according to biological data. Therefore, it can be considered that the higher one's "Self-Awareness" and "Relationship Management" is, the less the difference between emotion by biometric data and emotion by subjective evaluation is.

5 Conclusion

In this study, we conducted a validation study on the emotion evaluation using biometric data by the highs and lows of EQ quadrants. As a result, it was suggested that the "Self-Awareness" and "Relationship Management" are effective as an indicator of the credibility of the subjective evaluation of arousal degree. However, as an indicator of the credibility of the subjective evaluation of valence, none of the quadrants were suggested to be effective. The reason for this could possibly the use of image as the stimuli. Images are useful as a general stimulus, but it does not move and therefore lack dynamism, which proved to be insufficient as a stimulus for evoking emotion. To solve this, it is necessary to use stimuli that sufficiently evoke emotions to the extent where generality is not lost.

References

1. Apple Healthcare. https://www.apple.com/jp/ios/health/. Accessed 19 Jan 2019
2. Sony Lifelog. https://www.sonymobile.co.jp/myxperia/app/lifelog/. Accessed 19 Jan 2019
3. Schilit, B.N., Adams, N., Want, R.: Context-aware computing applications. In: Proceedings of Workshop Mobile Computing Systems and Applications, pp. 85–90 (1994)
4. Frantzidis, C., Bratsas, C., Papadelis, C.L., et al.: Toward emotion aware computing: an integrated approach using multichannel neurophysiological recordings and affective visual stimuli. IEEE Trans. Inf. Technol. Biomed. **14**(3), 589–597 (2010)
5. Mayya, V., Pai, R.M., Pai, M.M.M.: automatic facial expression recognition using DCNN. Proc. Comput. Sci. **93**, 453–461 (2016)
6. Frant, E., Ispas, I., Dragomir, V., Dascalu, M., Zoltan, E., Stoica, I.C.: Voice based emotion recognition with convolutional neural networks for companion robots. Rom. J. Signal Sci. Technol. **20**(3), 222–240 (2017)

7. Jack, R.E., Garrod, O.G.B., Yu, H., Caldara, R., Schyns, P.G.: Facial expressions of emotion are not culturally universal. PNAS **109**(19), 7241–7244 (2012)
8. Kanade, T., Cohn, J.F., Tian, Y.: Comprehensive database for facial expression analysis. In: Proceedings of International Conference on Automatic Face and Gesture Recognition, pp. 46–53 (2000)
9. Nasoz, F., Alvarez, K., Lisetti, C.L., Finkelstein, N.: Emotion recognition from physiological signals using wireless sensors for presence technologies. Cogn. Technol. Work **6**(1), 4–14 (2004)
10. Koelstra, S., et al.: DEAP: a database for emotion analysis using physiological signals. IEEE Trans. Affect. Comput. **3**(1), 18–31 (2012)
11. Kim, K.H., Bang, S.W., Kim, S.R.: Emotion recognition system using short-term monitoring of physiological signals. Med. Biol. Eng. Comput. **42**(3), 419–427 (2004)
12. Sakamatsu, H., et al.: A self-feedback interface using MMD model based on emotion identification method using multiple biometric information (Japanese). IPSJ Interact. 602–605 (2015)
13. Ikeda, Y., et. al.: Estimate emotion with biological signal for robot interaction. In: KES-2017, vol.112, pp. 1589–1600 (2017)
14. Hiramatsu, T., et. al.: Preliminary stage reaction analysis of audience with bio-emotion estimation method. In: EACIS 2018, COMPSAC 2018, pp. 601–605 (2018)
15. Mehrabian, A.: Basic Dimensions for a General Psychological Theory, pp. 39–53. Oelgeschlager Gunn & Hain, Cambridge (1980)
16. Russell, J.A.: A circumplex model of affect. J. Pers. Soc. Psychol. **39**(6), 1161–1178 (1980)
17. Tanaka, H., et al.: Emotional visualization based on nose thermal image processing (Japanese). Vis. Inform. **23** (2003)
18. NeuroSky Mindwave Mobile. https://store.neurosky.com. Accessed 19 Jan 2019
19. Sparkfun Pulse Sensor. https://www.sparkfun.com/products/11574. Accessed 19 Jan 2019
20. Lang, P.J., Bradley, M.M., Cuthbert, B.N.: International affective picture system (IAPS): affective ratings of pictures and instruction manual. Technical report A-8. University of Florida, Gainesville, FL (2008)
21. Goleman, D., Boyatzis, R., McKee, A.: Primal Leadership: Realizing the Importance of Emotional Intelligence. Harvard Business School Press, Brighton (2002)
22. Takayama, N.: EQ how to train your heart (Japanese). Toyo Keizai Inc. (2016)

Facial Expression Recognition for Children: Can Existing Methods Tuned for Adults Be Adopted for Children?

Zhi Zheng[1(✉)], Xingliang Li[2], Jaclyn Barnes[2], Chung-Hyuk Park[3], and Myounghoon Jeon[4]

[1] University of Wisconsin-Milwaukee, Milwaukee, WI 53211, USA
zheng36@uwm.edu
[2] Michigan Technological University, Houghton, MI 49931, USA
{xli17, jaclynb}@mtu.edu
[3] George Washington University, Washington, DC 20052, USA
chpark@gwu.edu
[4] Virginia Polytechnic Institute, Blacksburg, VA 24061, USA
myounghoonjeon@vt.edu

Abstract. Child facial expression recognition plays an important role in child-machine interactions. Recognition methods that were tuned for adults have been used for children in many studies without evaluating the applicability of these methods on children. This paper investigates this problem using a Support Vector Machine classification-based recognition algorithm, which is one of the most widely applied methods. We examined: (1) the difference in facial expressions between children and adults and (2) whether the classifiers trained on one group work for the other. Results show that the classifiers trained on child data were more accurate when tested on child data than adult data and the classifiers trained by adult data were more accurate when tested on adult data than child data. When the training and testing data were from the same group, the classifiers generally performed better for adults than children. Implications and future works are discussed with the results.

Keywords: Facial expression recognition · Differences between children and adults · Classification

1 Introduction

In many child-machine interactions, such as robotic companions for preschoolers [1] and adaptive tutoring through systems that respond to the student's emotional and cognitive state [2], the facial expression of the children is one of the most important interaction cues that need to be sensed [3].

Facial expression recognition is mostly used to indicate individuals' emotions, and the recognition is usually done using classification (among different emotions) algorithms, where datasets containing face images correspond with different emotions are used to train classifiers that can distinguish one or more emotions from others. These aspects have been thoroughly discussed in review articles [4–6]. Currently, most facial

M. Kurosu (Ed.): HCII 2019, LNCS 11567, pp. 201–211, 2019.
https://doi.org/10.1007/978-3-030-22643-5_16

expression recognition programs are trained using datasets collected from adults, due to the high accessibility of adult databases and the long history of designs for adults. Regarding applications for children, many works used recognition methods tuned for adults directly on children [7–9], while few of them conducted careful comparisons between adult and children [2] or trained child specific models [10]. However, since the facial morphology of children is different from that of adults [11], the recognition methods trained for adults may not work equally for children. To solve this problem, in the present work, we conducted a case study that carefully investigated whether a facial recognition algorithm works similarly for adults and children, and most importantly, whether models tuned for adults can be applied on children directly. To the best of our knowledge, this work is the first study exploring these questions specifically.

Therefore, ***the first contribution*** of this work falls on the investigation on the differences between children and adult when making facial expressions that corresponding with different emotions. We applied a Support Vector Machine (SVM) classification-based facial expression recognition algorithm, which is one of the most widely applied recognition methods [4, 6, 12], to evaluate how the same algorithm works for different groups. This algorithm was trained using both adult data and child data. Thus, ***the second contribution*** of this work includes the evaluation on: (1) whether the algorithm performs similarly for children as for adults and (2) whether classifiers trained by adult data can be used to classify child data, and vice versa. Finally, implications of this work and what needs to be done in the future are discussed.

2 Emotion Classification

2.1 Datasets

In this work, we focus on facial expressions that show neutral and six basic emotions including, anger, disgust, fear, happiness, sadness, and surprise. These six categories are considered prototypic expressions of emotions that have been focused by existing research [13, 14].

Data for this research are collected from public accessible databases that have been widely applied in research on facial expression. For adults, we collected frontal face images from three databases. Images of neutral, disgust, surprise and happiness are collected from the Multi-PIE database [15]. Images of anger, fear, and sadness came from the Extended Cohn-Kanade Dataset (CK+) [16] and Ohio Compound Facial Expressions of Emotion Database [13]. For children, very few datasets are available for public access. Here, we used the Child Affective Facial Expression (CAFE) set [17, 18], which contains frontal face images of 2- to 8-year-old children (M = 5.3 years; R = 2.7–8.7 years). This dataset contains facial expressions of all the seven emotions.

2.2 Feature Extraction

Geometric feature is one of the main effective features for facial expression recognitions [4, 5, 12, 19]. In this study, we applied this method and used the displacements of face landmarks to compose the feature vector as input of the SVM classification algorithm. We applied the constrained local neural fields method [20] embedded in the Openface system [21] for facial landmark detection. Sixty-eight landmarks that contour the eyebrows, eyes, nose, lips, and the chin line of a face (see Fig. 1) can be detected with reasonable accuracy using this method. The images that could not be properly detected by Openface were not used in this study. The numbers of images (i.e., data) of each emotion for both groups are listed in Table 1.

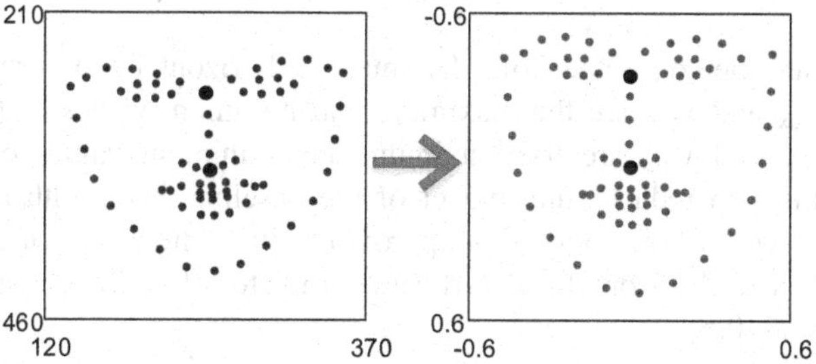

Fig. 1. Illustration of data normalization

When making the same facial expression, the landmark distribution of different person is different, due to the individual's unique facial structure (i.e., the positions of eyebrows, eyes, nose, and mouth), shape (e.g., some participants' faces are longer than the others), and size. In addition, even though all the images in the datasets show frontal faces, we can still observe slight head tilts on some images. Normalization is a common technique to solve such problems. Therefore, before feature extraction, we normalized the landmark coordinates on each face to reduce the impact of the aforementioned factors on classification. The normalization applied in this study includes three steps as follows and is illustrated in Fig. 1. Figure 1 shows the case for a real sample in the database. On the left image, the axes show the landmarks' position (number of pixels) on the original image, while the right image shows the landmarks of the same face after normalization.

Step 1: To eliminate the head tilts, faces are rotated to make the nose line (the connection between the upper and lower black dots in Fig. 1) completely vertical.
Step 2: The nose bottom (the lower black dot) is set as the origin, (0, 0), of the landmarks' coordinate frame, and the coordinates of all the other landmarks were shifted accordingly. Therefore, the landmarks' displacements in different expressions are all with respect to the same point so that the displacements only represent the change of geometric distribution and shape of eyes, nose, mouth and chin line, but not the position of the face on the image. Intuitively, the nose bottom of a face does not move in different facial expressions.
Step 3: Normalize the coordinates of landmarks using the following equations:

$$x' = x/(x_{\max} - x_{\min}), \tag{1}$$

Table 1. Number of images used in each emotion category.

	Anger	Disgust	Fear	Happiness	Neutral	Sadness	Surprise
Adults	268	224	246	312	329	228	160
Children	104	132	96	127	128	76	57

$$y' = y/(y_{max} - y_{min}) \qquad . \tag{2}$$

where x and y are the coordinates of a landmark in horizontal and vertical directions after Step 2, x_{max} and x_{min} are the maximum and minimum values of the horizontal coordinates, y_{max} and y_{min} are the maximum and minimum values of the vertical coordinates. This step reduces the impact of the baseline face width and length on classification. Since the nose bottom is approximately in the center of a face, Step 3 makes the landmarks' horizontal and vertical coordinates of all faces distribute around the range of [−0.5, 0.5].

The feature vector of each face consists of the normalized horizontal and vertical displacements of the 68 landmarks, i.e., $(x'_1, \ldots, x'_{68}, y'_1, \ldots, y'_{68})$.

2.3 Geometric Differences Between Children's and Adults' Faces

Before analyzing classification, it is helpful to observe the average faces of different emotions, which intuitively illustrate the differences among emotions. Figure 2 lists the average faces of children and adults. For each emotion, the average faces of children and adults are plotted in red and black, respectively. The landmarks of each eyebrow, each eye, bridge of the nose, contour below the nose, lips and chin line are linked with straight lines to facilitate visualization. We can see that none of the emotion has the two average faces exactly coincide with each other. Children made larger mouth movements than adults when showing anger, disgust, fear, and surprise. The positions of eyes and eyebrows of children are higher than those of adults when showing disgust, happiness, and neutral. The eyebrows of children are lower in anger, and the eyes of children are lower in fear. In addition, the chin line of children looks narrower than adults in most of these emotions.

As the feature vectors for classification are the displacements of landmarks from the bottom of the nose, we can expect different classification results for adults and children.

2.4 Training Classifiers

In this work, we applied the SVM classifier, which has been widely used for facial expression classification [4–6, 19, 22, 23]. Note that the aim of this study is not designing a new algorithm that is superior than existing methods, but applying a method that has been thoroughly studied to demonstrate the difference between adults and children as well as whether we can use classifiers trained by one group to classify data in another group. Base on research done by Jain et al. [23] and Suk et al. [22], we applied the linear kernel in the SVM classification. This kernel function has been

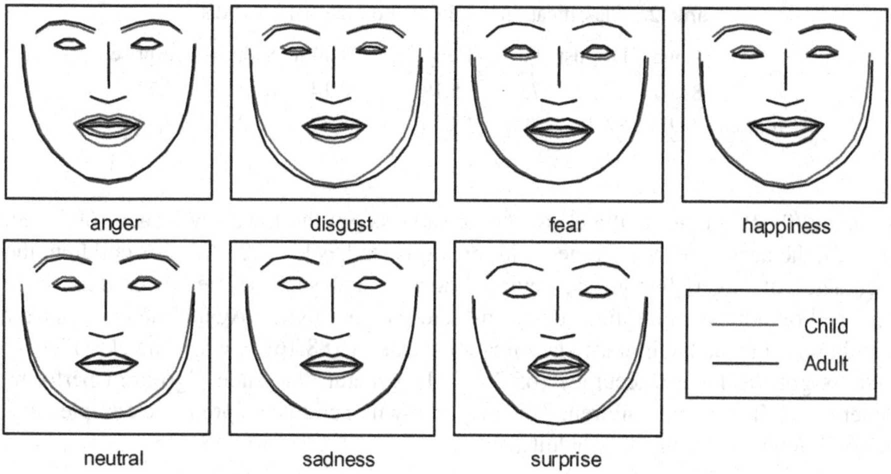

Fig. 2. Average faces of children and adults when making different facial expressions

shown to be flexible and suitable for applications that deal with data collected from people who were not in the training datasets.

For each emotion, a binary classifier was trained. The positive data are the ones in this emotion category (as discussed in datasets and feature extraction sections), and the negative data are randomly selected from the other six categories, which are called negative emotions. For example, if the classifier is trained for anger, then anger is the positive emotion. Disgust, fear, happiness, neutral, sadness, and surprise are the negative emotions. The number of samples randomly selected in each negative motion is rounded to the nearest integer of $N_j N_i / N_{sum}$, where N_j is number of positive samples, N_i is the number of samples in negative emotion i, and N_{sum} indicates the total number of samples in all the negative emotions. Therefore, the size of the negative data that were randomly selected equals to the size of the positive data approximately. In other words, the negative and positive data are balanced. The binary classifier was trained by 70% of the balanced data and was tested in two ways, one by the rest 30% of the balanced data and the other by all the data, as discussed in the following section.

2.5 Testing Classifiers

Classifiers' Performance on the Balanced Testing Data

The same algorithm was used for both adults and children. Table 2 lists the classification accuracy of each trained classifier on the 30% of the balanced testing data (i.e., the numbers of positive and negative samples are approximately equal as discussed in the last section) for each emotion. This is a conventional method that evaluates the classifiers' performance on data that were not included in training [24–26].

We can see that the classification method works for all the emotions but on different levels. There are both similarities and differences between the results of adults and children. For adults, the classifier for happiness achieved the highest classification

Table 2. Classification results (%) on the balanced data.

	Anger	Disgust	Fear	Happiness	Neutral	Sadness	Surprise
Adults	84.47	75.37	75.51	95.19	76.14	69.34	92.71
Children	79.03	82.28	79.31	88.16	68.42	65.22	79.41

accuracy (95.19%), while the classifier for sadness got the lowest accuracy (69.34%). Overall, the accuracies are aligned with previous studies [19, 22, 23]. For children, the accuracies of anger, happiness, neutral, sadness, and surprise are lower than those achieved on adults, while those of disgust and fear are higher. Again, the classifier for happiness achieved the highest classification accuracy (88.16%), while the classifier for sadness got the lowest accuracy (65.22%). In general, the same algorithm performs better on adults than on children. This may imply that child data are more complex and more difficult to classify than adult data.

Classifiers' Performance on all Data

This section evaluates: (1) how well a trained classifier recognizes data of its own category and (2) how much data from other emotions are misclassified as belonging to the classifier's category. Four tests that cover all the possibilities were conducted as follows:

Test 1 (adults vs. adults): the classifiers trained using adult data were used to classify adult data;
Test 2 (children vs. children): the classifiers trained using child data were used to classify child data;
Test 3 (adults vs. children): the classifiers trained using adult data were used to classify child data;
Test 4 (children vs. adults): the classifiers trained using child data were used to classify adult data;

Tests 1 and 2 evaluate the classifiers' performance within the adults and children groups, respectively. Tests 3 and 4 show whether the classifiers trained by one group can be used on another group. Test 3 demonstrates the common cases in recent research where classifiers trained on adults are used for children. Test 4 presents the only possibility beyond test 1 to 3, for the completeness of this study.

Tables 3, 4, 5 and 6 show the results of tests 1 to 4, respectively. For each number on a table, its label (on the left side) in the same row shows which emotion the classifier was trained for, and the label (on the upper side) in the same column indicates the emotion data this classifier was applied to classify. For example, in Table 3, the first row shows the results of the classifier trained for recognizing adults' anger. This anger classifier was tested using all the 268 anger data (see Table 1) and 86.94% of them were successfully recognized. In the same row, we can see that 23.21%, 10.57%, 1.6%, 3.95%, 42.54%, and 0% of all the adults' disgust, fear, happiness, neutral, sadness, and surprise data were recognized as anger, respectively. In other words, these numbers show the percentage of data that were wrongly classified as anger.

Ideally, the classifier trained for an emotion should recognize data in the same category and reject data in other categories. Therefore, Tables 3, 4, 5 and 6 are

Table 3. Results of test 1 (%, adults vs. adults).

		Testing data (Adult)						
		Anger	*Disgust*	*Fear*	*Happiness*	*Neutral*	*Sadness*	*Surprise*
Classifier (Adult)	*Anger*	**86.94**	23.21	10.57	1.60	3.95	42.54	0
	Disgust	29.48	**80.80**	0.81	18.91	11.85	10.96	3.75
	Fear	17.16	1.79	**78.86**	15.71	12.16	47.37	16.88
	Happiness	1.49	17.86	9.76	**95.51**	8.51	1.75	3.13
	Neutral	13.43	16.07	43.09	10.90	**75.68**	33.33	28.13
	Sadness	64.93	15.63	36.59	2.88	10.33	**67.10**	22.5
	Surprise	0.37	6.25	11.38	13.78	9.42	2.19	**93.13**

Table 4. Results of test 2 (%, children vs. children).

		Testing data (Children)						
		Anger	*Disgust*	*Fear*	*Happiness*	*Neutral*	*Sadness*	*Surprise*
Classifier (Children)	*Anger*	**82.69**	54.55	15.63	51.18	5.47	19.74	15.79
	Disgust	60.58	**71.97**	13.54	0.83	14.06	28.95	24.56
	Fear	13.46	21.21	**77.08**	32.28	39.84	28.95	66.67
	Happiness	31.73	12.88	20.83	**85.83**	4.69	6.58	15.79
	Neutral	10.58	18.94	29.17	15.75	**77.34**	38.16	43.86
	Sadness	30.77	42.42	42.71	22.05	35.94	**68.42**	64.91
	Surprise	5.77	15.15	38.54	4.72	34.38	13.16	**94.74**

analogous to (but not) confusion matrixes, where high numbers in the diagonal grids (shadowed) and low numbers in other grids indicate good classification results. To simplify description, here we name the numbers in the diagonal grids as recognition rates and the numbers in other grids as misclassification rates. Bold numbers in the tables represent the largest values in the same row. Form Fig. 2, we can see that the figures of some emotions look similar, such as adults' neutral and sadness, children's disgust and sadness, as well as adult's neutral and children's neutral. Therefore, the classification did NOT constrain how many emotion categories a sample can be classified into, to test all the possibilities.

For test 1 (adults vs. adults), Table 3 shows that each emotion's classifier recognized most data in its own category, which is expected. 86.94%, 80.80%, 78.86%, 95.51%, 75.68%, 67.10%, and 93.10% data in the anger, disgust, fear, happiness, neutral, sadness, and surprise categories are successfully recognized by their own classifiers, respectively. Misclassification rates range from 0% (0% surprise data were

Table 5. Results of test 3 (%, adults vs. children).

		Testing data (Children)						
		Anger	*Disgust*	*Fear*	*Happiness*	*Neutral*	*Sadness*	*Surprise*
Classifier (Adult)	*Anger*	51.92	**64.39**	14.58	14.96	57.81	57.89	5.26
	Disgust	29.81	**50.00**	1.04	7.87	1.56	11.84	1.75
	Fear	28.85	21.97	**77.08**	66.93	46.88	36.84	70.18
	Happiness	44.23	26.52	26.04	**84.25**	4.69	5.26	7.02
	Neutral	1.92	12.12	48.96	25.98	**52.34**	34.21	35.09
	Sadness	25.96	40.91	26.04	7.09	38.28	**46.05**	28.07
	Surprise	19.23	19.70	47.92	12.60	18.75	9.21	**91.23**

Table 6. Results of test 4 (%, children vs. adults).

		Testing data (Adult)						
		Anger	*Disgust*	*Fear*	*Happiness*	*Neutral*	*Sadness*	*Surprise*
Classifier (Children)	*Anger*	22.76	18.30	13.82	**53.53**	2.13	3.07	10.00
	Disgust	57.46	**87.95**	9.76	63.14	37.39	22.81	63.13
	Fear	4.10	29.46	50.41	48.40	54.71	21.93	**63.13**
	Happiness	0.75	9.38	6.10	**54.49**	3.34	0.44	2.50
	Neutral	14.93	0.89	21.14	0	6.38	**26.75**	6.25
	Sadness	**82.84**	33.48	60.16	20.19	23.71	71.93	38.75
	Surprise	1.12	0.45	6.50	0.32	2.13	1.75	**47.50**

recognized as anger) to 64.93% (64.93% anger data were recognized as sadness). While in most cases the misclassification rates are low or moderate, anger was misclassified as sadness with relatively high rates (>50%).

From test 2 (Table 4), we can see that 82.69%, 71.97%, 77.08%, 85.83%, 77.34%, 68.42%, and 94.74% data in the anger, disgust, fear, happiness, neutral, sadness, and surprise categories are successfully recognized by the corresponding classifiers, respectively. Misclassification rates range from 0.83% to 66.67%. In most cases the misclassification rates are low or moderate. Meanwhile, anger was misclassified as disgust, disgust was misclassified as anger, happiness was misclassified as anger, and surprise was misclassified as fear with relatively higher rates.

From test 3 (Table 5), we can see that although most of the child data can still be recognized by the adults' classifier trained for the same emotion, the recognition rates are much lower compared with test 1 and test 2. Only fear (77.08%), happiness (84.25%), and surprise (91.23%) were still recognized with high accuracies.

Misclassification rates range from 1.04% to 70.18%. While in most cases the misclassification rates are still moderate, disgust was misclassified as anger, happiness was misclassified as fear, neutral was misclassified as anger, sadness was misclassified as anger, and surprise was misclassified as fear with high rates. These results show that adults' classifiers perform worse for children than adults.

In Test 4 (Table 6), only disgust (87.95%) and sadness (71.93%) can be recognized with relatively high accuracies. Meanwhile, the misclassification rates are high in general. Anger are misclassified as disgust and sadness, fear was misclassified as sadness, happiness was misclassified as anger and disgust, neutral was misclassified as fear, and surprise was misclassified as disgust and fear with high rates. These results show children's classifiers do not work well for adults in most cases.

In summary, the classifiers trained using data from a group perform well on the testing data from the same group. The classifiers trained for adults classify child emotions with lower recognition accuracies and higher misclassification rates. This implies although adults' facial recognition classifiers may work for children in some applications, designing classifiers using child data may improve the performance of these applications. The classifiers trained using child data fail to recognize adult data for most emotions. Children's models are rarely applied for adults, and this case should be treated carefully.

3 Discussion and Conclusion

Careful and rigorous evaluations are critical in developing facial expression recognition applications for child-machine interactions. In this work, we studied whether facial expression recognition methods that were developed for adults can be applied on children, which has not been well investigated so far. We examined the differences between children and adults when making facial expressions and conducted a case study using a SVM classification-based facial expression recognition algorithm. The same algorithm was applied for both groups. Classifiers were separately trained by adult data and child data, and tested within and across groups. ***The most important results include: (1) the algorithm achieved higher accuracies when it is trained using adult data and tested by adult data than when it is trained using child data and tested by child data; (2) classifiers that are trained using adult data perform less accurately on child testing data than adult testing data; and (3) classifiers that are trained using child data perform poorly on adult testing data.***

The results presented in this paper are based on one exemplary algorithm and a moderate number of samples. As there are many algorithms and databases for facial expression recognition, more tests are necessary. In addition, compound emotions exist sometimes, which means a person may present multiple emotions at the same time, such as surprise combined with fear and anger combined with sadness, and thus more complex classifiers need to be designed and tested accordingly.

Nevertheless, this work shows that applying a facial recognition method that is tuned for adults directly on children may cause problems. Therefore, it is necessary to evaluate a method using child data thoroughly before application. Ideally, developing child-specific models is a better option. In this line, developing more child databases to support the design for children is critical, as there are less resources available for children compared with adults.

Acknowledgments. This project was supported by the National Institutes of Health under grant No.1 R01 HD082914-01 and the Institute of Computing and Cybersystems at Michigan Technological University.

References

1. Degiorgi, M., et al.: Puffy—an inflatable robotic companion for pre-schoolers. In: The 26th IEEE International Symposium on Robot and Human Interactive Communication (RO-MAN), pp. 35–41. IEEE (2017)
2. Littlewort, G.C., Bartlett, M.S., Salamanca, L.P., Reilly, J.: Automated measurement of children's facial expressions during problem solving tasks. In: 2011 IEEE International Conference on Automatic Face and Gesture Recognition and Workshops (FG 2011), pp. 30–35. IEEE (2011)
3. Yun, W. H., Kim, D., Park, C., Kim, J.: Facial expression recognition for detecting children's likes and dislikes. In: The 9th International Conference on Ubiquitous Robots and Ambient Intelligence (URAI), pp. 537–538. IEEE (2012)
4. Fasel, B., Luettin, J.: Automatic facial expression analysis: a survey. Pattern Recogn. **36**(1), 259–275 (2003)
5. Zhao, W., Chellappa, R., Phillips, P.J., Rosenfeld, A.: Face recognition: a literature survey. ACM comput. Surv. (CSUR) **35**(4), 399–458 (2003)
6. Zeng, Z., Pantic, M., Roisman, G.I., Huang, T.S.: A survey of affect recognition methods: audio, visual, and spontaneous expressions. IEEE Trans. Pattern Anal. Mach. Intell. **31**(1), 39–58 (2009)
7. Harrold, N., Tan, C.T., Rosser, D., Leong, T.W.: CopyMe: a portable real-time feedback expression recognition game for children. In: Proceedings of the Extended Abstracts of the 32nd Annual ACM Conference on Human Factors in Computing Systems, pp. 1195–1200. ACM (2014)
8. Obrist, M., Igelsböck, J., Beck, E., Moser, C., Riegler, S., Tscheligi, M.: Now you need to laugh!: investigating fun in games with children. In: Proceedings of the International Conference on Advances in Computer Enterntainment Technology, pp. 81–88. ACM (2009)
9. Jain, S., Tamersoy, B., Zhang, Y., Aggarwal, J.K., Orvalho, V.: An interactive game for teaching facial expressions to children with autism spectrum disorders. In: The 5th International Symposium on Communications Control and Signal Processing (ISCCSP), pp. 1–4. IEEE (2012)
10. Leite, I., Castellano, G., Pereira, A., Martinho, C., Paiva, A.: Modelling empathic behaviour in a robotic game companion for children: an ethnographic study in real-world settings. In: Proceedings of the Seventh Annual ACM/IEEE International Conference on Human-Robot Interaction, pp. 367–374. ACM (2012)
11. Fields, H.W., Proffit, W.R., Nixon, W., Phillips, C., Stanek, E.: Facial pattern differences in long-faced children and adults. Am. J. Orthodont. **85**(3), 217–223 (1984)
12. Tian, Y., Kanade, T., Cohn, J.F.: Facial expression recognition. In: Handbook of Face Recognition, pp. 487–519. Springer, London (2011)
13. Du, S., Tao, Y., Martinez, A.M.: Compound facial expressions of emotion. Proc. Natl. Acad. Sci. **111**(15), E1454–E1462 (2014)

14. Cohn, J.F., Zlochower, A.J., Lien, J., Kanade, T.: Automated face analysis by feature point tracking has high concurrent validity with manual FACS coding. Psychophysiology **36**(1), 35–43 (1999)
15. Gross, R., Matthews, I., Cohn, J., Kanade, T., Baker, S.: Multi-pie. Image Vis. Comput. **28** (5), 807–813 (2010)
16. Lucey, P., Cohn, J.F., Kanade, T., Saragih, J., Ambadar, Z., Matthews, I.: The extended cohn-kanade dataset (CK+): a complete dataset for action unit and emotion-specified expression. In: 2010 IEEE Computer Society Conference on Computer Vision and Pattern Recognition Workshops (CVPRW), pp. 94–101. IEEE (2010)
17. LoBue, V., Thrasher, C.: The child affective facial expression (CAFE) set: validity and reliability from untrained adults. Front. Psychol. **5**, 1532 (2015)
18. LoBue, V., Thrasher, C.: The child affective facial expression (CAFÉ) set. Databrary (2014)
19. Kotsia, I., Pitas, I.: Facial expression recognition in image sequences using geometric deformation features and support vector machines. IEEE Trans. Image Process. **16**(1), 172–187 (2007)
20. Baltrusaitis, T., Robinson, P., Morency, L.-P.: Constrained local neural fields for robust facial landmark detection in the wild. In: Proceedings of the IEEE International Conference on Computer Vision Workshops, pp. 354–361 (2013)
21. Baltrušaitis, T., Robinson, P., Morency, L.-P.: OpenFace: an open source facial behavior analysis toolkit. In: 2016 IEEE Winter Conference on Applications of Computer Vision (WACV), pp. 1–10. IEEE (2016)
22. Suk, M., Prabhakaran, B.: Real-time mobile facial expression recognition system-a case study. In: Proceedings of the IEEE Conference on Computer Vision and Pattern Recognition Workshops, pp. 132–137 (2014)
23. Jain, V., Aggarwal, P., Kumar, T., Taneja, V.: Emotion detection from facial expression using support vector machine. Int. J. Comput. Appl. **167**(8), 25–28 (2017)
24. Godbole, S., Sarawagi, S.: Discriminative methods for multi-labeled classification. In: Dai, H., Srikant, R., Zhang, C. (eds.) PAKDD 2004. LNCS (LNAI), vol. 3056, pp. 22–30. Springer, Heidelberg (2004). https://doi.org/10.1007/978-3-540-24775-3_5
25. Weinberger, K.Q., Saul, L.K.: Distance metric learning for large margin nearest neighbor classification. J. Mach. Learn. Res. **10**(Feb), 207–244 (2009)
26. Akay, M.F.: Support vector machines combined with feature selection for breast cancer diagnosis. Expert Syst. Appl. **36**(2), 3240–3247 (2009)

Eye-Gaze, Gesture and Motion-Based Interaction

An Application of Somatosensory Interaction for 3D Virtual Experiments

Si Chen[1(✉)], Chenqing Wang[2], and Jianping Huang[3]

[1] Fuzhou University of International Studies and Trade, Fuzhou 350202, Fujian, China
731553247@qq.com

[2] Fuzhou Institute of Technology, Fuzhou 350506, Fujian, China

[3] Graduate School of Creative Industry Design, National Taiwan University of Arts, New Taipei City, Taiwan

Abstract. Interaction based on natural limb movements is the so-called Somatosensory Interaction, which has multi-faceted and continuous features at the information transmission level. The dependence of the keyboard will be significantly weakened, and the learning subject will pay more attention to the corresponding learning tasks in this interactive mode, so that the learning comfort can be significantly improved in the three-dimensional virtual system. Situated in such technical context, more and more teachers and students are actively applying virtual experiment technology in their teaching and learning environment. human-computer interaction mode can directly affect the user's sense of sensation and immersion. In recent years, with the continuous development of digital media technology, the use of Somatosensory Interaction design and three-dimensional virtual experiment has practical improved the teaching effect and promoted transformation of teaching interaction mode. It not only saves a lot of animation problems involved in traditional virtual experiments, but also save costs significantly, and provide relevant innovation direction for the in-depth application of virtual experimental technology.

Keywords: Somatosensory Interaction design · 3D virtual experiment · Kinect

1 Preface

With the rapid development of information technology, the original two-dimensional plane has developed into a three-dimensional system, and further developed to virtual and augmented reality. In this technical context, more and more teachers and students are actively applying virtual experiment technology. The use of multimedia simulation and virtual reality (VR) and other related technologies to conduct analog simulation of traditional experiments through computer is the so-called virtual experiment. The technology of interacting with computer by means of a mouse, a remote control and other devices and through user gestures, body language, etc., is a so-called somatosensory interaction. Taking Kinect as an example, Kinect can capture and track user gestures and actions in real time. The main recognition modules of Kinect are infrared cameras, cameras, microphone arrays and color cameras [1]. Kinect emits

M. Kurosu (Ed.): HCII 2019, LNCS 11567, pp. 215–224, 2019.
https://doi.org/10.1007/978-3-030-22643-5_17

infrared rays by an infrared emitter. After these infrared rays are reflected by the human body, a random reflection spots are captured and analyzed by the infrared camera, and then the depth image of the human body and the object in the visible region can be created, thus achieving the recognition of the human movement. The color camera can capture the object in the visible region and correct the human body movement. The function of the microphone array is to collect the sound, and provide noise filtering and sound source localization functions to realize language recognition. At present, the role of virtual experiment is becoming increasingly significant in the process of teaching and research. However, the application of this technology has certain limitations in some aspects. For example, the truthfulness of the simulation is insufficient, the interactive operation is not user-friendly, and the virtual experimental materials are not readily available, and so on. This will inevitably make it difficult for teachers and students to immerse themselves in the experiment, and the related effects will be greatly reduced. However, with the combination of somatosensory interaction and the virtual experiment, and through the somatosensory interaction mode, the students can directly use their hands to manipulate the corresponding virtual instrument, which can improve the truthfulness of the virtual experiment, and also exercise students' flexibility in operation.

2 Principle of Somatosensory Interaction Design

The basis of somatosensory interaction is the real and natural interaction, while the core is the natural human-computer interaction technology. In this interactive mode, a high-simulation learning environment can be constructed by means of a three-dimensional virtual learning system, so that the corresponding situations can be easily created in traditional classroom, and thus the learning subject can learn through the problem situation. Generally, the main principles adopted in the design of the interactive technology are: first, consistency. That is, the design style of the relevant somatosensory interaction should be consistent, and the knowledge and concepts conveyed need to be consistent. In the specific design process, the designer should ensure the internal unity, so that the operator can understand thoroughly in the use of interaction mode, and the efficiency of learning the related interaction method will be significantly improved. Second, immediate feedback. This principle requires the device to feedback the relevant information involved in each step of the operation in real time, so that the user can quickly understand the results of his or her action, thereby the user interaction can be standardized and the learning effect can be improved. And the more complete the feedback information, the better the effect than the local feedback. Third, active reflections and guidance to migration of knowledge and techniques. Somatosensory interaction mainly covers three levels: reflection, action and senses. In the specific design process, it is necessary to pay attention to the psychological experience of the reflective level, strengthen the real problem situation design, guide the operator to self-think and explore, and thus realizing the migration of knowledge and skills.

3 Motion Capture Algorithm Design and Route Development Based on Somatosensory Interaction

3.1 The Working Principle of Kinect

Under this somatosensory interaction technology, the camera plays an important role in capturing the operator's limb movements, which can then be identified, stored, and processed using a computer program. The Kinect camera also captures the operator's gestures and then uses the background program to convert these gestures into manipulation commands. The somatosensory interaction technology discriminates and captures the operator's gestures, mainly using the camera and the Prime Sense system [2]. The captured dynamic video is then compared to the already stored mannequin. If the two human models are identical, the corresponding gestures can be created into a skeleton model that is consistent with them. With the support of this model, it is possible to identify up to 25 key parts of the human body. At present, based on this, the identification technology of human sitting and standing posture is further introduced [3] With the depth of field and RGB camera, the Kinect somatosensory interaction technology can project the recognized 3D object onto the corresponding display screen.

3.2 Human Motion Capture Algorithm

The motion capture implementation mechanism involved in Kinect somatosensory interaction technology is as follows: First, the infrared emitter will emit corresponding infrared light when the object is encountered, and then the light will be captured by the infrared camera integrated in the somatosensory interaction device, so that it can form the corresponding mathematical model. See Fig. 1 below for details. The purpose of constructing this model is to obtain the corresponding Zo, which is to calculate the distance between the object and the infrared emitter.

In Fig. 1, the focus of the infrared camera and the infrared emitter correspond to point C and point L, respectively, and perpendicular to the image depth direction, corresponding to the Z axis, and the farther apart from the camera, the corresponding Z axis value is larger. The X and Z axes are perpendicular to each other, which represent the baseline of the infrared camera and emitter, and their baseline distance is represented by b. It is assumed that there is an O reference plane in the specific space, and the distance between it and the infrared camera in the Z- axis is represented by Z_0, and that the object surface in the space is represented by K, and its distance from the infrared camera in the Z- axis is represented by Z_k. The distance from point C to the Z-axis is denoted by f, which corresponds to the focal length of the corresponding camera. For the same infrared light, it is reflected at points K and O, respectively, and projected on the depth image based on the point C, and then the measurement gap d can be obtained. When combined with principle of similar triangles, the following equation can be obtained:

$$\frac{D}{\mathrm{b}} = \frac{\mathrm{Z_o} - \mathrm{Z_k}}{Z_o} \tag{1}$$

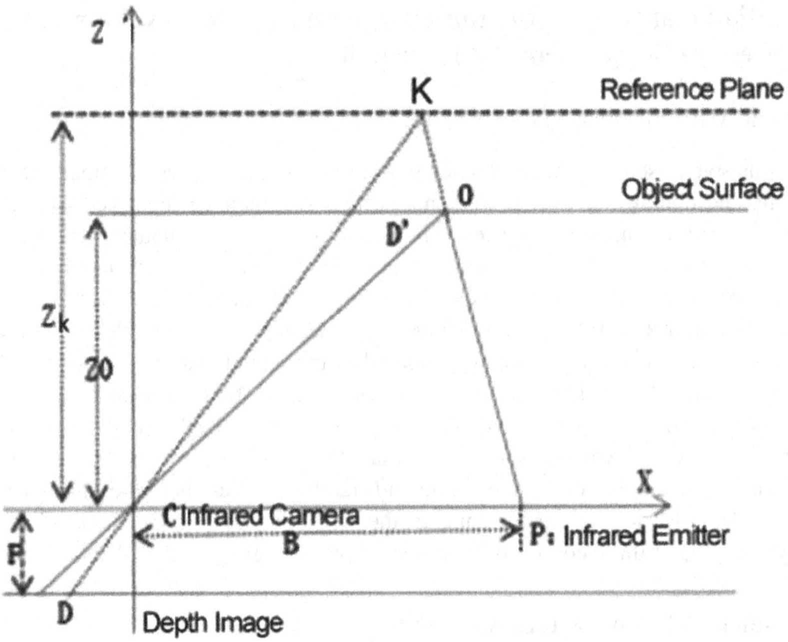

Fig. 1. Calculation of the spatial depth Z_0 based on the infrared spot

$$\frac{d}{f} = \frac{D}{Z_k} \tag{2}$$

Combining the two equations, the D parameter can be eliminated, so that:

$$\text{Zk} = \frac{Z_o}{1 + \frac{Z_o}{fb}\text{d}} \tag{3}$$

With this formula, the Zk mathematical model corresponding to the point K can be calculated, and the relevant parameters such as d, f, and Zo and b need to be corrected with the depth information. For the two parameters f and b, the relevant hardware can be provided. In the specific practice, based on the different spatial environment, the selection of O reference plane is often dynamic. Therefore, the Zo value is usually determined in conjunction with the correction. The d value is closely related to the Zo value. Therefore, it is necessary to perform linear regression of the above 3 formula, that is, linearly normalize the d parameter, and indicate this parameter by $md' + n$, wherein m and n are the parameters corresponding to the normalization process, and substitute it into the above formula (3), the following formula (4) can be obtained:

$$Zk^{-1} = (\frac{m}{fb})d' + (Z_o^{-1} + \frac{n}{fb}) \tag{4}$$

This formula shows the linear relationship between Zk and Zo. By means of a large number of samples and obtaining the corresponding regression coefficients by least square method, the spatial depth value of point k can be obtained.

The algorithm for recognizing human motion has been continuously optimized with the development of camera technology, which provides an important technical basis for the application of somatosensory interaction technology. Motion recognition can be completely converted into shape recognition, which obviously provides a new way of thinking. The core algorithm of this technology is mainly: in the following formula, the pixel point in the image is represented by x, and its eigenvalue f_θ is [4]:

$$f_\theta(I,x) = d_I(x + \frac{u}{d_I(x)}) - d_I(x + \frac{v}{dI(x)}) \tag{5}$$

Then use $d_I(x)$ to indicate the depth value of the pixel. When the user enters the image, the coordinates of his own attributes can be obtained by combining the position of user and the distance from the camera. Then you can start normalization by multiplying $d_I(x)$ and the offset values of the above coordinates to obtain two different depth values, which are then subtracted to obtain the eigenvalues f_θ. If this pixel belongs to the background image, then the value of $d_I(x)$ will be a maximum positive value, so that the shape of the human motion can be separated from the background image. After acquiring the silhouette of the human body, the motion represented by the silhouette can be recognized. Currently, the algorithm database has integrated up to 500,000 frames of human silhouette images, covering driving, dancing, walking, running and many other actions. Based on the database information, the corresponding classification device can be trained and the human skeleton can be further subdivided into 31 types of labels. Then, according to the Decision Tree algorithm, the x pixel points in the I image are assigned to the corresponding bone labels. The formula (6) indicates the decision forest consisting of T decision trees. In this decision tree, different leaf nodes exist f_θ and τ. The former corresponds to the eigenvalue and the latter to the threshold. And these decision trees can, based on $P_t(C|I, x)$, express associated pixel as the probability of belonging to a certain bone tag C.

$$P(C|I,x) = \frac{1}{T}\sum_{t=1}^{T} P(C|I,x) \tag{6}$$

In the following formula, the weight value of the pixel on the tag C is represented by w_{ic}. The pixel depth value $d_I(x)$ can ensure the stability of the corresponding weight value depth. Using the above formula, the correlation between the pixel and the tag C can be obtained:

$$w_{ic} = P(C|I,x) \cdot d_I(x)^2 \tag{7}$$

When many such pixels on the human silhouette are clearly identified and have their own structure tag, the mean shift algorithm can be used to integrate the pixels of different tags. When the weight value is greater than a certain threshold of the pixel point, it will be divided above the joint point to which this label is mapped. The total value of these weight values is the predicted value of the joint point confidence. When the joint point confidence exceeds a certain predicted value, the algorithm result can be included in the corresponding human silhouette image. With a large number of joint points, a complete human skeleton can be derived so as to identify the human movement.

3.3 Somatosensory Interactive Development Technology Route

Open natural interaction, the so-called OpenNI, the essence of it is openness. The application of this technology in the field of somatosensory interaction has been relatively mature and has been used widely. The development of this system is also the development of the overall architecture with this platform.

The following figure shows the interaction framework, where the top layer is the application layer, which corresponds to the application; the bottom layer is the hardware layer, represented by Hardware, which covers depth, color image cameras, and sound input; between the application layer and the hardware layer is the corresponding interface layer. The OpenNI, between applications and the hardware devices, provides the corresponding interfaces and middleware [5] (Fig. 2).

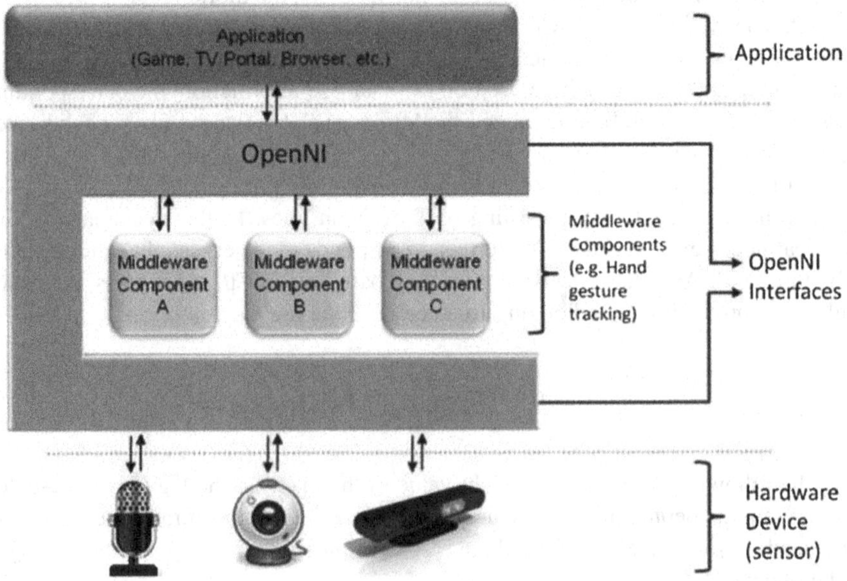

Fig. 2. OpenNI development framework

OpenNI defines the human skeleton frame, and each joint has two parameters, direction and position. Currently, in OpenNI, a total of 24 joint points are defined. With the middleware NITE, the human body motion can be captured, and at most 15 joint points of them can be obtained [5], as shown in detail in Fig. 3 below.

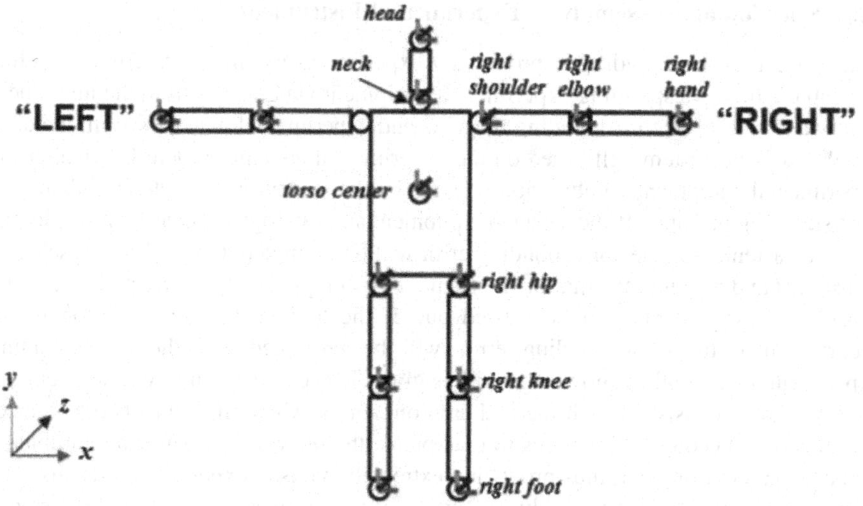

Fig. 3. Schematic diagram of joint points currently supported by OpenNI

In addition, the interactive technology also builds a category to serve the communication of software, which is called the production node category. To build an OpenNI framework, the role of production nodes is extremely important, that is, the development by means of OpenNI needs to apply production nodes. In addition, the technology defines other categories to make it more functional. These features are not necessary; developers can use them according to their own needs. Such categories are often referred to collectively as capability category. The technology uses OpenNI to realize the recognition of motions, and the core technology of it is the production node category, skeleton tracking and posture detection capability category.

4 Application of Somatosensory Interaction Design in 3D Virtual Experiment

4.1 Control of the Experimental Interface

The somatosensory interaction mode needs to be applied throughout the virtual experiment. Operators can use gestures to manipulate related windows and objects. For example, the selection and manipulation of menus, the choice of experiments, etc. At this point, the gesture can completely replace the operation of the mouse. In the Unity3D system, the gesture can replace the mouse for input by displaying the student's skeleton points recognized by Kinect and binding the coordinates x1, y1 and z1 of the mouse to the coordinates of the student's left hand or right hand (x2, y2, z2). For example, the algorithm of the abscissa: $x1 = x2 * a + b$, where b and a correspond to the position difference and the activity proportional coefficient of the arm relative to the screen area, respectively. In this way, the manipulation of the menu can be realized by means of gestures.

4.2 Selection and Assembly of Experimental Instruments

Students can conduct hydrogen production experiments in virtual experiments. They can capture the corresponding experimental equipment via gestures from the instrument library and select the corresponding reagents and experimental materials from the drug warehouse. The system will based on the experimental content to identify whether the experimental equipment combination selected by the student is accurate, and then give corresponding prompts. If the selected equipment and hydrogen preparation conditions are inconsistent, then the corresponding error will be prompted. Only when the selected instrument and reagent information are accurate, will it prompt the correct message and subsequent experiments will be carried out. If the logic judgment condition is not accurate, then the corresponding error will be prompted and the corresponding experimental preparation knowledge will be given. The corresponding virtual operating environment is consistent with the real environment in which the students are located. Students only need to use gestures to manipulate the relevant experimental equipment in the actual environment, thus producing extremely realistic experimental results. The animation interaction is detected by the vision of the distance between the bone nodes and devices and the collision between the object and the instrument. Students can use their hands to produce actions as performed in real experiments, complete the design of the relevant experimental principles, and add appropriate reagents, such as water and dilute sulfuric acid, into the corresponding containers, as shown in detail in Fig. 4 below.

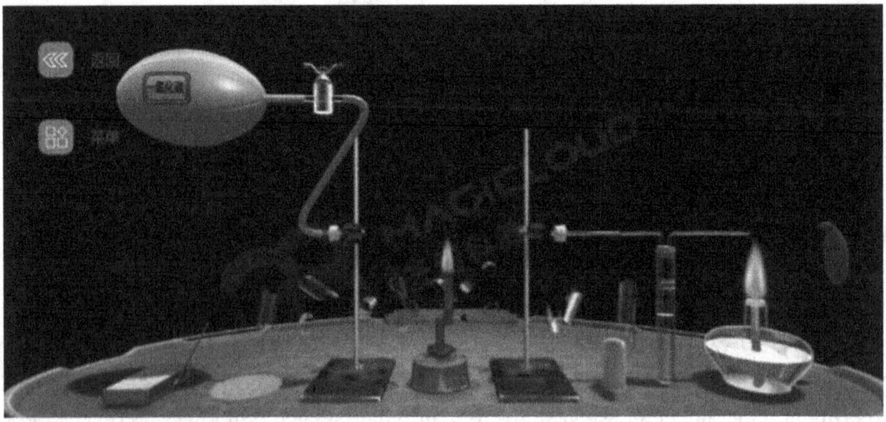

Fig. 4. Selection and assembly of experimental instruments

4.3 Operations in the Experimental Process

In the virtual experiment process, the instrument can be operated and corresponding experimental reagents can be added by means of gestures. When adding the corresponding reagents, it needs to be implemented as much as possible by animation. Using the arm bones, as well as the collision detection of the reagents and the calculation of the distance to stimulate the generation of related operation animations, and then the corresponding reagent weights are added according to the experimental requirements in order to complete the subsequent animation interactions, and display the corresponding experimental phenomena. For the demonstration of experimental animation, you can use the conditional statement to set up, so you can complete the virtual experiment of hydrogen production, as shown in detail in Fig. 5 below.

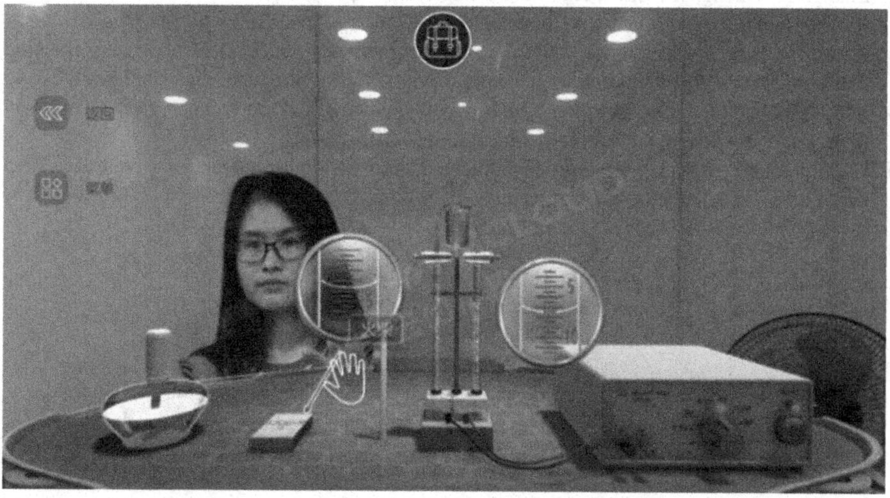

Fig. 5. Operations in the experimental process

4.4 Experimental Test

When the experiment is completed, the system will generate the corresponding experimental test results, and ask questions by taking into account of the experimental cautions, operational safety, experimental phenomena and equipment assembly based on experimental principles, while students can also use the virtual environment to answer questions by gestures. The system evaluates the results according to the students' answers and gives corresponding learning suggestions.

5 Conclusion

The implementation of virtual experiments using VR technology through the Kinect somatosensory technology allows students to perform experiments more realistically in a virtual environment. In this way, many sensory organs of students can be mobilized to participate in experiments and learning, so that it is better to help students improve their experimental ability. This technology can also save a lot of animation production problems involved in traditional virtual experiments, so it can greatly improve the efficiency of the Kinect-based virtual experiment, and save significant cost, providing corresponding direction of innovation on the in-depth application of virtual experimental technology.

References

1. Chen, G.: Virtual display system of process design based on somatosensory interaction technology. J. Xi'an Univ. Posts Telecommun. **21**(5), 76–79 (2016)
2. Zhang, Y., Cheng, X., Chen, H., et al.: Design and implementation of middleware based on Kinect somatosensory interactive development. Comput. Appl. Softw. **4**, 10–14 (2018)
3. Zhang, R., Liu, L., Zhang, G., et al.: Research on Kinect's method of accurately tracking multi-objectives in somatosensory interaction process. Mod. Manuf. Eng. **10**, 76–80 (2014)
4. Sun, B., Zhang, J., Cai, Y., et al.: Multiplayer online virtual experiment system based on Kinect somatosensory interaction. Comput. Sci. **43**(9), 284–288 (2016)
5. Gu, R., He, Y., Jin, L.: Design and implementation of intelligent teaching control system based on Kinect skeleton tracking technology. Comput. Appl. Softw. **30**(6), 276–280 (2013)

Using an Eye Tracker to Investigate the Effect of Sticker on LINE APP for Older Adults

Cheih-Ying Chen(✉)

Department of Product Innovation and Entrepreneurship,
National Taipei University of Business, Taipei City, Taiwan, R.O.C.
c.y.chen@ntub.edu.tw

Abstract. The aim of this study was to investigate the impact of the attractiveness or legibility of LINE stickers on the preferences and cognition of older adults. We conducted an eye tracking study with 10 senior participants. Participants were asked to compare and select two different LINE stickers in an eye tracker experiment. We examined (1) the preferences of two different LINE stickers, (2) the changes in older participation in cognition, and (3) the record of captured eye movement gaze and glance. The statistical results show a significant difference in the preferences of the two different LINE stickers. We are able to identify the unique behavior that older adults display in the user experience of LINE stickers.

Keywords: Older adults · Eye tracking · LINE stickers

1 Introduction

1.1 Older Adults and Communication App

Besides health issues, being alone, which causes the lack of the connection between society, is one of the problem of older adults. In the future, there would be more people in Taiwan become lonely and old due to their divorcement or spouse's death. Even those people could have children, however, these descendants usually unable or unwilling to live with their parents. One of the solutions is communication technology, which provides us more ways to keep in touch with others. According to the fact that these technologies improvement gives new forms of convenient communication methods that conquer far distance obstacles. On contrast, elder people most likely to use obsolete ways like chatting, telephone contact and letters. Thus, if old people can utilize smart phone properly, then they could communicate their relatives and community easily.

Due to physiological degradation, seniors have a hard time to learn how to operate each kinds of communication. Therefore, this study hopes to find out methods that old people acceptable and familiar with. By testing the user experience and eye tracking, to research how old people use instant messaging application stickers. The main goal is to make older adults use novel communication tools successfully, acquire the autonomy of controller's interface, interact with friends by using lively lovely stickers and connect to friends, family and social communities from instant messaging tools. Nevertheless, as

M. Kurosu (Ed.): HCII 2019, LNCS 11567, pp. 225–234, 2019.
https://doi.org/10.1007/978-3-030-22643-5_18

the elderly grows older, they gradually develop not only visual degradation, decline in learning ability and cognitive deterioration, but also, the negative effect of recognizing images, which affects their preference and application of stickers. Thence, this study explores the appealing factors and legibility of stickers for the elderly, and how to make instant messaging stickers become easy-to-use communication tools, also an aid for emotional interaction and social connections for elder people.

People from the elder generation have different lifestyles, the usages of technologies and the thoughts about virtual business from normal people. In 2016, Institute for Information Industry [1] implemented an older adult requirement investigation of the fourth generation of broadband cellular network technology. It points out that the proportion of elder people who have smartphones was 60.2%. Aside from that, the most used purpose of elder people using a smartphone is making a phone call. Moreover, social media applications such as Line Facebook are the most popular applications among seniors. LINE, which is a communication software used by around 60% of over 55 years old people, can advance interpersonal interaction. As for interactive video, more than half of elders usually interact with their children and grandchildren through video to get a closer bond. According to the investigation results of Institute for Information Industry, more and more people view "retirement" as a new start of life. High-tech products have gradually enriched the retirement life of the elders, so they can fully use their time to realize their dreams. They hope that they could keep up with the trend of technology in leisure activities, interaction or learning aspects. The survey also found that the elders' reliance on technology, especially smartphones, has gradually increased. In addition to the social media LINE, which is well-known for interpersonal communication and has high popularity among the elder people, other fields of elders' life like the most important health, long-distance interaction with relatives and friends, or drama, music, etc., are all expected to be improved or being improved through science and technology. By realizing their expectation of daily life, making seniors' life is not only brilliant, but also very elegant [2].

1.2 LINE and Stickers

The stickers of instant messaging software are one of the elements that drive the development of personalized mobile Apps. Nowadays, most of the instant messaging applications provide stickers function for users to send their messages, which means their messages no longer just presentation of words. The sending of sticker messages will enhance the cognition of both users and will motivate users to communicate through instant messaging software. At present, these stickers could not only be just simple images but also combined with sound effects or highlight, which make the symbolization more various and diverse. There are different categories of stickers on the market now, and this study will discuss two types of stickers, cartoon-stickers, and photograph-stickers:

(1) Cartoon-stickers:
The cartoon-sticker is a continuation of the traditional texture, mainly presents anthropomorphic style virtual images which designed by illustrators, so that it can vividly express the user's mood and message intonation, and text-assisted description,

thereby achieving the authenticity of the message. It is also the communication message symbol that is most popular among Taiwanese people in the LINE instant messaging application.

(2) Photograph-stickers:
The photograph-sticker is a type that has also been popular in LINE instant messaging application in recent years. The main forms are landscapes, people, animals, movie screens, etc., and the images or texts are added to the photos to display the messages meanings.

2 Related Studies

2.1 User Experience

Garrett [3] reported that the application of user experience on the website is more important than other products. User experience determines a product's impression and customer return. Kraft [4] points out that the user experience emphasizes the user's feeling of using a product. Therefore, it is necessary to avoid certain specific groups of users such as the older adults, the less educated, or the disabled, who refuse to use the product due to the bad user experience.

The picture can not only catch people's attention and transmit massive information but also go a step further in forming picture superiority effect. If the picture is texted, it can even convey the idea and achieve communication. Knutson's research on the sense of beauty and attraction of the website confirms that the presentation of the image is related to visual attraction [5]. Haig & Whitfield's site, presented by pictures, is more aesthetically pleasing than the site without image [6]. Djamasbi et al. pointed out that the application of the main image on the website's homepage can promote user's attractiveness, if the user is highly attracted to the image, the website will also receive a positive response from the user [7].

2.2 Eye Tracking Experiment

Eye tracking is a technique for a user to record and track the movement of his/her eye when a user views a stimulate object. The eyes are moving several times per second, containing micro-movements spanning sometimes only a few pixels. The eye tracker is a piece of equipment for collecting data, its purpose is to quantify the distribution of the user's visual attention and the behavior of the conversion, thereby analyzing the effects of different interface design versions and different user groups to adjust the design direction. Eye trackers include subjects such as Gaze Plot, Heat Map, and cluster, which are commonly used in eye tracker research. Eye tracking research can be operated whether it is a website, a picture, or a layout of a brick-and-mortar store, but the most important issue to understand is human behavior. Instead of relying on a machine for all the answers, the subject's ideas should be understood by reviewing the interview, with multi-quality and quantitative data for interactive verification.

Fixation is the maintaining of the visual gaze on a single location; Saccade is a quick, simultaneous movement of both eyes between patterns or other elements.

The most commonly used indicators of eye movement as research are fixation time, fixation frequency, saccade distance, and saccade path [8]. At first, the tracking record of eye movement behavior started for the purpose of studying the reading process, including total fixation time and fixation position from the reader's reading, which reflects the reader's reading psychological process [9].

3 Proposed Method

3.1 Research Purposes

This study explored the attractiveness of two type stickers, cartoon-stickers and photograph-stickers, for older adults and conducted research through eye tracking experiments to see if the graphics and text of the two type stickers affect the eye movements of elder users.

3.2 Participants

The participants in this study selected 10 Taiwanese elderly who were over 65 years old. Each older participant is familiar with LINE and has experience in sending LINE stickers to others. The vision of participants is able to see the screen graphic stimulus, and has regular Interpersonal communication.

3.3 Tools

The Pro X2 snaps into place on the laptop, providing a compact, highly-portable solution. The system enables us to perform cost-efficient studies in participants' homes or in an office – wherever your participants are. The Pro X2 shows exactly where people are looking and, with a sampling rate of 30 or 60 Hz, it is designed for fixation-based research. Participants can be tracked while moving their head freely positioned at a natural distance from the screen. This creates a distraction-free test environment, promoting natural human behavior.

3.4 Design of Stimulus

The research applied questionnaires and eye movement experiments, two of the most common Line stickers (Fig. 1) were designed and tested by older people's comparisons in this research.

3.5 Study Protocols and Data Collection Procedures

At the beginning of the study session, researchers briefed participants on the study protocol and the purpose of the study. Participants were given ample time to review the consent form and ask questions regarding the consent form, experiment procedures, or the research.

Participants were given pre-study and post-experiment questionnaires. A pre-study questionnaire was given at the beginning of the session to determine demographic

	The meaning of the stickers		
two types of stickers	Thank you	Happy Birthday	Good Moring
Photograph-stickers			
	1A	2A	3A
Cartoon-sticker			
	1B	2B	3B

Fig. 1. Two types of stickers (stimulus)

information and pretest. After eye tracking experiment, participants were asked to fill out a post-experiment questionnaire.

3.6 The Progress of the Experiment (4 Steps)

1. Eye tracker calibration and validation: At the beginning of the experiment, the elder respondents need to adjust their sitting position and height. Because elderly people could have presbyopia or cataract eye diseases, therefore, it is necessary to adjust the eye tracker and eye calibration and validation in more detail to ensure that there will be no problem when respondents gaze at the computer screen and the computer could capture eye movement as data.
2. Experiment description and guidance: Older people are unfamiliar with eye track experiments, so it is required to explain the experiment procedure more carefully, and let them simulate the test, familiar and can focus on the computer before testing with the simulated picture (stimulus).
3. Eye tracking test: Two types of textures (stimulus) appear on the computer screen at one time and the senior respondents watch two types of textures. The eye tracker also records the gaze and glance of the subject, allowing the elderly to be free and unconstrained while they watch two LINE stickers and compare them.
4. Questionnaire survey: After the test, the elder respondents compare the attractiveness of the two types of stickers and the legibility of the text, then answer the questionnaire.

According to Just and Carpenter [9], eye tracking represents an objective measure of a person's cognitive history. Compared with the post-test questionnaire to understand the subjects' opinion, eye tracking provides immediate records and objective test results for further analysis and study. Thereupon, this study can use both eye tracking record and post-test questionnaire at the same time, also set the AOI (where of interest) of the experimental picture to two different stickers for the following eye tracking data recording and analyzing. Afterward, the elders' cognition and attractiveness of the Line sticker can be comprehended by mutual examination between subjective and objective data.

4 Finding

Eye tracking experiments show that older people spend most of their time on pictures, and less than 10% of visual gaze time is on the text. In the process, 10 older participants were asked to test eye tracker. After the experiment was completed, these older participants were asked to recall important information about their comparison and selection process.

Interestingly, data shows that text was observed only for one-fifth of the time. Among them, some older participants watch the text in less than a second. Nonetheless, during the interview, more than half of the test older participants said that the Chinese text on the LINE stickers was "extremely" or "very" important. The cognitive psychology of the older participant thinks that the text is very important, but the text is easy to read and understand. The eyes of the older participants, however, tell us that the older participant is more attracted to the pictures, and the visual gaze will stay longer on them.

Eye tracking highlights the visual orbit of older people looking for certain information and the type of information that is most attractive when making comparative decisions. Since visual attention largely reflects our cognitive processes, valuable information about the motivations and influencing factors of cognitive behavior can be obtained. Eye tracking research can be used to study the sensitivity of some older participant to picture and text, the degree of their influence on the pictures clearly shows subjects' gaze stay longer on their preferences. Eye tracking can also improve the performance of texture messaging by capturing behavioral data that older participant interacts with textures, understanding how older participant are accustomed to searching for texture information.

4.1 Results of the Eye Tracking Experiment

Gaze plots, heat maps, and clusters are an easy way to visualize how people look at the interface, which key elements they look at, and what areas attract the most attention. This data visualization method can communicate the important aspects of visual behavior clearly and powerfully.

Gaze plots (Fig. 2) show the location, order, and time older adults looking at the stimulus. So the primary function of the gaze plot is to reveal the stickers of looking or where older adults look and when older adults look there. Older adults usually view people's photos, character images, main texts, and secondary texts in order. Time spent looking; most commonly expressed as fixation duration, and is shown by the diameter of the fixation circles. The longer the older adults look, the larger the circle. The circles of children's faces on the photograph-stickers are larger than the circles of character's faces on the cartoon-stickers, and then areas, children's faces, attract the most attention for older adults.

The meaning of the stickers	Gaze plots (10 older participants)
Thank you	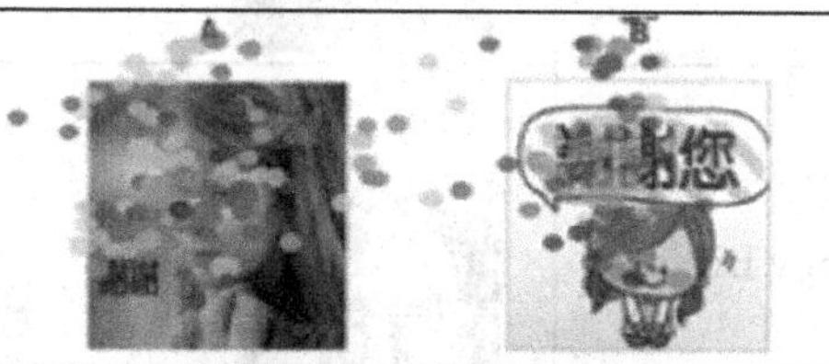
Happy Birthday	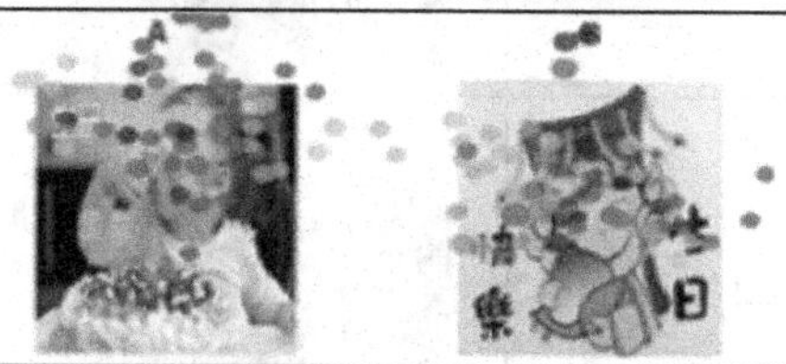
Good Morning	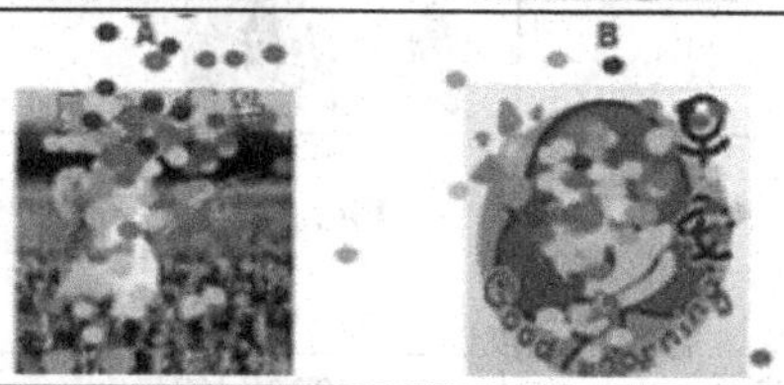

Fig. 2. Gaze plots

Heat maps (Fig. 3) are a visualization that can effectively reveal the focus of visual attention for 10 older participants at a time. Heat maps show how looking is distributed over the stimulus, and older participants look at the picture of stickers, which key elements they look at, and what areas attract the most attention. The colors on the heat maps indicate the spectrum of fixation intensity with red representing the longest fixation duration and green the shortest fixation duration. Areas not covered by colors were not viewed. Older adults usually pay attention to real children' photos for a long time, while cute characters have less gaze time, so they can discover the photos of the children and attract the attention of the older participants. Older adults had longer fixations on images of children or characters, particularly their faces.

Older participants spend less time watching word/text in the same picture than real people or cartoon characters. Older participants usually pay attention to characters/pattern for a long time, and the word/text is easy to read and understand for a short time. The stimuli of the pattern (Fig. 4) are also more attractive than the text.

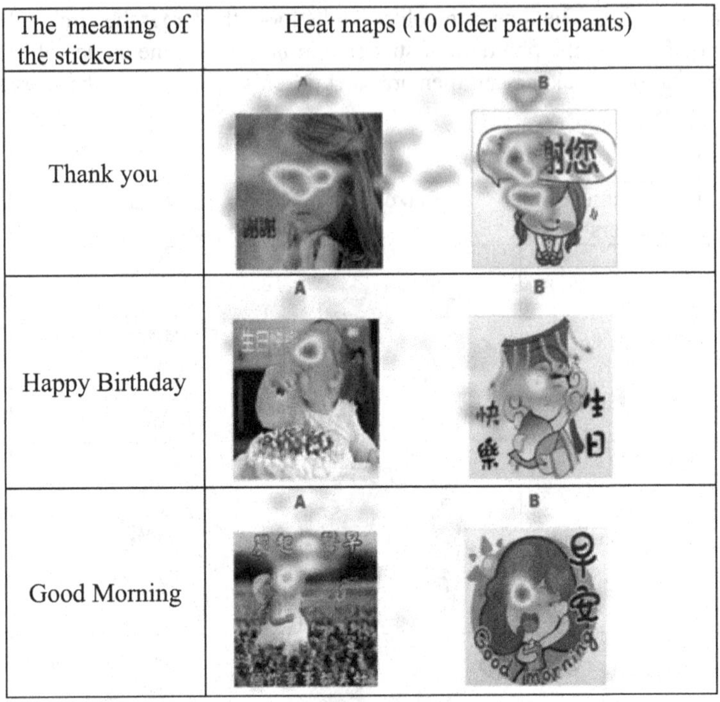
The meaning of the stickers
Heat maps (10 older participants)
Thank you
Happy Birthday
Good Morning
A
B

Fig. 3. Heat maps

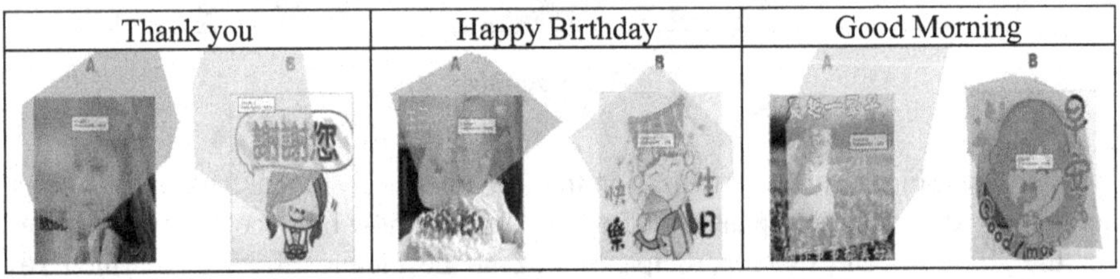
Thank you
Happy Birthday
Good Morning
A
B

Fig. 4. Clusters with 10 older participants

4.2 Results of the Questionnaire

The aim of this study was to investigate the impact of the attractiveness of LINE stickers on the preferences of older adults. After the test, the elder respondents compare the attractiveness of the two types of stickers and then answer the questionnaire. This survey, which was administered after viewing each sticker, asked participants to rate the visual appeal of the sticker on a 5 point Likert scale (1 = Not At All Appealing; 5 = Very Appealing).

Older adults had better attractiveness on images of children than characters. A recent study shows that images of people are particularly effective in drawing our attention [10]. The results also showed that images of photograph-stickers attracted more attention. These results show that suggests images of photograph-stickers, more than Cartoon-sticker, are effective in attracting older adults' attention.

The analytic results in Table 1 showed that 1A, 2A, 3A are more attractive to older adults than 1B, 2B, 3B; in other words, photograph-stickers are more attractive to older adults than cartoon-stickers. It can be deduced that photograph-stickers create more joyous and heart-warming for older adults.

Table 1. Results of the attractiveness of LINE stickers with chi-squared test

LINE stickers		M	SD	P-value	
Thank you-sticker	1A	4.2	0.79	0.051390835	$0.05 < p^* < 0.1$
	1B	2.5	0.53		
Happy birthday-sticker	2A	4.4	0.52	0.000273529	$p^{**} < 0.05$
	2B	2.7	1.16		
Good morning-sticker	3A	4.0	0.82	0.009997613	$p^{**} < 0.05$
	3B	2.1	0.57		

4.3 Conclusion

This study mainly evaluated two issues: First, we find older adults like photograph-stickers, and they also think the photograph-stickers design with some sense of attractive design. Older adults' attitudes towards photograph-stickers design are positively related to their experience, especially the image of cute children. Second, we find the children's faces on the photograph-stickers are more attractive than the character's faces on the cartoon-stickers, and then children's faces, attract the most attention for older adults.

Acknowledgments. The author would like to thank Yun-Cheng Lee and Yun-Shu Lee helping this experiment for data Collection.

References

1. Institute for Information Industry (III) (2016). http://www.iii.org.tw/Press/NewsDtl.aspx?nsp_sqno=1886&fm_sqno=14
2. Institute for Information Industry (III) (2015). http://www.iii.org.tw/Press/NewsDtl.aspx?nsp_sqno=1603&fm_sqno=14
3. Garrett, J.J.: The Elements of User Experience: User-Centered Design for the Web and Beyond, 2nd edn. New Riders, Indianapolis (2011)
4. Kraft, C.: User Experience Innovation: User Centered Design That Works. Apress, New York (2012)
5. Knutson, J.F.: The Effect of the User Interface Design on Adoption of New Technology. Dissertation Abstracts International: Section B: The Sciences and Engineering, vol. 59, no. 3-B, p. 1399 (1998)
6. Haig, A., Whitfield, T.W.A.: Predicting the aesthetic performance of web sites: what attracts people?. ACM (2001)

7. Djamasbi, S., Siegel, M., Tullis, T.: Can fixation on main images predict visual appeal of homepages?. In: HICSS, pp. 371–375 (2014)
8. Duchowski, A.: Eye Tracking Methodology: Theory and Practice, 2nd edn. Springer Science & Business Media, London (2007). https://doi.org/10.1007/978-1-84628-609-4
9. Just, M.A., Carpenter, P.A.: Eye fixations and cognitive processes. Cogn. Psychol. **8**(4), 441–480 (1976)
10. Djamasbi, S., Siegel, M., Tullis, T.: Faces and viewing behavior: an exploratory investigation. AIS Trans. Hum.-Comput. Interact. **4**(3), 190–211 (2012)

Development of Privacy Protection Monitoring Systems Using Skeleton Models and Their Evaluation on the Viewpoint of FUBEN-EKI

Hisashi Handa[1,2](✉), Shingo Ando[3], Tatsuhiro Ichikawa[1], Riku Yamamoto[1], and Miyu Otani[1]

[1] Faculty of Informatics, Kindai University, Higashi-Osaka 577–8502, Japan
handa@info.kindai.ac.jp
[2] Research Institute for Science and Technology, Kindai University, Higashi-Osaka, Japan
[3] Graduate School of Science and Engineering Research, Kindai University, Higashi-Osaka, Japan
https://www.info.kindai.ac.jp/handa

Abstract. In this paper, we propose a monitoring system using the pose estimation, which takes account of the protection of privacy. In order to cover a wider area, Region Correspondence Mechanism which associates skeletons of multiple cameras is introduced. In this paper, we examined the accuracy of association of the Region Correspondence Mechanism and verified the confidentiality of the skeleton model. Furthermore, qualitative consideration was made on the benefit of the inconvenience of the proposed system, i.e., FUBEN-EKI. We concluded that there are FUBEN-EKI such as "Enhance awareness", "Understand systems", and "Feel at ease".

Keywords: Pose estimation · Region Correspondence Mechanism · Privacy protected monitoring system · FUBEN-EKI

1 Introduction

In this study, skeleton models are constituted using pose estimation [1,2], and a monitoring system is constituted by depicting a skeleton in a background image. By constructing a monitoring system with a skeleton model, it is possible to infer the existence of a person and the action taken by the person, but it becomes difficult to identify a person. Hence, this monitoring system could be a privacy-protected system. Such a privacy protection monitoring system is useful in the fields of medical care, nursing care, and education. In these fields, monitors are often located in places that are seen by third parties. Since the developed privacy protection surveillance system is implemented using machine learning,

M. Kurosu (Ed.): HCII 2019, LNCS 11567, pp. 235–246, 2019.
https://doi.org/10.1007/978-3-030-22643-5_19

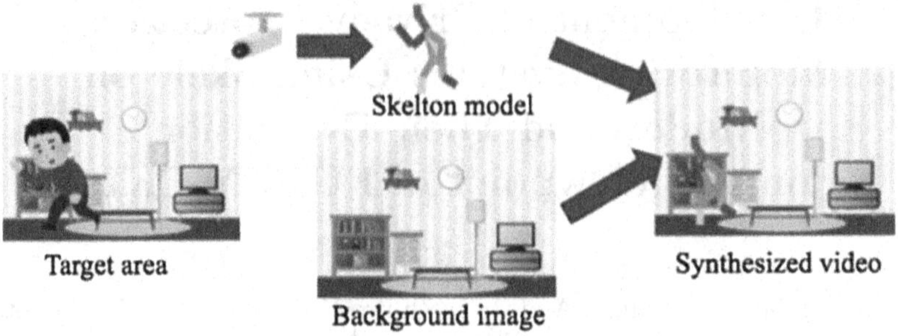

Fig. 1. A depiction of the developed systems

it is possible to display not only the skeleton model but also the full name of the worker in the text. From the viewpoint of FUBENE-EKI, this paper evaluates the effectiveness of the display of this monitoring system using skeleton models rather than text.

Figure 1 shows a depiction of the developed system: First, the network camera will take a video file the target area. Recorded videos are saved in the NAS. Moreover, the Pose estimation algorithms by Cao et al. is used to generate the skeleton models by applying to each frame in the recorded video file. Then, the system draws the generated skeleton model in the background image. The background image is taken in advance so that it is different with the one in live-streaming video. By sequentially displaying the synthesized images, the system can create a moving image in which persons are replaced with skeleton models.

2 Pose Estimation

This section introduces Cao's Pose Estimation Algorithms [2]. The method can detect poses in the image with CNN. There are two major approaches for the pose estimation: bottom-up and top-down approaches. In the bottom-up approach of pose estimation using images, it is difficult to join estimated human's parts [3]. On the other hand, in the top-down approach, there is a problem that the calculation cost increased in proportion to the number of people. Cao's Pose Estimation Algorithm is a bottom-up method that addresses these problems and can perform pose estimation with one inference. It enables high-speed processing in real time. Even when multiple people are shown in the input image, it can detect feature points of each person.

First, using the input image, Predict Part Confidence Maps are generated by detecting the position of the part of humans. Next, the Part Affinity Fields are generated, which includes the position information of each part and the skeleton direction information, encoding the degree of relevance between the parts. Based on Part Confidence Maps and Part Affinity Fields, a skeleton model is yielded by bipartite matching of plausible combinations of parts. Part Confidence Maps is a network that predicts position information of each part of the body in a heat

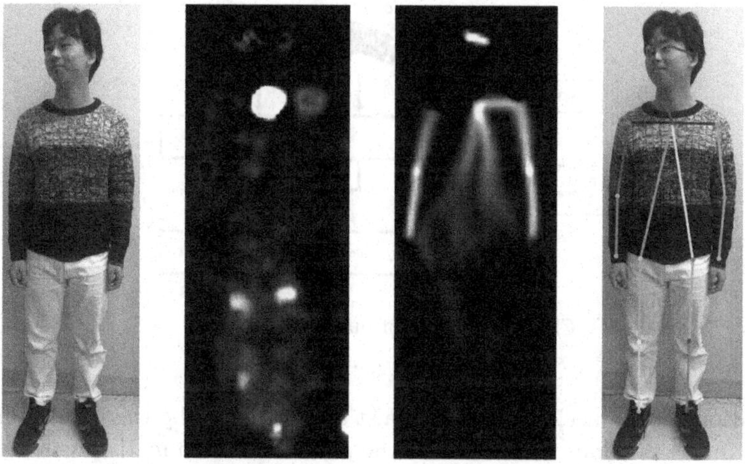

(a) Input image (b) Part Confidence Map (c) PAFs (d) Pose-esimated image

Fig. 2. An example of pose estimation

map. The Part Confidence Maps are generated for each part of a human. Part Affinity Fields represents the possibility of connecting each part. It is a network that predicts a vector map.

The error functions of Part Affinity Field and Part Confidence Maps are as follows:

$$f_{\mathbf{S}}^{t} = \sum_{j=1}^{J} \sum_{\mathbf{p}} \mathbf{W}(\mathbf{p}) \cdot \| \mathbf{S}_j^t(\mathbf{p}) - \mathbf{S}_j^*(\mathbf{p}) \|_2^2, \tag{1}$$

$$f_{\mathbf{L}}^{t} = \sum_{c=1}^{C} \sum_{\mathbf{p}} \mathbf{W}(\mathbf{p}) \cdot \| \mathbf{L}_c^t(\mathbf{p}) - \mathbf{L}_c^*(\mathbf{p}) \|_2^2, \tag{2}$$

Figure 2(b) represents Confidence Map: It shows coordinates with a high probability of neck positions. Figure 2(c) indicates Part Affinity Fields: It estimates the connections of each part. As a consequence of the pose estimation, 18 parts are detected as shown in Fig. 2(d).

3 Matching Persons Between Two Cameras

A diagram of a naive matching method of this research is shown in Fig. 3: For the cameras A and B, the skeleton information of the motion picture is obtained by the pose estimation model. We associate the positions of persons in the two video files with the region correspondence method.

3.1 Region Correspondence Between Two Cameras

As shown in Fig. 3, a model for region correspondence will be described. First, we prepare video files by two cameras with a set time. Then, for each video file,

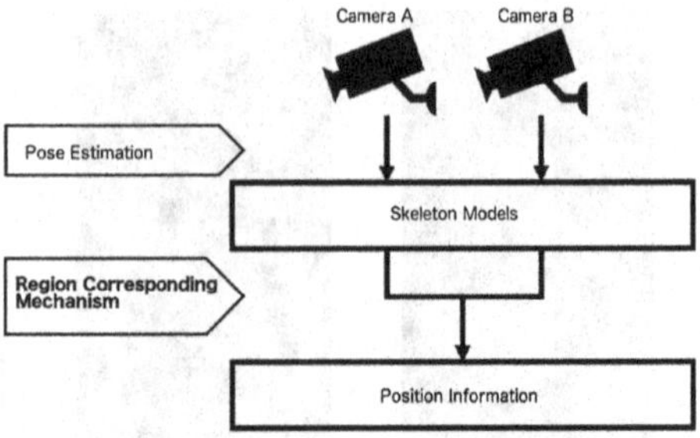

Fig. 3. Diagram of matching method

the positions of the neck, chest, and waist are estimated by the pose estimation method in the previous section. Since the pose estimation method can yield the position of the neck, the left-waist, and the right-waist, the following calculations to estimate the position of the chest and waist is adopted: The position of the waist was the coordinates of the middle point between the left-waist, and the right-waist. The coordinates of the point internally dividing the line segment connecting the neck and the waist into 1: 2 was used as the chest position. The reason for using the neck, chest, and waist is that the upper body is less incorrect estimation in pose estimation than the lower body.

The frame rate of pose estimation is 30 fps. The position of the neck, chest, and waist is given by the position in 19201080 pixels. The position on the pixel is sampled every 20 pixels. Each 2020 region is numbered sequentially from the upper left area of the image. As a consequence of the sampling, the position of the neck, chest, and waist is given by the region numbers.

The model is composed of maps of (the region number, the list of the number of another camera). For each camera, such a model is constituted. A list is used because there are multiple estimated regions in another camera for a certain region. Such multiple correspondences are caused by the height of a person and the time shift between cameras.

Region correspondence between two Cameras shown in Fig. 3 is described. As in Fig. 4, we employ video files that start at the same time, where two people are walking freely. First, the coordinates of the neck of two persons are estimated and converted into the region numbers. Figure 5 shows the region numbers of the two necks at the same time in cameras A and B.

As shown in Fig. 6(a), two persons are assumed to be person 1 and person 2. The list of region number of person 1 in the camera B is searched using the model of the camera A. Suppose that there are two persons in camera B: person I and person II. Let $d_{1,\mathrm{I}}$ be the distance between the region number of person I and the list of the region numbers of person 1 in the camera B, where distance metrics is used as the Manhattan distance in the region numbers in video image. As in Fig. 6(b), the correspondence of persons 1, 2 to persons I,

Fig. 4. An example of the video file: two persons walk around.

	Camera A				Camera B			
time	ID_a1	a1_id	ID_a2	a2_id	ID_b1	b1_id	ID_b2	b2_id
1	no1	a2084	no2	a2065	no1	b1386	no2	b1208

Fig. 5. Region numbers of two necks at the same time

II is made by comparison of the sum of distances: $d_{1,\mathrm{I}} + d_{2,\mathrm{II}} + d_{\mathrm{I},1} + d_{\mathrm{II},2}$ and $d_{1,\mathrm{II}} + d_{2,\mathrm{I}} + d_{\mathrm{II},1} + d_{\mathrm{I},2}$. If the sum $d_{1,\mathrm{I}} + d_{2,\mathrm{II}} + d_{\mathrm{I},1} + d_{\mathrm{II},2}$ is smaller than another sum, the method detects that person 1 in camera A corresponds the person I in camera B. Otherwise, the method detects that person 1 in camera A corresponds the person II in camera B.

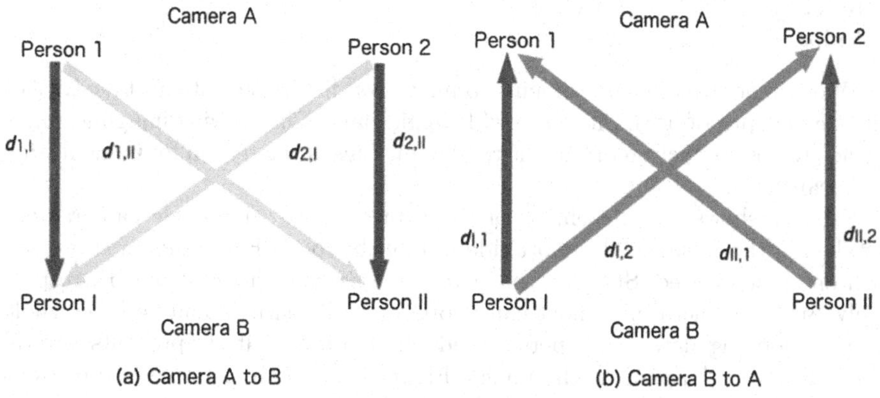

Fig. 6. Region correspondence

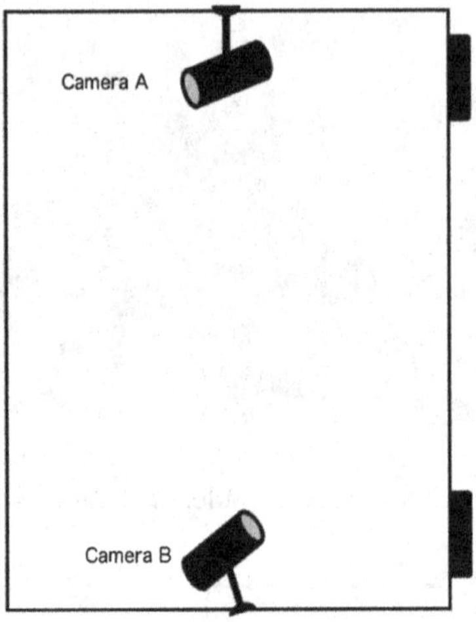

Fig. 7. Placement of cameras

4 Experiments

4.1 Experiental Configuration

We used a wide-angle network camera for the experiment. The specifications are summarized as follows:

- A fisheye lens that can display a wide range of about 180° horizontally
- Resolution: 1920 1080 pixel
- 15 fps

Wide-angle cameras are difficult to make low distortion but can take images with deep depth of field. Since the wide-angle camera has a wide imaging range, it leads to cost reduction of the entire system. This is the reason for using a wide angle camera.

Figure 7 shows the placement of the camera. Two wide-angle cameras are installed in the center of the short side wall of the room. Each camera stands up with one pole erected. Suppose that two cameras be cameras A and B, respectively. Such a camera placement can photograph the entire room and the whole body by looking down at a person and photographing it. It prevents several people from overlapping on the image. Figure 8 shows an example of images at the same time from each camera.

Table 1 shows three models used in this paper. Columns "A to B" and "B to A" stand for the number of the region numbers in the maps for each camera. Bigger models are expected to have better performance. Model 1 is a model generated using the region numbers at the neck and waist positions. Model 2 and 3 are of the region numbers at the neck and chest, and at the neck, chest, and waist, respectively.

Table 1. Models

Model	A to B	B to A
1: neck, and waist	1412	1532
2: neck, and chest	1235	1447
3: neck, chest, and waist	1479	1700

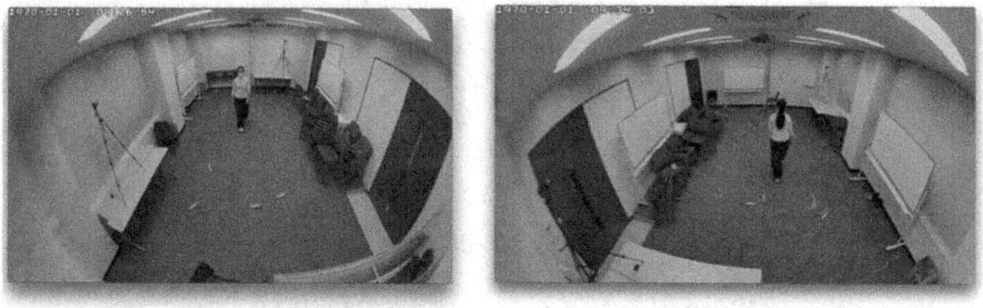

(a) snapshot of Camera A (b) snapshot of Camera B

Fig. 8. An example of images at the same time from each camera

4.2 Experiments on Person Tracking

The accuracy of estimating the data of 1171 necks for validation, according to the model of Table 1 is shown in the Table 2. The accuracy means that the ratio of correct detection over the number of the region numbers in the model, where the correct detection means that two persons in each camera are correctly estimated. The number of regional numbers indicates the number of times the region number of the validation set is found in the region number in the model.

We consider the relationship between the number of region numbers in Table 1 in Sect. 3.1 and the part used for the model. Model 2 using the neck and chest data has fewer searchable region numbers than model 1 using neck and waist data: 177 in "A to B", and 398 in "B to A." As a result, the number of estimable regions is 56 less.

Table 2. Accuracy of each model

Model	Accuracy	No. region numbers	No. uncorresponding region numbers
1: neck, and waist	98.96%	1158	13
2: neck, and chest	99.31%	1165	6
3: neck, chest, and waist	99.74%	1171	0

However, four of the 12 misdirected estimates in Model 1 are correctly estimated in Model 2, The number of incorrect estimates has been reduced to 8, and

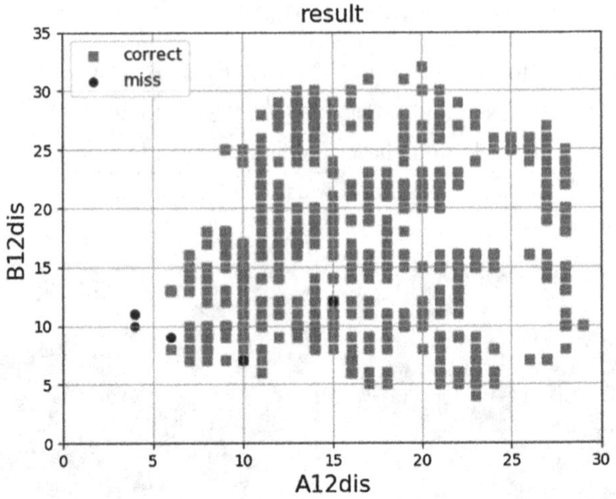

Fig. 9. Scater plots of distances (Model 1)

the accuracy is increased by 0.35 points. Also, in Model 3 including the neck, waist, and chest, it is possible to estimate all the validation data. From these results, it can be seen that even if the number of the region numbers increases and the number that can be estimated increases, the estimation accuracy is not necessarily improved. This is attributed to the difference in height between the parts used to generate the model, i.e. the waist, and the parts used in the validation, i.e., the neck. This is because, in one camera, in the case where the waist of a person is located in a certain region number, and in the case where the neck is positioned in that region number, the region number in the other camera is totally different.

To find out the cause of the incorrect estimations, Fig. 9 shows the experimental results for 900 frames of a verification movie of each model. The green square "correct" indicates that the correspondence of the persons to the walking of the two persons in the video frame is successful. On the other hand, the red circle "miss" denotes incorrect correspondence. The x-axis represents the Manhattan distance of the region number in camera A, and the y-axis represents the one in camera B. It is often the lower left area of the graph that makes incorrect estimations in any model. This means that the Manhattan distance in the cameras A and B is 10 or less for both cameras. That is, it shows that the two persons are close. The number of incorrect estimations of Model 1, 2, and 3 is 9, 6, and 3, respectively (Figs. 10 and 11).

Figure 12 is a scatter plot of performing region correspondence that two people pass each other at the viewpoint of a camera. The length of the video file is nine seconds. Model 3 is used for this scatter plot. This model correctly estimates the correspondence of people.

The images of cameras A and B at the time when the two Manhattan distances at Camera A are 4 and at Camera B is 30 are shown in Fig. 13. When the

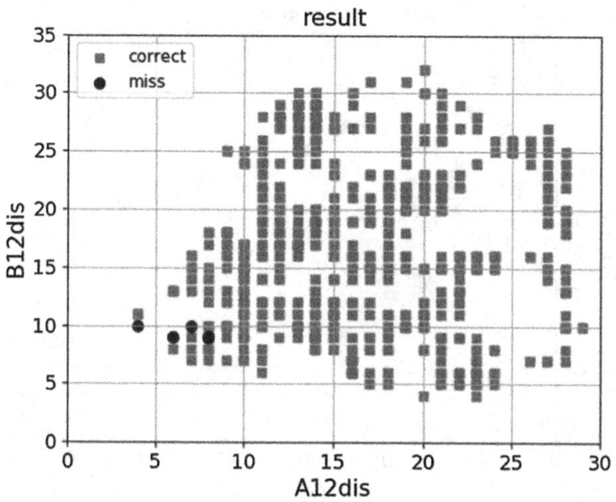

Fig. 10. Scater plots of distances (Model 2)

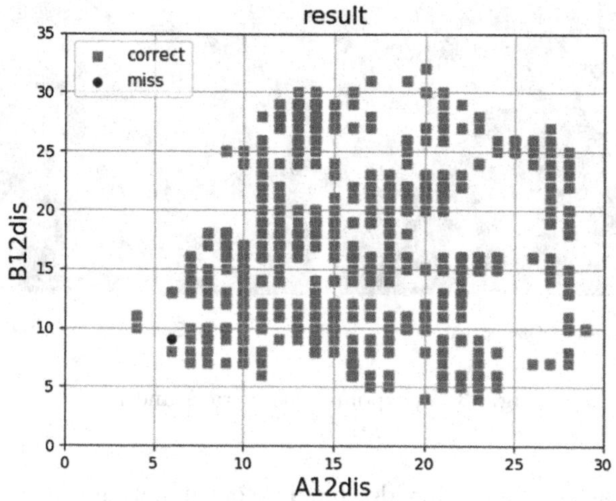

Fig. 11. Scater plots of distances (Model 3)

distance between the two Manhattan at Camera A was short, Camera B showed Manhattan distance and it was reflected. As a result, it is considered that a large distance difference occurred in the area to be estimated, and it was estimated correctly.

4.3 Experiments of Privacy Protection Monitoring Systems

As mentioned previously, by adding a skeleton model to the background image, we construct a monitoring system with privacy protection. Such overwriting is

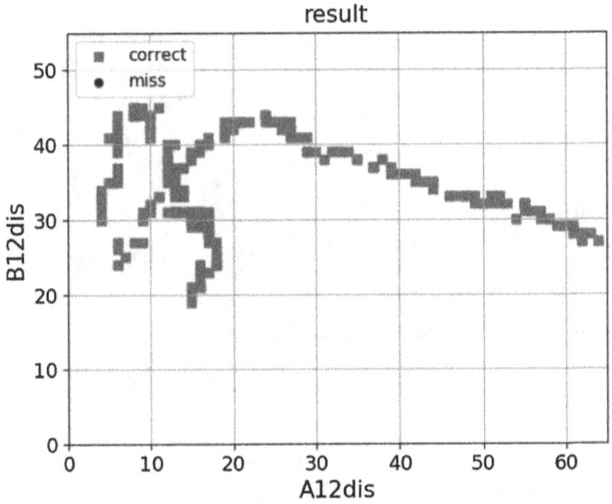

Fig. 12. Scatter plot of that two people pass each other

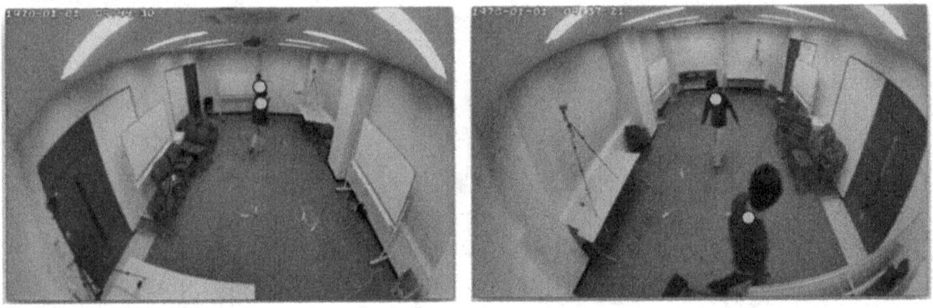

(a) Snapshot of Camera A (b) Snapshot of Camera B

Fig. 13. Viewpoint at camera A and B

performed for each frame of the video file. By concatenating the modified frames, it is possible to realize a monitoring system in which the skeleton model runs. Note that items and desks in images cannot move because only one background image is used. By linking with the region correspondence system in the previous section, monitoring can be performed while always tracking people in a wide area.

In this section, we examine the effectiveness of privacy protection by using the skeleton model. We ask four subjects to do muscle training. We take a video the muscle training. Then, the skeleton model is constituted by using the proposed system. Figure 14 shows snapshots of original video doing muscle training and corresponding skeleton video for the monitoring system. Obviously, the skeleton model contributes to privacy protection.

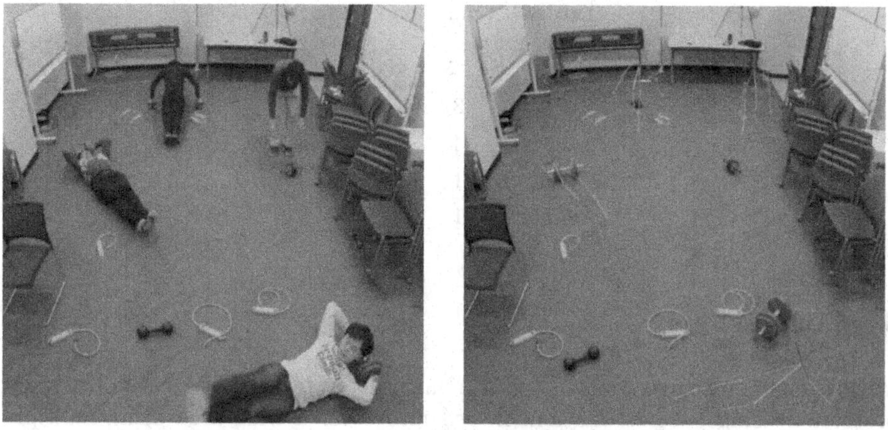

(a) original video (b) skeleton video

Fig. 14. Snapshots of original video doing muscle training and its skeleton video for the monitoring system

By watching skeleton video, the other nine subjects will guess who each of the four skeleton models is. They know the four subjects well but they do not know that the four subjects were doing muscle training. The nine subjects are told that the four subjects are being photographed, and one person is selected for each skeleton model from the four subjects. The length of the skeleton video is about 30 s. Table 3 shows the confusion matrix for the guess. Two of the four subjects, i.e., S, I, are shorter than the others. Hence, the nine subjects seem to be classified if they are tall or not.

5 Qualitative Discussion from the Viewpoint of the FUBEN-EKI

This monitoring system is considering use in nursing care facilities. If the latest machine learning methods are used, we could generate text information about when and who cares to someone when analyzing the video. The proposed systems introduced inconvenience, i.e., FUBEN, of "Less information", "Time consumption", and "Continuity." Such FUBENs not only contribute to privacy protection but also the benefit, i.e., FUBE-EKI, such as "Enhance awareness" and "Understand systems."

Person estimation from the skeleton model takes a very long time. But if you know the behavior and gesture of that person, its estimation will be easy. Furthermore, instead of converting actions into texts, by presenting them in an analog skeleton model, if the carer is ramped up or an accident occurs, it is easy to detect such abnormalities. That is, it also brings FUBEN-EKI "Feel at ease".

Table 3. Confusion matrix

	K	M	S	I
K	5	3	1	0
M	3	4	1	1
S	0	1	4	3
I	1	1	3	4

6 Conclusions

In this paper, we have constructed a monitoring system taking care of privacy protection using pose estimation. In order to cover a wide area using multiple cameras, we introduced a method of tracking people by the region correspondence mechanism. By combining Pose estimation and region correspondence system, it is possible to construct a system to monitor while protecting privacy. Section 4.2 examined the accuracy of the region correspondence mechanism. Although it was the correspondence between two cameras and two people, it was found that correspondence can be done with good precision. The confidentiality of the skeleton model was verified in Sect. 4.3. The benefits of the inconvenience, i.e., FUBEN-EKI, related to the proposed system were discussed in Sect. 5. "Less information", "Time consumption", and "Continuity" are introduced in the proposed system. As a result, FUBEN-EKI such as "Enhance awareness", "Understand systems", and "Feel at ease" are obtained.

Future works are summarized as follows: First, it is necessary to apply the proposed system to multiple cameras, multiple people environments, and to examine the tracking performance. We are considering introducing it to an actual care facility and conducting demonstration experiments.

References

1. Pishchulin, L., et al.: Deepcut: joint subset partition and labeling for multi person pose estimation. In: Proceedings of IEEE Conference on Computer Vision and Pattern Recognition (CVPR) (2016)
2. Cao, Z., Simon, T., Wei, S.-E., Sheikh. Y.: Realtime multi-person 2D pose estimation using part affinity fields. In: Proceedings of IEEE Conference on Computer Vision and Pattern Recognition (CVPR) (2017)
3. Simonyan, K., Zisserman, A.: Very deep convolutional networks for large-scale image recognition. In: Proceedings of International Conference on Learning Representations (ICLR) (2015)
4. Takahashi K.: Camera Calibration Based on Mirror Reflections (2018). http://hdl.handle.net/2433/232407

Improve Cutting Skill According to Skill and Difficulty Level

Takafumi Higashi(✉) and Hideaki Kanai

Japan Advanced Institute of Science and Technology, Ishikawa 923-1292, Japan
{htakafumi,hideaki}@acm.org

Abstract. In this paper, we aim to measure the cutting skill for creative paper cutting and increase practice effect. The practice effect changes according to the difficulty level of the cutting pattern and the skill level of the user. The cutting pattern of the picture consists of a straight line and a curved line, and we generalized the index of difficulty (ID) based on Steering law. One of cutting skills that shows the difference between novices and experts is time to cut. Besides, we developed a system consisting of a drawing display and a stylus with a knife to measure the cutting movement times (MT). The system measures MT according to the ID of the cutting pattern. We confirmed skill improvements by measuring changes in MT with various patterns from three experiments. In test 1, we confirmed the degree of conformity between the straight and curve pattern based on the steering law. In test 2, we measured skill improvement in repeatedly cutting patterns. In test 3, we compared the change in skill improvement of novices and artists. In these tests, we measured the reduction rate of MT to investigate the effectiveness of practice with various ID. As a result, we confirmed the difference in practice efficacy according to each ID.

Keywords: Cutting · Point task · Human motor performance · Steering law

1 Introduction

Currently, everyone can learn to create artistic designs from books and the Internet. However, it is difficult for novices to adapt motifs created by other artists, because of skill gaps between novices and experts. Therefore, novices satisfy their willingness to create themselves by improving their skills by repeating practice. Also, adjustment of the level of difficulty in practice is indispensable to enhance the effect. Practice at an appropriate level of difficulty leads novices to flow state. The flow state through creative and other activities yields fulfillment and happiness [12]. Paper-cutting is an art performed by controlling a knife and cutting paper. The creation of paper-cutting helps with concentration and has a relaxing effect. Actually, creating paper-cutting has a distraction effect of temporarily suppressing negative thinking [9]. When the difficulty level is inappropriate concerning the skill level, the effect of flow state decreases.

M. Kurosu (Ed.): HCII 2019, LNCS 11567, pp. 247–258, 2019.
https://doi.org/10.1007/978-3-030-22643-5_20

We focus on paper-cutting, which is a craft art. Paper-cutting is an art performed by controlling a knife and cutting paper. One of the creative skills in the paper-cutting is cutting pressure. Thus far, we have developed a system to support the improvement of skill to control cutting pressure [8]. Moreover, we have generalized the index of difficulty (ID) based on the steering law by patterning on straight lines and curves that compose a picture [7]. In this paper, we focus on cutting time which is one of the skills, confirm the skill improvement.

Our goal is to design difficulty levels suitable for skill improvement for novices. We show the relation between difficulty level and skill level by quantifying ID by width and distance. We generalize the index of difficulty (ID) based on the Steering law by patterning on straight lines and curves that compose the picture. We confirm practice effect based on the cutting time when novices cut various ID. The practice effect is affected by the difficulty level of the cutting pattern and the cutting skill of the user. One of the differences in cutting skill between novices and experts is the time to cut paper, so we compare the change of working time in each pattern. We developed a system to measure the cutting movement times (MT) by creating an improved drawing display and stylus. From three experiments, we evaluated the difficulty level of practice patterns to improve the skills of novices effectively. Test 1 confirms the degree of conformity between the straight and curve pattern based on the steering law. Test 2 measures skill improvement when participants repeatedly cut patterns of various difficulty levels. Test 3 compares the change in skill improvement when novices and artists cut the pattern with the same difficulty level. Finally, we discuss and summarize the improvement in cutting skill.

2 Related Work

Modeling human movement is a core theme in the field of human-computer interaction (HCI). Well-known models include Fitts Law [6], which predicts the time required for a one-dimensional pointing task, and a refined model for two-dimensional tasks by Accot and Zhai [3] or include modeling of the time to navigate a long, narrow path, known as the steering law [1]. All of these depict a linear relationship between the index of difficulty (ID) and the movement time (MT) of a task.

The difficulty level of a straight tunnel (ID_s) and a circular tunnel (ID_c) show the following calculation (Fig. 1).

$$ID_s = A/W \tag{1}$$

$$ID_c = 2\pi R/W \tag{2}$$

Where A and $2\pi R$ are the lengths of the tunnel and W is the tunnel width [1]. The Steering law can show as

$$MT = a + b \times ID \tag{3}$$

for both the straight and circular tunnels [2]. The a and b are empirically determined constants. In this paper, we adapted the ID and MT in the Steering law to the difficulty level and creative time required for the paper-cutting pattern.

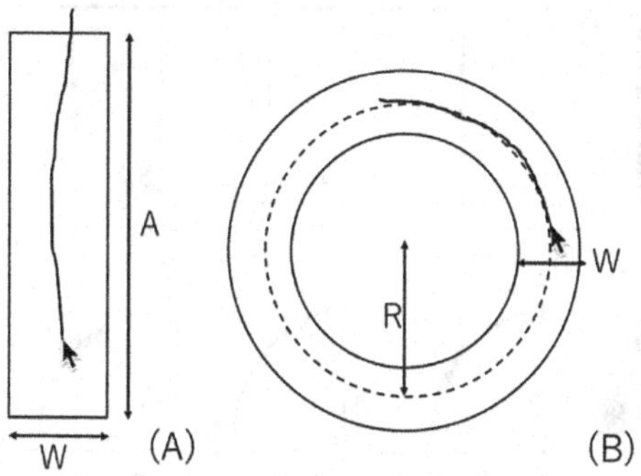

Fig. 1. For a straight tunnel, A is the length, and W its width (A). For a circular tunnel, the movement amplitude A is equal to the circle circumference $2\pi R$, where R is the circle radius (B).

Thus far, many researchers have measured the performance with various devices and for multiple shapes. For example, researchers have investigated operations with multiple types of input devices (mouse, stylus, touch panel, trackball) [2,5]. Moreover, several researchers have studied pen stroke gestures in letter writing [4] and the drawing of simple figures [10]. Curves contain many deformations according to the curvature, and [11] researchers have investigated the steering law that adapts to them. Additionally, shape-based differences have investigated in [13]. [14] modeled the cutting behavior by scissors. Many researchers have been examining intricate patterns based on the steering law.

3 Difficulty Level Measurements

3.1 Width for Novices

The artist cuts the border between a white and black area in a monochrome picture for creating a paper-cutting. In the paper-cutting, the width of the pattern constitutes the difficulty level; the narrower the width of the boundary, the more difficult it is for novices. We interviewed five instructors and artists to design the standards for two patterns (easy and difficult) for novices. These instructors are experts, with five years of experience for three of the experts and six years of experience for two of the experts. From the above result, we designed the width that the novice can cut allow plenty of time as 13 mm (SD = 0.89) and narrow width was 5.0 mm (SD = 0.31). In many workshops, the instructors modify the difficulty level of the motif according to the skills of the students from this range.

3.2 Pattern Design

We have measured the difficulty level for each straight line and curve pattern based on the steering law [7]. The steering law can measure the difficulty level

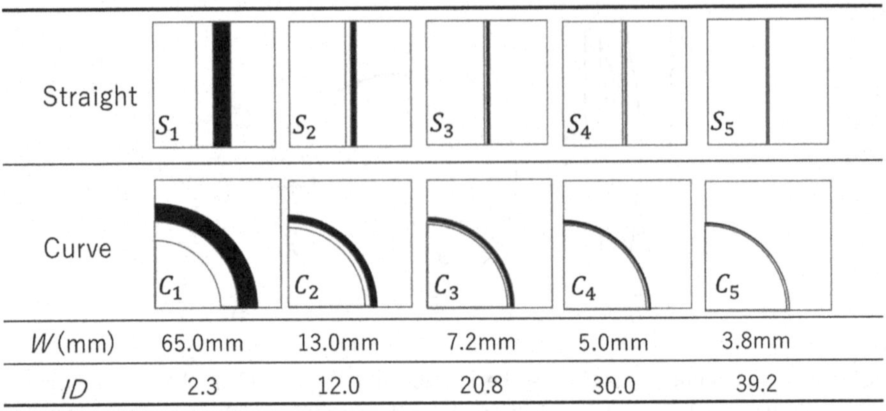

Fig. 2. Straight-line patterns and curve patterns were composed of the same width and ID.

based on the steering task in the tunnels of various widths and distances [1,2]. Based on the features above, we designed the level for each straight line or curve to cut paper.

In this paper, we designed 10 patterns with various widths from this range (Fig. 2). The difficulty level of these models monotonically increases based on Steering law. We designed each difficulty pattern lengths of 150 mm.

4 System for Measuring Skill Level

4.1 Stylus with Blade

Our device is designed to measure the cutting pressure. A blade is attached to the tip of the stylus. The user cut paper on the drawing display using our knife. The purpose of our system is to measure the cutting time with which the user cuts the paper.

We have modified the stylus to collect data by attaching a blade (NT BDC-200P) to the tip of the touch pen (Wacom PenPro2) (Fig. 3A). We have glued the tip of the knife and the stylus with ultraviolet resin (Fig. 3B). In our system, this stylus has a pressure sensor. It recognizes the cutting distance from 0.1 mm and the pressure from 0 to 500 g from 7000° at a response speed of 250 ms.

4.2 Display Unit

The drawing display (Wacom Cintiq Pro16, 3860 × 2140 pixels, 275 dpi) shows pictures (Fig. 4A). The system only responds when the stylus is in contact with the screen. Although the tip of the stylus and the surface of the screen are not in contact, the display can recognize the stylus's coordinates. It can obtain the location and angle data for the stylus via electromagnetic induction. Paper is

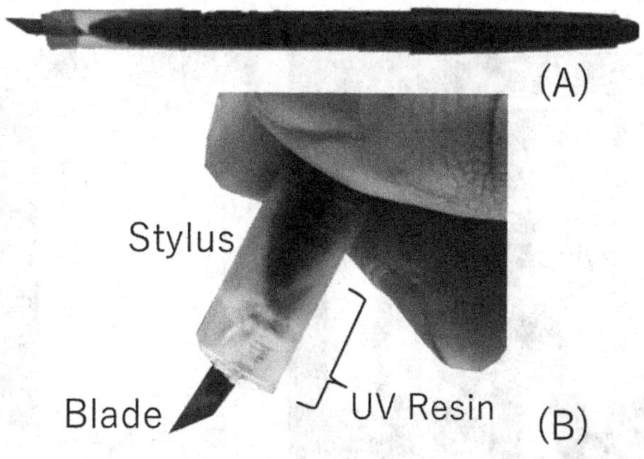

Fig. 3. A blade is attached to the tip of the stylus (A). The gap is covered with ultraviolet resin (B).

fixed on the screen, which is protected with tempered glass. The user cuts the paper with the device, and our system measures moving time and coordinates.

The user cuts the paper on the display at the start area, moves along the cutting line, and finishes at the end area (Fig. 4B). The timer starts when the knife passes the start line and stops when the blade crosses the end line. When the user cuts the paper beyond the width, the system beeps, signaling a failure. In that case, the user cuts the same pattern again. The participants were instructed to perform the required operation as quickly and accurately as possible in our experiments.

5 Test 1: Adaptable of Steering Law

5.1 Objective

In this test 1, we evaluate the adaptability of changes in the skills and Steering laws by novices. The purpose is to confirm the fitness as a motion of the paper cutting with the knife according to the steering law. We measure the cutting time and coordinates when participants cut the patterns using our knife device.

5.2 Sequence of Trials

The participants were 10 novices (average age: 27.2 years, SD: 1.15) who have never created paper-cutting. They exhibit visual acuity that does not interfere with creating paper-cuttings, and everyone was right-handed. First, they cut five types of straight lines, next cut five types of curves patterns (Fig. 2). They repeated these actions ten times.

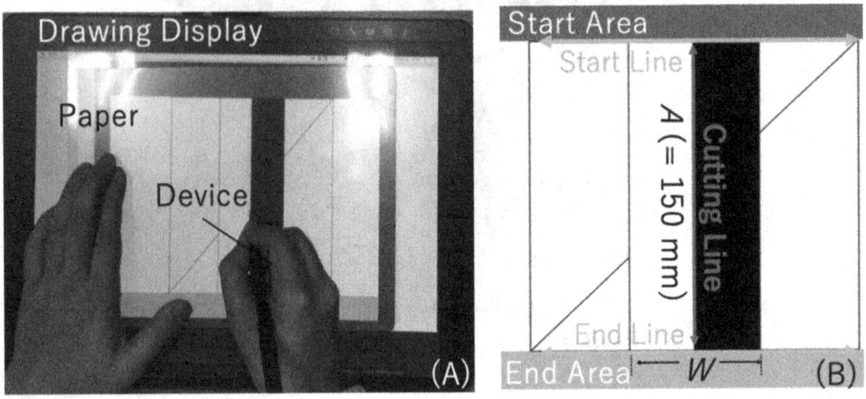

Fig. 4. Participants cut paper placed on the drawing display (A). The display shows images of six types of straight lines and curves (B).

5.3 Result on Change in MT According to ID

Cutting Time. Repeated measures ANOVA showed that significant effect of start position ($F_{4,45} = 4.229$; $p < .05$ for straight tasks, $F_{4,45} = 3.375$; $p < .05$ for curve tasks) upon steering time was observed. Figure 5 displays the relationship between ID and MT for straight and curve patterns. The plotted points represent the average of 500 trials each (5 widths × 10 frequency × 10 participants). The average operation time was 7458.3 ms for the straight and 9679.0 ms for the curve task. Figure 5 shows the interaction of the ID × MT on a straight line and a curve. All of the steering laws indicated a high degree of conformity ($R^2 > 0.9$, the number of data points is N = 5).

Error Rate. The error rate also increased as ID increased in both the straight and curved lines. By repeating the cutting, the error rate decreased. The error rate of each pattern is (Pattern in Fig. 2, Error rate) = (S1, 0.0%), (S2, 0.2%), (S3, 6.2%), (S4, 7.0%), (S5, 12.4%), (C1, 0.0%), (C2, 0.6%), (C3, 7.8%), (C4, 9.2%), (C5, 13.4%). Accordingly, even for identical paths, it was found that operational mistakes increased for the narrowing direction.

5.4 Conclusion of Test 1

From the above results, we confirmed the fitness between the straight line and the curve pattern and the steering law that make up the cutout. The Fig. 5 presents the relationship between MT and ID and R^2 is very high (straight: 0.967, curve: 0.932). There was no significant difference between the straight line and the curve pattern. Moreover, when novices cut these patterns, the error rate increased as the width became thinner for both beginners. As a characteristic point, the error

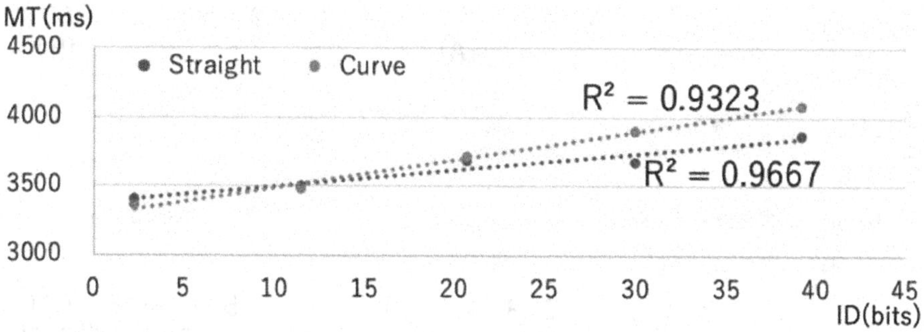

Fig. 5. Steering law fitness in straight and curve patterns.

rate of the curve was higher than the straight line at all difficulty levels. As a cause of this, cutting a straight pattern is a simple direction, but because cutting a curve requires a rotating motion of a wrist along an arc, we considered that the cutting operation has become complicated.

6 Test 2: Impact of the ID and Practice Effect

6.1 Objective

In this test 2, we confirm changes the skills to effective improve by practicing with the ID pattern corresponding to their abilities. The purpose is to compare the practice effects provided by various difficulty level. We measure the cutting time and coordinates when participants cut the patterns using our knife device.

6.2 Sequence of Trials

The participants were 20 novices. They (average age: 27.2 years, SD: 1.47) have previously never created paper-cuttings. They exhibit visual acuity that does not interfere with creating paper-cutting, and everyone was right-handed. They cut five types of straight lines, followed by five curves (Fig. 2). They repeated these actions 10 times. After the experiment, we interviewed the participants on the difficulty level of the patterns.

6.3 Result of Practice Effect

Cutting Time. The graph in Fig. 6 shows the average MT when participants cut 10 times repeatedly. The MT of the widest patterns (S1 and C1) were continuous for 5000 ms. Moreover, the MT in S2, S3, C2, and C3 converged to 5000 ms similarly. The participants cut the S4 line with the most reduced MT (59.8%) (Fig. 6A). The MT decreased with increasing difficulty, while the MT of S5 did not reduce as much as that of S4 (37.8%). Moreover, the curves demonstrated

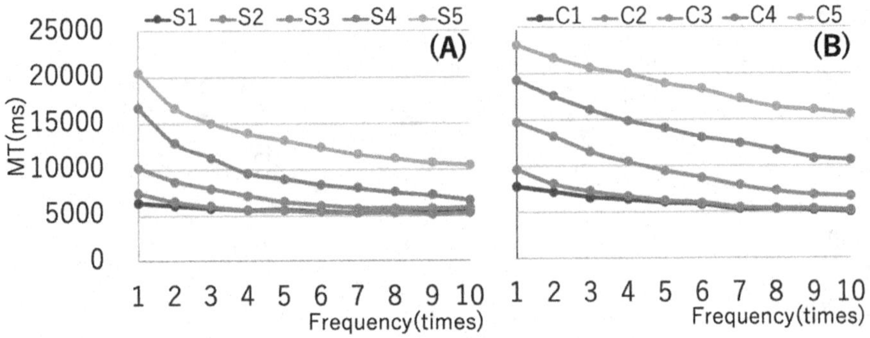

Fig. 6. Horizontal axis represents cutting frequency, and vertical axis represents MT in straight (A) and Curve pattern (B).

similar results (Fig. 6B). In the curve, the changes in MT reduced the most in the C3 line (54.9%). In addition, the amount of reduction in C4 and C5 decreased more than that in C3.

The MT decreased with increasing frequency. The decrease rate of each pattern is (Pattern in Fig. 2, Decrease Rate) = (S1, 10.3%), (S2, 25.7%), (S3, 36.7%), (S4, 59.8%), (S5, 37.8%), (C1, 30.1%), (C2, 34.8%), (C3, 54.9%), (C4, 48.2%), (C5, 33.8%).

Convergence. From the results above, the pattern in which the MT decreased the most among the 10 cuts by the novices is S4. Figure 5 shows the change in MT of the novices and experts in S4. The change of this MT synchronized with the improvement amount of the cutting skill, and the convergence of the MT signifies the mastery of the skill. The novices will improve their skills by acquiring considerable experience and converge to a MT cut of the experts.

6.4 Conclusion of Test 2

From the results above, we confirmed that MT changes according to ID. In particular, for low ID, the decrease in MT converged by repeating cutting. Additionally, for patterns with high ID, the reduction in MT is less pronounced than for low ID patterns. These causes are due to the difference between participant skill levels and design difficulty levels. From the above results, we measured the improvement of the skill from the change of MT.

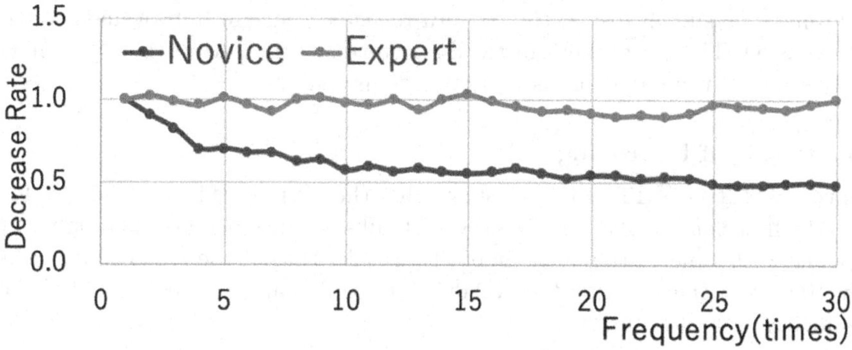

Fig. 7. The horizontal axis represents the cutting frequency, and the vertical axis represents the decrease rate for MT by novices and experts.

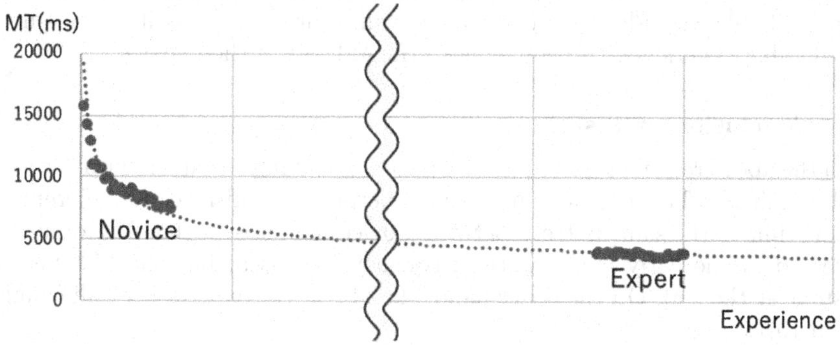

Fig. 8. Changes in skill improvement by novices and experts. X-axis is experiences.

7 Test 3: Change in MT Between Novices and Experts

7.1 Objective

In test 3, we compare the cutting skill between novices and experts. The purpose is to compare the practice effects provided by various difficulty level. We measure the cutting time and coordinates when participants cut the patterns using our knife device.

7.2 Method and Sequence of Trials

The participants were 10 novices and 10 experts. The novices (average age: 24.2 years, SD: 0.78) have never created paper-cuttings. Further, the experts (average age: 34.1, SD: 4.01) were either artists or instructors of paper-cutting. They exhibit visual acuity that does not interfere with creating paper-cuttings, and everyone was right-handed.

From the result in test 2, the pattern reflected the skill improvement of the novices as S4. Therefore, they cut the S4 pattern 30 times. After the experiment, we interviewed the participants regarding their skills.

7.3 Result of Improving

Decrease Rate of MT. Figure 7 shows that the novices' MT decreased by 44% from the first time to the time; however, it subsequently decreased to only 12% from the 20th time to the 30th time. Meanwhile, that of the experts decreased only 10% from the 1st time to the 30th time and changes as much as those of the novices were not observed.

Skill Improvement Model. Figure 8 shows the change in MT of the novices and experts in S4. The change in this MT is synchronized with the improvement amount of the cutting skill, and the convergence of the MT signifies the mastery of the skill. We consider that the novices will improve their skills by acquiring considerable experience and converge to the MT cut of the experts.

7.4 Conclusion of Test 3

From the above results, we compared changes in skill improvement with the same level of difficulty between beginners and experts. We confirmed the difference in cutting time in the same pattern between novices and artists. The MT of novices decreased in the early stage as the frequency increased, but the MT became constant at the end. On the other hand, the MT of the experts kept all changes within 10%.

8 Discussion

We verified the improvement in cutting skills from three tests in this paper. Our goal is to design each difficulty level for the creation paper-cutting. We designed the boundary pattern by white and black regions with 5 levels of ID. We measured the high adaptability of these patterns and Steering law. Moreover, we compared skill improvement with cutting patterns of various difficulty levels. We confirmed the change in the improvement amount of MT according to the ID by the difference between the beginner's skill level and the difficulty level to practice. In addition, we compared the change in skill when a novice and an artist cut off the same pattern. We measured the practice effects provided by various difficulty level. We showed the practice effect of each difficulty level on the change of cutting skill.

In these experiments, to improve the practice effect for novices, measurements were made by those who had no experience of cutting picture creation. Therefore, when targeting an intermediate person with experience of creation, the practice effect varies. Therefore, we measure the relationship between the skill level and the practice effect from the cutting action of the user. By doing this, we match the skill level according to users of various skills and give the user the best level of difficulty practice.

9 Conclusion

In this paper, we measured the improvement of participants' skills from the change of it MT. Therefore, we designed the difficulty level in the cutting pattern based on the steering law (Fig. 2). Moreover, we developed a system to measure the cutting time, which was one of the cutting skills. We confirmed the practice effect of each difficulty level on the change of cutting time. In test 1, the relationship with MT when the participants cut various ID patterns showed a high fitness to Steering law. In test 2, we compared the change in practice effect for novices by measuring the MT for each ID. As a result of cutting the low ID pattern, the change in MT was small, and the improvement effect was little. Moreover, the practice effect with the low ID pattern is small, the practice effect increases as the difficulty level rises. However, decreases when the width too hard for practicing, and the amount of MT decrease was small, and improvement of the skill of participants who performed with that pattern is also weak. In test 3, we compared the change in skill when a novice and an artist cut off the same pattern. From these experiments, we confirmed the change of novice's cutting skill according to difficulty level and the impact of practice effect according to skill level.

In future research, we will create a skill map to generalize the cutting skill. The skill map will be able to measures the difficulty level optimal for the skill level of the user, and the novices will be able to practice with optimal difficulty according to their changing his/her skills. We will try to adapt the combination of the artist's skill and painting difficulty.

References

1. Accot, J., Zhai, S.: Beyond fitts' law: models for trajectory-based HCI tasks. In: Proceedings of the ACM SIGCHI Conference on Human Factors in Computing Systems, pp. 295–302. CHI 1997. ACM, New York, NY, USA (1997). https://doi.org/10.1145/258549.258760, http://doi.acm.org/10.1145/258549.258760
2. Accot, J., Zhai, S.: Performance evaluation of input devices in trajectory-based tasks: an application of the steering law. In: Proceedings of the SIGCHI Conference on Human Factors in Computing Systems, pp. 466–472. CHI 1999. ACM, New York, NY, USA (1999). https://doi.org/10.1145/302979.303133, http://doi.acm.org/10.1145/302979.303133
3. Accot, J., Zhai, S.: Refining fitts' law models for bivariate pointing. In: Proceedings of the SIGCHI Conference on Human Factors in Computing Systems, pp. 193–200. CHI 2003. ACM, New York, NY, USA (2003). https://doi.org/10.1145/642611.642646, http://doi.acm.org/10.1145/642611.642646
4. Cao, X., Zhai, S.: Modeling human performance of pen stroke gestures. In: Proceedings of the SIGCHI Conference on Human Factors in Computing Systems, pp. 1495–1504. CHI 2007. ACM, New York, NY, USA (2007). https://doi.org/10.1145/1240624.1240850, http://doi.acm.org/10.1145/1240624.1240850

5. Cohen, O., Meyer, S., Nilsen, E.: Studying the movement of high-tech Rodentia: pointing and dragging. In: INTERACT 1993 and CHI 1993 Conference Companion on Human Factors in Computing Systems, pp. 135–136. CHI 1993. ACM, New York, NY, USA (1993). https://doi.org/10.1145/259964.260149, http://doi.acm.org/10.1145/259964.260149
6. Fitts, P.M.: The information capacity of the human motor system in controlling the amplitude of movement. J. Exp. Psychol. **47**(6), 381–391 (1954). https://doi.org/10.1037/h0055392
7. Higashi, T., Kanai, H.: Impact of practice effect on each difficulty of cutting skill. In: Proceedings of the 10th Nordic Conference on Human-Computer Interaction, pp. 904–909. NordiCHI 2018. ACM, New York, NY, USA (2018). https://doi.org/10.1145/3240167.3240236, http://doi.acm.org/10.1145/3240167.3240236
8. Higashi, T., Kanai, H.: Practice system for controlling cutting pressure for paper-cutting. In: Proceedings of the 2018 ACM International Conference on Interactive Surfaces and Spaces, pp. 363–368. ISS 2018. ACM, New York, NY, USA (2018). https://doi.org/10.1145/3279778.3281457, http://doi.acm.org/10.1145/3279778.3281457
9. Ishikawa, H., Koshikawa, F.: The effect of distraction with recalling objects of rumination on mood, and the evaluation of ruminative thoughts. J. Health Psychol. Res. **30**(2), 65–73 (2018). https://doi.org/10.11560/jhpr.160816047
10. Long, Jr., A.C., Landay, J.A., Rowe, L.A., Michiels, J.: Visual similarity of pen gestures. In: Proceedings of the SIGCHI Conference on Human Factors in Computing Systems, pp. 360–367. CHI 2000. ACM, New York, NY, USA (2000). https://doi.org/10.1145/332040.332458, http://doi.acm.org/10.1145/332040.332458
11. Nancel, M., Lank, E.: Modeling user performance on curved constrained paths. In: Proceedings of the 2017 CHI Conference on Human Factors in Computing Systems, pp. 244–254. CHI 2017. ACM, New York, NY, USA (2017). https://doi.org/10.1145/3025453.3025951, http://doi.acm.org/10.1145/3025453.3025951
12. Seligman, M.E.P.: Flourish: A Visionary New Understanding of Happiness and Well-being. Simon and Schuster, New York (2012)
13. Yamanaka, S., Miyashita, H.: Modeling the steering time difference between narrowing and widening tunnels. In: Proceedings of the 2016 CHI Conference on Human Factors in Computing Systems, pp. 1846–1856. CHI 2016. ACM, New York, NY, USA (2016). https://doi.org/10.1145/2858036.2858037, http://doi.acm.org/10.1145/2858036.2858037
14. Yamanaka, S., Miyashita, H.: Paper-cutting operations using scissors in Drury's law tasks. Appl. Ergon. **69**, 32–39 (2018). https://doi.org/10.1016/j.apergo.2017.12.018

Virtual Space Pointing Based on Vergence

Yuki Hirata[1(✉)], Hiroki Soma[1], Munehiro Takimoto[1], and Yasushi Kambayashi[2]

[1] Department of Information Sciences, Tokyo University of Science, Chiba, Japan
6315098@ed.tus.ac.jp, mune@is.noda.tus.ac.jp
[2] Department of Computer and Information Engineering, Nippon Institute of Technology, Saitama, Japan
yasushi@nit.ac.jp

Abstract. Recent virtual reality (VR) headsets make users perceive the three-dimensional (3D) virtual space through their parallax. The 3D space has been used for only passive use such as representing something put into intensive reality. We propose a new manner for pointing objects at specific locations in 3D space through vergence. In order to achieve this new manner, we have paid a close attention to the directions of eyes through parallax. Using the pointing manner, we cannot only drag icons or windows to any locations in 3D space, but also intuitively perform most desktop operations such as pilling up a pop-up menu and pushing a button. Because it is not easy for most people to control their vergence angle as they want, in our pointing manner, we present a feedback system of degree of vergence through an indicator appearing around a pointing cursor. In order to show the effectiveness of our proposal, we have implemented the pointing manner in a VR headset with an eye-tracker, and we have conducted numerical experiments. The experimental results show that our vergence based operations are feasible.

Keywords: Virtual reality · Eye tracking · Vergence · Indicator

1 Introduction

The virtual space is a three-dimensional (3D) space that a virtual reality (VR) headset presents. A user perceives the virtual space through his or her parallax [1]. Traditionally, the 3D space has been used for representing something put into intensive reality, but the expanse of the 3D space has not been used effectively [2]. We propose a new manner for pointing object at specific locations in 3D space. We focus attention on directions of eyes through parallax. For example, the eyes rotate towards each other for focusing on a closer object, and they rotate away from each other in focusing on a father object. These eye movements are respectively called convergence and divergence [3], which are collectively called vergence as shown in Fig. 1. Our pointing manner uses the vergence to specify a specific depth in virtual space. For example, a pop-up menu can be pulled out

M. Kurosu (Ed.): HCII 2019, LNCS 11567, pp. 259–269, 2019.
https://doi.org/10.1007/978-3-030-22643-5_21

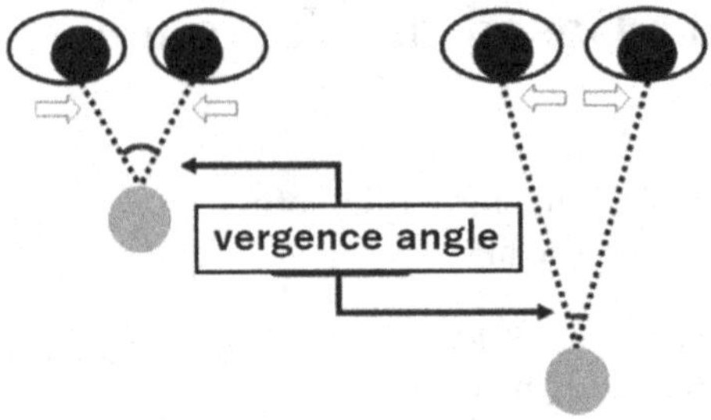

Fig. 1. Vergence: convergence in the left side and divergence in the right side.

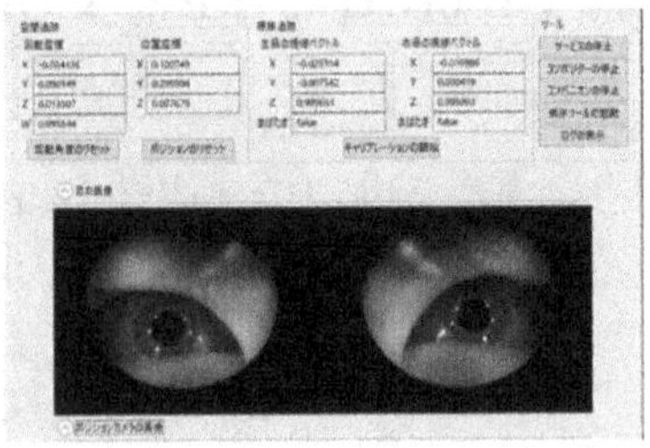

Fig. 2. Recognition of eyes.

through convergence on an icon or window. As well, a button can be pushed on through divergence on the button [4]. Furthermore, windows on a desktop can be arranged in any directions including their depth, and overlapped windows or desktops can be selected through vergence. Such a pointing manner is especially useful for handicapped people who cannot dexterously maneuver their hands and feet. On the other hand, most handicapped people can move their mouths and eyes quite precisely with their own will. Therefore, they can use them in order to operate computers. It is difficult for them, however, to talk to others during their mouth-based operations, and the behaviors of eyes used for PC operations are limited to only changing the directions or blinking for a few operations such as moving or clicking a mouse [5]. Also, the behaviors of eyes may cause a well-known Midas Touch problem [6].

In order to overcome these problems, we have implemented the pointing manner on a VR device with an eye-tracker. The device can measure directions of eyes of a user while he or she is watching a specific location. It is easy to check the degree of vergence with the device, because horizontal difference between the directions of eyes can be easily measured. However, it is not easy for most people to control their vergence. Therefore, we propose a cursor with indicator around it. Since the indicator feedbacks the degree of vergence to users, they can control not only convergence but also divergence of their eyes.

The structure of the balance of this paper is as follows. In the second section, we describe how to recognize vergence, and feedbacks the degree of the vergence to users. In the third section, we show the operations implemented on a VR device using our pointing manner. In the fourth section, we present some experimental results on the VR device with our pointing manner. Finally, we conclude our discussions in the fifth section.

2 Recognition and Feedback of Vergence

The vergence based pointing is requires an eye tracking VR headset such as FOVE. The headset can track user's eyes in addition to presenting users a virtual space through his or her parallax. Figure 2 shows a window to check the state of tracking eyes in FOVE. The headset can give vectors of left and right eyes from their directions through the position cameras. The information of the vectors can be used to specify the watching position as well as traditional usage of eye tracking. Additionally, letting the vectors of the left and right eyes $\boldsymbol{l}$ and $\boldsymbol{r}$ respectively, we can calculate the vergence angle θ using these vectors through the following equation:

$$\theta = \cos^{-1}(\frac{\boldsymbol{l} \cdot \boldsymbol{r}}{|\boldsymbol{l}||\boldsymbol{r}|})$$

The closer watching position is, the larger the angle becomes. Conversely, the further watching position is, the smaller the angle becomes. That is, convergence corresponds to the approaching of the pointing position, and divergence corresponds to the receding of it.

Thus, the vergence can be used for positioning or moving the cursor in the VR space with depth. Through several experiments, however, we have found that, for most people it is more difficult to perform divergence operations than to perform convergence operations. In order to overcome this problem of the vergence based pointing, in the early implementation, we decided to introduce a rotated pointing operation that takes advantage of only convergence for vergence based pointing. In the rotated pointing operation, the window to which a user is pointing is initially placed on a parent window in a window hierarchy. For example, windows on a desktop are initially placed on the background, and pop-up menus are initially placed on the window they operate. After that, as the angle of convergence increases, a pointed place moves closer to the user. This process causes movement closer to the user of pointed window, or selection of a window placed closer to the user. Notice that the pointed place never moves back. The pointed location finally reaches the closest point to the user immediately before his or her face. Once the pointed place becomes the closest to the user, the pointed place jumps to the initial location, i.e. the parent window or a background. The process of movement of pointed location can be repeated arbitrary times. Therefore, if the user makes some mistakes, he or she can simply retry the operation.

The rotated pointing operation works quite well. Once a user makes some mistakes for positioning or selection, however, he or she has to repeat the same operation. That is not only annoying, but also unintuitive. Therefore, we propose a more intuitive pointing operation based on an indicator. In the indicator based operation, as shown in Fig. 3, two circles, which are white in the left side and black in the right side, are displayed around the cursor as an indicator. The distance d between the two circles changes proportionally to the vergence angle θ, and it gives the user a feedback on the degree of vergence. The distance d is calculated as follows:

$$d = 1.0 + k * (\theta_0 - \theta)$$

In the equation, θ_0 denotes initial vergence, and k is a coefficient determined empirically. As shown by the equation, d is initially 1.0, and is increased or decreased k times as many as change of vergence angle. Our preliminary experiments show that $k = 10.0$ is the optimal. The enhanced feedback enables the

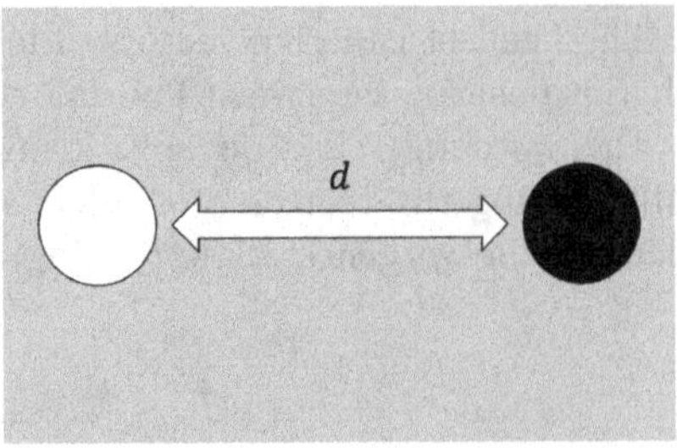

Fig. 3. Indicator based on the distance between two circles.

user to easily control divergence in addition to convergence. Therefore we can use the divergence to implement the pushing operations such as clicking. As a result, the user can intuitively operate most operations on a desktop through the indicator based operation.

3 Application of Vergence Based Pointing

In order to evaluate the feasibility of our pointing system, we have implemented the desktop operations on VR headset with eye-tracker as follows:

1. Window movement: places the window at a focused point on a line of sight on virtual space. The depth of the point is determined by the degree of vergence angle.
2. Pulling out: pulls out a pop-up menu.
3. Pushing: pushes a button.

The window movement starts active when the user points to a title bar of the window. The depth is separated to several partitions, of which a partition including the selected focus point. Actual depth of place is the farthest boundary of the partition. Since we have implemented the move based on the rotated pointing operation, a cursor moved too closely to a user is returned to the furthest point on the line of sight as shown in Fig. 4(a)–(c). Notice that two circles may be swapped by strong convergence. Similarly, a cursor moved too far from a user is returned to the closest point on a line of sight. Once the user points to the outside of the title bar, the window is held.

Also, we have implemented it based on an indicator based operation. As shown in Fig. 4, the indicator consisting of two circles is always displayed around the cursor. The distance between the circles shrinks by convergence, and stretches by divergence. The user can adequately adjust his or her vergence while watching the indicator, so that the user can make the cursor approach or leave through convergence or divergence. Once the convergence and divergence are available through the indicator, they can also intuitively be used for pulling up and pushing. Figure 5(a) shows a window is pulled out through convergence. Figure 5(b)–(c) shows the blue box among the four boxes behaves as a button and is pushed through divergence.

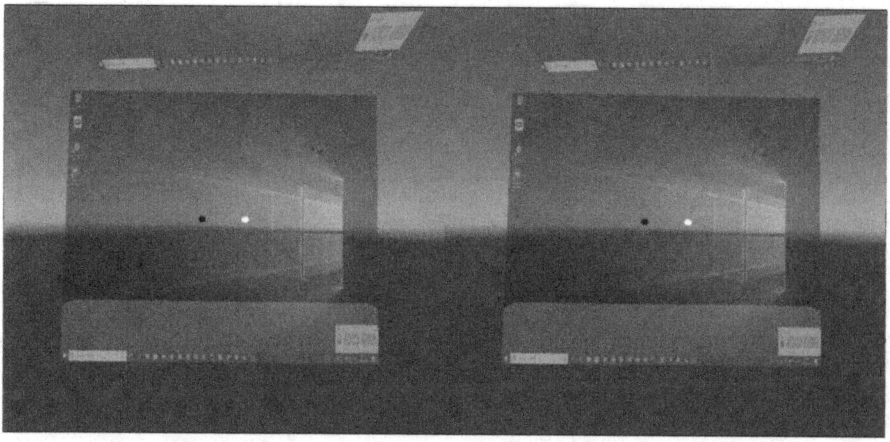

(a) Far point

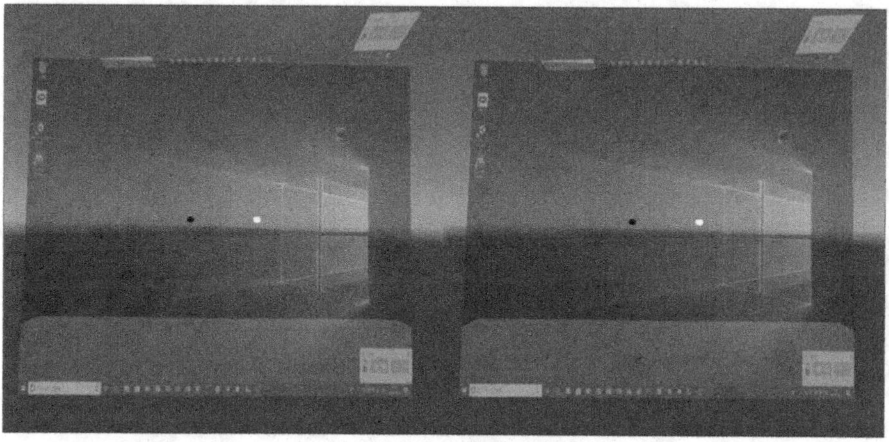

(b) Middle point

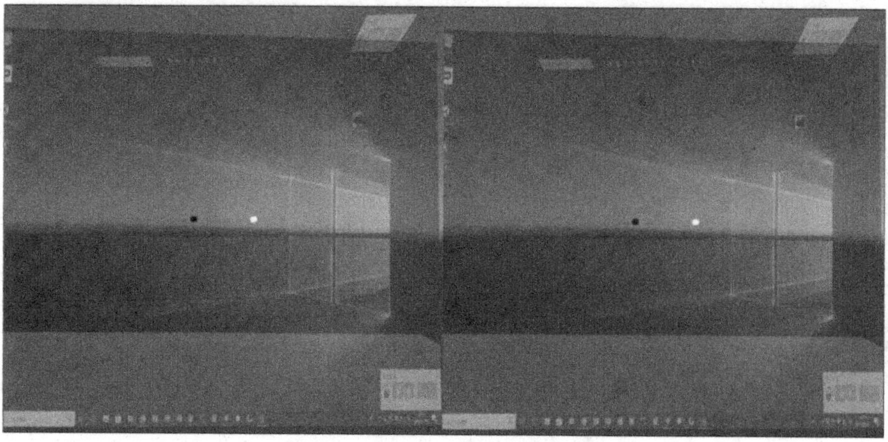

(c) Close point

Fig. 4. Rotated pointing operation

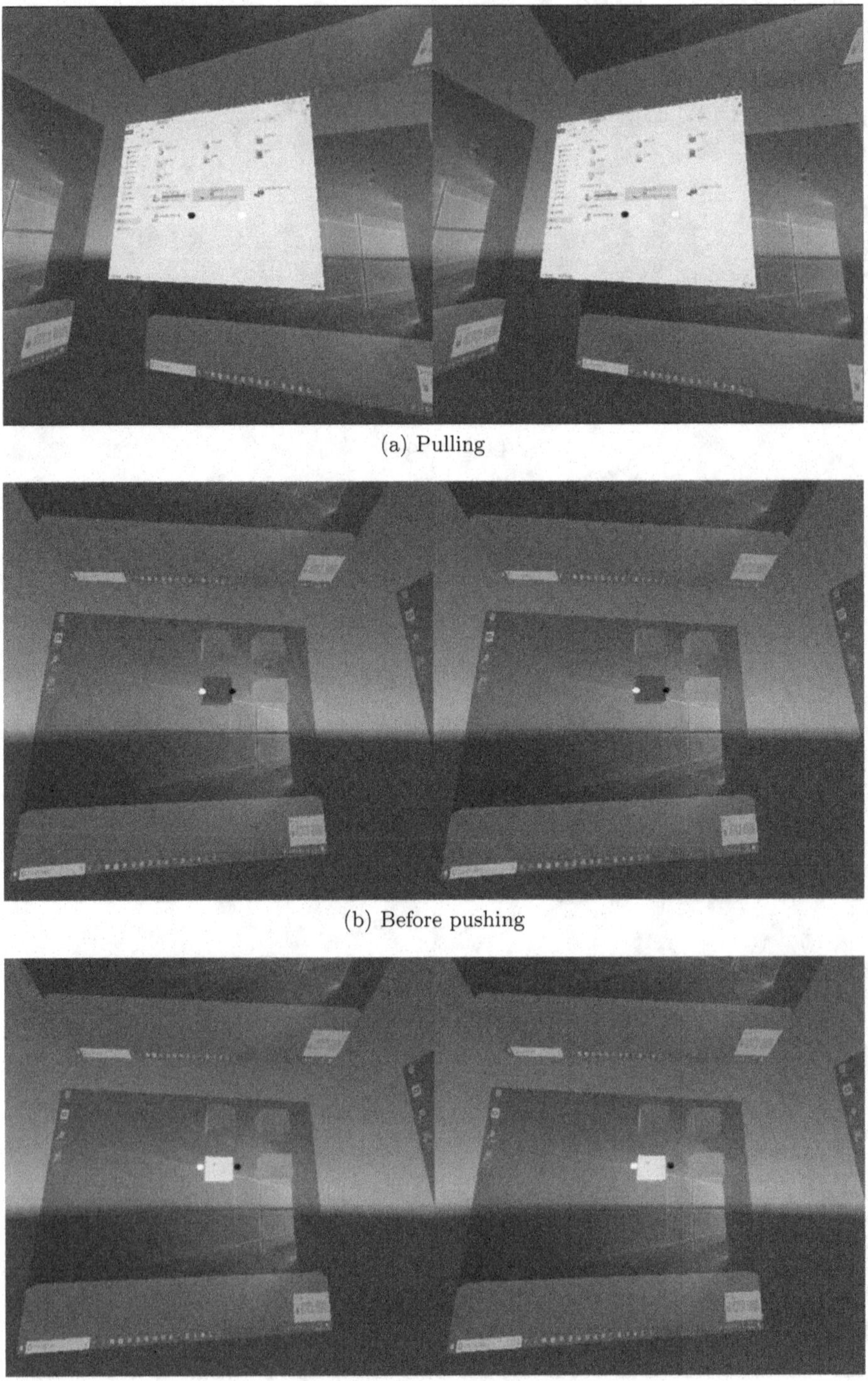

(a) Pulling

(b) Before pushing

(c) After pushing

Fig. 5. Pulling out a pop-up menu and pushing a button

4 Experimental Results

In order to evaluate the usability of the vergence based pointing manner for the desktop operations, we conducted numerical experiments. First, we selected eleven subjects, who have experiences for an eye-tracker and VR as respectively shown in Fig. 6(a) and (b), and had them perform experiments on moving windows, pulling out windows and pushing buttons.

In the experiment of the window movement, we use two sets of three windows with blue, green and red as shown in Fig. 7. The windows in one set are arranged as overlapping each other in the order of blue, green and red from the font. The other windows in the other set are arranged in the top side, the left side and the right side respectively, surrounding the front set. In the experiment, we have asked each subject to move the windows on the front in the following manners:

1. move back the front-most blue window to the rear-most position,
2. move back the front-most green window to the rear-most position,
3. move the front-most red window to another red window surrounding it,
4. move back the front-most blue window to the rear-most position,
5. move the front-most green window to another green window surrounding it, and
6. move the front-most blue window to another blue window surrounding it.

We have conducted these experiments twice. Figure 8 shows the total consumed time for the first and the second experiments. As shown in the figure, any subjects took shorter time, as they was getting used to our desktop operations.

In the experiments of pulling out and pushing, we evaluated usability of vergence based operation. As shown in Fig. 9, most subjects had mostly the same success rate for the convergence based operation regardless of the indicator. On the other hand, most subjects had higher success rate for the divergence based operation with the indicator than one without the indicator. This shows that the divergence based operation with the indicator has the potential to reaching operability close to convergence based operation through some trainings.

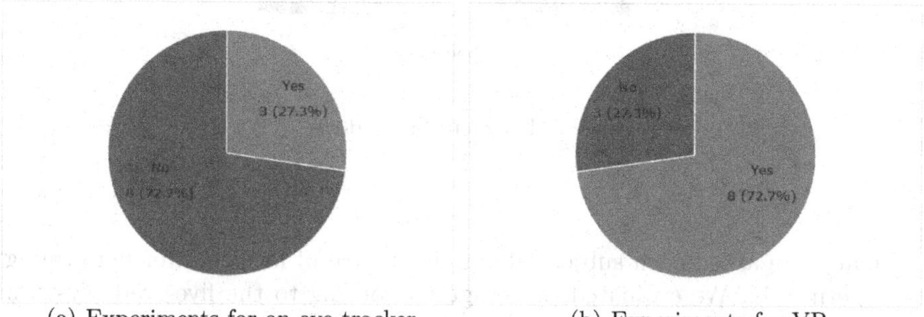

(a) Experiments for an eye-tracker (b) Experiments for VR

Fig. 6. Experiments of subjects

Fig. 7. The experimental environment for movement of windows

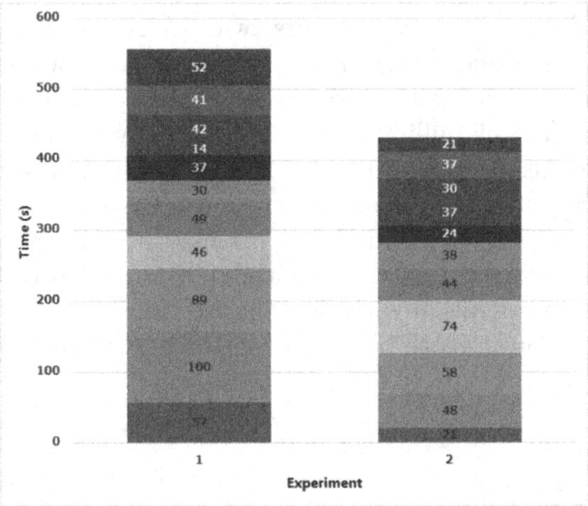

Fig. 8. Movement of windows

Finally, we asked each subject about the degree of fatigue after performing the experiments. We evaluated the fatigue according to the five-grade system. Figure 10 shows the number of subjects feeling each grade. As shown in the figure, the total number of grades 1 and 2 occupies more than a half of subjects. It shows that our vergence based pointing has the potential for practical use.

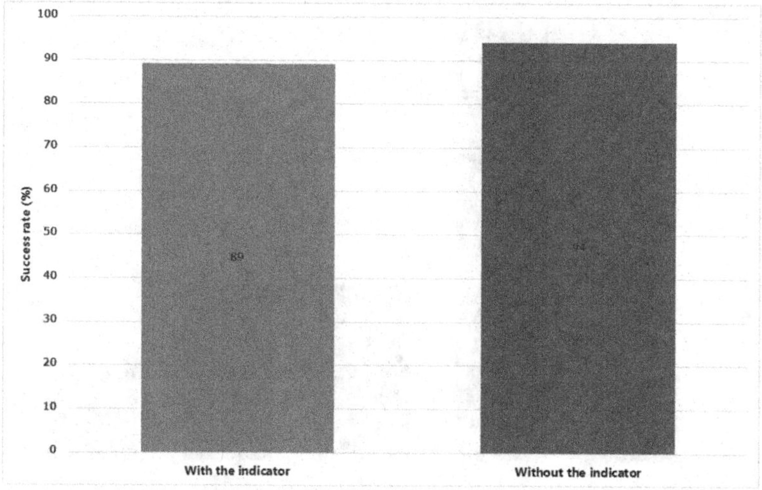

(a) Convergence

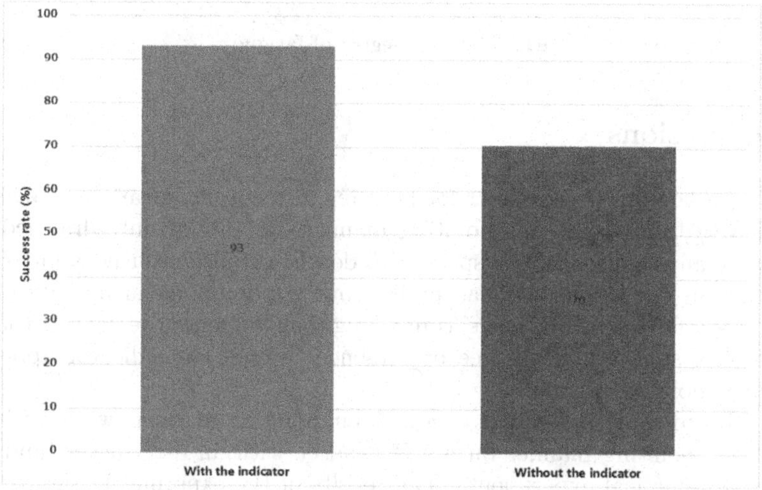

(b) Divergence

Fig. 9. Pulling out and pushing through vergence

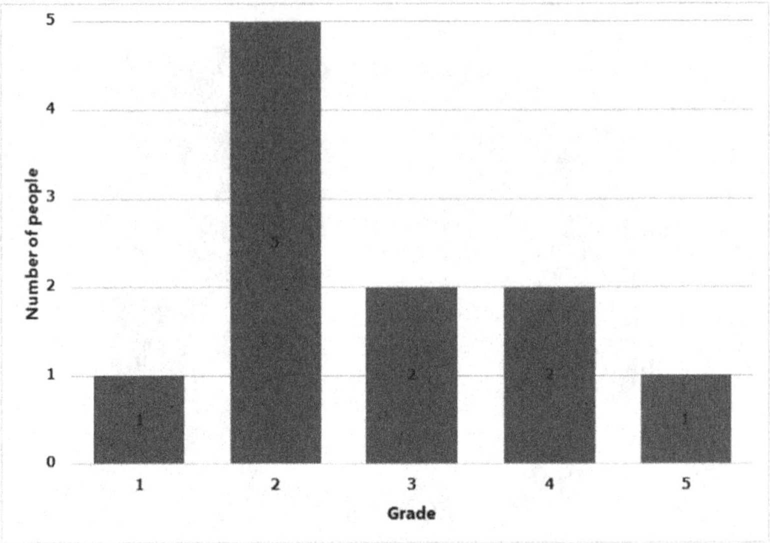

Fig. 10. The degree of fatigue

5 Conclusions

We have proposed a new manner for pointing at a specific location in 3D space through vergence. Using this pointing manner, we cannot only drag icons or windows to any locations in 3D space with depth, but also intuitively implement most desktop operations such as pulling out a pop-up menu and pushing a button. Also, for ease of the users' controlling their vergence, we have introduced a feedback system on the degree of vergence through an indicator appearing around the pointing cursor.

In order to show the effectiveness of our pointing manner, we have implemented our pointing manner on a VR headset with an eye-tracker, and then conducted numerical experiments. The results of the experiments showed that our pointing system had the potential for practical use. In future works, we will evaluate how the users improve their operations of our pointing system through trainings.

References

1. Konrad, R., Padmanaban, N., Cooper, E., Wetzstein, G.: Computational focus-tunable near-eye displays. In: ACM SIGGRAPH 2016 Emerging Technologies. SIGGRAPH 2016, New York, NY, USA. ACM 3:1–3:2 (2016)
2. Pfeiffer, T., Latoschik, M., Ipke, W.: Evaluation of binocular eye trackers and algorithms for 3D gaze interaction in virtual reality environments. J. virtual real. broadcast. **5**(16) (2008). https://www.jvrb.org/past-issues/5.2008/1660

3. Ukai, K.: Eye movement: characteristics and method of measurement. KOGAKU **23**(1), 2–8 (1994). (In Japanese)
4. Kudo, S., Okabe, H., Hachisu, T., Sato, M., Fukushima, S., Kajimoto, H.: Input method using divergence eye movement. In: CHI 2013 Extended Abstracts on Human Factors in Computing Systems. CHI EA 2013, New York, NY, USA, ACM, pp. 1335–1340 (2013)
5. Ohno, T.: Quick menu selection task with eye mark. Trans. Inf. Process. Soc. Jpn **40**(2), 602–612 (1999). (In Japanese)
6. Jacob, R.J.K.: What you look at is what you get: eye movement-based interaction techniques. In: Proceedings of the SIGCHI Conference on Human Factors in Computing Systems, CHI 1990, New York, NY, USA. ACM, pp. 11–18 (1990)

Applicability Study of Eye Movement Menu based on Analytic Hierarchy Process

Wen-jun Hou[1,2], Bo Zhang[1,2(✉)], Si-qi Wu[1,2], and Zhi-yang Jiang[1]

[1] School of Digital Media and Design Arts,
Beijing University of Posts and Telecommunications, Beijing 100876, China
935448078@qq.com
[2] Beijing Key Laboratory of Network System and Network Culture,
Beijing University of Posts and Telecommunications, Beijing 100876, China

Abstract. Eye movement interaction is more natural and intelligent than traditional input by mouse and keyboard, and has a wide range of application scenarios. Menu, as an important user input and selection mechanism, designed and interacted with eye movement input modality can greatly improve user interaction efficiency. An eye movement menu usability evaluation index system based on analytic hierarchy process was proposed in this paper. In addition, combined with experiments and questionnaires, a quantitative and qualitative combination study on eye movement types (fisheye linear menu, marking menu) and eye movement selection mechanisms (time delay selection mechanism, select sub-selection reconfirmation mechanism) was conducted. The problems of easy fatigue and "Midas Touch" in eye movement interaction were also discussed in the paper. The conclusions reached at the end of this paper have a guiding role in the design and evaluation of the eye movement menu.

Keywords: Human-computer interaction · Eye control selection · Menu design · Analytic hierarchy process

1 Introduction

1.1 Development, Principles and Applications of Eye Movement System

In the process of the development of human-computer interaction, compared with the diversified information such as text, image, audio and video transmitted to the user by the machine, the amount and form of the information input by the user is limited by the traditional GUI technology which is represented by the mouse and keyboard. However, multi-channel human-computer interaction technology can break through this limitation. This technology inputs information by acquiring multiple sensory information and physical behaviors of the user [1]. With the development of gaze tracking technology and the improvement of computer performance, the application research of gaze tracking technology in the field of human-computer interaction has emerged, and it has become an important research direction of intelligent human-computer interaction.

Eye movement interaction technology is based on gaze tracking and can transform eye movement data into gaze control commands. Gaze tracking technology is used to collect visual channel information, record eye gaze, beating, smooth trailing and other

M. Kurosu (Ed.): HCII 2019, LNCS 11567, pp. 270–282, 2019.
https://doi.org/10.1007/978-3-030-22643-5_22

activities. Gaze control technology provides the possibility of controlling the machine for eye movement interaction [2]. At present, the most common gaze tracking technology is the pupil-corneal reflection technique, which uses the infrared light to illuminate the cornea, and the high-light point that produces reflection on the cornea is called "Purkinje Image". According to the characteristics of the "Purkinje Image" changing with the movement of the eyeball, the camera is used to capture the distance of the pupil to the "Purkinje Image". After that, the image processing is performed. The gaze direction and gaze point of the user can be obtained after intersecting the vector with the plane of the screen [3].

Eye movement interaction is a natural interaction. From the perspective of interaction cost, eye movement interaction is the most relaxed and the most natural one. Besides, fast response speed and accurate tracking ability make eye movement interaction have a wide range of application scenarios. At present, new concepts are being developed in various fields, aiming to promote the application of eye tracking as an emerging human-computer interaction technology. In the field of disability medical care, eye movement interaction is used to serve people with physical disabilities, so that they can interact with computers, smart wheelchairs, mobile devices, etc. through eyes [4–6]. In the gaming world, with the help of gaze tracking and smartphone screens, it is already possible to activate icons or move game characters through line-of-sight contact. In the field of transportation, Delphi has developed an eye-moving system that allows the driver to control some functions in the car with simple eye movements, while monitoring the driver's eye movements to detect fatigue driving signals in a timely manner. In addition, Feng also researched and optimized the interaction of the car music application through the eye movement interaction for the driving scene [7].

1.2 Menu Form

After the menu was introduced into the computer software system, two main advantages were showed based on its features. The first advantage is that it allows the computer system to proactively present the current state and possible operations to the user, who manipulates the system by observing and exploring. The second advantage is that the input and display functions are separated and displayed with detailed software command information and data information. At the same time, users only need to spend the least effort to select the required commands and data. The existing mainstream menu forms are linear menus and marking menus [8].

The linear menu (see Fig. 1a) is the simplest and most intuitive menu that allows the user to quickly find the commands they need by browsing through the list of commands in the menu. But maybe because of containing too many commands so that the menu becomes very long, the user needs to move the cursor of the mouse a very long distance when selecting the menu command.

The marking menu (see Fig. 1b) is developed from the radial menu and the commands of the menu are executed by the selection of the direction. Marking menu provides the user with more visual feedback. As you move the cursor and select one of the commands on the menu, a "track" is left on the screen to display the cursor and the command executed. In addition, by marking the "track", the user can select a command without displaying the contents of the menu.

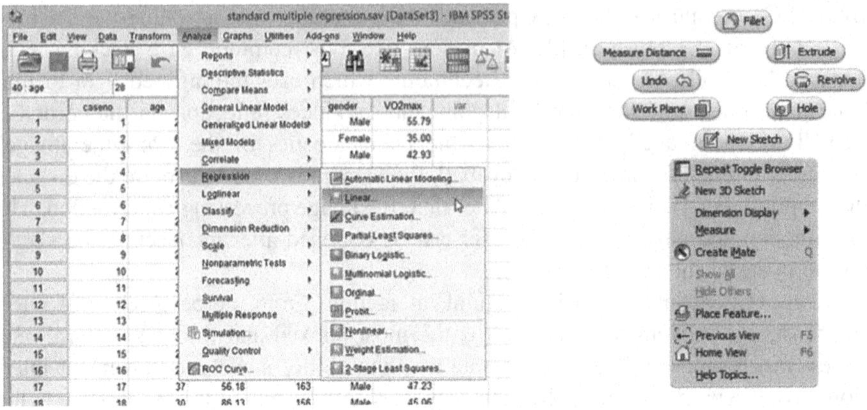

(a) (b)

Fig. 1. The existing mainstream menu forms. (a) Linear menu (b) Marking menu.

1.3 Eye Movement Selection Mechanism

The traditional eye movement menu selection mechanism has two options: time delay selection mechanism and selection sub-selection reconfirmation mechanism. The time delay selection mechanism uses gaze to make a selection of menu items. The selection sub-selection reconfirmation mechanism is to transfer the gazing object to the pop-up control corresponding to the target object, commonly known as the selector (usually the confirmation button) (see Fig. 2).

(a) (b)

Fig. 2. Two mainstream eye movement menu selection mechanisms. (a) Time delay selection mechanism requires focusing more than 600 ms. (b) Select sub-selection reconfirmation mechanism requires eye tracking to be placed in the first level menu and focusing on the sub-selection 300 ms.

In addition to the two mainstream eye movement selection mechanisms based on gaze input, there are other eye movement selection mechanisms that are used according to specific situations: blink selection and gaze gesture selection. Blink selection is done by judging the time of closing the eye or the times of eyes closed in a short time. By judging the trajectory of the eye moving on the interface, gaze gesture selection completes the selection task [9]. The following Table 1 shows the comparison of eye movement selection mechanisms.

Table 1. Comparison of eye movement selection input mechanisms

	Blink selection	Gaze selection	Gaze gesture selection
Index parameter	Continuous blinking times, blinking duration	Duration of fixation within a fixed range	Duration, amplitude, speed, direction, etc.
Requirements for interfaces	High requirements for space-time characteristics	High requirements for space-time characteristics	Low requirements for space-time characteristics
Interactive naturalness	Naturally, low cognitive load	Naturally, low cognitive load	Unnaturally, high cognitive load
Midas touch	High frequency of unconscious blinking, easy to make errors	Unconscious gaze behavior, easy to make errors	Specific sequences activate specific commands, not easy to make errors
Application status	Long research history, obvious shortcomings, less application	Long research history, currently widely used	Short research history, currently less applied

In the past, most of the application researches of eye movement technology in human-computer interaction are the introductions of realization principle of gaze tracking technology and its application value in the field of human-computer interaction. There are few systematic studies on the interface design and interaction mode of eye movement system. There is also no research to optimize the interface control design for eye movement scenarios. The mechanism and characteristics of eye movement selection were studied in this paper. Based on that, three eye movement menu design schemes were proposed. Then, by applying the analytic hierarchy process, we constructed an eye movement menu usability evaluation index system. Combined with experiments and questionnaires, the quantitative and qualitative analysis of the type of eye movement menu and the mechanism of eye movement selection was conducted. The conclusions reached at the end of this paper have a guiding role in the design and evaluation of the eye movement menu.

2 Eye Movement Menu Schemes Design

When using eye movement for menu selection, there is a big difference from traditional mouse and keyboard selection. Although the eye movement selection can achieve the goal of quick-seeking targets, there are also problems such as large information density, eye fatigue, accuracy, and false triggering. Therefore, eye movement menus need to be optimized.

According to the foregoing, the currently used menu categories include linear menu and marking menu. The selection mechanism includes time delay selection mechanism, selection sub-selection reconfirmation mechanism, blink selection and gaze gesture selection. By matching these menu forms and eye movement selection mechanisms, different types of eye movement menus can be formed. However, the user's operation on the eye movement menu should be an interactive behavior that does not require a lot of extra memory but requires a certain accuracy. Therefore the gaze gesture selection (increasing user memory burden) and the blink selection (affecting the eye movement recognition of the device easily [9]) are not suitable for the interaction of the menu. Therefore, at present, the operation modes selected by the subsequent design are the time delay selection mechanism and the selection sub-selection reconfirmation mechanism.

Compared with the time delay selection mechanism, the selection sub-selection reconfirmation mechanism can reduce the problem of "Midas Touch" to some extent [10]. However, for high-density operation menus, the selection sub-reconfirmation mechanism undoubtedly greatly reduces the efficiency of menu selection, and the interface construction of the sub-reconfirmation mechanism needs to add a sub-control in addition to the basic menu elements, so there are also requirements for menu interface itself. If the traditional linear menu is used in combination with the mechanism, the space of the selector will be greatly reduced, so the selection sub-confirmation mechanism is more suitable for the marking menu with less dense layout. Therefore, the design scheme is shown in Fig. 3.

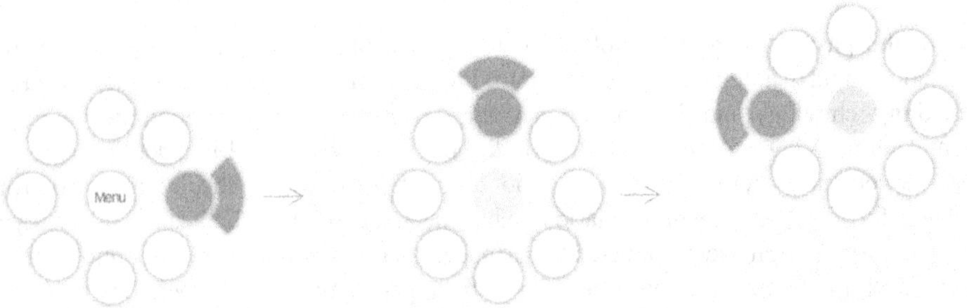

Fig. 3. Design scheme: marking menu with selecting sub-selection reconfirmation mechanism

The biggest problem with traditional linear menus is that the information density is too large, which exposes the "Midas Touch" problem. The fisheye menu is one of the solutions [8]. A long menu list can always be displayed in one window by using fisheye menus, so that users can see all the commands at all times. The menu item around the cursor is displayed in the full size, and other menu items that are far from the current cursor position are displayed in smaller sizes. The display mechanism can reduce the cursor movement distance when the user selects different commands. Although the method of combining the fisheye and the linear menu cannot completely avoid the "Midas Touch" problem, the false touch rate due to the excessive information density can be reduced to some extent. The design scheme is shown in Fig. 4.

According to the above two design schemes, another design scheme combining a marking menu and a linear fisheye menu can be derived. On the one hand, it reduces the operational fatigue caused by the single linear menu form when the menu selection level is too deep, and reduces the length of the eye movement track. On the other hand, it solves the problem that the marking menu has a small amount of information in a single level. The design scheme is shown in Fig. 5.

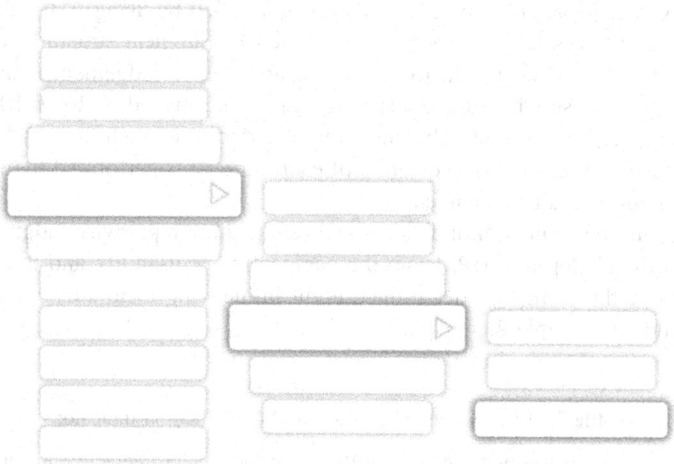

Fig. 4. Design scheme: fisheye menu with time delay selection mechanism

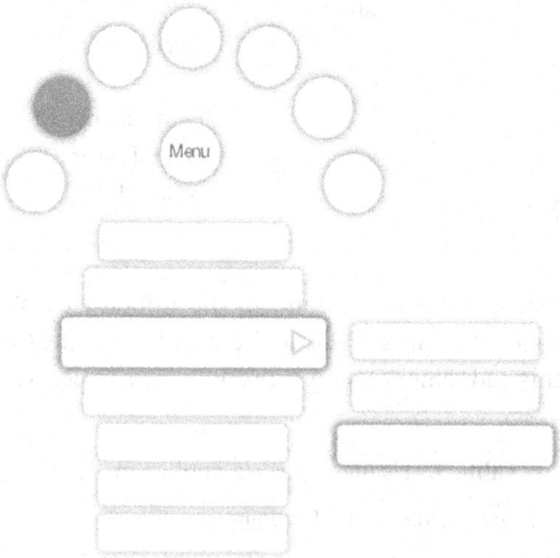

Fig. 5. Design scheme: marking menu combining with fisheye menu with time delay selection mechanism

3 Research Method

3.1 Analytic Hierarchy Process

Analytic Hierarchy Process (AHP) is a multi-objective evaluation method combining qualitative and quantitative analysis. It is a decision-making method for decomposing relevant elements of decision-making problems into goals, criteria and programs, etc. [11].

Complex decision-making processes can be quantified by using AHP. The method needs to subdivide a set of factors into an ordered hierarchical structure and experts should be invited to score the factors in pairs, and then a judgement matrix can be established. In the case where the consistency check is satisfied ($CR < 0.10$), weights are synthesized and the weight value and weight ordering of each factor are obtained. A comprehensive evaluation of indicators of each scheme is performed by user rating, and the evaluation result is obtained.

Determining the evaluation indicators and establishing a pairwise judgment matrix is the most critical step in AHP. From the perspective of usability and the functional requirements of the menu, we determined eight influencing factors of eye movement menus, as shown in Table 2.

Table 2. Eye movement menu usability evaluation indicator

Target	Compare performances of three eye movement interactive menu			
Primary indicators	Efficiency	Fatigue	Satisfaction	Expansibility
Secondary indicators	Task time consuming	Subjective fatigue	Learnability	Information capacity
			Accessibility	Information density
			Fault tolerance	
			Overall user satisfaction	

The judgement matrix refers to the ratio of the importance of each factor in each level to other elements of the same level, and the ratio is expressed in a matrix. AHP generally quantifies this judgement using a proportional scale, as shown in Table 3.

Table 3. Evaluation scale applied to AHP

Semantic differential	Scale value	Explanation
Same good	1	A is as important as B
Slightly better	3	A is slightly more important than B
Significantly better	5	A is significantly more important than B
Strongly better	7	A is strongly more important than B
Extremely better	9	A is extremely more important than B

It is easy to know from the table that the ratio of the importance of factor A to factor B is γ, and the ratio of the importance of factor B to factor A is $1/\gamma$.

3.2 Construction and Processing of Evaluation Matrix

AHP solves the problem of weight distribution of each indicator, but the following questions need to be considered when evaluating each indicator in practice:

1. Data trend requirements are different when quantifying various indicators
2. The dimensions of each indicator are different and difficult to unify

Lv et al. put forward an optimized method which can unify indicators' data trend, the order of magnitude of indicators and can eliminate the dimension [12]. Combined with the evaluation matrix unified by the method and the weight distribution of AHP, the comprehensive weighted scores of each design scheme can be finally obtained.

The method first needs to establish a design scheme evaluation matrix. Assuming that the number of design schemes is ***n***, the number of evaluation indicators is ***m***, and the evaluation matrix can be expressed as $A = \left(a_{ij}\right)_{n \times m}(i = 1, 2, \ldots, \mathrm{n}; \mathrm{j} = 1, 2, \ldots, \mathrm{m})$. Secondly, the indicators determined in AHP are classified into the following three categories, as shown in Table 4, to unify the trend requirements of the evaluation indicators. At the same time, the score trend of the optimal scheme is specified, and corresponding function mapping conversion is performed on each item in the evaluation matrix. Thirdly, using the calculation formula proposed in the method to unify the magnitude of the index and eliminate the dimension, a standardized evaluation matrix, expressed as $Z = \left(z_{ij}\right)_{n \times m}(i = 1, 2, \ldots, \mathrm{n}; \mathrm{j} = 1, 2, \ldots, \mathrm{m})$, is obtained. Finally, combined with the indicator weight matrix $\boldsymbol{W} = \left(w_1, w_2, \ldots, w_m\right)^T$, the comprehensive weighted score matrix $\boldsymbol{S}$ ($\boldsymbol{S} = \boldsymbol{Z} \times \boldsymbol{W}$) of ***n*** schemes can be obtained to complete complex decision-making.

Table 4. Three categories of indicator factors

Category index	Explanation
1	The smaller the data value, the better the indicator
2	The larger the data value, the better the indicator
3	The more stable the data value is at an ideal value, the better the indicator

4 Experimental Exploration

In the above method, the final evaluation of schemes needs to be explored experimentally to obtain the score of the corresponding scheme. An experimental platform was developed with eye-moving equipment. After that, users were recruited to test each design scheme and complete the questionnaire survey after the test. The objective quantitative data, user's subjective satisfaction and experimental values of other subjective indicators could be obtained through the above steps. Finally, the experimental data was processed and analyzed to complete the scientific evaluation of the design schemes.

4.1 Experimental Participants and Experimental Environment

A total of 10 participants with above 5.0 visual acuity and no astigmatism were recruited (age M = 23.0, 5 male and 5 female). In addition, the tested users did not wear all kinds of glasses during the experiment. Before the experiment, all users were tested by the eye tracker calibration. The calibration accuracy errors of X-axis and Y-axis were less than 0.5°, and the eye trajectories of the subjects were visible in the scope of the experimental platform during the experiment.

The experimental platform, developed based on Unity 2017.2.0f3, ran under Windows 10 OS. The eye control device used in the experience was Qing-Tech Eye Control and HTC Vive was used as the VR device. The experimental environment is shown in Fig. 6.

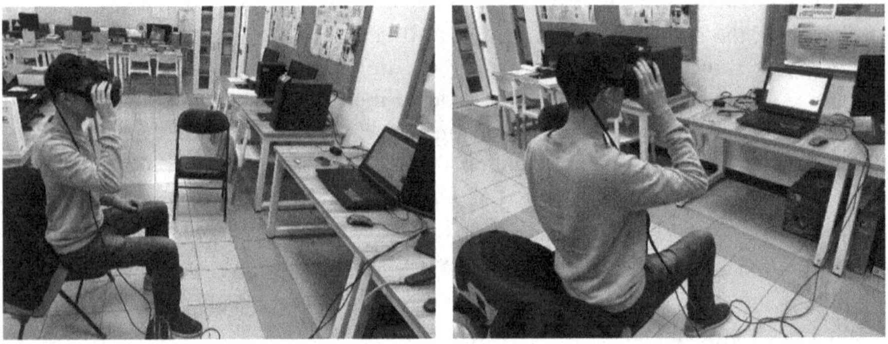

Fig. 6. Experiment environment

4.2 Variable Control and Experiment Task

Independent and dependent variables
The independent variable is menu form, and the dependent variables are task completion time and the score of subjective satisfaction evaluation, learnability, usability and fault tolerance. In order to eliminate the influence of unnecessary factors, the experimental task sequence of the tested users is arranged in the form of a Latin square.

Experiment Task
Indicate each user to locate and select a third level menu item under each design scheme (Task instructions such as: Please select {a third level menu item name} in {a second level menu item name} under {a first level menu item name}). Each design scheme requires the user to complete three selection tasks, that is, each user needs to complete 3 × 3 selection tasks. If the selection is correct, the task is judged to be successful. However, if the item is selected unsuccessfully or the user is difficult to select for other reasons, the task is judged to be unsuccessful. The host starts the timer after issuing the instructions of the experiment task. When the user clicks the third-level menu item, the timer is stopped and the time difference is recorded as the time spent by the user for the task.

4.3 Experiment Procedure

Before the user's formal test, the host will introduce the relevant content and the tasks of the experiment, guide the user to adjust the sitting posture and the experimental equipment to start the experiment. In the formal test, the training platform is first entered. In order to ensure the accuracy of the experiment, the text on the menu item of the test platform is hidden. After the eye movement calibration is successful, the host guides the user to familiarize and learn the eye control operation modes of the three design schemes. When the user can select third-level menu items in three successive times, it is considered that the learning is over and the formal test is entered. When entering the formal experimental platform, the eye tracking calibration is performed. The experiment will be started after the calibration meets the experimental requirements (the calibration accuracy errors in the X-axis direction and the Y-axis direction are less than 0.5°). The host issues the instructions in Latin square order, and the operator presents the corresponding design scheme for the user according to the instruction. After completing nine tasks, the experiment is over. After the test, the user is requested to fill out the post-test satisfaction scale. Seven-point scale, in which "-3" represents "very inconsistent" and "3" represents "very consistent" is used in the test.

5 Data Analysis and Evaluation Results

5.1 Weight Assignment of Indicators in AHP

According to the expert evaluation and literature survey in Sect. 3, the weight distribution of AHP indicators is shown in the Table 5:

Table 5. Weight values of indicators

Primary indicator	Secondary indicator	Level proportion	Overall proportion
Efficiency	Task time consuming	1.00	0.26
Fatigue	Subjective fatigue	1.00	0.08
Satisfaction	Learnability	0.05	0.031
	Accessibility	0.27	0.1674
	Fault tolerance	0.11	0.0682
	Overall user satisfaction	0.57	0.3534
Expansibility	Information capacity	0.67	0.0335
	Information density	0.33	0.0165

The following information was collected during and after the experiments:

1. Task completion time: the time difference between the time when the host issued the instruction and the time when the user completed the task.
2. Fatigue, learnability, usability, subjective satisfaction evaluation and fault tolerance: obtained from the score of the users' post-experimental questionnaire.

5.2 Data Analysis

According to the task completion time, data cleaning was carried out, and the data that didn't conform to the 3σ principle was cleared for subsequent data processing. One-way ANOVA was performed on the completion time of the task. The results showed that there were significant differences among the three schemes. The task completion time and the results of data processing of other indicators are shown in Table 6. Finally, the expert scoring method was used to quantify the information extensibility.

Table 6. Experimental value of each indicator

	Fisheye menu with time delay selection mechanism	Marking menu with selecting sub-selection reconfirmation mechanism	Marking menu combining with fisheye menu with time delay selection mechanism
Task time consuming	9.85954	18.09531	14.81510
Subjective fatigue	0.7	0.2	1.0
Learnability	2.3	1.9	2.0
Accessibility	1.6	0.3	1.2
Fault tolerance	−0.2	2.0	1.4
Overall user satisfaction	1.3	0.9	1.0

5.3 Evaluation Result

Based on the method mentioned in Sect. 3, the comprehensive weighted scores of three eye movement menu schemes were calculated, as shown in Table 7 below.

Table 7. Design schemes score

Scheme	Score
Fisheye menu with time delay selection mechanism	62.7627
Marking menu with selecting sub-selection reconfirmation mechanism	52.7849
Marking menu combining with fisheye menu with time delay selection mechanism	57.2677

5.4 Discussion

The experimental results show that the fisheye linear menu is more easily accepted by participants in the eye movement interactive selection than the marking menu and the mixed menu.

1. Learning costs of fisheye linear menu are relatively low, users can quickly operate it.

2. Although marking menu with selecting sub-selection reconfirmation mechanism has poor performance in terms of time using, learnability, accessibility and fatigue, the index of fault tolerance is significantly better than other menu types. The fault tolerance of such menu design can also effectively avoid " Midas Touch" to ensure accuracy of the selection.
3. Although the fault tolerance of marking menu with selecting sub-selection reconfirmation mechanism is relatively high, its user satisfaction is low. It proves that the user pays more attention to the indicators of efficiency, fatigue and ease-using when using the eye movement menu.
4. The combination of the linear menu and the marking menu can effectively improve the fault tolerance of the linear menu and the inefficiency of the marking menu with selecting sub-selection reconfirmation mechanism. However, the consistency of this menu is not strong, which results in users still need a large range of sights moving to find the first level of the task in the first step of selection process.

6 Conclusion

Compared with previous work, based on the eye tracking technology and eye control system, this study focused on the research and optimization of the interface control design in eye movement scenes. In addition, based on the optimized AHP, the evaluation index set of eye movement menu was constructed by expert evaluation and literature research. Afterwards, three eye movement menu schemes were evaluated by combining expert scoring and objective experiments. The preliminary conclusion is that the fisheye linear menu is more accepted by users. The fault tolerance of menu system can be effectively improved by marking menu with sub-selection reconfirmation mechanism.

However, there are still several shortcomings in the current work:

1. The number of users participating in the experiment is small and the group is single, so the data cannot reach universality.
2. There are actually many indicators for eye movement assessment, but there are not many indicators that can be detected due to hardware limitations. Therefore, the evaluation contains a large number of subjective scoring after the test, instead of acquiring some objective indicators related to eye movement.
3. There may be more possibilities for the design of the menu, and current research only explores the mainstream menu form.
4. In practical application, the size of menu itself and the proportion of interface will affect the experience of menu usage. In the next step, more stringent requirements should be put forward for the size of menu controls, and further in-depth evaluation should be carried out.

References

1. Wu, F., Ge, X., Wang, L., Ge, L.: Types and characteristics of eye-moving human-computer interaction technology. Chin. J. Ergon. **23**(04), 80–86 (2017)
2. Li, T.: Eye control interface design and case development. Master thesis, Zhejiang University (2012)
3. Lu, Y.: Eye tracking system for human-computer interaction on mobile devices. Master thesis, Zhejiang University of Technology (2016)
4. Päivi M.: Twenty years of eye typing: systems and design issues. In: Symposium on Eye Tracking Research & Applications, pp. 15–22 (2002)
5. Li, S., Pan, G., Li, S.: Eye-controlled painting system for disabled. Acta Electronica. Sinica. **39**(S1), 163–167 (2011)
6. Xin, Y.: The design and implementation of eye movement-based text input system. Master thesis, Nanjing University (2015)
7. Feng, F.: Study of eye-movement interaction based on the vehicle player. Master thesis, Hunan University (2014)
8. Liu, D.: The user experience research and design for marking menu and overflow menu integration in 3D mechanical software. Master thesis, Shanghai Jiao Tong University (2011)
9. Chen, K.: User interface design and research based on eye movement-based interaction. Master thesis, Beijing University of Posts and Telecommunications (2018)
10. Gong, X.: Research on headwear sight tracking method for human-computer interaction. Master thesis, University of Science and Technology of China (2010)
11. Kang, H., Zhao, K.: Evaluation model of automobile design scheme based on analytic hierarchy process. Packag. Eng. **35**(22), 53–57 (2014)
12. Lv, F., Tian, F., Du, Y., Chen, K., Hou, W., Ren, L., Dai, G.: NEM: a natural user interface evaluation method based on reality framework. J. Comput. Aided Des. Comput. Graphics **29**(11), 2076–2082 (2017)

Study on Spatiotemporal Characteristics of Gaze Gesture Input

Wen-jun Hou[1,2], Si-qi Wu[1,2(✉)], Xiao-lin Chen[1,2], and Kai-xiang Chen[1,2]

[1] School of Digital Media and Design Arts, Beijing University of Posts and Telecommunications, Beijing 100876, China
1519390005@qq.com
[2] Beijing Key Laboratory of Network Systems and Network Culture, Beijing University of Posts and Telecommunications, Beijing 100876, China

Abstract. The gaze gesture input has the advantages of high bandwidth, high efficiency, no misoperation and high customization, but it also has the disadvantages of high cognitive load and high fatigue degree. At present, few researches have thoroughly explored the regularity of gaze gesture input, which cause designers lack of design guidance, and it is difficult to reasonably apply gaze gesture input in interaction. This paper focuses on the study of the spatiotemporal features of the gaze gesture input. An experiment was designed so that the input region size, the feedforward type and the input gesture shape were within-subject experimental variables. By analyzing 1200 trajectory data of gaze gestures to exploring the effects of these three variables on the performance of and the subjective satisfaction of the gaze gesture input, the details of the three major characteristics of gaze gesture-based interaction were summarized, which are the input continuity, the implicit interaction and the real-time feedback. These may provide design guidance for gaze gesture interaction designers.

Keywords: Eye movement-based interaction · Gaze gesture input · Spatiotemporal feature · Feedforward

1 Introduction

The explosive growth of total information makes human-computer interaction more frequent and complex. Eye movement-based interaction has attracted more and more attention due to its high bandwidth, continuous input and natural interaction. As early as the early 1990s, the development of eye position input system based on eye tracking system has attracted much attention [1]. The improvement of accuracy and resolution of eye tracking technology makes eye movement-based input possible. Especially with the development of real-time eye tracking measurement technology, eye movement-based interaction has become a useful human-computer interaction mode [2, 3]. Many studies have confirmed that eye movement-based interaction has a faster targeting speed [2–4] than traditional interaction methods (such as mouse). Moreover, because it can only use eye movement to interact with machines, even people with limb defects

M. Kurosu (Ed.): HCII 2019, LNCS 11567, pp. 283–302, 2019.
https://doi.org/10.1007/978-3-030-22643-5_23

can easily use it, which also makes the research of eye movement-based interaction have high social value.

The essence of eye movement-based interaction is to record and recognize the movement mode of human eyes through devices, and take specific movement mode as input signal to control specific tasks. In human-computer interaction, blinking, gazing and saccade scanning are usually used as input signals.

At present, the application and research of eye movement-based interaction mainly focus on blink input [5, 6] and gaze input [7–9]. These two input modes require high spatiotemporal characteristics of user interface, and often accompanied by low efficiency, narrow bandwidth, easy misoperation and other usability problems. This also makes the related research of eye movement interaction stagnate, and fails to get real application and promotion from the lab to the market. The definition of gaze gesture comes from the direction or amplitude of the saccade, so the requirement for the spatiotemporal characteristics of the user interface is very low, which is not easy to cause Midas contact problem, and has the advantages of high bandwidth, high efficiency and high customization. However, gaze gesture input also has the remarkable characteristics of high cognitive load. If we can overcome these shortcomings, give full play to the advantages of gaze gesture input, and apply it reasonably to design, it will bring high application value and release the potential of eye movement-based interaction. Table 1 shows the difference between blink input, gaze input and gaze gesture input.

Table 1. Comparison of three input mechanisms for eye movement-based interaction

	Blink input	Gaze input	Gaze gesture input
Parameter	Blink duration/Blink frequency	Fixation duration/Fixation field	Saccade length/Saccade duration/Saccade velocity
Bandwidth	Low	High	Lowest
Efficiency	Fastest	Slow	Fast
Requirements for spatiotemporal characteristics of interfaces	High	Very high	Low
Naturalness	Quite natural	Natural	Not very natural
“Midas contact” problem	Appears often	Appears very often	Appears rarely
Application status	A long history, obvious shortcomings and few applications	A long history, many applications	A short history, few applications

However, the research on gaze gesture input is relatively less, and mainly focuses on the study of simple gaze gesture input symbols. The performance of experimental task completion is almost the only research indicator. No one has ever studied the appropriate input area size for gaze gesture, and no one has ever set the experimental conditions for gaze gesture input in the eye-friendly zone (ignoring the ergonomics to develop input performance). Moreover, few people have studied the effect of feed-forward types on gaze gesture input. To sum up, there are many factors that affect the performance of gaze gesture input, but many previous studies are too narrow to have broad practical significance.

In this paper, the spatiotemporal characteristics of gaze gesture input were focused. The effects of input area size, feedforward type and input gesture shape on the performance of gaze gesture input and the subjective satisfaction of users were synthetically explored. Then, the performance of gaze gesture input in the input continuity, the implicit interaction and the real-time feedback were summarized.

2 Related Work

Eye movement-based interaction takes vision as input channel and has the potential to replace traditional mouse-like pointing devices (such as mouse, stylus, finger touch screen). The difference in application between eye movement and mouse-like pointing devices makes the spatiotemporal characteristics of eye movement-based interaction significantly different from traditional ones. The time characteristic in eye movement-based interaction refers to the time threshold (residence time, blink time, etc.) required to trigger an interface instruction using eye movement data (including eye gaze, blink, eye gesture, etc.). The spatial characteristics in eye movement-based interaction refer to the spatial accuracy needed to select the interactive objects on the interface based on eye-movement interaction (including the size of the interactive objects, the distance between objects, the arrangement of objects, etc.).

In the study of spatiotemporal characteristics of eye movement-based interaction, Feng (2006) et al. found that for human-computer interface based on eye-movement gaze input technology, the horizontal arrangement of objects was significantly better than the vertical arrangement [10]. Zhu (2014) et al. found that in the touch screen interaction system, by observing the eye movement data, the user's visual focus in the operation process is mainly concentrated on the position of the object and the target, while only a small amount of attention is paid to the process, so there is enough data and time for eye movement behavior to be an input mechanism [11].

In addition to spatiotemporal characteristics, the study of feedback in eye movement-based interaction can also help to improve the availability of eye movement-based interaction. Feng (2004) et al. found that introducing visual feedback in eye movement-based interaction can improve the efficiency of searching, locating and activating the target objects on the interface, while introducing visual display of the border of the interactive objects in eye movement-based interaction interface has no significant impact on user's performance [12]. Zhu (2014) found that the availability of the touch screen interactive system has been significantly improved when the eye movement-based assisted operation was introduced. Moreover, if appropriate interference indication is introduced into the system, it will help users to establish target objects faster [11].

The above studies mainly focus on gaze gesture input. Gaze gesture input, also known as saccade input, is of great research value because of its advantages of fast speed, low requirement for spatiotemporal characteristics of the interface and difficulty in misoperation. Firstly, the fastest speed of saccade up to 400°–600° per second which means that gaze gesture input can reach 1° to 40° viewing angle within 30–120 ms which is much faster than a standard gaze input unit time 300–500 ms. Secondly, as gaze gesture input does not require specific interactive controls and elements on the interface, the interactive time is also relatively high robustness and it does not necessarily require an accurate response time, interface design will be easier and faster because of the low requirements of the spatiotemporal characteristics of the interface. Thirdly, since gaze gesture input is sequence-based and does not require a precise starting point and ending point, it is naturally more advantageous for Midas contact than blinking and gazing [12].

There are relatively few studies on spatiotemporal characteristics of gaze gesture input, and there is no decisive conclusion. Xin (2015) et al. studied the efficiency of gaze gesture and only analyzed the input performance of subjective defined short-range and long-range gaze gesture [13]. Møllenbach et al. found that short-range gaze gesture trajectories triggered faster than long-range gaze gesture trajectories, and the speed of horizontal trajectories performed better than vertical trajectories' [14]. However, there are some inaccuracies in this experiment. The experiment was carried out on a rectangular screen. In order to control the distance of gaze gesture in horizontal and vertical directions equally, the size of the trigger area of gaze gesture in these two directions is different, which may affect the validity of the experimental results. The flaws in this experimental design can be supported to a certain extent in the study by Heikkilä (2012) et al. In their study, similar experimental content has reached the opposite conclusion that gaze gesture moves faster in the vertical direction than in the horizontal direction [15]. Heikkilä et al. also found that there was no significant difference in time between short-range and long-range gaze gesture when eye movements were performed using closed eyes to end eye movement-based control. They think it is possible that in their experimental design, users only need to move their eyes in the right direction without precise eye movement control, which makes the conclusion different from that of Møllenbach [16]..

In fact, the gaze gesture input mechanism relies on saccade, and the speed of saccade is extremely fast, the fastest speed can reach 400°/s–600° /s. Therefore, if there is no significant difference in length between the same type of gaze gesture, performance should not vary too much. In ergonomics, there is a comfort zone when the human eye rotates. When rotating in the comfort zone, the muscle burden is small, it is not easy to fatigue, and the speed of eye movement is fast, and vice versa. However, previous researchers often neglected this point when they studied the performance of gaze gesture. We can assume that the reason for the significant difference in the performance of long-range and short-range gaze gesture in some experiments may not be simply because of the difference in the length of gaze gesture, but because long-range gaze gesture may have exceeded the comfort zone of gaze while short-range gaze gesture not. As shown in Fig. 1, there is a rotational comfort zone in eye rotation. The optimum upper and lower regions: upper 25° + lower 30° = 55°. The best left and right regions : left 15° + right 15° = 30°.

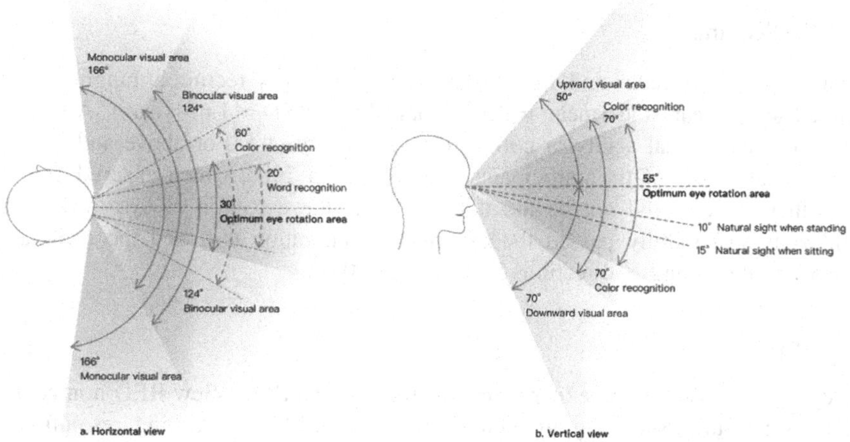

Fig. 1. Rotational comfort zones in eye rotation. a. horizontal view b. vertical view

Gaze gesture input has not been fully applied yet because of its obvious disadvantages. How to design gaze gestures as input symbols is a very difficult research topic. If the gaze gesture is too simple, it is easy to overlap with the unconscious eye movement, leading to misoperation; but if it is too complex, it will increase the user's learning cost, memory burden and cognitive load, which is contrary to the original intention of natural interaction. Previous studies have mostly focused on simple gaze gestures (single-step long gaze gestures), which are suitable for completing simple human-computer interaction tasks. Although multi-step gaze gesture (multi-step or radian gaze gesture) is difficult for users to learn and has a high degree of input fatigue, it is more suitable for completing complex human-computer interaction tasks because of its higher bandwidth. Istance et al. designed a series of composite gaze gestures for World of Warcraft games. Experiments have shown that the use of composite gaze gestures can interact more accurately than a single gaze gesture, but it will occupy a large number of cognitive channels [17]. Feedforward (giving guidance before the user performs the operation) as a special form of feedback, can reduce the user's learning burden and operating burden, so it is worth considering.

In summary, this article conducted research on the following four aspects:

(1) Gaze gesture input area size was taken as the control variable to study its influence on input performance.
(2) Input gesture type was taken as the control variable to study its influence on input performance.
(3) Feedforward type was taken as the control variable to study its influence on input performance.
(4) A multi-factor analysis of the above three factors and input performance was conducted to investigate whether there is a cross-effect effect.

3 Experiment

3.1 Participants

20 participants (10 males and 10 females) were voluntarily recruited, ranging in age from 20 to 25 years old (mean = 22.2 years old and SD = 1.67 years). All of the participants had visual acuity or corrected visual acuity of 5.0 or above and the corrected visual acuity of the participants was all within 200°, which ensured that the lenses they wore would not be too thick to affect the detection of eye tracker. All participants successfully passed the eye tracker calibration test, and the calibration accuracy in the X and Y directions was less than 0.5°.

3.2 Device

The eye tracker used in the experiment was the German SMI iView RED non-contact eye tracker with a sampling frequency of up to 500 Hz, a tracking resolution of 0.1 deg, and a gaze positioning accuracy of 0.5°–1°. The dedicated display for the eye tracker was a DELL 22-inch display. The physical size of the electronic screen was 475 mm long, 298 mm wide, and the resolution was 1680pi * 1050pi, with a ratio of 16:10. In terms of software, the software used to control the eye tracker device was iView X version and the analysis software was BeGaze. Experimental staff for the experimental included an operator, a recorded and a host.

3.3 Selection of Tasks

Firstly, the experimental level of input region size variables was determined. The relationship of human visual angle range is shown in Fig. 2 where α is the horizontal view size, β is the vertical view size, L is the horizontal view range length, W is the vertical view range length, and o is the center point of the screen. When the human eye's line of sight is perpendicular to o point in the center of the screen, H is called the line of sight distance from the human eye to the screen.

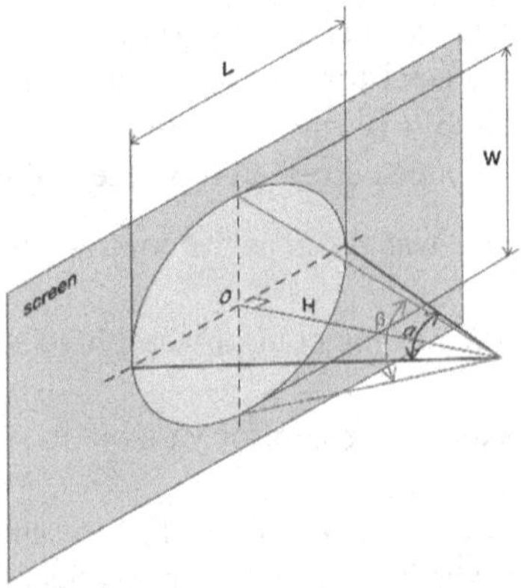

Fig. 2. View angle size and target size diagram

The relationship between the size of the perspective, the range of the perspective, and the line-of-sight distance is shown in formula 1 and formula 2.

$$\alpha = 2\mathrm{arctg}\frac{L}{2H} \tag{1}$$

$$L = 2H\mathrm{arctg}\frac{\alpha}{2} \tag{2}$$

According to the physical size and pixel size of the screen used for the observed materials in the experimental equipment, 10 levels of experiments as shown in Table 2 have been defined (the data have been rounded). The determination of the maximum viewing angle depends on the maximum height of the experimental screen, that is 298 mm. On the basis of 25°, the level of other variables is determined by decreasing the angle of view by 5°. When the angle is less than 5°, the decrease is changed to 1°. All horizontal viewing angles, both left and right rotation and up and down rotation, are in the comfortable region of rotation, as detailed in Table 2.

Table 2. Ten levels of the input area

Pixel (px)	View angel (°)	Physical dimension (mm)	Other instructions
1050 * 1050	27.89	298	The best eye movement area (within 30°)
937 * 937.37	25	266.03	The best eye movement area (within 30°)
745 * 745.54	20	211.59	The best eye movement area (within 30°)
556 * 556.65	15	157.98	The best eye movement area (within 30°)
369 * 369.92	10	104.99	The best eye movement area (within 30°)
184 * 184.61	5	52.39	Parafoveal (2°–5°)
147 * 147.65	4	41.90	Parafoveal (2°–5°)
110 * 110.72	3	31.42	Parafoveal (2°–5°)
73 * 73.80	2	20.95	Foreal area (1°–2°)
36 * 36.90	1	10.47	Foreal area (1°–2°)

Secondly, the experimental level of input gesture type variables was determined. Previous studies have been divorced from reality, and most of them were researches of single-step gaze gesture, and did not depend on specific application scenarios. The experimental level of the input symbol type variable in this experiment was derived from the action in the consensus set obtained in the previous experiment, from which the two representative inputs of square and circle were selected.

Finally, the experimental level of input feedforward type variables was determined. Considering the attention allocation mechanism of human eye movement, the experimental level was designed as follows: line-like feedforward, no feedforward and point-like feedforward.

In summary, there were three control variables in the experiment, including 10 levels, 2 levels and 3 levels, totaling 60 input tasks. In order to facilitate the experimental operation, during the actual experiment, the tasks were divided into 6 groups, as shown in Table 3.

Table 3. Details of 60 tasks in 6 groups

Group	Input gesture type	Feedforward type	Gaze gesture input area size
Group1	Square	Line-like feedforward	28°–1° (All ten levels:28°, 25°, 20°, 15°, 10°, 5°, 4°, 3°, 2°, 1°)
Group2	Square	No feedforward	28°–1° (All ten levels:28°, 25°, 20°, 15°, 10°, 5°, 4°, 3°, 2°, 1°)
Group3	Square	Point-like feedforward	28°–1° (All ten levels:28°, 25°, 20°, 15°, 10°, 5°, 4°, 3°, 2°, 1°)
Group4	Circle	Line-like feedforward	28°–1° (All ten levels:28°, 25°, 20°, 15°, 10°, 5°, 4°, 3°, 2°, 1°)
Group5	Circle	No feedforward	28°–1° (All ten levels:28°, 25°, 20°, 15°, 10°, 5°, 4°, 3°, 2°, 1°)
Group6	Circle	Point-like feedforward	28°–1° (All ten levels:28°, 25°, 20°, 15°, 10°, 5°, 4°, 3°, 2°, 1°)

According to the experiment task, 60 stimulating materials were developed. The stimulating materials were on the grey background, the input area was white background, the feed-forward reminder was located in the white background, and the inner margin was controlled between 0.5°–1°.

3.4 Procedure

Firstly, the participants adjusted their sitting posture to maintain a relatively comfortable sitting posture, with their eyes just perpendicular to the center of the display screen, and their heads aligned and fixed. The distance between their eyes and the screen was measured and determined to be about 600 mm. Specific experimental scenario is shown in Fig. 3.

The experiment was introduced to the participants before the experiment was officially started. A training opportunity was provided before each group of experiments begins. Between groups of experiments, three minutes' rest time was provided, and within each group, 20 s' rest time was provided.

After all the experiments were completed, participants were asked to fill in questionnaires to evaluate the overall satisfaction of each task, that was, "I feel satisfied with the overall performance of this gaze gesture input". Satisfaction refers to whether users feel it is easy, accurate and fast to complete the task with gaze gesture input. The design

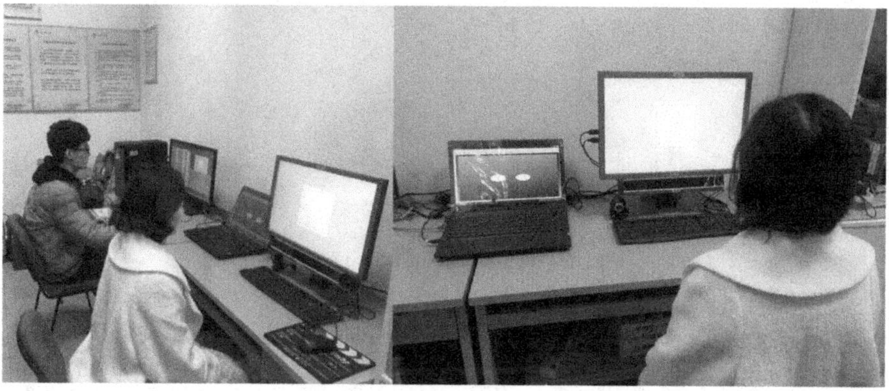

Fig. 3. Experimental scene

of the questionnaire was based on the Likert 10-point scale, with 10 representing "very satisfied" and 1 representing "very dissatisfied". The Likert 10-point scale can increase the rating, and the participants are more likely to give a score and improve the discrimination of the results [18], which is suitable for experiments with up to 60 samples in this evaluation. The whole experiment lasted about 60 min.

4 Results

The results of the experiment totaled 1200 input trajectories, of which 3 participants made obvious errors in the trajectory results of their individual tasks. There were two types of errors: one was systematic errors, that was, the device did not accurately record the input trajectory; the other was that users were distracted for a long time, and the characteristics of the input trajectory were obviously deviated from the whole. The number of valid input trajectories collected was 1020.

4.1 Qualitative Analysis of Input Trajectory

Rule1: It is most accurate to draw the square with gaze gesture input, when the feedforward form is point-like feedforward.
As shown in Fig. 4, the different feedforward types had very significant differences for the square trajectories ultimately drawn by the participants. The comprehensive performance of point-like feedforward was the best, while that no feedforward was the worst, mainly reflected in two points: first, the positioning of the four key points was not accurate; second, during the scanning process, there were a lot of additional fixation behaviors.

Rule2: The fourth step of drawing a square shows an offset.
When drawing a square, the fourth step of the trajectory generally showed an inclination of about 8° instead of vertical. When drawing a square, the trajectory of the fourth step was inclined about 8°, not vertical. The trajectory of the second step also showed a certain slope, but it was not obvious as the fourth step. The same situation did not occur in the first and third steps.

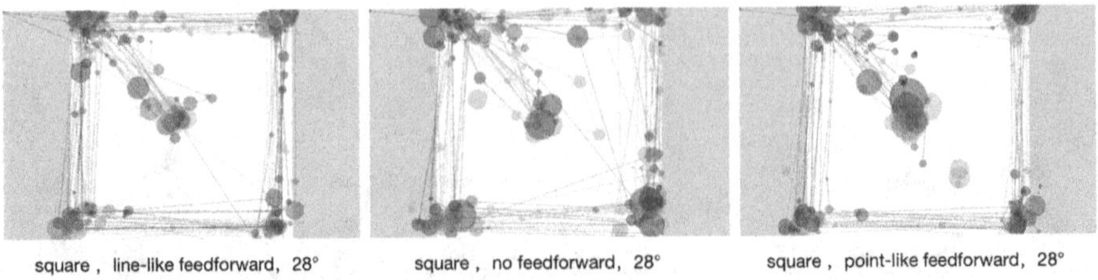

Fig. 4. All trajectories of the square

By analyzing the set of trajectory diagrams, we can find that there were two cases of b and c in Fig. 5b showed that when the third step was drawn, the position of the scanning end point exceeded the target position, and the participant added a fixation point to modify the figure in the fourth step. In the case of c, when the third step was drawn, the scanning end point positioning failed to reach the target position, and the participant added a fixation point for correction, but often the corrected point exceeded the target position. As a result, most of the graphs obtained in the final drawing present the situation of the fourth inclined step.

In conclusion, it can be speculated that the positioning accuracy of horizontal saccade is less than that of vertical saccade, while the positioning accuracy of left-to-right saccade is better than that of right-to-left saccade.

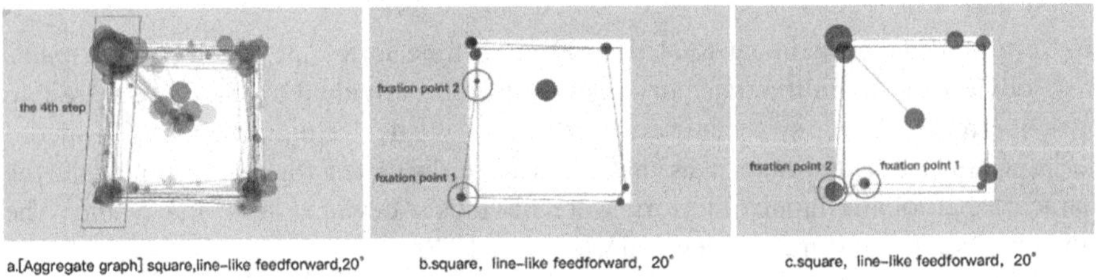

Fig. 5. An illustration of the fourth step of drawing a square to show the offset

Rule3: Point-like feedforward has a negative effect on the accuracy of drawing a circle.

Different feedforward types had a significant impact on the final circular trajectory. The performance of line-like feedforward was the best, while that of no feedforward was the worst. The fixation points of the circular trajectory drawn with line-like feedforward were evenly distributed on the circular border, compared with the figure drawn without feedforward, which deviates a lot from the circle. The result of point-like feedforward was like a diamond. After the experiment was completed, many of the participants bluntly stated that they needed to allocate extra attention to prevent them from simply connecting the points with straight lines, as shown in Fig. 6.

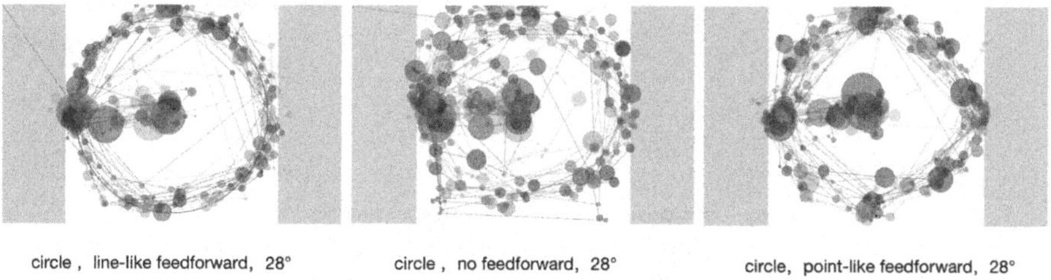

Fig. 6. All trajectories of the circle

Rule4: The participants automatically add key points to correct the drawing of the graph.

In Rule 3, point-like feedforward was counterproductive for guiding the user to draw an accurate circle. If we look at each participant's drawing process, as shown in Fig. 7, we can find that most of the participants unconsciously completed the presentation with one saccade, but also subconsciously added a fixation point between the two key points to correct their drawing.

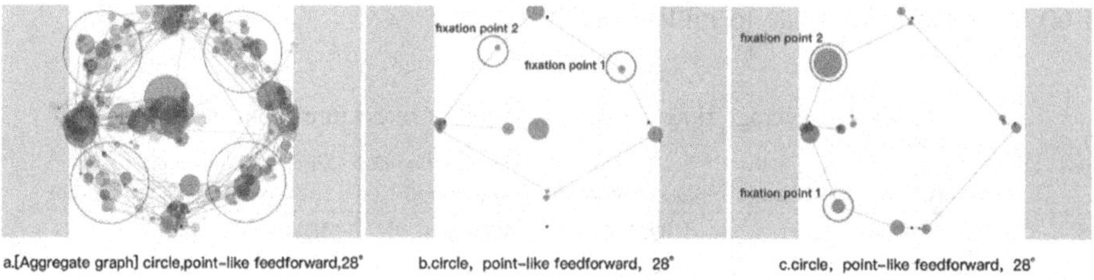

Fig. 7. An illustration that participants automatically add fixation points to correct their drawing

Rule5: The accuracy of symbol rendering decreases significantly when the input area is less than 5°.

The experimental results showed that when the input area decreased to less than 5°, the accuracy of drawing symbols decreased significantly, and the accuracy of drawing square was better than that of drawing circle. Usually when the input area droped to 3°, it was very difficult to distinguish the approximate figure from the trajectory (as shown in Fig. 8c and d). Of course, a small number of excellent participants also showed good accuracy when using gaze gestures to draw in small areas (as shown in Fig. 8c and d). Combined with the results of the loud thinking of the participants, when the input area was less than 3°, the participants felt that the input experience was extremely poor. First, it was necessary to concentrate a large amount of attention to control the unconscious shaking of the eyeball. Second, without feedback, participants felt frustrated if the drawing is inaccurate.

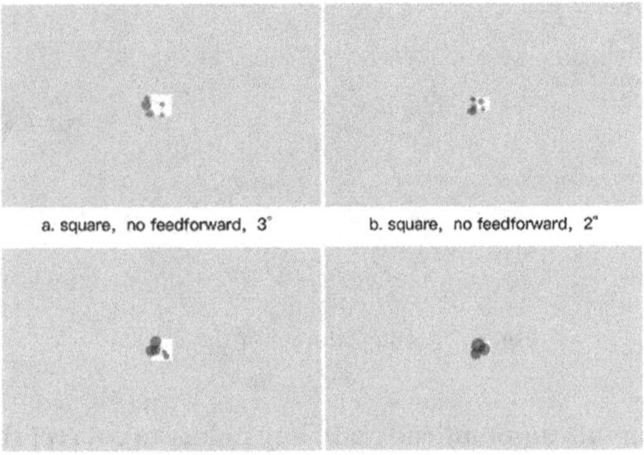

Fig. 8. Trajectory with too small input area

4.2 Quantitative Analysis of Input Trajectory

1020 valid sample data collected by eye movement equipment were quantitatively analyzed for input performance. Table 4 shows the average time-consuming statistics of 60 input tasks (accurate to milliseconds).

Table 4. Average time-consuming of 60 gaze gesture input tasks

(ms)	Square + line-like feedforward	Square + no feedforward	Square + point-like feedforward	Circle + line-like feedforward	Circle + no feedforward	Circle + point-like feedforward
28°	3716	3905	4109	4849	5590	5343
25°	3656	3958	3895	4860	5294	5395
20°	3577	3912	3895	4654	5324	5594
15°	3487	4188	3586	4022	4884	5236
10°	3105	3950	3642	3604	4662	4649
5°	3085	3808	3335	3461	4114	4270
4°	3066	3771	3272	3396	3923	4042
3°	3029	3614	3206	3216	3956	3820
2°	2870	3524	3016	3082	3759	3322
1°	2838	3410	2831	2785	3443	3070

Figure 9 was obtained by visualizing the above table data. From the results, as the input area became smaller, the overall input performance increases; the overall performance of the square input was better than the circular input; the performance of the line-like feedforward was the best. Simply analyzing the impact of each factor, we found that the three factors had significant impact on the input time (the P values of the three factors are less than 0.001).

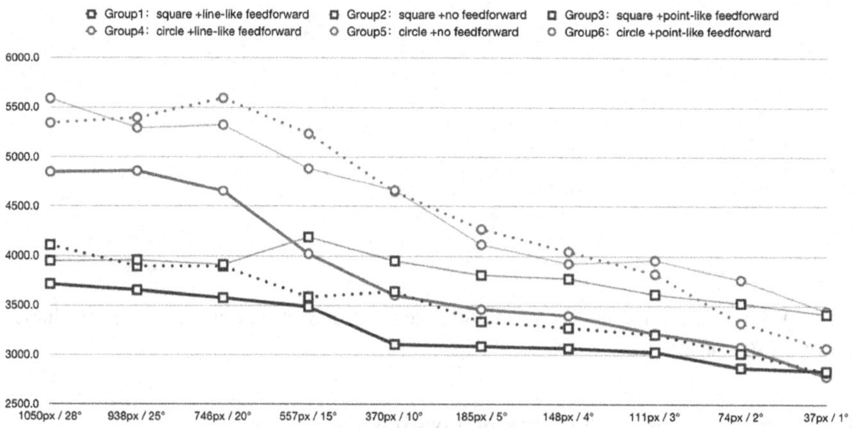

Fig. 9. Mean input time of six groups of tasks with different input area sizes

However, the eye movement-based speed (average eye movement angle per second) continued to decline as shown in Fig. 10. Eye movement-based speed reflects the degree of fatigue to a certain extent. The faster the eye movement-based speed is, the less effort the user pays to concentrate on the task, so user's fatigue is lower. When input area size was larger than 15°, the eye movement speed of the user was faster and would not cause obvious fatigue.

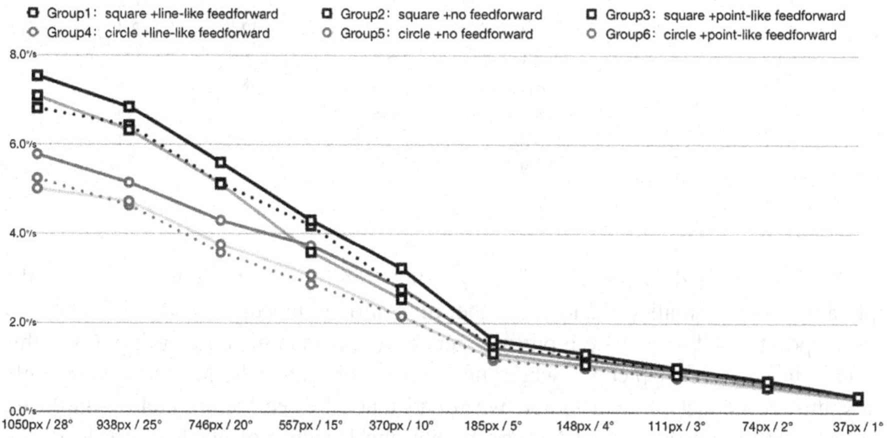

Fig. 10. Eye movement-based speed

In addition, it can be seen from the figure that each group of data had obvious variation rules and cross effects. In order to verify the above judgment, the data results were analyzed by univariate multivariate analysis of variance. The results are shown in Fig. 11.

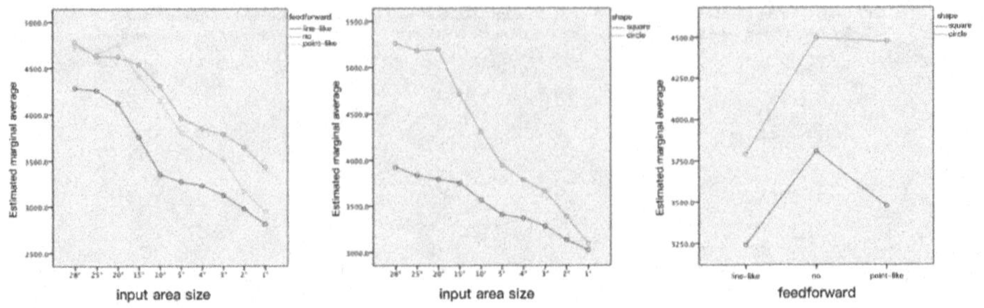

Fig. 11. Multivariate cross-effects of input time (a.size & feedforward b.size & shape c. feedforward & shape)

4.3 Change Law of the Number of Fixation Points

The variation of the number of fixation points was studied. Table 5 shows the statistics of the average number of fixation points for 60 input tasks.

Table 5. The average number of fixation points for 60 input tasks

(number)	Square + line-like feedforward	Square + no feedforward	Square + point-like feedforward	Circle + line-like feedforward	Circle + no feedforward	Circle + point-like feedforward
28°	13.1	11.9	13.4	16.8	18.9	18.4
25°	11.2	12.4	11.6	16.9	17.6	18.2
20°	10.5	12.5	11.3	16.1	16.8	18.1
15°	10.6	11.8	10.1	13.6	15.3	16.2
10°	9	14.1	9.4	11.2	12.5	12.4
5°	7.3	8.6	8.1	8.9	9.4	9.2
4°	7.1	8.1	7.5	7.2	8.2	7.8
3°	6.1	7	6.6	6.8	7.2	6.5
2°	3.1	5.3	3.8	4.8	6.2	4.4
1°	2.8	4.1	2.9	4.8	4.9	3.8

The above table data was visualized and shown in Fig. 12. From the results, as the input area became smaller, the total number of fixation points decreased; the number of fixation points used for square input was generally less than the circular input, but this situation became inconspicuous when the input area began to be less than 5°. Simply analyzing the impact of each factor, we found that all three factors had a significant impact on the number of input fixation points (the P values of all three are less than 0.05).

In addition, it can be found from the figure that each group of data had obvious variation rules and cross effects. In order to verify the above judgments, the data results were analyzed by univariate multivariate analysis of variance. The results are shown in Fig. 13.

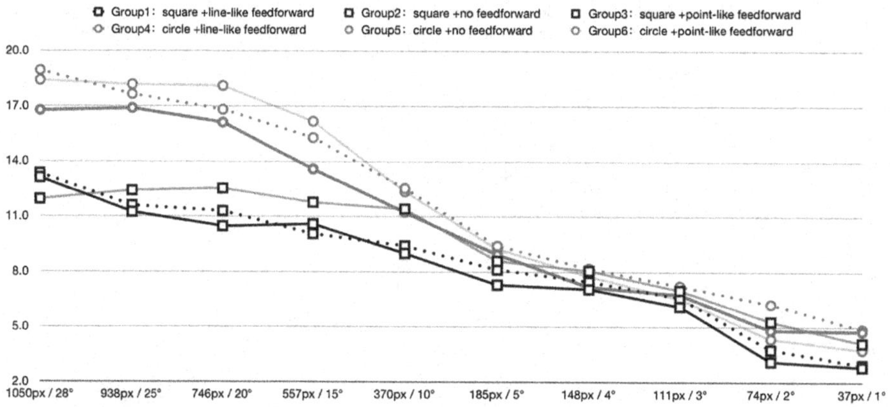

Fig. 12. The mean number of fixation points for six tasks with different input sizes

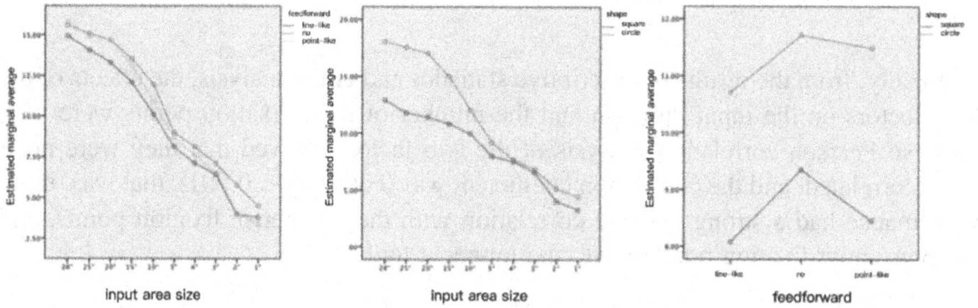

Fig. 13. Multivariate cross-effects of fixation points (a.size &feedforward b.size &shape c. feedforward &shape)

The results of multivariate cross-analysis are as follows:

Firstly, there was no significant cross-effect between feedforward and input area size ($p = 0.974 > 0.05$). In general, no matter what kind of feedforward, their trend of the number of fixation points changed consistently, which decreased with the decrease of the size of the input area.

Secondly, there was a significant cross-effect between shape and size of input area ($p = 0.000 < 0.001$). When the input area size was greater than 5°, the number of square input fixation points was less than that of the circular input; when the input area startedto be less than 5°, the difference of the input symbols had little effect on the number of fixation points.

Thirdly, there was no significant cross-effect between feedforward and shape ($p = 0.405 > 0.05$). Generally speaking, both line-like feedforward and point-like feedforward could reduce the number of fixation points used in input, which was not affected by the type of input shape.

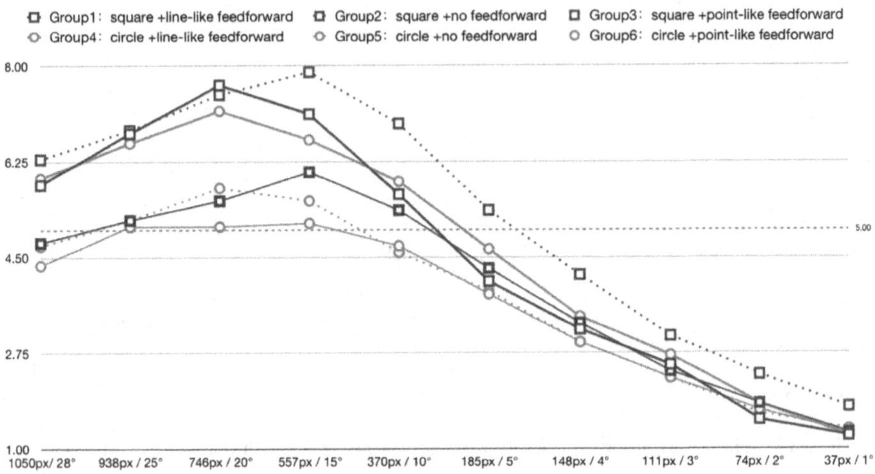

Fig. 14. Mean satisfaction of six tasks with different input sizes

Finally, from the results of descriptive statistics and cross-analysis, the effects of the three factors on the input duration and the number of input fixation points were very close, so Pearson correlation analysis of the two factors showed that they were positively correlated, and the correlation coefficient was 0.0651 ($p < 0.001$), that was, input performance had a strong positive correlation with the number of fixation points, and the more input fixation points were, the longer it took.

4.4 Subjective Satisfaction Evaluation

The data of 17 users collected were summarized and counted to obtain the comparison chart of the average satisfaction in Fig. 14. It was found that the overall satisfaction was higher when the input area was between 10°–20°. When the input area began to be less than 5°, the satisfaction decreased rapidly. The overall satisfaction of square input was better than that of circular input, but this phenomenon was not obvious when the input area was less than 5°. Point-like feedforward improved the satisfaction of square input but reduced the satisfaction of circular input. Simply analyzing the impact of each factor, we found that all three factors had a significant impact on satisfaction (the P values of all three are less than 0.001).

In addition, it can be found from the figure that each group of data had obvious variation rules and cross effects. In order to verify the above judgments, the data results were analyzed by univariate multivariate analysis of variance. The results are shown in Fig. 15.

Firstly, feedforward and input area size had significant cross-effects ($p = 0.009 < 0.001$). When the size of the input area was larger than 10°, the satisfaction when there was feedforward was much higher than that without feedforward, and the satisfaction of point-like feedforward was higher than that of line-like feedforward. When the input area began to be less than 10°, the existence of feedforward had little effect on the input satisfaction.

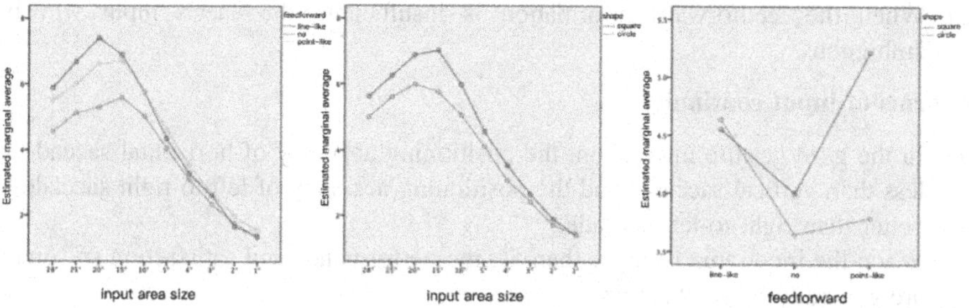

Fig. 15. Multivariate cross-effects of satisfaction (a.size & feedforward b.size & shape c. feedforward & shape)

Secondly, there was no significant cross-impact effect between shape and input area size ($p = 0.15 > 0.05$). In general, whether the input is square or circular, their satisfaction trends are consistent, and they all change with the size of the input area.

Thirdly, the feedforward and shape factors had significant cross-effects ($P = 0.000 < 0.001$). When there was line-like feedforward, the satisfaction of circle and square had little difference; when there was no feedforward, the satisfaction of square was obviously higher than that of circle; when there was point-like feedforward, the satisfaction of square was much higher than that of circle. In general, feedforward can improve the user's satisfaction at gaze gesture input, but different feedforward types have different help for different graphics. For example, point-like feedforward plays a great role in promoting input square, but it has very limited help for input circle.

5 Conclusion

In this paper, the spatiotemporal characteristics of gaze gesture input were focused. The conclusions of this study include the following aspects:

In terms of real-time feedback:

(1) Feedforward is very important, which can reduce the number of fixation points and improve performance.
(2) Drawing straight lines with point-like feedforward is more accurate, while drawing curves with line-like feedback has better accuracy.
(3) When the user's eye movements have sight deviates or the number of points in the point-like feedforward is insufficient to describe feature of the gaze gesture, the user will automatically correct the data by adding fixation points.

In terms of implicit interaction:

(1) When user performs gaze gesture, it is easier to lead to visual fatigue which tend to cause fuzzy input which has low accuracy.
(2) When the input area is smaller than 5°, the drawing accuracy of gaze gesture is degraded, and the satisfaction is very low.

(3) When the feedforward information is insufficient, the user's input will be ambiguous.

In terms of input continuity:

(1) In the gaze gesture interaction, the positioning accuracy of horizontal saccade is less than vertical saccade, and the positioning accuracy of left-to-right saccade is better than right-to-left saccade.
(2) When the input area is larger than 5°, the performance and satisfaction of square are generally better than circle.
(3) With the decrease of input area size, the number of fixation points decreased significantly, and the performance of gaze gesture interaction also increased significantly. However, the eye movement-based speed (average eye movement angle per second) continued to decline. Eye movement-based speed reflects the degree of fatigue to a certain extent. The faster the eye movement-based speed is, the less effort the user pays to concentrate on the task, so user's fatigue is lower. When input area size is larger than 15°, the eye movement speed of the user is faster and will not cause obvious fatigue. Satisfaction is higher when the gaze gesture interaction area is 10°–28°.

According to the research on the spatiotemporal characteristics of gaze gesture interaction, the following reference points in the gaze gesture interaction design are obtained:

(1) Considering the accuracy of gaze gesture, the vertical saccade accuracy is better than the horizontal saccade, and the positioning accuracy of left-to-right saccade is better than right-to-left saccade.
(2) Gestures consisting of only straight lines should be adopted as far as possible in the design of gaze gesture, and feedforward with sufficient information should be used to guide users.
(3) When the gestures consisting of curves have to be drawn, line-like feedforward or point-like feedforward with sufficient information should be used to reduce the cognitive burden of user.
(4) It is not advisable to set the eye gesture interaction area smaller than 5°, and the gaze gesture interaction task should be designed as far as possible between 10° and 28°.

Through interviews with the participants, one of the reasons for the influence of the gaze gesture input performance was that once the user is psychologically aware that he was using the gaze gesture to input, the spirit would be tightened. In order to pursue the accuracy of the input, the user's eye fatigue would increase dramatically, and the psychological pressure would double, which in turn would affect the performance of continuous gaze gesture input.

According to the experimental results, the relationship between the degree of eye load and the degree of attention distribution is roughly described as shown in Fig. 16. The Y-axis represents load, including physiological load and psychological load. When the user is in unconscious eye movement, the load is very low, and is not affected by the complexity of eye movement. When the user is in the subconscious eye movement area, the load is affected by the complexity of the eye movement. The X-axis represents attention resources. When users realize that they are using gaze gesture to input, they begin to allocate attention resources, and the allocation is affected by the complexity of the eye movement. The unconscious eye movement area, which is the user's natural eye movement area, is usually used as the data source for the implicit input of eye movement in human-computer interaction. Subconscious eye movement area is usually used as a data source for explicit input in human-computer interaction.

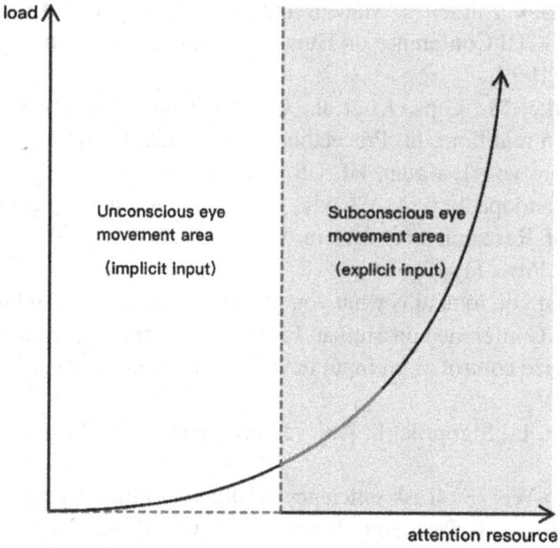

Fig. 16. Relationship between attention distribution of gaze gesture input and load

Not all eye movements are suitable as input instructions. The blue line in Fig. 16 is used to represent the appropriate input state. In the specific application process, we should follow the principle of attention distribution and reasonably consider the complexity of input symbols.

There is a long way to go in gaze gesture input and eye movement interaction interface research. The work done in this paper is only a little bit. Specifically, inspired by the research results of this paper, there are already several clear directions, which are worthy of further research:

(1) The input performance can be studied when the input area is larger than 30° (outside the comfort zone of the eyeball rotation).
(2) It is possible to explore whether there is a better performance feedforward type for input symbols such as circles.
(3) It is possible to define the "complexity" metric for eye movements and the range of complexity metrics that are appropriate for eye movement explicit input.

References

1. Farwell, L.A., Donchin, E.: Taking off the top of your head: toward a mental prosthesis utilizing event-related brain potentials. Electroencephalogr. Clin. Neurophysiol. **70**(6), 510–523 (1988)
2. Sibert, L.E., Jacob, R.J.K.: Evaluation of eye gaze interaction. In: Proceedings of CHI2000, The Hague, The Netherlands, 281–288 (2000)
3. Murata, A.: Eye-gaze input versus mouse: cursor control as a function of age. Int. J. Human-Computer Interact. **21**(1), 1–14 (2006)
4. Zhai, S., Morimoto, C., Ihde, S.: Manual and gaze input cascaded (MAGIC) pointing. In: Proceedings of SIGCHI Conference on Human Factors in Computing Systems, pp. 246–253, New York, USA (1999)
5. Grauman, K., Betke, M., Gips, J., et al.: Communication via eye blinks - detection and duration analysis in real time. In: Proceeding of IEEE Conference on Computer Vision and Pattern Recognition, vol. 1, Kauai, HI, USA (2001)
6. Kaufman, A.E., Bandopadhay, A., Shaviv, B.D.: An eye tracking computer user interface. In: Proceedings of Research Frontiers in Virtual Reality Workshop, pp. 120–121. IEEE Computer Society Press (1993)
7. Jacob, R.J.K.: What you look at is what you get: eye movement- based interaction technique. In: Proceedings of Conference on Human Factors in Computing Systems, pp. 11–18 (1990)
8. Hyrskykari, A.: Gaze control as an input device. In: Proceeding of ACHCI 1997, University of Tempere (1997)
9. Corno, F., Farinetti, L., Signorile, I.: An eye-gaze input device for people with severe motor disabilities (2002)
10. Cheng-Zhi, F., Mo-Wei, S.: Task efficiency of different arrangements of objects in an eye-movement based user interface. Acta Psychol. Sin. **04**, 515–522 (2006). (in Chinese)
11. Zhu, H.-J.: Research on eye movement control of mobile terminal system and prototype design of interaction framework. Master thesis, Shanghai Jiao Tong University (2014) (in Chinese)
12. Feng, C.-Z., Shen, M.-W., Chen, S., Su, H.: Influence of border and eye cursor on task performance in eye movement interaction, Chinese J. Appl. Psychol. **01**, 9–12+17 (2004) (in Chinese)
13. Xin, Y.-X.: Design and implementation of text input system based on eye movement. Master thesis, Nanjing University (2015) (in Chinese)
14. Møllenbach, E., Lillholm, M., Gail, A., et al.: Single gaze gestures. In: Proceedings of the 2010 Symposium on Eye-Tracking Research & Applications, pp. 177–180 (2010)
15. Heikkilä, H.: Simple gaze gestures and the closure of the eyes as an interaction technique. In: Symposium on Eye Tracking Research and Applications, vol. 85, pp. 147–154 (2012)
16. Mollenbach, E., Hansen, J.P., Lillholm, M., et al.: Single stroke gaze gestures. CHI 2009 Extended Abstracts on Human Factors in Computing Systems. ACM, pp. 4555–4560 (2009)
17. Istance, H., Hyrskykari, A., Immonen, L., et al.: Designing gaze gestures for gaming: an investigation of performance. In: Proceedings of the 2010 Symposium on Eye-Tracking Research & Applications, pp. 323–330 (2010)
18. Yu-Hui, L., Bei-Ping, T., Yun, W., Liang, S.: Comparative study on variant degree likert scale on satisfaction research. J. Data Anal. **1**(2), 159–173 (2006). (in Chinese)

Angle and Load Measurement Method for Ankle Joint Using Active Bone-Conducted Sound Sensing

Atsutoshi Ikeda[1(✉)], Shinichi Kosugi[2], and Yasuhito Tanaka[3]

[1] Kindai University, 3-4-1 Kowakae, Higashiosaka, Osaka, Japan
ikeda@mech.kindai.ac.jp

[2] Nara Prefectural Seiwa Medical Center, 1-14-16 Mimuro, Ikoma Gun Sango Cho, Nara, Japan

[3] Nara Medical University, 840 Shijo-Cho, Kashihara, Nara, Japan

Abstract. In this paper, we present a kinematic and dynamic measurement method of an ankle using an active bone-conducted sound sensing system. This sensing method is minimally invasive because the vibration which is propagated in a leg, mainly a tibia, is only used. First, we describe about the active bone-conducted sound sensing system. Second, we show the best measurement setup using proposed system. Then the relationships between the load on the leg, the ankle joint angle and the frequency characteristics of the vibration are presented. The experimental results show that the vibration characteristics are changed in heavy load and extension condition.

Keywords: Active bone-conducted sound sensing · Ankle biomechanics · Internal measurement

1 Introduction

Measurement and analysis techniques of the gait become important clinical tools for the quantitative evaluation of human locomotion ability. Both the kinematic and the dynamic measurement are necessary for understanding of the mechanical function of the feet and the legs.

Three dimensional motion capture system is widely employed for the kinematic measurement of the gait in the research field (joint angle, stride, swing speed and so on). However, accurate motion capture systems are costly and need large space and a lot of setup time. The Microsoft Kinect (Microsoft) also applies for kinematic measurement of gait. Pfister et al. were reported accuracy comparison between the Microsoft Kinect and Vicon motion capture system (Vicon) during sagittal plane gait kinematics [1]. They said that the Microsoft Kinect has basic motion capture capabilities but still needs improvements of the software and the hardware before it is used in clinical field. Hondori et al. were reported the technical and the clinical impacts of the Microsoft Kinect in physical therapy and rehabilitation fields [2]. In this paper, the number of the rehabilitation system using the Microsoft Kinect is increased. Also, many papers which are reported evaluation of the Microsoft Kinect's accuracy and

M. Kurosu (Ed.): HCII 2019, LNCS 11567, pp. 303–313, 2019.
https://doi.org/10.1007/978-3-030-22643-5_24

reliability were published. Müller et al. were presented the high accuracy motion capture system using multiple the Microsoft Kinect v2 [3]. They said that the proposed motion capture system is easy to setup, flexible with respect to the sensor locations and delivers high accuracy for the gait measurement.

These motion capture systems are using the Microsoft Kinect/v2 provide low cost and accurate measurement environment in the clinical field. However, the measurement range of the sensor and the system setup is still need some improvements before using clinicians.

Various sensors are proposed to measure the contact force between the foot and the floor during the gait. Taborri et al. were reported the review paper of a variety of sensors for the gait phase partitioning [4]. These sensors can be classified into the two types, wearable or non-wearable. Foot switches or insole pressure sensors are standard for the wearable type sensing system, but the wearable type sensors have some inherent limitations. Therefore, inertial measurement systems were presented instead. Valuable results are reported using the electromyography, electroneurography and ultrasonic sensors. However, the internal measurement methods are necessary to improve for clinical applications.

The force plate with the optical three dimensional motion capture system, the most accurate system for the gait analysis, is widely used in an indoor environment. However, subject is required to step on the force plate for the contact force measurement during gait motion. This causes difficulties or unnatural motion for the subjects.

Therefore, accurate and simple measurement technique which is easily use for clinicians is needed. In vibrational science field, the nondestructive inspection method is widely used to measure the internal condition of a building construction [5]. We use this methodology to human gait measurement. In this paper, we present the relationship between the ankle joint angle, the load on the leg and the frequency characteristics of propagating vibration.

Figure 1 shows a conceptual image of proposing sensing method. We actively add vibration to a leg and measure propagated vibration at other point of the leg. This sensing method is minimally invasive because vibration which is propagating in a leg, mainly the tibia, is only used. Kato et al. were presented the hand pose estimation method using the active bone-conducted sound sensing and the support vector machine to classify the hand pose [6]. Funato et al. were proposed the three axis contact force estimation method using the active bone-conducted sound sensing and a support vector regression [7]. The vibration which is propagated in-vivo tissue can be used for the joint angle estimation and the force estimation of the end-effector. However, it is still unclear the possibility of the joint angle and the force estimation at the same time.

In this paper, we present measurement method of the propagated vibration in the leg under different the ankle joint angle and the loading force on the ankle. Firstly, we compare the sensor position and the distance between the oscillator and the microphone for stable measurement of the vibration. Then the frequency characteristics of the propagated vibration under different condition are analyzed. We discuss the experimental result from the view point of biomechanics.

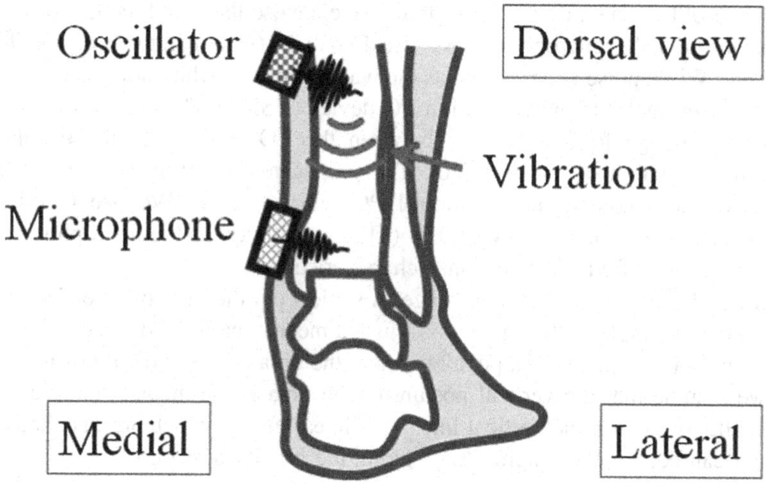

Fig. 1. Internal propagation of the vibration using active bone conducted sound sensing system on the leg (the tibia)

2 Measurement System

The active bone-conducted sound sensing system is consisting from three components which are a control PC, an oscillator and a microphone. Figure 2 shows the measurement system which we use in this paper.

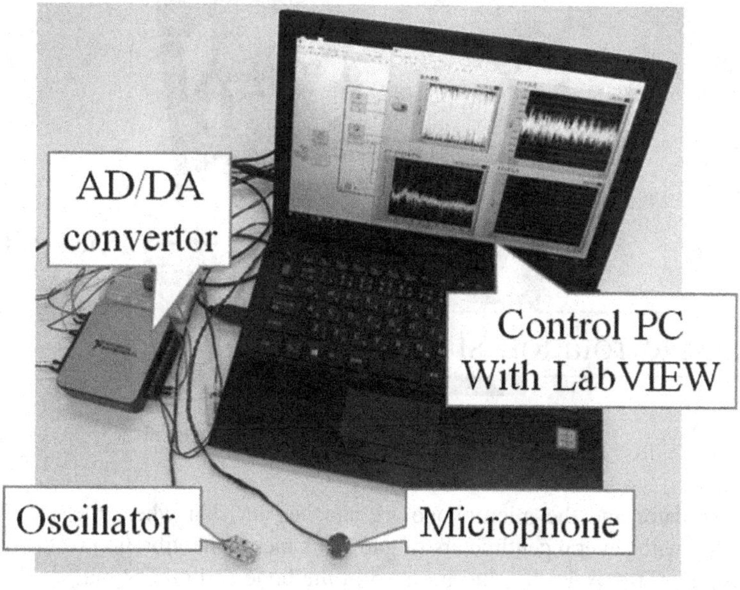

Fig. 2. Active bone-conducted sound sensing system

The control PC generates a waveform to drive the oscillator and records propagated vibration through the microphone. We use LabView (National Instruments) for the programing. White noise is employed as the waveform. The white noise is outputted to the oscillator through the multi-function I/O device (USB-6002,National Instruments). We insert a voltage follower circuit between the I/O device and the oscillator to stabilize the operation of the oscillator. The propagated vibration is received by the microphone and recorded in the control PC with 4 [kHz]. We use COM-10917 (SparkFun) as the oscillator and CM-01B (TE connectivity) as the microphone. These devices has enough frequency response characteristic.

Figure 3 shows the measurement stage. A subject put the right bare foot on the foot plate. Ankle joint angle of the subject is adjusted mechanically by the accurate rotation stage. Then foot is adjusted to a position where the tibia is in a vertical posture. In this paper, we assume that the vertical posture of the tibia is the medial condyle and the medial malleolus are on the vertical line. Two linear guides which are installed on the upper part can control the loading force along the gravity direction.

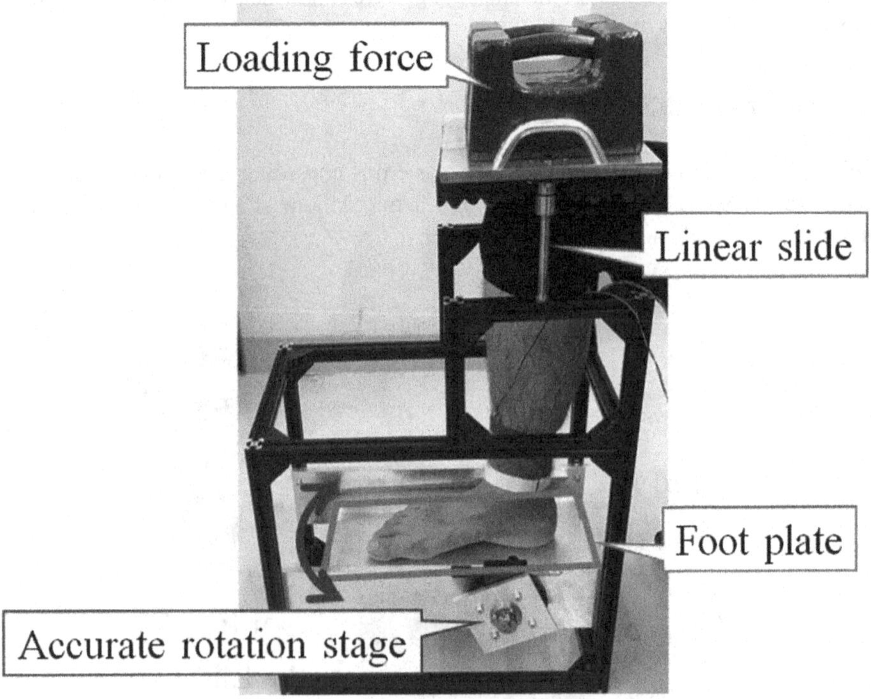

Fig. 3. Adjustable stage for stable measurement

The oscillator and the microphone are attached on skin where the subcutaneous tissue is thin with several centimeters of gap. This means the vibration of the oscillator is transmitted not only in the skin but also in the bone and other tissues.

3 Sensor Position Comparison

3.1 Sensor Position Patterns

First, we compare the sensor positions to find the best measurement setup. Figure 4 and Table 1 describe the sensor position patterns. Again, we focus on an ankle joint mechanical property. Therefore, we try to measure directly an ankle joint mechanical property with the pattern A. However, there are many tissues, skin, the bones, the tendons, the cartilage, etc., in an ankle joint. There is a possibility of that these tissues affect as a noise to the measurement.

The pattern B is most close to the contact area during gait motion. And the area around the heel has the smallest organization type, almost the bone (the calcaneu) and skin. This means that a noise from tissues is less than the other patterns.

In the pattern C, the sensors are attached on the tibia which is one of the most important bones to support the weight. The tibia is also important for the power transmission during gait. The vibration by the oscillator easily propagates in the tibia because the shape of the tibia is long and thin.

We use a hook-and-loop fastener band to fasten the sensors in the pattern A and C. In the pattern B, we use an extensionless taping tape to avoid the ankle joint movement limitation.

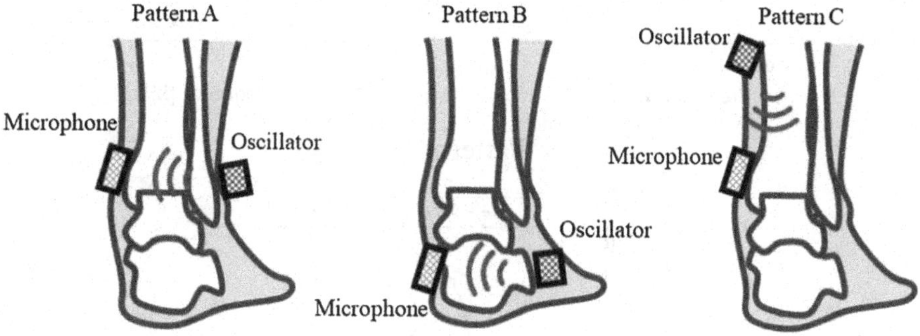

Fig. 4. Sensor position patterns

Table 1. Sensor attached bones

	Oscillator	Microphone
Pattern A	Lateral malleolus	Medial malleolus
Pattern B	Lateral process	Medial process
Pattern C	Tibia (medium)	Medial malleolus

One healthy subject volunteered to participate the sensor comparison experiment. The subject was received the explanation of the detail of this research and gave written informed consent before the experiment. We measure the vibration under the two load condition, 0 [kg] and 50 [kg], in each pattern. The ankle joint angle was kept 0 [deg]. We did five trials under respective conditions.

3.2 Result

Recorded voltage data from the microphone were fast Fourier transformed (FFT) for the frequency analysis. Figure 5 shows the average FFT data of pattern A, B and C. The blue dash line means the no-load condition (no weight) and the red line means the maximum load condition (the log + 50 [kg] weight).

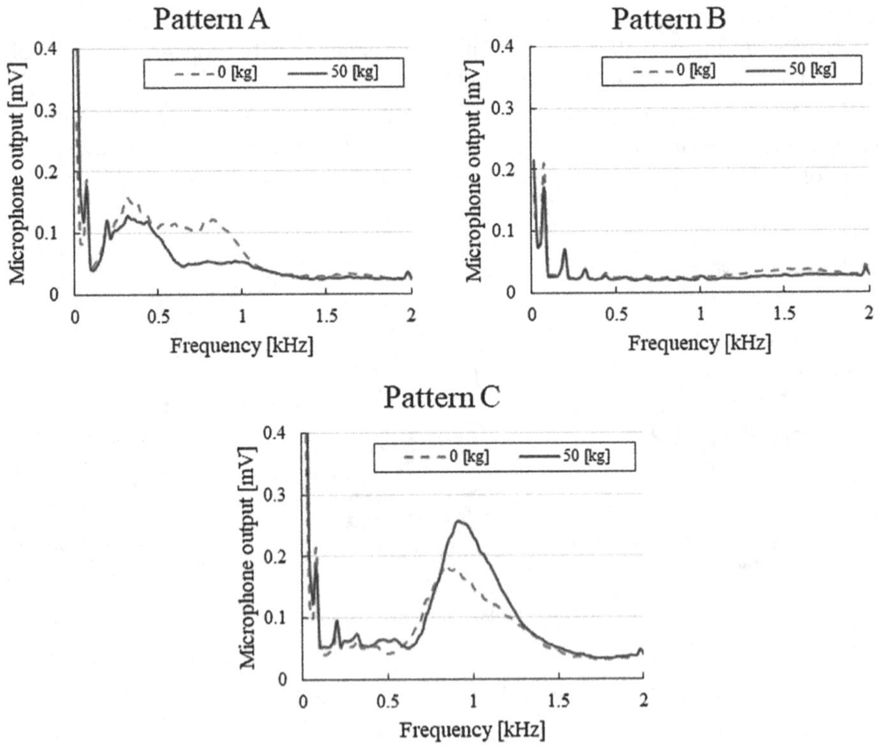

Fig. 5. Frequency characteristics under different loading conditions (Color figure online)

We cannot observe any significant change of the frequency characteristics in the pattern B. In pattern A, the frequency components from 600 to 1000 [Hz] are decreased when the weight was loaded. In pattern C, the frequency components from 800 to 1300 [Hz] are increased the weight was loaded. Also, the peak frequency was changed from 840 [Hz] to 920 [Hz] when the weight was loaded.

We observe the biggest difference of the frequency characteristics between the no-load condition and the maximum load condition in the pattern C. This means that the mechanical characteristics of the tibia is most.

3.3 Distance Between Sensors

Second, we compare the distance between the oscillator and the microphone. The sensor's relative distance affect the strength and the path of the vibration. If the sensors attached close place, we can observe the strong vibration signal. However, the vibration mostly path through the surface of the body. On the other hand, the signal strength become weaker according to the sensor's relative distance. In this case, the vibration signal includes a lot of noise.

In our preliminary experiment, the relative distance around 6 to 12 [cm] performed better signal-to-noise ratio. Accordingly, we compare three relative distance of the sensors. Figure 6 shows the sensor attached position with the relative distance 6, 9 and 12 [cm]. The sensor positions are as same as the pattern C in the previous subsection. The microphone is attached on the medial malleolus (the white band in Fig. 6) and the oscillator is attached on the tibia (the blue band in Fig. 6).

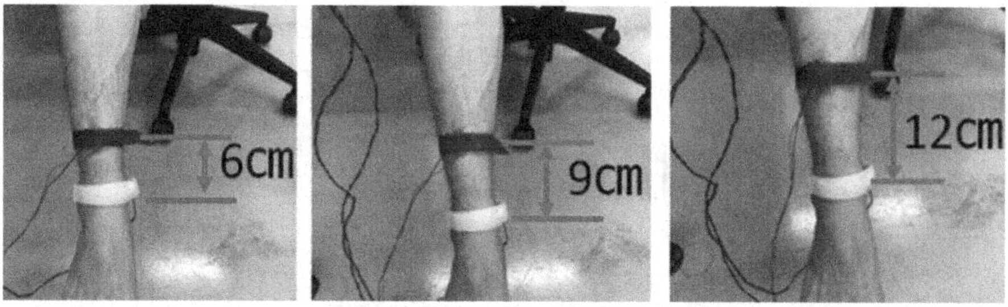

Fig. 6. Distance between the oscillator and the microphone (Color figure online)

In this experiment, we participate other healthy subject. The subject was received the explanation of the detail of this research and gave written informed consent before the experiment. We measure the vibration under the two load condition and the one ankle joint angle condition as same as previous subsection. We did three trials under respective conditions.

3.4 Result

Recorded voltage data from the microphone were fast Fourier transformed for the frequency analysis. Figure 7 shows the average FFT data of three relative distances. The blue dash line means the no-load condition (no weight) and the red line means the maximum load condition (the log + 50 [kg] weight).

We observe that the vibration signal of 12 [cm] much weaker than the other distance. Under the no-load condition, the waveforms of 6 and 9 [cm] have similar shape and amplitude. When the maximum load condition, the vibration signal of 9 [cm] is much bigger than 6 [cm]. Also, the peak frequency is slightly increased.

These results indicates that the best distance between the oscillator and the microphone is around 9 [cm]. However, this result depends on the subject's physical parameter of the leg.

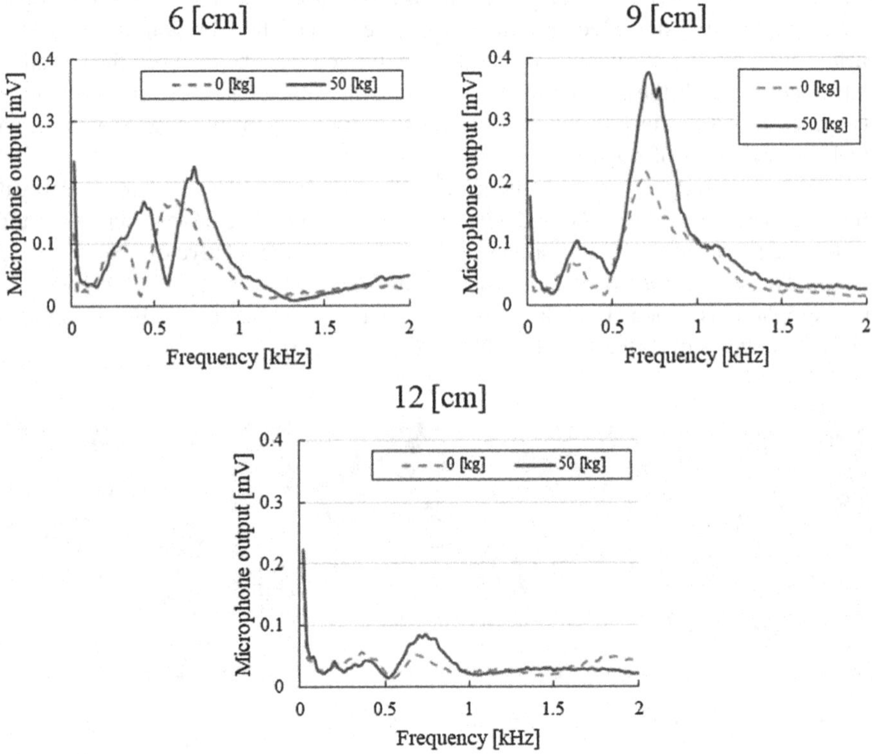

Fig. 7. Frequency characteristics with difference relative distance of the sensors (Color figure online)

4 Frequency Characteristics Under Different Load and Joint Angle Condition

4.1 Experimental Setup

In this experiment, we measure the vibration using proposed system under 30 different conditions. Experimental conditions are composed of combination of the joint angle (−10 (plantar flexion), 0, 10, 20, 30 (dorsal flexion) [degree]) and the load (0, 10, 20, 30, 40, 50 [kg]). We did three trials in each condition. One healthy subject volunteered for this experiment. The subject was given the experimental protocol information and he gave his consent to participate.

The subject was sitting and put the right foot on the foot plate then keep relaxing during the experiment. Recorded vibration data are transformed to frequency data by FFT.

4.2 Result

Figure 8 shows the average FFT data of different ankle joint angle under the no-load condition. We observe the biggest amplitude when the ankle joint angle is 10 [deg] flexion. The amplitude of the vibration signal is decreased according to the ankle joint bending or flexing. On the other hand, the frequency peak does not change dynamically.

This result indicates that the vibration frequency component from 700 to 1160 [Hz] are also changed according to the ankle joint angle.

Figure 9 shows the average FFT data of different load condition with the maximum flexion posture. We observe the same amplitude level under all load condition. On the other hand, the frequency peak is slightly increased according to the weight number.

Figure 10 shows the average FFT data of different load condition with the small flexion posture. We observe the same amplitude level under all load condition. On the other hand, the frequency peak is slightly increased according to the weight number.

These results show the different trend from the experimental result in the Sect. 3.

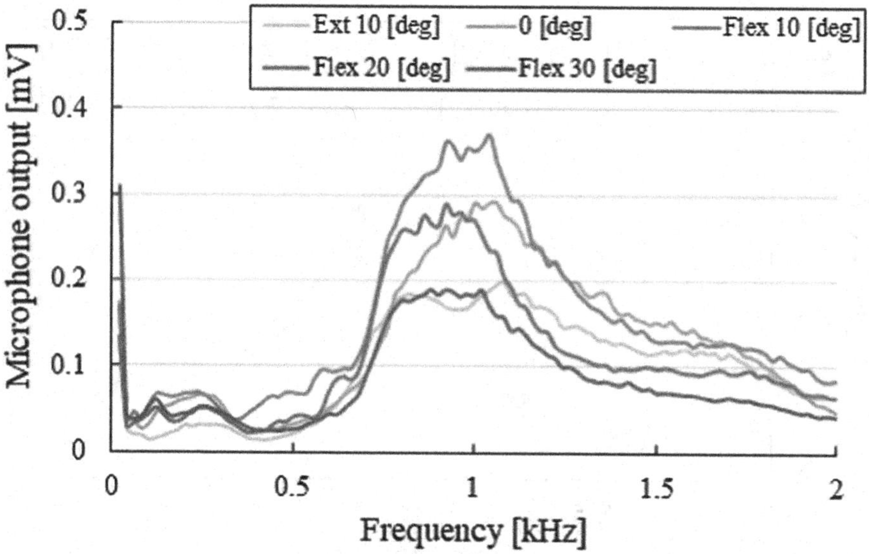

Fig. 8. Ankle joint angle comparison under the no-load condition (50 [kg])

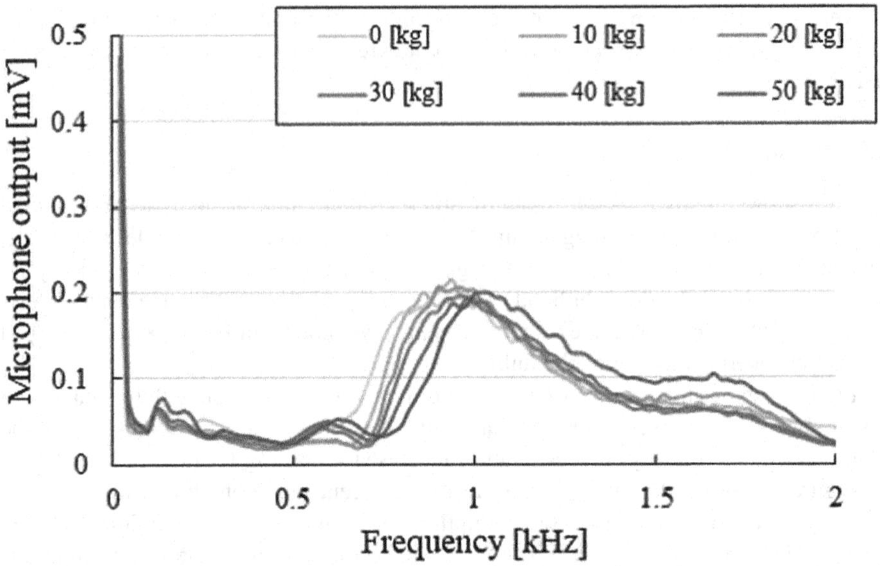

Fig. 9. Load comparison under the maximum flexion condition (30 [deg])

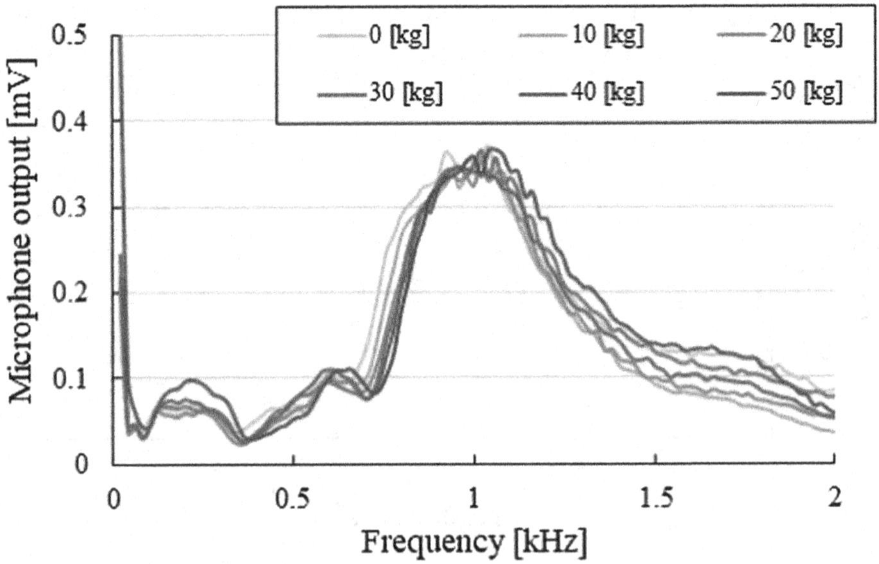

Fig. 10. Load comparison under the small flexion condition (10 [deg])

5 Discussion

According to the experimental results of the Sect. 3, the vibration amplitude of the middle range frequency (around 600 to 1200 [Hz]) are increased to depend on the load condition. However, the experimental results of the Sect. 4 shows the different trend. This difference of the data trend is caused by the difference between the subjects. Because the data of each experiment are very stable.

The data trend from one subject, we can observe the trend of the amplitude and the frequency peak according to the ankle joint angle and the load. We believe that the possibility of the estimation of the joint angle of the ankle and the load on the leg at the same time.

6 Conclusion

We propose the kinematic and dynamic measurement method for the ankle using the active bone-conducted sound sensing system. The relationships between the ankle joint angle, the load on the leg and the frequency components of the vibration are discussed. Future work will include correcting more data from variable subjects and compare the data trend.

Acknowledgment. This research was supported by the SCOPE #162103009.

References

1. Pfister, A., West, A.M., Bronner, S., Noah, J.A.: Comparative abilities of Microsoft Kinect and Vicon 3D motion capture for gait analysis. J. Med. Eng. Technol. **38**(5), 274–280 (2014)
2. Hondori, H.M., Khademi, M.: Review on technical and clinical impact of microsoft kinect on physical therapy and rehabilitation. J. Med. Eng. **2014**, 846514 (2014)
3. Müller, B., Ilg, W., Giese, M.A., Ludolph, N.: Validation of enhanced kinect sensor based motion capturing for gait assessment. PLoS One **12**(4), e0175813 (2017)
4. Taborri, J., Palermo, E., Rossi, S., Cappa, P.: Gait partitioning methods: a systematic review. Sensors **16**(1), 66 (2016)
5. Rehman, S.K.U., Ibrahim, Z., Memon, S.A., Jameel, M.: Nondestructive test methods for concrete bridges: a review. Constr. Build. Mater. **107**, 58–86 (2016)
6. Kato, H., Takemura, K.: Hand pose estimation based on active bone-conducted sound sensing. In: Proceedings of the 2016 ACM International Joint Conference on Pervasive and Ubiquitous Computing: Adjunct, pp. 109–112. ACM (2016)
7. Funato, N., Takemura, K.: Estimating three-axis contact force for fingertip by emitting vibration actively. In: Proceedings of the 2017 IEEE International Conference on Robotics and Biomimetics (ROBIO2017), pp. 406–411 (2017)

The Study of Teleoperation Technology Based on Hand Gesture Recognition

Wanhong Lin[1,2](✉), Yu Zou[1], Jin Yang[1], Jiangang Chao[1,2], and Ying Xiong[1]

[1] China Astronaut Research and Training Center, Beijing, China
acclwh@hotmail.com
[2] National Key Laboratory of Human Factors Engineering, China Astronaut Research and Training Center, Beijing, China

Abstract. Background: To solve the traditional manual teleoperation problems, this project explores a more natural method of manipulator teleoperation, sets up a fusion virtual teleoperation scene, uses hand gesture recognition technology to convert the operator's hand action to the manipulator's execution instruction, avoids the complexity which is caused by the operation translation and the posture handle control respectively. The three-dimensional scene reconstruction enables the operator to have a clear understanding of the three-dimensional situation of the whole teleoperation scene, and can perceive the spatial relationship between the operator, the manipulator and the target in real time, thus improving the execution efficiency of the teleoperation. **Methods:** This project used mature commercial depth camera devices (such as Kinect, Leapmotion, Intel Creative, ZED camera, etc.) as input device to identify operator's hand movements and used a manipulator with multiple joints for teleoperation. The camera was installed on the wrist of manipulator or other related parts to obtain the images of operational objectives without changing the robot arm control system. The location and attitude of operational objectives was achieved by measuring the depth of data image, manipulator space location identification. After the completion of the operational objectives identification, the virtual hand, manipulator and the target were generated in the same virtual scene by using virtual reality technology and augmented reality technology to provide a stereoscopic display to the operator through the 3D display device. Based on stereo video image display technology, the position relation of manipulator and operational objectives in space was restored in virtual reality system, and the visual space location was realized by SLAM method. The operator will get the visual perception of the teleoperation scene with large field of view. The mapping relationship between the hand model and the manipulator was established to get the precise control, which can enhance the perception ability of the operator. Finally, an experimental system was formed to evaluate the applicability and effectiveness of interaction, which was modified according to the feedback results. An effective human-machine interaction method was proposed based on visual gesture recognition. **Conclusion:** Experiments show that the accuracy of the gesture operation is slightly lower than that of the handle operation, but it is easier to operate, and the operation is natural and smooth, which accords with the advantages of human-computer interaction habits. For scenes with low precision requirements, the advantages of gesture operation are

M. Kurosu (Ed.): HCII 2019, LNCS 11567, pp. 314–331, 2019.
https://doi.org/10.1007/978-3-030-22643-5_25

obvious. It can be used as an operation mode of teleoperation. It has wide application prospects in the field of teleoperation system or task, such as space station, extraterrestrial exploration, robots, UAV and so on.

Keywords: Hand gestures · Depth sensor cameras · Augmented cognition · Teleoperation technology

1 Introduction

The purpose of this study was to explore a more natural method of manipulator teleoperation to optimize productivity and usability.

This subject solved the three-dimensional spatial position recognition between the operator's hand and the operation target, and integrates the spatial position of the manipulator, the operation target and the hand action to form a unified mixed reality scene. uses hand gesture recognition technology to convert the operator's hand action to the manipulator's execution instruction, avoids the complexity which is caused by the operation translation and the posture handle control respectively.

According to the characteristics of hand and manipulator, the human in the teleoperation control circuit model and an immersed virtual operation scene was established, sets up a fusion virtual teleoperation scene, which was used to find the suitable visual gesture recognition method and teleoperation control model. The three-dimensional scene reconstruction enables the operator to have a clear understanding of the three-dimensional situation of the whole teleoperation scene, and can perceive the spatial relationship between the operator, the manipulator and the target in real time, thus improving the execution efficiency of the teleoperation.

2 System Design

The research of this subject is based on the interactive technology of computer vision, including hand motion recognition, mapping relationship between hand and manipulator, target space position relationship and information enhancement in virtual scene. It uses mature commercial depth camera equipment (such as Kinect, Leapmotion, Intel Creative, ZED camera, etc.) as recognition input equipment to track hand motion. uses a manipulator with multiple joints, and installs a camera on the wrist or other related parts of the manipulator to obtain the depth image of the operating target. The spatial position recognition of the operating target (non-cooperative target) is accomplished through the depth image and the measurement data output from the manipulator.

Using virtual reality technology, the operator's virtual hand action, virtual manipulator and virtual operation target are generated in a unified virtual scene, and provided to the operator in a stereoscopic way. The operator can realize the visual perception of the operation scene through the 3D large field of view display helmet or desktop 3D display device.

According to the above technical route and based on the basic principle of teleoperation, an experimental system based on visual recognition interaction is established.

The operator's hand is recognized by computer vision, and the three-dimensional model of hand action is established on the basis of the most optimized algorithm. Through the augmented reality technology and the measurement data of the manipulator itself, the position of the operation target in space is identified. A unified scene is formed by the fusion of manipulator, manipulation target space position and hand movement. The operator perceives the operation scene by observing the virtual scene, recognizes the human hand by computer vision, and finally drives the manipulator of the terminal to complete the manipulator operation on the target object. The principle can be shown in the following Fig. 1.

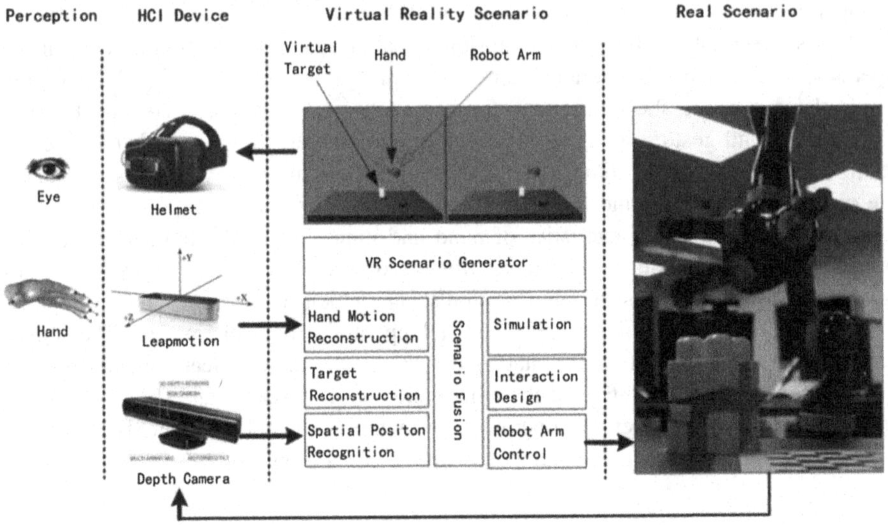

Fig. 1. Manipulator operating prototype based on machine vision.

In the above-mentioned system, through the interactive equipment of visual recognition, the control consistency expression of both ends of manual and manipulator operation is completed, and a complete man-in-loop teleoperation control system is formed.

3 Hand Motion Recognition

There are many devices that provide hand pose data such as Intel RealSense, Leapmotion, Kinect etc. Due to the high accuracy of Leapmotion and its compatibility with the Oculus Rift [1], we chose the pose data provided by the Leapmotion for gesture recognition.

3.1 Gesture Recognition Algorithm

As previously reported, although the Leapmotion device provides only a limited set of relevant points and not a complete description of the hand shape [2], the device provides enough relevant points for gesture recognition, avoiding complex computations required when extracting gesture recognition from depth and color data.

The grabbing recognition algorithm proposed in this project supported two types of gestures [3]. The first grabbing gesture was the grab, in which the user curled his/her fingers inwards towards the palm center C as depicted in Fig. 2. The grab value of the grab gesture g_c was determined by the following algorithm:

$$g_c = \frac{\sum_{i=1}^{5} |F_i - C|}{5} \tag{1}$$

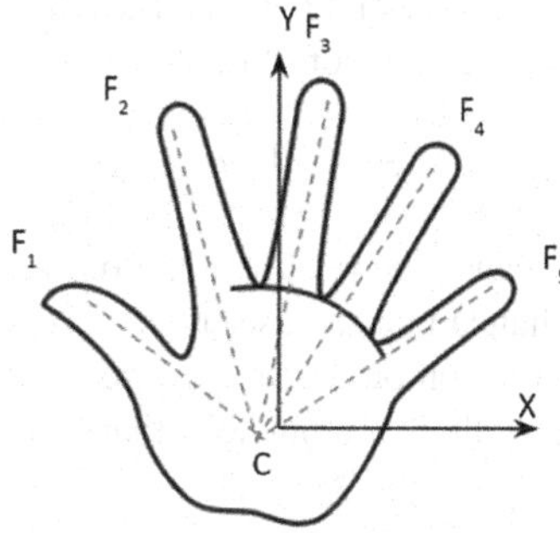

Fig. 2. The features of hand (Grab)

The other grabbing gesture modeled a pinching pose, in which the user clumped the fingertips together (Fig. 3). The algorithm used to determine grab value of the pinch gesture g_p was computed in a similar fashion:

$$g_p = \frac{\sum_{i=2}^{5} |F_i - F_1|}{4} \tag{2}$$

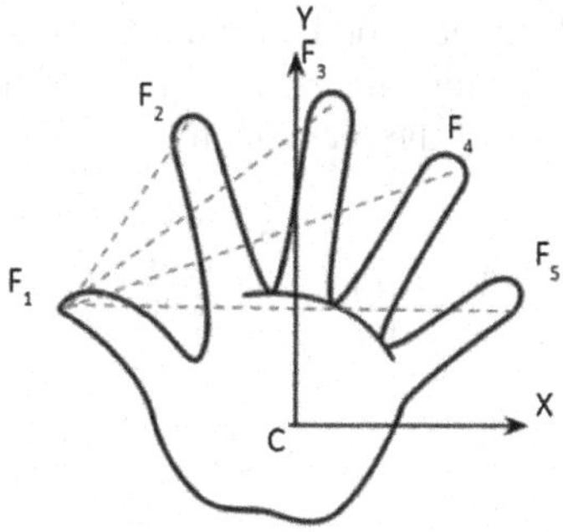

Fig. 3. Pinch gesture (Color figure online)

This algorithm simply calculated the average distance (Fig. 3, blue dashed lines) of the thumb tip to each of the other fingertips. Hence, if the finger types were spread out, then g_p would be large. If the fingertips were clumped together then g_p would be small.

In order for the FSM to transition into the gesture state, g_c and g_p must have been below a trigger threshold. For this research, the grab G_T threshold (G_T) was the same for both the grab gesture and the pinch gesture. was calculated by multiplying the length of the metacarpal bone of the thumb finger (m) by a grab threshold constant α:

$$G_T = \alpha \cdot m \tag{3}$$

The length of the metacarpal bone was extracted directly from data provided by the Leapmotion sensor. Hence, the grab threshold value is different for each user. Users with bigger hands had a higher threshold and vice versa.

The release threshold (R_T) dictated when the hand transitioned out of the grabbing state. This is similar to the grab threshold in such a way that it was determined by multiplying m by the release threshold constant β.

$$R_T = \beta \cdot m \tag{4}$$

For this research $\beta \geq \alpha$, because the release threshold needed to be greater than the grab threshold reducing the chance that the user might inadvertently change their hand pose and cause the FSM to transition out of the gesture state (i.e. grab value $\geq R_T$). If the grabbing value was greater than G_T but less than R_T the FSM remained in the gesture state.

3.2 Noise Suppression

Although, in theory, the tracking accuracy of Leap Motion is less than submillimeter, environmental noise causes the Leapmotion to incorrectly detect the hand pose state and position. Noise signals include room lighting, shadows, hand jumping [4], and visual and numerical block singular value solvers. Prior research [5] has proposed an adaptive cut-off frequency of the low pass filtering method; therefore, this study used the real-time speed of palm to remove hand pose states whose velocity is above a certain threshold. As an example, consider a time frame that includes a history of all the hand states where H_i represents the hand state at time frame i in a set H. The hand state included properties such as hand position P_i, hand rotation R_i, and hand velocity V_i. V_i is determined by taking the absolute difference in hand position from the current time frame and the average position of the previous five hand frames (including itself):

$$V_i = \left| P_i - \frac{\sum_{n=i-4}^{i} P_n}{5} \right| \tag{5}$$

The low pass filtering method filtered out all the hand states H_i in which their corresponding V_i is above a cutoff threshold V_{cutoff}. The new set of hand states $\widehat{H}$ were rendered and used for gesture recognition:

$$\widehat{H} = \{H_i | V_i < V_{cutoff}\} \quad (6)$$

The lower filter cutoff is used to filter out any noise detected by the Leap Motion that caused the hand to jump to a completely different location in the virtual environment. For example, consider a set of five time frames of hand state H_1, H_2, H_3, H_4, H_5, where all hand states were correctly detected by the Leap Motion except for H_5, which was completely off from where the users hand position was. V_5 will be very high (greater than V_{cutoff}), and hence the low pass filtering algorithm will not include H_5 in the $\widehat{H}$ set to be rendered for the gesture recognition process.

3.3 Snapback Method

Implementing separate thresholds for the Gesture State (S1) and the Release State (S2) has its drawbacks. When the subject was in the act of releasing (going from S1 to S2) there was a period of time in which the object inadvertently shifted since R_T had not been exceeded yet. During the period required to release the object (exceed R_T), the object was still attached to the virtual hand and adhered to the Move State manipulation rules (S3); hence if the hand moved during the act of releasing, the object moved too.

To solve this issue and facilitate object stability during release, a snapback algorithm was designed to return an object to its position when the release was first initiated.

As shown in Figs. 4 and 5, a set of parameters was defined to implement the snapback algorithm: Grab Value (G_V), Release Threshold (R_T), Grab Threshold G_T), Slope value (S_V), and Slope Threshold (S_T). As previously described, when G_V fell below G_T during grabbing, the program would move into the gesture state. A similar approach was used for releasing, except a different threshold was used, R_T. $S_V$measured how fast the grab value changed during any single frame. S_T was used as a breakpoint in the snapback algorithm. Throughout the duration of the program, a history kept a list of the previous N hand states, call this H. Hence, H_{N-1} would be the hand state one frame before the current hand state because it is the last index in the list of histories. Consequently H_0 would be the hand state N frames before. During the act of releasing, at the moment the grab value of the current hand frame was above the release threshold, the program triggered a snapback which retraced movement back through the previous N hand states stored in H (indexcounter starts at N − 1, then decrements) until one of the follow conditions are met:

$$H_{index}[G_V] < G_T$$

$$H_{index}[S_V] < S_T$$

$$index = 0$$

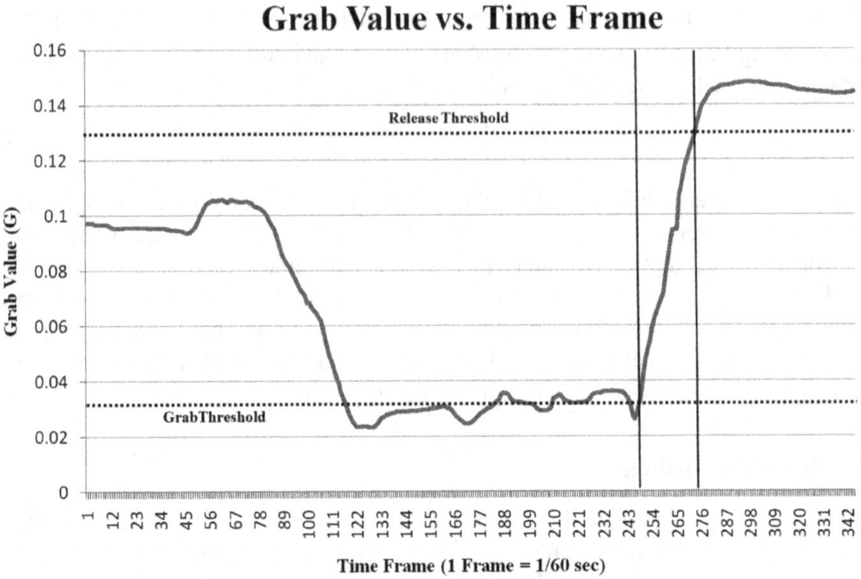

Fig. 4. Snapback graphical representation. Top dashed line represents R_T, bottom dashed line represents G_T, and the two vertical lines represent the start and end of the releasing phase.

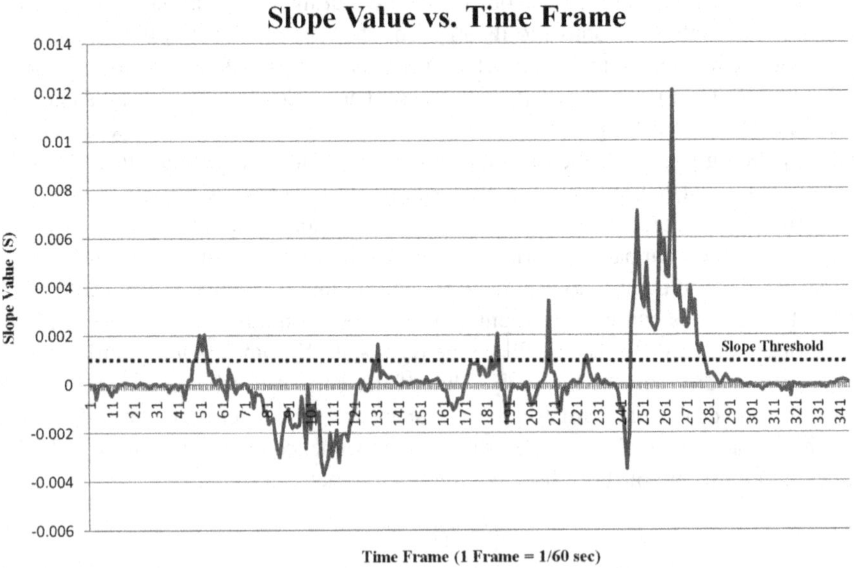

Fig. 5. Snapback graphical representation of slope. In general, the S_V will be above the S_T during the act of releasing.

Condition one assessed whether the grab value of the hand state at that specific index was less than the grab threshold. Condition two assessed whether the slope value was less than the slope threshold. Lastly, condition three assessed whether the program reached the end of the history (cannot retrace further back). When any of these three conditions were met, say at index = T, the object was returned (snapback) to the position and rotation state at the time frame associated with H_T. This is done by calculating the deviation in position (dP) and deviation in angle (dA) between the current hand state (Current) and the hand state it was snapped back to (H_T):

$$dP = H_T[position] - Current[position] \tag{7}$$

$$dA = Quaternion.inverse(H_T[rotation], Current[rotation]) \tag{8}$$

where dP, and dA were used rotate and translate the object back to the state corresponding to H_T:

$$Object_{new}[position] = Object_{old}[position] + dP \tag{9}$$

$$Object_{new}[rotation] = Quaternion.rotate(Object_{old}[rotation], dA) \tag{10}$$

For example, in Fig. 4, $R_T = .13$, $G_T = .03$, and $S_T = .001$. The program retraced back through the time frames (Fig. 4, section between two vertical lines), until $G_v < G_T$ at time frame 248. The object being grabbed snapped back to the position and rotational values corresponding to time frame 248. Other times, if condition two was met before condition one, then the breakpoint would occur when $S_v < .001$.

4 Grasp Rules

When grasping objects in virtual system, some grasping rules must be established to ensure the natural grasping operation. When the grasping rules are satisfied between virtual hand and virtual object, it is considered that virtual hand grasps the object. From then on, virtual hand and virtual object maintain the grasping relationship, that is, the base coordinate system of the object is attached to the virtual hand, so that the movement of virtual hand and other operations can control the movement or other states of the virtual object. When the operation is completed, the state of virtual hand is switched, such as loosening fingers to make the virtual hand and the virtual object detached. The grasping rules are no longer satisfied between the simulated objects, thus the grasping relationship is released.

4.1 Grasp Rules Based on Normal Vector of Point Contact Plane

According to the relationship between grasping posture and grasping stability, combined with the geometry and material characteristics of the object, this paper formulates an improved virtual hand grasping rule based on normal vector of point contact plane. This rule guarantees the correctness and naturalness of grasping. The rule includes the following two parts:

(1) Position Judgment of Point Contact Method. Two or more fingers must be in contact with the object, including the thumb, or three or more fingers must be in contact with the object, and at least three of them are not in a straight line.
(2) Normal Vector Judgment of Point Contact Method. The normal vector between planes in contact with objects must be greater than a threshold angle, which is temporarily defined as 90°.

As shown in the Fig. 6 below, there are three fingers (thumb, index finger and middle finger) in contact with the cube (satisfying Rule 1), three normal vectors of the contact plane N_1, N_2, N_3 (N_3, the normal vectors of the edge of the object, is assumed to be over-centroid point G), and there are three angles q_{12}, q_{13}, q_{23} between the two, which are greater than 90° (satisfying Rule 2), so the object is considered to be grabbed.

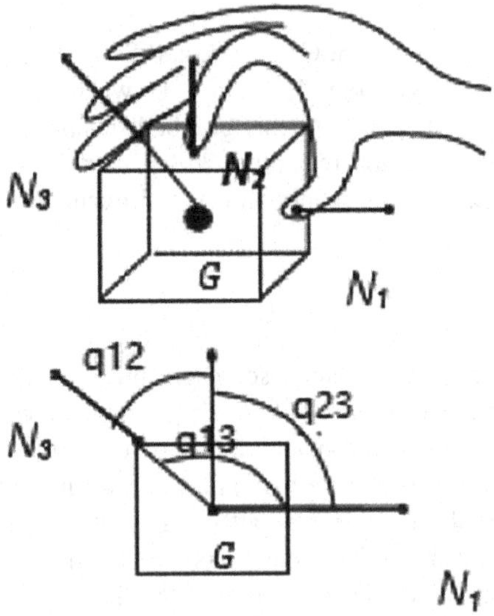

Fig. 6. Grasp rules based on geometry

Grasp rules based on geometry can basically guarantee natural interaction and meet the immersion requirements of virtual reality system. The virtual hand grasping rules based on normal vector of point contact plane have the following characteristics:

(1) It can effectively avoid some misoperations. Because virtual hand inevitably contacts with other objects in the process of motion. Only Rules 1 and 2 are satisfied at the same time the object can be grasped. And Rule 2 can avoid misoperations.

(2) The complexity of calculation is avoided. Rule 2 is judged only when Rule 1 is satisfied. Normal vector and angle of contact plane are not need real-time calculation in the whole process.
(3) The stability of grasping is improved. When virtual hand grasps an object, the hand will inevitably shake slightly. The judgment rules allow this kind of shaking slightly, avoiding misrelease.
(4) According to the material of the object, the threshold is set to improve the reality of grasping the object.
(5) Rule 2 only deals with normal vector and angle of contact plane. This rule applies not only to grasping simple objects, but also to grasping complex objects.

4.2 Research on Normal Vector Threshold of Point Contact Plane

Firstly, the concept of anti-interference and stable grasping is proposed. As shown in the Fig. 7, taking two finger grasping as an example, the force provided by fingertips is expressed by friction cone, which is the resultant force range of pressure and friction. F_e, the resultant force of external forces, i.e. interference force, is exerted on an object other than the force exerted on the hand. The maximum component of fingertip contact force along the opposite direction of F_e is recorded as anti-interference force f_1 and anti-interference force f_2 respectively. If $f_1 + f_2 \geq F_e$ satisfied, the object can be grasped steadily with two fingers, otherwise it can't be grasped. In the m fingers grasp, the interference force $f_1, f_2 \cdots, f_m$ are the maximum component of the contact force along the opposite direction of the interference force F_e. If $f_1 + f_2 \cdots + f_m \geq F_e$ satisfied, the stable grasp of anti-interference is satisfied, otherwise, the stable grasp of anti-interference is not satisfied.

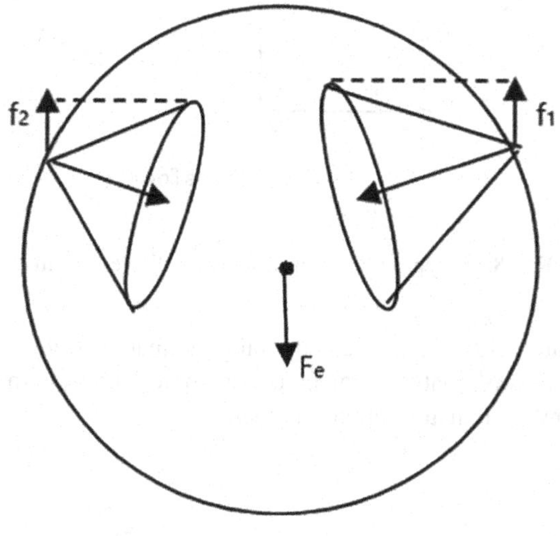

Fig. 7. A simple judgment of grasp force

5 Manipulator Mapping

The attitude estimation method is used to calculate hand attitude when interact with the manipulator. The motion of the manipulator is controlled by palm information (including position and posture), and the motion of the robot hand is controlled by finger posture. After obtaining the relative coordinates of the hand, coordinate transformation is carried out, and the hand coordinates are mapped to the manipulator. The coordinate system satisfies the right hand principle. The incremental information of hand motion is used to control the end movement of the manipulator. It only needs to rotate the coordinates directly without paying attention to the initial deviation. The coordinate transformation relationship is shown in the following Fig. 8.

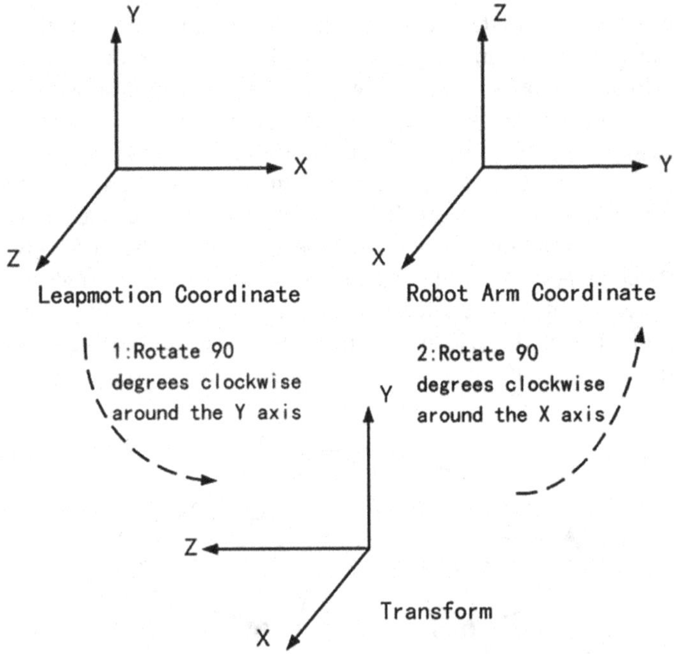

Fig. 8. Mapping diagram of two coordinate systems

Define the point coordinates in Leapmotion coordinate system as (x, y, z) and the corresponding point coordinates in manipulator coordinate system as (x1, y1, z1), satisfying the following transformation relations:

$$
\begin{aligned}
\begin{bmatrix} x1 \\ y1 \\ z1 \end{bmatrix} &= \begin{bmatrix} 1 & 0 & 0 \\ 0 & \cos(-\pi/2) & \sin(-\pi/2) \\ 0 & -\sin(-\pi/2) & \cos(-\pi/2) \end{bmatrix} \times \begin{bmatrix} \cos(-\pi/2) & 0 & -\sin(-\pi/2) \\ 0 & 1 & 0 \\ \sin(-\pi/2) & 0 & \cos(-\pi/2) \end{bmatrix} \\
&= \begin{bmatrix} 1 & 0 & 0 \\ 0 & 0 & -1 \\ 0 & 1 & 0 \end{bmatrix} \times \begin{bmatrix} 0 & 0 & 1 \\ 0 & 1 & 0 \\ 0 & 0 & 0 \end{bmatrix} = \begin{bmatrix} 0 & 0 & 1 \\ 1 & 0 & 0 \\ 0 & 1 & 0 \end{bmatrix} \begin{bmatrix} x \\ y \\ z \end{bmatrix} = \begin{bmatrix} z \\ x \\ y \end{bmatrix}
\end{aligned} \tag{11}
$$

6 Scene Fusion

This paper solves the problem of three-dimensional rendering based on video stream. The discrete frame images of left and right eyes in the video captured by the camera are processed and sent to the left and right display screens of the 3D helmet respectively to form the three-dimensional image.

When rendering, the projection axes must be parallel to each other and the left and right views are completely independent. In addition to the special settings required for the position relationship between the camera and the eye, the other parameters of the camera are very similar to those used in conventional non-stereo rendering.

In the process of rendering, it is found that when full-screen rendering is performed with high resolution, the frame rate may be below 60, which seriously affects the use effect. This paper improves the rendering performance by reducing FOV and queuing ahead of time.

Reducing the cross-pixel of FOV to improve performance may shrink the field of view and reduce immersion, but if the frame rate is not enough, it may lead to vertigo and other problems. This paper uses the way of reducing filling rate to reduce FOV and improve performance. For a fixed pixel density on the retina, smaller FOVs have fewer pixels. When there are fewer visible objects in each frame, there will be fewer animations, fewer state changes, and fewer calls to draw.

In order to improve the parallelism of CPU and GPU and enhance the frame processing ability of GPU, the time-ahead queuing method is used in rendering process. When the advance queue is disabled, the CPU starts processing the next frame immediately after the last frame is displayed. If the GPU cannot process it in time, the previous frame will be displayed. This will cause the picture to jitter. When queuing ahead of time is available, CPU can start earlier, which provides GPU with more time for frame processing and makes scene display more smoothly (Fig. 9).

Fig. 9. Three-dimensional rendering based on video stream

7 Experiments

7.1 Subjects

A total of 15 subjects participated in the experiment, including 10 males, with an average age of 32 years. Two of them had experience in using virtual reality systems.

7.2 Task and Experimental Setup

The experiment of manipulator manipulation based on visual gesture is to test the availability and effectiveness of manipulator manipulation based on visual gesture.

The experimental system uses two modes:

(1) Leapmotion for hand data acquisition and Oculus CV1 for scene display.
(2) Second, the handle controls data acquisition and display by helmet or flat panel display.

The composition of the experimental system is shown in the following Fig. 10.

The subjects controlled the manipulator to shoot at the fixed target paper by teleoperation. Record the shooting time and accuracy to evaluate the accuracy and effectiveness of the operation process. The teleoperation mode based on visual gesture is compared with that based on traditional handle. The experimental scenario is shown in the following Fig. 11.

Standard target images were used in the experiment, which consisted of 10 rings. The center of the target was a solid black circle with a diameter of 4 mm, and the radius of the outer rings was increased by 2 mm in turn.

The experiment is divided into two parts. 1. Use the handle and helmet to control the manipulator to shoot. 2. Use gestures and helmet to control the manipulator to shoot. The experimental results are recorded in the following Table 1.

Each participant completed two groups of experiments: gesture operation and handle operation, each group operated 10 times.

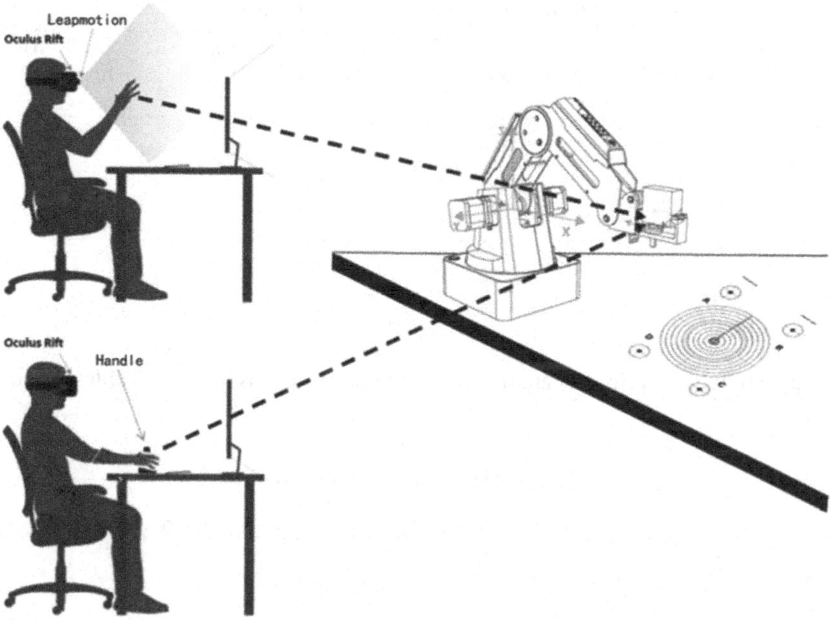

Fig. 10. Schematic diagram of experimental system

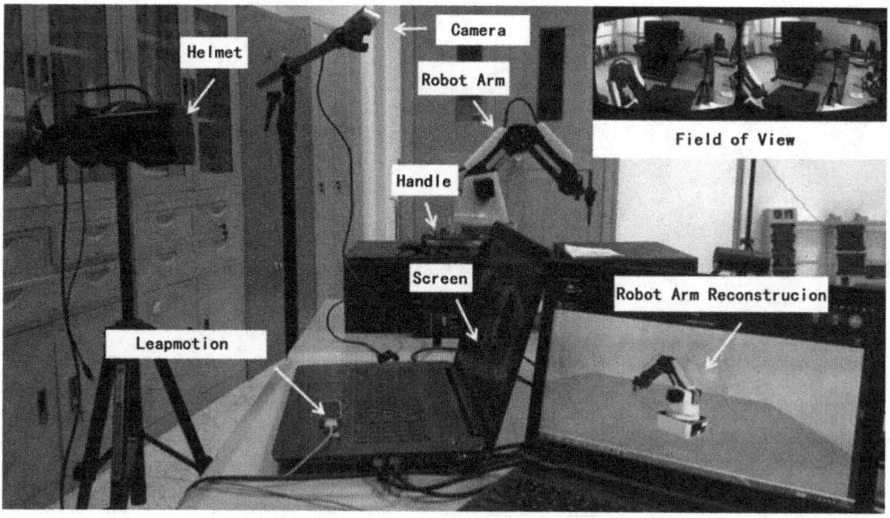

Fig. 11. Experimental scenario

Table 1. Test result record table template

Subject SN	Gender	Device	Image matching degree	Combined load	Learning difficulty	Result 1	Time 1	……	Result 10	Time 10
1										
2										
……										
15										

7.3 Results

The results of two experiments are obtained. The details are as follows (Tables 2 and 3).

Table 2. The result of gesture group

SN	Gen	Device Type	IMD	Load	Learning	R1	T1	R2	T2	R3	T3	R4	T4	R5	T5	R6	T6	R7	T7	R8	T8	R9	T9	R10	T10
1	Male	Gesture	★★★★☆	★☆☆☆☆	★☆☆☆☆	7	18	10	16	10.2	19	10.1	21	10.1	17	8.5	15	10.4	11	10	16	9.8	12	10.7	10
2	Female	Gesture	★★★☆☆	★★★★☆	★★☆☆☆	10.2	20	9.2	22	8.5	20	9.5	22	10.9	22	10.5	20	10.4	26	9.9	23	10.3	21	10.6	25
3	Female	Gesture	★★★☆☆	★★★☆☆	★★★★☆	8.5	41	8.9	17	8.8	9	7	8	3.8	25	10.4	21	9.5	29	8.8	17	8.5	13	9.8	18
4	Female	Gesture	★★★★☆	★★☆☆☆	★☆☆☆☆	9.4	43	8.8	22	9.8	19	7.8	15	10.2	17	9.2	16	9.8	10	7.8	10	9.2	15	9.0	21
5	Male	Gesture	★★★★☆	★★☆☆☆	★☆☆☆☆	10.3	16	2.5	11	9.8	12	9.8	14	10.2	11	10.6	17	7.5	13	10.6	13	10.6	12	9.5	11
6	Male	Gesture	★★★★☆	★★☆☆☆	★☆☆☆☆	10.2	13	9.5	12	10.3	17	10.3	12	10.2	11	10.7	14	10.7	12	10.3	17	10.8	13	10.2	10
7	Female	Gesture	★★★★☆	★★☆☆☆	★★☆☆☆	4	13	7.5	19	9.5	12	10.7	15	10.7	21	9.8	14	10.6	24	9.5	15	9.5	17	10.7	15
8	Male	Gesture	★★★★☆	★☆☆☆☆	★★★☆☆	10.6	21	10.6	13	9.6	28	10.2	12	9.5	15	10.4	14	9.2	24	10.3	13	10.6	17	9.3	15
9	Male	Gesture	★★★★★	★☆☆☆☆	★★★☆☆	10.6	26	10.2	23	10.3	29	10.7	33	10.3	34	10.3	18	10.6	19	10.5	10	10.6	17	10.4	17
10	Male	Gesture	★★★★☆	★★☆☆☆	★★★☆☆	10.2	25	10.6	10	10.4	37	10.2	16	10.7	18	10	13	10.4	12	10.1	14	10.8	12	10.6	12
11	Male	Gesture	★★★★☆	★☆☆☆☆	★☆☆☆☆	9.9	15	10.2	11	10.2	15	9.6	14	10.5	11	10.2	8	10.3	7	9.8	7	10.1	12	10.6	16
12	Male	Gesture	★★★★★	★★☆☆☆	★☆☆☆☆	10.4	20	8.9	25	10.2	16	10.2	24	10.8	23	9.8	32	10	19	10.2	25	9	18	9.5	17
13	Male	Gesture	★☆☆☆☆	★☆☆☆☆	★☆☆☆☆	10.8	18	10.2	7	8.5	6	10.2	10	7	9	8.5	11	8.5	11	9	11	10.3	9	9.1	8
14	Female	Gesture	★★★★☆	★☆☆☆☆	★★☆☆☆	10.4	34	9.6	22	9.8	13	10.5	18	10.5	14	10.9	19	10.7	11	10.2	12	8.6	10	9.8	15
15	Male	Gesture	★★★★☆	★★★☆☆	★★★☆☆	9.5	30	8.9	20	9.7	13	9.9	21	10.7	28	9.5	17	9.4	28	8.9	22	8.9	27	10	31
AVG			3.8	1.866667	1.9333	9.4133333	23.066667	9.94	17.06667	9.486667	16.26667	9.78	16.93333	9.74	18.4	9.953333	16.53333	9.986667	17.33333	9.866667	15.26667	9.853333	15	10.04	16.06667
Female			3.6	2.4	2.2	8.5	30.2	8.8	20.4	8.62	14.6	9.1	15.6	9.22	19.8	10.16	17.8	10.2	21.2	9.48	16	9.22	13.2	10.14	18.8
Male			3.9	1.8	1.8	10.01	22.3	9.1	16.5	9.88	16.9	10.71	16.1	10	16	9.92	17	9.74	15.6	10.12	15.4	10.07	14.7	9.91	16.6

Table 3. The result of handle group

SN	Gen	Device Type	IMD	Load	Learning	R1	T1	R2	T2	R3	T3	R4	T4	R5	T5	R6	T6	R7	T7	R8	T8	R9	T9	R10	T10
1	Male	Handle	★★★★☆	★☆☆☆☆	★★☆☆☆	10.2	46	10.4	34	10.0	27	10.2	26	10.2	25	3	13	10.5	32	10.2	24	10.3	23	10.9	10
2	Female	Handle	★★★☆☆	★★★☆☆	★☆☆☆☆	10.8	62	10.5	31	10.7	20	10.3	30	10.3	30	10.3	27	10.5	23	10.9	32	10.7	23	10.7	28
3	Female	Handle	★★★☆☆	★☆☆☆☆	★☆☆☆☆	9.2	57	10.3	31	10.4	31	10.1	27	9.9	38	10.2	33	10.7	48	10.5	40	10.3	29	10.8	35
4	Female	Handle	★★★★☆	★☆☆☆☆	★☆☆☆☆	10.3	42	10.8	36	10.5	25	10.4	17	10.1	36	10.1	29	10.2	22	9.5	21	10.8	28	9.9	26
5	Male	Handle	★★★★☆	★☆☆☆☆	★☆☆☆☆	10.4	51	10.5	25	10.8	18	10.7	24	10.7	22	10.7	21	9.6	23	10.6	50	10.5	21	10.2	34
6	Male	Handle	★★★★☆	★★★☆☆	★☆☆☆☆	10.2	35	10.2	24	10.7	28	10.5	26	10.6	25	10.7	16	10.2	20	10.8	14	10.5	26	10.7	21
7	Female	Handle	★★★★☆	★★☆☆☆	★★★☆☆	7.5	28	10.8	49	10.8	60	10	38	10.6	31	10.5	32	10.9	26	10.3	30	10.1	26	10.2	24
8	Male	Handle	★★★★☆	★☆☆☆☆	★☆☆☆☆	9.2	29	9.5	18	8.5	20	9.8	24	9.5	30	10.6	15	10.1	22	10.5	18	10.3	16	10.1	14
9	Male	Handle	★★★★★	★★☆☆☆	★☆☆☆☆	10.9	36	10.3	39	10.4	36	9.6	36	10.7	26	10.7	31	10	40	10.8	21	10.9	38	10.8	26
10	Male	Handle	★★★★☆	★☆☆☆☆	★☆☆☆☆	10.2	28	10.9	21	10.8	19	10.3	18	10.9	17	10.9	20	10.9	17	10.8	15	10.9	17	10.8	14
11	Male	Handle	★★★★☆	★★☆☆☆	★★☆☆☆	9.9	42	9.9	30	10.2	29	10.8	39	10.4	26	10	20	10.6	18	10.3	21	10.7	22	10.5	28
12	Male	Handle	★★★★★	★☆☆☆☆	★☆☆☆☆	10.8	32	10.4	29	10.8	25	10.6	24	10	27	10.6	24	10.7	28	10.5	36	10.6	21	10.5	20
13	Male	Handle	★☆☆☆☆	★☆☆☆☆	★☆☆☆☆	9.8	29	7.5	41	10.4	18	9.2	27	9.9	16	9.3	14	10.4	23	10.8	38	10.8	23	10.6	21
14	Female	Handle	★★★★☆	★☆☆☆☆	★☆☆☆☆	10.7	29	10.4	21	10.6	28	10.4	34	10.2	18	10.8	16	10.6	24	10.6	17	10.4	24	10.2	23
15	Male	Handle	★★★★☆	★★★☆☆	★★★★☆	9.1	34	10.2	38	10.1	42	9.3	39	9.8	42	10.3	34	10.5	32	10.6	26	10	29	10.3	32
AVG			3.8	1.6	1.467	9.933333	37.2	10.17333	31.93333	10.43333	29.13333	10.18	28.6	10.25333	26.4	9.69	23	10.41333	26.53333	10.51333	26.66667	10.5	26.13333	10.48	24.13333
Female			3.6	1.6	1.4	9.7	43.4	10.56	33.6	10.6	34.8	10.36	29.2	10.22	30.2	10.38	27.4	10.56	28.6	10.36	28	10.46	30	10.30	27.2
Male			3.9	1.6	1.5	10.13	32.7	10.03	29	10.39	26.2	10.08	27.9	10.25	23.7	9.71	20.4	10.34	26.1	10.62	25.9	10.49	24.4	10.51	22.1

As shown in Fig. 12, the task completion time of the handle operation and the gesture operation decreases and tends to be stable with the increase of operation times. The gesture operation is always about 13 s faster than the handle operation. As shown in Fig. 13, the number of hits increases and tends to be stable with the increase of the number of experiments. Hit rings of the handle operation are always higher than those of the gesture operation. As shown in Table 4, gesture operation is more difficult and loaded.

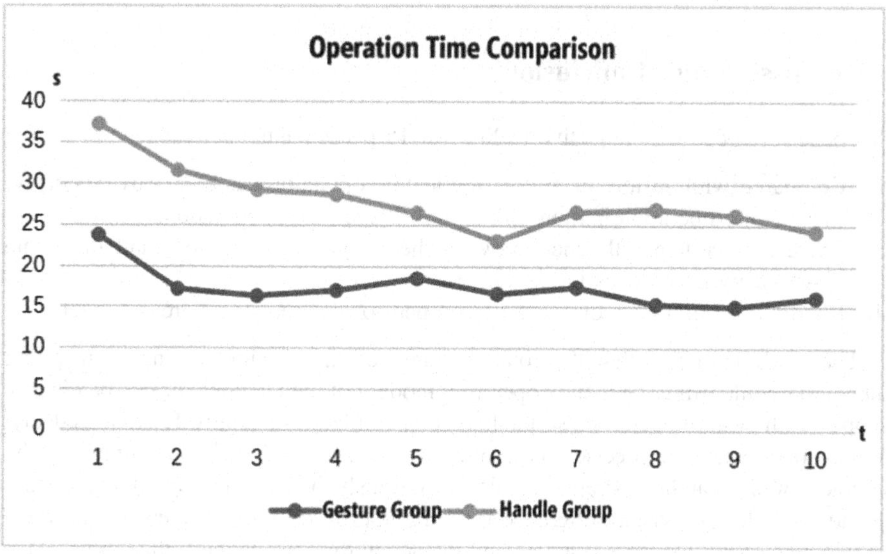

Fig. 12. Operation time comparison diagram

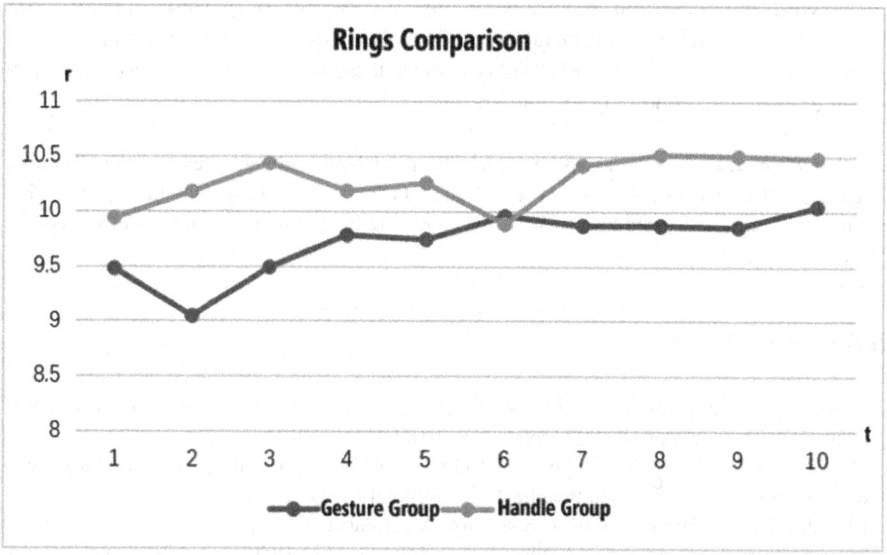

Fig. 13. Rings comparison diagram

Table 4. Comparison of operation load and experimental difficulty

Load	Gesture group	1.8667
	Handle group	1.6
Difficulty	Gesture group	1.933
	Handle group	1.467

8 Discussion and Conclusion

This paper recorded the subjective feelings of 15 participants, including:

(1) Compared with gesture operation, the handle operation has more obvious delay.
(2) The gesture operation is more intuitive than the handle operation.
(3) There is a certain difference between the image seen in HMD and the scene observed by naked eyes in reality.
(4) Handle operation can control the movement of manipulator more accurately.

The analysis shows that the rotation angle of the manipulator needs mapping calculation while using the handle operation mode, but the manipulator can be directly mapped with gesture operation, so the handle operation has a relatively obvious delay; the manipulator can be precisely controlled by keys in the handle operation, and the accuracy of the handle operation mode is obviously better than that of the gesture operation mode. The visual difference in HMD is caused by the discrepancy between the two cameras of the stereo camera and the actual distance between the human eyes.

Experiments show that the accuracy of the gesture operation is slightly lower than that of the handle operation, but it is easier to operate, and the operation is natural and smooth, which accords with the advantages of human-computer interaction habits. For scenes with low precision requirements, the advantages of gesture operation are obvious. It can be used as an operation mode of teleoperation. It has wide application prospects in the field of teleoperation system or task, such as space station, extraterrestrial exploration, robots, UAV and so on.

Acknowledgments. This work was supported by the China Astronaut Research and Training Center and National Key Laboratory of Human Factors Engineering within the following research programs: Advanced Space Medico-Engineering Research Project of China (SYFD1600 51807).

References

1. Weichert, F., Bachmann, D., Rudak, B., Fisseler, D.: Analysis of the accuracy and robustness of the leap motion controller. Sensors **13**(5), 6380–6393 (2013)
2. Marin, G., Dominio, F., Zanuttigh, P.: Hand gesture recognition with jointly calibrated Leap Motion and depth sensor. Multimedia Tools Appl., 1–25 (2015)
3. Lin, W., Du, L., Harris-Adamson, C., Barr, A., Rempel, D.: Design of hand gestures for manipulating objects in virtual reality. In: Kurosu, M. (ed.) HCI 2017. LNCS, vol. 10271, pp. 584–592. Springer, Cham (2017). https://doi.org/10.1007/978-3-319-58071-5_44

4. Vaillancourt, D.E., Newell, K.M.: Amplitude changes in the 8–12, 20–25, and 40 Hz oscillations in finger tremor. Clin. Neurophysiol. **111**(10), 1792–1801 (2000)
5. Casiez, G., Roussel, N., Vogel, D.: 1€ filter: a simple speed-based low-pass filter for noisy input in interactive systems. In: Proceedings of the 2012 ACM Annual Conference on Human Factors in Computing Systems, pp. 2527–2530 (2012)
6. Feng, Z., Yan, B., Xu, T., et al.: 3D direct human-computer interface paradigm based on free hand tracking. Chin. J. Comput. **37**(6), 1309–1323 (2014)
7. Sen, F., Diaz, L., Horttana, T.: A novel gesture-based interface for a VR simulation: re-discovering Vrouw Maria. In: 2012 18th International Conference on Virtual Systems and Multimedia (VSMM), pp. 323–330 (2012)
8. Sato, Y., Saito, M., Koike, H.: Real-time input of 3D pose and gestures of a user's hand and its applications for HCI. In: Proceedings of the Virtual Reality 2001, pp. 79–86. IEEE (2001)
9. Ming, A., Yuqing, L., Bohe, Z., Fuchao, H.: Study on real-time interactive simulation of rotating top in weightlessness. Manned Spaceflight, March 2014

The Assessment of Sencogi: A Visual Complexity Model Predicting Visual Fixations

Maria Laura Mele[1,2,3(✉)], Silvia Colabrese[1], Luca Calabria[1], Damon Millar[1], and Christiaan Erik Rijnders[1]

[1] COGISEN Engineering Company, Rome, Italy
{marialaura, silvia, luca, damon, chris}@cogisen.com
[2] Department of Philosophy, Social and Human Sciences and Education, University of Perugia, Perugia, Italy
[3] ECONA, Interuniversity Centre for Research on Cognitive Processing in Natural and Artificial Systems, Sapienza University of Rome, Rome, Italy

Abstract. This paper investigates whether a frequency-domain model of complexity can accurately predict human visual salience maps. The Sencogi model uses the frequency domain to calculate maps of spatial (i.e., static) and temporal (i.e., dynamic) complexity. This study compares the complexity maps generated by Sencogi to human fixation maps obtained during a visual quality assessment task on static images. This work is the first part of an ongoing multi-step study designed to assess whether fixation maps are an accurate representation of saliency for spatio-temporal scenes. A supporting experiment confirmed that top-down factors, such as scene type, task or emotional states, did not affect human fixation maps. Results show that the Sencogi visual complexity model estimates human eye fixations of images with prediction scores that are significantly above a Chance baseline and is able to compete with a Single Observer baseline. We conclude that the Sencogi visual complexity model is able to predict human fixations in the spatial domain. The next studies will focus on the assessment of Sencogi's performance predicting visual fixations in the spatio-temporal domain.

Keywords: Visual complexity · Visual saliency · Spatio-temporal saliency models · Computer vision

1 Introduction

Visual saliency is "an abstract representation of attentional priority" [1, 2]. The literature commonly uses the term "saliency" as a synonym for the total time of foveal fixations. Most computational saliency models are designed as an estimate of the overall probability that each image area influences fixations. The close relationship between fixation length and visual saliency has led to a common methodology to assess visual saliency models, by using human fixation maps as a ground truth to estimate image saliency [3].

Visual saliency processes are driven by both bottom-up and top-down perceptual processes. Bottom-up saliency is data-driven, i.e., it is based on the intrinsic features of

M. Kurosu (Ed.): HCII 2019, LNCS 11567, pp. 332–347, 2019.
https://doi.org/10.1007/978-3-030-22643-5_26

visual scenes and is an automatic and implicit perceptual process. Top-down saliency is guided by cognitive processes rather than the features of visual stimuli, meaning that environmental and psychological components (e.g., nature of the task, context, previous-knowledge or expectations) guide the spatio-temporal deployment of eye fixations and attention over visual scenes [4]. State of the art saliency models mostly embrace the bottom-up approach to visual saliency.

Computational saliency maps are usually compared with human fixation maps created by free-viewing tasks [5]. However, free-viewing tasks are not able to control top-down influences because there is no explicit task, thus causing idiosyncratic gaze behaviors depending on subjective factors such as expectancies, mood, language and gender [6, 7]. In a study by Köehler and colleagues, the authors studied the effects of both free viewing and targeted tasks on the ability of saliency models to predict human fixations. They showed that saliency models more accurately predicted human fixations on judgement tasks than the widely used free viewing tasks [8].

Visual saliency prediction is a topic of broad and current interest in the field of computational neuroscience and computer vision. The main challenge of visual saliency prediction is to develop architectures that are able to model how human attention behaves in visual scenes. More accurate visual saliency prediction models would benefit fields such as image and video compression [4], as in the case of the Sencogi model. Most saliency models for compression aim to predict visual saliency of images and videos from the spatial properties of the visual frames [9]. These models consider only the saliency properties within a video frame (i.e., spatial saliency), thus excluding the influence of motion between frames in saliency (spatio-temporal saliency). Until now, spatio-temporal saliency models have been mainly proposed in the cognitive science research field for modelling perceptual processes (e.g., [10]), and in spectral analysis research for extending frequency domain use of phase data (e.g., [11]).

Spatial models for video saliency do not take into account the fact that regions of consecutive frames have a spatio-temporal correlation that may affect saliency (e.g., a moving object has higher salience) [12]. Spatio-temporal models that process both within-frames and between-frames information in dynamic visual scenes are rarely used for compression applications (e.g., [12–16]) because discriminating salient motion from noise is still one of the most challenging issues in this field [17].

This work is part of an ongoing multi-step study for the assessment of Sencogi. It describes the assessment of the spatial component of Sencogi on static images. Sencogi is a bottom-up spatio-temporal model for visual compression applications (see [19–21]). The model calculates visual complexity maps using a frequency-domain remapping of the visual complexity of blocks of pixels. The aim of the model is to predict visual fixations on scenes in the spatial and temporal domain. The model has been validated on subjective quality scores with both images and videos for compression applications [19–21]. In this study, the evaluation of the spatial component of Sencogi model was conducted by comparing Sencogi visual complexity maps with human fixation maps derived from a judgment task on an image database. Commonly used metrics for the assessment of saliency models were used to compare Sencogi's maps with human fixation maps. Two additional models were computed to compare the Sencogi model performance with (i) a Chance baseline with visual fixations maps randomly assigned and (ii) a Single Observer baseline with visual fixations maps as predicted by a model computing a single observer performance.

Saliency maps are affected by top-down factors such as interest and mood. Some of the factors that influence top-down salience can be measured using biometric sensors, to determine whether the top-down motivations of all participants are similar. Eye fixations, EEG correlates of decision making and motivation, and facial expressions of emotional states have been studied. Frontal EEG asymmetry in alpha oscillations is an important decision-making marker related to approach/withdraw processes [22]. The Frontal Alpha Asymmetry (FAA) power indicates subjects' approach/withdraw from unexpected or affective stimuli. Facial expressions coded by the Facial Action Coding System (FACS) [23] are patterns of involuntary muscular movements related to affective valence (positive, negative and neutral) and the seven universal basic emotions proposed by Ekman, i.e., joy, sadness, anger, contempt, disgust, fear, and surprise [23].

1.1 Sencogi: A Visual Complexity Model

Sencogi is a frequency-domain algorithm which extracts from input images (or videos) a number of features and combines them linearly. It models the variations of brightness between pixels of a visual frame in order to create a map called a "visual complexity map". Sencogi's visual complexity map represents predictions of which parts of the input image is perceptually relevant and might be affected by visual distortions if heavily compressed. The visual complexity model is able to estimate the degree that a portion of the input image is visually relevant. Visual complexity maps can be used to compress images, by removing data from areas that have low visual complexity.

In order to avoid visual degradation due to information removal, Sencogi's architecture is comprised of four independent visual complexity maps. They are simultaneously computed on the real-time visual scene stream and combined to drive the compression task. The four visual complexity maps are: (1) "Static image visual complexity", measuring visual complexity within each video frame. (2) "Spatio-temporal saliency", measuring visual complexity between multiple frames. (3) "Delta-quality", that detects when quality changes to the image quality introduce artefacts that might be subjectively perceived by the human visual system, thus affecting scene saliency [24]. (4) "Pixel noise detection" that differentiates between scene motion and sensor pixel noise.

The four visual complexity maps are weighted by tunable thresholds, and then combined to return a final visual complexity map driving compression. In this paper, the result of this combination, i.e., the final visual complexity map, has been tested. More details on Sencogi model can be found in [25].

2 Method

The study evaluates the performance of Sencogi, a visual complexity model for predicting human visual fixations. Typically, fixation prediction models are compared to human fixation datasets provided by MIT [26]. However, MIT ground truth datasets are based on free viewing tasks. As Sect. 1 explains, explicit tasks are better at controlling top-down influences, to avoid subjective factors. A judgement task has been used as described in Sect. 2.3. An analysis investigating whether scene type and cognitive factors related to the test affect human performance was performed through eye tracking and EEG. As visual fixations can be affected by emotional states [6], an emotion recognition method based on facial expressions was used to ascertain whether the test affected emotions.

2.1 Apparatus

The Sencogi Visual Complexity model was evaluated by three psychophysiological tools synchronized together using a biometric research platform called iMotions. The evaluation test was conducted with an MSI laptop computer, CPU Intel(R) Core(TM) i7-7820HK CPU @2.90 GHz, RAM 32.0 GB. A second screen was used at native resolution (HP 22vx IPS Monitor 546 × 305 mm, 21.5-in. LED backlight, full HD 1920 × 1080) to present images to the participants. The eye tracker, the electroencephalography (EEG) and the facial expression recognition software specifications are detailed as follows.

Eye Tracker. A Tobii X3, with 120 Hz gaze sample rate, 0.4° accuracy, 0.24° precision, headbox size 500 × 400 mm, affixed to the second screen.

Electroencephalograph. We used a 256 Hz B-Alert (Advanced Brain Monitoring, CA, USA) X10 EEG, a wireless EEG headset recording up to 9 channels of monopolar EEG based on the international 10–20 system [27] and one optional channel of electrocardiography (ECG) data. The FAA index was calculated as the difference between the alpha EEG power right electrode (in this study, F4) and the alpha EEG power left (in this study, the F3 electrode) [28].

Facial Expression Recognition Software. The Affectiva Affdex technology was used. The Affdex algorithm uses an index of facial expressions, called Facial Action Coding System (FACS) [23] to classify the fundamental actions of muscles involved in facial expressions, called Action Units [29]. The Action Units processed by Affdex are unconscious psychomotor processes corresponding to emotional valence rated from −100 (Negative valence) to 100 (Positive valence), and the seven universal human emotions rated from 0 (absent) to 100 (present). Measures were computed with a 20% confidence threshold. The facial expressions that fall outside the threshold were assigned with a "neutral" valence or "lack of facial expressions".

2.2 Methods for Data Representation

Human Visual Fixations Representation. Human fixations can be represented in different formats, either preserving their discrete nature or smoothing the fixation locations to have a continuous representation, called a heatmap. Common practice is to use a Gaussian to blur the points and spread them to mimic visual acuity at one degree [30].

Sencogi Visual Complexity Representation. Sencogi maps have a blocky nature: the model measures the visual complexity per region of neighboring pixels. Those regions, hereafter called macroblocks, can have configurable size (8 × 8, 16 × 16 or 32 × 32, depending on the compression). Each pixel within a macroblock has the same visual complexity value. Visual complexity values are independently computed for each macroblock, meaning that visual complexity can greatly vary among nearby macroblocks.

Common Representation. To fairly compare Sencogi maps to visual fixation heatmaps, a common representation was needed. First, the Gaussian heatmaps were computed according to Le Meur and colleagues [30], then the Gaussian heatmaps were transformed into a macroblock version by adopting the maximum heatmap value within the covered area. Gaussian heatmaps are commonly compared to the blurred version of saliency maps, however blurring a Sencogi map would lead to the loss of neighboring values' independence. In order to not blend independently-computed information, we opted for a subsequent blocky transformation on the visual fixation heatmaps. Heatmaps were computed with the code provided by Bylinskii and colleagues [26], using a cut off value (fc = 8) which corresponds to a Gaussian width of 37 pixels (roughly 1° of visual angle). Each Sencogi macroblock dimension (8×8, 16×16, 32×32) falls within the Gaussian width, thus the blocky transformation does not introduce artefacts that may affect the information conveyed by heatmaps values due to exceeding 1° of visual angle.

2.3 Metrics

A Chance baseline and a Single Observer baseline were computed. The Chance baseline was calculated by assigning a random value to image pixels and using it as a saliency map [26]. We used the Chance baseline as a reference bound for each metric and macroblock combination (see Sect. 4) in order to calculate whether Sencogi predicts eye fixations of participants significantly above chance. The Single Observer baseline was computed by calculating how well a fixation map from a baseline of a single human observer predicts all the subjects of the test, averaged over all images and five variations of observers per image. The Single Observer baseline was computed by following the procedure described by Judd and colleagues [31]. The Single Observer baseline was created in order to understand how a fixation map of one observer predicts fixations of the other observers' fixations. The literature shows that the Single Observer baseline provides values "about as accurate as the best saliency models" ([31], p. 12). The performance of Sencogi Visual Complexity models in predicting the average visual fixations of our cohort, was compared with both the Chance baseline and Single Observer baseline.

The performance assessment of both the Sencogi model and the Single Observer baseline was measured by four of the most used saliency evaluation metrics chosen according to the recommendations provided by Bylinskii and colleagues in a recent paper [26]. Although using only one metric is considered enough for assessing one saliency model, the same metric may be not appropriate for comparing its performance with a model designed with different assumptions and for different applications, as in this study. For our purposes, we chose to use metrics that differ in the way they consider fixation locations (i.e., location based or distribution based) and how they compare saliency maps with fixation maps (i.e., similarity or dissimilarity). Three similarity measures, i.e., Linear Correlation Coefficient (CC), Shuffled AUC (sAUC), and Similarity (Sim), and one dissimilarity measure, i.e., Kullback–Leibler divergence (KL) were used. CC is a correlation coefficient metric returning a measure of the linear correlation between two maps. A CC value of one reflects a total correlation between the maps. KL is a nonlinear measure often used in machine learning and neuroscience to calculate the overall dissimilarity between two probability distributions. KL range is from zero to infinity, where a value close to zero indicates a higher similarity. Area Under the ROC curve (AUC) uses fixation and non-fixation points. The shuffled-AUC (sAUC) uses gaze fixations from other images to sample non-fixation distribution. While in AUC the sampling of non-fixation points is random, in sAUC there is more control on the sampling strategy, meaning that points are taken from regions of other images that are highly fixated. sAUC values of one indicates a perfect correlation.

Sim measures the similarity between two distributions, which are considered as histograms. Sim is calculated as the sum of the minimum values at each pixel, after normalizing the input maps [26]. Sim values close to one indicate a higher similarity of distributions, while Sim values close to zero indicate no correlation.

These are the most commonly used metrics for the evaluation of saliency maps and they are reported in the MIT Saliency Benchmark [32].

2.4 Procedure

A selection of forty images taken from the MIT1003 database [33] was used. The database consists of a collection of 1003 random images from Flickr creative commons and LabelMe [33]. The images were selected by dimension (selected pictures were all 1024 × 768 pixels), format (images were all landscape format) and scene type (ten pictures were selected according to four scene types: closeup, indoor, outdoor and subjects). The selected pictures were used for an image quality judgment test using the Single Stimulus Continuous Quality Scale [34] procedure. The test consists of showing a series of single images and asks participants to rate their subjective perceived quality on a slider numerically marked from one to one hundred and divided into five equal portions, which are labelled as "Bad", "Poor", "Fair", "Good", and "Excellent". The image quality ratings that the participants provide in their judgement task are not used - its role is only to provide a judgement task for the participants. The test was administered to participants using the iMotions platform. Subsequent images were interleaved with a central fixation stimulus displayed for 300 ms. Each image was displayed for 5000 ms at screen native resolution. After the image was displayed, the participant was asked to rate the perceived quality on a dim-grey page lasting at least 300 ms. The experimental task of judging the quality of forty images lasted about 10 min. The test was conducted under an artificial constant dim light. Participants were seated at about 600 mm from the screen and equipped with the EEG headset. Before starting the test, the electrodes impedance was assessed, EEG benchmark data was acquired, and a 16-point eye-tracking calibration was conducted. The whole pre-setting phase required about 20 min per participant.

3 Results

This part reports the results of comparisons between the Sencogi model, a Chance baseline and a Single Observer baseline, compared to human eye fixation data obtained from our cohort on a selection of pictures taken from MIT1003 database. Results on eye tracking data, facial expression recognition and electroencephalography are also described.

3.1 Subjects

An experimental test with twenty right-handed subjects was conducted. Participants (40% female, mean age 28.75 years old) declared normal or corrected-to-normal vision, no color blindness, and no professional experience in the field of video systems. Participants were rewarded for performing the test. One outlier was excluded by the eye tracking dataset.

3.2 Experimental Eye Tracking Ground Truth

Fixation number (total mean number of fixations for the entire test = 5.79, S.D. = 174.36) and fixation duration (total mean time of fixations for the entire test = 174.37, S.D. = 31) were calculated for all participants and for each type of image (closeup, indoor, outdoor, subjects). We discarded the first fixation from eye tracking data of each image in order to avoid adding irrelevant information from the initial center fixation [33]. For each measure, comparisons by image type were conducted. The one way analysis of variance (ANOVA) found no significant difference for both fixation number ($F(3,72) = 0.144$, $p > 0.05$) and fixation duration ($F(3,72) = 0.427$, $p > 0.05$) among all image types.

3.3 Performance Assessment of the Sencogi Visual Complexity Model

An analysis was performed to see whether visual complexity could be a predictor of human fixations. An example of fixation and visual complexity maps is given by Fig. 1.

Performance Assessment Metrics. To test the hypothesis that visual complexity is a predictor of human gaze, four metrics were performed for comparisons with human fixations: Pearson's Correlation Coefficient (CC), Kullback–Leibler divergence (KL), Shuffled AUC (sAUC), and Similarity or histogram intersection (Sim) (see Sect. 3.1). Table 1 shows the results of metrics for visual complexity maps calculated for 8×8, 16×16 and 32×32 macroblocks size. A Chance baseline and a Single Observer baseline were calculated as explained in Sect. 3.1 (Table 1).

Comparisons Between the Sencogi Model Performance Scores and Chance: Chance values and visual complexity values were calculated for each metric. Results of paired t-test show a highly significant difference for all the metrics at each macroblock size (Table 2).

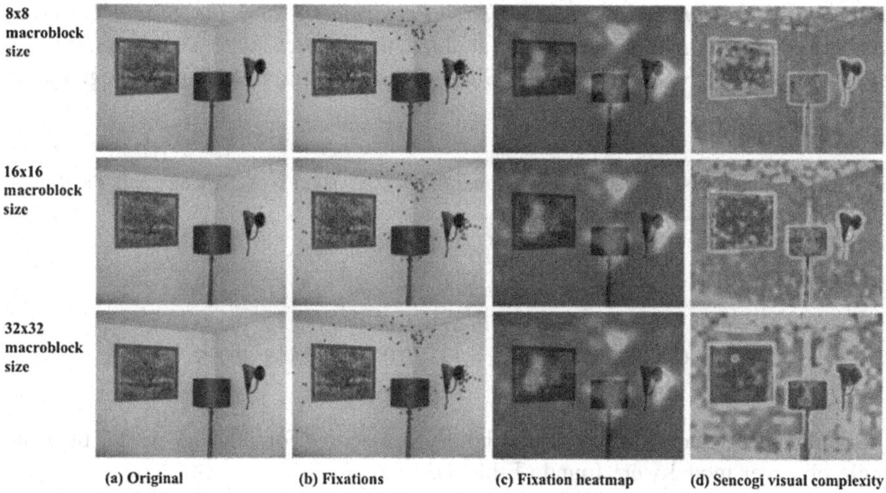

Fig. 1. Figure shows an example of (a) original picture, (b) fixations of all the participants measured with the eye tracking methodology, (c) fixations heatmap mapped into the same range of values of Sencogi maps, (d) Sencogi visual complexity heatmaps according to the three different macroblock sizes (8 × 8, 16 × 16, 32 × 32).

Table 1. Table shows the results obtained by the Sencogi model, the Single Observer baseline, and the Chance baseline at each macroblock size.

	CC ↑	KL ↓	sAUC↑	Sim↑
Single observer 8 × 8	0.396	8.030	0.582	0.313
Sencogi 8 × 8	0.121	1.127	0.542	0.409
Chance 8 × 8	0.001	1.496	0.501	0.375
Single observer 16 × 16	0.413	7.800	0.587	0.328
Sencogi 16 × 16	0.128	1.036	0.543	0.433
Chance 16 × 16	0.000	1.439	0.501	0.390
Single observer 32 × 32	0.447	7.328	0.599	0.360
Sencogi 32 × 32	0.132	0.913	0.539	0.469
Chance 32 × 32	0.000	1.320	0.496	0.417

Table 2. Comparisons between the Sencogi model performance scores and the chance baseline for each macroblock size.

	8 × 8		16 × 16		32 × 32	
	t(201)	*p-value*	*t(201)*	*p-value*	*t(201)*	*p-value*
CC	−11.657	0.000	−11.741	0.000	−12.187	0.000
KL	30.181	0.000	33.897	0.000	31.925	0.000
sAUC	−9.011	0.000	−9.217	0.000	−8.373	0.000
Sim	−12.091	0.000	−17.882	0.000	−24.512	0.000

Comparisons Among the Sencogi Model Performance and the Single Observer Baseline Performance: Comparisons at three macroblock sizes show significantly better CC and sAUC scores for the Single Observer baseline than Sencogi model (Table 3).

Table 3. Comparisons between the CC and the sAUC scores of Sencogi and the Single Observer baseline for each macroblock size.

	8 × 8		16 × 16		32 × 32	
	t(201)	*p-value*	*t(201)*	*p-value*	*t(201)*	*p-value*
CC	15.126	0.000	15.671	0.000	17.279	0.000
sAUC	6.733	0.000	6.733	0.000	9.109	0.000

Significantly better KL scores and better Sim scores for Sencogi model than the single observer model were found (Table 4).

Table 4. Comparisons between the KL and the Sim scores of Sencogi and the Single Observer baseline.

	8 × 8		16 × 16		32 × 32	
	t(201)	*p-value*	*t(201)*	*p-value*	*t(201)*	*p-value*
KL	29.468	0.000	29.358	0.000	28.702	0.000
Sim	−9.213	0.000	−9.853	0.000	−10.048	0.000

The Effect of Scene Type on the Sencogi Model Performance: Visual complexity maps were calculated for 8 × 8 macroblock resolution. No significant difference among metric values for image type was found (KL, $F(3, 36) = 1.213$, $p > 0.05$; sAUC, $F(3, 36) = 0.860$, $p > 0.05$; Sim, ($F(3, 36) = 1.367$, $p > 0.05$), except for CC where outdoor images have significantly better CC values than closeup images (CC, $F(3, 36) = 2.962$, $p = 0.042$). Visual complexity maps were calculated for 16 × 16 macroblock resolution. No significant difference among metric values for image type was found (CC, $F(3, 36) = 2.704$, $p > 0.05$; KL, $F(3, 36) = 0.874$, $p > 0.05$; sAUC, $F(3, 36) = 0.615$, $p > 0.05$; Sim, $F(3, 36) = 0.746$, $p > 0.05$). Visual complexity maps were calculated for 32 × 32 macroblock resolution. No significant difference among metric values for image type was found (CC, $F(3, 36) = 1.733$, $p > 0.05$; KL, $F(3, 36) = 0.520$, $p > 0.05$; sAUC, $F(3, 36) = 1.068$, $p > 0.05$; Sim, $F(3, 36) = 0.417$, $p > 0.05$).

3.4 Facial Expression Recognition

The Effect of the Test on Participants' Affective Valence and Basic Emotions Responses. The mean time percent of both valence and basic emotions related to test pictures, out of the total time recorded for all the whole test, was calculated (Table 2).

Emotions were calculated by iMotions[1] as the mean of 100* (count frames in which emotion appears/count frames in stimulus) (Table 5).

Table 5. Comparisons between the KL and the Sim scores of Sencogi and the Single Observer baseline.

Affective valence	MTP	S.D.
Neutral valence	58.039	4.060
Positive valence	0.089	0.330
Negative valence	1.820	3.270
Basic emotions	MTP	S.D.
Contempt	0.562	2.562
Fear	3.280	9.298
Surprise	2.239	7.799
Joy	0.092	0.541
Disgust	0.012	0.089
Sadness	0.002	0.014
Anger	0.013	0.103

The one way ANOVA on affective valence means shows significant differences among neutral, positive and negative affective values ($F(2, 119) = 19840.4$, $p = 0.000$). The post-hoc test (Bonferroni corrected) shows a meantime percent of facial expressions related to neutral affective states that is significantly longer at $p < 0.01$ than both negative and positive valence values. A multivariate analysis of variance (MANOVA) was performed on affective valence mean time percent, showing no significant difference among image types (subjects, outdoor, indoor, closeup) for neutral, positive and negative affective values (Wilks' Lambda $F(9, 180) = 0.387$, $p > 0.05$).

Significant time differences among basic emotions were found with respect to each other ($F(6, 279) = 70.735$, $p = 0.000$). The post-hoc test (Bonferroni corrected) shows a meantime percent of facial expressions related to fear (mean time = 3.281%) and surprise (mean time = 2.240%) that is significantly higher at $p < 0.01$ than the other measured basic emotions.

A paired t-test comparison among the subsections of the test composed by center-fixation slide, image slide, and image quality rating slide shows significantly higher values of emotions of fear and surprise during the image slides (fear $t(39) = 4.380$, $p = 0.000$; surprise $t(39) = 3.177$, $p = 0.003$) and quality rating slides (fear $t(39) = -4.954$, $p = 0.000$; surprise $t(39) = -4.737$, $p = 0.001$) compared to center-fixation slides. No significant differences were found for emotions of fear and surprise between the image slides and quality rating slides (fear $t(39) = -0.187$, $p > 0.05$; surprise $t(39) = -0.137$, $p > 0.05$)

[1] www.imotions.com.

The Effect of Scene Type on Participants' Basic Emotions. A MANOVA was performed on emotions mean time percent, showing no significant difference among image types (subjects, outdoor, indoor, closeup) for basic emotions (Wilks' Lambda $F_{(21, 201)} = 0.565$, $p > 0.05$).

Eye Tracking Data Compared to Facial Expression Recognition. No correlation between fixation number, affective valence, and basic emotions was found. A negative correlation was found between fixation duration and fear (Pearson's $r = -0.383$, $p = 0.015$) and disgust (Pearson's $r = -0.324$, $p = 0.041$). No other correlation between fixation duration, affective valence, and basic emotions was found.

3.5 EEG

The Effect of the Test on Participants' Approach/Avoidance States. After a previous automatic decontamination process for artefact removal, the Frontal Alpha Asymmetry (FAA) mean values were calculated (Table 6).

Table 6. FAA mean value for each scene type.

Scene type	FAA
Closeup	79.915
Indoor	82.761
Outdoor	81.488
Subjects	81.693

The one way ANOVA on mean FAA values shows no significant differences among image types ($F_{(3, 72)} = 0.001$, $p > 0.05$).

Eye Tracking Data Compared to EEG Frontal Alpha Asymmetry. No significant correlation between fixations and FAA was found (Pearson's $r = 0.066$, $p > 0.05$).

4 Discussion

The aim of this work was to investigate whether the Sencogi model of visual complexity can accurately predict human foveal vision, and to control for factors that might affect salience. Three experimental investigations were performed to verify (i) whether Sencogi visual complexity predicts visual fixations, (ii) whether saliency prediction performs better with certain types of visual scenes than others, and (iii) whether the experimental test introduces top-down factors affecting foveal fixations.

(i) Does Sencogi visual complexity predict visual fixations? Sencogi visual complexity maps were compared to human visual fixation maps using four of the most suitable, commonly used assessment metrics (CC, KL, sAUC, and Sim).

Statistical comparisons of the results with a Chance baseline were performed. The Chance baseline assigns saliency values to random pixels (chance). The results show that Sencogi has significantly better scores than chance (i.e., they are closer to human fixations).

Sencogi performs better than the Single Observer baseline at predicting overall visual saliency in two assessment metrics, i.e., Kullback–Leibler divergence and Similarity, likely because they both penalize sparser sets of predictions such as the Single Observer baseline, which might miss fixations that emulate average fixation behavior [26]. Comparisons were made between the Sencogi model performance and the Single Observer baseline performance in predicting visual fixations. The Single Observer baseline obtained significantly higher scores for the Pearson's Correlation Coefficient (CC) metric and for the shuffled AUC metric. These results can be explained by the nature of the metrics used for assessing the two models. As the CC metric does not assume that saliency models are probabilistic [26], it will produce a worse score for models such as Sencogi that don't include any possible systematic bias of observers. The other metric in which Sencogi received significantly lower values than the Single Observer baseline is sAUC. sAUC is not invariant to center bias. A model with high central predictions is ranked lower than a model with more peripheral predictions [26].

Sencogi received significantly lower sAUC scores than the Single Observer baseline, meaning that the Single Observer baseline could have sets of predictions that are too sparse to emulate average viewing behavior in the central part. In this perspective, the Single Observer baseline is not penalized by the sAUC metric because it does not account for the central predictions of all the observers' fixations as Sencogi does. Therefore, for most measures that are not biased, Sencogi correctly predicts visual fixations.

(ii) Is Sencogi visual saliency prediction sensitive to scene type? The experimental images shown during the test were divided into four groups according to the type of scene depicted, i.e., images showing closeup, indoor, outdoor, and subject scenes in order to investigate whether image type influences the Sencogi performance scores. We found no significant difference for 16×16 and 32×32 visual complexity maps. Only maps with 8×8 pixels macroblocks had significantly higher linear correlation scores (CC) for images showing outdoor scenes compared to the other scene types, in particular closeup scenes. This result might be related to the nature of outdoor scenes, in which subjects are usually smaller than other scene types. However, this result is related to a barely detectable statistically significant difference that happens only for one of the four metrics (CC). The other assessment metrics (KL, sAUC, and Sim) do not seem to be sensitive to any difference among scene types. A new in-depth investigation on the effects of scene type on Sencogi performance is needed.

(iii) Does the experimental test introduce top-down factors affecting eye foveal fixations? Eye fixation duration reflects how much the fixated information is processed by cognitive processes [35]. The more a visual stimulus requires the allocation of the analysis process, the more fixation time is prolonged [36] because of the increase in mental load. In this work, the average eye fixation lasts about 180 ms per image, which is about 20% of the presentation time, meaning that the nature and the duration of the task did not cause any significant increase in cognitive workload to participants. No differences among visual scene type were found for fixation numbers and fixation duration, meaning that in this study, scene type did not affect eye fixations in a significant way.

During the presentation of experimental images, the overall neutral emotional state in participants was significantly higher than positive and negative emotional states. Both emotional valence and basic emotions were not affected by scene type, confirming that the type of content in the images used for this study did not affect the emotional quality of the interaction. However, if we analyze only the longitudinal differences among basic emotions, participants' facial expressions related to fear and surprise were significantly higher than the others (joy, sadness, anger, contempt and disgust). This result suggests that the emotions of fear and surprise might be due to the nature of the task, which is a time-based trial (participants have five seconds to examine the quality of each image) that does not provide any feedback to let the participant know whether they are correctly performing the assigned task. This assumption is supported by significantly higher scores of fear and surprise during both images and scoring slides presentation, compared to neutral areas where participants are not asked to perform a judgment task, such as the center fixations period. Emotional states do not correlate with the number of fixations, but the duration of eye fixations negatively correlates with emotions of fear and disgust, confirming that the more observers feel negative emotions, the less likely they are to keep gazing at a certain fixation point [37].

Findings on EEG measures showed no differences in FAA mean values among image types, nor the number and the duration of fixations, meaning that participants' approach/withdraw psychophysiological processes did not significantly change during the test. These findings highlight that no intervening top-down factor related to test or to the material affected eye foveal fixations in a significant way.

5 Conclusion

In this paper, we validated the performance of the Sencogi visual complexity model for predicting visual fixations of static frames. Visual complexity maps were compared with human fixations derived from a judgment task. Findings show that Sencogi significantly surpasses Chance and performs better than the model of a single observer for metrics that penalize models that are too sparse to emulate average viewing behavior (in particular, the KL metric and the Sim metric). We found no noteworthy differences in predicting visual saliency among the four scene types of the images (closeup, indoor, outdoor, and subjects).

Investigations of psychophysiological measures during the test excluded the possibility that, in this test, cognitive and affective psychological factors such as approach/withdraw processes, emotional valence or basic emotions relate to fixation number and/or duration. This lack of emotional correlation suggests that psychological factors did not affect the participants' performance. Observers' mental load and affective valence (overall neutral) were not influenced by task-related factors such as scene type. The only basic emotions seen during the test (fear and surprise) were not significantly present over the whole test. Fear and surprise are most likely related to the demand of assigning a quality score rather than to the image content. Future work will focus on comparisons between the performance in predicting saliency of Sencogi and traditional state of the art saliency methods. This study has shown that Sencogi can produce visual complexity maps that predict visual fixations for static images, but Sencogi can also produce spatio-temporal visual complexity maps, so future studies on video databases will be conducted in order to validate the temporal components of the Sencogi model.

References

1. Treisman, A.M., Gelade, G.: A feature-integration theory of attention. Cogn. Psychol. **12**(1), 97–136 (1980). https://doi.org/10.1016/0010-0285(80)90005-5
2. Koch, C., Ullman, S.: Shifts in selective visual attention: towards the underlying neural circuitry. In: Vaina, L.M. (ed.) Matters of Intelligence. Synthese Library (Studies in Epistemology, Logic, Methodology, and Philosophy of Science), vol. 188, pp. 115–141. Springer, Dordrecht (1987). https://doi.org/10.1007/978-94-009-3833-5_5
3. Kummerer, M., Wallis, T.S., Gatys, L.A., Bethge, M.: Understanding low-and high-level contributions to fixation prediction. In: Proceedings of the IEEE International Conference on Computer Vision, pp. 4789–4798 (2017). https://doi.org/10.1109/iccv.2017.513
4. Itti, L., Koch, C.: Computational modelling of visual attention. Nat. Rev. Neurosci. **2**(3), 194 (2001). https://doi.org/10.1038/35058500
5. Zhang, Y.Y., Zhang, S., Zhang, P., Zhang, X.: Saliency detection via background and foreground null space learning. Sig. Process. Image Commun. **70**, 271–281 (2019). https://doi.org/10.1016/j.image.2018.10.005
6. Shen, J., Itti, L.: Top-down influences on visual attention during listening are modulated by observer sex. Vision. Res. **65**, 62–76 (2012). https://doi.org/10.1016/j.visres.2012.06.001
7. Borji, A., Sihite, D.N., Itti, L.: What stands out in a scene? A study of human explicit saliency judgment. Vision. Res. **91**, 62–77 (2013). https://doi.org/10.1016/j.visres.2013.07.016
8. Koehler, K., Guo, F., Zhang, S., Eckstein, M.P.: What do saliency models predict? J. Vis. **14**(3), 14 (2014). https://doi.org/10.1167/14.3.14
9. Zhang, W., Borji, A., Wang, Z., Le Callet, P., Liu, H.: The application of visual saliency models in objective image quality assessment: a statistical evaluation. IEEE Trans. Neural Netw. Learn. Syst. **27**(6), 1266–1278 (2016). https://doi.org/10.1109/TNNLS.2015.2461603
10. Muddamsetty, S.M., Sidibe, D., Tremeau, A., Meriaudeau, F.: Spatio-temporal saliency detection in dynamic scenes using local binary patterns. In: 2014 22nd International Conference on Pattern Recognition (2014). https://doi.org/10.1109/icpr.2014.408
11. He, X. (ed.): IScIDE 2015. LNCS, vol. 9243. Springer, Cham (2015). https://doi.org/10.1007/978-3-319-23862-3
12. Yubing, T., Cheikh, F.A., Guraya, F.F.E., Konik, H., Trémeau, A.: A spatiotemporal saliency model for video surveillance. Cogn. Comput. **3**, 241–263 (2011). https://doi.org/10.1007/s12559-010-9094-8
13. Mu, N., Xu, X., Zhang, X.: A spatial-frequency-temporal domain based saliency model for low contrast video sequences. J. Vis. Commun. Image Represent. **58**, 79–88 (2019). https://doi.org/10.1016/j.jvcir.2018.11.012
14. Rapantzikos, K., Avrithis, Y., Kollias, S.: Dense saliency-based spatiotemporal feature points for action recognition (2009). https://doi.org/10.1109/cvpr.2009.5206525

15. Mahadevan, V., Vasconcelos, N.: Spatiotemporal saliency in dynamic scenes. IEEE Trans. Pattern Anal. Mach. Intell. **32**(1), 171–177 (2010). https://doi.org/10.1007/978-3-642-37431-9_41
16. Oikonomopoulos, A., Patras, I., Pantic, M.: Spatiotemporal salient points for visual recognition of human actions. IEEE Trans. Syst. Man Cybern. Part B (Cybernetics) **36**(3), 710–719 (2005). https://doi.org/10.1109/tsmcb.2005.861864
17. Dhiman, C., Vishwakarma, D.K.: A review of state-of-the-art techniques for abnormal human activity recognition. Eng. Appl. Artif. Intell. **77**, 21–45 (2019). https://doi.org/10.1016/j.engappai.2018.08.014
18. Achanta, R., Hemami, S., Estrada, F., Susstrunk, S.: Frequency-tuned salient region detection. In: IEEE Conference on Computer Vision and Pattern Recognition, CVPR 2009, pp. 1597–1604. IEEE, June 2009. https://doi.org/10.1109/cvpr.2009.5206596
19. Mele, M.L., Millar, D., Rijnders, C.E.: The web-based subjective quality assessment of an adaptive image compression plug-in. In: 1st International Conference on Human Computer Interaction Theory and Applications, HUCAPP, Porto, Portugal (2017). https://doi.org/10.5220/0006226401330137
20. Mele, M.L., Millar, D., Rijnders, C.E.: Using spatio-temporal saliency to predict subjective video quality: a new high-speed objective assessment metric. In: Kurosu, M. (ed.) HCI 2017. LNCS, vol. 10271, pp. 353–368. Springer, Cham (2017). https://doi.org/10.1007/978-3-319-58071-5_27
21. Mele, M.L., Millar, D., Rijnders, C.E.: Sencogi spatio-temporal saliency: a new metric for predicting subjective video quality on mobile devices. In: Kurosu, M. (ed.) HCI 2018. LNCS, vol. 10902, pp. 552–564. Springer, Cham (2018). https://doi.org/10.1007/978-3-319-91244-8_43
22. Schneirla, T.C.: An evolutionary and developmental theory of biphasic processes underlying approach and withdrawal (1959). https://doi.org/10.1177/000306517001800210
23. Ekman, P., Friesen, W.V.: Manual for the Facial Action Coding System. Consulting Psychologists Press (1978). https://doi.org/10.4135/9781483381411
24. Redi, J., Liu, H., Zunino, R., Heynderickx, I.: Interactions of visual attention and quality perception. In: Human Vision and Electronic Imaging XVI (2011). https://doi.org/10.1117/12.876712
25. Rijnders, C.E.: U.S. Patent Application No. 15/899,331 (2018)
26. Bylinskii, Z., Judd, T., Oliva, A., Torralba, A., Durand, F.: What do different evaluation metrics tell us about saliency models? IEEE Trans. Pattern Anal. Mach. Intell. (2018). https://doi.org/10.1109/tpami.2018.2815601
27. Jasper, H.H.: The ten-twenty electrode system of the International Federation. Electroencephalogr. Clin. Neurophysiol. **10**, 370–375 (1958). https://doi.org/10.1080/00029238.1961.11080571
28. John, E.R.: Neurometrics: clinical applications of quantitative electrophysiology, vol. 2. Wiley (1977). https://doi.org/10.1177/002076407902500222
29. Ekman, P.: Facial action coding system (FACS). A human face (2002)
30. Le Meur, O., Baccino, T.: Methods for comparing scanpaths and saliency maps: strengths and weaknesses. Behav. Res. Methods **45**(1), 251–266 (2013). https://doi.org/10.3758/s13428-012-0226-9
31. Judd, T., Durand, F., Torralba, A.: A benchmark of computational models of saliency to predict human fixations (2012)
32. Bylinskii, Z., Recasens, A., Borji, A., Oliva, A., Torralba, A., Durand, F.: Where should saliency models look next? In: Leibe, B., Matas, J., Sebe, N., Welling, M. (eds.) ECCV 2016. LNCS, vol. 9909, pp. 809–824. Springer, Cham (2016). https://doi.org/10.1007/978-3-319-46454-1_49

33. Judd, T., Ehinger, K., Durand, F., Torralba, A.: Learning to predict where humans look. In: 2009 IEEE 12th International Conference on Computer Vision, pp. 2106–2113. IEEE, September 2009. https://doi.org/10.1109/iccv.2009.5459462
34. BT.500: Methodology for the subjective assessment of the quality of television pictures (n. d.). http://www.itu.int/rec/R-REC-BT.500-7-199510-S/en. Accessed 9 Oct 2017
35. Yarbus, A.L.: Eye Movements and Vision, New York (1967). https://doi.org/10.1007/978-1-4899-5379-7
36. Jacob, R.J.: The use of eye movements in human-computer interaction techniques: what you look at is what you get. ACM Trans. Inf. Syst. (TOIS) **9**(2), 152–169 (1991). https://doi.org/10.1145/123078.128728
37. Mele, M.L., Federici, S., Dennis, J.L.: Believing is seeing: fixation duration predicts implicit negative attitudes. PLoS ONE **9**(8), e105106 (2014). https://doi.org/10.1371/journal.pone.0105106

Evaluation of Orientation Correction Algorithms in Real-Time Hand Motion Tracking for Computer Interaction

Nonnarit O-larnnithipong(✉), Neeranut Ratchatanantakit, Armando Barreto, and Sudarat Tangnimitchok

Department of Electrical and Computer Engineering, Florida International University, Miami, FL, USA
{nolar002,nratc001,barretoa,stang018}@fiu.edu

Abstract. This paper outlines the evaluation of orientation correction algorithms implemented in a hand motion tracking system that utilizes an inertial measurement unit (IMU) and infrared cameras. Thirty human subjects participated in an experiment to validate the performance of the hand motion tracking system. The statistical analysis shows that the error of position tracking is, on average, 1.7 cm in the x-axis, 1.0 cm in the y-axis, and 3.5 cm in the z-axis. The Kruskal-Wallis tests show that the orientation correction algorithm using gravity vector and magnetic North vector can significantly reduce the errors in orientation tracking in comparison to fixed offset compensation. Statistical analyses show that the orientation correction algorithm using gravity vector and magnetic North vector and the on-board Kalman-based orientation filtering produced orientation errors that were not significantly different in the Euler angles, Phi, Theta and Psi, with the p-values of 0.632, 0.262 and 0.728, respectively.

Keywords: Inertial measurement unit · Gyroscope drift · Orientation correction algorithm · Bias offset error · Quaternion correction using gravity vector and magnetic north vector · 3D hand motion tracking interface

1 Introduction

Recent studies on human-computer interaction have been leading towards the development of systems in which humans would be able to interact with computers more naturally [15,16,22]. For example, there are several developments on integrating voice commands into the computer systems or personal mobile devices in order to request information or to command actions. There is also an increasing popularity for the uses of Virtual Reality (VR) and Augmented Reality (AR) in several applications so that the users can interact with immersive environments. The users must perceive themselves in a state of presence in order to achieve the key goal of VR and AR systems [6,10,17,18]. Thus, a

M. Kurosu (Ed.): HCII 2019, LNCS 11567, pp. 348–365, 2019.
https://doi.org/10.1007/978-3-030-22643-5_27

hand motion tracking system was proposed and developed [13, 14] as one of the alternative ways for human to interact more naturally within 3D environments. The hand motion tracking system utilizes an inertial measurement unit (IMU) to determine the orientation of the user's hand, and infrared cameras to determine the position of the hand in 3-dimensional space, in real-time. This paper will focus on the implementation and evaluation of orientation correction algorithms that were used to improve orientation tracking using IMUs.

The gyroscopes in IMUs provide the inertial measurement in the form of angular velocity. Theoretically, the orientation (angle) can be calculated by mathematical integration. However, most commercial-grade Microelectromechanical Systems (MEMS) gyroscopes may generate output signals that deviate from zero even when there is no rotational input applied on them, called "bias offset error". This error is a cause of the common phenomenon in orientation tracking called "drift", which can grow proportional to time. The drift severely causes problems in navigation and other applications that utilize commercial-grade MEMS gyroscopes to determine the orientation [3, 19]. Kalman-based orientation filtering is a common method to improve orientation tracking and eliminate gyroscope drift in inertial measurement units [9, 20, 21]. In addition, several studies employ sensor fusion approaches, in which the measurements from accelerometers, gyroscopes, and magnetometers are combined to determine the orientation [2, 7].

This paper statistically evaluates the effects of three different orientation correction algorithms on the orientation output errors in the form of Euler Angles (Phi, Theta and Psi). The three orientation correction algorithms are: (1) the orientation correction using fixed bias offset (FB), (2) the correction using the Kalman-based orientation filtering streamed directly from the Yost Labs 3-Space sensor module (KF), and (3) the proposed orientation correction algorithm using the gravity and magnetic North vectors (GMV).

2 Methodology and Materials

2.1 Hand Motion Tracking System

The 3D hand motion tracking system shown in Fig. 1 is capable of determining the hand position and orientation in 3-dimensional space. The infrared cameras V120: Trio in Fig. 1(a) located above the computer screen can be used to track the position of an infrared dot marker attached on the glove. The 3D coordinate of the marker represents the position of the wrist of the hand. The orientation of the hand is determined by Yost Labs 3-Space sensors attached at the back of the hand, as shown in Fig. 1(b). Yost Labs 3-Space module consists of tri-axial accelerometer, gyroscope and magnetometer, and can be connected to the host computer via a USB cable.

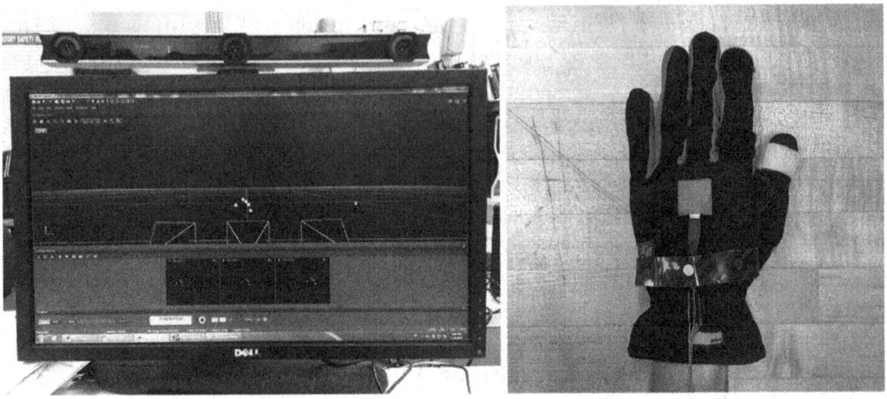

(a) (b)

Fig. 1. Hand motion tracking system using (a) infrared cameras for position tracking and (b) inertial measurement unit for orientation tracking.

2.2 Orientation Correction Using the Gravity and Magnetic North Vectors

A gyroscope should ideally generate the output signal of zero angular velocity when it is not in motion. However, a commercial-grade gyroscope can generate a non-zero erroneous reading, called "the bias offset error", under those circumstances. This error produces a major distortion of the orientation measurement, called "drift" [3,19]. An algorithm to improve the orientation estimation using the gravity and magnetic North vectors (GMV) was previously proposed [12–14] and implemented in this evaluation. The orientation correction algorithm using the gravity and magnetic North vectors, as shown in Fig. 2, consists of 4 steps, as described below.

(1) Prediction of the Bias Offset Error. When the sensor is static, the gyroscope in the IMU is expected to provide zero readings in all axes. However, for commercial-grade MEMS, they could generate the output signals that deviate from zero, called "bias offset error". The bias offset error in IMU consists of deterministic and stochastic components [1], resulting in the change of bias randomly through time. Thus, the bias offset error should be re-calculated for every period of time. The new bias offset error will be estimated and updated only when the IMU is static. For real-time implementation, the bias offset of gyroscope ($\hat{b}$) is calculated from the mean of five consecutive gyroscope samples that have magnitudes smaller than predefined thresholds. The unbiased angular velocity ($\boldsymbol{\omega}_B$) is then calculated by subtracting the calculated bias offset error ($\hat{b}$) from the raw gyroscope reading ($\boldsymbol{\omega}_0$) as described in Eq. 1.

$$\boldsymbol{\omega}_B = \boldsymbol{\omega}_0 - \hat{b} \tag{1}$$

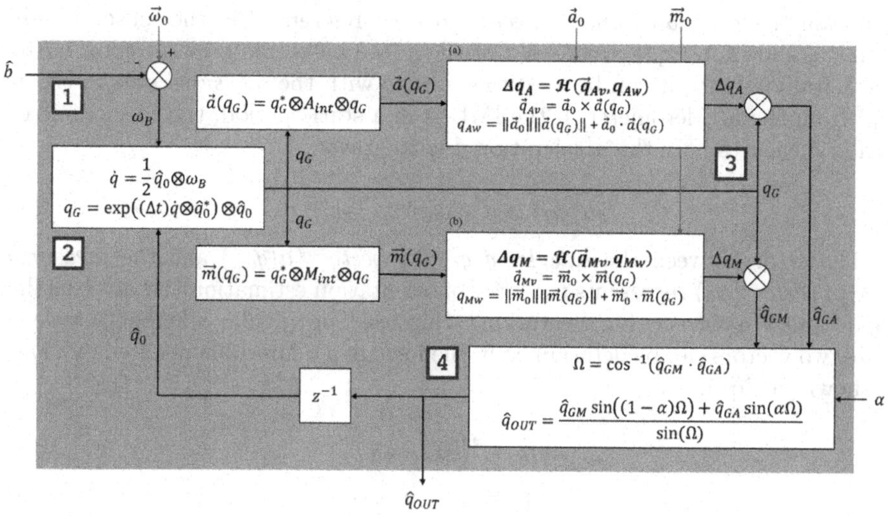

Fig. 2. Block diagram of the orientation correction algorithm using the gravity vector and the magnetic North vector correction (GMV).

(2) Estimation of a Quaternion Orientation. The rotation or orientation in this work is represented by quaternion notation, having its real part in the forth component. Quaternion is a 4-dimensional quantity which is a commonly used to describe orientation of an object in computer graphics because it prevents singularity and gimbal lock problem [8]. The quaternion rate ($\dot{q}$) in Eq. 2 can be calculated by using the unbiased angular velocity ($\boldsymbol{\omega}_B$) and the quaternion estimation of the orientation from the previous iteration ($\hat{q}_0$). At the initial stage, $\hat{q}_0$ is set to $[0, 0, 0, 1]$, indicating zero-degree rotation.

$$\dot{q} = \frac{1}{2}\hat{q}_0 \otimes \boldsymbol{\omega}_B \tag{2}$$

$$q_G = exp((\Delta t)\dot{q} \otimes \hat{q}_0^*) \otimes \hat{q}_0 \tag{3}$$

The quaternion q_G in Eq. 3 represents the estimated orientation, which can be calculated from the quaternion rate ($\dot{q}$), the quaternion estimation of the orientation from the previous iteration ($\hat{q}_0$), and the sampling interval used by the IMU for recording data (Δt). This estimated quaternion (q_G) can be used to describe the orientation of the sensor module or the object that the IMU is attached to.

(3) Quaternion Correction. In the Earth frame, the gravity vector always points towards the Earth's center. The estimated orientation q_G from Eq. 3, which represents the orientation of the sensor module with respect to the Earth frame, can be used to rotate the gravity vector in the Earth frame in order to obtain the *calculated gravity vector* ($\boldsymbol{a}(q_G)$) referenced in the sensor's body frame, as shown in Eq. 4, where $\boldsymbol{A}_{int}$ is the initial measured gravity vector in the Earth frame. Then, it can be used to compare with the *measured gravity vector* ($\boldsymbol{a}_0$) from the accelerometer. If the IMU is in a static period, the accelerometer ideally measures only the acceleration due to gravity.

$$\boldsymbol{a}(q_G) = {q_G}^* \otimes \boldsymbol{A}_{int} \otimes q_G \tag{4}$$

The error between the *calculated gravity vector* ($\boldsymbol{a}(q_G)$) and the *measured gravity vector* ($\boldsymbol{a}_0$) represents the error of orientation estimation and gives us the opportunity to correct the orientation estimates. The angular difference between these two vectors can be determined in the form of a quaternion denoted by Δq_A, as shown in Eq. 5.

$$\Delta q_A = \mathbb{H}(\boldsymbol{q}_{Av}, q_{Aw}) \tag{5}$$

$$\boldsymbol{q}_{Av} = \boldsymbol{a}_0 \times \boldsymbol{a}(q_G) \tag{6}$$

$$q_{Aw} = \|\boldsymbol{a}_0\|\|\boldsymbol{a}(q_G)\| + \boldsymbol{a}_0 \cdot \boldsymbol{a}(q_G) \tag{7}$$

To correct the orientation estimation, q_G is multiplied by Δq_A since the product of 2 quaternions implies compounding of their rotations. The estimated quaternion with gravity vector correction ($\hat{q}_{GA}$) is described in Eq. 8. Note that $\hat{q}_{GA}$ needs to be normalized before using it as a rotation operator.

$$\hat{q}_{GA} = q_G \otimes \Delta q_A \tag{8}$$

Similarly, the magnetic North vector at a certain location always points towards the Earth's magnetic North pole in the Earth frame. The estimated orientation q_G from Eq. 3 which represents the orientation of the sensor module with respect to the Earth frame, can also be used to rotate the magnetic North vector in the Earth frame in order to obtain the *calculated magnetic North vector* ($\boldsymbol{m}(q_G)$) referenced in the sensor's body frame, as shown in Eq. 9, where $\boldsymbol{M}_{int}$ is the initial measured magnetic North vector in the Earth frame. Then, it can be used to compare with the *measured magnetic North vector* ($\boldsymbol{m}_0$) from the magnetometer.

$$\boldsymbol{m}(q_G) = {q_G}^* \otimes \boldsymbol{M}_{int} \otimes q_G \tag{9}$$

The error between the *calculated magnetic North vector* ($\boldsymbol{m}(q_G)$) and the *measured magnetic North vector* ($\boldsymbol{m}_0$) represents the error of orientation estimation and gives us a second opportunity to correct the orientation estimates. The angular difference between these two vectors can be determined in the form of a quaternion denoted by Δq_M, as shown in Eq. 10.

$$\Delta q_M = \mathbb{H}(\boldsymbol{q}_{Mv}, q_{Mw}) \tag{10}$$

$$\boldsymbol{q}_{Mv} = \boldsymbol{m}_0 \times \boldsymbol{m}(q_G) \tag{11}$$

$$q_{Mw} = \|\boldsymbol{m}_0\|\|\boldsymbol{m}(q_G)\| + \boldsymbol{m}_0 \cdot \boldsymbol{m}(q_G) \tag{12}$$

To correct the orientation estimation, q_G is multiplied by Δq_M. The estimated quaternion with magnetic North vector correction ($\hat{q}_{GM}$) is described in Eq. 13. Note that $\hat{q}_{GM}$ needs to be normalized before using it as a rotation operator.

$$\hat{q}_{GM} = q_G \otimes \Delta q_M \tag{13}$$

(4) Adaptive Quaternion Interpolation. Adaptive quaternion interpolation is the last step to be implemented in the orientation correction algorithm, which determines the final quaternion estimate based upon the current conditions of the sensor. In some circumstances, when the IMU is moving rapidly, the accelerometer does not measure only acceleration due to gravity. Thus, the accelerometer is no longer a reliable reference for orientation correction. For the magnetometer, the rapid movement of the hand does not directly affect its measurement. Spherical Linear Interpolation (SLERP) or great arc interpolation [4] is proposed as an approach to determine the final orientation estimates ($\hat{q}_{OUT}$) from two quaternions by using an adaptive weight (α).

$$\hat{q}_{OUT} = \frac{\hat{q}_{GM} sin((1-\alpha)\Omega) + \hat{q}_{GA} sin(\alpha\Omega)}{sin(\Omega)} \tag{14}$$

$$\Omega = cos^{-1}(\hat{q}_{GM} \cdot \hat{q}_{GA}) \tag{15}$$

From Eq. 14, when α equals to 1, the final estimated quaternion orientation ($\hat{q}_{OUT}$) is equal to the orientation estimation using only the gravity vector correction ($\hat{q}_{GA}$). This is appropriate, because $\alpha = 1$ implies that the sensor is in a static period. When α equals to 0, the final estimated quaternion orientation ($\hat{q}_{OUT}$) is equal to the orientation estimation using only the magnetic North vector correction ($\hat{q}_{GM}$). The adaptive weight (α) is the parameter that indicates the stillness of the sensor module and can be used to linearly interpolate the two quaternions. When the sensor is in static period, the value of α is equal to 1. While the sensor is in rapid motion, the value of α drops towards zero.

3 Implementation

Thirty human subjects were asked to participate in the evaluation experiment. Each of the subjects wore the instrumented glove on his/her left hand and performed specific hand movement tasks. While the tasks were being performed, the marker coordinate from OptiTrack V120: Trio and the data from an inertial measurement unit attached at the back of the hand, were recorded. The orientation correction algorithm, described in Sect. 2, was implemented to calculate the estimated orientation. The orientation estimates obtained with the orientation correction algorithm using the gravity vector and magnetic North vector algorithm (GMV) were compared to orientation estimates obtained with a fixed bias offset compensation (FB), and the quaternion output from the Kalman-based orientation filtering streamed directly from the Yost Labs 3-Space sensor module (KF).

3.1 Testing Environment Setup

For this evaluation, each subject was asked to wear on his/her left hand the glove with an inertial measurement unit attached at the back of the hand. The subject was sitting on a chair, having his/her face looking towards a computer screen in which the OptiTrack V120: Trio was installed (sensor bar placed above the screen). Between the subject and the computer screen, a rectangular frame with referenced position markers was placed with a fixed distance from the computer screen. The testing environment was set up as shown in Fig. 3.

Fig. 3. Hand motion tracking system testing environment setup.

3.2 Virtual 3D Environment

A virtual 3D environment was created with Unity, for this evaluation. The virtual 3D environment consists of a 3D hand model and the rectangular frame with referenced position markers. A C# script was written and attached to the 3D hand model so that a sequence of 10 pre-defined movements of the 3D hand model were visualized as the hand movement guide for the subjects to perform the tasks. A sequence of 10 pre-defined movements of the 3D hand model were visualized (as shown in Fig. 4), and each subject was asked to replicate the movements with his/her left hand, wearing the instrumented glove, trying to match in each pose the position and orientation of the virtual hand shown on the screen. The position and orientation estimates from the system were recorded with the 3 orientation correction methods: FB, GMV and KF being applied in parallel fashion.

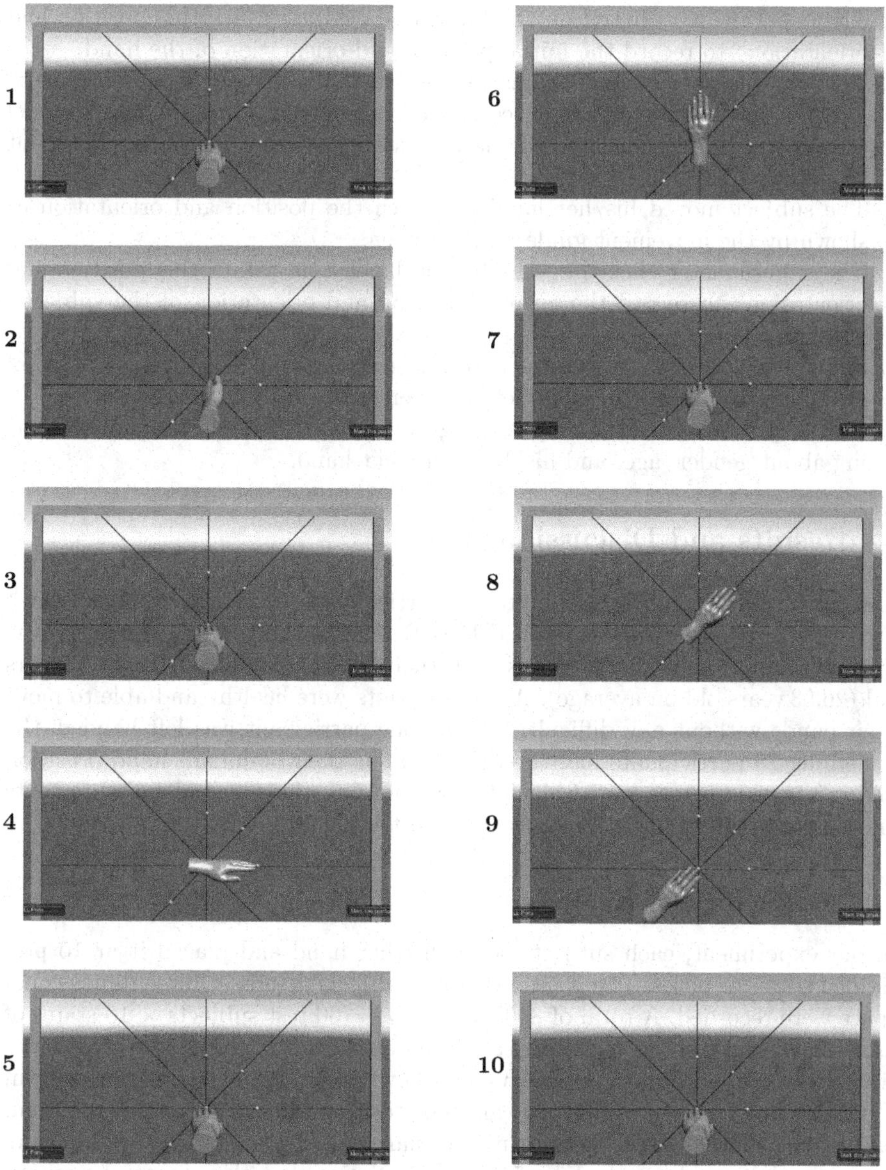

Fig. 4. The sequence of the 3D hand model movement (poses 1 to 10).

3.3 Experiment Procedure

1. Each subject was asked to wear the glove on his/her left hand and put the hand into the initial position and orientation. (Pose 1 in Fig. 4)
2. The experimenter clicked on the button labeled as "Mark this position and orientation" to record the initial position and orientation of the hand.
3. The experimenter clicked on the button labeled as "Show hand movement" located on the bottom right corner of the screen. The 3D hand model then rotated and translated to the next state (pose) of the hand movement sequence.
4. The subject moved his/her hand to match the position and orientation as shown by the movement guide on the screen.
5. The experimenter clicked on the button labeled as "Mark this position and orientation" to record the current position and orientation of the subject's hand.
6. Steps 3 to 5 of this procedure were repeated until all 10 states or poses of movement of the 3D hand model had been performed by the subject.
7. The subject was asked to remove the glove and answer a questionnaire inquiring about gender, age, and his/her dominant hand.

4 Results and Discussion

A total of 30 test subjects voluntarily participated in our experiment, which had been previously approved by FIU IRB board. There were 10 female participants and 20 male participants with their ages ranging from 19 to 55 years old (26.53 years old on average). All participants were healthy and able to move their hands without any difficulties. Only one participant was left-handed, the remaining 29 participants had the right hand as their dominant hand. Position and orientation errors were calculated considering the physical measurements and angles in the guiding frame as "ground truth".

4.1 Position Error Analyses

In our experiment, each subject moved his/her hand and placed it at 10 prescribed states or poses. The positions of the subjects' hands in three-dimensional space were recorded. A total of 300 rows of data (30 test subjects $\times$ 10 states of hand movement) were statistically analyzed using SPSS. The descriptive statistics for the errors in position tracking are shown in Table 1. The position error in the x-axis is 1.7 cm on average, the mean of position error in the y-axis is 1.0 cm, and 3.5 cm for the z-axis. The estimated marginal means of the position errors in x, y and z are shown in Figs. 5, 6 and 7. Notice that the means of position errors for the 4th, 8th and 9th states or poses in all axes are relatively higher than other states in the movement sequence. This could be because of the less natural hand movements required for those states, which caused difficulties for the test subjects in trying to exactly match the pre-defined positions of the hand that were requested.

Table 1. Descriptive statistics for errors in position tracking (in meter)

	N	Mean (m)	Std. deviation (m)
Error in x	300	.01722576	.042859991
Error in y	300	.01031162	.025989994
Error in z	300	.03526925	.095968643

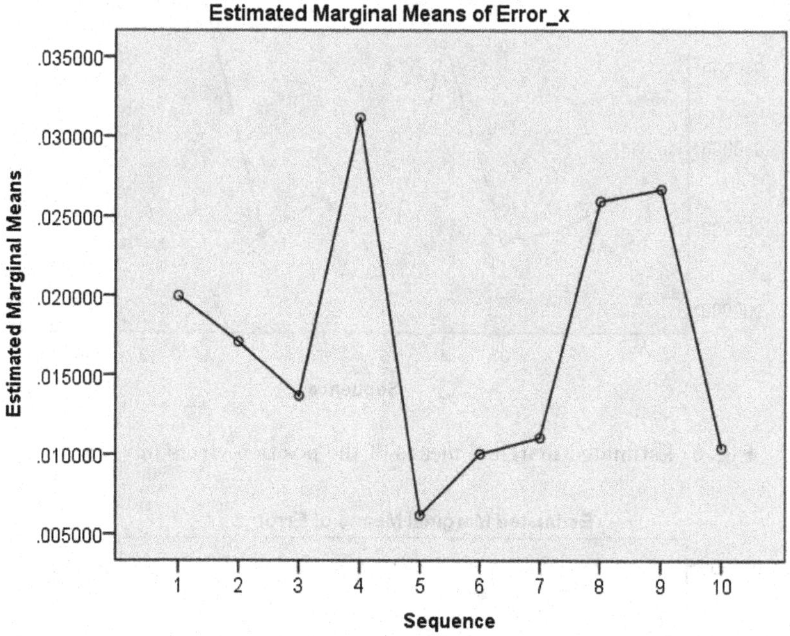

Fig. 5. Estimated marginal means of the position errors in x (m).

4.2 Orientation Error Analyses

In our experiment, each subject moved his/her hand through a sequence of 10 hand poses, or states, while three different orientation correction algorithms were running simultaneously to estimate the orientations. The purpose of this experiment is to evaluate the effects of three different orientation correction algorithms on the orientation output errors. The orientation errors were calculated under the assumption that the subjects oriented their hands exactly as required in each pose, aided by the frame provided. The orientation output errors in the form of Euler Angles (Phi, Theta and Psi) were calculated for the three orientation correction algorithms which are: (1) The orientation correction using fixed bias offset (FB), (2) The correction using the Kalman-based orientation filtering streamed directly from the Yost Labs 3-Space sensor module (KF), and (3) The proposed orientation correction using gravity and magnetic North vector (GMV).

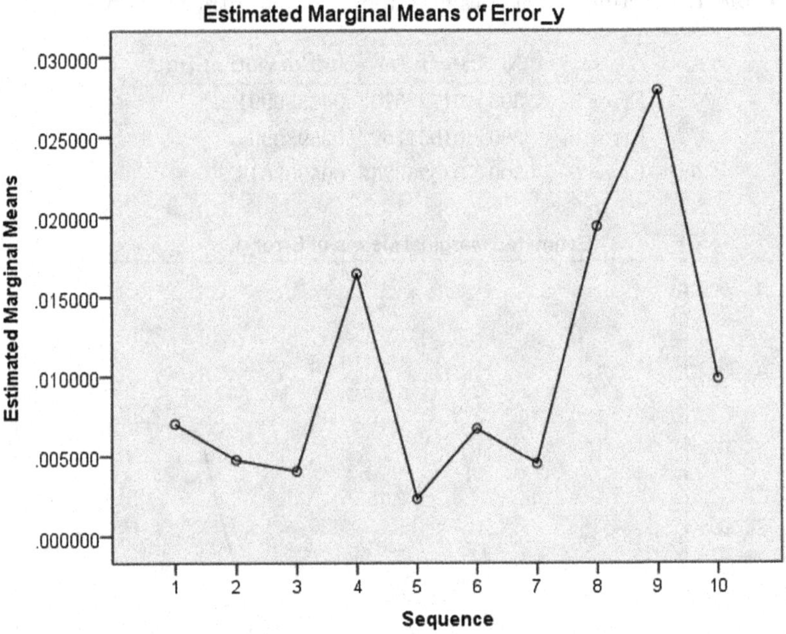

Fig. 6. Estimated marginal means of the position errors in y (m).

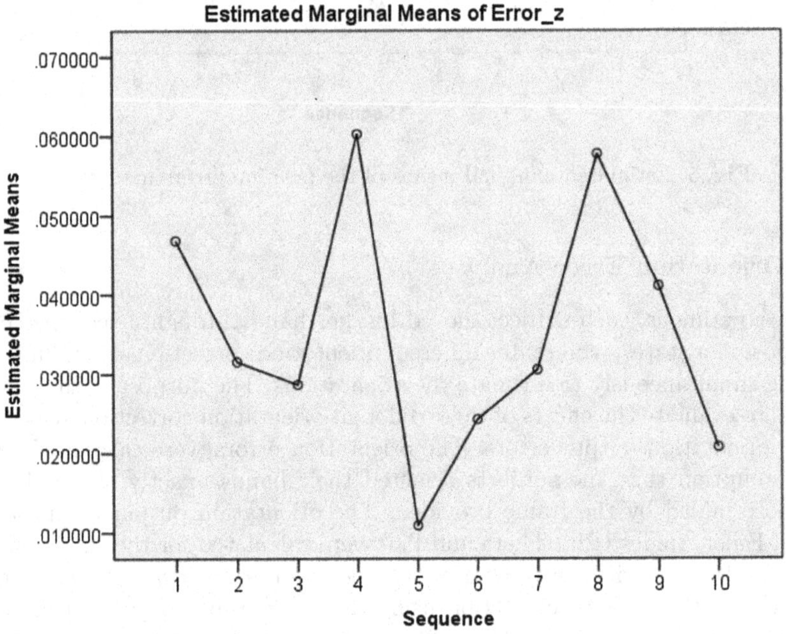

Fig. 7. Estimated marginal means of the position errors in z (m).

A total of 900 rows of data (30 test subjects × 10 states of hand movement × 3 algorithms) were recorded and statistically analyzed using SPSS. Table 2 shows the estimated means of the orientation errors in all Euler angles. Notice that the means of the orientation errors for GMV and KF are less than those for FB in every Euler angle. The means of the orientation errors for GMV are similar to the means of the orientation errors for KF in every Euler angle. The estimated marginal means of the orientation errors for Phi, Theta and Psi are shown in Figs. 8, 9 and 10, respectively.

Table 2. Estimated means of the orientation output errors (in degree)

Dependent variable	Algorithm	Mean (deg)
Phi	FB	11.505
	GMV	5.24
	KF	5.171
Theta	FB	9.288
	GMV	4.646
	KF	4.258
Psi	FB	11.137
	GMV	4.854
	KF	4.799

Table 3. Tests of normality

Dependent variables	Algorithm	Kolmogorov-Smirnov			Shapiro-Wilk		
		Statistic	df	Sig.	Statistic	df	Sig.
Phi	FB	.156	300	.000	.836	300	.000
	GMV	.151	300	.000	.876	300	.000
	KF	.182	300	.000	.862	300	.000
Theta	FB	.114	300	.000	.923	300	.000
	GMV	.159	300	.000	.842	300	.000
	KF	.180	300	.000	.817	300	.000
Psi	FB	.139	300	.000	.889	300	.000
	GMV	.182	300	.000	.814	300	.000
	KF	.185	300	.000	.820	300	.000

To test for the effects of three algorithms on the orientation output errors, a multivariate analysis of variance (MANOVA) was initially suggested. Before performing an analysis of variance, the data has to be validated on two assumptions, which are normality of the error and equal variances across treatments.

Table 4. Levene's test of equality of error variances

Dependent variables	F	df1	df2	Sig
Phi	29.352	29	870	.000
Theta	21.847	29	870	.000
Psi	26.455	29	870	.000

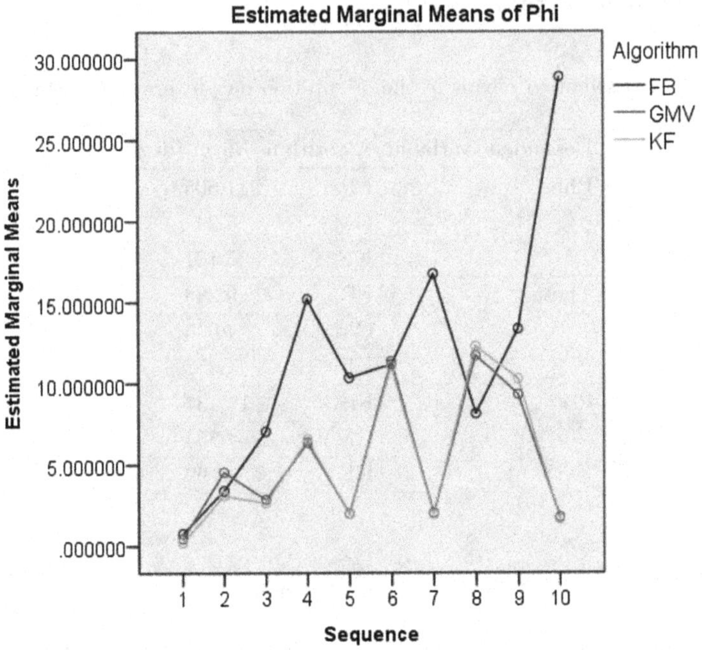

Fig. 8. Estimated marginal means of the orientation errors for Phi (deg).

The normality test is the test for the null hypothesis that the data are normally distributed within each treatment group. Table 3 shows the results of the test statistics Kolmogorov-Smirnov and Shapiro-Wilk, having the p-values for testing normality of 0.000 (the null hypothesis is rejected), which indicates strong evidence that the orientation output errors are not normally distributed. Table 4 shows the results of the test statistics for the null hypothesis that the error variance of the dependent variable is equal across treatment groups. The p-values of the test of homogeneity of variances are 0.000 (the null hypothesis is rejected) for all three dependent variables (Phi, Theta and Psi), indicating strong evidence that the error variances are not equal among the three treatment groups (three algorithms). Since the normality and the homogeneity of variance assumptions are not met, the multivariate analysis of variance (MANOVA) cannot be used as a statistical test model on these data.

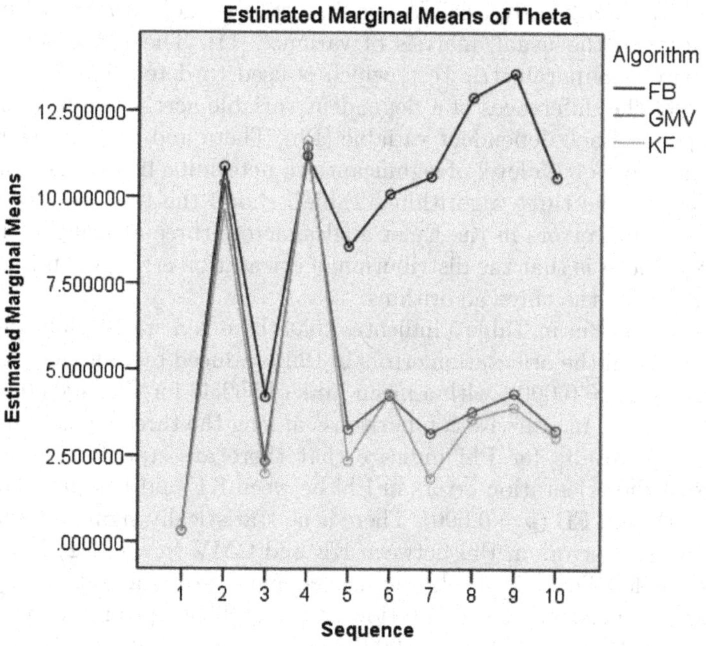

Fig. 9. Estimated marginal means of the orientation errors for Theta (deg).

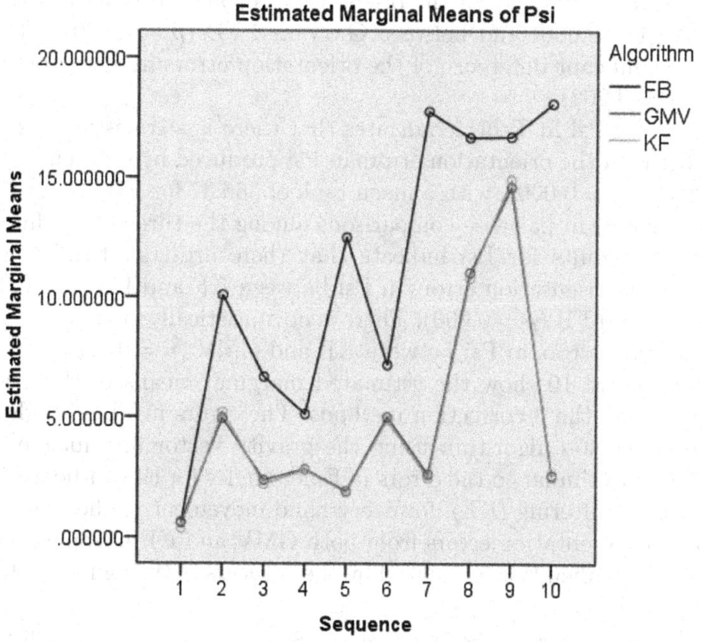

Fig. 10. Estimated marginal means of the orientation errors for Psi (deg).

In this situation, the Kruskal-Wallis H test is suggested as a nonparametric alternative to the usual analysis of variance [11]. The Kruskal-Wallis test is a rank-based nonparametric test, which is used to determine the statistical significance of the differences of a dependent variable across two or more treatment groups [5]. Each dependent variable (Phi, Theta and Psi) was tested with Kruskal-Wallis on a 0.05 level of significance to determine if there is a difference in means across the three algorithms. Table 5 shows the test statistics for the orientation output errors in the Euler angles, across three algorithms, in which the null hypothesis is that the distribution of orientation errors in an Euler angle is the same across the three algorithms.

The result for Phi in Table 5 indicates that there is a statistically significant difference between the orientation errors in Phi produced by different algorithms ($H(2) = 80.773, p = 0.000$), with a mean rank of 560.48 for FB, 400.60 for GMV and 390.43 for KF. In pairwise comparisons[1] among the three algorithms, shown in Table 6, the results for Phi indicate that there are statistically significant differences of the orientation errors in Phi between KF and FB ($p = 0.000$) and between GMV and FB ($p = 0.000$). There is no statistically significant difference of the orientation errors in Phi between KF and GMV ($p = 0.632$).

The result for Theta in Table 5 indicates that there is a statistically significant difference between the orientation errors in Theta produced by different algorithms ($H(2) = 89.439, p = 0.000$), with a mean rank of 565.57 for FB, 404.86 for GMV and 381.06 for KF. In pairwise comparisons among the three algorithms, shown in Table 6, the results for Theta indicate that there are statistically significant differences of the orientation output errors in Theta between KF and FB ($p = 0.000$) and between GMV and FB ($p = 0.000$). There is no statistically significant difference of the orientation errors in Theta between KF and GMV ($p = 0.262$).

The result for Psi in Table 5 indicates that there is a statistically significant difference between the orientation errors in Psi produced by different algorithms ($H(2) = 89.528, p = 0.000$), with a mean rank of 566.37 for FB, 396.26 for GMV and 388.87 for KF. In pairwise comparisons among the three algorithms, shown in Table 6, the results for Psi indicate that there are statistically significant differences of the orientation errors in Psi between KF and FB ($p = 0.000$) and between GMV and FB ($p = 0.000$). There is no statistically significant difference of the orientation errors in Psi between KF and GMV ($p = 0.728$).

Figures 8, 9 and 10 show the estimated marginal means of the orientation errors found using the 3 correction methods. The errors in Euler angles for the orientation correction algorithm using the gravity vector and magnetic North vector (GMV) are similar to the errors in Euler angles for the on-board Kalman-based orientation filtering (KF), for every hand movement in the sequence. The large amount of orientation errors from both GMV and KF in some poses could be caused by the difficulty experienced by the subjects in trying to exactly match

[1] Each row tests the null hypothesis that the Sample 1 and Sample 2 distributions are the same. Asymptotic significance (2-sided tests) are displayed. The significance level is .05.

Table 5. Kruskal-Wallis test for orientation errors in the Euler angles

Dependent variable	Algorithm	N	Mean rank	Test statistic	df	Asymp.Sig.
Phi	FB	300	560.48	80.773	2	.000
	GMV	300	400.60			
	KF	300	390.43			
Theta	FB	300	565.57	89.439	2	.000
	GMV	300	404.86			
	KF	300	381.06			
Psi	FB	300	566.37	89.528	2	.000
	GMV	300	396.26			
	KF	300	388.87			

Table 6. Pairwise comparison among three algorithms for orientation errors in the Euler angles.

Dependent variable	Sample1-Sample2	Test statistic	Std. Error	Std. test statistic	Sig.	Adj.Sig.
Phi	KF-GMV	10.170	21.225	.479	.632	1.000
	KF-FB	170.050	21.225	8.012	.000	.000
	GMV-FB	159.880	21.225	7.533	.000	.000
Theta	KF-GMV	23.800	21.225	1.121	.262	.786
	KF-FB	184.510	21.225	8.693	.000	.000
	GMV-FB	160.710	21.225	7.572	.000	.000
Psi	KF-GMV	7.390	21.225	.348	.728	1.000
	KF-FB	177.500	21.225	8.363	.000	.000
	GMV-FB	170.110	21.225	8.015	.000	.000

the pre-defined orientations of the hand requested on the computer screen. It is possible that the amount of orientation errors for both algorithms could in fact be smaller, and both algorithms could estimate the actual orientation of the hand.

5 Conclusion

The statistical analyses show that the orientation correction algorithm using gravity vector and magnetic North vector can significantly reduce the errors in orientation tracking when comparing to the orientation correction algorithm using fixed bias offset correction. The orientation correction algorithm using gravity vector and magnetic North vector and the on-board Kalman-based orientation filtering produced orientation errors that were not significantly different in Phi, Theta and Psi. The development of hand motion tracking systems using

IMUs and infrared cameras can be a significant contribution to the improvement in the realism of natural human-computer interactions within a 3D virtual environment.

Acknowledgments. This research was supported by National Sciences Foundation grants HRD-0833093 and CNS-1532061 and the FIU Graduate School Dissertation Year Fellowship awarded to Dr. Nonnarit O-larnnithipong.

References

1. Aggarwal, P.: MEMS-Based Integrated Navigation. Artech House, Norwood (2010)
2. Bachmann, E.R., Duman, I., Usta, U.Y., McGhee, R.B., Yun, X.P., Zyda, M.J.: Orientation tracking for humans and robots using inertial sensors. In: Proceedings of 1999 IEEE International Symposium on Computational Intelligence in Robotics and Automation CIRA 1999, pp. 187–194. IEEE (1999)
3. Borenstein, J., Everett, H.R., Feng, L., Wehe, D.: Mobile robot positioning sensors and techniques. Naval Command Control and Ocean Surveillance Center RDT and E DIV San Diego, CA (1997)
4. Dam, E.B., Koch, M., Lillholm, M.: Quaternions, interpolation and animation, vol. 2. Datalogisk Institut, Kbenhavns Universitet (1998)
5. Field, A.: Discovering Statistics using SPSS. Sage publications, London (2009)
6. Heeter, C.: Being there: the subjective experience of presence. Presence: Teleoperators Virtual Environ. **1**(2), 262–271 (1992). https://doi.org/10.1162/pres.1992.1.2.262
7. Kong, X.: INS algorithm using quaternion model for low cost IMU. Robot. Auton. Syst. **46**(4), 221–246 (2004)
8. Kuipers, J.B.: Quaternions and Rotation Sequences: A Primer with Applications to Orbits, Aerospace, and Virtual Reality. Princeton University Press, Princeton (1999). ID: 024971770; Includes bibliographical references (p. 365–366) and index
9. Marins, J.L., Yun, X., Bachmann, E.R., McGhee, R.B., Zyda, M.J.: An extended kalman filter for quaternion-based orientation estimation using MARG sensors. In: Proceedings of 2001 IEEE/RSJ International Conference on Intelligent Robots and Systems, vol. 4, pp. 2003–2011. IEEE (2001)
10. Mccall, R., O'Neil, S., Carroll, F.: Measuring presence in virtual environments. ACM (2004). ID: acm985934; ACM Digital Library; ACM Digital Library (Association for Computing Machinery); KESLI (ACM Digital Library)
11. Montgomery, D.C.: Design and Analysis of Experiments. wiley, New York (2017)
12. O-larnnithipong, N., Barreto, A.: Gyroscope drift correction algorithm for inertial measurement unit used in hand motion tracking. In: 2016 IEEE SENSORS, pp. 1–3 (2016)
13. O-larnnithipong, N., Barreto, A., Ratchatanantakit, N., Tangnimitchok, S., Ortega, F.R.: Real-time implementation of orientation correction algorithm for 3D hand motion tracking interface. In: Antona, M., Stephanidis, C. (eds.) UAHCI 2018. LNCS, vol. 10907, pp. 228–242. Springer, Cham (2018). https://doi.org/10.1007/978-3-319-92049-8_17
14. O-larnnithipong, N., Barreto, A., Tangnimitchok, S., Ratchatanantakit, N.: Orientation correction for a 3D hand motion tracking interface using inertial measurement units. In: Kurosu, M. (ed.) HCI 2018. LNCS, vol. 10903, pp. 321–333. Springer, Cham (2018). https://doi.org/10.1007/978-3-319-91250-9_25

15. Pavlovic, V.I., Sharma, R., Huang, T.S.: Visual interpretation of hand gestures for human-computer interaction: a review. IEEE Trans. Pattern Anal. Mach. Intell. **19**(7), 677–695 (1997)
16. Roh, M.-C., Kang, D., Huh, S., Lee, S.-W.: A virtual mouse interface with a two-layered bayesian network. Multimedia Tools Appl. **76**(2), 1615–1638 (2017). ID: Roh 2017
17. Slater, M., Usoh, M., Steed, A.: Depth of presence in virtual environments. Presence: Teleoperators Virtual Environ. **3**(2), 130–144 (1994)
18. Slater, M., Wilbur, S.: A framework for immersive virtual environments (five). Presence: Teleoperators Virtual Environ. **6**(6), 603 (1997)
19. Sukkarieh, S., Nebot, E.M.: A high integrity IMU/GPS navigation loop for autonomous land vehicle applications. IEEE Trans. Robot. Autom. **15**(3), 572 (1999)
20. Yun, X., Bachmann, E.R.: Design, implementation, and experimental results of a quaternion-based kalman filter for human body motion tracking. IEEE Trans. Robot. **22**(6), 1216–1227 (2006)
21. Yun, X., Lizarraga, M., Bachmann, E.R., McGhee, R.B.: An improved quaternion-based kalman filter for real-time tracking of rigid body orientation. In: Proceedings of 2003 IEEE/RSJ International Conference on Intelligent Robots and Systems. (IROS 2003), vol. 2, pp. 1074–1079. IEEE (2003)
22. Zhang, X., Liu, X., Yuan, S.-M., Lin, S.-F.: Eye tracking based control system for natural human-computer interaction. Comput. Intell. Neurosci. (2017)

Translating the Pen and Paper Brainstorming Process into a Cognitive and Immersive System

Matthew Peveler[1(✉)], Shannon Briggs[1], Jaimie Drozdal[1], Lilit Balagyozyan[1], Chang Sun[1], Michael Perrone[2], and Hui Su[2]

[1] Rensselaer Polytechnic Institute, Troy, NY 012180, USA
{pevelm,briggs3,drozdj3,balagl,sunc4}@rpi.edu
[2] IBM Thomas J Watson Research Center, Yorktown Heights, NY 10598, USA
{mpp,huisuibmres}@us.ibm.com

Abstract. Within this work, we introduce a digital sticky note tool to be used by analysts for a brainstorming session within a cognitive and immersive system (CAIS). This tool was setup to mimic and enhance the traditionally pen-and-paper process. By utilizing a digital interface, we allow for more feature-rich note taking including pictures and hyperlinks in addition to just text, as well as an increased amount of captured meta-data about each created note. To achieve parity with the non-digital process, our interface allows for both individual usage via personal devices (e.g. tablets, laptops) as well as for coming together as a group and collaborating via a multi-modal interface, supporting commands through a mixture of voice and gestures.

Keywords: Human–centered computing · Collaborative and social computing systems and tools, technology · Gesture and eye—gaze based interaction, technology · Second screen (multi screen scenario)

1 Introduction

Much of contemporary research and design into tools for intelligence analysts focus around the use of tools aimed at individuals. However, much of the analysis is done within a social environment, with analysts working in groups to come to a conclusion about the data under review. While it is still possible to utilize these tools, this often comes at the price of having to email data around so that each analyst can use the tool, or by grouping around a single workstation that is then driven by a single person through the use of keyboard and mouse, or a single touchscreen. However, often times the best solution is to fallback to a more traditional "pen-and-paper" version of the tool such that all members of the group can then participate simultaneous.

One such tool that we examined for this work is sticky notes, and their use in the brainstorming technique for intelligent analysts. The brainstorming

M. Kurosu (Ed.): HCII 2019, LNCS 11567, pp. 366–376, 2019.
https://doi.org/10.1007/978-3-030-22643-5_28

structured analytic technique is a cognitive tool used by analysts to help generate new ideas and opinions about materials relevant to their job. In addition, it is one of the earliest techniques that can be carried out during the analysis process [2]. The brainstorming technique is a multi-step process that involves data collection, analysis, and then group discussion. The purpose of the exercise is to reduce cognitive bias, and to allow a diversity of perspectives to be taken into consideration when dealing with a problem or scenario. For this work, we utilize a multi-step process for a brainstorming session, wherein there are at least two analysts and a discussion facilitator. The process starts with the analysts operating independently to analyze and document the salient details of a scenario onto notes. The analysts then come together as a group, synthesizing a final result of notes as well as creating categories to group them.

In this paper, we present a full description of the pen-and-paper brainstorming process, including a list of the primary high level actions that are taken. We then describe what is a cognitive and immersive system, and how we utilize it to allow and accomplish handling both multi-users and multi-inputs for a group of analysts. In the next section, we describe the digital tool that we've created and how it can be used by analysts. We then present the results of a user study that we conducted comparing and contrasting the two methods. We then conclude the paper with a discussion of the results and promising future lines of work.

1.1 Prior Work

Electronic sticky notes have been proposed before in digital brainstorming literature, and varieties of such a tool have been implemented. Prior research has examined the application of sticky note tools in group and collaborative settings [5], in mediated group work accomplished remotely, and how sticky notes can be used to define affinity groups in collaborative work [10]. Jensen et al. [6] conducted a study comparing the use of traditional analog sticky notes to a digital sticky-notes tool, and concluded that the digital sticky notes were superior in terms of increased note interaction, clustering, and labelling. Existing digital sticky note tools can be found in examples such as Discusys [10], ECO-Pack [9], Padlet, and Quickies [7]. These tools demonstrate the power of moving to the digital medium, in allowing for embedding of digital content (e.g. pictures, videos, hyperlinks) alongside the text, which is not possible in the the analog version. However, these tools focus on individual usage for making and taking sticky notes, and not necessarily a collaborative group interface.

2 The Pen and Paper Brainstorming Process

Traditionally, analysts utilize a "pen-and-paper" process to conduct their brainstorming process (though they may use a whiteboard, or some other tool instead of paper). We focus on the usage of sticky notes through the process. During the initial portion of the brainstorming process, analysts utilize a personal workspace to generate notes that they think are relevant to what they're studying. After some time spent generating these notes and potential categories for them, the analysts then come together as a group to generate a final working set of notes. At first, the analysts would put up all their ideas together on a board, removing duplicates. The analysts would then discuss what potential categories they think the notes could fall under. After deciding on a set number of categories, the analysts then assign categories to each note. This process can be derived into the following number of high level actions:

- Generate notes in a private workspace
- Share notes in an uncategorized workspace
- Create and delete categories for notes
- Assign notes to categories

These actions are then inline with prior work done on how experts and non-experts approach this task, and the process they go through [1].

3 Cognitive and Immersive System

To support the translation into a digital process, we utilize a cognitive immersive room architecture [4] in building our cognitive and immersive system (CAIS). At its core, we have lapel microphones (one per user) that pick up what participants say to the system and each other. We utilize the IBM Bluemix Speech-to-Text service to then transcribe the speech to a textual representation, and then Watson Assistant to generate an intent and entities for each utterance that contain our "trigger word" for the system. In addition to the microphones, we utilize a Kinect camera to monitor users' actions, primarily focusing on what the users might be pointing at as well as simple (open, closed, and pointing) gestures the user might do with their hand. These intents and gestures are fed into a central executor that then drives an action within the room. The system then has available to it several displays (projectors or screens) as well as speakers.

The system utilizes the Electron framework (in what's called the *display-worker* to show content on the screens, allowing for showing websites that are placed within a grid defined within the available display space, allowing us to show both internally developed websites. The speakers are used to play synthesized voice from the system utilizing the IBM Bluemix Text-to-Speech service. The diagram of components are shown in Fig. 1. The modules that are connected via red lines utilize RabbitMQ to send and receive JSON objects. The blue lines represent communication via HTTP GET/POST methods. The purple lines represent communication through websockets. The yellow lines represent connections to physical hardware.

The components that were developed for this work were the *spatial-context-bridge*, *live-frame-server*, and the *sticky-note-displayer*. We describe the first two components below, and the final is covered in Sect. 4.

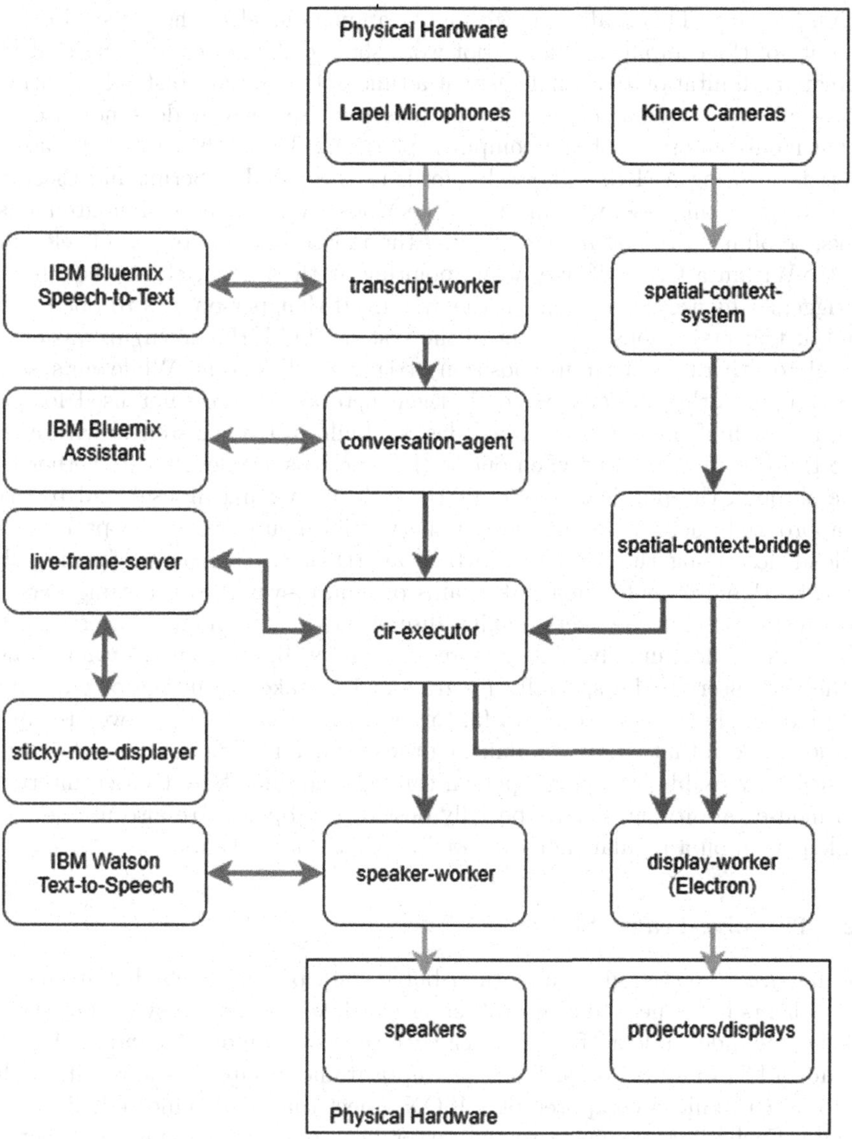

Fig. 1. Diagram of the cognitive and immersive system

3.1 The Spatial-Context-Bridge

The *spatial-context-bridge* takes input from the spatial context system [11] that creates a semantic encoding of the data the kinect sensors are receiving. This positional and gesture data is then used to alert the executor when a gesture changes (e.g. going from an open hand to a closed hand) as well as to push the relevant information to the display-worker to show the user's hand positions within Electron. This is all done without wrapping ourselves the physical mouse interface of the computer. While prior work showed the power of doing that [3], it created a limitation of a single user at a time of the system. Instead, we utilize a concept of a "virtual mouse" that exists per user, which does not use the actual mouse interface of the computer platform. To do this, we make use of the rich scripting API that the web affords us through JavaScript and Electron framework. In this case, we can utilize the MouseEvent APIs to simulate mouse clicks, scrolling with the mouse, holding the mouse button down and releasing it, etc. Within a CAIS, if one, while pointing at the screen, closes their hand, it triggers a mouse down event in the system. If that person was to open their hand, it triggers a mouse up event in the system, and if the down/up was quick enough together (and in similar position), triggers a click event. While our system does support other actions, we omit them here as they are not used for our tool. For each of these generated actions, we build in EventListeners within the page to react in some way when one of these actions are detected (whether it's done through the physical mouse, or through our virtual mouse) and to take an appropriate action. In the case of the virtual mouse events, as part of the payload describing the event, we attach an ID of the person performing the event, so that we could then link chains of mouse events to the same person, and thus allow multiple users making discrete actions without interfering with each other. Unfortunately, this does require any webpage that we want to use as multiple users to be specially programmed to take advantage of our extra metadata in the events. However, for any webpage that does not, we are equal to prior work in that as we're mimicking the events a real mouse does, the pages are still fully usable by a single person through the same kinect based interface as a mouse. Additionally, our specially designed webpages are also usable by a single person on a regular mouse as well by that same token.

3.2 The Live-Frame-Server

The *live-frame-server* gives us a distributed data pattern such that it enables many clients to connect to a central server which keeps them in-sync. The server holds many independent "frame", each with their own unique ID and are backed by MongoDB to allow for picking back up a frame in later sessions within the CAIS. Each frame is composed of a JSON object that any connected client can update. Each client connects to the server via websocket passing in a specific frame ID that it is interested in. When one client sends an update to the server, the server calculates the diff of the change, and then pushes both that diff as well as the new JSON object for the frame to all other clients, keeping everyone in-sync with all changes. The final component is the *sticky-note-displayer* which houses the display logic for our clients. Each client that connects through the displayer is connected to the same frame, allowing us to give multiple views as well as allow users to utilize their own personal devices.

4 The Digital Brainstorming Tool

The digital version of the brainstorming tool was designed to try to follow the traditional pen-and-paper process as closely as possible, while taking advantage of the additional capabilities that the CAIS provides. To accomplish this, we drew mock-ups and designs for how the high level actions taken in the pen and paper process in a digital tool that took advantage of the space offered by the CAIS. To accomplish this, we developed two separate interfaces for interacting with the system. The first is the "personal view" which is displayed to users via a personal device (such as laptop or tablet), shown in Fig. 2 and is linked to a specific user (though the same user could connect to the "personal view" on multiple devices at the same time).

Within the view, the user sees all categories that have been created within the system as well as all of the notes belonging to each category. The first section however contains a "personal" category such that any notes within it are only viewable and editable by that user. Users are free to create as many categories as they want, as well as many notes as they want per category. The users can then delete any category, which would include the notes in that category, except for their personal category. Any created category or note within any of the non-personal categories are then synced to any other connected "personal views". The interface is used through tapping on the icons (such as the plus icon within a category to create a note, or the x icon to delete the category) and the keyboard. When a user clicks to create a category or note, a prompt appears which allows the user to type into it to fill the category title or note content. To move a note from a category, the user clicks on the note, and then clicks on a category to move it to.

The other interface for the system is the "global view", shown in Fig. 3. This view was split in two with the left half used for the notes in the "uncategorized" category, and the right half containing all the of the created categories and the notes within those categories. Interaction with this display is done through a combination of voice and gestures for commands, as well as picking up any changes done via any open "personal view". The allowed voice commands are:

1. Create a note that reads "text"
2. Create a category named "title"
3. Rename the category named "title" to "new title"
4. Move note "ID" to category named "title"
5. Delete note "ID"
6. Delete category named "id"

For commands 3–6, the one of the blanks can be substituted by a pointing gesture at the item you're attempting to operate on. An example of would be saying, "Move that note to category named foo." In parsing this command, the executor is given a move note intent by the user which requires a note and category, however the speech only supplies the category. The system then contacts the "spatial-context-bridge" to find out where that user is currently pointing, which is given as an x-y coordinate on the screen. The executor then

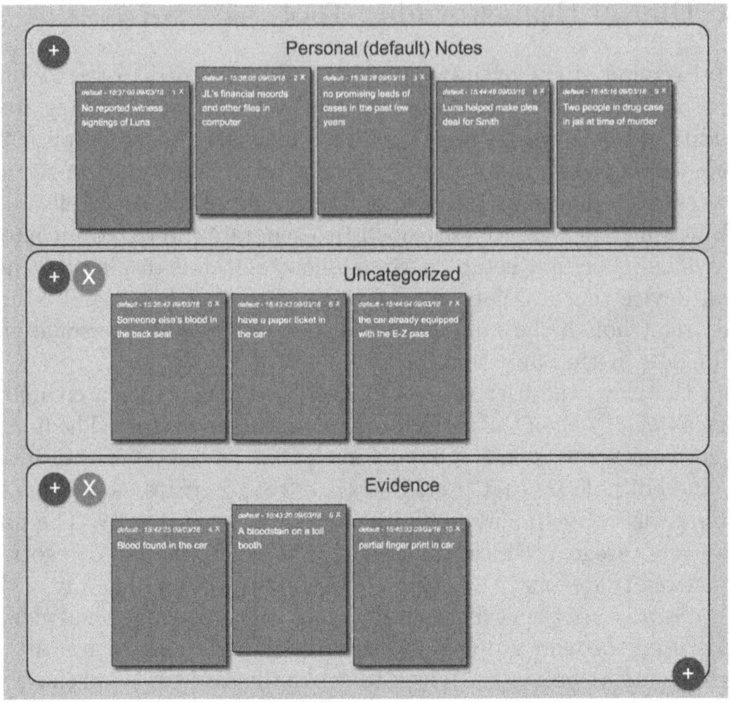

Fig. 2. Personal view of brainstorming tool

Fig. 3. Global view on panoromic display

translates that into a relative x-y coordinate within a given webview, which is then used to get the elements that are at that coordinate within the webview, and to check if any of the elements match the type we're looking for. By getting all elements at the coordinate, and not just the top-most, we can handle resolution of moving a note via its ID while pointing at an existing note within a category, such that the category element is underneath the note element we're pointing at, but we're referencing the category.

5 User Study

An ongoing user study uses participants from a local university to test the usability of our digital brainstorming tool in comparison to the more traditional pen and paper tool. The study is run via a within-subjects design where participants go through two brainstorming sessions in groups of three. In both sessions, the participants go through the same brainstorming process, which is broken up into several five minute sections. To start with, the participants are given the same one-page excerpt of a murder case to read. Following the reading phase, participants are asked to individually create notes about the most relevant details of the excerpt. The next phase involves the participants coming together as a group and then putting all of their created notes into a shared workspace. After all notes are in the workspace, the participants are asked to start grouping the notes based on similarity into categories. Finally, the participants have a discussion phase about the case, as well as if they feel that they may have missed any important details in the grouping, or if there are some notes that do not fall into one of their categories. To finish the session, the participants are then asked to fill out a brief survey as well as conduct a question and answer session on what they thought about a given tool. The first session involves using the pen and paper approach as described in Sect. 2. The second session involves using the digital tool, both the overall CAIS and global workspace, as well as the personal view on a tablet that each participant has as described in Sect. 4.

6 Discussion

The preliminary user studies conducted gives us valuable feedback on how we may improve the tool and its functionality. We conducted two rounds of our study, implemented improvements to the system based on their feedback, and then conducted another round.

From the first two rounds, the biggest criticism that we received was that the tool was not as easy to grasp as we had originally supposed going in. While we provided users with a brief introduction to all technology, many felt it hard to remember all of the commands to the system, as well as how to mix voice and gestures. The feedback from the users was that they would have liked an extended video, tutorial, or sheet of commands to the system. Following this, we implemented a view to the right of their primary workspace that listed all commands that could be issued to the system with some slight variations in how they could say it. The final group found this useful and was able to use the system more fluently without having to ask us questions on commands.

When using the tool, while participants did find the live transcription of what they were saying useful, they were consistently frustrated by the strictness of some commands as they attempted to leave out words from the phrases we had inputted. An example of this is the command "Move the note into the category named foo" to move a note. Users would often times leave out the "named" part of the command, which messed up our parser in finding the category name in the sentence. However, the system did not make it obvious that the command was not properly parsed, and users were left wondering what had went wrong. In addition, users identified various features that they thought were missing from the digital tool. The most significant feature was the ability to undo a deletion of a note or category. Whereas in the pen-and-paper version, removed notes were just placed off to the side, and could be quickly and easily re-put up on the wall if necessary, notes that were removed from the digital tool had to be recreated from scratch. Categories that were deleted that contained notes would also delete all notes underneath that category, which surprised users who were expecting the notes to automatically go back to being "uncategorized".

With the gesture system, we found mixed results with participants. Several found the system easy to use, while others found it difficult. The biggest issue we found was that the system was designed for a person to be gesturing with one hand while their other hand was at their side. When that other hand was holding a tablet, it caused the system to mistakenly classify the hand as holding the tablet as a gesture in addition to the hand actually making a gesture.

Most startling was the mixed feedback on the collaborative benefits of the digital tool with some subjects stating that they felt more involved in the discussion and another stating that they felt disconnected from the other participants. It was not clear with the negative response whether their disconnect from other participants was principally due to the platform, or mostly do the problems they had with using the tool. For future user studies with an improved version of the tool, it will be important to monitor engagement of participants in the group discussion phase of the digital tool session compared to the pen and paper process, and attempting to pinpoint why a disconnect might exist.

7 Conclusion

We now quickly summarize our work and present promising lines of future work. Our primary contribution is in the development of an integrated sticky notes application used for brainstorming which easily allows for both individual and group usage. Our paper describes contributions that we've made in components necessary in a cognitive and immersive system to support this work, as well as for future work, especially for the design of the virtual mouse interface. This provides a generalized interface that can be attached to any use-case within our cognitive and immersive system in both providing for interaction via gestures of webpages, both specialized to take advantage of normal users, as well as normal webpages supporting single users.

However, as shown in Sect. 6, thoughts of our tool by users were mixed. At this stage, we plan to look to address many of these concerns, before conducting future user studies as we continue to believe that the digital tool has the potential to become invaluable to this process. To accomplish this, we plan to add in a new "trash" section within the tool that stores notes that have been deleted, and through which users can recover notes. For categories that are deleted, any note under it should go into the "uncategorized" section of the screen, instead of being deleted as well. A more substantial change is in loosening the parsing of commands to allow for more formats of each command (as well as missing words in the command), while also adding in the capacity of our system to prompt the user for information it could either not find in the command or did not understand. An example of this is that the system would sometimes incorrectly transcribe someone when they attempted to say a category's name, and then do nothing, which would force the user to look at the live transcript and parse it to see what went wrong. The system should at the very least prompt the user for the information it was missing, giving the user a notion that their previous command got messed up, as well as just requiring the user to say the missing information, and not the entire, potentially lengthy command. In addition, for commands that referenced a category, if the category name did not exist, the system could then check to see if any of the existing names were similar (an example of this would be using the levenshtein distance) and if so, prompt the user to see if that was what they meant, requiring just a yes or no response from the user. This would hopefully help to relieve frustration with the system when it messed up, as well as make it clearer to the user what went wrong. In addition, we plan to look into how we may allow users to better utilize the digital format in attaching non-text content to their notes as part of the brainstorming process, and how this content could then be showed to the users on demand. A primary consideration as well is needed in making the tool feel more intuitive to the users such that using it does not detract from the sense of discussion of the topic at hand.

Future work will consist of expanding the work to be used to drive future stages of a sense-making model [8]. The next stage of the model is that of dealing with alternative competing hypothesises, utilizing the notes created in the brainstorming session for evidence that might support or contradict any created hypothesis. In addition to the sense-making direction, we hope to apply the sticky notes application as something we can utilize within other domains to help capture whatever it is that users are discussing and to help them categorize and share their thoughts with their colleagues.

References

1. Baber, C., Attfield, S., Conway, G., Rooney, C., Kodagoda, N.: Collaborative sense-making during simulated intelligence analysis exercises. Int. J. Hum.-Comput. Stud. **86**, 94–108 (2016)
2. Beebe, S.M., Pherson, R.H.: Cases in Intelligence Analysis: Structured Analytic Techniques in Action. CQ Press, Thousand Oaks (2012)

3. Brooks, R.A.: The intelligent room project. In: Proceedings of the 2nd International Conference on Cognitive Technology (CT 1997), p. 271. IEEE Computer Society, Washington (1997)
4. Divekar, R.R., et al.: CIRA: an architecture for building configurable immersive smart-rooms. In: Arai, K., Kapoor, S., Bhatia, R. (eds.) IntelliSys 2018. AISC, vol. 869, pp. 76–95. Springer, Cham (2019). https://doi.org/10.1007/978-3-030-01057-7_7
5. Dornburg, C.C., Stevens, S.M., Hendrickson, S.M.L., Davidson, G.S.: Improving extreme-scale problem solving: assessing electronic brainstorming effectiveness in an industrial setting. Hum. Factors **51**(4), 519–527 (2009). pMID: 19899361
6. Jensen, M., Thiel, S., Hoggan, E., Bødker, S.: Physical versus digital sticky notes in collaborative ideation. Comput. Support. Coop. Work **27**(3–6), 609–645 (2018)
7. Mistry, P., Maes, P.: Intelligent sticky notes that can be searched, located and can send reminders and messages. In: Proceedings of the 13th International Conference on Intelligent User Interfaces IUI 2008, pp. 425–426. ACM, New York (2008)
8. Pirolli, P., Card, S.: The sense making process and leverage points for analyst technology as identified through cognitive task analysis. In: Proceedings of International Conference on Intelligence Analysis (2005)
9. Saleh, M., Abel, M.H., Misséri, V., Moulin, C., Versailles, D.: Integration of brainstorming platform in a system of information systems. In: 8th International ACM Conference on Management of Digital EcoSystems (MEDES2016), pp. 166–173. Hendaye, France, November 2016
10. Widjaja, W., Yoshii, K., Haga, K., Takahashi, M.: Discusys: multiple user real-time digital sticky-note affinity-diagram brainstorming system. Procedia Comput. Sci. **22**, 113–122 (2013)
11. Zhao, R., Wang, K., Divekar, R., Rouhani, R., Su, H., Ji, Q.: An immersive system with multi-modal human-computer interaction. In: The IEEE Conference on Automatic Face and Gesture Recognition, May 2018

Consistency Study of 3D Magnetic Vectors in an Office Environment for IMU-based Hand Tracking Input Development

Neeranut Ratchatanantakit(✉), Nonnarit O-larnnithipong, Armando Barreto, and Sudarat Tangnimitchok

Electrical and Computer Engineering Department, Florida International University, 10555 W Flagler St, Miami, FL 33174, USA
{nratc001,nolar002,barretoa,stang018}@fiu.edu

Abstract. This paper reports our study of the distortion of the Magnetic North Vector in an office environment, which affects the use of commercial-grade Inertial Measurement Units (IMUs) for orientation tracking in a 3D hand motion tracking interface. The study includes data collected for 30 days to analyze the effect that may occur in terms of error and consistency. The Magnetic North Vector is one of the data sets used in orientation correction algorithms to reduce the bias offset error in IMUs. A non-ferromagnetic frame was made to define 125 points inside a cubic space in an office. Data was recorded for 30 days and analyzed to define the variation of errors. Experiment results show that the metal from a desk creates a magnetic distortion. In some areas the deviation of the Magnetic North Vector is severe and the amount of variation error is not uniform.

Keywords: Magnetic field · Magnetic North Vector · Sensors · Inertial Measurement Unit · Gyroscope drift · Orientation correction algorithm · Bias offset error · Magnetic distortion

1 Introduction

There is currently heightened interest in developing alternative computer input mechanisms, beyond general input devices (e.g., keyboard and mouse). Hand motion tracking is an interesting choice for a user to interact with 3D interfaces in augmented reality and virtual reality environments [8]. Natural hand movements could be used to indicate translations and rotations in a 3D environment. One emerging approach for hand motion tracking involves the use of miniaturized MEMS Inertial Measurement Units (IMUs) [1] as shown in Fig. 1.

Originally, IMUs track orientation accumulating orientation changes ("Dead Reckoning") measured by gyroscopes. However, commonly present offsets in the

M. Kurosu (Ed.): HCII 2019, LNCS 11567, pp. 377–387, 2019.
https://doi.org/10.1007/978-3-030-22643-5_29

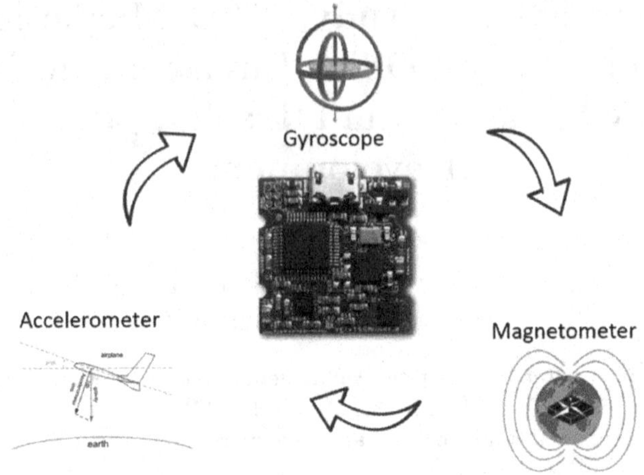

Fig. 1. Orientation tracking system provided by three different sources of vector information from commercial-grade IMU (Yost Labs 3-Space Sensor)

gyroscopes create "drift" errors in the orientation results. The orientation needs to be corrected periodically measuring the gravity vector with accelerometers or the magnetic North vector with magnetometers, also included in many IMUs [5,7,10]. However, the corrections are based on the assumption that the gravity and magnetic North vectors have constant orientation throughout the operation of the hand tracker. Since the early 15th Century, researchers have been aware of the magnetic declination, especially in Europe. [4] For example, Gilbert observed a tilt in the magnetic field of more than 10° [6]. Beyond the earth's magnetic declination, the local magnetic field can, additionally, be distorted in the proximity of large ferromagnetic objects [2,9,11].

The purpose of the research described in this paper is to study the distortion of the magnetic field in a general office environment [3] to better understand how the magnetic North vector may be distorted by ordinary objects (e.g., desk) and to study the level of consistency of those distortions through time (over weeks). This knowledge may inform future approaches to compensate magnetic disturbances in the development of IMU-based hand trackers for human-computer interaction.

2 Methodology and Materials

2.1 Non-ferromagnetic Frame

The positioning frame built for this study was constructed with wood and wood glue, to ensure that no metal from the frame itself would affect the magnetic field during the experiment. Only metal or ferromagnetic objects in the office environment are the causes of the observed distortion in the Magnetic North Vector. The frame was built to make measurements in a 5' × 5' × 5' grid with

1 foot separation between nodes in each direction, defining 125 measurement locations as shown in Fig. 2. This grid will be referred as the "Dense Grid" and can be visualized as in Fig. 3. The mean vector components averaged over the 125 measurements in the Dense Grid, were considered as the (true) reference Magnetic North Vector, Ref(X,Y,Z), as shown in Eq. (1).

$$Ref.(X,Y,Z) = \frac{\Sigma_{i=1}^{125} X_i}{125}, \frac{\Sigma_{i=1}^{125} Y_i}{125}, \frac{\Sigma_{i=1}^{125} Z_i}{125} \quad (1)$$

Additionally, to assess how consistent the configuration of the magnetic vector in our measuring space is, we conducted periodic measurements (every Monday, Wednesday and Friday) in a "Sparse Grid". This grid spans the same overall measurement volume, but with a separation of 2' between nodes in all directions, i.e., containing 3 recordings in each direction, for a total of 27 measurement locations.

Fig. 2. Office environment space where the experiment took place

2.2 Magnetic North Vector Recording Using Yost Labs 3-Space Sensors

The MEMS Inertial Measurement Unit used to collect data for testing the distortion of the magnetic field is the Yost Labs 3-Space sensor, which is a low-cost MEMS IMU. This IMU provides 3 types of data, which are gyroscope, accelerometer and magnetometer measurements. Each of the units give the result in three

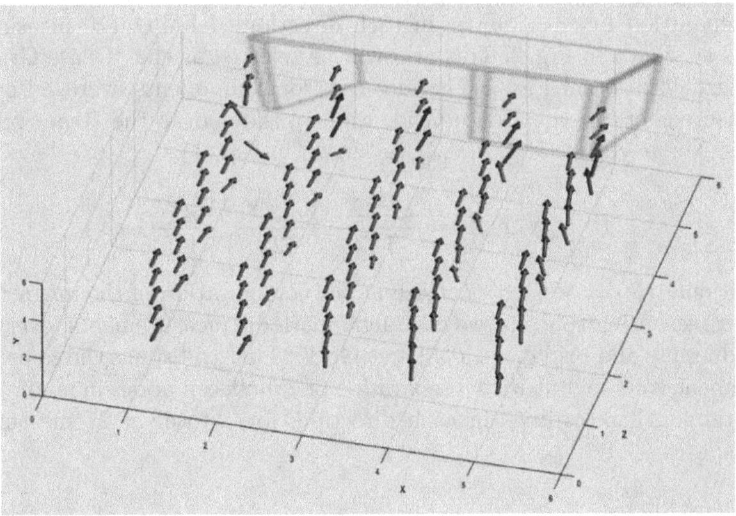

Fig. 3. 3D plot of Magnetic Vector recordings in the 5 × 5 × 5 Dense Grid (separation between nodes is 1' in all directions)

orthogonal axes labeled as X-axis, Y-axis and Z-axis. The IMU is connected to a PC through a USB cable. A C# script was created to receive the data from the Yost Labs 3-Space IMU. The recorded data were stored for further analysis in a MATLab program.

Error Calculation. The Magnetic Vector will be analyzed separately for each one of the X, Y, Z components. In this paper, the data recorded on each day is compared to the Reference Magnetic North vector from the dense grid (Ref.(X,Y,Z)) to yield the error values for each day, as shown in Eq. (2).

$$Err.(X,Y,Z) = RawData(X,Y,Z)_{Day(n)} - Ref.(X,Y,Z) \tag{2}$$

3 Implementation

Data from the Sparse Grid were collected for 30 days (every other day) from the beginning of October until the end of December. The variation (i.e. error) at each measurement point is calculated by subtracting Ref(X,Y,Z) from the raw data each day, individually for each coordinate. The populations of deviations (errors) in X, Y and Z are then analyzed separately (Fig. 4).

$$Avg.Data(X,Y,Z) = \frac{\Sigma_{i=1}^{n} Err.X_i}{n}, \frac{\Sigma_{i=1}^{n} Err.Y_i}{n}, \frac{\Sigma_{i=1}^{n} Err.Z_i}{n} \tag{3}$$

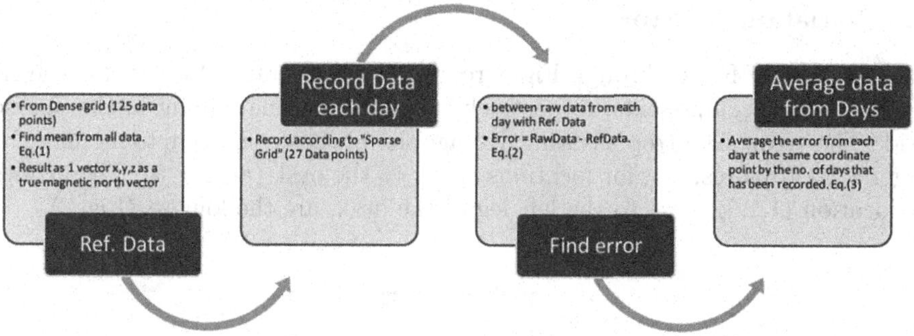

Fig. 4. The flow chart of how the data were analyzed

4 Results and Discussion

4.1 Visualization of Superimposed Measurements

The superimposed 3D vectors of raw data from 30 days are plotted on the Sparse Grid as shown in Fig. 5. This figure seems to indicate that the magnetic field close to the desk is also more variable. The arrow directions show more variation at the coordinate (1,1,5) compared to other points which showed more consistency throughout the several weeks spanned by the study.

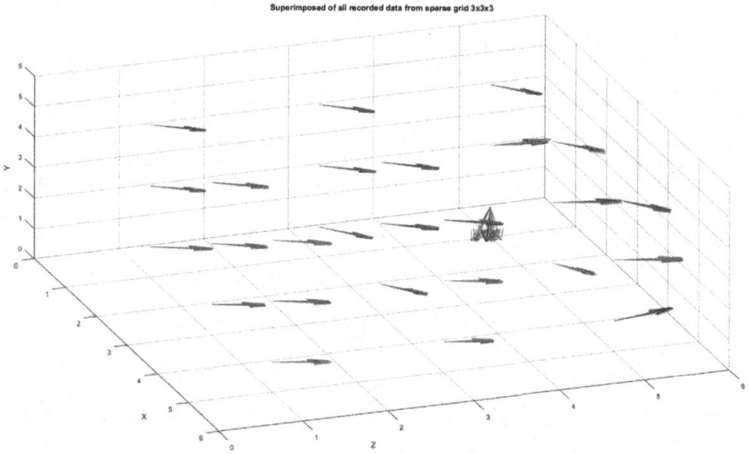

Fig. 5. Superimposed plot of 30 days of recorded data from the Sparse Grid ($3 \times 3 \times 3$), where Z = 5 is the plane closest to the desk.

4.2 Variation of Error

The 3D plots of Fig. 6 through Fig. 8 represent the average of errors for the X, Y and Z vector components, respectively, at each coordinate point in the Sparse Grid . The arrow sizes (representing average size of the error) seem to increase for larger Z coordinates, i.e., for locations closer to the desk (at Z = 5). The arrows for location (1,1,5), next to the left leg of the desk, are the longest (Fig. 7).

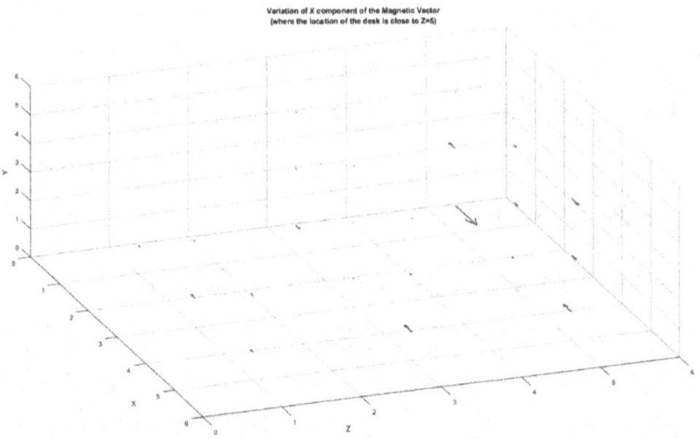

Fig. 6. 3D plots of variation of the Magnetic Vector for the X component

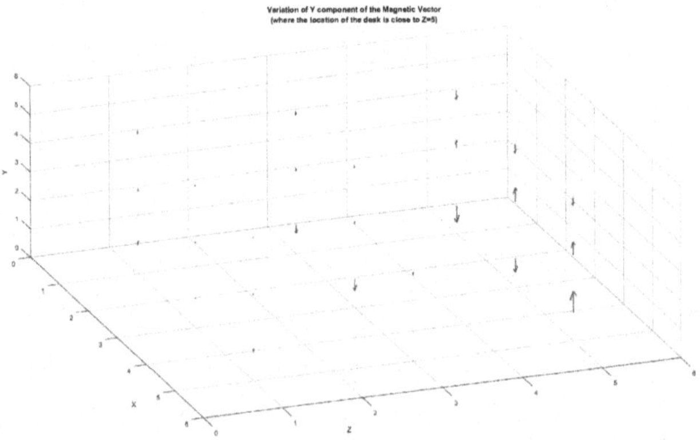

Fig. 7. 3D plots of variation of the Magnetic Vector for the Y component

The bar graph in Fig. 9 represents the mean error (30 days) at 27 measurement points, showing the 3 error components in X, Y and Z order. It is clearly seen that mean errors grow as the Z coordinate increases and the errors in the Y direction seem to be consistently larger than the errors in X and Z (the triad of

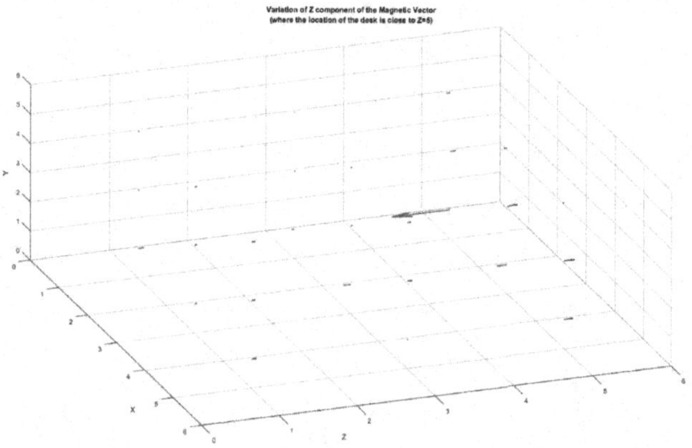

Fig. 8. 3D plots of variation of the Magnetic Vector for the Z component

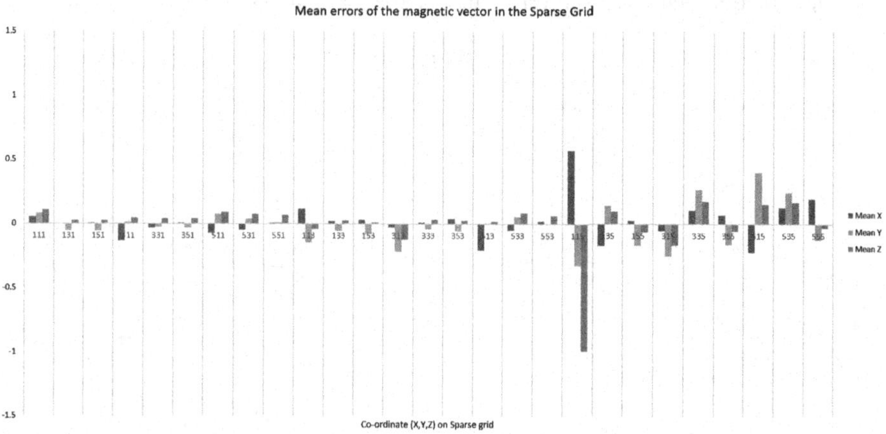

Fig. 9. Bar chart of mean (30 days) X, Y and Z errors, by location.

numbers, e.g., "351", under each cluster of 3 bars encodes the XYZ coordinates of each spatial location).

To confirm this observation, Fig. 10 through Fig. 12 display the progression of average errors constraining the scope to just one vertical plane, at X = 1. To obtain clear displays we show separate bar graphs of the average errors at 3 different vertical levels, separately. Figure 10 shows the evolution of average error at the top level (Y = 5). Here average errors increase for larger values of the Z coordinate, i.e., as the location is closer to the desk. The increasing trend is more noticeable in Fig. 11, corresponding to the intermediate height, Y = 3, and even more pronounced in Fig. 12, representing locations at floor level (Y = 1).

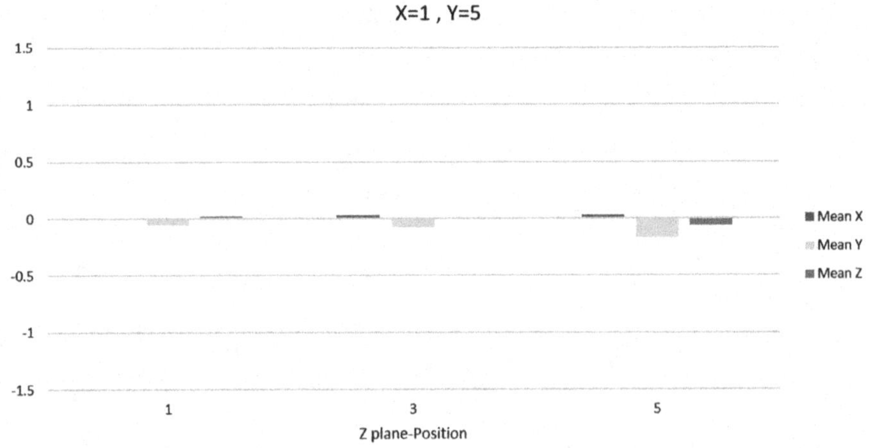

Fig. 10. Bar chart of mean errors in Plane X = 1, at the top level (Y = 5)

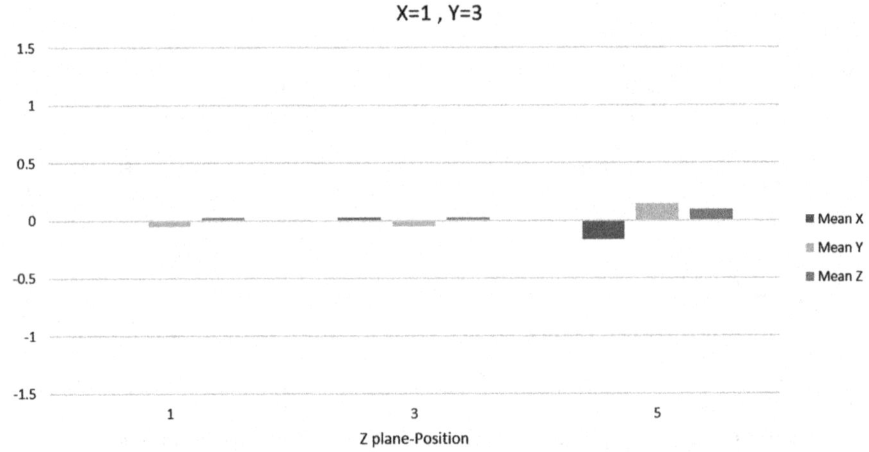

Fig. 11. Bar chart of mean errors in Plane X = 1, at the middle level (Y = 3)

4.3 Consistency Comparison

The specific point at (1,1,5), which was found to have the most distortion, was analyzed in the long-term (30 measurements, within 3 months), comparing it to the point that seemed to show the lowest risk of magnetic distortion. The point at coordinates (3,5,1) was chosen for this, as it seems to be away from any objects in the office environment. The graph in Fig. 13 shows that the mean error at coordinate (1,1,5) fluctuates widely during the 30 days, with averages of 0.6, −0.3 and −1.0 in X-axis, Y-axis and Z-axis respectively, while the mean error at point (3,5,1) varies only within 0 to 0.05 for all axes as shown in Fig. 14.

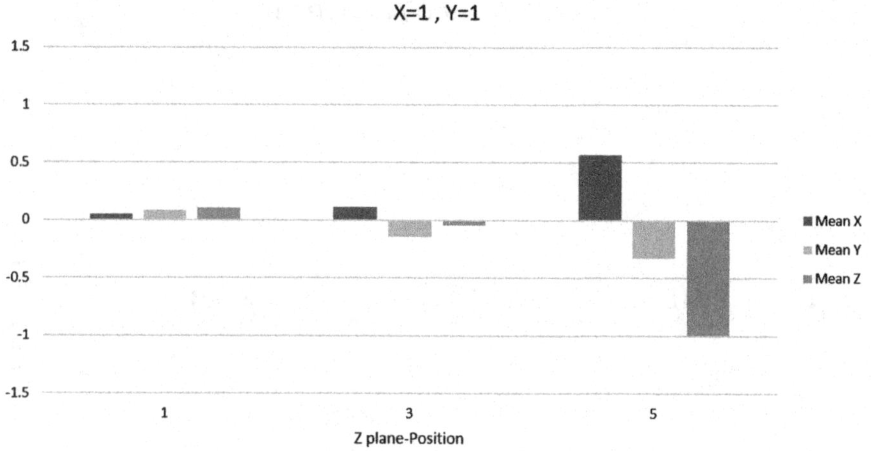

Fig. 12. Bar chart of mean errors in Plane X = 1, at the low level (Y = 1)

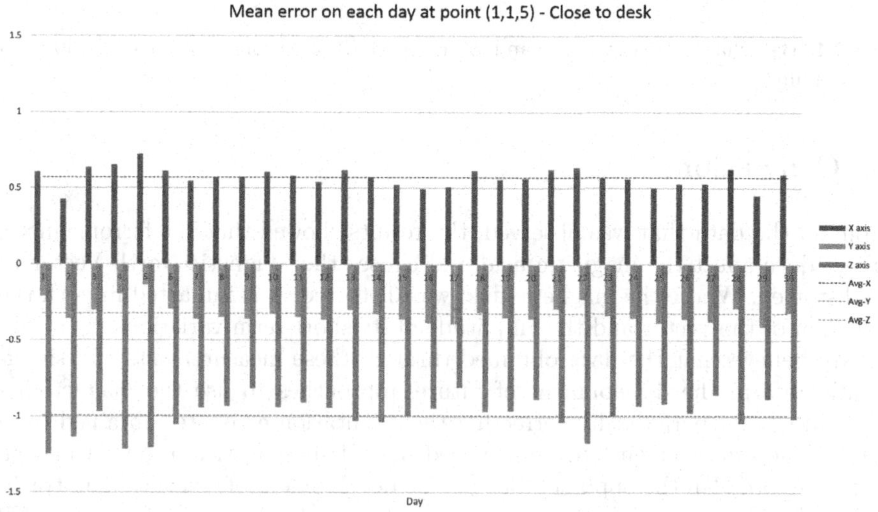

Fig. 13. Bar chart of mean X, Y and Z errors at (1,1,5) from day 1 to day 30 with average lines.

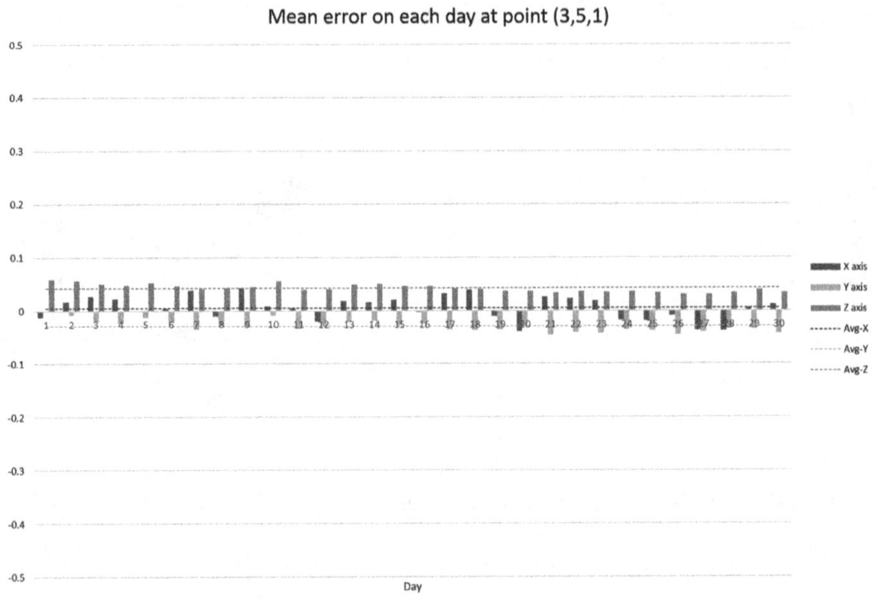

Fig. 14. Bar chart of mean X, Y and Z errors at (3,5,1) from day 1 to day 30 with average lines.

5 Conclusion

From all the data that was observed, the results showed that the ferromagnetic object does affect the magnetic field and causes the Magnetic North Vector to be distorted. Where the magnetic field was distorted, it is impacted in both the direction of the vector and the amplitude of its short-term variations.

We believe that the data obtained through these measurements will significantly inform the development of future approaches to use the magnetometer readings for periodically correcting the orientation estimates obtained from IMUs. The improvements to be achieved in IMU-based orientation estimation will likely broaden the opportunities for the development of efficient hand tracking mechanisms which may propel the near-future development of practical 3D spatial computer interfaces.

Acknowledgments. This research was supported by National Sciences Foundation grants HRD-0833093 and CNS-1532061.

References

1. Bachmann, E.R.: Inertial and magnetic tracking of limb segment orientation for inserting humans into synthetic environments. Technical report, Naval Postgraduate School Monterey CA (2000)

2. Bachmann, E.R., Yun, X., Peterson, C.W.: An investigation of the effects of magnetic variations on inertial/magnetic orientation sensors. Technical report, Naval Postgraduate School Monterey CA Department of Electrical and Computer Engineering (2004)
3. De Vries, W.H.K., Veeger, H.E.J., Baten, C.T.M., Van Der Helm, F.C.T.: Magnetic distortion in motion labs, implications for validating inertial magnetic sensors. Gait Posture **29**(4), 535–541 (2009)
4. Jackson, A., Jonkers, A.R.T., Walker, M.R.: Four centuries of geomagnetic secular variation from historical records. Philos. Trans. R. Soc. Lond. A: Math. Phys. Eng. Sci. **358**(1768), 957–990 (2000)
5. Madgwick, S.O.H., Harrison, A.J.L., Vaidyanathan, R.: Estimation of IMU and MARG orientation using a gradient descent algorithm. In: 2011 IEEE International Conference on Rehabilitation Robotics (ICORR), pp. 1–7. IEEE (2011)
6. Merrill, R.T., McElhinny, M.W.: The Earth's magnetic field: its history, origin and planetary perspective, vol. 401. Academic Press, London (1983)
7. Nonnarit, O., Barreto, A., et al.: Gyroscope drift correction algorithm for inertial measurement unit used in hand motion tracking. In: SENSORS 2016 IEEE, pp. 1–3. IEEE (2016)
8. O-larnnithipong, N., Barreto, A., Ratchatanantakit, N., Tangnimitchok, S., Ortega, F.R.: Real-time implementation of orientation correction algorithm for 3D hand motion tracking interface. In: Antona, M., Stephanidis, C. (eds.) UAHCI 2018. LNCS, vol. 10907, pp. 228–242. Springer, Cham (2018). https://doi.org/10.1007/978-3-319-92049-8_17
9. Roetenberg, D., Luinge, H.J., Baten, C.T.M., Veltink, P.H.: Compensation of magnetic disturbances improves inertial and magnetic sensing of human body segment orientation. IEEE Trans. Neural Syst. Rehabil. Eng. **13**(3), 395–405 (2005)
10. Sabatini, A.M.: Quaternion-based extended kalman filter for determining orientation by inertial and magnetic sensing. IEEE Trans. Biomed. Eng. **53**(7), 1346–1356 (2006)
11. Wan, H.: System for using a 2-axis magnetic sensor for a 3-axis compass solution. US Patent 6,836,971, 4 Jan 2005

Body Movements for Communication in Group Work Classified by Deep Learning

Hiroaki Sakon and Tomohito Yamamoto(✉)

Department of Information and Computer Science, College of Engineering, Kanazawa Institute of Technology, 7-1 Oogigaoka, Nonoichi, Ishikawa 921-8501, Japan
b6400561@planet.kanazawa-it.ac.jp, tyama@neptune.kanazawa-it.ac.jp

Abstract. In recent years, interactive educational methods called "Active Learning" have often been introduced in educational institutions such as universities. However, active learning activities such as group work are sometimes difficult to evaluate because it is uncertain what types of outcome should be considered good or bad. To approach this problem, using sensors on a smartphone, we developed a support system visualizing situations such as group work activity or the degree of understanding of students. In this study, we focus on body movements that appear frequently in this group work and classify them to understand the group work situation more clearly. To classify body movements, we created a dataset consisting of 10 movements appearing in group work, such as "Nodding." Using this dataset, we investigated whether the movements could be identified by the method of deep learning. As a result, it was found that body movements with few individual differences could be identified with relatively high accuracy.

Keywords: Active learning · Deep learning · Body movement · Communication · Smartphone · Human sensing

1 Introduction

In recent years, educational methods called "Active Learning" have been introduced in education, from primary schools to universities; students are supposed to learn more subjectively and interactively by this method. For example, in active learning, students often discuss a certain theme in groups and present the groups' conclusions to other students. It is argued that this type of subjective activity has a higher educational value than the traditional "knowledge transfer" type of education [1, 2].

In an actual class, it may be difficult for teachers to evaluate whether group work is going well or whether students are acquiring the ability to communicate knowledge outside of a specific field. From this point of view, our research group developed a system to measure the group work situation using smartphone sensors so that teachers, as facilitators, can evaluate the activities of students and give better advice to students [3]. The developed system could speculate about body movements related to communication and the state of a dialogue situation [4]. This measurement system currently

M. Kurosu (Ed.): HCII 2019, LNCS 11567, pp. 388–396, 2019.
https://doi.org/10.1007/978-3-030-22643-5_30

only acquires values from an acceleration sensor, and the evaluation of the body movements is performed manually after the data acquisition. In the future, we will develop a system that can evaluate group work in real time using measured data. To realize such a system, it is necessary to identify body movements in real time and to evaluate group work from a time series of body movements.

Several previous studies have measured body movements in the education field. One of these studies analyzed the body movements of primary school students during classes using sensors like name tags [5]. In that research, relatively large movements such as "Standing upright and seating" and "Moving desk" were focused on and analyzed. In contrast, in the group work that we focus on, body movements related to communication such as "Nodding" or "Turning around" are considered essential; these have often been observed in our previous research [4]. In addition to these movements, casual body movements such as "Crossing legs" or "Touching face" have also often been confirmed in previous research [4]. If these various body movements appearing in group work can be identified in real time, the group work can be evaluated from the viewpoint of nonverbal communication, that constitutes most of human communication [6]. Therefore, in this research, we create datasets of body movements appearing in group work and investigate whether they can be identified by deep learning.

2 Methods

2.1 Body Movements Related to Group Work

In this research, we investigated the recorded video from a previous study [4] again and selected 10 types of body movements to identify. Table 1 shows these movements. Identification numbers, M01–M10, are assigned to each of the 10 movements. M01–M05 were considered to be body movements related to communication, whereas M06–M10 were casual body movements appearing in group work.

Table 1. Ten types of body movements in group work.

Movement ID	Movement name
M01	Remaining stationary
M02	Clapping
M03	Raising hand
M04	Nodding
M05	Turning around
M06	Stretching
M07	Crossing legs
M08	Crossing arms
M09	Resting elbow on a desk
M10	Touching face

2.2 Data Measurement of Body Movements

Measurement of body movement data for deep learning was conducted with 11 university students (average age 21.7 years) using the system developed in the previous study [3] (Fig. 1). Measurement of five body movements were conducted as one session and the body movements related to communication were measured at first. Then, five casual body movements were measured.

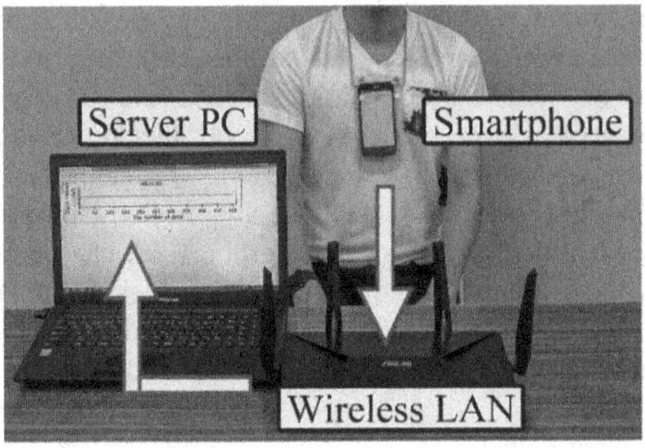

Fig. 1. Measurement system.

The measurement time was set to 1 min for each body movement, and each session lasted approximately 15 min including explanation and break time. Nine types of body movements—all except "Remaining stationary"—were repeated in accordance with the buzzer, which sounded at intervals of 5 s.

2.3 Preprocessing of Measured Data

In this research, the measured data from the acceleration sensor were used for learning using a convolutional neural network (CNN), which is one of the deep learning methods. In the CNN (Fig. 2), the following preprocessing was performed on the measured data.

1. Extract 4096 ms data (the norm of triaxial acceleration data) from 6000 ms data, which contain one body movement.
2. Apply Hanning window to the 4096 time series data and apply Fast Fourier Transform to the data.
3. Extract the power spectrum in the low frequency region (0–25 Hz) where the features of body movements appear.
4. The maximum value is found within each sample and normalization is performed to scale the input data to the range 0–1.

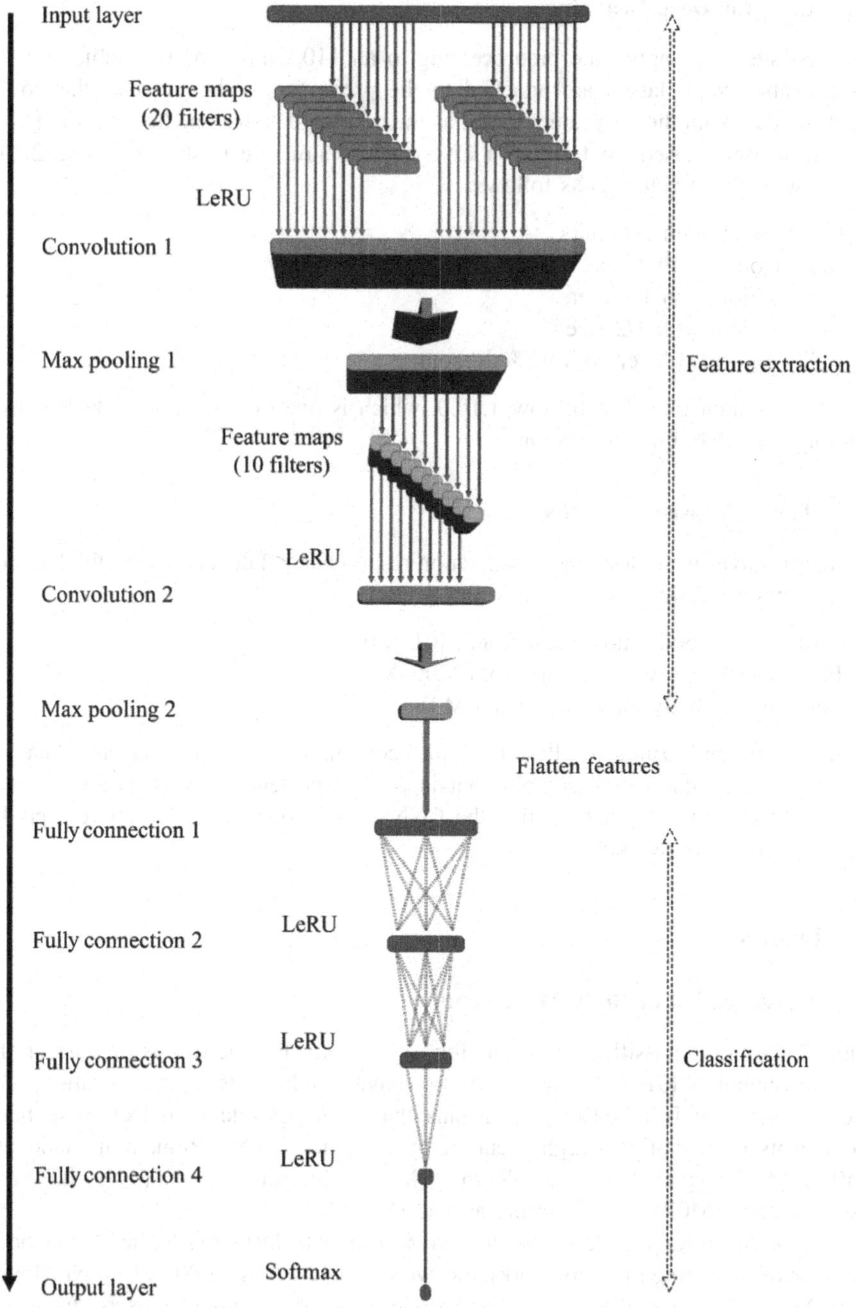

Fig. 2. Overview of CNN.

2.4 CNN for Deep Learning

The first step is to apply the preprocessing to all 110 data items (11 subjects × 10 movements). Next, labels are attached to the preprocessed data to pair the power spectrum data with the movement name, as the training data for one hot encoding. The created dataset is used for training a CNN, whose structure is shown in Fig. 2. An overview of the structure is as follows:

1. Convolution with 20 filters.
2. Max pooling with 1/8 size.
3. Convolution with 10 filters.
4. Max pooling with 1/2 size.
5. Fully connected layer with 90% dropout.

This research uses TensorFlow 1.10.0, which is one of the frameworks for deep learning, for CNN implementation.

2.5 Three Datasets for CNN

In order to investigate how the classification result changed depending on the learning data, we prepared three types of learning dataset:

1. Five types of body movement from M01–M05.
2. Five types of body movement from M06–M10.
3. Ten types of body movement from M01–M10.

To verify the learning results, 11 samples combining 10 items of training data and one item of test data (each sample contained 11 data items) were prepared in each dataset. In other words, we verified the CNN with learning data for 10 subjects by inputting one unknown subject.

3 Results

3.1 Classification of Body Movements

Table 2 shows all classification results for each dataset. For the results of learning the five movements M01–M05 (the body movements related to communication), the average accuracy is 87.64%. This means that it is possible to detect these body movements with relatively high accuracy by using the CNN. "Remaining stationary (M01)," "Clapping (M02)," and "Nodding (M04)" give better results (over 90%) than "Raising hand (M03)" and "Turning around (M05)."

As for the results of learning the five movements M06–M10 (the casual body movements appearing in group work), the average accuracy is 68.00%. Compared with M01–M05, it is more difficult to classify these five body movements by using the CNN. "Crossing legs (M07)," "Crossing arms (M08)," and "Resting elbow on a desk (M09)" give the best results. However, "Stretching (M06)" and "Touching face (M10)" are often classified as other movements.

Table 2. Results of classification using three datasets.

Subject	Accuracy for each dataset (%)		
	M01–M05	M06–M10	M01–M10
S01	84.00	84.00	68.00
S02	84.00	64.00	50.00
S03	80.00	68.00	56.00
S04	96.00	60.00	64.00
S05	92.00	72.00	62.00
S06	100.00	68.00	70.00
S07	88.00	72.00	68.00
S08	92.00	64.00	56.00
S09	80.00	52.00	50.00
S10	84.00	80.00	60.00
S11	84.00	64.00	66.00
Average	87.64	68.00	60.91

Finally, for the results of learning all 10 types of movement, the average accuracy is 60.91%. Of the three datasets, these types of data give the worst results. "Remaining stationary (M01)," "Clapping (M02)," and "Nodding (M04)" give better results than the other seven movements, which are often misclassified.

3.2 Verification of CNN Using Actual Group Work Data

The trained CNN was verified with the data about body movements in actual group work. For this, a real group work (20 min) involving three subjects was carried out three times; the three subjects learned one topic by teaching each other. In this research, movements by the nine subjects were identified with the learned CNN. Figure 3 shows a picture of the actual group work.

Fig. 3. Sample of actual group work.

Within the three 20-min group work sessions, the section where the discussion was held was extracted and this section was divided into 10-s segments. Next, the body movements of each subject were visually inspected and labeled by a human analyzer, using the labels for the 10 types of body movements (M01–M10). As a result, 440 movements in the group work sessions were labeled. Table 3 shows the number of occurrences of each body movement.

Table 3. Number of movements that appeared in actual group work.

Movement ID	Number of samples
M01	32
M02	0
M03	0
M04	133
M05	18
M06	32
M07	4
M08	6
M09	53
M10	162

For verification, body movements in the actual group work were identified by the trained CNN for every 10-s segment. The CNN trained with the data of M01–M05 was used for the identification of M01–M05. Similarly, the CNNs trained with the data of M06–M10 and M01–M10 were used for the identification of M06–M10 and M01–M10, respectively.

Table 4 shows the results of the five movements from M01–M05. In this case, the total accuracy is 75.41% (138/183). This means that it is possible to detect the body movement of actual group work with high accuracy.

Table 4. Results of classification of movements M01–M05.

Input	M01	M02	M03	M04	M05
M01	***19***	0	0	13	0
M04	14	0	0	***119***	0
M05	8	0	0	10	***0***

Table 5 shows the results of M06–M10. In this case, the total accuracy is 63.81% (164/257). As with the test data, these five body movements are more difficult to classify in actual group work. In particular, "Crossing legs (M07)," "Crossing arms (M08)," and "Resting elbow on a desk (M09)" are often misclassified as other body movements.

Finally, Table 6 shows the results of body movements M01–M10. The accuracy was 46.82% (206/440). In this case, the answer rate is the worst, as with the test data.

Among these movements, only "Nodding (M04)" and "Touching face (M10)" give the best results, but even these movements are often misclassified.

Table 5. Results of classification of movements M06–M10.

Input	M06	M07	M08	M09	M10
M06	***10***	0	0	0	22
M07	1	***0***	0	0	3
M08	0	0	***0***	0	6
M09	4	0	0	***0***	49
M10	8	0	0	0	***154***

Table 6. Results of classification in movement M01–M10

Input	M01	M02	M03	M04	M05	M06	M07	M08	M09	M10
M01	5	0	0	11	0	0	0	0	0	16
M04	1	0	0	***74***	0	0	0	0	0	58
M05	0	0	0	5	***0***	0	0	0	0	13
M06	0	0	0	14	0	***0***	0	0	3	15
M07	0	0	0	3	0	0	***0***	0	0	1
M08	0	0	0	3	0	0	0	***0***	0	3
M09	1	0	0	14	0	0	0	0	***0***	38
M10	2	0	0	33	0	0	0	0	0	***127***

4 Discussion

The results showed that the accuracy, for data consisting of five body movements related to communication, was 87.64% with test data and 75.41% with real data. This means that analyzing the frequency of acceleration data and learning its distribution with the CNN make it possible to identify body movements related to communication in group work with high accuracy.

Meanwhile, the accuracy for five casual body movements was 68.00% with test data and 63.81% with real data, which is more than 10% lower than the movements related to communication. This difference is caused by the individual differences in the casual body movements. For example, the "Stretching" movement was different depending on the subject, and such data would dirty the learning data for CNN. In contrast, "Clapping" and "Raising hand" varied in rhythm and speed depending on the subject, but the basic movement did not change between subjects. This explains why they could be learned by the CNN.

In this research, the dataset consisted of only 11 people, but if the dataset is enlarged, it is possible that the individual differences can be canceled. However, if only the quantity of training data is increased, overfitting may occur and the classification rate cannot be improved. To solve this problem, ensemble learning would be a better approach. For example, in the case of preparing data on 40 people, it is better to create

10-person data for one classifier and to prepare four weak classifiers than to prepare one classifier using all 40-person data. Using this method, even if there are data groups with a large amount of noise, its influence can be reduced. In addition, when increasing the quantity of data, it is possible to grow existing classifiers only by increasing their number.

5 Conclusions

In this research, to identify the body movements in group work for understanding the situation of active learning, the datasets of body movements appearing in group work were created and classified by deep learning. It was found that data groups composed of body movements with little individual differences can be identified with relatively high accuracy.

In future work, further learning data will be added while using an ensemble learning method, as explained above. At the same time, we will identify the body movements in more samples of actual group work. In this case, it is not clear whether the body movements used in this research necessarily yield good results. Therefore, we will further investigate the dataset of body movements and the structure of the classifier that can yield the best results. Furthermore, we will develop a system to evaluate the group work in real time using data classified by CNNs so that facilitators can realize better active learning class.

Acknowledgments. This work was supported by JSPS KAKENHI Grant Numbers 16H0322500 and 18K1141200.

References

1. Dale, E.: Audio-Visual Method in Teaching. The Dryden Press, New York (1946)
2. Crawley, F.E., Malmqvist, J., Östlund, S., Brodeur, R.D., Edstrom, K.: Rethinking Engineering Education: The CDIO Approach. Springer, London (2014). https://doi.org/10.1007/978-0-387-38290-6
3. Kimura, M., Kato, Y., Hagisawa, T., Yamamoto, T., Miyake, Y.: Measuring system of communication between a lecturer and students in a class. Correspondences Hum. Interface **18**(2), 113–118 (2016)
4. Harada, N., Kimura, M., Yamamoto, T., Miyake, Y.: System for measuring teacher–student communication in the classroom using smartphone accelerometer sensors. In: Kurosu, M. (ed.) HCI 2017, Part II. LNCS, vol. 10272, pp. 309–318. Springer, Cham (2017). https://doi.org/10.1007/978-3-319-58077-7_24
5. Yamamori, K., Ito, T., Nakamoto, K., Haggiwara, Y., Tokuoka, M., Oouchi, Y.: Recording elementary school students' academic engagement or on-task behavior using accelerometers. Jpn. J. Educ. Technol. **41**(2), 501–510 (2018)
6. Birdwhistell, R.L.: Kinesics and Context: Essays on Body Motion Communication. University of Pennsylvania Press (1970)

Eliminating the Pupillary Light Response from Pupil Diameter Measurements Using an RGB Camera

Sudarat Tangnimitchok(✉), Nonnarit O-larnnithipong, Neeranut Ratchatanantakit, and Armando Barreto

Florida International University, Miami, FL 33174, USA
{stang018,nolar002,nratc001,barretoa}@fiu.edu

Abstract. This paper describes our approach to remove the effect of the Pupillary Light Reflex (PLR) component from pupil diameter signals obtained by an Eye-Gaze Tracking device (Eyetech Digital TM3) using the RGB camera from Kinect as a way to measure the illuminance around the eyes of the user. The purpose of this study is to obtain filtered pupil diameter signals that mainly contain the Pupillary Affective Response (PAR) used to estimate the arousal level in the response of a human subject to affective stimuli. The approach includes using the Adaptive Interference Canceller (AIC) technique to filter out the Pupillary Light Reflex (PLR) from pupil diameter signals (PD). We also present the empirical method followed to replace a stand-alone light meter with the RGB camera from Kinect to measure illuminance.

Keywords: Digital Signal Processing · RGB-D camera · Eye-Gaze Tracking

1 Introduction

Previous research has shown that the pupil diameter (PD) is inherently controlled by the Autonomic Nervous System (ANS) [1,2]. There is evidence that, in constant light conditions, the pupil diameter is increased when a subject is presented with stress stimuli. The reasons behind this phenomenon lies in a mechanism that modifies the balance between the Sympathetic and Parasympathetic divisions of the ANS [2]. This article describes a subtask under the main project called "AffectiveMonitor" (Fig. 1) which is a system for the evaluation of a computer user's affective state based on the Circumplex Model of Affect [3].

Despite all that, pupil diameter changes are not only caused by affective reactions, but also by the amount of light that falls upon the retina, causing the Pupillary Light Reflex (PLR), which can be viewed as a process to regulate the retina light flux [4], to occur. This effect causes the contraction of the pupil and is superimposed to the changes in pupil diameter caused by affective responses, and hindering our study. Thus, we seek to remove the PLR component from the

M. Kurosu (Ed.): HCII 2019, LNCS 11567, pp. 397–406, 2019.
https://doi.org/10.1007/978-3-030-22643-5_31

pupil diameter signals we measure. In our previous work from the same research group [1], we have already presented our approach, using Adaptive Interference Canceller (AIC) to remove the PLR component from the PD signal. That previous work utilized the AIC canceller to implement a stress detector tested on the reactions of the subject to "Incongruent Stroop Segments". The study showed promising results in the PD-based system's performance as evaluated by the Receiver Operating Characteristic curve (ROC). The PD-based stress detector exhibits an area under the curve (AUROC) of 0.9331, indicating robust performance after the PLR was removed.

Fig. 1. An entire system including Kinect V2 (on top of the screen) and TM3 (in front of the computer)

There are also other physiological signals that can act as an indicator of arousal changes such as the Galvanic Skin Response (GSR), the Blood Volume Pulse (BVP), the Heart Rate (HR), and etc.; however, the pupil diameter is more suitable to estimate the arousal level and assess the affective state of a computer user because it can be observed non-intrusively, which is critical due to the nature of the study itself. In this kind of experiment, it is highly desirable that the subject is to be at his/her normal state as much as possible, without any unnecessary distracting factor. This issue is also the reason why we chose to use the RGB camera from Kinect, which is already a part of the AffectiveMonitor system [3], to measure the illumination around the subject's eye. Previously, a light meter was used to obtain illuminance signals to play the role of the required noise reference in the AIC algorithm. The light meter requires the placement of a sensor at the desired area where we would like to measure the illumination and it causes some distraction to the subject during the experiment.

In the following sections, we will discuss the AIC strategy in detail and describe how we obtain the illuminance signals around the eye area of the subject's face using images from the RGB camera as a mean to measure the illumination.

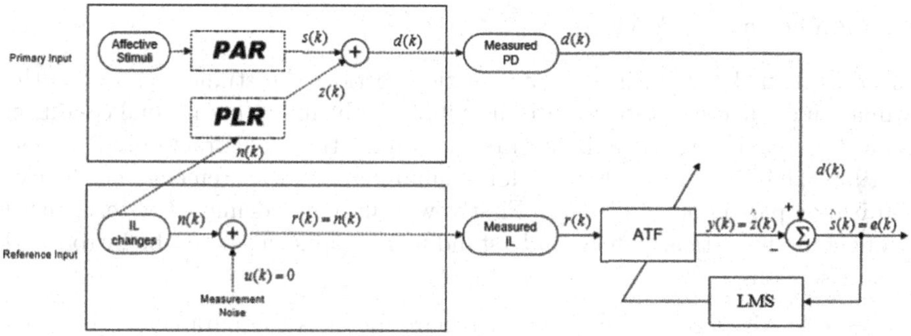

Fig. 2. Diagram of Adaptive Interference Canceller (AIC) (from [1])

2 Methodology

2.1 Adaptive Interference Canceller

The Adaptive Interference Canceller (AIC) is a system that is often used in Digital Signal Processing (DSP) to remove an unwanted interference component that pollutes a signal of interest [5]. The best way to explain how the system work is to walk through its diagram (Fig. 2). The concept here is to measure the signal of interest $s(k)$ that is corrupted with an uncorrelated noise $z(k)$ as the primary input signal $d(k)$. The reference input signal $r(k)$ is a signal that is correlated with the corrupting noise $z(k)$ but uncorrelated with our target signal $s(k)$. The adaptive algorithm, the Least Mean Square (LMS), in this case, will adjust the parameters in an Adaptive Transversal Filter (ATF) to bring the reference input signal $r(k)$ to be as close as possible to the interference signal $z(k)$ in order to bring the error $e(k)$, down to a minimum value (in a mean squares sense). By doing so, we can obtain our signal of interest, i.e., the filtered signal $\hat{s}(k)$, with the attenuated interference signal. In order to apply the theory to our application, we can think of the pupil diameter signal (PD) obtained from the TM3 Eye-Gaze Tracker as the primary input signal $d(k)$ while the measured illumination around the subject's eye area, from the RGB camera (Kinect) is used as the reference input signal $r(k)$. After the filtering process, we expect to obtain the output signal $e(k)$ that mainly contains the Pupillary Affective Response (PAR) component without the Pupillary Light reflex (PLR), which is removed by the adaptive filter.

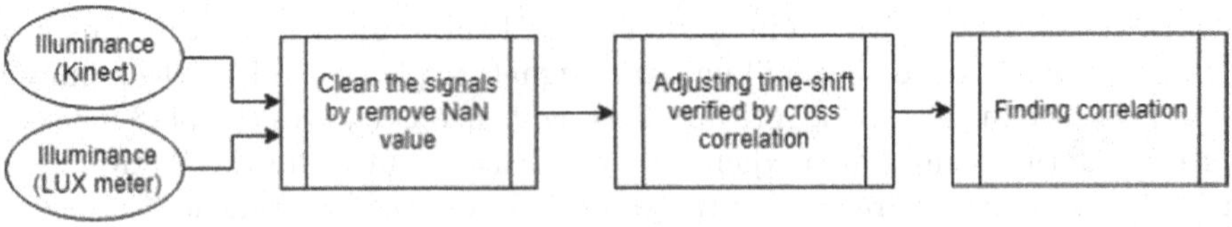

Fig. 3. Diagram showing the process of finding correlation between Kinect and LUX meter signals

2.2 Kinect as LUX Meter

As we explained earlier, in the introduction section, the studies related to the evaluation of affective state require the subject to be in his/her normal condition as much as possible to minimize extraneous stimulation or distractions. We chose to utilize the RGB camera (Kinect) for an illumination measurement since Kinect is already a part in our system [3]. Firstly, we will briefly define a few terms used throughout this article to help understanding concepts which will be introduced in later sections.

Luminance: Measured in candela per square meter is the parameter perceived by humans as the brightness of a light source.

RGB Camera: Captures the incoming light rays and turns them into electrical signals enabling many pieces of electronic equipment to act as light detectors. The incoming color and brightness of an image are converted to numbers, preserving those characteristics of the image and breaking it up into millions of pixels, depending on the camera resolution.

For the purpose of eliminating the unwanted PLR factor from the pupil diameter signal using the RGB camera, we only compute the pixel values around the eye area, using a cropping rectangle image that always has its center between the left and the right eyes (Fig. 4).

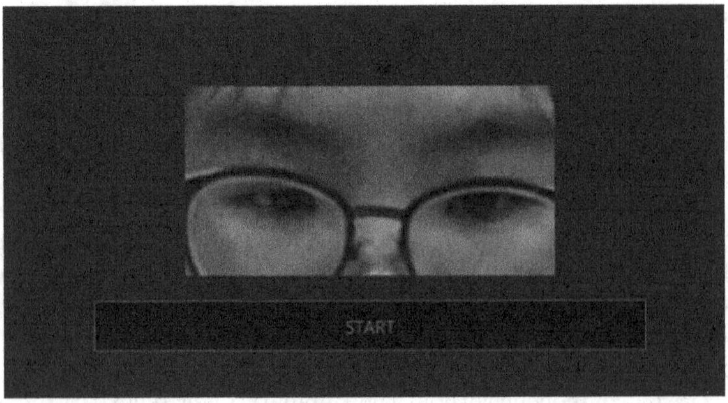

Fig. 4. Cropped video used to compute luminance around the eye area

The pixel values in an image from the RGB camera are proportional to the luminance, because the light sensors convert the intensity of light falling upon them to electrical signals whose strength depends on the brightness of the received light. That is why an RGB camera can act as a luminance meter [6]. Equation 1 is used to calculate the luminance from RGB values in the image, according to a color model based on human physiological characteristics [7]. Note that, R is Red, B is Blue, and G is green.

$$Y' = 0.299R' + 0.587G' + 0.114B' \quad (1)$$

However, the sensitivity of the sensors may be different for different RGB cameras. The relationship shown above may vary depending on the camera specifications. For this reason, we need to find out if the luminance values measured via our implementation followed the same trends as the luminance values measured using a luminance meter. To verify this hypothesis, we performed simultaneous light measurements in our experimental setup using the RGB camera from Kinect and a stand-alone LUX meter (Extech 401036 Datalogging Light Meter), while introducing strong illumination changes. Subsequently, after some processing, we computed the correlation between the two signals. If our hypothesis is correct, the luminance values obtained from Kinect should have a high correlation with the luminance value measured from the lux meter. A summary diagram of how we confirm our hypothesis is shown in Fig. 3

Table 1. Correlation coefficient between Kinect and LUX meter

	Kinect	LUX meter
Kinect	1.00000	0.922234
LUX meter	0.922234	1.00000

We can notice that the plots in Fig. 5a are not synchronized because of the different delays in the measurement systems. To circumvent this problem, we performed a correlation analysis to determine the delay time and then re-align the two signals. After the aligning process, now we can calculate the correlation between the two signals. Figure 5b shows the plot of luminance after the preprocessing and shifting of one signal to align it with the other. Then we computed the correlation between these signals. The correlation coefficients of illuminance signals measured from Kinect and the LUX meter are shown in Table 1. The pairs of measurements are shown in a scatter plot in Fig. 6, which also includes a "best fit" line. The result indicates strong correlation between the two signals, confirming that our hypothesis is correct and that we can use the luminance signal from our implementation as the reference input $r(k)$ (see Fig. 2) to filter out the PLR from the pupil diameter measured signal.

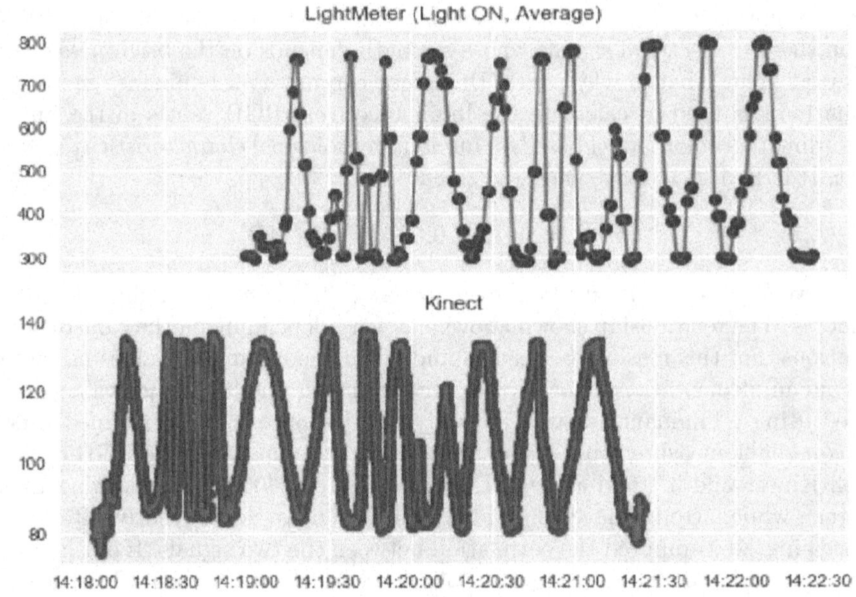

(a) Data before pre-processing

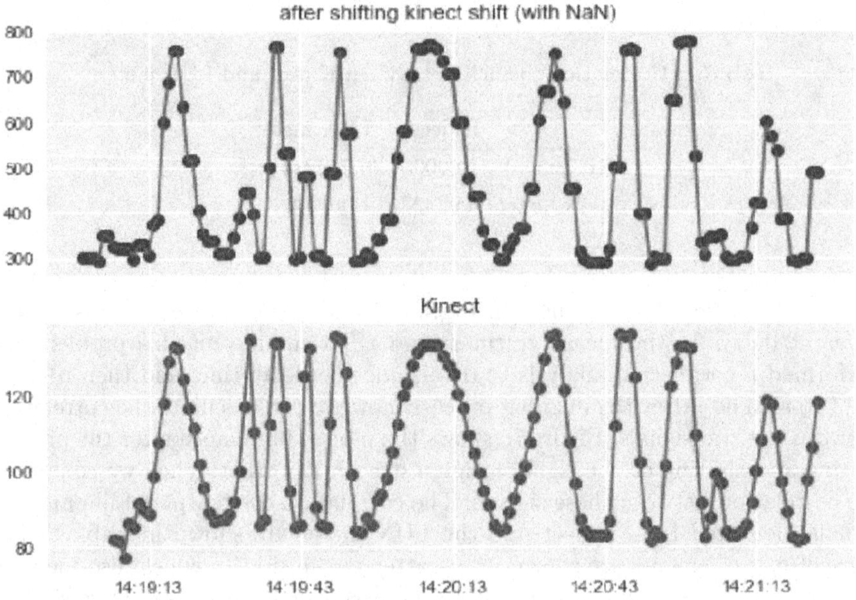

(b) Data after pre-processing

Fig. 5. Pre-processing of luminance signals obtained from LUX meter (blue) and Kinect (red) (Color figure online)

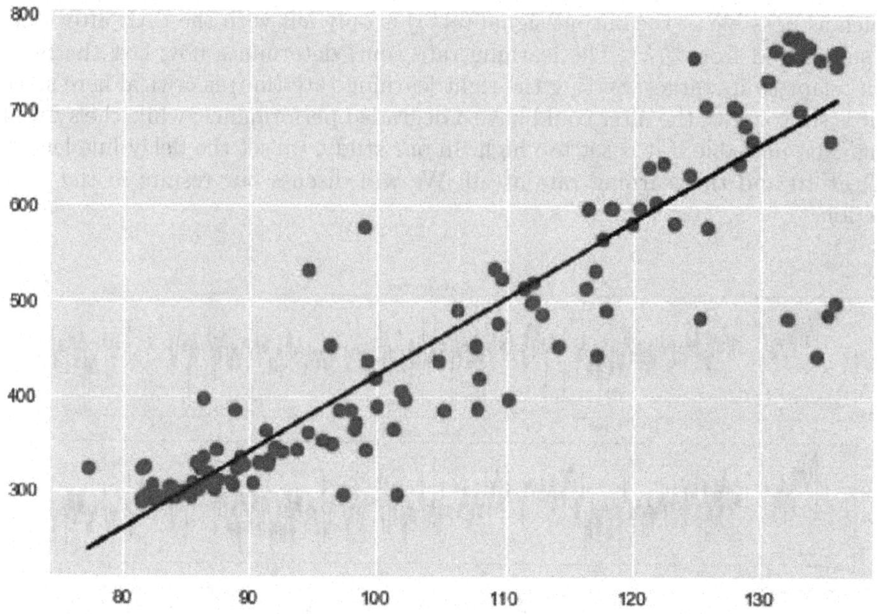

Fig. 6. Scatter plot and correlation (m = 8, b = –386)

2.3 Removing the Pupillary Light Reflex

As we have explained, we use an adaptive interference canceller (AIC) to filter out the Pupillary Light Response (PLR) and obtain a result, an output signal, containing only the Pupillary Affective Response (PAR). The first step is to pre-process the pupil diameter signal (PD); for instance, substituting missing samples due to eye blinks with an average value of the samples recorded in the neighborhood of the missing samples, and normalizing the pupil diameter as well as the illuminance signal before the filtering process. The signals we record are pupil diameter values obtained from the TM3 Eye-Gaze Tracking device from both left and right eyes containing about 7000 samples recorded at a sampling rate of 1 sample/sec. The illuminance signals are recorded using the RGB-camera (Kinect) at the same sampling rate. An example plot of pupil diameter signals after pre-processing along with the illuminance signal is shown in Fig. 7.

To develop the adaptive interference canceller (AIC), we follow the theory and practice from [8] as our guideline to implement an LMS adaptive filter. Both recorded pupil diameter signals that are impacted by the pupillary light response ($d(k)$) and the illuminance signal ($r(k)$) are normalized before they are processed by the LMS adaptive filter. There are two hyperparameters that affect the performance of the adaptive filter. They are the length of the delay line (L) and the learning rate (mu). The longer the delay line is, the slower and smoother the modified reference input signal ($y(k)$) becomes. In this case, we would like $y(k)$ to imitate the PLR component in the primary input ($d(k)$) as much as possible so the output signal ($e(k)$) is only left with the PAR after $y(k)$ is subtracted from $d(k)$. The learning rate (mu) determines how fast the filter can adapt to its target. Setting the right learning rate (mu) is critical here since if it is set too low, the filter could have a degraded performance; while the system might be unstable if it is set too high. In our study, we set the delay line length (L) at 10 and the learning rate at 50. We will discuss our results in the next section.

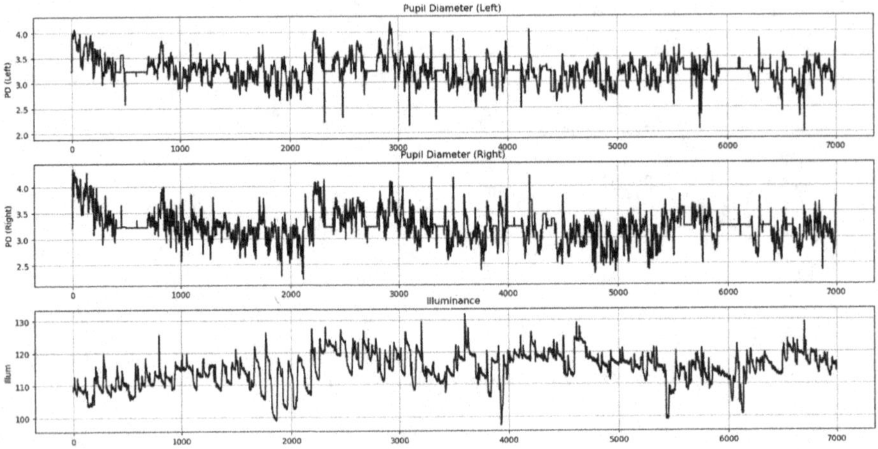

Fig. 7. Plots from top to bottom: Pupil diameter (Left), Pupil diameter (Right), Illuminance

3 Result

Our results are shown in Fig. 8, which consists of two plots. The first one (Fig. 8a) shows signals $d(k), r(k), y(k)$, and $e(k)$, respectively, from top row to bottom row. Figure 8b shows some of these same signals superimposed for an easier visualization. Here each signal is shown in a different line style. The primary input signal ($d(k)$) is represented in solid black line at the top part of the graph; this signal is the left pupil diameter signal. Our output signal ($e(k)$) is also in solid black line but located at the bottom of the graph. The reference signal ($r(k)$), illuminance, is shown here in light color and, lastly, the modified reference signal ($y(k)$) is plotted in dotted line. It is possible to observe, in this figure, how each signal behaves based on the nature of the pupillary response. The basic idea is that when the illuminance is low, the pupil diameter is increased in order to adjust the amount of light that reaches the retina. That is why when the reference signal is lower, the pupil diameter signal is shifted upward.

The purpose of the implementation of the adaptive filter is to eliminate this effect and shift the pupil diameter down to the baseline when the interference from pupillary light response produced by illumination changes occur. In Fig. 8b,

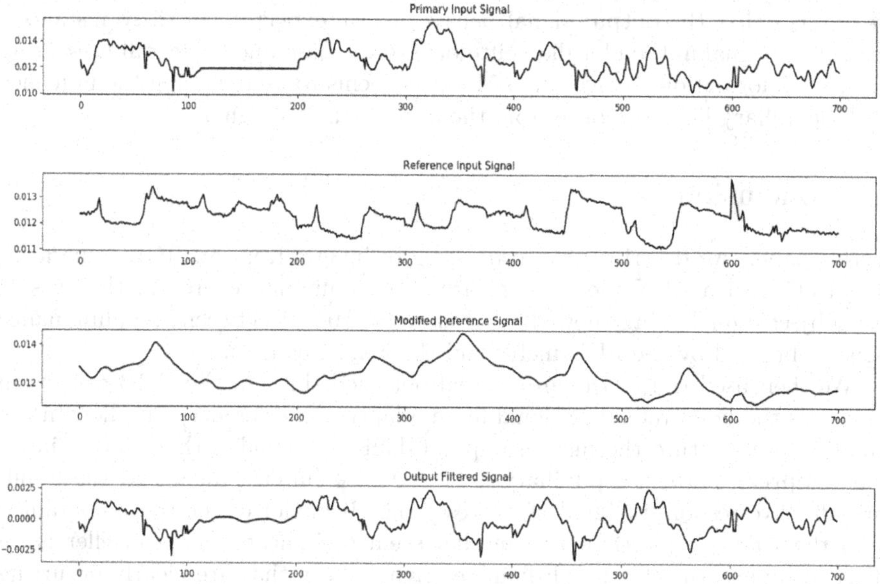

(a) Signals plotted separately

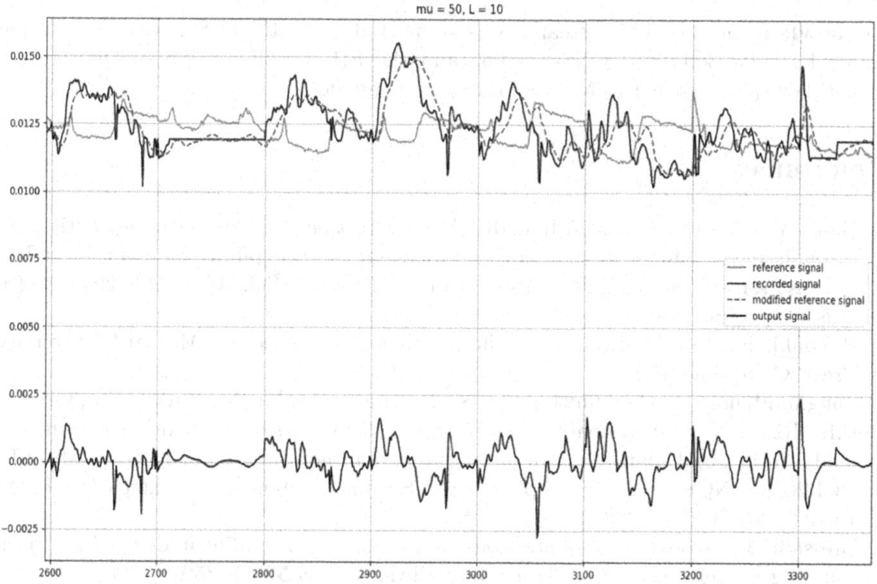

(b) Signals plotted in one graph

Fig. 8. Plot of signals processed in removing PLR using AIC

we observe that the output signal behaves as we expected. In these instances, the output signal in the plot did shift down to the base line while still preserving the PAR information. Hence, the LMS filter seems to be removing the influence of the pupillary light response from the pupil diameter signal.

4 Conclusion

In this paper, we described the processing of images from an RGB-camera for substitution of a LUX meter to measure the illuminance around the eyes of the subject. Our testing showed a correlation of 0.922 between the illuminance signals obtained by the LUX meter and the Kinect camera.

We then used the illuminance signal obtained through the RGB camera in Kinect as the noise reference signal in an adaptive interference canceller. In the canceller architecture the measured pupil diameter signal is the primary input and comprises both, the pupillary light response (interference) and the pupillary affective response (signal of interest). The behavior of the results obtained from the adaptive interference canceller seem to indicate that canceller is, in effect, compensating for pupil diameter signal shifts that are clearly occurring in response to illumination changes.

Acknowledgments. This research was supported by National Sciences Foundation grants HRD-0833093 and CNS-1532061 and the FIU Graduate School Dissertation Year Fellowship awarded to Ms. Sudarat Tangnimitchok.

References

1. Gao, Y., Barreto, A., Adjouadi, M.: Detection of sympathetic activation through measurement and adaptive processing of the pupil diameter for affective assessment of computer users. Am. J. Biomed. Sci. **1**(4), 283–294 (2009). pdfs.semanticscholar.org
2. Hugdahl, K.: Psychophysiology: The Mind-Body Perspective. Harvard University Press, Cambridge (1995)
3. Tangnimitchok, S., O-larnnithipong, N., Ratchatanantakit, N., Barreto, A., Ortega, F.R., Rishe, N.D.: A system for non-intrusive affective assessment in the circumplex model from pupil diameter and facial expression monitoring. In: Kurosu, M. (ed.) HCI 2018. LNCS, vol. 10901, pp. 465–477. Springer, Cham (2018). https://doi.org/10.1007/978-3-319-91238-7_38
4. Bressloff, P., Wood, C.: Spontaneous oscillations in a nonlinear delayed-feedback shunting model of the pupil light reflex. Phys. Rev. E **58**(3), 3597 (1998)
5. Strum, R.D., Kirk, D.E.: First Principles of Discrete Systems and Digital Signal Processing. Addison-Wesley, Reading (1988)
6. Hiscocks, P.D., Eng, P.: Measuring luminance with a digital camera, vol. 16. Syscomp Electronic Design Limited (2011)
7. Arts, J.S.G., Meeting, P.o.t.s.A.: Color measurement with an RGB camera (2009). researchgate.net
8. Tan, L., Jiang, J.: Digital Signal Processing: Fundamentals and Applications. Academic Press, London (2018)

Interaction in Virtual and Augmented Reality

Digital Design and Research of Ink Art Based on Infrared Interactive Projection Technology - Taking the Work of "Listen to the Ink" as an Example

Yarong Deng(✉), Lihong Luo, and Xiaoying Tang

Guangdong University of Technology,
No. 729 Dongfeng Road, Yuexiu District, Guangzhou, Guangdong, China
dyr806800257@qq.com

Abstract. In the interactive desktop projection "Listening to Ink", through the appreciation of the existing digital ink art, we try to use the infrared interactive projection technology to combine the ink art and the interactive device, to achieve a new interactive way, breaking through the traditional inertial cognition in ink art.

The infrared interactive desktop projection system of "Listen to the Ink" works includes a projection module, an infrared transmitting module and a sensing module. Firstly, an infrared interactive desktop projection system consisting of three modules was built; the infrared light reflected by the finger touch or the laser pen was illuminated by the camera; then the information was transmitted to the image processing module, and multi-point positioning and analysis were performed; After judging the operation intention, the processing result was transmitted to the corresponding application in a standard form, and corresponding operations were performed. Finally, a digital ink art based on interactive projection was completely realized, which provided new ideas for exploring ink digital art.

Keywords: Ink digital art · Infrared interaction · Desktop projection

1 Introduction

Chinese ink painting is a natural and poetic cultural carrier. It is one of Chinese national quintessence culture and plays an important role in Chinese art history.

In the era of multicultural development and collision, in the process of wide application of various media materials, digital technology has also participated in ink art with its unique charm. When ink painting entered the creation of contemporary digital art, works began to combine new media technologies with ink symbols. From simple ink digital animation, photography, digital painting to ink art behavior, ink art installations and other multi-dimensional virtual space art forms. In the experimental art combining new media technology and ink symbols, try to break through the boundaries of ink art [2].

M. Kurosu (Ed.): HCII 2019, LNCS 11567, pp. 409–418, 2019.
https://doi.org/10.1007/978-3-030-22643-5_32

At present, there are two main ways to express ink art using digital technology: One is based on planes. From the perspective of the drawings, there is an ink expression that depicts the digital image purely using ink media; and there also have an ink art performance that refers to composite materials and digital technology. For example, Huang Yihan's "New Generation" and "Cartoon Generation" series; Mao Donghua's "Cloudy to Sunny"; Dan Zheng's "One Day of Alice" and so on. The second is the creation of behaviors, images, and installations. Liu Xuguang's "Sound"; Image "Ink Drop"; Wang Chuan's installation "Zero"; Wang Tianyi's installation "Ink Table", "Digital Series • Lonely Mountain", etc.; Barbara Edelstein's image "Tree of The Life" series and the Leaf Book series and more [3].

The ink art work "Listening to Ink" was realized by infrared interactive desktop projection interactive method, and the interactive content was divided into three scenes: The first act of "Listen to the Ink" was to bring the audience into the ink scene. The audience began with the brush to draw the ink point, followed by the ink waterfall, the fishing boat and the lotus flower, then bring the audience into the ink world. The second act was the String Song Interaction. The interactor used the brush to play the ink string, and the string changed with the sound into a splash, a crane, a dragon, etc., to achieve audio-visual interaction. The third act was the interaction between the fish and the disks. The patterns are respectively put into three white disks by interactive projection. The color changed the pattern with difference music, the interactor held the brush to touch the plate to appear ink dots. Then the ink dots changed into a swimming fish, complete the interaction. This form of interaction breaks the one-way spread of traditional ink, giving viewers a more impactful form of expression, and further innovation in culture through creative attempts combining modern technology with traditional art.

2 Creative Innovation of Ink Art

2.1 New Way of Viewing

"Ideology" is an important part of Chinese classical aesthetics, and it is also the aesthetic standard of a unique Chinese art painting of traditional Chinese ink painting. Many Chinese painters regard "Ideology" as the creative principle of Chinese ink painting, and use "Ideology" as the appreciation principle of works. Environment and imagination are the source of artistic conception [4].

The traditional Chinese ink paintings are mainly created on the table, and they are created on the flat paper or enamel. The table and the creator are in a vertical angle. The creator's charm is vivid, and the bone method is integrated into the flat paper.

In the traditional form of viewing, Chinese ink painting is mostly displayed in vertical static art, and it also determines the audience's single and passive viewing angle.

The first act of "Listening to Ink" is to introduce the ink rhyme. The audience starts with the ink brush to draw the ink point. The desktop projection method realizes the change of the ink culture viewing angle, transforming the audience from a quiet parallel angle to ink painting. The vertical angle of the countertop is appreciated, and the innovation of dynamic display form and interactive viewing mode is realized.

The creation of "Listening to Ink" is a work with unique artistic conception, which integrates the environment and creative content into a whole, making the work extremely vital and inspiring the audience's imagination. These abilities are called work's vitality (Figs. 1 and 2).

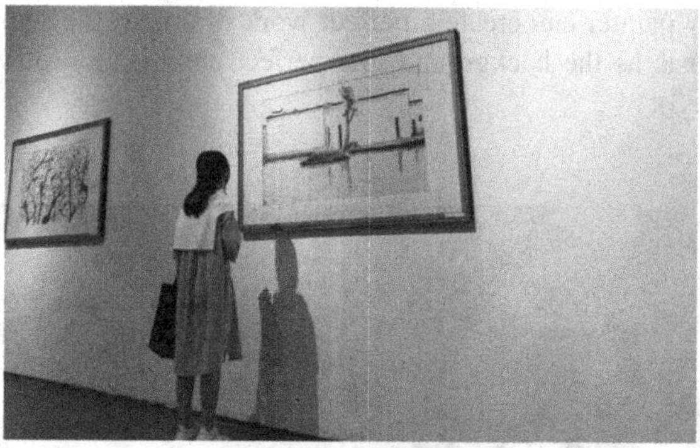

Fig. 1. Traditional ink painting form.

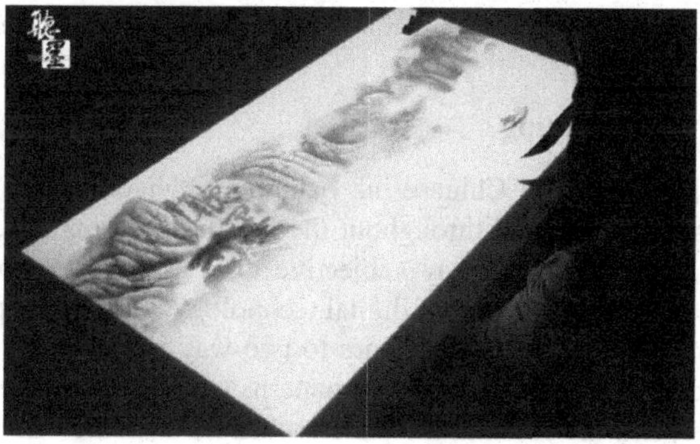

Fig. 2. 《Listen to the ink》 form.

2.2 New Way of Viewing

In the second act of the ink art "Listen to the Ink", the audience used the brush to move the ink strings, the strings changed with the sounds, and the creators tried to blend the Chinese ancient string music with the Chinese ink elements. Using digital media technology to change the viewer's inertia cognition when watching ink painting, emphasizing the connection between hearing and ink painting art, and realizing the synchronous experience of visual and auditory ink painting.

The view of the form and spirit of Chinese ink painting is a contradictory concept. It is the most frequently used concept in Chinese ink painting to express aesthetic thoughts and is also part of Chinese traditional aesthetics. Gu Kaizhi's "Theory of

Painting" laid the view of the unification of Chinese ink painting. "Shape" is a depiction of the external shape of a thing, and "Spirit" is a depiction of the inner ideological activity or characteristics of a thing [5]. In the second act of "Listening to Ink", the audience was quickly substituted into the artistic conception of ink in a dim environment, and the pen in the hands was forgotten, the external identity was forgotten, and the spirit was concentrated in the creation of ink art. Every audience is a painter, and every painter can create a perfect work of art. At the same time, with the ancient string music as the background, the perfect combination of visual sense and touch sense (Fig. 3).

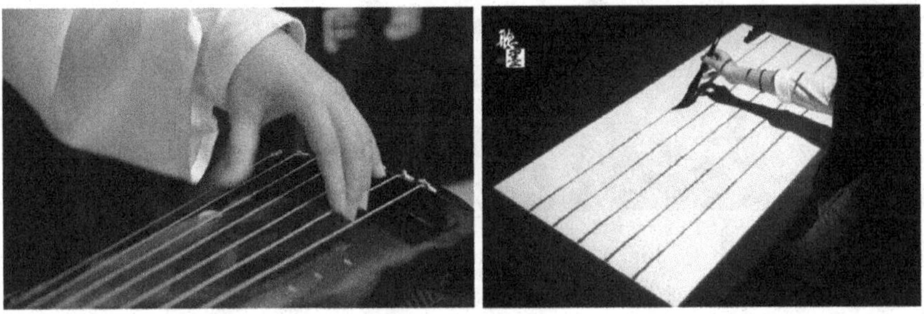

Fig. 3. The second act of "Listen to the Ink"—New sensory experience.

2.3 New Way of Interacting

One of the artistic essences of Chinese ink painting is "vigorous and vivid" [6]. The charm of the work is distributed throughout the creative environment. The traditional Chinese ink art is mostly a one-way subjective taste and artistic conception of the creator. With the rapid development of digital technology, the digital application of ink art attempts to spread from one-way culture to two-way interaction.

In the third act of "Listening to Ink", the patterns are placed in three white discs in a projection manner, and the color of the pattern changes with the music. The audience held the brush and the fish jumped between the plates as the audience touched. The creators have enriched the sensory experience of ink culture with the combination of audio and sound. The desktop projection ink creation table has broken through the single and boring display method of ink. Using new media technology to realize the interaction between the real ink creation tool (brush) and the virtual pen and ink creation table (desktop projection), creating a complete ink and wash creation immersion space. It perfectly presents the "vibrant and vivid" of Chinese ink painting (Fig. 4).

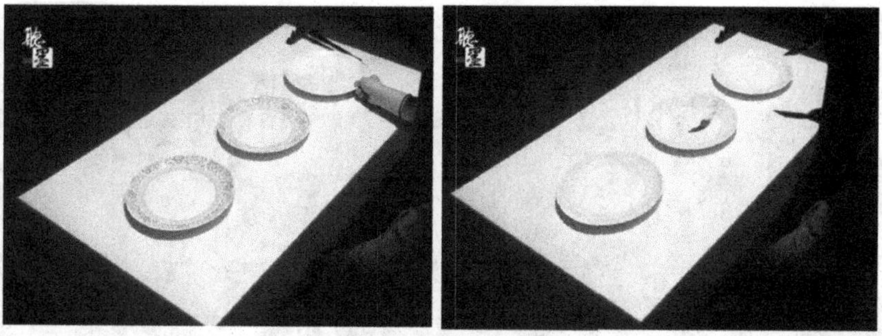

Fig. 4. The digital creativity of "Listen to the Ink"

3 The Digital Technology of Ink Art

The interactive projection system is a combination of dynamic capture technology and virtual reality technology. It is a technology that generates three-dimensional or two-dimensional images from a computer and provides users with a virtual space image and interacts with it. By mixing reality, the user can also touch the real environment while manipulating the virtual image, thereby enhancing the sensory experience. Allows the experiencer to better participate and immerse in the projected image for a more intense and realistic interactive experience. The operation principle of the interactive projection system is firstly to capture and capture the target image (such as the participant) through the capture device (sensor), and then analyze by the image analysis system to generate the motion of the captured object, the motion data combined with the real-time image interaction system. To create a close interaction between the participants and the screen [7].

In 2009, at the American International Consumer Electronics Show in Las Vegas, USA, a light-touch interactive projector won the applause of visitors and experts. It can turn all the common plane into a touch screen, and realize the interaction of the screen by dancing the limbs. This marks the official application of interactive projection technology and has caused great repercussions in the market.

Desktop projection is a product derived from the application of interactive projection technology. As a new high-tech product, desktop projections have been paid attention to in the mainland, and many investors have poured in, which has accelerated the development of the desktop projection industry, and related application fields have been continuously developed. Desktop projection games are currently mainly used in entertainment venues such as KTV, bars, nightclubs, etc., which enhances the entertainment experience of consumers to a certain extent, and can also drive additional operating income of the business premises (Fig. 5).

Fig. 5. Desktop interactive projection

3.1 Ink Effect Rendering Technology for 3D Models

The movement of the three-dimensional models in the "Listen to the Ink" works is achieved through the bound bones in C4d. The ink effect of the model is based on the material ball of the C4d software. In addition to adjusting the color and transparency properties of the Shader, the texture is added to the color and transparency channels to achieve the subtle ink effect of the 3D model. After attaching the 3D model to the ink effect material, you need to add the TFD plug-in application to complete the random generation of the ink (Fig. 6).

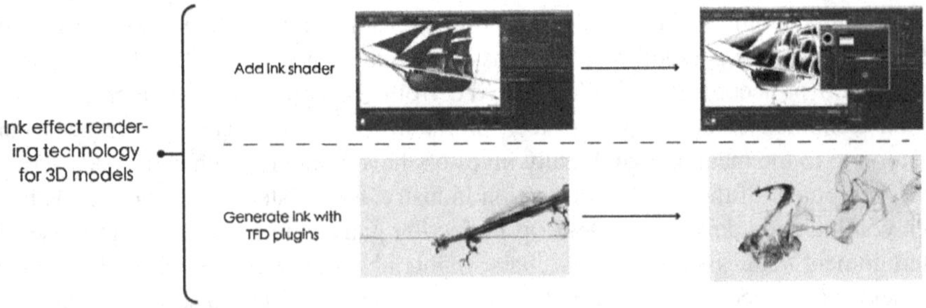

Fig. 6. The digital creativity of "Listen to the Ink"

3.2 Infrared Interactive Desktop Projection Technology

In the aspect of interactive equipment construction of "Listen to the Ink", after comparing and analyzing various technologies for realizing desktop interactive projection, the infrared interactive desktop projection technology was adopted to realize the digital innovation of ink art.

The light projected by the projector is visible light, and its infrared part is filtered by the filter film inside it [8]. Therefore, it can't see the projector's projected content for the camera. If the infrared light is strong, the camera can see the human body. How to enhance the image of the object seen by the camera? Fortunately, the infrared active emission technology in the market is very mature. For example, the night vision camera sold on the surveillance market can emit near-infrared (850 nm), which is more powerful. There is a special long-range infrared light, and the camera can reach 5 m without overnight, so it is not needed.

The night vision camera actively emits infrared, and then the ccd sensor accepts infrared. Then the most difficult part of the interactive projection, the segmentation of the human body and the background virtual object is solved, and the camera obtains a black and white monochrome background including the image of the person. Next, to detect the movement of the human body, the image difference technique is adopted. The difference is to subtract the images of two consecutive frames obtained by the camera, then what is obtained, and the obtained part is the movement, so if the person is moving the difference will intercept the moving part.

The next step is to analyze the data obtained, and then project the virtual part. Of course, complex interactive projection is not just these technologies. These are just the most basic principles. In the meantime, it involves the calibration of the camera, the optical flow method to find the direction of motion, the optimization of performance, and the special effects

The complete hardware device of the infrared interactive desktop projection system includes a projection module, an infrared transmitting module and a sensing module. A new projection system based on multi-touch, gesture recognition and other technologies, captures the infrared light reflected by the finger touch or the laser pen when the projection screen is illuminated by the camera, transmits the information to the image processing module, and performs multi-point positioning and analysis thereon [1]. After judging the operation intention, the processing result is transmitted to the corresponding application in a standard form, and corresponding operations are performed to realize the digital creation of the "Listen to the Ink" work (Fig. 7).

The target image (such as the participant) is captured by the capture device (sensor) and then analyzed by the image analysis system to generate an action of the captured object. The motion data is combined with the real-time image interaction system to enable the participant and the screen. Produce a tightly integrated interaction [9].

To detect the movement of the human body, the image difference technique is adopted. The difference is to subtract the images of two consecutive frames obtained by the camera to obtain the moving part, so that as long as the person is moving, the difference will intercept the moving part. The next step is to analyze the data obtained, and then project the virtual part. Then simulate the mouse message to the window in the foreground.

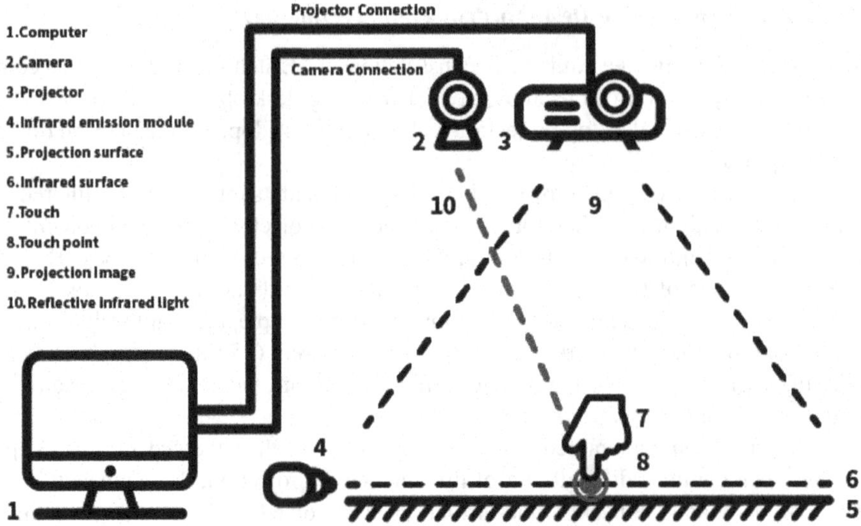

Fig. 7. Infrared interactive desktop projection system

4 The Innovative Significance of Ink Art

4.1 Creative Meaning

As one of the representatives of China's national quintessence, ink art plays an important role in Chinese art history. The traditional ink art combines the human spirit and the natural realism with a touch of ink, which arouses the viewer's resonance. However, the limitations of traditional ink painting have created a sense of distance on the path of communication, which conflicts with the characteristics of today's "interactive" and "autonomy". Under the current aesthetic cognition that emphasizes the combination of multiple sensory experiences, the ink painting presented in the form of plane vision needs to be passed through [10].

There are still many ink paintings in the museum or private collections for a hundred years, which have failed to let the world appreciate their beauty. Therefore, the digital media art has given the deep meaning of innovation to the display of traditional ink paintings. Yang Chun, who graduated from the Central Academy of Fine Arts, came to the Oscar Film Awards in the United States for his work on the theme of the Song Dynasty fan painting "Red Dragonfly Waterfowl". The national painting style impressed the judges and was nominated for an Oscar [11].

As early as during the Shanghai World Expo, a classic Chinese ink painting "The Riverside Scene at Qingming Festival", which was moved by the exhibition, was a sensation. So far, the "Qingming Shanghe Map" made by digital media technology is still on display in the Forbidden City. It is hard to find a ticket every day.

With the continuous development of cross-media technology integration, the trend of integration and mutual penetration of art and technology is increasing, and the new media art has brought about the change of aesthetic style, that is, the viewers are more eager to participate in the physical state. The creation of "Listening to Ink" works to let the traditional ink art show to the audience in the form of static to dynamic, visual and auditory and more sensory.

In the context of new media art, we combine modern technology with traditional art to create new forms of expression. In this way, we use the audio-visual interaction method to re-create and re-expose the ink-and-wash works, break through the inertia cognition of the ink-and-wash art with visual as the main body, emphasize the connection between the auditory and the ink art, and finally achieve the win-win of artistic expression and bring the viewers a win-win situation. It not only has cultural heritage but also brings visual impact to the artistic expression, and realizes a new analysis and experience of ink and wash, and expands the new field of traditional cultural heritage (Fig. 8).

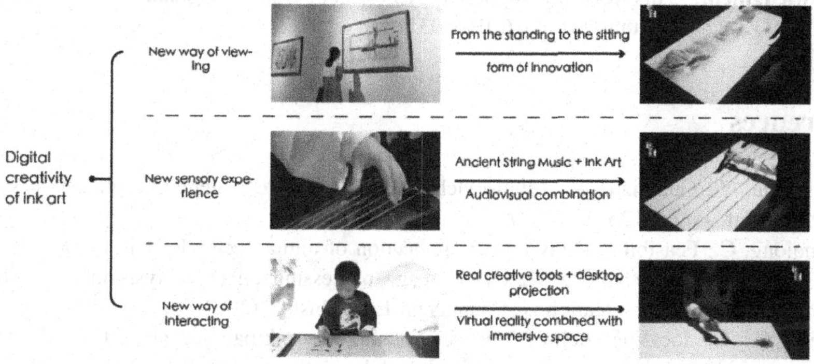

Fig. 8. The creative meaning of "Listen to the Ink"

4.2 Social Significance

The desktop projection ink interactive work "Listen to Ink" was selected in October 2018 to participate in the Beijing International Design Week "The 2nd Contemporary International Ink Design Exhibition" exhibition and won the gold medal. "Contemporary International Ink Design Exhibition" is an important component of Beijing International Design Week. It is the leading brand of "Ink Design" at home and abroad. The works exhibited include various forms of information such as information, concept, design, experiment and media. Among the more than 2,200 pieces of the works, only 3 gold medals were selected. The desktop projection interactive work "Listen to Ink" stood out in many works and won the gold medal. It is also the only gold award in the media design category. The exhibition and award-winning information were reported by many domestic media such as NetEase, Sohu, Phoenix.com and today's headlines. At the same time, the exhibition works will be invited to tour in Mexico. The "new interpretation" and "new proposition" of ink design will go to the international stage.

5 Conclusion

The continued development of digital media art, continuous creation and re-creation, innovation and innovation, it is not only limited to the film and television we have seen, but has penetrated our lives. From traditional ink painting to ink animation to modern interactive new media, it can influence the art of ink painting to influence our ethics, aesthetics, politics, and our everyday feelings and perceptions. The culture of digital media art is an open culture, allowing people to review and think, and to provide feedback. The future of digital media art will not be limited to ink animation or other forms of animation. It is slowly expanding into the cross-disciplinary field, in the environment of graphics, space, sound, film and television, contemporary art, advertising culture, etc.

Acknowledgment. This work was supported by Project of Guangdong Science and Technology Department of China (Grant No. 2016a040403110).

References

1. Shaohua, Y., Guanjian, W.: Multi-touch intelligent infrared interactive projection system. Autom. Inf. Eng. **5**, 26–30 (2017)
2. Yuqiong, C.: Feasibility study on the application of digital technology in ink art (2017)
3. Weipeng, C.: Application research of image processing effect analysis in contemporary Chinese ink painting creation. J. Changchun Educ. Inst. **7** (2014)
4. Ying, C.: The local research of Chinese contemporary ink painting art (2016)
5. Hao, L.: The modern pursuit of radical and breakthrough–on the cultural position and linguistic features of modern ink and wash (2010)
6. Ping, Z.: Exploring the boundary of ink and wash - the experimental art of combining new media technology with ink symbols operation. Fine Art (2008)
7. Qiang, F.: Research on the application of traditional ink art in digital media art works. Comput. Prod. Circ. 129–130 (2017)
8. Li, T.: Application and research of Chinese ink texture in graphic design (2012)
9. Qiwang, L.: Analysis of the significance of ink animation to the inheritance and innovation of ink painting art. J. News Res. 137–138 (2017)
10. Lihua, D.: Research on the artistic conception and language limitation based on ink animation. Art Educ. Res. **99** (2016)
11. Ping, Z.: Comparison of Chinese experimental ink and other modern ink art forms. Art 100 (2008)
12. Zijian, F.: Interactive projection Chinese painting works - Chunjiang plumbing (2018)

Text Entry in Virtual Reality: A Comprehensive Review of the Literature

Tafadzwa Joseph Dube(✉) and Ahmed Sabbir Arif

Human-Computer Interaction Group,
University of California, Merced, CA 95343, USA
{tdube, asarif}@ucmerced.edu

Abstract. The availability of consumer-ready Virtual Reality (VR) Head-Mounted Displays (HMDs) has resulted in a surge in VR applications. It has also prompted the design and development of numerous text entry techniques for the paradigm. However, it is difficult to understand the mechanism of these techniques and extract meaningful average performance data from this body of work since they were evaluated in diverse experiment conditions and report different performance metrics. To remedy this, this paper classifies the existing text entry techniques for VR based on their input mechanism and discusses their strengths, limitations, and performance.

Keywords: Virtual Reality · Text entry · Review · Performance · Input

1 Introduction

Virtual Reality (VR) is rapidly growing in popularity due to the availability of affordable consumer-ready products [1]. Although initially branded as a technology for entertainment and simulation, nowadays its being used for office work [2, 3], collaboration [4], and training and education [5]. These newfound applications have rendered a need for efficient and effective text entry techniques for VR as inputting text is an essential part of these experiences. Many recent works have attempted to meet this need by developing novel, as well as customizing the existing text entry techniques for VR. However, it is often difficult to comprehend the mechanism of these techniques and extract meaningful average performance data from this body of work as they were evaluated in different experiment conditions and report different performance metrics. This makes it difficult for the researchers to use and apply these findings, causing re-exploration of design philosophies, and as a result slowing down the overall development process. To address this, this paper reviews the existing text entry techniques for VR. It categorizes these techniques based on their input mechanism and discusses their strengths, limitations, and performance. It also provides design recommendations for researchers to facilitate the development of more user-friendly and effective text entry techniques. This work does not include speech recognition.

M. Kurosu (Ed.): HCII 2019, LNCS 11567, pp. 419–437, 2019.
https://doi.org/10.1007/978-3-030-22643-5_33

2 Physical Techniques

Adapting the standard physical Qwerty keyboard for VR is difficult for several reasons. Numerous studies have established that both novice and expert typists look down at the keyboard to verify their hand position [6, 7]. Since users wearing a Head-Mounted Display (HMD) cannot see their hands (Fig. 1), it is almost impossible for them to input text as fast and accurate as in the real world. The size of the keyboards and the need for a supporting surface also make physical Qwerty harder to use in scenarios where users are required to move around. Although some have proposed miniature Qwerty layouts, the smaller key size makes it impossible to touch-type, which further affects entry speed and accuracy [8]. This section reviews all techniques that use a physical keyboard or a keypad in VR. Table 1 presents the entry speed and error rates [9] of these techniques from the literature.

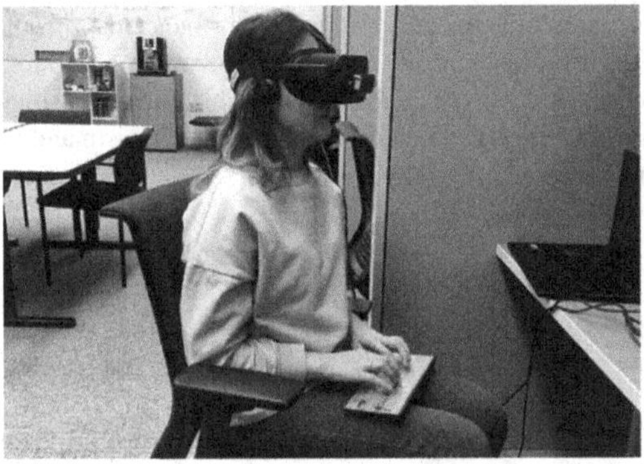

Fig. 1. A user entering text in VR using a physical Qwerty keyboard.

2.1 Physical Qwerty

Many have used a physical Qwerty or its variants, particularly Qwertz and Azerty, in VR to bank on their widespread use and familiarity [10–12]. Most of these techniques track the keyboard and hands with external depth cameras to display their virtual representations in VR [2, 10, 13, 14] to enable users to enter text with a physical keyboard through its animated representation. In an evaluation, this approach yielded 34.0 wpm and 12% error rate [13].

Bovet et al. [14] used the Logitech BRIDGE SDK [15] with an HTC Vive Pro HMD [16] and a Logitech G810 Orion Spectrum keyboard to display an animated representation of the keyboard and hands in VR. In a user study, this method reached an average entry speed of 44.4 wpm from an initial speed of 34.5 wpm. It also yielded negligible mental and physical demand scores. Grubert et al. [2] argued that this method can retain at least 50% of users' desktop typing skills. This method's effectiveness, however, is dependent on the reliability of its tracking sensors.

Kim and Kim [17] tracked the keyboard and hand positions to display a visual representation of the keyboard and hands. Unlike the previous approach, they did not track fingers, instead displayed finger positions based on the last keypress. That is, they calibrated finger positions based on the assumption that specific fingers were used to press specific keys, which is a cheaper, but a less accurate approach compared to using depth cameras. In an evaluation, users retained at least 60% of their desktop typing speed and 80% of accuracy with this method.

A different method embedded a live video stream of the real world onto the virtual world to afford the use of a physical Qwerty in VR [11, 12]. It displayed the full and a partial view of the keyboard and hands. In a user study, the full view yielded 36.7 wpm and 10.4% error rate [12]. Partial view that displayed only the keyboard and the hands yielded comparable results. McGill et al. [12] also proposed a partial blending option that displays parts of the keyboard but did not evaluate its performance. Although this method demonstrates competitive speed and accuracy, it breaks the immersion by displaying the real world. It also requires the use of additional cameras, increasing the cost of development and installation. To remedy this, Walker et al. [18] proposed a software solution for predicting finger positions. They argued that when expert users are provided with adequate visual feedback, they can use their sense of proprioception to correctly (re)position their hands on the keyboard for the next key. They used a decoder [19] for auto-correction. In a user study, this approach reached 43.7 wpm and 92.6% accuracy rate. Although the performance of this approach is promising, its reliance on a decoder can potentially frustrate users. Its dependence on the sense of proprioception can also increase the cognitive load.

It is clear from this section that physical Qwerty remains an essential method for text entry in immersive environments. Researchers have proposed the use of various sensors, cameras, and decoders to facilitate reasonably fast and accurate text entry in VR with physical Qwerty, which may not be feasible in all scenarios and for low-income groups.

2.2 Mobile Keypads

Some immersive systems allow users to move around within a limited space. Since physical Qwerty restricts this ability, researchers have proposed using mobile keypads.

Bowman et al. [20] and González et al. [21] used Twiddler in VR. Twiddler is a 12-key chorded keypad, with which users enter characters by pressing either one or a combination of keys simultaneously (called a chord). This approach was evaluated in a user study, where a virtual layout of the keypad was displayed in VR. In the study, Twiddler yielded 3.0 wpm and 82% accuracy rate. Although Twiddler enables users to be mobile, it is substantially slower than the other techniques. Besides, it requires extensive training to learn the chords, which may discourage many to try it [6].

González et al. [21] also evaluated a 9-key mobile keypad that has three characters on each key. They embossed the keys to provide users with haptic feedback. To enter characters with this keypad, users press the key containing the intended character once or multiple times, respective to the position of the character on the key, just like Multi-tap [6]. For instance, to enter the letter "c", users press the "2" key containing the letters "a", "b", and "c" three times. This method yielded 12.1 wpm and 95% accuracy rate. Although relatively slow, this method could be useful for short-term text entry, such as while entering a password or a search keyword.

Table 1. Physical text entry techniques with their entry speed in words per minute (wpm) and error rate (%). "Char" signifies "character". Sensors are not considered as auxiliary devices.

Method	Short description	Input unit	Auxiliary devices	Bimanual	Hand tracking	Participant	Session	Entry speed (wpm)	Error rate (%)
Qwerty [12]	*Displays full* and partial† view of the keyboard and the hands*	Char	Keyboard Camera	✓	✓	16	1	36.6* 38.5†	10.4* 9.2†
Qwerty [18]	*Visual feedback on keypress without* & with† auto-correction*	Char	Keyboard	✓	✗	24	2	43.7	8.4* 2.6†
Qwerty [13]	*Displays an animated view of the keyboard without* & with† hands*	Char	Keyboard	✓	✓	13	1	34.0* 31.2†	12.0* 13.4†
Qwerty [17]	*Calibrates virtual finger position based on the last keypress*	Char	Keyboard	✓	✓	✗	1	✗	✗
Qwerty [14]	*Displays an animated view of the keyboard and hands*	Char	Keyboard	✓	✓	12	1	44.4	0.4
Qwerty [22]	*Tests four feedback conditions: none*, animated keyboard†, animated keyboard & hands‡, & video inlay of keyboard & hands§*	Char	Keyboard Keyboard Camera	✓	✓	16	1	28.1* 24.3† 27.4‡ 27.8§	0.3* 0.2† 0.2‡ 0.2§
Qwerty [10]	*Tests four feedback conditions: none*, animated fingertips†, animated abstract hands ‡, & animated realistic hands§*	Char	Keyboard Keyboard Camera	✓	✓	16	1	31.8* 32.2† 38.8‡ 37.5§	14.0* 7.5† 7.7‡ 7.6§
	Same four conditions evaluated with experienced typists whose entry speed is over 53.3 wpm		Keyboard Keyboard Camera			16	1	61.8* 68.5† 67.0‡ 66.6§	7.3* 4.4† 5.1‡ 5.0§
Qwertz [11]	*Tests four feedback conditions: keypress only*, animated fingertips†, animated hands‡, & video inlay of keyboard & hands§*	Char	Keyboard Camera	✓	✓	24	1	26.1* 36.4† 34.4‡ 38.7§	15.2* 6.3† 11.5‡ 5.1§
Qwertz [2]	*Users look straight* or down† to see the keyboard*	Char	Keyboard Camera	✓	✓	24	1	25.3* 26.3†	2.4* 2.1†
Chorded [20, 21]	*Displays an animated view of the chorded keyboard*	Char	Twiddler	✗	✗	10	1	3.0 [21]	17.0
Keypad [21]	*Uses a custom embossed keypad to provides haptic feedback*	Char	X-keys [23]	✗	✗	10	1	12.1	4.0

2.3 Discussion

One can see in Table 1, Knierim et al. [10], Grubert et al. [11], Hoppe et al. [13], Bovet et al. [14], and Lin et al. [22] all investigated physical Qwerty with animated keyboard and hands as visual feedback, yet reported diverse results, summarized in Table 2. Bovet et al.'s [14] study yielded the highest entry speed (roughly16% faster than the next fastest result). The fact that the baseline condition of this study also yielded a relatively high entry speed suggests that this is likely due to a more experienced sample. The fact that this study used a sophisticated tracking apparatus optimized for text entry in VR may have contributed towards this as well. This presumably impacted the accuracy rate of the method too since Bovet et al. [14] and Lin et al. [22] reported substantially lower error rates than the others (0.4% vs. > 7.6%).

Table 2. Studies investigating physical Qwerty with animated keyboard and hands. Best and worst results are highlighted in bold and italic, respectively.

Reference	Entry speed (wpm)	Error rate (%)
Knierim et al. [10]	37.5	7.6
Grubert et al. [11]	34.4	11.5
Hoppe et al. [13]	31.2	*13.4*
Bovet et al. [14]	**44.4**	0.4
Lin et al. [22]	*27.4*	**0.2**

Unfortunately, Table 1 does not provide a clear indication of whether users perform better (in terms of speed) with animated representation of the keyboard and hands. In the studies conducted by Hoppe et al. [13] and Lin et al. [22], users performed much better without any visual feedback compared to when animated keyboard and hands were displayed (34.0 wpm vs. 31.2 wpm [13]; 28.1 wpm vs. 27.4 wpm [22]). However, in the studies conducted by Knierim et al. [10] and Grubert et al. [11], users performed substantially better with visual feedback (31.8 wpm vs. 37.5 wpm [10]; 26.1 wpm vs. 34.4 wpm [11]). We speculate, this is due to the unreliability of the feedback provided in the former studies. It was reported that visual feedback in the former studies was not always accurate or available. Hoppe et al. [13] used a Leap Motion [24] to track hands and reported that it was able to display the hands for about 70% of the time.

Walker et al. [18] and Grubert et al. [11] both provided visual feedback on key-press. However, Walker et al. reported a 40% higher entry speed than Grubert et al. This is likely because Walker et al. used a decoder to enhance the accuracy of their system. They also included an extensive training session before the actual study. Further, in addition to highlighting the currently pressed key like Grubert et al. [11], Walker et al.'s [18] system also highlighted other recently pressed keys to aid in users' sense of proprioception. These could also help explain a 45% lower error rate (15.2% [11] vs. 8.4% [18]). In fact, Walker et al.'s system yielded even a lower error rate with auto-correction (2.6%).

Studies comparing visual feedback through animated fingertips and full hand representation revealed that fingertips yield a slightly higher accuracy rate than full hand [10, 11]. This gain in accuracy is likely due to the obstruction of keys when a full hand is displayed as opposed to fingertips. Interestingly, Grubert et al. [11] identified this difference to be statistically significant ($p < .05$), while Knierim et al. [10] did not.

Table 3. Error rate metrics reported in the literature.

Error metrics	References
Error rate	[2, 10, 11, 13, 14, 21]
Total error rate	[18, 22]

Table 3 presents the error rate metrics reported in the literature. As one can see, most studies reported either the Error Rate (ER) or the Total Error Rate (TER) metrics. However, text entry studies often use different methods to calculate the same error metrics. For instance, Knierim et al. [10] used the Minimal String Distance (MSD) algorithm to count the total number of errors, when Rajanna et al. [25] counted the total number of backspaces. A previous work [9] analyzed these performance metrics and demonstrated how different metrics yield different results. Yet, unfortunately, most studies do not report how they calculate errors.

3 Virtual Qwerty

Numerous virtual text entry techniques have been developed for VR to enable mobility and eliminate the dependence on physical keyboards and keypads. Most of these techniques use the Qwerty layouts or its variants to facilitate the transference of knowledge from the physical to virtual keyboards. These techniques exploit a variety of interaction methods, including head pointing, finger, wrist, and hand gestures, game controllers, touch, eye gazing, and handwriting. The following sections reviews these techniques. Table 4 displays the entry speed and error rates [9] of these techniques from the literature.

3.1 Head Pointing

Since head pointing is the default interaction method for most HMDs, it has been widely used in text entry. Head pointing text entry techniques cast a ray into the scene that is controlled by head movements. A virtual Qwerty keyboard floats in front of users (Fig. 2). To enter a character, users first move the cursor over a key, then select the respective character by either dwelling on it for a predetermined amount of time (a timeout period) [26] or pressing a controller key [26, 27].

Yu et al. [26] evaluated a head pointing technique that used a 400 ms dwell time. It yielded a 10.6 wpm entry speed and 95.8% accuracy rate. Since dwelling can affect the overall entry speed, Majaranta et al. [28] suggested using customizable dwell time. Yu et al. [26] also evaluated a different approach that enables users to select characters by pressing a controller key in place of dwelling. They reported a 15.6 wpm entry speed and 98% accuracy rate by the 6th session. This suggests that head pointing is faster with

Fig. 2. Text entry through head pointing [27].

keypress than with dwelling. Although these approaches could cause physical discomfort since they force users to constantly move their heads around, could be effective in short-term text entry, such as entering a password or a search keyword [26].

3.2 Finger, Wrist, and Hand Gestures

Many have explored text entry with finger, wrist, and hand gestures in VR. These methods usually use external cameras, sensors, and gloves to track fingers, wrists, and hands.

Bowman et al. [29] developed a digital glove that maps the Qwerty layout to the fingers. Such as, it maps the second-row letters "a", "s", "d", and "f" to the left little, ring, middle, and index fingers, respectively. With this approach, users first rotate their hands to select a row, then enter a character by pinching the thumb and another finger. This method was evaluated in a user study, where it reached on average 6.1 wpm entry speed and 90% accuracy rate [20, 21]. The fact that it lacks haptic feedback may have contributed towards its relatively low speed and accuracy. The KITTY keyboard [30] uses a similar approach, but instead of using hand rotation, it uses the thumb with six degrees of freedom to select a row. Three positions in the front and three in the back of the thumb are assigned to different rows. For example, a pinch between the left little finger and the middle inner thumb enters the letter "a". This method also lacks haptic feedback. Wu et al. [31] designed a different approach that uses micro speakers to simulate haptic feedback on keypress. With this approach, users wear two data gloves on each hand and enter a character by bending a finger beyond a predetermined threshold.

The main challenge of these techniques is that they demand a substantial amount of time and effort to master. The use of digital gloves makes them a costly solution for both manufacturers and consumers and restricts users from using their hands for secondary tasks. Further, they can strain the fingers when used for an extended period.

Ishii et al. [32] proposed a fist-pointer method, where hand movements and fist gestures are used to select characters. First, users move the pointer by moving the hand in a thumbs-up position. Once the pointer is over the intended character, they select it by folding the thumb. Ishii et al., however, did not evaluate this approach.

Some have also explored mid-air gestures that enables users to select characters by performing hand gestures and finger postures [27, 33]. This technique, too, does not provide haptic feedback. In an evaluation, it yielded a relatively low 9.8 wpm and 92.5% accuracy rate. It was also mentally and physically demanding.

3.3 Controllers

Some techniques enable users to enter text using handheld controllers augmented with motion trackers.

Speicher et al. [27] evaluated four such techniques. The first enables users to use a controller as a laser pointer. Users move the cursor over a keyboard by pointing the controller, then select a character when the cursor is over it by pressing a key. Speicher et al. allowed users to hold two controllers in two hands to facilitate bimanual input. It yielded on average 15.4 wpm and 99% accuracy rate. The second enables users to use a controller as a stylus. Users tap the controller on a character to enter it. It yielded 12.7 wpm and 98.1% accuracy rate. The third enables users to use a controller as a joystick. Users navigate the cursor over a keyboard by pressing the four directional keys, i.e., the four edges of a touchpad, then select a character when the cursor is over it by pressing a key. It yielded 5.3 wpm and 77.2% accuracy rate. The fourth is identical to the third but uses continuous cursor control instead of a discrete movement selection. It yielded 8.4 wpm and 87.8% accuracy rate. While these four techniques are competitive in terms of speed and accuracy, they can cause physical stress in extended use. Results revealed that the latter two techniques were the least physically demanding but the most frustrating due to slower entry speed.

Min et al. [34] designed an ambiguous Qwerty keyboard that arranges the keys into a 3 × 3 grid (Fig. 3). With this approach, users first select a cell by pressing a button, then select the target character by pressing the button once or multiple times, respective to the position of the character in the cell (like Multi-tap [6]). For instance, to enter the letter "p", users first select the top-right cell, then press the button twice. This method saves space due its smaller size, leaving extra space for work, which is rather important in immersive environments [8]. This method has not yet been evaluated.

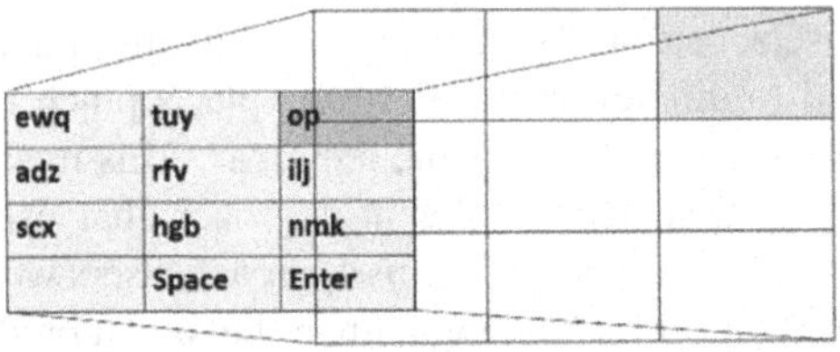

Fig. 3. An ambiguous Qwerty that arranges the keys into a 3 × 3 grid [34].

3.4 Touch-Based Techniques

Some have exploited the popularity of touch-based interaction in VR.

Gugenheimer et al. [35] augmented a 17.78 cm capacitive touchpad on the back of an HMD. They enabled users to enter text by selecting characters on a floating virtual keyboard using the touchpad. They argued that users can use their sense of proprioception to select the correct keys. In an informal evaluation, this approach reached 10 wpm. The challenge with this approach is that it requires users to interact with a trackpad on the back of the HMD, limiting its use to a few scenarios. This method can also cause physical stress when used for an extended period.

Kim and Kim [36] used the hover functionality of a Samsung Galaxy S4 smartphone [37] to enable text entry through its touchscreen. This approach senses the finger using the hover sensor to display its position over a virtual keyboard. Users select a character by either touching the touchscreen or moving the finger beyond the range of the sensor. The former approach enables users to reposition their fingers to correct a selection before leaving the touchscreen. In a user study, these methods reached 7.8 and 9.0 wpm and 79.5% and 92.6% accuracy rate, respectively. The latter approach was more accurate since it enabled users to correct their selections, but at the same time, caused additional physical stress. Although entry speed of these techniques is relatively low, the concept of using hover for text entry in VR is promising.

3.5 Eye Gazing

Many recent HMDs are equipped with eye trackers, making it possible to use eye movements to control the cursor.

Hajana and Ransen [25] studied gaze typing in VR for flat and curved virtual keyboards. They enabled users to select characters by either dwelling on a virtual key for 520 ms or pressing a controller key. The former approach yielded 9.4 and 7.5 wpm, while the latter yielded 10.2 and 9.2 wpm for the flat and curved keyboards, respectively. Accuracy rate for both were over 99%. No significant difference was identified between the curved and flat keyboards.

Ma et al. [38] incorporated a Brain Computer Interface (BCI) with eye gaze for text entry in VR. They combined electric signals from the brain with eye gaze to determine cursor position and selection. Unlike most methods reviewed in this work, this method did not use Qwerty, instead designed an alphabetic layout with 3 rows with 8 characters per row (i.e., first row includes the letters from "a" to "h"). An informal study reported an entry speed of 10.0 wpm, which is relatively low. Yet, this approach could be useful to users with physical disabilities.

3.6 Word-Level Techniques

Word-level text entry techniques have also been explored in VR [26, 39].

Yu et al. [26] investigated gesture typing [40], where users press down a controller key to indicate the start of a gesture, perform the gesture using head movements, then release the button to indicate the end of the gesture. In a user study, this approach reached 24.7 wpm with 94.2% accuracy rate by the 8th session. The accuracy rate of this approach, however, is reliant on the efficiency of its decoder. Further, it has a high physical demand since it requires users to define gesture using expressive head movements.

Popriev et al. [41] and Gonzalez et al. [21] explored handwriting in VR, where users write on an actual tablet using a stylus and the output is displayed on a virtual notepad. This method, however, yielded a low entry speed and accuracy rate, 2.3 wpm and 77%, respectively [21].

4 Novel Virtual Techniques

Many have designed novel keyboard and keypad layouts to facilitate text entry in VR. This section reviews all such techniques.

4.1 Circular and Cubic Layouts

Gonzalez et al. [21] evaluated a circular layout that organizes the letters in an alphabetic order. The keyboard is displayed on a tablet. First, users select a character on the circle using the stylus, then confirm the selection by dragging it to the center of the circle. This approach yielded an entry speed of 4.4 wpm and 98% accuracy rate.

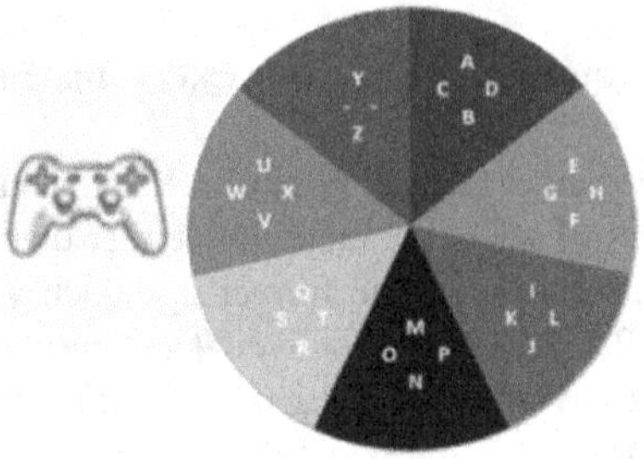

Fig. 4. With the PizzaText keyboard [42], users traverse the keyboard using the right thumbstick and select characters using the left thumbstick.

Yu et al. [42] developed PizzaText, which divides a circle into 7 slices, each containing 4 characters (Fig. 4). Users use the dual thumbsticks of a joystick to interact with this layout [43]—the right thumbstick is used to move around the circular keyboard and the left thumbstick is used to select characters. In a user study, this approach reached 15.9 wpm and 94.6% accuracy rate by the end of the 5th session. Yu et al. [42] evaluated this layout in three different sizes, however, failed to identify a significant difference between the three in terms of speed and accuracy.

4.2 3D Layouts

Most keyboards for VR are in 2D, although virtual environments are in 3D. The Cubic keyboard [44] is a 3D keyboard that arranges the letters in a 3 × 3 × 3 (H × W × D) 3D array. It has 27 cells, 26 for the 26 letters of the English language and a blank cell at the center. Users use a controller to navigate through the cells to select a character. In a pilot study, this approach yielded a competitive entry speed of 21.7 wpm, demanding further exploration of 3D keyboard layouts for VR.

4.3 Hand-Based Techniques

Some have proposed hand-based approaches that map characters onto fingers to reduce the reliance on external hardware.

The BlueTap keyboard [45] maps the letters onto the fingers in an alphabetic order, with at most 4 characters per finger (Fig. 5). Users tap on different parts of the fingers with the thumbs to select characters. This approach uses a wrist worn camera to detect the taps.

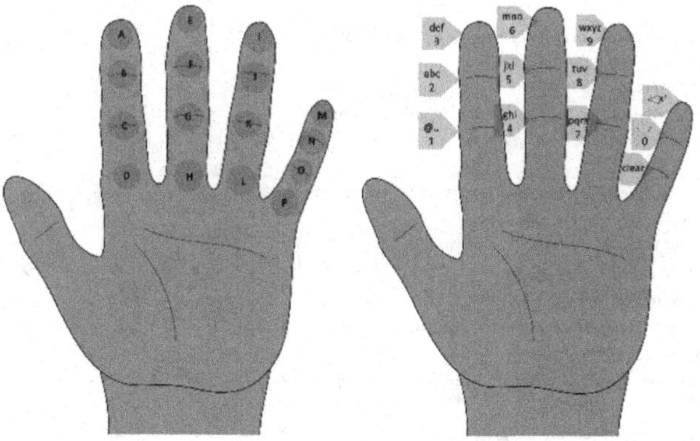

Fig. 5. From left, the BlueTap [45] and the standard 12-key mobile keypad [46] mapped onto the fingers.

Pratorious et al. [46] proposed another approach that maps the standard mobile keypad to the index, middle, and ring fingers. Each knuckle or fingertip includes up to 4 letters (Fig. 5). Like Multi-tap [6], users tap on the knuckle or fingertip once or multiple times, respective to the position of the character. This approach uses a wrist worn camera and an accelerometer to detect the taps. In a pilot study, it yielded 10 wpm.

Ogitani et al. [47] designed a 12-key mobile keypad layout that maps up to 4 characters to each key. With this layout, users tap on the key containing the target character, then swipe towards the direction of the character to enter it (similar to an existing tablet keyboard [48]). They evaluated two techniques using the keypad. The first projects the keypad on the palm and users use the index finger of the other hand to select characters. The second displays the keypad in mid-air and users use their hands to select characters. Both techniques display an animated representation of the hand in the virtual world. These techniques yielded 5.6 wpm and 8.2 wpm, respectively. Interestingly, the authors reported that a projected Qwerty yielded a better entry speed than the keypad, however, did provide further insights into it. We speculate that could be because all participants were familiar with the Qwerty layout.

Although hand-based techniques do not require external devices to function and free up virtual real estate, they do not provide haptic feedback and can cause physical stress. Besides, these techniques force users to perform multiple actions to enter one character, which is a slow approach by design, thus can affect one's overall text entry experience.

Table 4. Virtual text entry techniques with their entry speed in words per minute (wpm) and error rate (%). "Char" signifies "character". Sensors are not considered as auxiliary devices.

Method	Short description	Input unit	Auxiliary devices	Bimanual	Hand tracking	Participant	Session	Entry speed (wpm)	Error rate (%)
Qwerty [26]	*Users move the cursor over a key via head movement, dwell to enter the respective letter*	Char	✗	✗	✗	6	6	10.6	4.2
	Users move the cursor over a key via head movement, enter the respective char by a keypress		Controller					15.6	3.7
	Users gesture type by moving the cursor via head movement while holding down a key	Word	Controller			12	8	24.7	5.8
Qwerty [20, 21, 29]	*Users enter a char by pinching between a thumb and a finger on the same hand, change rows via hand gestures*	Char	Glove	✓	✓	10	1	6.0 [21]	10.0
Qwerty [30]	*Users enter a char by pinching between a thumb and a finger on the same hand*	Char	Glove	✓	✗	✗	✗	✗	✗
Qwerty [31]	*Provides haptic feedback via a glove on each keypress*	Char	P5 Data Glove	✓	✓	✗	✗	✗	✗
Qwerty [35]	*Users select and enter chars via a touchpad behind the HMD*	Char	Touchpad	✗	✗	3	1	10.0	✗
Qwerty [32]	*Users select a key by moving the hand in a thumbs-up position, enter the respective char by folding the thumb*	Char	✗	✗	✓	✗	✗	✗	✗
Qwertz [27]	*Users enter chars by freehand typing in mid-air*	Char	✗	✓	✓	24	1	9.8	7.6
	Users point at keys using controllers, enter a char by pressing a button* or performing a push gesture†		Controller					15.4* 12.7†	1.0* 1.9†
	Users point at keys via direction buttons* or a touchpad†, select a char by pressing a button							5.3* 8.4†	2.8* 2.2†
	Users point at a key by pointing to it with their head & enter it by pressing a button			✗	✗			10.2	1.2
Qwertz [2]	*Users look straight* or down† to see the keyboard*	Char	Camera	✓	✓	24	1	8.8* 11.0†	3.6* 2.7†
Qwerty [36]	*Users select a key by hovering over the keyboard, enter the respective char by touching* or leaving† the screen*	Char	Phone	✗	✗	10	1	9.0* 7.8†	✗ ✗
Qwerty, Cirrin, Pen [21]	*Users use a pen and tablet to enter chars using Qwerty*, Cirrin†, & handwriting‡*	Char	Pen & Tablet	✗	✓	10 28	1	8.2* 2.3† 4.4‡	8.0* 23.0† 2.0‡
Circular PizzaText [42]	*Users use thumbsticks of a controller to enter chars from a circular keyboard containing 7 slices, each with 4 chars*	Char	Controller	✗	✗	10	5	15.9	5.5
BlueTap [45]	*At most four chars are mapped onto all fingers but the thumb, users input by selecting the chars using the thumb*	Char	✗	✓	✓	✗	✗	✗	✗
Qwerty [25]	*Users move the cursor over a flat* and a curved† keyboard via eye movements, enter a char by dwelling for 550 ms*	Char	✗	✗	✗	16	4	9.4* 7.5†	0.02* 0.06†
	Users move the cursor over a flat* and a curved† keyboard via eye movements, enter a char by pressing a button		Controller					10.2* 9.2†	0.07* 0.03†
Mobile Qwerty [34]	*Keys are arranged in a 3 × 3 cell. Users point at a cell via mouse, enter a char using Multi-tap*	Char	Rotational mouse	✓	✓	✗	✗	✗	✗

(continued)

Table 4. (*continued*)

Method	Short description	Input unit	Auxiliary devices	Bimanual	Hand tracking	Participant	Session	Entry speed (wpm)	Error rate (%)
A-Z [38]	*Keys are arranged in 3 rows, each containing 8 chars. Eye movements and electric signals from the brains are combined to enter a char*	Char	EEG	✗	✗	✗	✗	10.0	✗
Cubic [44]	*Keys are arranged in a 3 × 3 × 3 (height, width, and depth) grid. Users enter chars using a tracked controller*	Char	Controller	✓	✗	✗	✗	21.6	✗
12-Key Keypad [47]	*Freehand Multi-tap typing in mid-air using a keypad*	Char	✗	✗	✓	6	5	5.2	16.0
	Keypad is projected on one hand, users Multi-tap using the other hand							5.6	22.0
12-Key Keypad [46, 49]	*Keypad is mapped onto the index, middle, ring fingers, users enter chars by tapping on the fingertips & knuckles with the thumb*	Char	✗	✗	✓	✗	✗	10.0	✗

4.4 Discussion

We can see in Table 4 that both Speicher et al. [27] and Yu et al. [26] investigated head pointing coupled with a controller but Yu et al. reported a 35% faster entry speed than Speicher et al. (15.6 wpm vs. 10.2 wpm). We believe the use of a predictive system contributed towards this—Yu et al. augmented their system with predictive features, including word suggestion and completion. They both reported comparable error rates.

Eye gazing [25] and head pointing [26] coupled with dwelling yielded comparable entry speed (9.4 wpm and 10.6 wpm). Eye gazing was slightly faster (11%), most probably due to the use of a shorter dwell time (400 ms vs. 550 ms). The similarly between the two is further established when coupled with a controller. Eye gazing [25] and head pointing [27] both yielded 10.2 wpm when coupled with a controller. This is most probably because both techniques use similar methods for moving the cursor—one uses the head and the other uses eyes. However, it is worth noting that eye gazing has a lower physical demand than head pointing. Yu et al. [25] showed that word-based input using head gestures increases text entry speed by ~40%, it would be worth investigating how this method performs with eye gazing.

Both Speicher et al. [27] and Yu et al. [42] used directional control—the former used thumbsticks with a circular keyboard and the latter used a directional pad with Qwerty. Although the techniques are different, it is worth mentioning that the circular keyboard yielded a 67% higher entry speed than Qwerty (15.9 wpm vs. 5.3 wpm). This is likely due to the compact nature of the circular keyboard layout, which makes it suitable for navigation using directional control. However, the higher error rate of the circular keyboard (5.5% vs. 2.8%) is likely due to the unfamiliarity with the novel layout.

Interestingly, an embossed mobile keypad [21] yielded a 26% faster entry speed than a smartphone virtual Qwerty [36] (12.1 wpm vs. 9 wpm), regardless of the fact that the keypad used Multi-tap. We believe this result could be attributable to the familiarity of feature phones at that time (2009) and the haptic feedback afforded by the keypads.

Table 5. Error rate metrics reported in the literature.

Error metrics	References
Error rate	[2, 21, 25]
Total error rate	[26, 34, 40]
Corrected error rate	[27]

Table 5 presents the error rate metrics reported in the literature. Evidently, most studies reported either the Error Rate (ER) or the Total Error Rate (TER) metrics. The studies that reported TER also reported the Corrected Error Rate (CER) and Uncorrected Error Rate (UER) metrics. Only one study reported only CER [25]. However, text entry studies often use different methods to calculate the same error metrics. Knierim et al. [10], for instance, used the Minimal String Distance (MSD) algorithm to count the total number of errors, when Rajanna et al. [25] counted the total number of backspaces. A prior work [9] analyzed these metrics and showed how different metrics yield different results. Nevertheless, most studies do not report how they calculate errors.

5 Hand Representation

Grubert et al. [11] investigated the effects of different hand representation on text entry in four conditions: none, animated hands, fingertips, and video inlay of the hands. They failed to identify a significant effect of hand representation on entry speed. However, fingertips and video inlay were significantly more accurate. The task load scores for video inlay were also significantly lower. McGill et al. [12] reported similar results. Knierim et al. [10] also compared different hand representations in four conditions: none, realistic hands, abstract hands, and fingertips. Surprisingly, they found out that hand representation did not affect entry speed or accuracy for experienced typists; but affected entry speed for the inexperienced ones. Evidently, inexperienced typists were significantly slower with no hand representation compared to abstract hand representation.

A different study [50] compared male, female, and robotic hand representations. Results revealed that female participants preferred female hands than male and robotic hands, while male participants were mostly neutral.

6 Conclusion

This paper categorized the existing text entry techniques for VR based on their input mechanism. It discussed their strengths, limitations, and the overall performance. It also highlighted important design considerations for the development of more effective text entry techniques. The goal of this paper is to help researchers to comprehend the mechanism of these techniques, compare their performance, and finally identify and address the gaps in this body of work.

6.1 Future Work

This work highlighted the fact that most existing text entry techniques for VR are adaptations of techniques that were designed and optimized for different form factors. As a result, these techniques fail to address all needs and challenges of the paradigm [27]. In VR, speed and accuracy alone do not entirely reflect the effectiveness of a text entry method—usability, learnability, fatigue, and space requirement must also be taken into consideration. Further, as we continue to seek solutions for virtual office spaces, it is important to consider methods that are not only efficient but also portable.

Due to the unviability of an effective text entry technique, physical Qwerty remains an important tool in VR [8]. Although it is substantially faster than most alternatives, it compromises mobility. Further, it relies on expensive sensors to track hands and fingers for visual feedback, which hinders its widespread use. The reliability of the sensors also poses a challenge [13, 27] as most popular tracking devices are error prone [47]. Hence, there is a need for developing cheaper and more reliable tracking devices for physical Qwerty to be fully embraced in VR. Embedding live video streams of the keyboard and hand in VR is an effective alternative [11, 12]. However, further investigation is needed to identify the optimal level of video stream that does not compromise the immersion. The methods for seamlessly blending the virtual and real worlds must also be explored.

In addition, the effects of various keyboard properties have not yet been fully studied. Yu et al. [42] investigated the effects of different sized circular keyboards and Rajana and Hansen [25] investigated different shaped keyboard in gaze typing. However, the effects of the size, position, type (3D vs. 2D), and shape (flat vs. curved) of different types of keyboards in virtual space is still unexplored.

Good user experience is an important ingredient in successful technologies. This review showed that different approaches can be effective in different scenarios [21, 27]. Hence, the possibility of using different text entry solutions for different scenarios must be explored. For instance, users could use a pointing-based or an ambiguous technique for short-term text entry, then switch to a physical keyboard for heavy text entry sessions. It is also essential that we design alternative text entry techniques specifically for 3D environments, such as the Cubic keyboard [44]. Circular and touch-based keyboards also demand further exploration [36, 42].

References

1. 2019-2024 Global and regional augmented reality and virtual reality industry production sales and consumption status and prospects professional market research report. https://www.360marketupdates.com/2019-2024-global-and-regional-augmented-reality-and-virtual-reality-industry-production-sales-and-consumption-status-and-prospects-professional-market-research-report-13733991
2. Grubert, J., Witzani, L., Ofek, E., Pahud, M., Kranz, M., Kristensson, P.O.: Text entry in immersive head-mounted display-based virtual reality using standard keyboards, pp. 1–8 (2018)
3. Grubert, J., Ofek, E., Pahud, M., Kristensson, P.O.: The office of the future: virtual, portable, and global. IEEE Comput. Graph. Appl. **38**, 125–133 (2018). https://doi.org/10.1109/MCG.2018.2875609

4. Nguyen, C., DiVerdi, S., Hertzmann, A., Liu, F.: CollaVR. In: Proceedings of the 30th Annual ACM Symposium User Interface Software Technology - UIST 2017, pp. 267–277 (2017). https://doi.org/10.1145/3126594.3126659
5. Ma, C., Du, Y., Teng, D., Chen, J., Wang, H., Dai, G.: An adaptive sketching user interface for education system in virtual reality. ITME2009 – Proceedings of the 2009 IEEE International Symposium on IT Medical Education, pp. 796–802 (2009). https://doi.org/10.1109/ITIME.2009.5236314
6. Arif, A.S.: Predicting and reducing the impact of errors in character-based text entry (2013). http://hdl.handle.net/10315/28170
7. Salthouse, T.A.: Effects of age and skill in typing. J. Exp. Psychol. Gen. **113**, 345–371 (1984). https://doi.org/10.1037/0096-3445.113.3.345
8. LaViola Jr., J.J., Kruijff, E., McMahan, R.P., Bowman, D., Poupyrev, I.P.: 3D User Interfaces: Theory and Practice. Addison-Wesley Professional, Boston (2017)
9. Arif, A.S., Stuerzlinger, W.: Analysis of text entry performance metrics. In: Proceedings of the IEEE Toronto International Conference - Science and Technology for Humanity - TIC-STH 2009, pp. 100–105. IEEE (2009). https://doi.org/10.1109/TIC-STH.2009.5444533
10. Knierim, P., Schwind, V., Feit, A.M., Nieuwenhuizen, F., Henze, N.: Physical keyboards in virtual reality: analysis of typing performance and effects of avatar hands. In: Proceedings of the 2018 CHI Conference on Human Factors Computing Systems, pp. 1–9 (2018). https://doi.org/10.1145/3173574.3173919
11. Grubert, J., Witzani, L., Ofek, E., Pahud, M., Kranz, M., Kristensson, P.O.: Effects of hand representations for typing in virtual reality, pp. 1–8 (2018)
12. McGill, M., Boland, D., Murray-Smith, R., Brewster, S.: A Dose of Reality: Overcoming Usability Challenges in VR Head-Mounted Displays. In: Proceedings of the SIGCHI Conference on Human Factors in Computing Systems, pp. 2143–2152 (2015). https://doi.org/10.1145/2702123.2702382
13. Hoppe, A.H., Otto, L., van de Camp, F., Stiefelhagen, R., Unmüßig, G.: qVRty: virtual keyboard with a haptic, real-world representation. In: Stephanidis, C. (ed.) HCI 2018. CCIS, vol. 851, pp. 266–272. Springer, Cham (2018). https://doi.org/10.1007/978-3-319-92279-9_36
14. Bovet, S., Curran, N., Kehoe, A., Gutierrez, M., Rouvinez, T., Crowley, K.: Using traditional keyboards in VR: SteamVR developer kit and pilot game user study. In: The 2018 IEEE Games, Entertainment, Media Conference - GEM 2018, pp. 131–134. IEEE (2018)
15. Introducing the Logitech BRIDGE SDK. https://blog.vive.com/us/2017/11/02/introducing-the-logitech-bridge-sdk/
16. VIVE Pro - The Professional-grade VR Headset. https://www.vive.com/us/product/vive-pro
17. Kim, S., Kim, G.J.: Using keyboards with head mounted displays. In: Proceedings of the VRCAI 2004 - ACM SIGGRAPH International Conference on Virtual Reality Continuum and its Applications in Industry, pp. 336–343 (2004). https://doi.org/10.1145/1044588.1044662
18. Walker, J., Li, B., Vertanen, K., Kuhl, S.: Efficient typing on a visually occluded physical keyboard. In: Proceedings of the 2017 CHI Conference on Human Factors in Computing Systems - CHI 2017. pp. 5457–5461. ACM Press, New York (2017). https://doi.org/10.1145/3025453.3025783
19. Vertanen, K., Memmi, H., Emge, J., Reyal, S., Kristensson, P.O.: VelociTap: investigating fast mobile text entry using sentence-based decoding of touchscreen keyboard input. In: Proceedings of the 33rd Annual ACM Conference on Human Factors in Computing Systems - CHI 2015, pp. 659–668 (2015). https://doi.org/10.1145/2702123.2702135

20. Bowman, D.A., Rhoton, C.J., Pinho, M.S.: Text input techniques for immersive virtual environments: an empirical comparison. In: Proceedings of the Human Factors and Ergonomics Society Annual Meeting, vol. 46, pp. 2154–2158 (2002). https://doi.org/10.1177/154193120204602611
21. González, G., Molina, J.P., García, A.S., Martínez, D., González, P.: Evaluation of text input techniques in immersive virtual environments. In: Macías, J., Granollers Saltiveri, A., Latorre, P. (eds.) New Trends on Human-Computer Interaction, pp. 109–118. Springer, (2009). https://doi.org/10.1007/978-1-84882-352-5_11
22. Lin, J.-W., et al.: Visualizing the keyboard in virtual reality for enhancing immersive experience. In: ACM SIGGRAPH 2017 Posters - SIGGRAPH 2017, vol. 1, pp. 1–2 (2017). https://doi.org/10.1145/3102163.3102175
23. P.I. Engineering: X-keys Computer Input Devices. https://xkeys.com/xkeys.html
24. Leap Motion. https://www.leapmotion.com/
25. Rajanna, V., Hansen, J.P.: Gaze typing in virtual reality: impact of keyboard design, selection method, and motion. In: Proceedings of the 2018 ACM Symposium on Eye Tracking Research and Applications - ETRA 2018, pp. 1–10. ACM Press, New York (2018). https://doi.org/10.1145/3204493.3204541
26. Yu, C., Gu, Y., Yang, Z., Yi, X., Luo, H., Shi, Y.: Tap, dwell or gesture?: exploring head-based text entry techniques for HMDs. In: Proceedings of the 2017 CHI Conference on Human Factors in Computing Systems - CHI 2017, pp. 4479–4488. ACM Press, New York (2017). https://doi.org/10.1145/3025453.3025964
27. Speicher, M., Feit, A.M., Ziegler, P., Krüger, A.: Selection-based text entry in virtual reality. In: Proceedings of the 2018 CHI Conference on Human Factors in Computing Systems - CHI 2018, pp. 1–13. ACM Press, New York (2018). https://doi.org/10.1145/3173574.3174221
28. Majaranta, P., Ahola, U., Špakov, O.: Fast gaze typing with an adjustable dwell time. In: Proceedings of the 27th international conference on Human factors in computing systems - CHI 2009, p. 357. ACM Press, New York (2009). https://doi.org/10.1145/1518701.1518758
29. Bowman, D.A , Ly, V.Q., Campbell, J.M.: Pinch keyboard: natural text input for immersive virtual environments. Virginia Tech Department of Computer Science Technical report (2001)
30. Mehring, C., Kuester, F., Singh, K.D., Chen, M.: KITTY: keyboard independent touch typing in VR. In: Proceedings - Virtual Reality Annual International Symposium, pp. 243–244 (2004). https://doi.org/10.1109/VR.2004.1310090
31. Wu, C.-M., Hsu, C.-W., Lee, T.-K., Smith, S.: A virtual reality keyboard with realistic haptic feedback in a fully immersive virtual environment. Virtual Real. **21**, 19–29 (2017). https://doi.org/10.1007/s10055-016-0296-6
32. Ishii, A., Adachi, T., Shima, K., Nakamae, S., Shizuki, B., Takahashi, S.: FistPointer: target selection technique using mid-air interaction for mobile VR environment. In: Proceedings of the 2017 CHI Conference Extended Abstracts on Human Factors in Computing Systems, p. 474 (2017). https://doi.org/10.1145/3027063.3049795
33. Markussen, A., Jakobsen, M.R., Hornbæk, K.: Selection-based mid-air text entry on large displays. In: Kotzé, P., Marsden, G., Lindgaard, G., Wesson, J., Winckler, M. (eds.) INTERACT 2013. LNCS, vol. 8117, pp. 401–418. Springer, Heidelberg (2013). https://doi.org/10.1007/978-3-642-40483-2_28
34. Min, K.: Text input tool for immersive vr based on 3 × 3 screen cells. In: Lee, G., Howard, D., Ślęzak, D. (eds.) ICHIT 2011. LNCS, vol. 6935, pp. 778–786. Springer, Heidelberg (2011). https://doi.org/10.1007/978-3-642-24082-9_94

35. Gugenheimer, J., Dobbelstein, D., Winkler, C., Haas, G., Rukzio, E.: FaceTouch: enabling touch interaction in display fixed uis for mobile virtual reality. In: Proceedings of the ACM User Interface Software and Technology (UIST 2016), 49–60 (2016). https://doi.org/10.1145/2984511.2984576
36. Kim, Y.R., Kim, G.J.: HoVR-type: smartphone as a typing interface in VR using hovering. In: 2017 IEEE International Conference on Consumer Electronics, ICCE 2017, pp. 200–203 (2017). https://doi.org/10.1109/ICCE.2017.7889285
37. Petrovan, B.: Galaxy S4 to feature floating touch, highly efficient AMOLED display. https://www.androidauthority.com/galaxy-s4-floating-touch-display-167326/
38. Ma, X., Yao, Z., Wang, Y., Pei, W., Chen, H.: Combining brain-computer interface and eye tracking for high-speed text entry in virtual reality. In: Proceedings of the 2018 Conference on Human Information Interaction - IUI 2018. Part F1351, pp. 263–267 (2018). https://doi.org/10.1145/3172944.3172988
39. Jimenez, J.G., Schulze, J.P.: Continuous-motion text input in virtual reality. Electron. Imaging 450-1–450-6 (2018). https://doi.org/10.2352/ISSN.2470-1173.2018.03.ERVR-450
40. Alvina, J., Malloch, J., Mackay, W.E.: Expressive keyboards: enriching gesture-typing on mobile devices. In: Proceedings of the 29th Annual Symposium on User Interface Software and Technology - UIST 2016, pp. 583–593. ACM Press, New York (2016). https://doi.org/10.1145/2984511.2984560
41. Poupyrev, I., Tomokazu, N., Weghorst, S.: Virtual notepad: handwriting in immersive VR. In: Proceedings of the IEEE 1998 Virtual Reality Annual International Symposium (Cat. No.98CB36180), pp. 126–132 (1998). https://doi.org/10.1109/VRAIS.1998.658467
42. Yu, D., Fan, K., Zhang, H., Monteiro, D., Xu, W., Liang, H.: PizzaText: text entry for virtual reality systems using dual thumbsticks. IEEE Trans. Vis. Comput. Graph. **24**, 2927–2935 (2018). https://doi.org/10.1109/TVCG.2018.2868581
43. Wilson, A.D., Agrawala, M.: Text entry using a dual joystick game controller. In: Proceedings of the SIGCHI Conference on Human Factors in Computing Systems, pp. 475–478. ACM, New York (2006). https://doi.org/10.1145/1124772.1124844
44. Yanagihara, N., Shizuki, B.: Cubic keyboard for virtual reality. In: Proceedings of the Symposium on Spatial User Interaction - SUI 2018, pp. 170–170. ACM Press, New York (2018). https://doi.org/10.1145/3267782.3274687
45. BlueTap—The Ultimate Virtual-Reality (VR) Keyboard. https://medium.com/eunoia-i-o/bluetap-the-ultimate-virtual-reality-vr-keyboard-77f1e3d57d6f
46. Prätorius, M., Valkov, D., Burgbacher, U., Hinrichs, K.: DigiTap: an eyes-free VR/AR symbolic input device. In: Proceedings of the 20th ACM Symposium on Virtual Reality Software and Technology, pp. 9–18. ACM, New York (2014). https://doi.org/10.1145/2671015.2671029
47. Ogitani, T., Arahori, Y., Shinyama, Y., Gondow, K.: Space saving text input method for head mounted display with virtual 12-key keyboard. In: 2018 IEEE 32nd International Conference on Advanced Information Networking and Applications, pp. 342–349 (2018). https://doi.org/10.1109/AINA.2018.00059
48. Arif, A.S., Pahud, M., Hinckley, K., Buxton, B.: Experimental study of stroke shortcuts for a touchscreen keyboard with gesture-redundant keys removed. In: Proceedings of the 2014 Graphics Interface Conference - GI 2014, pp. 43–50. Canadian Information Processing Society (2014). https://doi.org/10.20380/GI2014.06

49. Prätorius, M., Burgbacher, U., Valkov, D., Hinrichs, K.: Sensing thumb-to-finger taps for symbolic input in VR/AR environments. IEEE Comput. Graph. Appl. **35**, 42–54 (2015). https://doi.org/10.1109/MCG.2015.106
50. Schwind, V., Knierim, P., Tasci, C., Franczak, P., Haas, N., Henze, N.: These are not my hands! In: Proceedings of 2017 CHI Conference on Human Factors in Computing Systems - CHI 2017, pp. 1577–1582 (2017). https://doi.org/10.1145/3025453.3025602

Evaluation of the Degree of Heat Conduction with the da Vinci Surgical System

Akihiro Hamada[1], Atsuro Sawada[1], Jin Kono[1], Masanao Koeda[2], Katsuhiko Onishi[2], Takashi Kobayashi[1], Toshinari Yamasaki[1], Takahiro Inoue[1], Hiroshi Noborio[2], and Osamu Ogawa[1](✉)

[1] Department of Urology, Graduate School of Medicine, Kyoto University, Kyoto, Japan
{ahamada, ogawao}@kuhp.kyoto-u.ac.jp

[2] Department of Computer Science, Osaka Electro-Communication University, Osaka, Japan

Abstract. Laparoscopic surgery enabled surgeons to perform more minimally invasive surgery compared with conventional open surgery. Besides, robotic surgery has become more common in many fields, thus, facilitating performance of more precise procedures. As the performance of the devices improved, surgeons aim at not only cure of the disease, but also at preservation of the organ function. One of the causes of damage to normal tissue is "heat" generated during tissue dissection or hemostasis. However, there are few reports that analyzed the amount of heat generated by surgical devices and the associated tissue damage.

We evaluated the degree of heat conduction and tissue damage using electrical devices of the da Vinci Xi Surgical System (dVSS). Cauterized samples were obtained using dVSS monopolar curved scissors with the setting on cut or coagulation mode. We measured the range of heat conduction in the area by thermography. We also evaluated the damage to tissue, based on macroscopic findings and pathological features.

In point cauterization using the coagulation mode, macroscopic tissue damage was greater ($p = 0.012$) and tissue damage was deeper ($p = 0.011$) than those on the cut mode. Maximum tissue temperature was higher for the coagulation mode than for the cut mode. Time to cool down from the maximum temperature to 60 °C and 40 °C was longer in the coagulation mode.

These results suggested that the use of cut mode for a short time may be acceptable in situations where minimal heat-induced tissue damage is required in the robotic surgery.

Keywords: Robotic surgery · Heat conduction · Thermography

1 Introduction

The primary aim of surgery, especially in cancer treatment, is curing the disease. To increase the possibility of curing the disease, extended radical operation with adequate surgical margin is needed. However, when resecting extensively, the damage to the surrounding normal tissue may lead to functional disorder and may have a significant

M. Kurosu (Ed.): HCII 2019, LNCS 11567, pp. 438–446, 2019.
https://doi.org/10.1007/978-3-030-22643-5_34

impact on the patient's quality of life. As the performance of the devices has improved, surgeons aim at not only cure of the disease, but also at preservation of the organ function. Especially in robotic surgery, the improvement of the visual field by 3D cameras and precise motion by articulated arms enable a fine procedure, which is useful for both curing the disease and preserving the organ function. However, it is still challenging to achieve early recovery of urinary continence in robot assisted radical prostatectomy (RARP) or to preserve renal function in robot assisted partial nephrectomy (RAPN).

One of the causes of damage to normal tissue is the heat generated during tissue dissection or hemostasis. Several studies report that athermal procedures around important organs, such as vessels or nerves, are needed to avoid heat damage [1–4]. The evaluation of energy devices focused on thermal spread and tissue damage have been reported in some fields. For example, Kwak et al. and Coughlin et al. reported thermal injury of the laryngeal nerve during thyroid surgery using intraoperative neuromonitoring [5, 6]. However, how the robotic energy devices damage the surrounding tissue is still not known.

The aim of the present study was to evaluate the degree of heat conduction and the associated tissue damage when using the robotic electrical devices by thermography and pathological examination.

2 Materials and Methods

2.1 Selection of Tissue

The liver of cows was chosen as the sample tissue since both macroscopic and microscopic findings can be easily be evaluated with liver tissue. Each sample was cut into 15 × 15 × 20 mm sized pieces. The tissue was then placed on a stainless steel board covered by gauze soaked in saline. We attached a return electrode to the back of the board.

2.2 Devices

da Vinci Surgical System. We used the da Vinci Xi Surgical System (dVSS, Intuitive Surgical, CA, U.S.) electrical devices (Fig. 1) [7]. The energy generator was the ERBE VIO system. The output of energy was fixed at Effect 2 during the whole experiment.

Infrared Thermography. We used the Optris infrared thermometer system Xi400 model (Optris GmbH, Berlin, Germany). The thermometer was set 20 cm above the tissue and monitored the degree of heat conduction. The change in tissue temperature over time were analyzed. The device configurations are as follows:

Model: Optris Xi400: 382 × 288 Pixel/80 Hz
Lens: 29° × 22°lens/f = 12.7 mm
Temperature range: −20–100 °C
Measurement accuracy: ±2 °C or ±2%

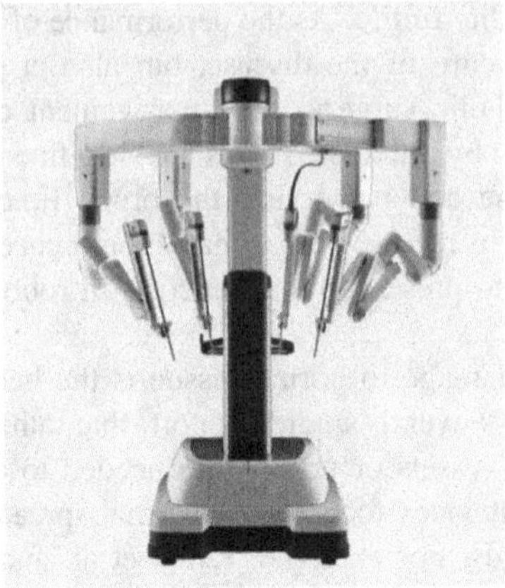

Fig. 1. da Vinci Xi Surgical System (dVSS).

2.3 Group Setting

Cauterization of sample tissues was performed using dVSS monopolar curved scissors in the setting of cut mode or coagulation mode. Tissue was cauterized for one second using the tip of the blade (point cauterization group) or the back face of the blade (back face cauterization group) (Fig. 2). The tissue samples were divided into four groups: Mode setting: cut or coagulation; Cauterization style: point or back face. Five pieces of tissue were examined in each group.

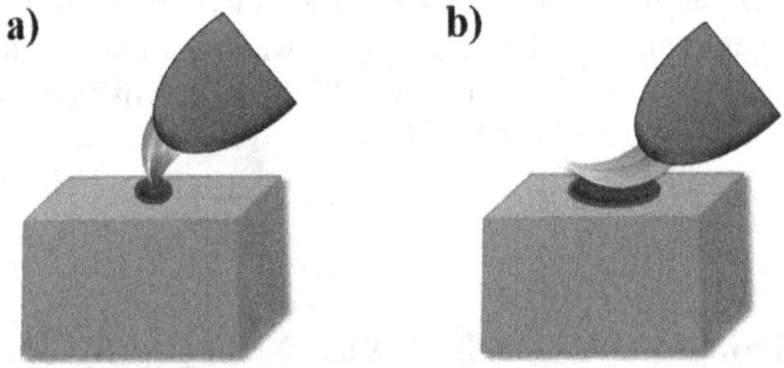

Fig. 2. Technique for tissue cauterization. (a) Point cauterization (b) Back face cauterization

2.4 Evaluation of Outcomes

Macroscopic Evaluation. We assessed the macroscopic findings in each groups. After cauterization, tissues were denatured macroscopically and the tissue color changed. Therefore, the long diameter (a) and short diameter (b) of the color changing area were measured (Fig. 3).

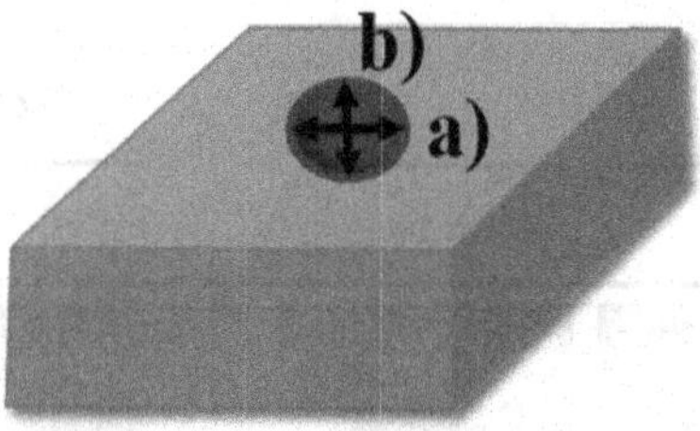

Fig. 3. Macroscopic findings: (a) Long diameter (b) Short diameter

Evaluation of Temperature. We recorded tissue temperature changes by thermography and measured the long diameter of the area at a temperature >60 °C. We compared the temperature-changing area with the macroscopic findings. We also evaluated the maximum tissue temperature and time to cool down from maximum temperature to 60 °C and to 40 °C.

Microscopic Evaluation. Tissues were formalin-fixed and stained with hematoxylin and eosin. We measured the depth of the area of tissue damage and assessed the surface feature after cauterization in each group.

2.5 Statistical Methods

Statistical analysis was performed using JMP®, Version 14.0 (SAS Institute., Cary, NC, U.S.). Mann-Whitney U test was performed to assess continuous variables. All statistical analysis consisted of two-tailed tests with a statistical significance of $p < 0.05$.

3 Results

3.1 Macroscopic Findings of Tissue Damage Compared with the Rise of Temperature

In the point cauterization groups, the color changing tissue area and the area of the tissue at a temperature >60 °C were greater in the coagulation mode than in the cut mode. In the coagulation mode, carbonization (black coagulation) was found macroscopically on the surface (Fig. 4).

In the back face cauterization groups, heat spread unevenly in the cut mode, while it spread evenly in the coagulation mode. The edge of the cauterization area was irregular in the cut mode and regular in the coagulation mode.

3.2 Evaluation of the Length and Area

We showed the comparison of the long diameter in each group (Table 1). The long diameter of the macroscopic color changing area and of the area at a temperature >60 °C were approximately the same for each condition.

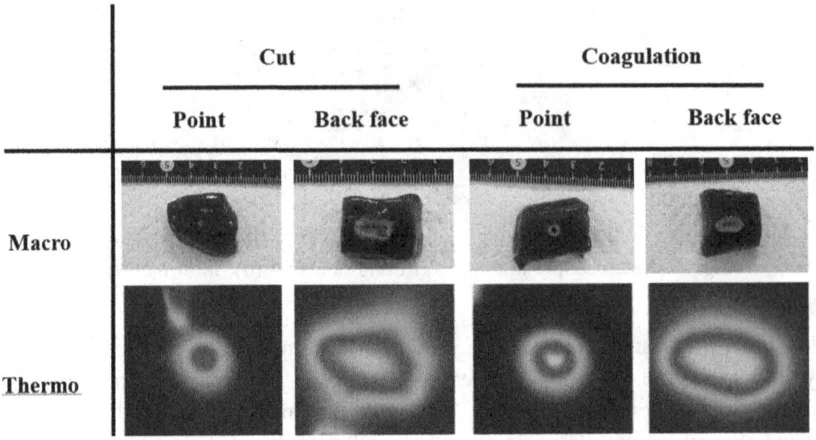

Fig. 4. Macroscopic and thermography findings in each group.

Table 1. Length of long diameter in each group (mean value is shown)

		Cut	Coagualtion
Point	Macroscopic (mm)	2.3	4.1
	Thermography (mm)	2.7	4.5
Back face	Macroscopic (mm)	10	10.8
	Thermography (mm)	10.5	10.8

In the point cauterization groups, macroscopic long diameter of tissue damage was longer ($p = 0.011$) and area of tissue damage (long diameter × short diameter) was larger ($p = 0.012$) in the coagulation mode than in the cut mode. In addition, also the depth of tissue damage was longer ($p = 0.011$) in the coagulation mode than in cut mode (Fig. 5).

In the back face cauterization groups, macroscopic long diameter of tissue damage, area of tissue damage and depth of tissue damage were not significantly different between both modes (Fig. 6).

3.3 Maximum Temperature and Time to Cool Down

We evaluated the maximum tissue temperature and the respective cool down time from the maximum temperature to 60 °C or 40 °C (Fig. 7). In the point cauterization groups, maximum tissue temperature of the center area was higher for the coagulation mode than for the cut mode. In both cauterization groups, time to cool down from maximum temperature to 60 °C or 40 °C was longer in the coagulation mode than in the cut mode (Table 2).

1) Macroscopic long diameter of tissue damage.

2) Macroscopic area of tissue damage (long diameter × short diameter).

3) Depth of tissue damage.

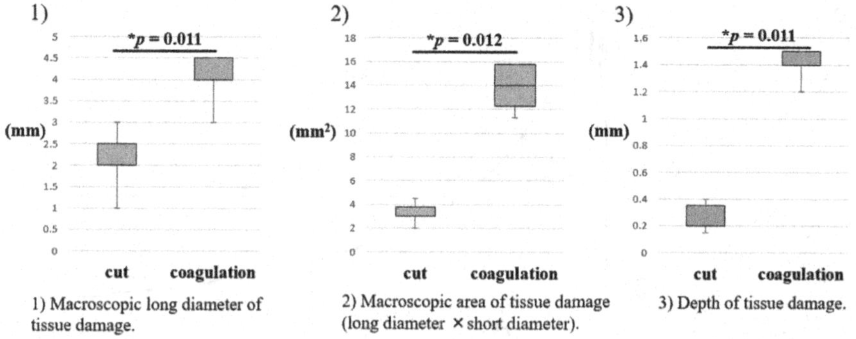

Fig. 5. Graphic representation of each of the setting parameters in the point cauterization groups. (1) Macroscopic long diameter of tissue damage; (2) Macroscopic area of tissue damage (long diameter × short diameter); (3) Depth of tissue damage.

1) Macroscopic long diameter of tissue damage.

2) Macroscopic area of tissue damage (long diameter × short diameter).

3) Depth of tissue damage.

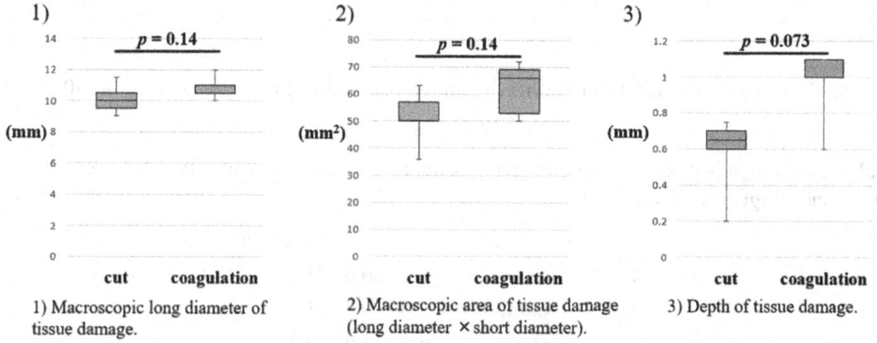

Fig. 6. Graphic representation of each of the setting parameters in the back face cauterization groups. (1) Macroscopic long diameter of tissue damage; (2) Macroscopic area of tissue damage (long diameter × short diameter); (3) Depth of tissue damage.

3.4 Comparison of Microscopic Features

The surface after cauterization was regular and sharp in the point cauterization by cut mode group. Instead, in the point cauterization by coagulation mode group, the edge was irregular and presented carbonization (what is called "black coagulation"), in which protein denaturation was reached greatly by heat conduction.

In the back face cauterization groups, the surface was retained in both cut and coagulation mode, but tissue damage was seen in deep area. The tissue damage was more severe in the coagulation mode than in the cut mode (Fig. 8).

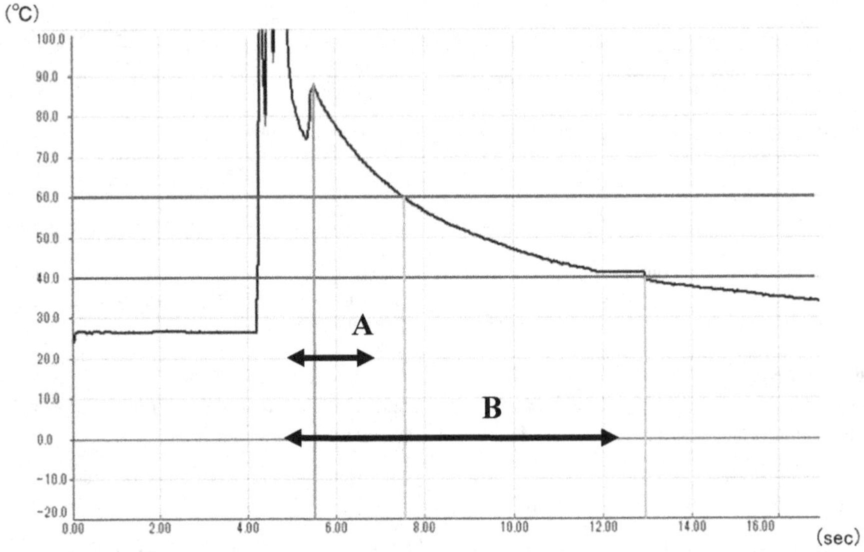

Fig. 7. Cool down time from the maximum temperature (A) to 60 °C and (B) to 40 °C.

Table 2. Comparison of the maximum temperature and time to cool down between the cut mode and coagulation mode groups.

		Cut	Coagualtion
Point	Max temp. (°C)	60.6	81.9
	Time to 60 °C (s)	0.3	1.8
	Time to 40 °C (s)	1.4	6.5
Back face	Max temp. °C (s)	83.7	87.7
	Time to 60 °C (s)	3.7	6.8
	Time to 40 °C (s)	17.3	23.5

4 Discussion

In this study, the long diameter of macroscopic denaturation and of the area at a temperature >60 °C in thermography was approximately the same in all groups. This means that tissue denatured macroscopically at temperatures >60 °C, as described previously [8]. In point cauterization method, macroscopic area of tissue damage was significantly larger and deeper by coagulation mode than by cut mode. The thermography showed that maximum tissue temperature was higher on coagulation mode than on cut mode in both point and back face cauterization methods. Besides, time to cool down from the maximum temperature to 60 °C and to 40 °C was longer for the coagulation mode than for the cut mode.

The reason for the differences between cut mode and coagulation mode is thought to result from patterns of output waveform. On cut mode, waveform is continuous and

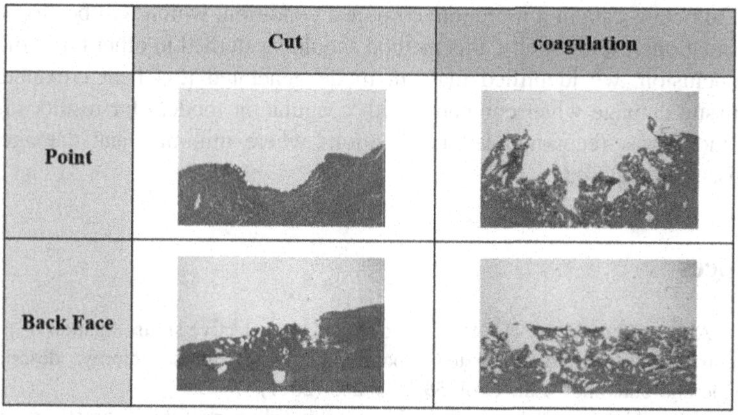

Fig. 8. Pathological findings after tissue cauterization in each mode.

low voltage, while on coagulation mode, it is intermittent and high voltage. Continuous waveform causes the rapid increase of tissue temperature, which is suitable for tissue vaporization and tissue cutting. On the other hand, because the duration of the current flowing in intermittent waveform is shorter, the cutting effect decreases on coagulation mode. Furthermore, it is considered that the thickness of coagulation layer (or tissue damage) depends on the voltage [9]. Our microscopic findings supported this theory. On cut mode, tissue damage of cutting edge is small due to the low voltage, while tissue damage of cutting edge is large due to the high voltage on coagulation mode. As a result, we should select cut mode if we want to keep tissue damage to a minimum or, select coagulation mode if hemostasis is needed. In our study, back face cauterization retained the surface and showed less cutting effect when compared with point cauterization. It is supposed that when the contact area of the energy device is wide, the current spread out to the tissue and cutting effect was then reduced.

Especially in robotic-assisted laparoscopic surgery, effective hemostasis leads to a reduction of blood loss keeping the operation field clear, and allowing a more precise procedure, which consequently shortens the operation time, and reduces complications and necessary preservation of organ function. Therefore, surgeons are required to use properly cut mode and coagulation mode in monopolar, being the latest the most commonly used in several surgical situations. There is no report that describes the rise of tissue temperature and the degree of tissue damage according to the mode setting of dVSS. Consequently, this study is a first step towards a good understanding of dVSS energy devices.

There are some limitations in this study. First, electric resistance of cow liver tissue was different from real tissues in the human body, because of the difference of distance between cauterization and return electrode. Thus, this study shows only relative comparisons between cut and coagulation. Secondly, thermography only measured surface temperature of the tissue, and another device is needed to assess temperature in the deep tissue. Lastly, the ability of hemostasis on either mode was not evaluated.

We need to obtain data in a more intracorporeal condition, which will be closer to real surgery situations. Additionally, this method should be studied in other types of tissues.

In conclusion, we identified that cut mode generated less heat conduction and smaller tissue damage when compared with coagulation mode. Our results suggested that cut mode was recommended in situations where minimal heat damage to the normal tissue is required.

References

1. Lei, Y., Alemozaffar, M., et al.: Athermal division and selective suture ligation of the dorsal vein complex during robot-assisted laparoscopic radical prostatectomy: description of technique and outcomes. Eur. Urol. **59**, 235–243 (2011)
2. Tewari, A.K., Ali, A., et al.: Functional outcomes following robotic prostatectomy using athermal, traction free risk-stratified grades of nerve sparing. World J. Urol. **31**, 471–480 (2013)
3. Tewari, A., Takenaka, A., et al.: The proximal neurovascular plate and the tri-zonal neural architecture around the prostate gland: importance in the athermal robotic technique of nerve-sparing prostatectomy. BJU Int. **98**, 314–323 (2006)
4. Coughlin, G., Dangle, P.P., et al.: Athermal early retrograde release of the neurovascular bundle during nerve-sparing robotic-assisted laparoscopic radical prostatectomy. J. Robot. Surg. **3**, 13–17 (2009)
5. Kwak, H.Y., Dionigi, G., et al.: Thermal injury of the recurrent laryngeal nerve by THUNDERBEAT during thyroid surgery: findings from continuous intraoperative neuromonitoring in a porcine model. J. Surg. Res. **200**, 177–182 (2016)
6. Yang, X., Cao, J., et al.: Comparison of the safety of electrotome, Harmonic scalpel, and LigaSure for management of thyroid surgery. Head Neck **39**, 1078–1085 (2017)
7. Intuitive HP. https://www.intuitive.com/en/products-and-services
8. Thomsen, S.: Pathologic analysis of photothermal and photomechanical effects of laser-tissue interactions. Photochem. Photobiol. **53**, 825–835 (1991)
9. Electrosurgery Use and practical tips. Erbe Elektromedizin GmbH (2017)

A Design of Augmented-Reality Smart Window Using Directive Information Fusion Technology for Exhibitions

Chun-Yen Huang[1(✉)], Li-Hung Wang[1], Wei-Lin Hsu[1], Kuo-Ping Chang[1], Fu-Ren Lin[2], Heng-Yin Chen[1], Kuan-Ting Chen[1], and Jia-Chong Ho[1]

[1] Industrial Technology Research Institute (ITRI), Hsinchu, Taiwan (R.O.C.)
{CYHuang0427,LiHungWang,WayneHsu,KPChang,che0319,william0917,jcho}@itri.org.tw

[2] Institute of Service Science, National Tsing Hua University, Hsinchu, Taiwan (R.O.C.)
frlin@iss.nthu.edu.tw

Abstract. In this paper, we present a design of augmented-reality (AR) smart window with directive information fusion technology. Typically, a showcase used in exhibitions is a glass cabinet used to display exhibits for viewing. However, if visitors want to get more information about the exhibit or identify a specific object in the showcase, they need to check label cards attached beside the showcase, which seriously distracts their attention to the exhibit at the moment. In order to create a more intuitive user's experience for museum visitors, an AR smart window system has been established. By the use of flexible transparent AMOLED display, the window is not only a case to display exhibits, but also a display to show their description. What's more, the AR smart window is integrated with directive information fusion technology which is based on eye tracking and object recognition technique, enabling the information to always show on the user's eyesight to the exhibit no matter how the user moves. This novel system not only makes exhibitions more intelligent and user-friendly but also brings a whole new interactive experience for visitors in exhibitions.

Keywords: Augmented-reality · Smart window · Transparent display · Eye tracking · Object recognition

1 Introduction

Display is an important issue in exhibition design. The typical way to display exhibits is to put them in showcases with transparent glass or plastic [1, 2]. However, although the showcases function as good protection for the exhibits, the poor design of current showcases indirectly intervenes the interaction between visitors and the exhibits, resulting in much negative visiting experience to users. For instance, if a visitor wants to get the description of an exhibit while observing it, normally he needs to check a label card with description attached beside the showcase, which distracts his attention

M. Kurosu (Ed.): HCII 2019, LNCS 11567, pp. 447–457, 2019.
https://doi.org/10.1007/978-3-030-22643-5_35

from the exhibit [2]. This negative experience will be even more serious in large showcases. Mostly, large showcases are used to display plentiful of exhibits [1, 3]. However, it will cause a visitor to feel difficult to distinguish and identify a specific exhibit while reading the description. In these situations, not only the visitor's experience is negatively influenced, but the information of the exhibits is also hardly conveyed to the visitor.

In order to improve visitor experience in exhibitions, an AR smart window system using directive information fusion technology is developed. The window is integrated with a transparent AMOLED display on its front side, and visitors can select any object behind the AMOLED display to make object-related information show on the display [4, 5]. In this way, visitors can check the description directly while observing the exhibits [1, 6, 7]. Moreover, the AR smart window combines the function of directive information fusion technology. This is the technology that allows the information of exhibits to be placed at a proper position which is always aligned with a visitor's eyesight and the object. When a visitor selects an exhibit behind the AMOLED display and touches the display, directive information fusion technology makes the touch point directive by connecting the location of the touch point, visitor's eyes and the display. Through the directive touch point, the information of the exhibit will always show at the correct place no matter how the visitor moves, which is a more intuitive way to get the information of the exhibit [6].

2 Related Work

The science fiction movies revealed many applications for the transparent display system such as communication, advertisement, and entertainment etc. As a result, a lot of studies emerged to explore the possibilities of the potential amplifications. Heo et al. proposed the TransWall which is a transparent display that can show the information on the both sides of the display [6]. Its touch function enables the user to interact with the other one on the opposite side. Li et al. proposed a two-sided collaborative transparent display that the users on the both sides of the transparent display can work on the same project using the gesture, gaze and touch etc. [4]. Moreover, the information shown on the display is also available for the two users. Kim et al. presented the TransLayer, which is a transparent touch display floating of a large display table [8]. Through the TransLayer, the user can interact with the display table by touch. Xi et al. introduced the interactive lecture system using the transparent display that it makes the instructor to seem being in the same place with the students [9].

Based on an intensive market research and evaluation process, Li et al. revealed that the interactive show-window is a designed solution that the connection between the customer and the product is reinforced by emphasizing customized product visualization and direct interactivity [10]. To select an object behind the display, the relative distance between the length of the arm and the height of the eye are used by Hirakawa et al. [5]. However, the length of the arm and the height of the eye are different between each person, and it leads to the inaccuracy of the selection. To avoid the binocular parallax, Lee et al. proposed a quantitative measure called Binocular Selectability Discriminant (BSD) [11]. However, the working distance is fixed and therefore the user is confined to a fixed range. Yoshimura et al. proposed binocular interface for the far working distance that the user is unable to reach the transparent display [12]. Its prototype uses the basis of the positions of eyes and a finger detected by an RGB-D camera to achieve pointing positions.

Augmented reality (AR) technology was first introduced in 1990. It refers to the position and angle of image acquired through the camera. Through image analysis technology, virtual objects are combined with real-world scenes on the display device to provide interaction. Milgram and Kishino proposed a concept of Reality-Virtuality Continuum, which treats the real environment and the virtual environment as two ends of a continuous system [13]. Virtual reality is combined virtual object in a totally virtual environment, while augmented reality is superimposed virtual object into a real environment. Azuma proposed that augmented reality should include three characteristics: combining virtual objects with the real environment, instant interaction, and presenting in three dimensions [14]. Augmented reality technology requires both hardware and software support. The hardware part contains the processor, display, sensor and input device. The software part is mainly the algorithm of coordinate operation and virtual object interaction that has many software development kits as support, such as Unity Vuforia, ARKit, ARCore, ARToolKit etc.

Due to the increase in processor computing, the application of augmented reality is becoming more diverse. The application of augmented reality is spread across industries such as military [15], industry [16], education [17] and game [18]. Andersen et al. proposed the STAR which is a novel surgical AR system that using a virtual transparent display with telementoring to train the skills of trainee on surgeons [19]. Selvam, Yap, Ng, Tong, and Ho developed an information application that using AR technology to enhance users' experience in museum exhibition [20]. Their system provided an interactive experience to users who could hold the smartphone to see the information of a specific marker. But the tracking of the markers is unreliable when the system doesn't have 3D tracking. Rodrigues et al. proposed the adaptive user interface (UI) for implementing AR museum. In their study presented a framework and an initial object recognition of the marker for the museum which was integrated AR technology [21].

3 Method

3.1 Implementation

In this section, we will elaborate how the AR smart window system operates and how directive information fusion technology is adopted in the system. The construction of the window system is also illustrated as below.

Software. Figure 1 shows the software structure of the AR smart window. Two important functions are adopted in the AR smart window system using directive information fusion technology: object recognition and eye tracking. The system keeps recognizing objects behind the AMOLED display and calculating their locations. After their locations are identified, the system will create initial region of interest (ROI) areas of the objects by the process of coordinate transformation. Meanwhile, the system is also detecting users in front of the AMOLED display, and calculating the eye position of a user. The calculated eye position will be used as a variable to calibrate the ROI areas of the objects. Next, the system matches the user's touch point on the display and the accurate ROI areas of the objects to show the information of the objects at a proper position on the display. In doing so, the user will always see the information on his eyesight to the object no matter how he moves.

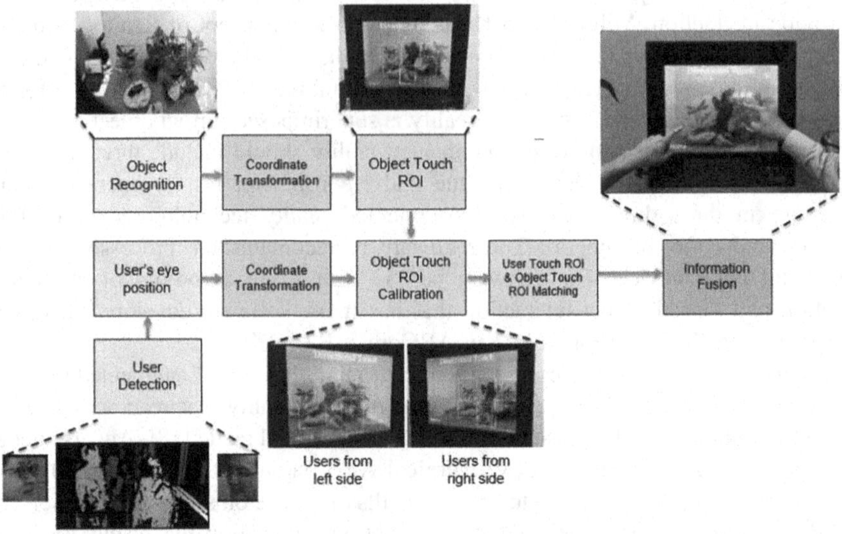

Fig. 1. The software structure of the AR smart window

As shown in Fig. 2, A user from left side wants to realize more about the butterfly, and another user from right side wants to get the information of the dragonfly. After they both touch the display, the system is able to respond correct information to the corresponding users because the users' eye positions are also calculated. Hence, although the positions of their touch point are close, due to the difference of the eye positions, the information will also be different and show to its correspondent target users.

Hardware. The AR smart window consists of two camera modules, one touch module, a display module and a host. The first camera module is called in-camera module, which is used to detect user's eye position; the other camera, or out-camera module, functions as a module to process object recognition. These two are 3D stereo OV-580 camera. The touch module used in the system is Airbar, which is an optical touch sensor. The physical arrangement of hardware modules used in the AR smart window as shown in Fig. 3. The display module is a transparent AMOLED display, whose size is 17 inch with a resolution of 640 * 480 and a frame rate of 60 Hz. The host is a gaming computer with RAM of 16G and GPU of 6G. The integration of the AR smart window system is shown in Fig. 4.

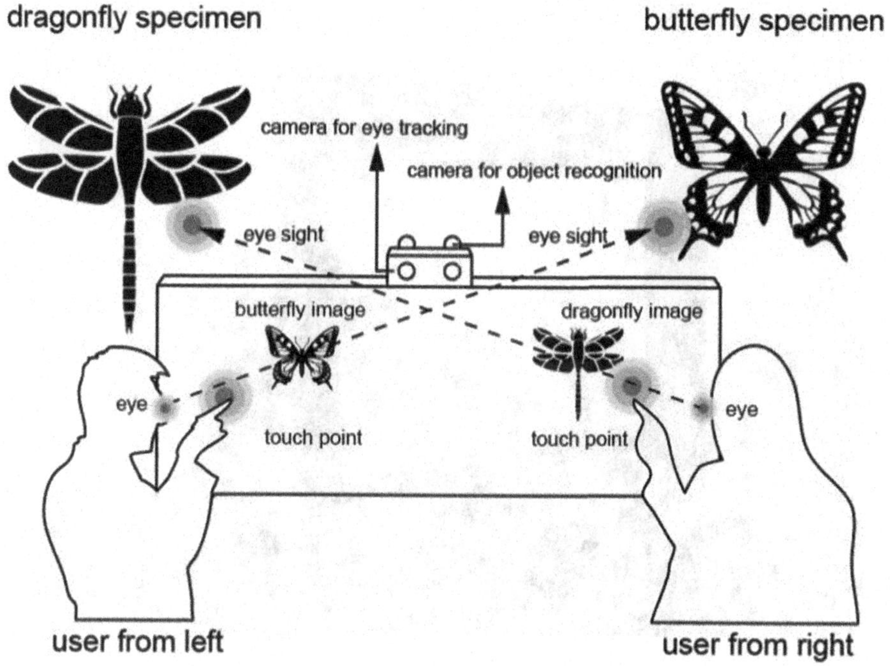

Fig. 2. User interaction of the AR smart window system

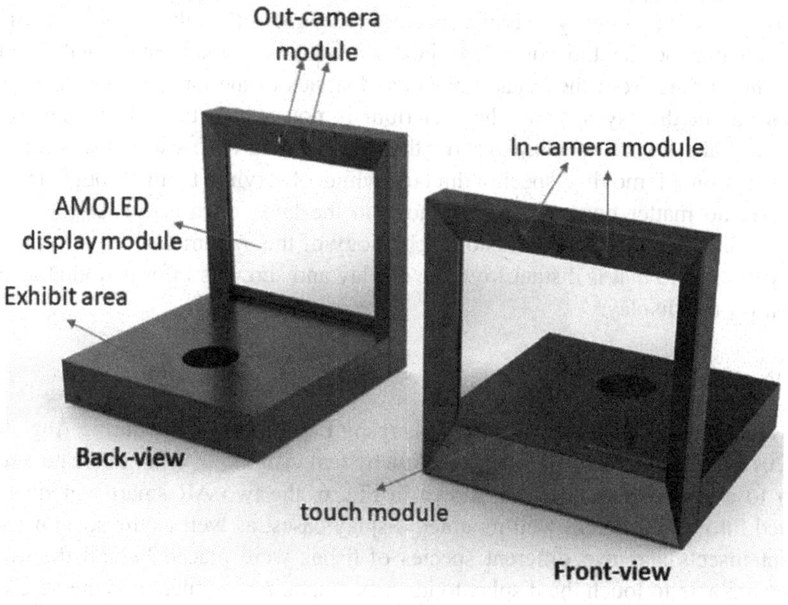

Fig. 3. The physical arrangement of hardware modules used in the AR smart window system

Fig. 4. The integration of the AR smart window system

Another good application of the system is aquariums, as shown in Fig. 5. Users might find it hard to identify a certain species in an aquarium tank only by checking the labels attached beside the aquarium since the aquatic animals are usually moving around and hiding from the aquatic plants and stones in the tank. However, by using the transparent display system, the aquarium is not only a tank to display aquatic species, but also a smart display to show their description. In this way, users can check the description of moving species directly while observing them through the tank. Therefore, no matter how the species move in the tank, once a user selects each of them, the directive information fusion technology of the system enables it to precisely identify the specie that is distant from the display and show its information at a correct position on the display.

3.2 Evaluation

The evaluation was conducted at Taipei Nangang Exhibition Center during Aug 29th to 31th, 2018 to evaluate the AR smart window by real visitors. In order to create a setting similar to a science exhibition as shown in Fig. 6, the two AR smart windows were designed into two different wall-mounted display cases, as well as the specimens of 6 different insects and two different species of fishes were placed behind the display. Visitors are able to touch the display to identify a certain specimen, and the description of the specimen will directly show on the display, as shown in Fig. 7.

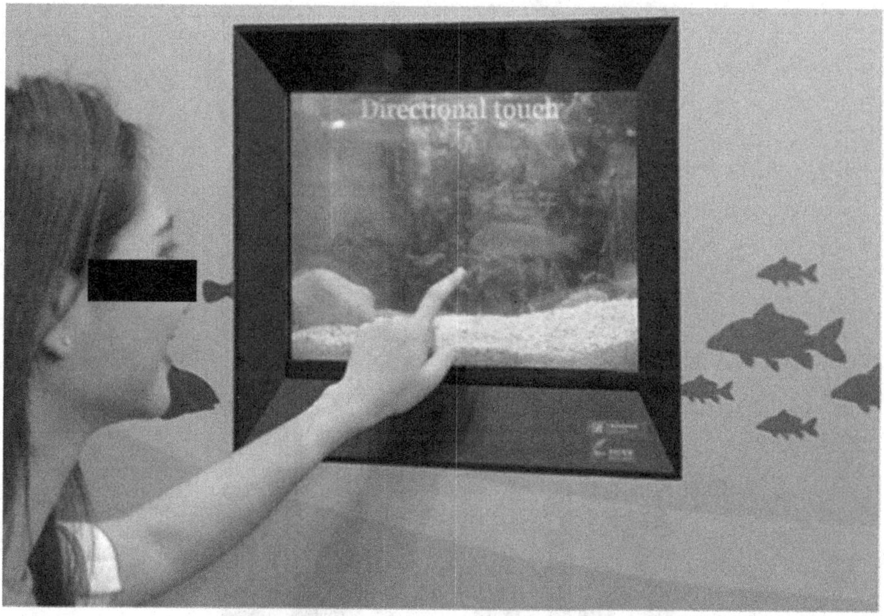

Fig. 5. The AR smart window system of aquariums

Experiment Settings. 32 visitors in an age of 25–40 were invited to take the evaluation test. 18 of them were male, and 14 were female. These visitors were asked to finish a subjective questionnaire after they had tried the AR smart window system. The questionnaire was divided into 3 sections: overall review of the system, guiding function of the system and system stability. Each section consisted of 4 to 7 items, and each item was a five-scale rating scheme ranging from "very disagree (1)" to "very agree (5)".

4 Findings

Results of the questionnaire are shown in Fig. 8. The average scores for the system stability, the guiding function and the overall review were 3.27, 4.4, and 4.34 respectively. The scores above 4.0 indicated that the visitors had a positive attitude toward the AR smart window system. The visitors were satisfied with the guiding function of the system. It might attribute to a fact that the AR smart window supported an intuitive and simple way for the visitors to get the information of the exhibits. They could directly get the information of the exhibits on the display rather than move beside to check label cards. Moreover, since the system was able to detect a visitor's eye position, the information was always showing at a proper position, which was a strength they agreed the most.

"the information is always showing at the intersection of my eyesight to the exhibit I am looking at and the display", a 29-year-old male visitor said.

Fig. 6. One of the AR smart window system in the exhibition center

However, the system stability might be a concern for the visitors. The touch function didn't work very fluently. Users might need to touch more than once to enable the information to show on the display successfully. Also, some visitors replied it was hard for them to focus on both the information on the display and the exhibits behind the display.

"I feel a bit dizzy to focus on the information and the exhibit simultaneously", a 32-year-old female visitor said.

5 Discussion

In general, the AR smart window system serves as a great display tool for exhibitions and museums. The directive information fusion technology of the system makes it easier and smarter for visitors to get the information of the exhibits.

On the other hands, there are some issues to be solved to improve the system stability. First, the insensitive touch function of current system might rest on the use of Airbar. Airbar is an optical touch senor which relies on infrared ray (IR) to send and receive signal. However, the sensitivity of IR sensor is unstable due to physical factors

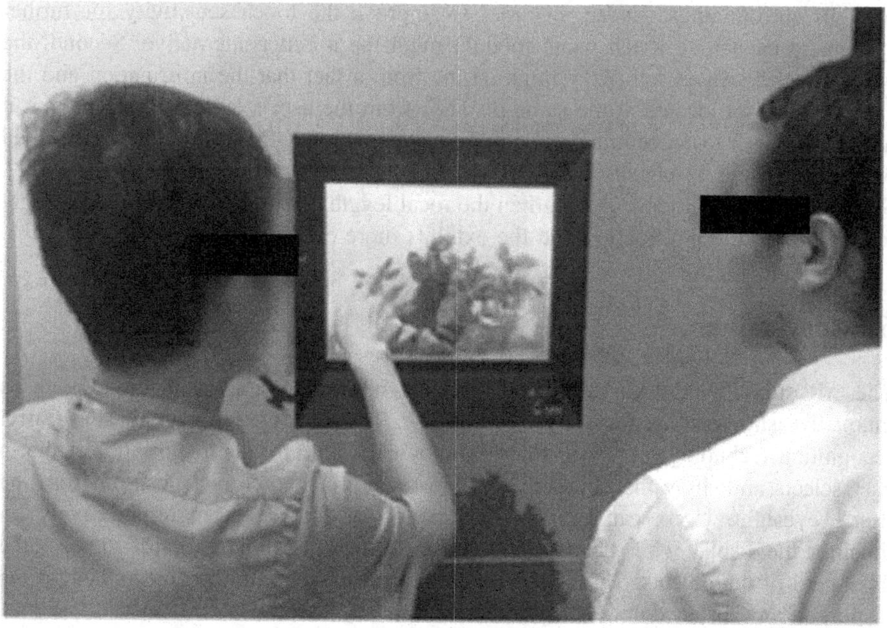

Fig. 7. Evaluation of the AR smart window system in the exhibition center

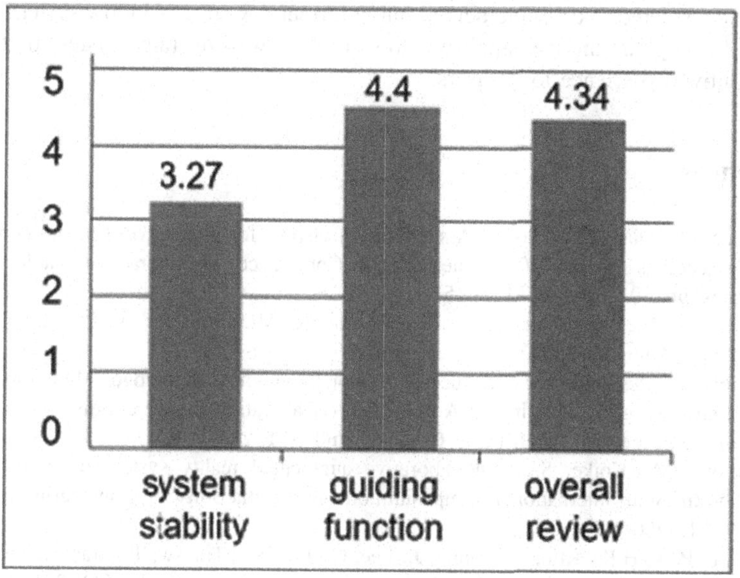

Fig. 8. The result of the questionnaire

from its surroundings. Hence, in order to improve the touch sensitivity for further systems, a capacitive touch panel module might be a better alternative. Second, the issue that the visitors felt dizzy might come from a fact that the information and the exhibit were not located at the same distance from the user's eye position, making it hard for the user to concentrate on both. To solve this issue, the display can be attached with Fresnel lens to change the focal length of the information on the display [22]. Since Fresnel lens are able to lengthen the focal length of the information, users might focus on both the information and the exhibits more easily.

6 Conclusion

The AR smart window system with directive information fusion technology is an innovative showcase design for exhibition use. Through the eye-tracking and object recognition technology, the AR smart window was able to identify the object that a user selects and show the object-related information at the correct position from the user's eyesight. Users can get the information of the object more intuitively by touching the display while observing the object, rather than moving beside to check the label card of the objects. Therefore, the users can interact with the objects behind the display in any distance and at any direction.

For further improvement of the AR smart window system, we might replace the current modules with the ones that meet the requirements of different exhibits and exhibitions. For instance, a capacitive touch panel and a wider-angle camera module might be considered to be implemented into a further AR smart window system. In this way, we believe that the AR smart window can be a well-operated system that brings more intuitive experience to its users.

References

1. Bellucci, A., Diaz, P., Aedo, I.: A see-through display for interactive museum showcases. In: Proceedings of the 2015 International Conference on Interactive Tabletops and Surfaces, pp. 301–306. ACM (2015)
2. Black, G.: The Engaging Museum: Developing Museums for Visitor Involvement. Routledge, Abingdon (2012)
3. Roppola, T.: Designing for the Museum Visitor Experience. Routledge, Abingdon (2013)
4. Li, J., Greenberg, S., Sharlin, E.: A two-sided collaborative transparent display supporting workspace awareness. Int. J. Hum. Comput. Stud. **101**, 23–44 (2017)
5. Hirakawa, M., Koike, S.: A collaborative augmented reality system using transparent display. In: Sixth International Symposium on Multimedia Software Engineering, pp. 410–416. IEEE (2004)
6. Heo, H., Park, H.K., Kim, S., Chung, J., Lee, G., Lee, W.: Transwall: a transparent double-sided touch display facilitating co-located face-to-face interactions. In: CHI 2014 Extended Abstracts on Human Factors in Computing Systems, pp. 435–438. ACM (2014)
7. Woods, E., et al.: Augmenting the science centre and museum experience. In: Proceedings of the 2nd International Conference on Computer Graphics and Interactive Techniques in Australasia and South East Asia, pp. 230–236. ACM (2004)

8. Kim, C.M., Nam, T.J.: Exploring the layered use of transparent display on a large tabletop display. In: Proceedings of the 2016 CHI Conference Extended Abstracts on Human Factors in Computing Systems, pp. 2555–2562. ACM (2016)
9. Xi, Y., Cho, S., Fong, S., Lee, B.K., Um, K., Cho, K.: Interactive lecture system based on mixed reality with transparent display. In: Park, J., Jin, H., Jeong, Y.S., Khan, M. (eds.) Advanced Multimedia and Ubiquitous Engineering. LNEE, vol. 393, pp. 223–228. Springer, Singapore (2016). https://doi.org/10.1007/978-981-10-1536-6_30
10. Li, J., Hamacher, A., Waghorn, D., Barnes, D., Wang, S.J.: Interact with show-window at stores: exploratory study and design solution for physical retailers' product demonstration. In: Brooks, A.L., Brooks, E., Vidakis, N. (eds.) ArtsIT/DLI -2017. LNICST, vol. 229, pp. 116–126. Springer, Cham (2018). https://doi.org/10.1007/978-3-319-76908-0_12
11. Lee, J.H., Bae, S.H., Jung, J., Choi, H.: Transparent display interaction without binocular parallax. In: Adjunct Proceedings of the 25th Annual ACM Symposium on User Interface Software and Technology, pp. 97–98. ACM (2012)
12. Yoshimura, K., Ogawa, T.: Binocular interface: interaction techniques considering binocular parallax for a large display. In: IEEE Virtual Reality (VR), pp. 315–316. IEEE (2015)
13. Milgram, P., Kishino, F.: A taxonomy of mixed reality visual displays. IEICE Trans. Inform. Syst. **77**(12), 1321–1329 (1994)
14. Azuma, R.T.: A survey of augmented reality. Presence **6**(4), 355–385 (1997)
15. LaViola, J., Williamson, B., Brooks, C., Veazanchin, S., Sottilare, R., Garrity, P.: Using augmented reality to tutor military tasks in the wild. In: Proceedings of the Interservice/Industry Training Simulation and Education Conference, Orlando, Florida (2015)
16. Malý, I., Sedláček, D., Leitao, P.: Augmented reality experiments with industrial robot in industry 4.0 environment. In: 2016 IEEE 14th International Conference on Industrial Informatics (INDIN), pp. 176–181. IEEE (2016)
17. Sanusi, A.N.Z., Abdullah, F., Kassim, M.H., Tidjani, A.A.: Architectural history education: students' perception on mobile augmented reality learning experience. Adv. Sci. Lett. **24**(11), 8171–8175 (2018)
18. de Gortari, A.B.O.: Empirical study on game transfer phenomena in a location-based augmented reality game. Telemat. Inform. **35**(2), 382–396 (2018)
19. Andersen, D., et al.: Medical telementoring using an augmented reality transparent display. Surgery **159**(6), 1646–1653 (2016)
20. Selvam, A., Yap, T.T.V., Ng, H., Tong, H.L., Ho, C.C.: Augmented reality for information retrieval aimed at museum exhibitions using smartphones. J. Eng. Appl. Sci. **100**(3), 635–639 (2016)
21. Rodrigues, J.M.F., et al.: Adaptive card design UI implementation for an augmented reality museum application. In: Antona, M., Stephanidis, C. (eds.) UAHCI 2017. LNCS, vol. 10277, pp. 433–443. Springer, Cham (2017). https://doi.org/10.1007/978-3-319-58706-6_35
22. Clement, C.E., Thio, S.K., Park, S.Y.: An optofluidic tunable Fresnel lens for spatial focal control based on electrowetting-on-dielectric (EWOD). Sens. Actuators B: Chem. **240**, 909–915 (2017)

Proposal and Evaluation of AR-Based Microscopic Brain Surgery Support System

Masanao Koeda(✉), Sana Nishimoto, Hiroshi Noborio, and Kaoru Watanabe

Department of Computer Science, Osaka Electro-Communication University, Kiyotaki 1130-70, Shijonawate, Osaka 575-0063, Japan
koeda@osakac.ac.jp

Abstract. In this study, we describe an augmented reality (AR) support system that superimposes a three-dimensional computer graphics (3DCG) brain model image on an intraoperative microscopic image using simultaneous localization and mapping (SLAM). First, we extract regions such as tumor and blood vessel from computed tomography (CT) images or magnetic resonance images (MRI) of real patients, where data is stored in the digital imaging and communications in medicine (DICOM) format. Then, the entire brain and identified regions are converted into three-dimensional computer graphics (3DCG) model with a standard triangulated language (STL) format. The motion of the camera is estimated from the surgical video using SLAM. Based on the movement, the 3DCG brain model can be moved according to the movement of the real brain. Finally, we verified the estimation accuracy of the camera movement using SLAM.

Keywords: Microscopic brain surgery · Simultaneous localization and mapping · Augmented reality · Surgical navigation

1 Introduction

The brain is surrounded by the skull and is covered by meningeal cells. It is composed of nerve cells (neurons) that send signals to various parts of the body. According to a survey by the Ministry of Health, Labor and Welfare, the first leading cause of death in Japan in 2017 was malignant neoplasm (cancer), and the proportion of total deaths was 27.8% [1].

The number of the brain tumor resection surgeries conducted in Japan in 2016 was approximately 14,000 [2]. The brain tumor resection surgery is carried out according to the following approximate process.

Fix the patient's head.
Open the scalp.
Remove a part of the skull.
Remove the tumor in the brain.
Close the skull and suture the scalp.

M. Kurosu (Ed.): HCII 2019, LNCS 11567, pp. 458–468, 2019.
https://doi.org/10.1007/978-3-030-22643-5_36

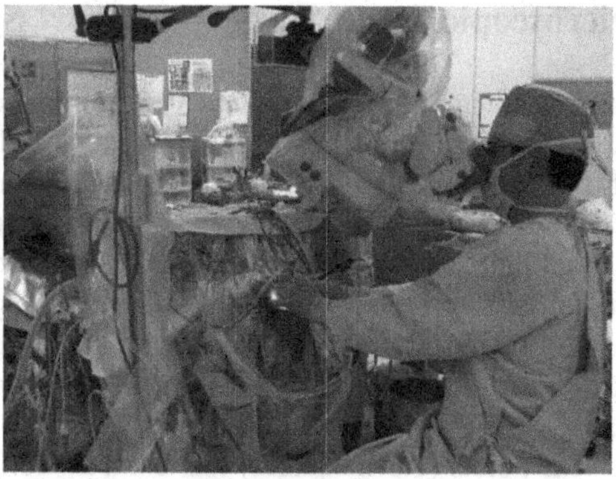

Fig. 1. Microscopic brain surgery

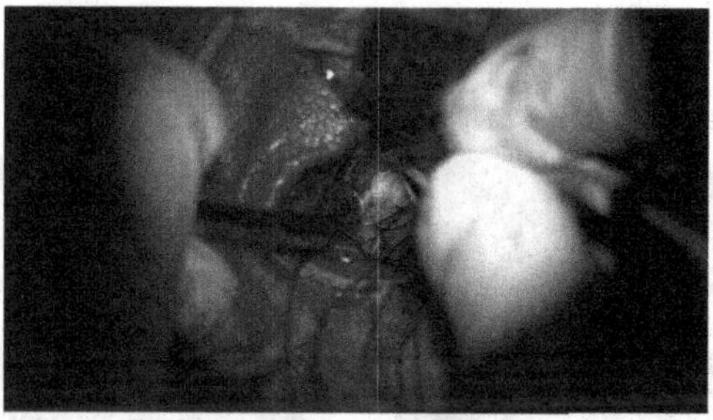

Fig. 2. Removing a tumor in the deep part of the brain

Brain surgery is performed using a microscope, and it needs precise and careful operation (Fig. 1). If the tumor is in a deep part of the brain, it is difficult to remove the whole tumor completely. This approach involves carefully opening the gaps of the brain and removing the tumor gradually (Fig. 2). Brain damage during the surgery can cause memory impairment and paralysis.

Several surgical support and navigation systems are commercially available. Brainlab has developed a microscope navigation system [3], which superimposes a digital imaging and communications in medicine (DICOM) image on the microscopic image. However, the user needs to mount a large number of markers on the patient's head. Both the microscope and the markers must be monitored with an external stereo camera. Attaching the markers is complicated process, and the markers are a hindrance for the medical personnel at the time of surgery. Additionally, the user needs to calibrate the external camera and the markers in advance.

We are developing a surgical support system for the safe and accurate extraction of tumors in the brain for the purpose of reducing the risk of damage in microscopic brain surgeries [4, 5]. In this paper, we describe an augmented reality (AR) support system that superimposes a three-dimensional computer graphics (3DCG) brain model image on an intraoperative microscopic image using simultaneous localization and mapping (SLAM).

2 AR-Based Microscopic Brain Surgery Support System

The proposed system is a microscopic brain surgical operation support system with AR, that can be used during surgical operations removing a part of the patient's skull. A 3DCG model of the brain created from DICOM data obtained by computed tomography (CT) or magnetic resonance imaging (MRI) is superimposed on the microscopic image in real time, and the resulting system can check the position of the blood vessels and the tumor during the surgery. In order to automatically update the 3DCG model according to the microscopic image, we analyze the image using simultaneous localization and mapping (SLAM) to obtain the motion of the camera.

Our system consists of a SLAM system (Fig. 3(a)) and AR system (Fig. 3(b)). The SLAM system tracks points (green squares) that exhibit strong image features of the microscopic image and estimates the camera position/orientation. The AR system superimposes a translucent 3DCG brain model on the microscopic image. The 3DCG brain model is controlled according to the camera position/orientation estimated by the SLAM system.

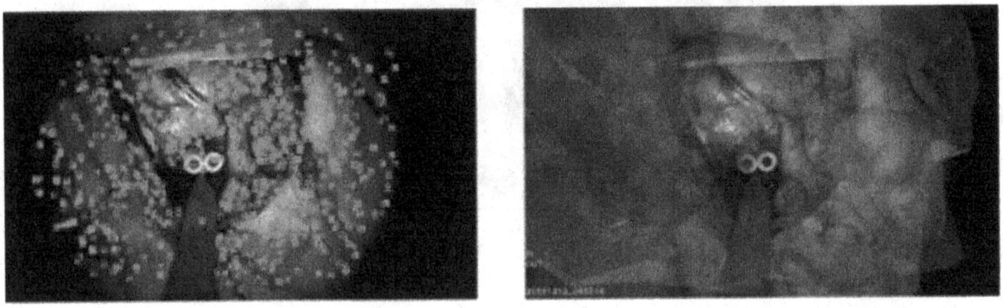

(a) Microscopic image and tracking points (b) AR image

Fig. 3. Snapshot of AR-based microscopic brain surgery support system

2.1 SLAM System

SLAM is a method to grasp the shape of the surrounding environment and estimating its own position/orientation based on the shape data. In our system, we used partially modified ORB-SLAM2 [6] as a SLAM library. In ORB-SLAM2, three threads of tracking, local mapping, and loop closing run in parallel. In the tracking thread, the camera position/orientation is estimated by tracking the oriented FAST and rotated BRIEF (ORB) image features [7] in the input videos (Fig. 4(a)). In the local mapping thread, a global map and a camera position is displayed as shown in Fig. 4(b). In the loop closing thread, the accumulation of the camera position and orientation error is eliminated.

The input image to the SLAM system and the camera position and orientation estimated by the SLAM system are transmitted to the AR system using the shared memory.

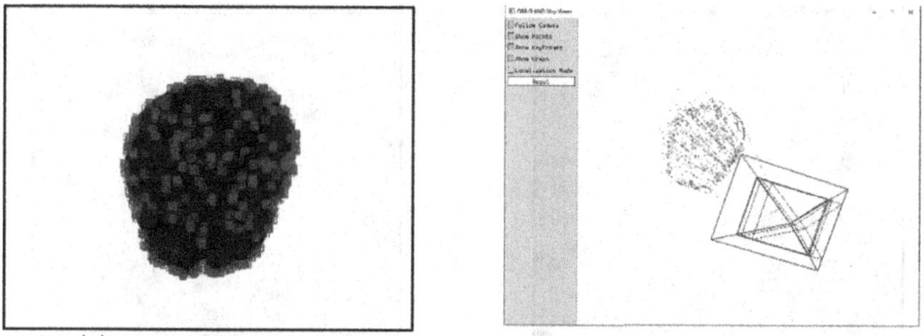

(a) Tracking thread (b) Mapping thread

Fig. 4. Snapshots of ORB-SLAM2 process

2.2 AR System

In the AR system, a 3DCG model of the brain is superimposed on the microscopic image during the brain surgery. The initial position and orientation of the 3DCG model are set manually, and then its position and orientation are determined based on the data received from the SLAM system. The 3DCG model is composed of brain parenchyma and the tumor. The color and transparency of each model can be changed. OpenGL is used for displaying 3DCG models. The 3DCG model of the brain used in this system was a part of BodyParts3D [8]. BodyParts3D is a free 3D whole-body model of an adult human male. The following files related to the brain were selected from Body-Pars3D and merged into a single STL format file (Fig. 5, Tables 1 and 2).

Table 1. The details of the merged 3DCG model of brain.

FJ1732.obj,	FJ1733.obj,	FJ1734.obj,	FJ1735.obj,	FJ1736.obj,	FJ1738.obj,
FJ1739.obj,	FJ1740.obj,	FJ1741.obj,	FJ1742.obj,	FJ1743.obj,	FJ1744.obj,
FJ1745.obj,	FJ1746.obj,	FJ1747.obj,	FJ1748.obj,	FJ1749.obj,	FJ1750.obj,
FJ1751.obj,	FJ1752.obj,	FJ1753.obj,	FJ1754.obj,	FJ1755.obj,	FJ1756.obj,
FJ1757.obj,	FJ1758.obj,	FJ1759.obj,	FJ1760.obj,	FJ1761.obj,	FJ1762.obj,
FJ1763.obj,	FJ1764.obj,	FJ1766.obj,	FJ1767.obj,	FJ1768.obj,	FJ1770.obj,
FJ1771.obj,	FJ1772.obj,	FJ1773.obj,	FJ1774.obj,	FJ1775.obj,	FJ1776.obj,
FJ1777.obj,	FJ1778.obj,	FJ1779.obj,	FJ1780.obj,	FJ1781.obj,	FJ1782.obj,
FJ1783.obj,	FJ1784.obj,	FJ1785.obj,	FJ1786.obj,	FJ1787.obj,	FJ1788.obj,
FJ1789.obj,	FJ1790.obj,	FJ1791.obj,	FJ1792.obj,	FJ1793.obj,	FJ1794.obj,
FJ1795.obj,	FJ1796.obj,	FJ1797.obj,	FJ1798.obj,	FJ1799.obj,	FJ1800.obj,
FJ1801.obj,	FJ1802.obj,	FJ1803.obj,	FJ1804.obj,	FJ1805.obj,	FJ1806.obj,
FJ1807.obj,	FJ1808.obj,	FJ1809.obj,	FJ1810.obj,	FJ1811.obj,	FJ1812.obj,
FJ1813.obj,	FJ1814.obj,	FJ1815.obj,	FJ1816.obj,	FJ1816M.obj,	
FJ1817.obj,	FJ1818.obj,	FJ1819.obj,	FJ1820.obj,	FJ1821.obj,	FJ1822.obj,
FJ1823.obj,	FJ1824.obj,	FJ1825.obj,	FJ1826.obj,	FJ1827.obj,	FJ1828.obj,
FJ1829.obj,	FJ1830.obj,	FJ1832.obj,	FJ1833.obj,	FJ1834.obj,	FJ1835.obj,
FJ1836.obj,	FJ1837.obj,	FJ1838.obj,	FJ1839.obj,	FJ1840.obj,	FJ1841.obj,
FJ1842.obj,	FJ1844.obj				

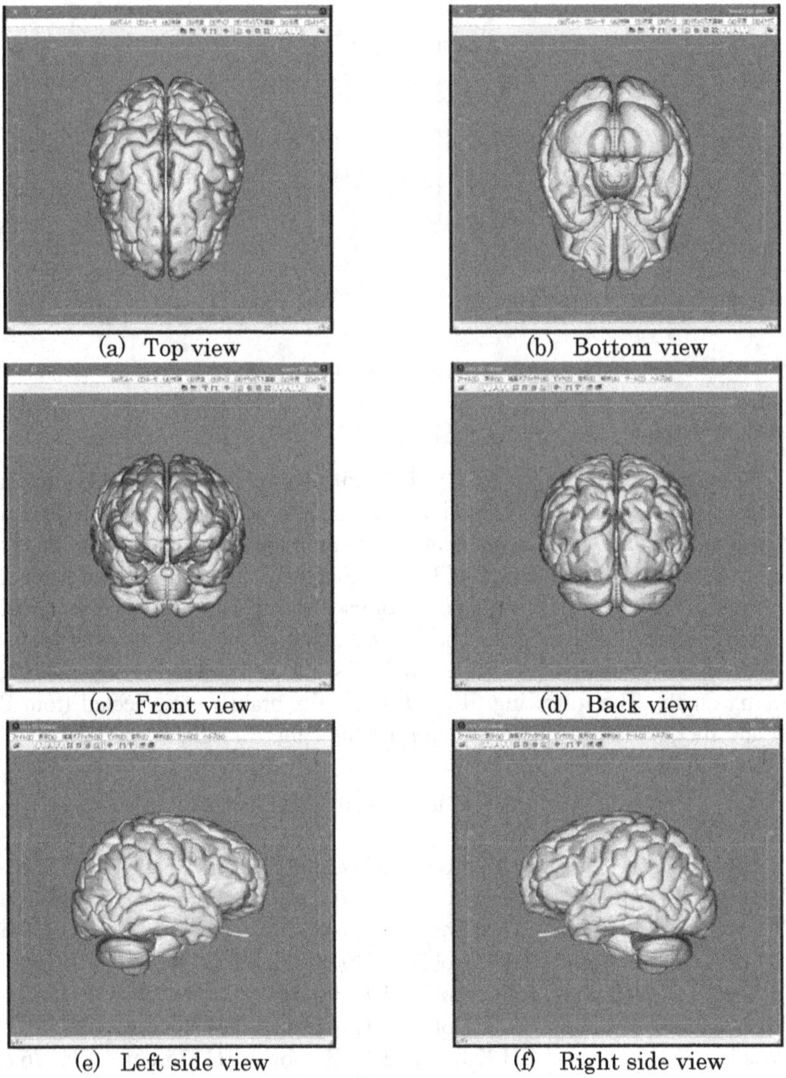

Fig. 5. Merged 3DCG brain model displayed in Hira 3D Viewer

Table 2. Details of the merged 3DCG brain model

Length	140.85 mm
Width	180.01 mm
Height	143.22 mm
Volume	1385.08 mm
Area	5355.01 mm
Polygons	4498888

3 Experimental Environment and Conditions

The specifications of the PC used for the experiments are Windows 10 Enterprise 64bit OS, Intel Core i7-4930K 3.4 GHz CPU, 16 GB memory, and NVIDIA GeForce GTX TITAN Black GPU. The development environment is Microsoft Visual Studio Professional 2015 (Ver. 14.0.25431.01 Update 3), Microsoft.NET Framework (Ver. 4.6.0 1586), and OpenCV 3.2.0.

The input image of the SLAM system was generated using our software described in [9], which can freely change the position/orientation of the camera and the 3DCG model (hereinafter referred to as a *simulator*). The displayed 3DCG model is the merged STL format file shown in the previous section, and the initial position of the STL is the center of the screen. The resolution of the image is 960 × 540 pixels, and the angle of view is 60°. Figure 6 shows the coordinate system of the simulator.

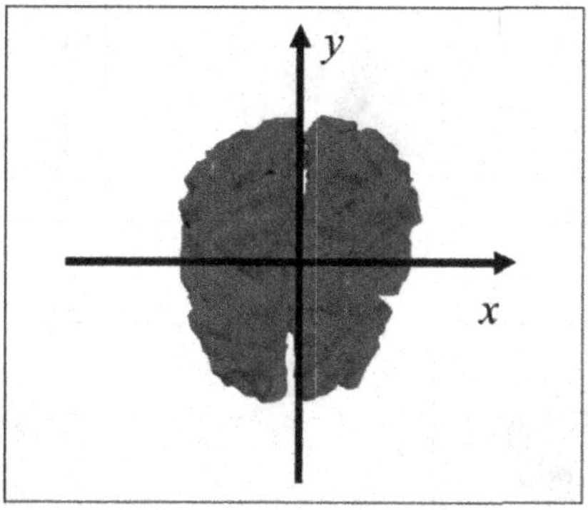

Fig. 6. Coordinate system of the simulator

The parameters required for SLAM were set as follows. Because the simulator generates ideal camera video, the center position of the image (cx, cy) is set to half of the resolution and all the lens distortion parameters (k1, k2, p1, p2) are set to 0.

- Camera.fx: 1000
- Camera.fy: 1000
- Camera.cx: 480
- Camera.cy: 270
- Camera.k1:0
- Camera.k2: 0
- Camera.p1: 0
- Camera.p2: 0
- ORBextractor.nFeatures: 4000
- ORBextractor.scaleFactor: 1.2
- ORBextractor.nLevels: 12
- ORBextractor.iniThFAST: 10
- ORBextractor.minThFAST: 5

4 Experiments and Results

By moving the position of the camera laterally and vertically by a certain distance using the simulator, we generated input videos for the SLAM system. The position of the camera estimated by the SLAM system is compared with the true value.

4.1 Lateral Movement

Using the simulator, we created a video in which the position of the camera was moved in lateral direction, and the motion of the camera was estimated from the video using SLAM. The movement of the camera in the simulator is (x, y) = (0, 0), (100, 0), (0, 0), (−100, 0), (0, 0) at a constant speed of 1 mm/frame as shown in Fig. 7.

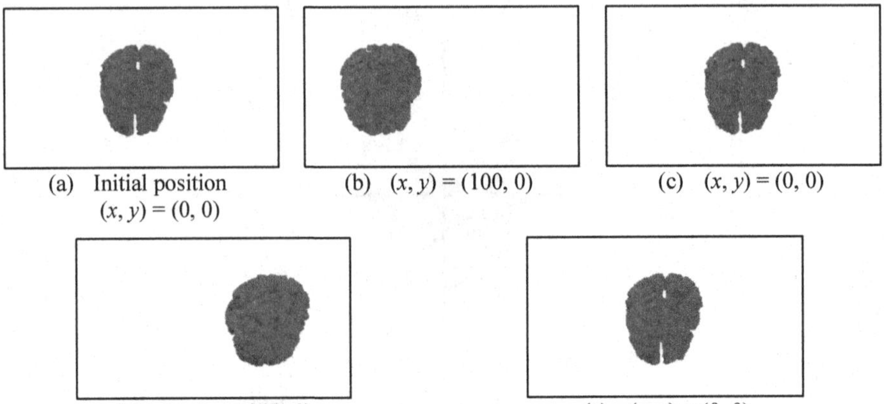

(a) Initial position $(x, y) = (0, 0)$ (b) $(x, y) = (100, 0)$ (c) $(x, y) = (0, 0)$

(d) $(x, y) = (-100, 0)$ (e) $(x, y) = (0, 0)$

Fig. 7. Snapshots of the video of lateral movement of the camera in the simulator

The resulting camera position estimated by the SLAM system is shown in Fig. 8. The blue and the red line in Fig. 8 represent estimated positions of the camera in the x and y directions, respectively. Because the lines are not discrete, the SLAM estimation ca continue during the camera movement. The maximum and minimum values of the estimated position in the x direction are 106.9 and −113.9 mm, respectively. The error is 13.9 mm at maximum. The average value in the y direction is 0.0 mm, and the standard deviation was 0.57 mm. Therefore, the estimation of y direction is almost correct.

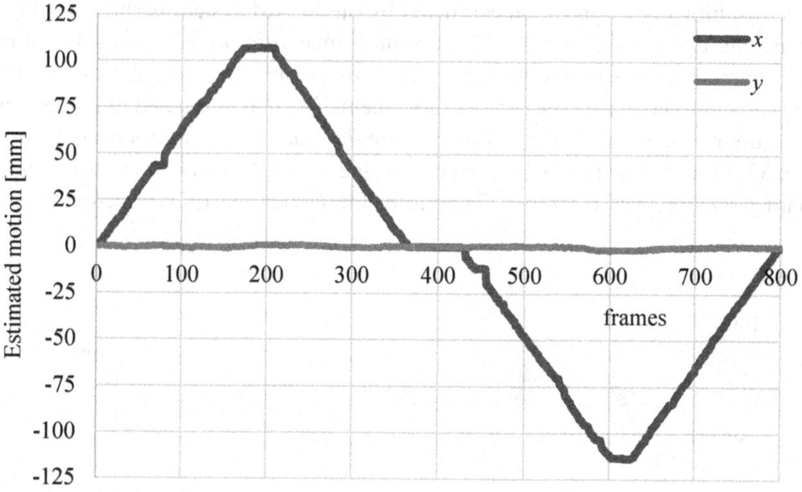

Fig. 8. Experimental result of the estimated position of the camera in lateral movement (Color figure online)

4.2 Vertical Movement

Using the simulator, we created a video in which the position of the camera was moved in vertical direction, and the motion of the camera was estimated from the video using the SLAM system. The movement of the camera in the simulator is $(x, y) = (0,0)$, $(0, 50)$, $(0, 0)$, $(-50, 0)$, $(0, 0)$ at a constant speed of 1 mm/frame as shown in Fig. 9.

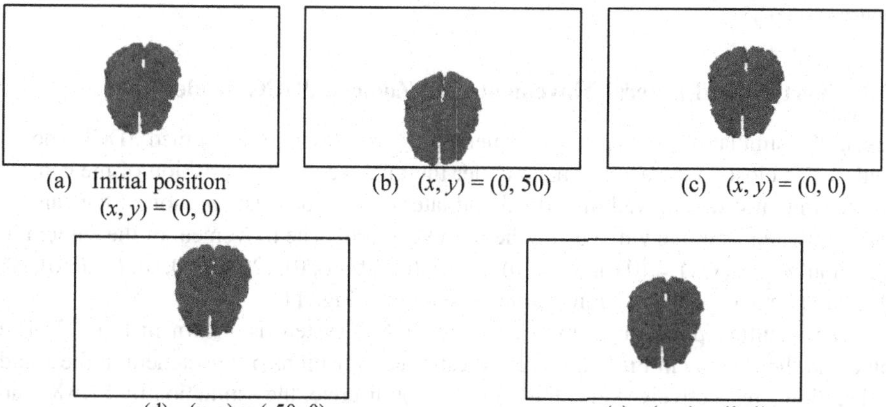

(a) Initial position $(x, y) = (0, 0)$ (b) $(x, y) = (0, 50)$ (c) $(x, y) = (0, 0)$ (d) $(x, y) = (-50, 0)$ (e) $(x, y) = (0, 0)$

Fig. 9. Snapshots of the video of vertical movement of the camera in the simulator

The resulting camera position estimated by the SLAM system is shown in Fig. 10. The blue and the red line in Fig. 10 represent estimated positions of the camera in the x and y directions, respectively. Since the lines are not discrete, the estimation by SLAM can continue during the camera movement. The maximum and minimum values of the estimated position in the y direction are 77.2 and −83.9 mm, respectively. The error is 33.9 mm at maximum. The average value in the x direction is 0.2 mm, and the standard deviation was 0.66 mm. Therefore, the estimation of x direction is almost correct.

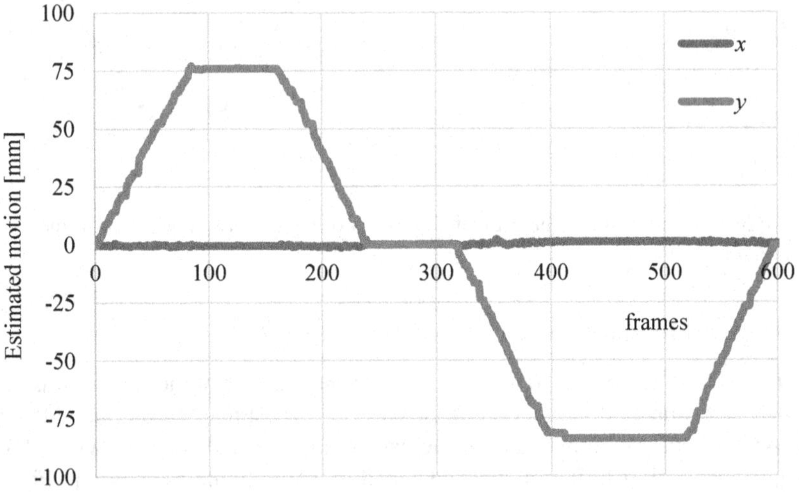

Fig. 10. Experimental result of the estimated position of the camera in vertical movement (Color figure online)

4.3 Vertical and Lateral Movement with Zoomed 3DCG Model

Using the simulator, the video was generated by displaying the zoomed 3DCG model with a size close to the actual image under the microscope. The position of the camera in the simulator was moved in vertical and lateral directions. The motion of the camera was estimated from the video using the SLAM system. The movement of the camera in the simulator is (x, y) = (0,0), (0, −20), (0, 0), (0, 20), (0, 0), (20, 0), (0, 0), (−20, 0), (0, 0) at a constant speed of 1 mm/frame as shown in Fig. 11.

The resulting position estimated by the SLAM system is shown in Fig. 12. The blue and the red line in Fig. 12 represent estimated positions of the camera in the x and y directions, respectively. Since the lines are not discrete, the estimation by SLAM can continue during camera movement. The maximum and minimum values of the estimated position in the x direction are 116.8 and −114.1 mm, respectively. The maximum and minimum values of the estimated position in the y direction are 114.5 and −118.4 mm, respectively. As a result, a large error occurred in both direction.

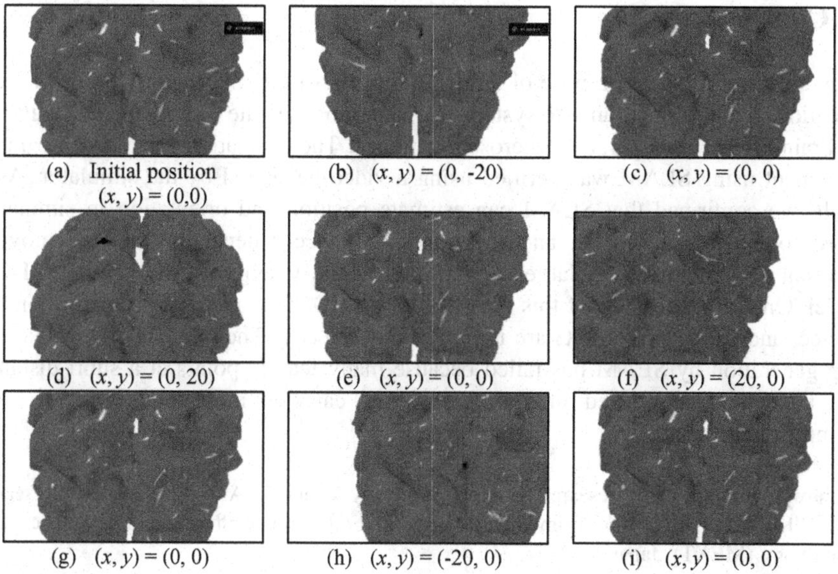

Fig. 11. Snapshots of the video of vertical and lateral movements of the camera with the zoomed 3DCG model in the simulator

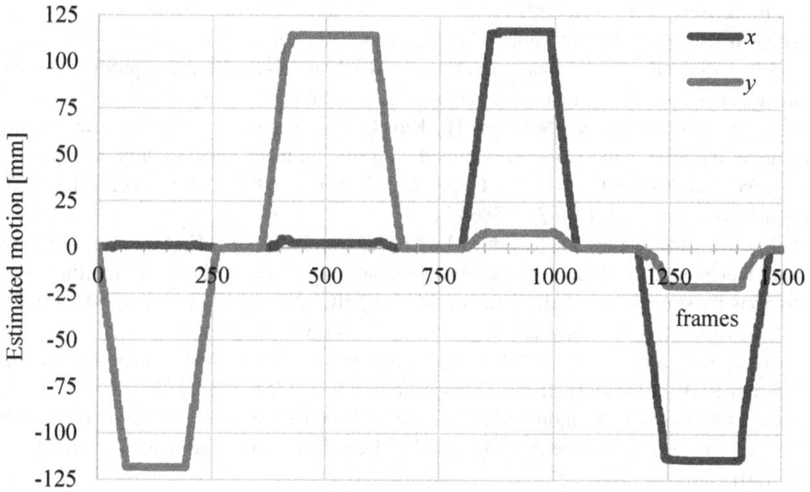

Fig. 12. Experimental result of the estimated position of the camera in vertical and lateral movements with the zoomed 3DCG model (Color figure online)

5 Conclusion

In this research, for the purpose of reducing the risk of the microscopic brain surgical operation, we described an AR system that superimposes the 3DCG model image of the brain on the intraoperative microscopic image. The estimation accuracy of camera movement using SLAM was verified using a video generated by the simulator. As a result, we confirmed that SLAM can estimate position and orientation in simulated microscopic surgical image, and the errors may occur depending on the moving direction of the camera. A large error occurs in the video with the zoomed 3DCG model. One of the reasons of this error is that the 3DCG model has no texture on the surface, and the feature points are not detected correctly. The other reason is that the map generation by SLAM has failed because many feature points at a short distance from the camera are tracked. In the future, we will carry out more detailed experiments to improve the accuracy.

Acknowledgement. This research was supported by Grants-in-Aid for Scientific Research (No. 17K00420, 18K11496) from the Ministry of Education, Culture, Sports, Science and Technology (MEXT), Japan.

References

1. Vital statistics in Japan. https://www.mhlw.go.jp/toukei/saikin/hw/jinkou/geppo/nengai17/index.html. Accessed 30 Jan 2019
2. Hospital Intelligence Agency. https://hospia.jp/dpc. Accessed 30 Jan 2019
3. Brainlab Microscope Navigation. https://www.brainlab.com/surgery-products/overview-neurosurgery-products/microscope-navigation/. Accessed 30 Jan 2019
4. Nonaka, M., Watanabe, K., Noborio, H., Kayaki, M., Mizushino, K.: Capturing a surgical area using multiple depth cameras mounted on a robotic mechanical system. In: Marcus, A., Wang, W. (eds.) DUXU 2017. LNCS, vol. 10289, pp. 540–555. Springer, Cham (2017). https://doi.org/10.1007/978-3-319-58637-3_42
5. Nonaka, M., Chikayama, Y., Kayaki, M., Koeda, M., Tachibana, K., Noborio, H.: A useful robotic-mechanical system for measuring a surgical area without obstructing surgical operations by some surgeon. In: Kurosu, M. (ed.) HCI 2018. LNCS, vol. 10902, pp. 43–52. Springer, Cham (2018). https://doi.org/10.1007/978-3-319-91244-8_4
6. Mur-Artal, R., Tardós, J.D.: ORB-SLAM2: an open-source SLAM system for monocular, stereo and RGB-D cameras. IEEE Trans. Robot. **33**(5), 1255–1262 (2017)
7. Rublee, E., Rabaud, V., Konolige, K., Bradski, G.R.: ORB: an efficient alternative to SIFT or SURF. In: Proceedings of the 2011 International Conference on Computer Vision, pp. 2564–2571 (2011)
8. Mitsuhashi, N., Fujieda, K., Tamura, T., Kawamoto, S., Takagi, T., Okubo, K.: BodyParts3D: 3D structure database for anatomical concepts. Nucleic Acids Res. **37**, D782–D785 (2009)
9. Noborio, H., et al.: Fast surgical algorithm for cutting with liver standard triangulation language format using z-buffers in graphics processing unit. In: Fujie, Masakatsu G. (ed.) Computer Aided Surgery, pp. 127–140. Springer, Tokyo (2016). https://doi.org/10.1007/978-4-431-55810-1_11

Walking in the Head: Methods of Sonic Augmented Reality Navigation

Andreas Kratky(✉)

Interactive Media and Games Division, School of Cinematic Arts,
University of Southern California, 3470 McClintock Ave., SCI 201Q,
Los Angeles, CA 90089-2211, USA
akratky@cinema.usc.edu

Abstract. This paper describes an experimental method for the navigation of immersive sonic augmented reality experiences. The focus is on tight integration of the audio experience with the real environment in conjunction with high quality immersion in both the real space as well as the augmented information presented throughout the experience. Drawing from lessons learned from two projects that present narrative content pertaining to the historic layers of two places in the form of location-specific immersive audio experiences embedded in the current, real environment, we discuss techniques of sonic immersion and auditory spatial navigation strategies. With custom-developed headsets the realization and performance of bone-conducted spatial sound is explored and design considerations for such experiences are formulated.

Keywords: Audio Augmented Reality · Spatial audio · Bone conduction · HRTF

1 Introduction

Immersive audio and Audio Walk experiences have regained new attention. Since the early walks of Janet Cardiff in 1991, which used a portable cassette player [1], and the classic museum audio guide, which was first deployed in 1952 using a short-wave broadcasting technology [2], the medium of a guided audio tour has become an established format for museums and tourist guides as well as for artistic experiences since many years. The new spark in attention in this format emerges at a convergence point of widespread availability of personal mobile media (specifically smartphones), tourism, AR-gaming (such as Ingress [3] or Pokemon-Go [4]) and mobility applications for navigation or in support of people with various impairments to their ability to navigate real space.

This convergence, and in particular the strong interest in virtual and augmented reality (VR and AR) platforms, such as the Oculus Rift VR headset [5] and the HTC Vive [6], as well as augmented reality platforms such as Microsoft's Hololens [7], has supported the development of audio technologies that lend themselves to such audio tours. These VR and AR platforms stimulate a need for immersive audio formats that are able to deliver spatial audio mapped to the visual experience of space. For example, the long neglected format of ambisonic encoding and decoding for spatial sound has been revitalized as

M. Kurosu (Ed.): HCII 2019, LNCS 11567, pp. 469–483, 2019.
https://doi.org/10.1007/978-3-030-22643-5_37

Google LLC adopted the format for its own VR platform. Originally developed in the early 1970s [8], the format allows the recording and rendering of a complete soundfield surrounding the listener. Despite the fact that VR and AR experiences are predominantly targeting the visual sense, experience designers and hardware companies have realized the importance of convincing spatial audio to realize better immersive qualities for their products. This realization has resulted in several new products and software libraries that specifically target spatial audio, such as Sennheiser AMBEO [9] and Bose AR [10], as well as several audio spatialization toolkits.

The focus on spatial sound-only experiences that developed alongside with the visually-oriented formats, instantiated for example by the new Bose AR device, a pair of glasses with integrated stereo speakers, indicate that an interest and market viability for such audio-focused experiences beyond the traditional museum or tourist tours is expected. We can see a mutual stimulation between visual and auditive immersive experiences, which, on one hand, leads to new research and the development of new technologies, and, on the other hand, to a demand for a certain form of experience, that realizes a combination of narrative and spatial immersion as we know it from visually oriented VR experiences, and the experience of real space with additional content layers as we know it from AR experiences. Both experience forms relate to traditional cinematic and sonic experiences but also move beyond the established languages of those experiences [11, 12].

2 Immersiveness and Integration of Real and Augmented Environments

The two projects discussed in this paper are implementing two different approaches to audio-only immersive experiences. The aim of the two projects is to develop a quality of immersiveness as we know from VR experiences, but without transporting the user into a completely fictional environment. The intention of the projects is to realize a compelling rootedness in the real environment. Both projects engage with complex historical and political events that happened in the places in which they are deployed and, in order to allow the users to be highly engaged with the reading of the real environment according to the perspectives provided by the experiences, they aim to create an unencumbered and seamless connection between the real space and the augmented information in which the user can be deeply immersed without feeling any form of experiential dissociation of the two aspects of the experiences. The first project, "Weeping Bamboo," engages with the colonial past and the destruction of indigenous cultures by the Spanish conquest of certain parts of Colombia; and the second project, "Ghost Letter," excavates the past of a mental asylum on the Island of San Servolo in the Venetian Lagoon in Italy.

The intention for these two projects was to implement an augmented reality approach that is apt to combine the experience of real space with an additional augmentation layer. Nevertheless, the classic AR experience model suffers, similar to VR experiences, from experiential dissociation between reality and the additional information layers. VR experiences are characterized by a complete experiential dissociation between virtual environment and reality in which it is experienced. By putting on the

VR headset the user sensorially and mentally "leaves" the real environment and steps into the experiences, ideally as fully immersed as possible. Sinking into this dissociation, and "leaving reality behind" was the main promise when the current wave of VR interest and products began [13, 14]. In cases where the experiential dissociation (ED) of the virtual experience delivered through the visual and aural senses and the real environment experienced through the haptic senses was perceived as too abrupt and harsh, multiple attempts have been made to mitigate the ED between the two colliding experiences. The concepts of passive haptics and substitutional reality have been developed for this purpose [15, 16].

Augmented Reality has less ED between real space and added information since it does not fully take over the visual and aural sense impressions. Nevertheless, by using screens, lenses and headphones to communicate the additional information overlaid on the real environment, both sense modalities are encumbered such that the user cannot have direct access to the real environment. The interfering media technologies can be more or less encumbering, typically using either smartphone screens, the single focal-depth display of the Hololens or the double focal-depth display of devices such as Magic Leap [17]. While the smartphone screen is clearly a foreign element held up in the field of view by the user, which does not easily merge with the real environment to provide an immersive experience, AR headsets provide more seamless integration between the real and augmented information layers. By using multi-focal displays, such as in the Magic Leap headset, a more natural and haptically correct experience can be achieved, because the problem of vergence accommodation conflict can be addressed, which in headsets with a single visual plane leads to possible nausea [18, 19]. Addressing both passive haptics as well as active haptics like vergence accommodation are attempts to create a more natural and comfortable experience.

Valkov et al. [20] have investigated the process of transition between a real and a virtual environment and developed techniques for a smooth transition in order to avoid the negative psychological effects that stem from the perceptual system's inability to cope with a sudden and disruptive transition from one spatial experience to another that is completely different and does not have any relationship to the first. Their concept of smooth immersion aims to ease the transition of the user from one environment to the other by user into the virtual environment by using replicas of objects in the real environment that slowly morph into the virtual environment.

2.1 Sonic Immersion

Audio-only experiences forego any kind of ED on the visual level as they keep the visual environment continuous as additional information is communicated only via auditive signals. Nevertheless, Sonic AR experiences often have different forms of ED. Most experiences use headphones to transmit the additional auditory information, which can follow different construction principles. We can distinguish headphones that allow an adjustment of the relationship between the auditory information pertaining to the Sonic AR experience and those that do not provide this option. Even though early examples such as the work of Cardiff mentioned above has used headphones without adjustment options, most current implementations of Sonic AR follow the principle of wearable and mobile augmented reality audio (WARA) employing a combination of microphones and headphone transducers with active adjustment between ambient and augmented audio signals as well as head-tracking devices that determine the position and orientation of the head [21]. Headphone constructions for this purpose cover the ear and close the ear canal so that ambient sounds are more or less blocked from directly entering the ear canal. The headphones either have an open or closed back, where an open back allows a degree of ambient sounds to permeate the ear cup and membrane in such a way that the additional auditory information of the experience always layers with the ambient sounds. Closed back headphones provide a stronger insulation against ambient sounds. Two kinds of possible sound mixing between ambient and augmented sounds can be used in these scenarios, physical mixing of sound permeating the open back headphones and electronic mixing, where all sounds are transmitted by the headphone transducers after having been mixed electronically [22]. An additional degree of insulation against ambient noise are active noise-controlled headphones that employ a combination of microphones and phase inverting circuitry to actively cancel ambient noises in the path of transmission to the user's ear [23].

Due to the use of headphones in most Sonic Augmented Reality experiences an ED between real and augmented environment exists in so far as the auditory continuity is interrupted by the intervention of a device covering the ear. Various types of filtering can be applied to mitigate this ED and realize a close to natural hearing experience [24]. Our tests indicated, though, that any form of interference of a headphone tends to make the users feel more separated from the environment and "more in their head" than in an open ear experience.

3 Theoretical Background for Proposed Approach

The intention of the two projects discussed in this paper is to stimulate an active engagement with the environment within which the experiences are situated and to reexamine the places according to the information presented in the experience. The complexity of the historic and political information and the attempt to really encourage users to draw parallels to the current environment in consideration of the presented information made it seem most appropriate to realize an unencumbered experience quality that avoids any form of ED separating users from their environment. Instead, all presented information is intended to link back directly to the environment and the current events in the space at the time of the visit.

3.1 Audio Only Experience

The first decision we made was to go for an audio only experience to avoid the ED of Visual AR. This decision was informed by the fact that it is established from cinematic experiences that sound contributes significantly to the emotional impact and the overall engagement of an experience [25]. Spatially rendered sound has also been recognized as particularly suitable to seamlessly merge real and virtual content, and thus avoid or realize a very low degree of ED [26].

While the specific qualities of sound to deliver emotional experiences have been explored in depth in the realm of cinema, there is also evidence that sound-only experiences have similar capabilities. In respect to audio drama experiences it has been stated that they are at least as powerful as visual sources and that they are particularly stimulating on a psychological and imaginative level [27, 28].

Sound stands out as a way of communicating specific experience qualities that cannot or only with difficulty be delivered through visual experiences. In particular the emotional quality of sonic experience has been highlighted [29]. Helmreich [30] introduces the term "transduction" as a way of going beyond immersion and speaks of "analytic of transduction—the transmutation and conversion of signals across media that, when accomplished seamlessly, can produce a sense of effortless presence." Akiyama discusses composed soundscapes as media that can "stand in or 'speak' for a place" and as having a double structure combining aesthetic with rational scientific power [31].

3.2 Bone Conduction

The second decision in the implementation of the two projects was to choose bone conducted sound instead of using air conducted sound through headphones. Humans can perceive sonic phenomena in several ways; in most cases we hear sound waves that travel through the air, enter the ear canal and, from there, travel via the middle and inner ear to the cochlea. Bone conducted sound takes a different path to the cochlea; the sound travels as vibration transmitted through the bone structure of the skull to the cochlea, where it is perceived as sound. Bone conduction normally occurs in direct contact with a source of vibration or sound; for example, when hearing our own voice, we hear both air and bone conducted parts of our voice, perceiving our own voice significantly differently than other listeners who only hear the air conducted component. To perceive bone conducted sound the ear canal can remain open and receptive to any air conducted sound. Bone conduction transducers are used in hearing aids, military and emergency communication devices for situations in which it is important that the ear canal remains open. Besides those specialized applications bone conduction is suitable for augmented reality experiences since a seamless layering of real ambient and augmented sounds can be achieved by using the different transmission mechanisms in parallel.

The use of bone conduction for Audio Augmented Reality has been examined and speech recognizability as well as the ability to transmit spatial information and handling of ambient sounds have been tested [32]. The performance of bone conduction transducers has been found comparable to air conducted sound in terms of speech recognizability; in terms of ambient sound handling bone conduction transducers are superior, but air conducted sound transducers can be equalized to perform similarly (this was studied in respect to speech recognizability in [33]).

3.3 Spatial Sound

Audio Augmented Reality experiences rely on a spatial registration of the virtual sound source location. Sounds are located through interaural level differences (ILD) and interaural time differences (ITD) in how sounds are perceived by the ears. From these differences the brain computes locational information. In addition to the ILD and ITD the spectral reflection pattern of the pinna is used to infer sound source locations. When listening with headphones or with bone conduction transducers these cues are not delivered because there is no interaction of the sound waves with the listener's head or ears. But the interference patterns, head related transfer functions (HRTF) can be measured and applied as filters to the reproduced sounds as filters in order to communicate information about the location of the sound sources [34]. The use of HRTFs can achieve compelling results in terms of sound source location but only under specific circumstances. The specific transfer function is dependent on the individual shape of the head and ears of the listener, i.e. to achieve the best result, HRTFs need to be established for every listener individually. As this process is very time intensive (proposals for alternative processes have been developed [35]), it is common practice to use generic HRTFs established for an "average" ear for purposes of navigating an VR experience and utilize cross modal information stemming from auditory as well as visual cues [36]. For complex spatial tasks individualized HRTFs improve the task precision and speed [37]. In AR experience that have no visual component, or even conflicting visual information stemming from the real-world environment navigated by the user, a good spatial rendering and spatial coherence is important.

Another difficulty with HRTF functions lies in the fact that they are established for air conducted hearing and only transferable to bone conducted sound transmission with certain limits. [38] argues that, with appropriate adjustment, bone conducted sound source localization performance can be indistinguishable from that in air conducted sound transmission. The frequency spectrum of sound transmitted through the bone structure of the skull differs from the model of air conduction. As [39] has shown, through specifically determined transfer functions this difference can be corrected. But this correction is a rather complicated process, because not only are the HRTFs specific to the individual listener's head, but also the correction transfer functions between air and bone conducted sound. In addition, these transfer functions also depend on the location of the bone conduction transducer on the head of the listener. Different placements have significantly different sensitivity and transduction characteristics [40]. It is possible to make sensitivity mappings of bone conduction transducer placement for the different locations on the skull and, based on this mapping, as well as based on certain predictive models of the tissue composition of the head [41], implement basic corrections. In this correction process, ILD is the most important parameter to correct the perceptual pattern of bone conducted (BC) sound [42].

4 Implementation

The two projects discussed in this paper employ custom headsets that have been specifically developed for the purpose of the experiences. Both headset iterations share major components: The are both worn on the head and attached with an elastic strap that run around the head. They employ a four-channel audio processing unit, a GPS, compass and inertial measurement unit. GPS and compass are used for acquisition of the position of the user and to determine which part of the audio experience has to be played. All these components are mounted on a plate situated above the head (Fig. 1).

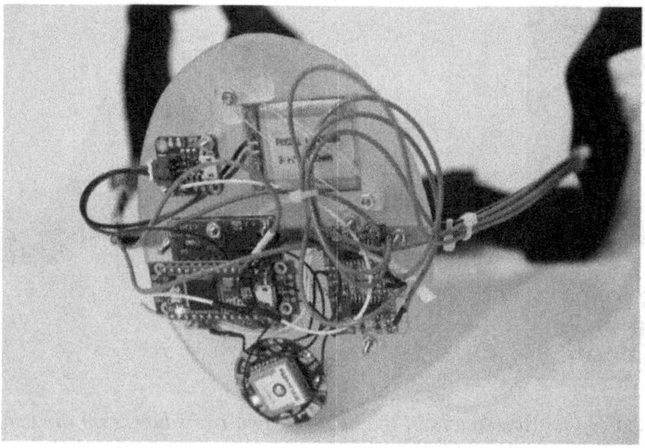

Fig. 1. Picture *of the electronic components of the headset*

The headset employs 4 bone conduction transducers placed on different parts of the listener's skull. Two transducers are placed on the left and right temples, one in the center of the forehead and one in the center of the back of the head. The four positions correspond to the four major directions of left, right, front and back to represent sound source locations. The implementation makes use of the level, time and spectral differences of sound cues coming from different locations of the skull. Listeners can associate different locations with the different patterns of level, time and spectral characteristics and identify different locations of the sound sources in correspondence with their head orientation (Figs. 2 and 3).

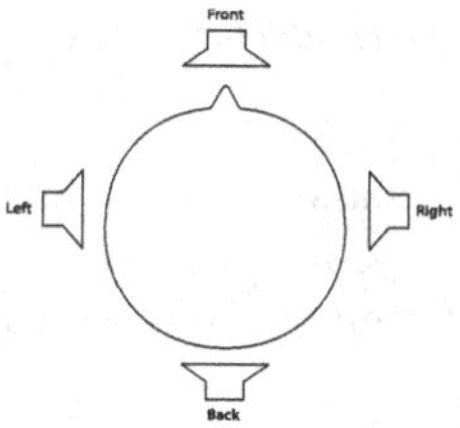

Fig. 2. Bone *conduction transducer placement on the head.*

The headset is adjustable so that the placement of transducers can be fit to the individual listener's heads. Front and back transducers are embedded into an elastic strap that wraps around the head and the temple transducers have an adjustable flexible placement case so that they can be fit to various head anatomies (Fig. 4).

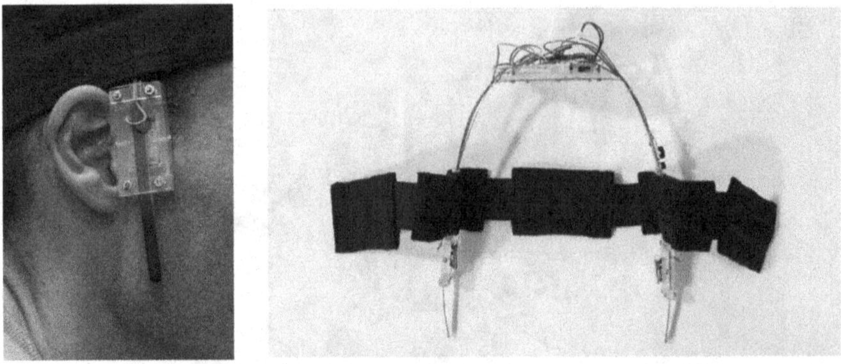

Fig. 3. Placement *of the transducers in the headset: two transducers on the temples, one at the forehead and one at the back of the head.*

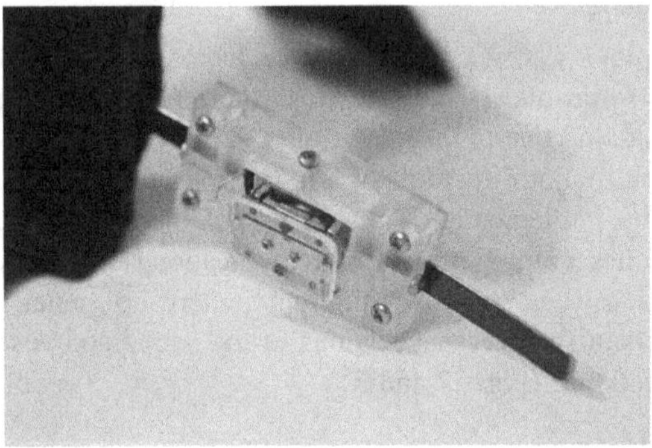

Fig. 4. Picture *of the bone conduction transducer for the temple area.*

The GPS unit, IMU, and compass are used to keep the soundscape in correct registration with the surrounding geography. The compass is used to pan sounds according to head movement between the four transducers so that a spatially correct representation is created (Fig. 5).

The second iteration of the headset includes a microphone to record environmental sounds that can be dynamically mixed into the soundscape in order to increase the connection between real environment and the augmented information. This function was integrated based on our experience of the first iteration in the "Weeping Bamboo" project. We realized that a dynamic addition of sounds from the real environment that are processed such that they become sound effects within the audio experience significantly increases the immersion into both the real space as well as the narrative layers added to it through the audio augmented reality (AAR) experience.

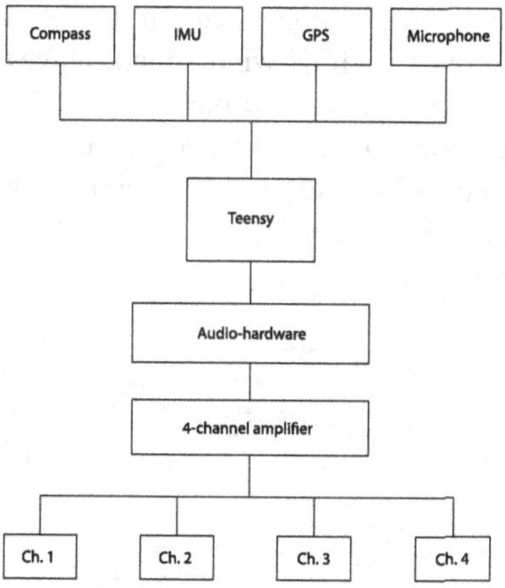

Fig. 5. Diagram *of the electronic components*

4.1 Experience 1: Weeping Bamboo

The first iteration of our investigation in AAR and the first project with the title "Weeping Bamboo" was designed for the city of Manizales in Colombia. The experience is situated at the Plaza Simon Bolivar, the central square in the old city center of Manizales. It explores the complex historic layering of the city and aims to make these layers an experiential part of the modern-day city. Even though nothing is left of the Pre-Columbian times, the area was a fertile and highly developed cultural center of the indigenous cultures of Quimbaya and Carrapa. They had a broad economic base with robust trade activities among various native nations and sophisticated agricultural and technical knowledge about irrigation systems. The culture of the native peoples did not construct lasting monuments or buildings, despite their sophistication of other areas of cultural production, such as the utilization of natural irrigation routes, bridge systems, and an abundant agricultural production [43]. Cultural expression was in harmony with nature, focused on living with and preserving naturally salient places and processes. The culture of the Quimbaya has disappeared by 1700 beyond recognizable presence and without wider knowledge of their language [44]. The city of Manizales was founded in 1849 and now constitutes a center of traces from the Spanish colonial times and modern-day Colombia, which is the stage for our project and the point of departure to excavate the cultural history of the native cultures inhabiting this area for several thousand years before the Spanish conquest.

The "Weeping Bamboo" AAR experience is set on the main part of the Simon Bolivar square. Participants put on the headset at a dedicated starting point and from there can wonder freely across the square. The area is subdivided into four quadrants (titled Earth, Wind, Water and Condor) which are associated with four different parts of the experience. A loose narrative thread, which can be suspended and resumed whenever a listener crosses the boundaries between the quadrants. The application keeps track of the user's position and of the parts of the experience that have been heard in order to avoid duplications and make sure a coherent and meaningful experience emerges from the navigational pattern of the listeners. Along with the narrator voice locational sounds such as wind sound, leaves rustling in wind, creeks gurgling, birds, insects etc. are presented to build a soundscape evocative of the narrative of the indigenous cultures. The Condor quadrant is the concluding part of the experience which ends at the foot of the condor monument in the square. At this point the listener hands back the headset (Fig. 6).

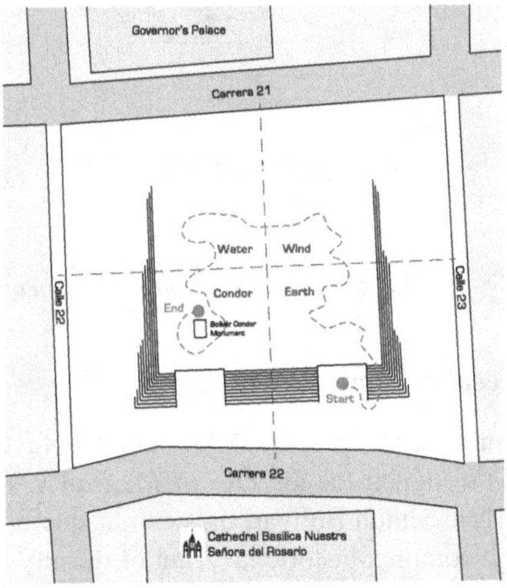

Fig. 6. Layout *of the Manizales experience in four quadrants covering the Bolivar square.*

The structure of the experience is designed such that the users can freely explore the square and the get invited to imagine the narrative elements presented in the experience. The quadrants are delimited atmospherically through different types of soundscape designs, but they can flow into each other as users transition between them. All sounds are fixed in space and users can navigate between them. There is no explicit path users have to follow, the narrative builds dynamically as they spend time in the different quadrants. The experience uses a composite of current day landmarks, namely the cathedral and the condor monument and merges them with imaginary landmarks that appear sonically and as part of the narrative.

4.2 Experience 2: Ghost Letter

The second experience, titled "Ghost Letter," is situated on the Island San Servolo in the Venetian Lagoon in Italy. Also, this project explores the past history of the place, which, between 1725 and 1978, served as a mental asylum for the city of Venice. In a richly layered collage, the experience describes the situation of the mentally ill with examples from both the late 19th century and leading up to 1978, when a new law changed the practice of mental health care in Italy. Written as an undelivered letter to a patient in San Servolo, the story unfolds as a walk across the island with a soundscape that is tailored to deliver a superposition of the environmental sounds and the audio experience. Through the additional microphones added to the headset the surrounding sounds are integrated into the experience and shaped in response to the movement and gestures of the listener in order to establish a tight connection between the AAR experience and the real-world environment. The narrative of the letter is the main line that can be followed across the island. The narrative is stretched along a series of GPS coordinates and thus closely rooted in the space. If the listener veers off this path they encounter other voices, which are ghostly voices of other patients as well as descriptions of patients states from the historic hospital files. Different voices a reading these parts, which are located close to the main narrative part, so that, if listeners follow not exactly on the main path, they would encounter these voices. The voices are distracting from the main narrative and invite to explore the island more closely, encounter more sound effects and ghosts (Fig. 7).

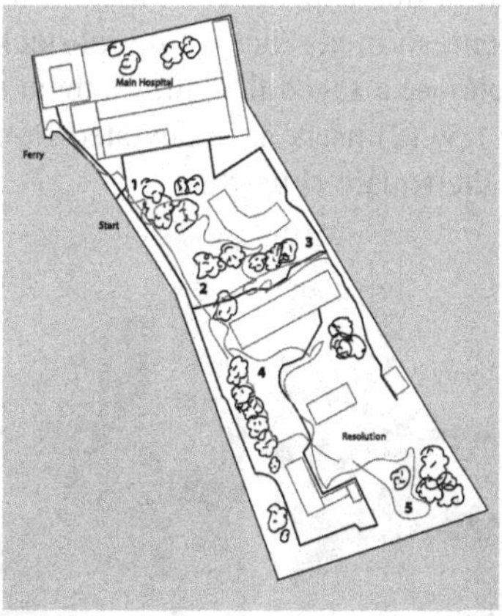

Fig. 7. Layout of the San Servolo experience covering the entire island

In the "Ghost Letter" experience listeners encounter numerous obstacles along their way, which guides them past trees and bushes, houses, walls etc. So here the navigation pattern is more complex and designed to "get lost" and distracted. In this sense the navigational pattern is very different from the first "Weeping Bamboo" experience, which was situated on a free square without any encumbrances.

5 Evaluation

Our main questions to evaluate the two described experiences are regarding the degree of immersion and the navigation patterns, testing if our approach to spatial sound rendering through bone conduction transducers was successful. In order to formulate an appropriate measure for the degree of immersion we have to understand the nature of the tasks solved by listeners in the experiences. Our goal is to realize a full spatial mapping experience connecting the augmented soundscape and real space; we are not aiming to present extraneous information in register with space, but to stimulate listeners to explore and scan the real space, to make direct connection of the narrative augmented content with actual space. Success criteria in this sense would be a tendency to deviate from the straight path and venture into an explorative motion; in distinction from other studies that measure time spent on visual search tasks and measure a shorter amount of time spent on those tasks as a criterium for efficient navigational guidance [45]. In our case the measure of success would be the opposite: the more time spent on exploring details of the space and spending more time with the narrative and soundscape should be interpreted as success.

Our observations reveal that in the "Weeping Bamboo" experience users spend approximately 20 min, which is the amount of time it takes complete the main narrative. The exploration of the soundscape is limited, and users follow more or less similar paths, even though no direct guidance is provided. The path follows a line from one quadrant to the next, following a nearly circular path from the beginning to the end. The variability of time spent in this experience is max. 8 min. The start end points of the experience are very salient, so in absence of any obstacles users seem to be taking the most efficient path and choose a speed that allows them to complete the experience in the minimum time. Only few (2) users have deviated from this pattern and spent an additional 8 min exploring the square (Fig. 8).

Fig. 8. Plaza Simon Bolivar in Manizales, Colombia

Listener behavior in the "Ghost Letter" experience was significantly different. Even though in this experience the narrative followed a clearly laid out path, the time spent in the experience was significantly longer. the main narrative has a similar running time of 26 min, but listeners spent up to 42 min exploring the island. The amount of available material in terms of soundscape and additional voices was larger and allowed for longer exploration; nevertheless, we have to relate the difference in exploration time not to the length of possible experience time, because in "Weeping Bamboo" none of the listeners even came close to exhausting the available material. Our interpretation for this behavior is twofold: First, the atmosphere of the San Servolo island is a lot more secluded and sheltered, so listeners feel more comfortable to spend time here than in the open public square in Manizales. Odd navigational movements or gestures would not be noticed by many other bystanders, so listeners feel safe and encouraged to follow their inclinations. A second explanation has to do with the presence of numerous obstacles in the island experience, which made it possible that voices could emerge behind bushes and force listeners to follow more complex paths. Lastly, the composite nature of multiple voices and sound effects in the San Servolo experience made it more fitting to veer off the main path and explore (Fig. 9).

Fig. 9. Exploration *in the natural landscape setting of San Servolo Island*

A preliminary test comparing the bone conduction headset with closed, noise-canceling headphones in transparent listening mode (Sony MDR 1000X, setting "ambient sound normal"), which allowed ambient sounds to come in through the microphones of the headphones and be mixed to the augmented audio layer with filtering applied, clearly favored the bone conduction version due to less ED and a more natural experience of the location.

6 Discussion and Future Work

The presented study is a first explorative study that mainly aims to establish general feasibility of the chosen implementation and explores in broad strokes several possible design choices. In comparing the two experiences, our results are influenced by the nature of the narrative design, the nature of the locations and other variables extraneous to the exact set-up of the bone conduction headset and the navigational guidance, GPS area dimensions etc. Another, more controlled study should yield more precise quantitative results in the future. Due to the fact that we had only one prototype headset we were not able to test a representative number of listeners. Further study of navigational behavior will be necessary with more isolated variables. Our conclusion is that we will test another iteration of the headset construction that make placement of temple transducers easier and reduces the procedure of putting on the headset to one act of fixing the elastic headband to the head; in the current version we encountered a few problems with fit for significantly smaller heads and with the forward- and backward adjustability of the temple transducers. After a successful test with this new iteration we will be able to produce several headsets and test a larger amount of people. Our intention is to use the "Ghost Letter" experience for further testing and to develop a revised version for this purpose.

References

1. Christov-Bakargiev, C.: Janet Cardiff: a survey of works including collaborations with George Bures Miller. P.S. 1 Contemporary Art Center, New York (2002)
2. Tallon, L., Walker, K. (eds.): Digital Technologies and the Museum Experience. Altamira Press, Lanham (2008)
3. Niantic: Ingress Prime – Ingress Prime. https://ingress.com/. Accessed 15 Mar 2019
4. Nintendo: Homepage. Pokémon Go. https://www.pokemongo.com/en-us/. Accessed 15 Mar 2019
5. Oculus. https://www.oculus.com. Accessed 15 Mar 2019
6. HTC Vive. https://www.vive.com/. Accessed 15 Mar 2019
7. Microsoft Hololens. https://www.microsoft.com/en-US/hololens. Accessed 15 Mar 2019
8. Gerzon, M.A.: Periphony: with-height sound reproduction. J. Audio Eng. Soc. **21**, 2–10 (1973)
9. Sennheiser AMBEO. http://sennheiser-ambeo.com. Accessed 15 Mar 2019
10. Bose AR. https://www.bose.com/en_us/better_with_bose/augmented_reality.html. Accessed 15 Mar 2019
11. Nielsen, L.T., et al.: Missing the point: an exploration of how to guide users' attention during cinematic virtual reality. ACM, New York (2016)
12. Knorr, S., Ozcinar, C., Fearghail, C.O., Smolic, A.: Director's cut: a combined dataset for visual attention analysis in cinematic VR content. ACM, New York (2018)
13. Looking at the reality of virtual reality: Dreamscapes on demand - Chicago Tribune. https://www.chicagotribune.com/news/opinion/editorials/ct-virtual-reality-oculus-rift-facebook-edit-0328-jm-20160325-story.html. Accessed 15 Mar 2019
14. Kim, M.: The Good and the Bad of Escaping to Virtual Reality. The Atlantic (2015)
15. Suzuki, K., Wakisaka, S., Fujii, N.: Substitutional reality system: a novel experimental platform for experiencing alternative reality. Sci. Rep. **2**, 459 (2012). 2017 7:1
16. Simeone, A.L., Velloso, E., Gellersen, H.: Substitutional Reality: Using the Physical Environment to Design Virtual Reality Experiences. ACM, New York (2015)
17. Leap, Magic: Welcome. Magic Leap. https://www.magicleap.com/. Accessed 15 Mar 2019
18. Kramida, G.: Resolving the Vergence-Accommodation Conflict in Head-Mounted Displays. IEEE Trans. Visual Comput. Graphics **22**, 1912–1931 (2015)
19. Koulieris, G.-A., Bui, B., Banks, M.S., Drettakis, G.: Accommodation and comfort in head-mounted displays. ACM Trans. Graphics (TOG) **36**, 11 (2017). 87
20. Valkov, D., Flagge, S.: Smooth immersion: the benefits of making the transition to virtual environments a continuous process. In: SUI 2017, pp. 12–19 (2017)
21. Karjalainen, M., Lokki, T., Nironen, H., Harma, A., Savioja, L., Vesa, S.: Application scenarios of wearable and mobile augmented reality audio (2004)
22. Higa, K., Nishiura, T., Kimura, A., Shibata, F., Tamura, H.: A two-by-two mixed reality system that merges real and virtual worlds in both audio and visual senses. Presented at the 2007 6th IEEE International Symposium on Mixed and Augmented Reality (ISMAR) (2007)
23. Miljkovic, D.: Active noise control: from analog to digital—last 80 years. Presented at the 2016 39th International Convention on Information and Communication Technology, Electronics and Microelectronics (MIPRO) (2016)
24. Ranjan, R., Gan, W.-S.: Natural listening over headphones in augmented reality using adaptive filtering techniques. IEEE/ACM Trans. Audio Speech Lang. Process. **23**, 1988–2002 (2015)
25. Sider, L.: If you wish to see, listen. J. Media Pract. **4**, 5–16 (2003)

26. Sodnik, J., Tomazic, S., Grasset, R., Duenser, A., Billinghurst, M.: Spatial sound localization in an augmented reality environment. Presented at the Proceedings of the 18th Australia Conference on Computer-Human Interaction: Design: Activities, Artefacts and Environments, New York, NY, USA (2006)
27. Crook, T.: Radio Drama. Routledge, London, New York (1999)
28. Cory, M., Haggh, B.: Horspiel as music: music as horspiel: the creative dialogue between experimental radio drama and avant-garde music. Ger. Stud. Rev. **4**, 257 (1981)
29. Berrens, K.: An emotional cartography of resonance. Emot. Space Soc. **20**, 75–81 (2016)
30. Helmreich, S.: Listening against soundscapes. Anthropol. News **51**, 10 (2010)
31. Akiyama, M.: Transparent listening: soundscape composition's objects of study on JSTOR. RACAR revue dart canadienne Canadian Art Review **35**, 54–62 (2010)
32. Lindeman, R.W., Noma, H., de Barros, P.G.: An Empirical study of hear-through augmented reality: using bone conduction to deliver spatialized audio. Presented at the 2008 IEEE Virtual Reality Conference (2008)
33. Kondo, K., Anazawa, N., Kobayashi, Y.: Characteristics comparison of two audio output devices for augmented audio reality. Presented at the 2013 Asia-Pacific Signal and Information Processing Association Annual Summit and Conference (APSIPA) (2013)
34. Zhang, W., Samarasinghe, P.N., Chen, H., Abhayapala, T.D.: Surround by sound: a review of spatial audio recording and reproduction. Appl. Sci. **7**, 532 (2017)
35. Hai, N.D., Chaudhary, N.K., Peksi, S., Ranjan, R., He, J., Gan, W.-S.: Fast HRFT measurement system with unconstrained head movements for 3D audio in virtual and augmented reality applications. Presented at the 2017 IEEE International Conference on Acoustics, Speech and Signal Processing (ICASSP) (2017)
36. Berger, C.C., Gonzalez-Franco, M., Tajadura-Jiménez, A., Florencio, D., Zhang, Z.: Generic HRTFs may be good enough in virtual reality. Improving source localization through cross-modal plasticity. Front. Neurosci. **12**, 441 (2018)
37. Poirier-Quinot, D., Katz, B.F.G.: Impact of HRTF individualization on player performance in a VR shooter game II (2018)
38. MacDonald, J.A., Henry, P.P., Letowski, T.R.: Spatial audio through a bone conduction interface. Int. J. Audiol. **45**, 595–599 (2009). PubMed - NCBI
39. Ogiso, S., Mizutani, K., Zempo, K., Wakatsuki, N.: Measurement of the differential transfer function between bone-conduction and air-conduction for sound localization. Presented at the 2015 IEEE 4th Global Conference on Consumer Electronics (GCCE) (2015)
40. Dobrev, I., et al.: Sound wave propagation on the human skull surface with bone conduction stimulation. Hear. Res. **355**, 1–13 (2017)
41. Ogiso, S., Mizutani, K., Zempo, K., Wakatsuki, N.: Analysis of sound propagation in human head for bone-conduction headphones using finite element method. Presented at the 2014 IEEE 3rd Global Conference on Consumer Electronics (GCCE) (2014)
42. Iwaki, M., Chigira, Y.: Compensation of sound source direction perceived through consumer-grade bone-conduction headphones by modifying ILD and ITD. Presented at the 2016 IEEE 5th Global Conference on Consumer Electronics (2016)
43. Llano, A.V.: Manizales en la dinámica colonizado. Universidad de Caldas, Manizales (1990)
44. Adelaar, W.F.H.: The Language of the Andes. Cambridge University Press, Cambridge, New York (2004)
45. Hoeg, E.R., Gerry, L.J., Thomsen, L., Nilsson, N.C., Serafin, S.: Binaural sound reduces reaction time in a virtual reality search task. Presented at the 2017 IEEE 3rd VR Workshop on Sonic Interactions for Virtual Environments (SIVE) (2017)

Gamification-Based VR Rowing Simulation System

Xuecheng Li[1], Zhengyu Wu[2], and Ting Han[1](✉)

[1] School of Design, Shanghai Jiao Tong University, Shanghai, China
hanting@sjtu.edu.cn

[2] School of Electronic Information and Electrical Engineering, Shanghai Jiao Tong University, Shanghai, China

Abstract. Rowing is an efficient sport that exercises all major muscle groups. Considering the physical restrictions (i.e. rowable bodies, water, weather conditions) of rowing, indoor rowing machines are used alternatively to simulate the rowing action. But despite their popularity, rowing machines fail to produce the immersive experience and may make the exercise tedious with repetitive movements. Based on the gamification theory, this study designed the game mechanics that involved the incentive and competitive mechanisms and developed a virtual reality (VR) simulation system for indoor rowing training. In the control experiment, an improved rowing performance (i.e. finishing time, heart rate, stroke rate) and higher motivation levels were observed in the immersive VR environment. Results of the study showed that the gamification-based VR rowing simulation system could produce an improvement in exercise intensity and quality, and that the application of gamification theory could improve exercisers' enjoyment and motivation.

Keywords: Gamification · VR rowing simulation system · Rowing machine

1 Introduction

1.1 Rowing Training

As pointed out by Guangju (2017), rowing training in China now faces problems such as physical restrictions, closed training patterns and limited training venues [1]. In the study on the characteristics of rowing beginner's training, Zaihang (2018) suggested that indoor rowing machine training should be carried out as the basis of on-water training [2]. Xiaoyan (2017) proposed an intelligent visualization improvement of rowing machines and conducted comprehensive analysis and evaluations of rowers' training indicators [3].

1.2 Training in VR Environment

In recent years, virtual reality technology has developed as a popular tool that has brought changes in many fields. Xu (2018) found that VR technology in physical education and training could produce immersive experiences for students and enhance the teaching effect [4]. Qing and Yuanfei (2016) pointed out that physical requirements

M. Kurosu (Ed.): HCII 2019, LNCS 11567, pp. 484–493, 2019.
https://doi.org/10.1007/978-3-030-22643-5_38

(i.e. venues, equipment and environments) in physical education (PE) restricted the conduction of many courses, and that a VR environment could create immersive experiences in a visual world and serve for the teaching purposes [5]. Jingyu (2017) designed a VR-based serious game for Rococo art teaching, combining technology, education and gamification [6]. The study of Murray et al. (2016) proved that VR could improve performance and the affective response to aerobic exercise [7]. Hoffmann et al. (2013) highlighted the importance of VR technology as a means to learn an energy-related skill and improve performance [8]. Brett et al. (2018) emphasized that challenge levels should be considered in the design of VR-based exercise programs and in matching competitive interactions among exercisers in virtual environments [9].

1.3 Gamification Theory

Gamification is the application of game-related elements in non-game contexts. Gamification has been applied to many fields such as business, marketing, management, health and education [10]. Many studies have explored the effectiveness of gamification in education and training. In the study on the effect of gamification-based task design on self-regulated learning, Dongjian (2018) demonstrated gamification's effect in enhancing learners' motivation, participation and learning outcomes [11]. Rob (2018) and others proved the motivational effects of gamification theory in education [12]. Lihua (2011) pointed out that motivational measures, as an important incentive mechanism in gamification, could stimulate the trainees and thereby improve the quality of military training [13]. In terms of gamification design, Werbach (2012) proposed the PBL (points, badges, leaderboards) method of gamification design [14], and ten of the most common game mechanics were perfected by Schell (2014): challenges, opportunities, competition, collaboration, feedback, resource acquisition, rewards, trading, rules, and winning conditions [15]. In rowing training, Wenzheng (2012) designed a rowing machine game in terms of both hardware and software [16].

Many experiments have been conducted to test sport training within a VR-based simulated environment, and almost all suggested that VR environment could effectively improve the training performance. The VR simulation experiences of rowing at present, however, are mostly generated using projectors or screens to produce dynamic virtual environments of simulated outdoor rowing, which does not necessarily have the desired effect. This study built on the Unity platform a VR rowing environment that applies to the HTC Vive and rowing machines (i.e. ergometers), allowing exercisers to feel fully immersed in a simulated rowing environment. Based on the motion principles and competition formats of rowing and the game mechanics in gamification theory, the study gave an in-depth analysis of the contents and logic of the rowing game, and extracted suitable game contents such as competition, leaderboard and resource acquisition.

2 Method

2.1 Participants

20 university students completed the International Sports Activity Questionnaire (IPAQ-SF) [17] and constituted the convenience sample. There were no significant differences in participants' age, BMI, physical activity level and physical health.

2.2 Apparatus

Hardware

The experiment was completed in a 5 m × 4 m light-controlled room set with a temperature of 15°C. The hardware equipment included physical equipment, control center and VR equipment. Participants rowed on the Concept 2 Model D Indoor Rowing ergometer fitted with Performance Monitor 4 set with a distance of 300 m and a 1-level drag factor. The control center was a computer with Unity4 installed. And the VR devices consisted of HTC Vive, VR controllers and two laser position sensors (as shown in Fig. 1.).

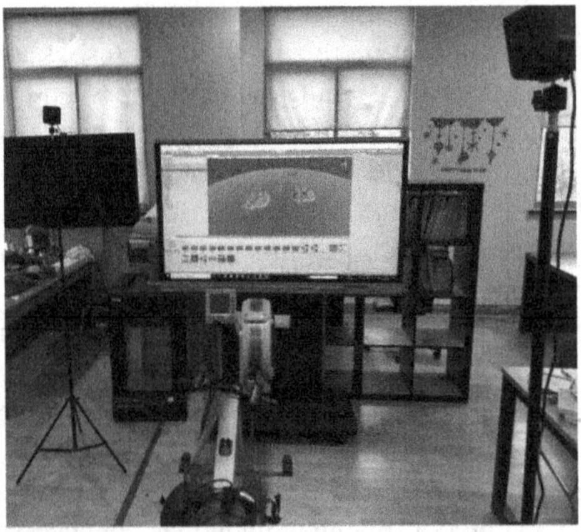

Fig. 1. Hardware equipment for gamification-based VR rowing simulation system

Software

This study built on the Unity platform a VR rowing game that applies to the HTC Vive and rowing ergometers. The HTC Vive controller was connected to the rowing ergometer handle to obtain real-time physical position of the VR headset and the handle, detect position changes of the ergometer and the participant, and based on the changes construct a rowing movement model. As participants rowed on the ergometer wearing a VR headset and holding the oars with controllers, the computer would record the position of the VR headset and oars and compare it with the previous position to infer participants' movements and simulate human and boat movements in the VR environment, creating simulated rowing process for participants in the VR game.

Specifically, first the tracks, boats, end signs, landscapes and other objects were drawn in Unity. Then, the boat was set as the main object, and the headset and controllers the sub-objects on the boat. Code scripts were bound on these objects to obtain their position of each frame.

This experiment established a series of incentive and reward mechanisms in the game. A number of boats with the speed set to a random number within a certain range would compete with the participants. The game levels had progressively increasing difficulty (i.e. the speed of competing boats increases) to appeal to participants. Real-time ranking and speed were displayed and participants would be awarded according to the ranking when the game ended. Besides, rowing scores would appear on the leaderboard, and the points could be accumulated to redeem different items in the game shop, such as boat skins and modification tool.

2.3 Measures

International Physical Activity Questionnaire – Short Form (IPAQ-SF)
The International Physical Activity Questionnaire – Short Form (IPAQ-SF) was used to classify participants into one of three categories of physical activity (low, medium, and high). The IPAQ-SF has seven items asking participants about the amount of time spent engaging in various forms of exercise over the last 7 days. The IPAQ-SF is positively correlated with exercise level and physical fitness.

Physical Activity Enjoyment Scale (PACES)
Physical Activity Enjoyment Scale [18] was used to measure the enjoyment of physical activity. The scale consists of 16 statements relating to physical activity. Participants respond to the statements on a Likert scale. PACES contains 9 positively-keyed questions and 7 negatively-keyed questions which are summed to produce the total enjoyment score. Higher scores suggest higher level of enjoyment.

User Experience Questionnaire (UEQ)
User Experience Questionnaire (UEQ) was used to obtain a preferably comprehensive impression of the product user experience. The 26-item questionnaire includes six factors: Attractiveness, Perspicuity, Efficiency, Dependability, Stimulation, and Novelty.

2.4 Procedure

On arrival, 20 participants provided informed consents and health certificates and then completed the IPAQ-SF. The height, weight and BMI of participants were measured. Participants on normal rowing ergometers were set as the control group, and those using VR rowing simulation system as the experimental group. Professional coaches gave participants instructions on correct rowing techniques. All participants were given a 5-min warm-up period rowing on the ergometer for familiarization with the equipment and performance feedback.

The experiment began after a 10-min rest. All participants were asked to row 300 m on the ergometer and were informed every 100 m. After the 300-m rowing, participants' heart rate in 30 s as well as the rowing time and stroke rate shown on PM4 were recorded. Then participants complemented the PACES and the UEQ.

To eliminate the influence of drops in energy levels, 20 participants were constructed to complete the row in VR simulation system after 24-h rest. The experimenters explained to participants the VR environment and game rules. Next, participants were fitted with VR headsets and completed a 5-min free rowing for warm up and familiarization with the equipment and performance feedback.

The experiment began after a 10-min rest. All participants were asked to row 300 m in a gamification-based VR simulation environment (as shown in Fig. 2.) and were informed every 100 m. After the 300-m rowing, participants' heart rate in 30 s as well as the rowing time and stroke rate shown on PM4 were recorded. Then participants complemented the PACES and the UEQ.

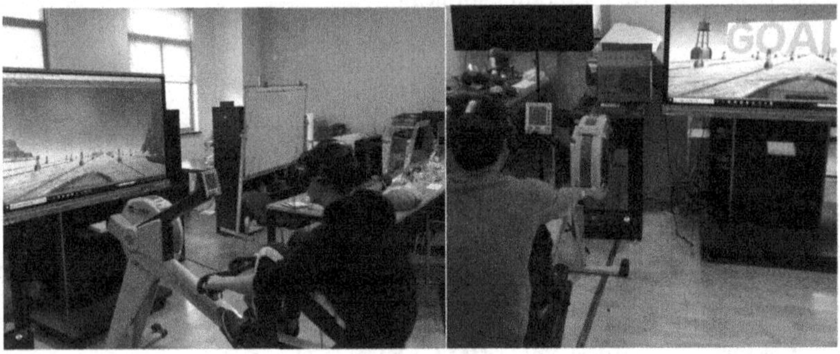

Fig. 2. Participants in the experiment

2.5 Scoring and Statistical Analysis

Prior to statistical analysis, time data were converted to seconds for analysis. Next, Paired-Samples T-tests were conducted to compare the heart rate, finishing time and stroke rate in the control group and the experimental group. In all analyses, α was set as 0.05.

3 Results

3.1 Physiological Indicators

Heart Rate
Null hypothesis: the heart rate of participants in a gamification-based VR rowing simulation system (experimental group) would not be higher than those rowing on normal ergometers (control group).

Alternative hypothesis: the heart rate of participants in a gamification-based VR rowing simulation system (experimental group) would be higher than those rowing on normal ergometers (control group).

As shown in Table 1, $t = -9.723$, $p < 0.001$, $df = 19$, the null hypothesis was rejected. In terms of heart rate, significant differences between the control group ($M = 69.25$) and the experimental group ($M = 78.70$) were found as the difference between the two means statistically significantly different from zero at the 5% level of

Table 1. T-test results of heart rate

(a) Paired samples statistics

		Mean	N	Std. Deviation	Std. Error Mean
Pair 1	cg	69.2500	20	8.34061	1.86502
	eg	78.7000	20	6.13103	1.37094

(b) Paired samples correlations

	N	Correlation	Sig.
Pair 1 cg & eg	20	.863	.000

(c) Paired samples test

	Paired Difference					t	df	Sig. (2-tailed)
	Mean	Std. Deviation	Std. Error Mean	95% Confidence Interval of the Difference				
				Lower	Upper			
Pair 1 cg -eg	-9.45000	4.34650	.97191	-11.48423	-7.41577	-9.723	19	.000

significance. Specifically, the results suggest that the experimental group experienced higher exercise intensity and quality compared with the control group that had lower heart rate.

Finishing Time

Null hypothesis: the finishing time of participants in a gamification-based VR rowing simulation system (experimental group) would not be shorter than those rowing on normal ergometers (control group).

Alternative hypothesis: the finishing time of participants in a gamification-based VR rowing simulation system (experimental group) would be shorter than those rowing on normal ergometers (control group).

As shown in Table 2, $t = 8.852$, $p < 0.001$, $df = 19$, the null hypothesis was rejected. In terms of finishing time, significant differences between the control group ($M = 102$) and the experimental group ($M = 89.3$) were found as the difference between the two means statistically significantly different from zero at the 5% level of significance. Specifically, the results suggest that compared with participants in the control group, participants in the experimental group experienced enhanced exercise performance with improved speed and body strength.

Stroke Rate

Null hypothesis: the stroke rate of participants in a gamification-based VR rowing simulation system (experimental group) would not be higher than those rowing on normal ergometers (control group).

Table 2. T-test results of finishing time

(a) Paired samples statistics

	Mean	N	Std. Deviation	Std. Error Mean
Pair 1 cg	102.0000	20	16.42847	3.67352
eg	89.3000	20	13.70401	3.06431

(b) Paired samples correlation

	N	Correlation	Sig.
Pair 1 cg & eg	20	.925	.000

(c) Paired samples test

	Paired Difference							
	Mean	Std. De-viation	Std. Error Mean	95% Confidence Interval of the Difference		t	df	Sig. (2-tailed)
				Lower	Upper			
Pair 1 cg -eg	12.70000	6.41626	1.43472	9.69710	15.70290	8.852	19	.000

Alternative hypothesis: the stroke rate of participants in a gamification-based VR rowing simulation system (experimental group) would be higher than those rowing on normal ergometers (control group).

As shown in Table 3, $t = -7.738$, $p < 0.001$, $df = 19$, the null hypothesis was rejected. In terms of stroke time, significant differences between the control group ($M = 102$) and the experimental group ($M = 89.3$) were found as the difference between the two means statistically significantly different from zero at the 5% level of significance. Specifically, the results suggest that the experimental group experienced showed better exercise quality and motivation compared with the control group with lower stroke rate.

3.2 Psychological Indicators

Physical Activity Enjoyment

Null hypothesis: the physical activity enjoyment of participants in a gamification-based VR rowing simulation system (experimental group) would not be greater than those rowing on normal ergometers (control group).

Alternative hypothesis: the physical activity enjoyment of participants in a gamification-based VR rowing simulation system (experimental group) would be greater than those rowing on normal ergometers (control group).

As shown in Table 4, $t = -12.040$, $p < 0.001$, $df = 19$, the null hypothesis was rejected. In terms of physical activity enjoyment, significant differences between the control group ($M = 102$) and the experimental group ($M = 89.3$) were found as the

Table 3. T-test results of stroke rate

(a) Paired samples statistics

	Mean	N	Std. Deviation	Std. Error Mean
Pair 1 cg	102.0000	20	16.42847	3.67352
eg	89.3000	20	13.70401	3.06431

(b) Paired samples correlation

	N	Correlation	Sig.
Pair 1 cg & eg	20	.925	.000

(c) Paired samples test

	Paired Difference							
	Mean	Std. Deviation	Std. Error Mean	95% Confidence Interval of the Difference		t	df	Sig. (2-tailed)
				Lower	Upper			
Pair 1 cg -eg	12.70000	6.41626	1.43472	9.69710	15.70290	8.852	19	.000

Table 4. T-test results of physical activity enjoyment

(a) Paired samples statistics

	Mean	N	Std. Deviation	Std. Error Mean
Pair 1 cg	102.0000	20	16.42847	3.67352
eg	89.3000	20	13.70401	3.06431

(b) Paired samples correlation

	N	Correlation	Sig.
Pair 1 cg & eg	20	.925	.000

(c) Paired samples test

	Paired Difference							
	Mean	Std. Deviation	Std. Error Mean	95% Confidence Interval of the Difference		t	df	Sig. (2-tailed)
				Lower	Upper			
Pair 1 cg -eg	12.70000	6.41626	1.43472	9.69710	15.70290	8.852	19	.000

difference between the two means statistically significantly different from zero at the 5% level of significance. Specifically, the results suggest that the VR rowing simulation system could greatly improve participants' physical activity enjoyment, raise their exercise motivation and reduce their anxiety levels.

User Experience Impression

Results of the UEQ showed significant differences among the control group and the experiment group, as the average score of each item in two groups suggested ($p = 0.001 < 0.05$). Specifically, compared with traditional rowing machines, the gamification-based VR rowing simulation system could provide better user experiences especially in interestingness and ingenuity.

4 Discussion

Findings of the present experiment show that rowing in a gamification-based VR simulation environment increased performance as measured by finishing time, heart rate and stroke rate when compared to rowing without VR input, which indicates that the VR rowing simulation system can produce an improvement in exercise intensity and quality. The results of the PACES show that the application of gamification theory can improve the participants' enjoyment and motivation in the exercise. And the UEQ results show that the VR rowing simulation system provides better user experience in terms of interestingness and ingenuity.

Although participants of the present study were all university students, the findings could apply to professional rowing athletes. Long practices on the rowing ergometer would cause stronger anxiety for athletes, and the VR rowing simulation system could reduce their anxiety and improve their training enjoyment and motivation.

The findings of this study are likely to generalize to other training and exercises. For example, a VR parkour game could be designed for running on the treadmill, which requires new research paths and design principles.

This study designed a gamification-based VR rowing simulation system that innovatively combined the rowing machine and VR headset to produce greater immersion. With VR technology, rowing exercise is no longer subject to on-water training requirements, and the gamification-based game contents enhance the playability of rowing. The use of VR simulation system could be expanded in rowing training to promote the development of rowing and national fitness.

Several limitations of the present study need to be considered when interpreting the results. First, the game content richness and the virtual environment reality could be further improved. In addition, the relatively short rowing distance and small sample size may affect the experiment results.

The present study is an interdisciplinary study in the industrial design and sports field. The gamification-based VR rowing simulation system is a Human-Computer Interaction (HCI) product that explores new paths in rowing training using new technologies and is of great relevance in the application of gamification theory in sports training. Findings of this research could be further generalized to other sports.

Acknowledgement. The research is supported by Science Foundation of Ministry of Education of China (Grant No. 17YJAZH029).

References

1. Guangju, L.: Rowing training in China: problems and solution. Sport. **19**, 14, 29 (2017)
2. Zaihang, Y.: A study on the training characteristics of male rowers in university and middle school students: Taking Tianjin Student Rowing Union as an example. Master. Tianjin Normal University (2018)
3. Xiaoyan, H.: Design of multi-functional intelligent test training system of rowing visualization. Youth Sports **50**, 53–54 (2017)
4. Xu, H.: Study on the feasibility of VR technology in college physical education and training. Contemp. Sports Technol. **8**(21), 3, 11 (2018)
5. Qing, W., Yuanfei, Y.: Study on the feasibility of VR technology in physical education and training. Youth Sports **44**, 7–9 (2016)
6. Jingyu, Y.: Design and development of VR-based serious game: a case study of rococo art teaching. Master. Beihua University (2017)
7. Murray, E.G., Neumann, D.L., Moffitt, R.L., Thoma, P.R.: The effects of the presence of others during a rowing exercise in a virtual reality environment. Psychol. Sport Exerc. **22**, 328–336 (2016)
8. Hoffman, C.P., Filippeschi, A., Ruffaldi, E., Bardy, B.G.: Energy management using virtual reality improves 2000-m rowing performance. J. Sports Sci. **32**, 501–509 (2014)
9. Brett, J.P., David, L.N.: The effects of competitiveness and challenge level on virtual reality rowing performance. Psychol. Sport Exerc. **41**, 191–199 (2018)
10. Dicheva, D., et al.: gamification in education: a systematic mapping study. J. Educ. Technol. Soc. **18**(3), 75-88 (2015)
11. Dongjian, Z.: Study on the effect of gamification-based task design on undergraduate's self-regulated learn. Northeast Normal University, Master (2018)
12. Rob, V.R., Bieke, Z.: Need-supporting gamification in education: An assessment of motivational effects over time. Comput. Educ. **127**, 283–297 (2018)
13. Lihua, W.: Motivational measures in military fitness training. Sports Art. **10**, 151 (2001)
14. Werbach, K., Hunter, D.: For the Win: How Game Thinking Can Revolutionize Your Business. Wharton Digital Press, Philadelphia (2012)
15. Schell, J.: The Art of Game Design: A book of lenses. AK Peters/CRC Press, Natick (2014)
16. Wenzheng, X.: A Design and Implementation of Rowing Fitness Equipment Games. Master. Sun Yat-sen University (2012)
17. Craig, C.L., et al.: International physical activity questionnaire: 12-country reliability and validity. Med. Sci. Sports Exerc. **35**(8), 1381–1395 (2003)
18. Motl, R.W., Dishman, R.K., Saunders, R., Dowda, M., Felton, G., Pate, R.R.: Measuring enjoyment of physical activity in adolescent girls. Am. J. Prev. Med. **21**(2), 110–117 (2001)

Analysis of the Mixture of Linear and Circular Vections in Immersive Visual Space

Comparison of Forward and Backward Moving Visual Stimuli

Ayumi Matsuda[1(✉)], Yuma Koga[2], Miki Matsumuro[1], Fumihisa Shibata[1], Hideyuki Tamura[3], and Asako Kimura[1]

[1] College of Information Science and Engineering, Ritsumeikan University, 1-1-1 Noji-Higashi, Kusatsu, Shiga 525-8577, Japan
a_matuda@rm.is.ritsumei.ac.jp
[2] Graduate School of Information Science and Engineering, Ritsumeikan University, 1-1-1 Noji-Higashi, Kusatsu, Shiga 525-8577, Japan
[3] Research Organization of Science and Engineering, Ritsumeikan University, 1-1-1 Noji-Higashi, Kusatsu, Shiga 525-8577, Japan

Abstract. Vection is a visually induced, self-motion illusion caused by observing a moving pattern in certain direction. Vection is classified into two types based on its moving direction: linear vection (LV; rectilinear motion sense) and circular vection (CV; rotational motion sense). Most studies focus on either LV or CV, and the mutual effects between LV and CV remain uninvestigated. Therefore, in this study, we aim to reveal the relationship between LV and CV by analyzing; whether or not each vection was perceived independently from visual stimuli with a spiral motion. From the results of our two experiments, we demonstrate that, as vection in one direction that is perceived from a visual stimulus with the spiral motion is strengthened, the vection in another direction is weakened. In other words, the strengths of both LV and CV have a negative correlation. Additionally, we explain that the influence degree of LV strength on the evaluation of CV is different between backward and forward LV.

Keywords: User interface · Ego-motion · Optic flow

1 Introduction

Vection is a visually induced, self-motion illusion caused by observing a moving pattern in a certain direction [1]. For instance, when a train on the opposite track begins to move, an observer inside a stationary train perceives his/her own train as moving in the opposite direction [2]. When the participants observed radial optic flow (Fig. 1(a)), they perceived their bodies as moving backward or forward (linear vection [LV]); when they observed rotational optic flow (Fig. 1(b)), they perceived as their bodies rotating (circular vection [CV]).

Vection can be used to express and produce rectilinear and rotational motion sense without actually moving. For this reason, many videos are designed to induce vection.

M. Kurosu (Ed.): HCII 2019, LNCS 11567, pp. 494–505, 2019.
https://doi.org/10.1007/978-3-030-22643-5_39

Discovering features to produce stronger vection or elucidate its mechanism improve its expression and immersion in videos.

Some previous studies investigated the relationship between the velocity of visual stimulus's motion and the vection strength. Berthoz et al. [3] demonstrates that the faster the linear velocity becomes, the stronger the strength of LV becomes based on the analysis of the relationship between the radial forward movement velocity of a visual stimulus and the LV strength. Similarly, Held et al. [4] explains that CV becomes stronger as the rotational velocity of a roll rotating stimulus increases. These studies reveal that the vection strength is related to the velocity of the corresponding movement in the visual stimulus; however, these studies used visual stimuli that had either linear motion or rotational motion (i.e., Fig. 1(a) or (b)).

Some studies have analyzed vection with a stimulus moving spirally, where the radial and circular movement were presented simultaneously (see Fig. 1(c)) [5–7]. For example, Palmisano et al. examined the influence of the presentation methods of visual stimuli with radial, circular of roll rotation, and spiral motions on the vection's strength. The authors measured the vection strength with one question that inquired into the overall strength of the of self-motion feeling.

The spiral motion contains both radial and rotational movement and the velocity of each movement can be manipulated independently. An observer can perceive the linear and rotational self-motions from such a stimulus; therefore, each strength varies according to the velocity of the corresponding movement direction.

Meanwhile, whether the velocities of each movement influences the strength of vection for the no-corresponding direction remains uninvestigated-namely, the effect of the linear movement's velocity on the CV strength and vice versa. We aim to demonstrate the mutual effects of LV and CV using spiral motion stimuli (Fig. 1(c)). Additionally, we compare the effects of LV on CV strength wherein the linear motion is forward and backward.

2 Experimental Setup

2.1 Wide-Field-of-View Display System

A human's viewing angle is more than 180° in the horizontal direction. Therefore, it is important to present a visual stimulus in the participants' entire visual field investigate

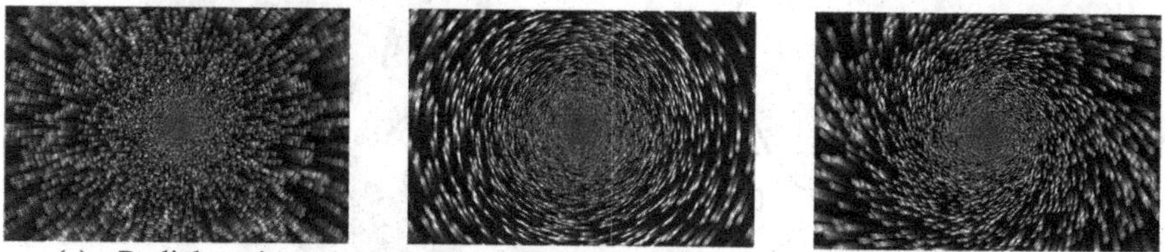

(a) Radial motion (b) Circular motion (c) Spiral motion (combined radial and circular)

Fig. 1. Image of movement of visual stimulus

vection. In this study, we construct an immersive display system to present a visual stimulus to participants' entire fields of view.

The 360-degree-view videos can be presented using three projectors. The projector light dazzled participants' eyes and casted their shadows on the screen because our display system uses front projection. To solve these problems, we projected a black circle on each participant's head position, meaning the projector provided no direct light to participants' eye [8]. The participants observed the visual stimulus from a certain upright position to prevent their shadows from appearing on the screen (Fig. 2).

2.2 Visual Stimulus

In our experiments, we used a flow of random dots. This method is used in many vection studies, and participants can recognize both radial and circular motions of the visual stimulus. The vection strength is influenced by the visual stimulus's depth information [7]. Therefore, we prepared a virtual cylinder with a random dot image and moved it into the rectilinear and rotational directions, for which Fig. 3 illustrates the simulated visual environment. In this way, participants were able to observe the visual stimulus (i.e., radial, rotational or spiral flow) along the identical motion in depth.

In all experiments, the rotation direction was clockwise, and participants felt as though their bodies were rotating counterclockwise. We moved the cylinder from front to back in Experiment 1 and from back to front in Experiment 2; thus, participants felt as though they were moving forward in Experiment 1 and backward in Experiment 2.

2.3 Evaluation Methods of Vection Strength

We evaluated the vection strength using onset latency, duration, and vection strength rating. The onset latency was the time until the participants started experiencing self-motion, and a shorter onset latency indicated stronger vection. The duration was the sum of the time during which the participants experienced self-motion, where longer duration indicated stronger vection. The vection strength rating was a self-reported value of how strongly the participants felt they were moving.

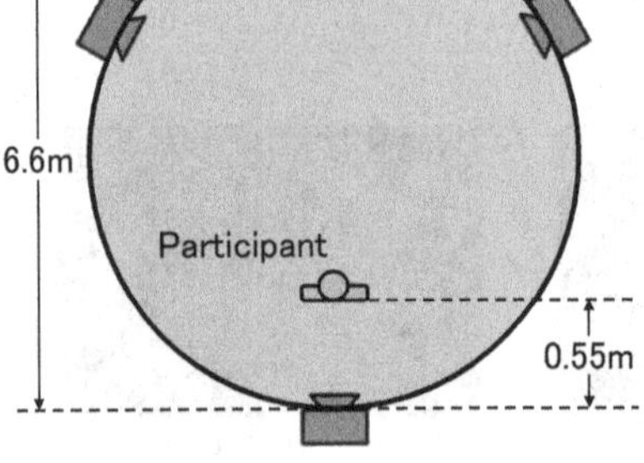

Fig. 2. Observation position of participant

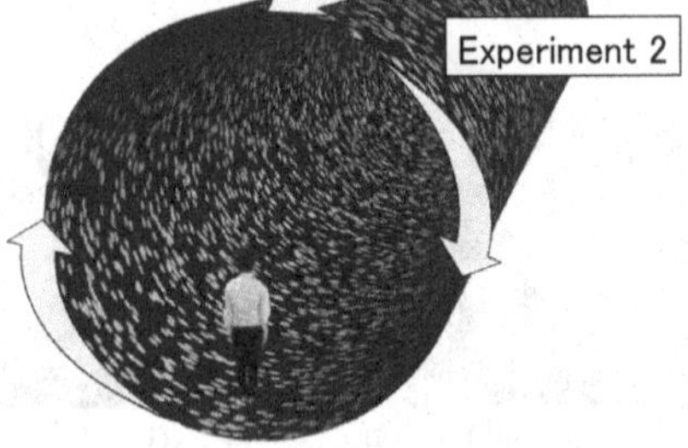

Fig. 3. Simulated visual environment

We used a Wii Remote controller to acquire the onset latency and duration. The controller was connected to the PC using the Bluetooth adapter, which transmitted data stably at 100 Hz. The participants kept the button of the Wii Remote depressed for the duration of the vection experience. The time at which the controller's button was first pressed was used for the onset latency, and the sum of how long the button was pressed was used for the duration. As soon as the visual stimulus presentation was finished, participants reported the vection strength using a 101-point rating scale ranging from 0 = "no vection" to 100 = "very strong vection".

3 Experiment 1

We investigated whether or not forward LV and counter-clockwise CV affect each other. In order to achieve this objective, the LV strength was acquired in Experiment 1a and the CV strength was acquired in Experiment 1b. If each vection did not affect the other, the acquired strength would be constant regardless of the other vection's strength. Each vection's strength was manipulated by changing the cylinder's velocity in each direction.

3.1 Experiment 1a

We acquired the LV strength by changing the radial and rotational velocity.

Experimental Condition
We manipulated the linear and rotational velocities of the visual stimulius. Each velocity factor possessed four levels. The prepared levels in the linear velocity factor were 0.0 m/s, 4.0 m/s, 8.0 m/s and 16 m/s and the prepared levels in the rotational velocity factor were 0.0°/s, 4.0°/s, 8.0°/s and 16°/s. Experiment 1a had twelve conditions combined with three linear velocities and four rotational velocities with the exception of 0.0 m/s.

Participants
Ten males and three females participated in this experiment, all of whom had normal or corrected-to-normal vision.

Experimental Procedure
The participants evaluated the LV strength while observing the spiral motion. The procedure for one trial is explained below.

There existed the possibility that participants neglected the circular motion due to excess concentration while evaluating LV. To avoid this possibility, the visual stimulus was presented with only rotational motion at the start of each trial. We waited to add linear motion until the participants indicated that they perceived CV by pressing the button. As soon as the button was pressed, we added the radial motion to the visual stimulus and presented a spiral motion. The participants were asked to keep the button depressed as long as the LV experience continued during the spiral motion's presentation. After observing of the spiral motion for 40 s, participants reported the vection strength using a 101-point rating scale.

The number of all trials was 36 per participant because we conducted three trials for each condition, and the order of trials was randomized for each participant.

Results

Figure 4 illustrates the onset latency for CV before the radial motion was added. A repeated-measures ANOVA revealed the significant main effects of the rotational velocity ($F_{(2,24)} = 19.654$, $p < 0.001$). A post hoc analysis using Bonferroni correction revealed significant differences illustrated in Fig. 4. Thus, CV was strengthened as the rotational velocity increased.

Figures 5, 6 and 7 illustrate the onset latency, duration, and strength for LV. For all indices, 3 (linear velocity) × 4 (rotational velocity) ANOVAs revealed the significant main effects of the linear velocity (onset latency $F_{(2,24)} = 33.529$, $p < 0.001$; duration: $F_{(2,24)} = 40.638$, $p < 0.001$, strength rating: $F_{(2,24)} = 98.484$, $p < 0.001$) and the rotational velocity (onset latency: $F_{(3,36)} = 7.251$, $p < 0.001$, duration: $F_{(3,36)} = 9.279$, $p < 0.001$, strength rating: $F_{(3,36)} = 5.469$, $p = 0.003$). The interaction was significant for the onset latency and duration (onset latency: $F_{(6,72)} = 6.521$, $p < 0.001$, duration: $F_{(6,72)} = 8.533$, $p < 0.001$); but insignificant for the strength rating ($F_{(6,72)} = 1.099$, $p = 0.372$). For the onset latency and duration, there was a significant, simple main effect of rotational velocity at 4.0 m/s (onset latency: $F_{(3,108)} = 19.459$, $p < 0.001$, duration: $F_{(3,108)} = 24.344$, $p < 0.001$). Post hoc analyses using Bonferroni correction

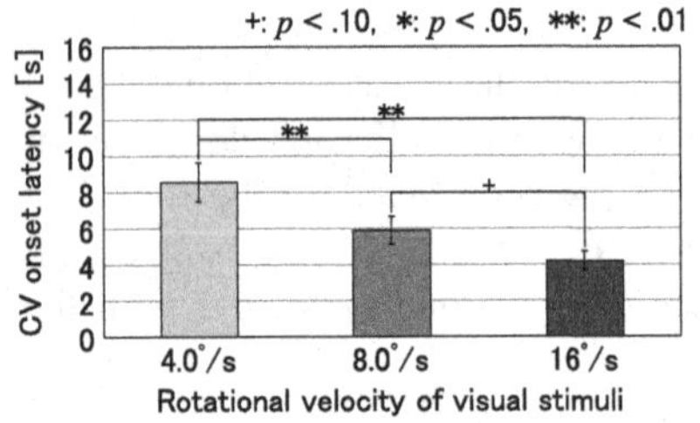

Fig. 4. CV onset latency before adding linear flow

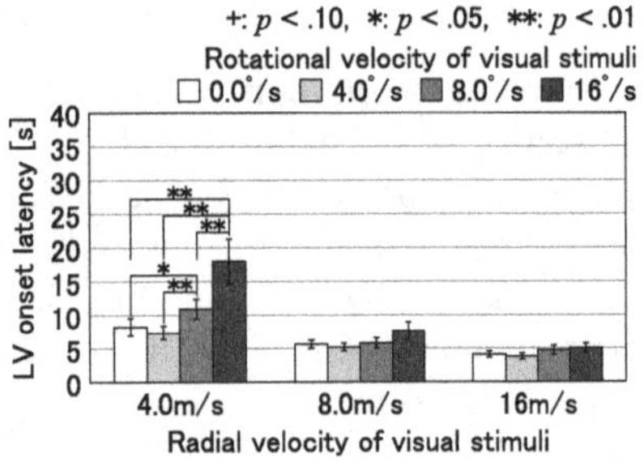

Fig. 5. LV onset latency after adding linear flow

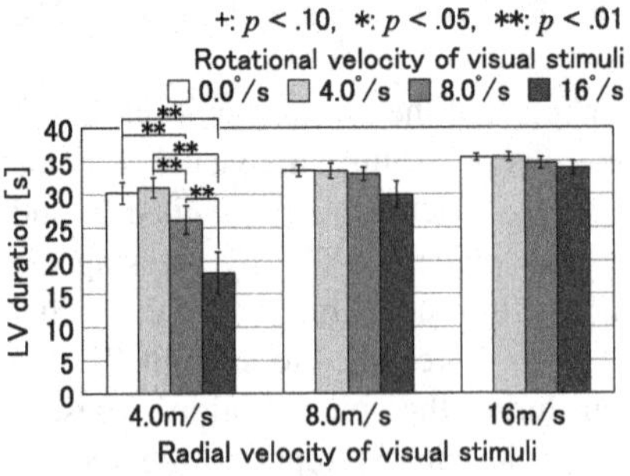

Fig. 6. LV duration after adding linear flow

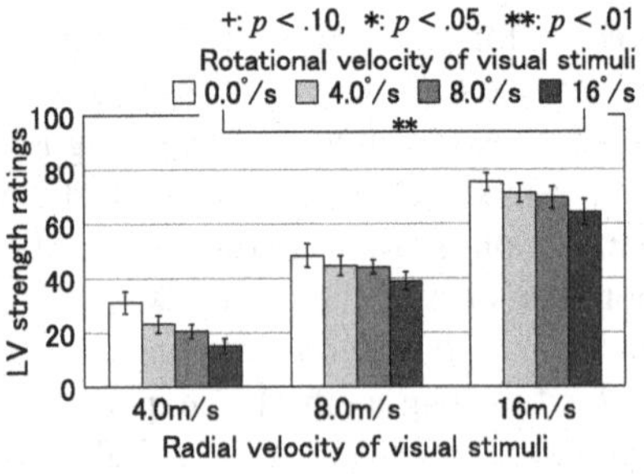

Fig. 7. LV strength ratings after adding linear flow

revealed significant differences shown in both Figs. 4 and 5. We found that LV was weakened as the rotational velocity of the visual stimulus became faster only when the radial velocity was slow.

In addition, a multiple comparison by Bonferroni correction was executed to investigate the effect of rotational velocity on the LV strength rating (Fig. 7). As a result, there was a significant difference between the 0.0°/s and the 16°/s condition ($p = 0.002$). This result indicates the LV strength decreased as the rotational velocity increased in the self-report following the observation; however, different from the onset latency and duration, the influence of linear velocity was constant under all linear velocity conditions.

3.2 Experiment 1b

We acquired the CV strength by changing the radial and rotational velocities.

Experimental Condition

Experiment 1b had twelve conditions combined four radial velocities (0.0 m/s, 4.0 m/s, 8.0 m/s and 16 m/s) and three rotational velocities (4.0°/s, 8.0°/s and 16°/s).

Participants

The same ten males and three females who participated in Experiment 1a also participated in Experiment 1b.

Experimental Procedure

With the exception of the presentation order of radial and circular motion, the procedure was identical to that used in Experiment 1a. The participants observed the visual stimulus with only the radial motion and pushed the button when they felt their bodies were moving (i.e., the LV onset latency). Next, we added circular motion to the visual stimulus and acquired the onset latency, duration, and strength for CV.

Results

Figure 8 illustrates the onset latency for LV before adding the circular motion to the visual stimulus. A repeated-measures ANOVA revealed the significant main effect of the radial velocity ($F_{(2,24)} = 22.490$, $p < 0.001$), and post hoc analyses revealed significant differences displayed in the Fig. 8. LV was strengthened as the radial velocity increased.

Figures 9, 10 and 11 illustrate the onset latency, duration, and strength rating for CV. For all indices, 4 (linear velocity) × 3 (rotational velocity) ANOVAs revealed the significant main effects of the radial velocity (onset latency: $F_{(3,36)} = 18.624$, $p < 0.001$, duration: $F_{(3,36)} = 30.948$, $p < 0.001$, strength rating: $F_{(3,36)} = 33.117$, $p < 0.001$) and the rotational velocity (onset latency: $F_{(2,24)} = 18.624$, $p < 0.001$, duration: $F_{(2,24)} = 90.274$, $p < 0.001$, strength rating: $F_{(2,24)} = 280.232$, $p < 0.001$), and the significant interaction (onset latency: $F_{(6,72)} = 10.391$, $p < 0.001$, duration: $F_{(6,72)} = 9.523$, $p < 0.001$, strength rating: $F_{(6,72)} = 3.520$, $p = 0.004$). In the onset latency and duration, significant, simple main effects of the radial velocity at 4.0°/s (onset latency: $F_{(3,108)} = 33.372$, $p < 0.001$, duration: $F_{(3,108)} = 40.860$, $p < 0.001$) and 8.0°/s (onset latency: $F_{(3,108)} = 9.752$, $p < 0.001$, duration: $F_{(3,108)} = 15.082$, $p < 0.001$). In the strength rating, significant, simple main effects of radial velocity at all levels of

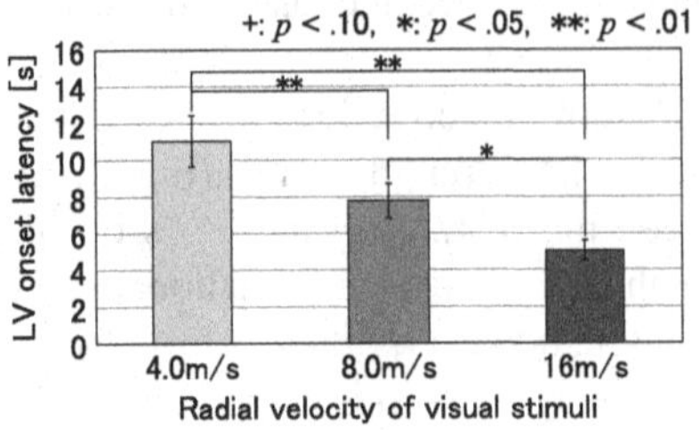

Fig. 8. LV onset latency before adding rotational flow

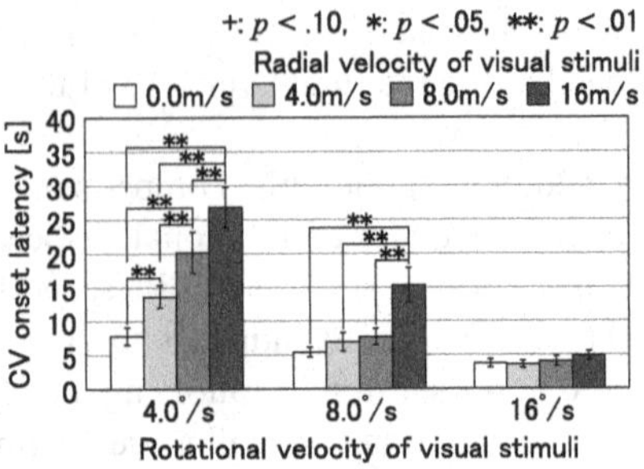

Fig. 9. CV onset latency after adding rotational flow

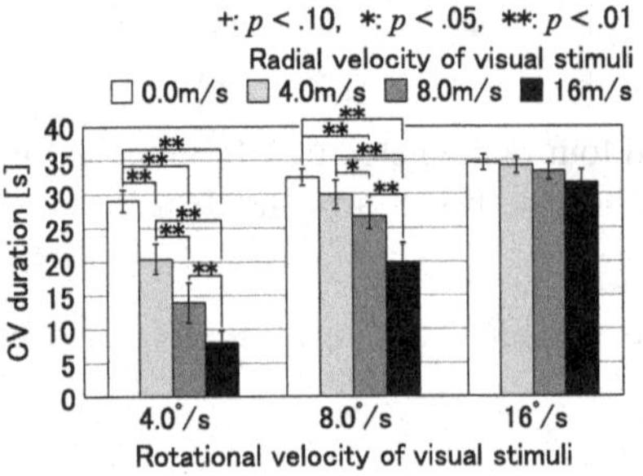

Fig. 10. CV duration after adding rotational flow

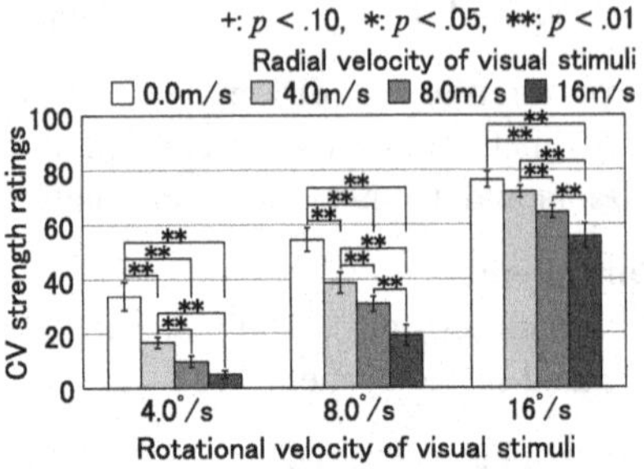

Fig. 11. CV strength ratings after adding rotational flow

rotational velocity (4.0°/s: $F_{(3,108)} = 22.186$, $p < 0.001$, 8.0°/s: $F_{(3,108)} = 30.649$, $p < 0.001$, 16°/s: $F_{(3,108)} = 11.626$, $p < 0.001$). Post hoc analyses using Bonferroni correction revealed significant differences that may be observed in Figs. 9, 10 and 11.

Discussion

The results of Experiment 1a demonstrate that the LV strength decreased as the rotational velocity increased; and, this influence of the rotational velocity on the LV strength was observed only when the radial velocity was slow. Considering that the CV strength increased as the rotational velocity increased, the visual stimulus of spiral motion producing stronger CV weakened the LV strength, which was perceived simultaneously. However, in some indices, such an effect of the CV strength disappeared when the participants observed the spiral motion with the faster radial velocity producing the stronger LV.

The results of Experiment 1b reveal the same tendency observed in Experiment 1a. As the radial velocity increased, the LV strength increased and the CV strength decreased. Therefore, it can be argued that the stronger the LV vection becomes, the weaker the CV strength becomes-an effect that decreases as the rotational velocity increases. From the results of Experiment 1, we found a negative correlation between the CV and LV strengths perceived from the spiral motion.

4 Experiment 2

To generalize the results of Experiment 1, we investigated whether backward LV and counter-clockwise CV affect each other. To achieve this objective, the LV and CV strengths were acquired in Experiments 2a and 2b.

4.1 Experiment 2a

We acquired the LV strength by changing the radial and rotational velocities.

Experimental Condition
We used the same twelve conditions used in Experiment 1a.

Participants
Ten males and two females different from those in Experiment 1 participated in Experiment 2a, all of whom had normal or corrected-to-normal vision.

Experimental Procedure
The experiment procedure was identical to that applied in Experiment 1a, with the exception of the radial movement's direction.

Results
Figure 12 illustrates the onset latency for CV before adding the radial motion to the visual stimulus. A repeated-measures ANOVA revealed the significant main effects of the rotational velocity ($F_{(2,22)} = 8.023$, $p = 0.002$), and a post hoc analysis using Bonferroni correction revealed significant differences that can be observed in Fig. 12. Stronger CV was produced from the visual stimulus with faster rotational velocity, and the onset latency and its trend were almost identical to those observed in Experiment 1a.

Figures 13, 14 and 15 show the onset latency, duration, and subject strength for LV. For all indices, 3 (linear velocity) × 4 (rotational velocity) ANOVAs revealed the significant main effects of the radial velocity (onset latency: $F_{(2,22)} = 24.115$, $p < 0.001$, duration: $F_{(2,22)} = 46.856$, $p < 0.001$, subject strength: $F_{(2,22)} = 37.077$, $p < 0.001$), the rotational velocity (onset latency: $F_{(3,33)} = 3.550$, $p = 0.025$, duration: $F_{(3,33)} = 7.643$, $p < 0.001$, subject strength: $F_{(3,33)} = 5.914$, $p = 0.002$), and the significant interactions (onset latency: $F_{(6,66)} = 4.508$, $p < 0.001$, duration: $F_{(6,66)} = 4.575$, $p < 0.001$, subject strength: $F_{(6,66)} = 2.720$, $p = 0.020$). For the onset latency, the significant, simple main effects of rotational velocity at 4.0 m/s ($F_{(3,99)} = 11.597$, $p < 0.001$); for the duration and subjective strength, the significant, simple main effects of the rotational velocity at 4.0 m/s (duration: $F_{(3,108)} = 14.720$, $p < 0.001$, subject strength: $F_{(3,108)} = 9.042$, $p < 0.001$) and 8.0 m/s (duration: $F_{(3,108)} = 3.351$, $p = 0.022$, subject strength: $F_{(3,108)} = 3.373$, $p = 0.022$). Post hoc analyses using Bonferroni correction revealed significant differences that can observed in Figs. 13, 14 and 15.

As with Experiment 1a, we found that LV was weakened when the visual stimulus's rotational velocity increased. Considering that the strength of CV increased as the rotational velocity increased, the CV strength perceived from the spiral motion increased and the LV strength perceived from the same motion decreased. Additionally, this effect disappeared when the linear velocity was fast.

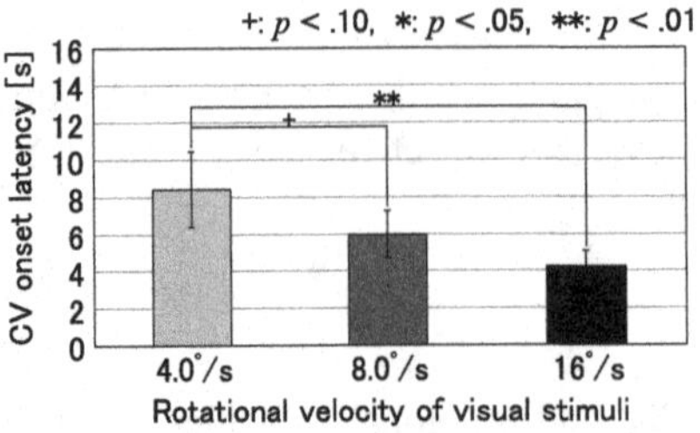

Fig. 12. CV onset latency before adding linear flow

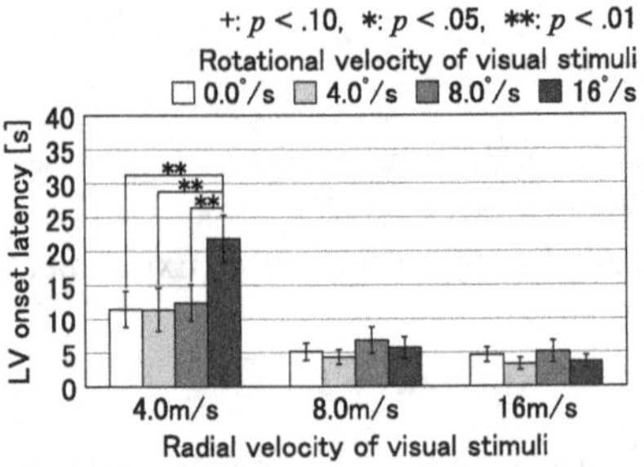

Fig. 13. LV onset latency after adding linear flow

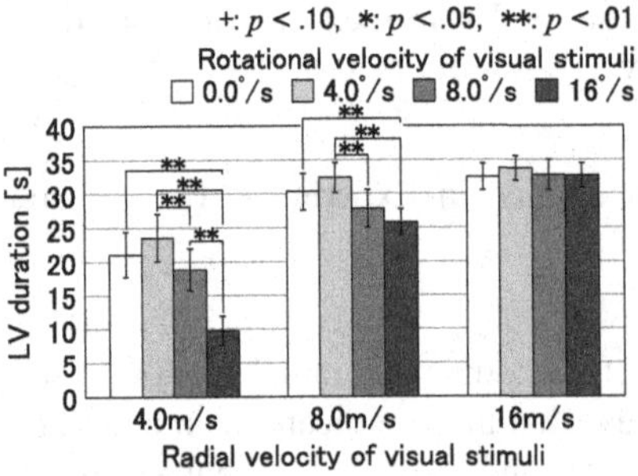

Fig. 14. LV duration after adding linear flow

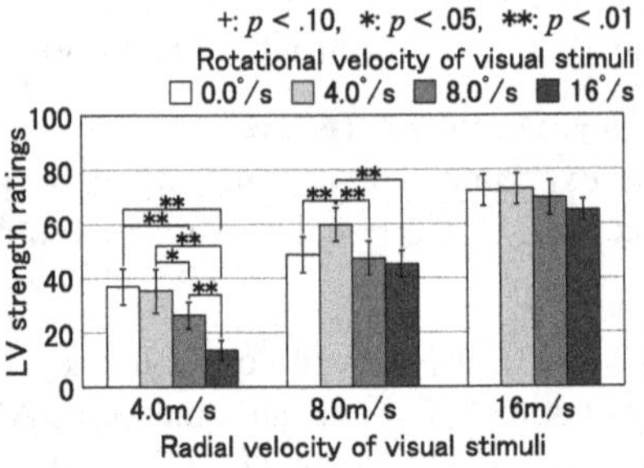

Fig. 15. LV strength ratings after adding linear flow

4.2 Experiment 2b

We acquired the CV strength by changing the radial and rotational velocities.

Experimental Condition
We adopted the same twelve conditions used in Experiment 1b.

Participants
The same ten males and two females who participated in Experiment 2a also participated in Experiment 2b.

Experimental Procedure
The experiment procedure was identical to that used in Experiment 1b, with the exception of the radial movement's direction.

Results
Figure 16 shows the onset latency for LV before adding the circular motion to the visual stimulus. A repeated-measures ANOVA revealed the significant main effect of linear velocity ($F_{(2,22)} = 6.995$, $p = 0.005$), and a multiple comparison using Bonferroni correction revealed the significant differences illustrated in Fig. 16. LV was strengthened as the radial velocity increased. Compared with the results of Experiment

1b (Fig. 8), the onset latency was slightly shorter. From this result, the backward LV was demonstrated to be perceived more easily than the forward LV.

Figures 17, 18 and 19 show the onset latency, duration, and strength rating for CV. For all indices, 4 (radial velocity) × 3 (rotational velocity) ANOVAs revealed the significant main effects of the radial velocity (onset latency: $F_{(3,33)} = 26.461$, $p < 0.001$, duration: $F_{(3,33)} = 47.215$, $p < 0.001$, strength rating: $F_{(3,33)} = 33.442$, $p < 0.001$), the rotational velocity (onset latency: $F_{(2,22)} = 50.183$, $p < 0.001$, duration: $F_{(2,22)} = 111.006$, $p < 0.001$, strength rating: $F_{(2,22)} = 93.366$, $p < 0.001$), and the significant interactions (onset latency: $F_{(6,66)} = 4.412$, $p < 0.001$, duration: $F_{(6,66)} = 6.068$, $p < 0.001$, strength rating: $F_{(6,66)} = 3.423$, $p = 0.005$). Significant, simple main effects of the radial velocity in all rotational velocities for the onset latency (4.0°/s: $F_{(3,99)} = 22.621$, $p < 0.001$, 8.0°/s: $F_{(3,99)} = 13.939$, $p < 0.001$, 16°/s: $F_{(3,99)} = 3.217$, $p = 0.026$), duration (4.0°/s: $F_{(3,99)} = 27.380$, $p < 0.001$, 8.0°/s: $F_{(3,99)} = 29.603$, $p < 0.001$, 16°/s: $F_{(3,99)} = 6.012$, $p < 0.001$), and strength rating (4.0°/s: $F_{(3,99)} = 12.108$, $p < 0.001$, 8.0°/s: $F_{(3,99)} = 24.768$, $p < 0.001$, 16°/s: $F_{(3,99)} = 18.944$, $p < 0.001$). Post hoc analyses using Bonferroni correction revealed the significant differences that can be observed in Figs. 17, 18 and 19.

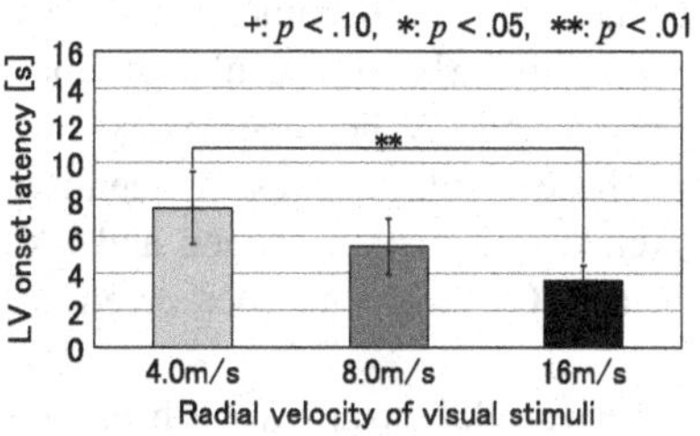

Fig. 16. LV onset latency before adding rotational flow

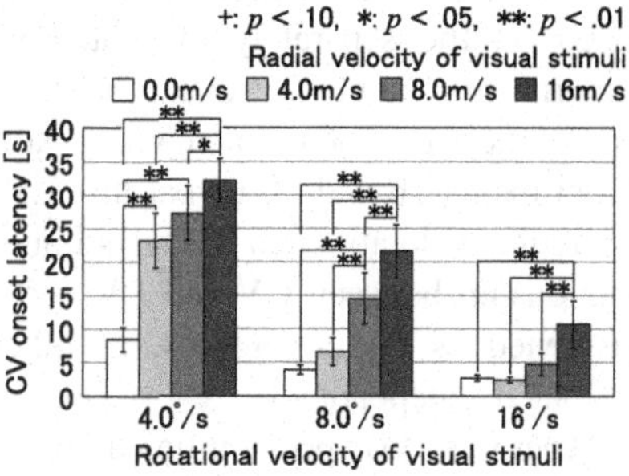

Fig. 17. CV onset latency after adding rotational flow

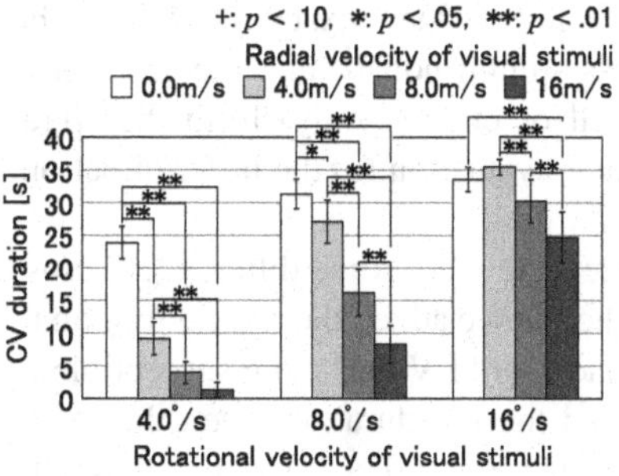

Fig. 18. CV duration after adding rotational flow

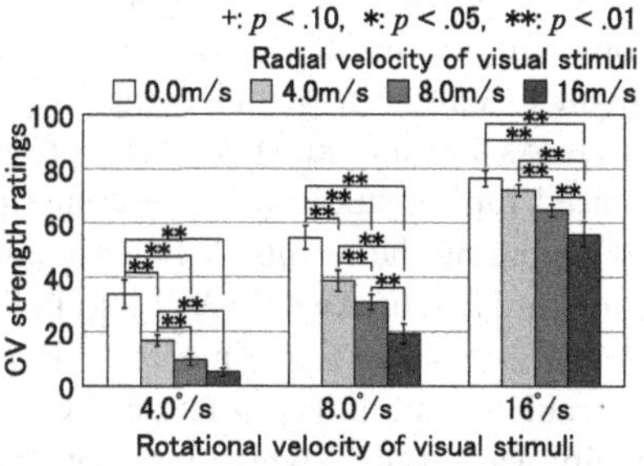

Fig. 19. CV strength ratings after adding rotational flow

As with Experiment 1b, we found that CV was weakened when the radial velocity of the visual stimulus increased. Considering that the strength of LV increased as the radial velocity increased, the LV strength perceived from the spiral motion increased, and the CV strength perceived from the same motion decreased. As illustrated in Figs. 17, 18 and 19, the differences between each radial velocity lessened as the rotational velocity increased; namely, the effect of radial velocity was more remarkable when the rotational velocity was slower.

Discussion

We confirmed the negative relation between CV and LV through Experiment 2. The results of both Experiments 2a and 2b reveal that increasing the velocity of one direction increase the strength of the corresponding vection and decreases the strength of the noncorresponding vection. However, when the velocity of one direction is fast, the influence from the other directiotn's velocity weakens or disappears.

5 General Discussion

We investigated the relationship between LV and CV perceived from the spiral motion based on the separately evaluated strength of each vection. The results of both Experiments 1a and 2a reveal that CV becomes stronger and LV becomes weaker as the rotational velocity of a visual stimulus increases. Similarly, the results of both Experiments 1b and 2b reveal that LV becomes stronger and CV becomes weaker as the radial velocity of a visual stimulus increases. These results suggest a negative relationship between CV and LV because CV weakened as LV strengthened and LV weakened as CV strengthed. In other words, LV and CV were not perceived or evaluated independently.

There are two possibilities as to why such a negative relationship was observed. The first possibility is the limitation of the cognitive resource. The faster motion draws more attention; therefore, observers tend to spend more cognitive resources processing it. As spared resource for another slower motion becomes small, and as a result, the faster motion prevents observers from experiencing the self-motion in another direction. The second possibility is that the observer cannot evaluate exactly how long the stimulus moves in each direction. Humans process stimuli holistically; therefore, it is difficult to extract a partial component (i.e., radial or circular only) from the spiral motion. As a result, humans simply provide a greater evaluation for the faster direction. We need further studies to investigate these possibilities.

Comparing the results of Experiments 1 and 2, there were some differences across the forward and backward LV. First, in the case wherein we added the radical motion to the circular motion (Experiments 1a and 2a), the backward LV was more susceptible to the circular motion. The rotational velocity affected the LV duration when the radial velocity was 8.0 m/s, which was not observed for the forward LV (Figs. 6 and 14). In addition, the onset latency was slower and the duration was shorter for the backward LV than were those for the forward LV, especially when the radial velocity was slow. On the other hand, when the rotational motion was added to the radial motion (Experiments 1b and 2b), the influence of the backward LV was stronger than that of the forward LV.

When the radial motion produced backward LV, the effect of the radial velocity was observed even if the rotational velocity was faster (Figs. 17 and 18), and the onset latency was shorter for backward LV than that for forward LV (Figs. 8 and 16).

The comparison of the two experiments' results reveals that backward LV is easily perceived and has stronger effects on CV than does forward LV. However, backward LV is susceptible to rotational velocity than is forward LV. One of possible reasons for this contradictory result is the frequency of everyday movements we experience. Generally, the opportunities to move forward are more frequent than those to move backward. We are accustomed to processing visual information for forward movement; therefore, we can easily neglect or pay attention to and then process such information. However, this is not the case for backward movement; we cannot adjust the sensitivity to visual information for backward movement. As a result, backward LV is susceptible to CV strength in some situations, while it is easily perceived and strongly influences CV strength in other situations.

6 Conclusion

From the results of our experiments, we determined there exists a negative correlation between the strengths of LV and CV. According to the visual stimulus wherein the strength of one vection was high, the strength of another vection became weak. Additionally, there were some differences in the effect of the forward and backward LV that imply what effect everyday observations of scenery produced by our movement have on the strength of perceived vection.

References

1. Palmisano, S., Allison, R.S., Schira, M.M., Barry, R.J.: Future challenges for vection research: definitions, functional significance, measures, and neural bases. Front. Psychol. **6**, 1–15 (2015). Article 193
2. Seno, T., Fukuda, H.: Stimulus meanings alter illusory self-motion (vection) - experimental examination of the train illusion. Seeing Perceiving **25**, 631–645 (2012)
3. Berthoz, A., Pavard, B., Young, L.R.: Perception of linear horizontal self-motion induced by peripheral vision (linearvection) basic characteristics and visual-vestibular interactions. Exp. Brain Res. **23**, 471–489 (1975)
4. Held, R., Dichgans, J., Bauer, J.: Characteristics of moving visual scenes influencing spatial orientation. Vis. Res. **15**(3), 357–365 (1975)
5. Pitzalis, S., et al.: Selectivity to translational egomotion in human brain motion areas. PLoS ONE **8**(4), 1–13 (2013)
6. Kim, J., Khuu, S.: A new spin on vection in depth. J. Vis. **14**(5), 1–10 (2014)
7. Palmisano, S., Summersby, S., Davies, R.G., Kim, J.: Stereoscopic advantages for vection induced by radial, circular, and spiral optic flows. J. Vis. **16**(14), 1–19 (2016)
8. Tamaki, J., Murakami, K.: A proposal of non-dazzling projector system. IPSJ SIG Tech. Rep. **2008-CVIM-163**(36), 43–46 (2008)

Multi-camera Coordinate Calibration and Accuracy Evaluation for Robot Control

Masahiro Nonaka[1], Hiroshi Noborio[1,2,3(✉)], Katsuhiko Onishi[1,2,3], Katsunori Tachibana[1,2,3], Kaoru Watanabe[2], and Kiminori Mizushino[3]

[1] Kansai Medical University, Hirakata, Osaak 573-1010, Japan
[2] Osaka Electro-Communication University, Shijo-Nawate, Osaka 575-0063, Japan
noborio@osakac.ac.jp
[3] Embedded Wings Co., Minoh, Osaka 562-0015, Japan

Abstract. In this study, our goal is to create a surgical navigation system that takes stable measurements of a surgical area using RGB/depth cameras without obstructions, such as the surgeon's head or hands. We mounted three cutting-edge D435 Intel RealSense Depth Cameras onto a ring and photographed the surgical area from three directions. We also installed a robotic mechanical system that can move the camera ring up and down so that the surgery can proceed smoothly. First, we calibrated the coordinate systems so that the coordinate systems of the three cameras (three-dimensional XYZ coordinate system) align and their Y-axis (vertical axis) aligns with the moving axis of the robot slider. Next, we captured an ArUco marker with each camera and visualized its position within the camera coordinate system. After verifying that the initial positions of the ArUco marker captured by the three cameras match, we moved the robot slider up by 50 mm thrice and investigated the degree of change in the measured position of the ArUco marker measured by the three cameras. The results show that as the ArUco marker moves farther away, the extent of error in the measured position of the ArUco marker increases. Additionally, the measured position of all the ArUco markers varied owing to the digital pixel error in the two-dimensional images (the pixel in which the ArUco marker is visible moves between neighboring pixels). Future work includes checking that the calibration pattern and ArUco marker are parallel to the camera ring and perpendicular to the robot slider using a level instrument; packing the calibration pattern and ArUco marker horizontally with vinyl; and implementing a moving average in the program to reduce pixel digital error in the calculations to sub-pixel level.

Keywords: Neurosurgery · Navigation system · Intel RealSense Depth Camera D435 · Organ deformation and movement · Brain shift

M. Kurosu (Ed.): HCII 2019, LNCS 11567, pp. 506–523, 2019.
https://doi.org/10.1007/978-3-030-22643-5_40

1 Introduction

In recent years, we have constructing surgical navigation systems for brain, kidney, liver and so on. There are many navigation systems in the field of orthopedic surgery because bones have few variations. In addition, we have a lot of navigation systems for neurosurgery and otolaryngology [1, 2]. These include endoscopic and/or lap-aroscopic surgery systems [3, 4] and robot surgery systems [5].

We have supported doctors by designing a sensor-based surgical operation navigator for brain, kidney, liver and so on [6–13]. For these, it was essential to accurately measure the surgical area with a depth camera to obtain a depth image. To accomplish this, last year we built a new surgical area-measuring robot-mechanical system and assessed the correlation between the distance the robot traveled and the change in distance of the depth image [14–17].

In neurosurgery, doctors create surgery plans in conferences held beforehand based on DICOM images from CT/MRI captured before the surgery. Doctors use the DICOM images for neuronavigation during brain surgery to ensure that brain tumors are accurately removed by the scalpel. However, cerebrospinal fluid may drain from the brain or its surroundings during the surgery, which can cause displacement or deformation of the brain. This is referred to as brain shift. Therefore, there may be some displacement between the brain in the preoperative DICOM image and the intraoperative actual brain for both the interior and the exterior. This could result in failure to completely remove the tumor, even if the surgery is performed according to the navigation system. There is also a possibility that the brain will become damaged due to pressure applied to the bottom of the brain from brain shift. To overcome this issue, we are constructing an advanced neurosurgery navigation system that enables doctors to visualize the brain. The system photographs the movement and deformation of the brain surface using sensors and simulates the brain movement and deformation in real-time. In this study, we calibrate and align the coordinate systems of three cameras for measuring the surgical area. We aligned the three 3-dimensional XYZ frames-of-reference of the three cameras and aligned their Y axis (vertical axis) with the moving axis of the robot slider. In general, the surgical area being measured is often obstructed by the doctor's head or hands, and it is often not possible to measure the surface of the organ in the surgical area. However, our system photographs the surgical area using three cameras with different poses. Therefore, at least one of the cameras can photograph the surgical area. By superimposing the video captured by one to three cameras, it becomes possible to tell the surgical navigation system that the organ has moved or deformed. It is important for the doctor to perform surgery in the way that is easiest. Therefore, we installed a robot slider on the navigation system which moves the camera ring as far up as needed when the camera ring interferes with the doctor's ability to operate accurately. In general, as the camera becomes closer to the surgical area, the accuracy of the measurements of the movement and deformation increases. Finally, the system performs a high-speed simulation of the brain shift in the DICOM image based on the measurement of the organ displacement and movement, visualizes the brain shift in the navigation system in real-time, and provides support for the doctor performing the surgery by helping the doctor accurately detect the locations of malignant tumors and blood vessels. As a result, the system can decrease the surgery time and improve the accuracy for neurosurgery.

In Sect. 2 of this study, we will explain our robotic-mechanical system including three depth/RGB cameras for measuring some surgical area. In Sect. 3, we will focus on calibration software of three cameras for capturing the surgical area precisely. In succession, in Sect. 4, we will show calibration results using three depth/RGB cameras controlled by the robotic-mechanical system. Finally, in Sect. 5, we will summarize this result and discuss future improvements.

2 Experiment System

2.1 Overview

First, we used a ChArUco board to align the coordinate axes of three cameras and to align the moving axis of the robot slider with the Y-axis. Next, we measured the coordinates of the ArUco markers. After verifying that the measurements of the marker positions measured by the three cameras match, we raised the robot slider, and confirmed that the coordinates of the ArUco markers changed by the same amount as the amount of movement.

2.2 Preparations

Equipment used in this experiment:

- Intel Real Sense Depth Camera D435 (Fig. 1): Measures the location of the markers and captures RGB and depth images of the organs. The former measurement measures feature points on the organ surfaces and amount of movement through SLAM (Simultaneous Localization and Mapping). The latter directly measures the changes in the shape of the organ surface. The measurements are used to update the movement and deformation of the organ model in the surgical navigation system.

Fig. 1. Intel Real Sense Depth Camera D435

- Robot slider: moves the camera ring up and down
- ChArUco board (7 × 5): Performs calibration of the camera coordinates (for aligning the three-dimensional XYZ camera coordinate system of the three cameras, and for aligning their Y axis (vertical axis) with the robot slider's moving axis)
- ArUco markers: To be installed at the location that we want to measure after performing calibration of the camera coordinates.

About the Intel Real Sense Depth Camera D435

The Intel Real Sense Depth Camera D435 is a stereo vision depth camera that can measure the distance to an object. The D435 includes an RGB camera and two depth sensors (infrared sensors). The specifications are listed in Table 1.

Table 1. Intel RealSense Depth Camera D435 Specifications

Items	Explanation
Use environment	Indoor/indoor
Depth technology	Active IR stereo (global shutter)
Main Intel RealSense component	Intel RealSense Vision Processor D4, Intel RealSense module D430
Depth sensor field of view (horizontal × vertical × diagonal)	91.2° × 65.5° × 100.6° (±3°)
Output resolution (depth Stream)	Up to 1280 × 720
Output frame rate (depth Stream)	Up to 90 fps
Minimum depth distance (min-Z)	0.2 m
Shutter type	Global shutter
Maximum range	Approximately 10 m (varies depending on calibration, scene, and lighting conditions)
Resolution and frame rate (RGB sensor)	1920 × 1080@30 fps
RGB sensor field of view (horizontal × vertical × diagonal)	69.4° × 42.5° × 77° (±3°)
Camera dimensions (length × depth × height)	90 mm × 25 mm × 25 mm
Connectors	USB3.0 Type-C
Mounting mechanism	1 × 1/4-20 UNC thread mounting point, 2 × M3 thread mounting points

Robot Slider

The system which moves the ring with the three cameras mounted onto it up and down accurately is an RS1 single-axis robot from Misumi (Fig. 2). The specifications are listed in Table 2.

ArUco Markers

ArUco markers are used for estimating position and pose using a camera (Fig. 3). We use the ArUco markers included in OpenCV Contrib in OpenCV. ArUco markers are black and white squares in a binary format. Advantages of ArUco markers include that they are easy to detect and that they are fast to calculate.

ChArUco Board

A ChArUco board is a combination of a chessboard and ArUco markers (Fig. 4). ArUco markers can be rapidly detected and have a diverse variety of patterns. However, one issue with ArUco markers is that the accuracy of the detection of the corner position is low. Therefore, the corner accuracy is compensated by combining the markers with a black and white chessboard. We used the ChArUco board sample in OpenCVContrib.

Fig. 2. RS1 robot slider used in the experiment (manufactured by Misumi)

Table 2. Robot slider RS1 specifications

Items	Explanation
Type	Slider
Drive method	Rolled ball-screw
Input power	DC24V
Position detector	Resolver incremental method
Table width	41 mm
Table length	58 mm
Positioning repeatability	±20 μm
Motor mounting direction	Straight

Fig. 3. ArUco marker

Fig. 4. ChArUco board

3 Experiment Content

In this experiment, we mounted three D435 cameras to a ring-shaped fixture attached to the single-axis robot, as shown in Fig. 5. The cameras were mounted such that the entire ChArUco board was visible from all the cameras. Because the angles of the sensor cameras are fixed by the fixture, we adjusted the size of the ChArUco board and adjusted its height by pasting it onto a box.

Fig. 5. Single-axis robot used in the experiment setup

First, we used the ChArUco board to calibrate the coordinate systems of the three cameras and the robot coordinate system. Next, we captured the ArUco markers in the cameras, and verified whether the three cameras could accurately measure their coordinates [18]. To verify this, we captured 9 ArUco markers simultaneously with the cameras as shown in Fig. 6 and verified whether the coordinates of the 9 markers were on a plane (Fig. 7). If the 9 measurement points are not on a plane, then we check the code in the program in Figs. 8 and 9 and change the settings for the ChArUco board and the ArUco markers to enable the accurate detection of coordinates. Once it can detect accurate coordinates, we move the single-axis robot up by 50 mm, 100 mm, and 150 mm, measure the coordinates of the ArUco markers, and evaluate the amount of error.

The procedures for our experiment are described below. The camera calibration described above refers to finding the intrinsic parameters, which are unique to the camera, and the extrinsic parameters, which represent the pose of the camera in the world coordinate system. After completing camera calibration, it is possible to calculate the pixel within the camera image onto which an arbitrary point in the 3-dimensional XYZ coordinate system will be projected, and to calculate the position within the 3-dimensional coordinate system that corresponds to projection points in multiple cameras. It is also possible to compensate for distortion (tangential and radial directions) unique to each camera. In general, the calibration method that can be applied depends on the number of cameras and the available equipment. OpenCV implements the method proposed by [19].

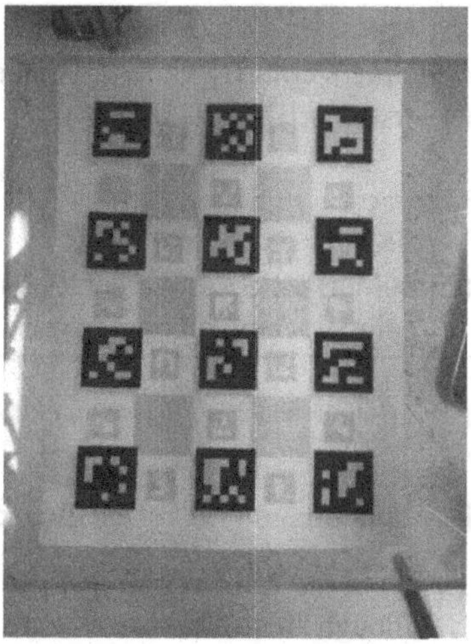

Fig. 6. Measurement of 9 ArUco markers

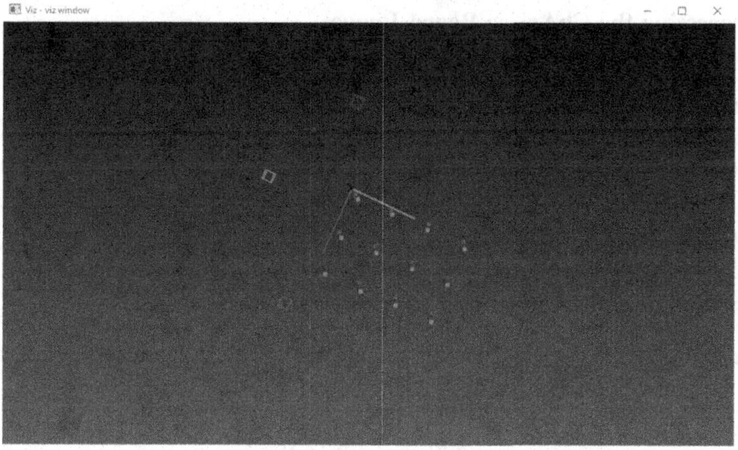

Fig. 7. 9 ArUco markers on the 3D monitor

```
CCameraParameterscameraParameters;
cameraParameters.load("../../data/camera_parameters.xml");

CCharucoBoardcharucoBoard(5, 7, 28.0, cv::aruco::DICT_4X4_50);
CArucoMarkerarucoMarker(cv::aruco::DICT_5X5_100);
```

Fig. 8. Source code for ChArUco board settings

```
float z = 0.0f;
if (arucoMarker.detectMarkers(color[i], cameraParameters)) {
arucoMarker.drawMarkers(color[i]);

std::vector<cv::Vec3d>rvecs;
std::vector<cv::Vec3d>tvecs;
arucoMarker.estimatePoseMarkers(33.0f, cameraParameters, rvecs, tvecs);
arucoMarker.drawAxis(color[i], cameraParameters);
```

Fig. 9. Source code for ArUco markers.

3.1 Reading in the Calibration Image (ChArUco Board)

We attached three D435 cameras to the camera ring and captured the ChArUco board (7×5) in all the cameras. Although there is no rule that determines the number of static images that should be captured, capturing several tens of images will give sufficient calibration accuracy.

3.2 Processing the ChArUco Board Image

Here, we scan the corners of the ChArUco board from the lower left to the upper right corner and detect them. To increase the calibration accuracy, we edit the corners to sub-pixel accuracy (units of 0.5 pixels). Once all the corners have been detected correctly, the corners are drawn in 7 internally-defined colors. If not, all the corners are drawn in red. Therefore, we perform this process until all the corners are draw in the 7 internally-defined colors.

3.3 Formulation of Intrinsic and Extrinsic Parameters

First, we estimate the camera intrinsic parameters and the distortion coefficients. The intrinsic parameters correspond to A in the equation below.

$$s\,m = A\,[R|t]\,M$$

- m: Coordinates of the point projected onto the image plane
- A: Camera intrinsic parameter matrix
- R|t: Translation/rotation homogeneous coordinate matrix (extrinsic parameter matrix)
- M: 3-dimensional coordinates in the world coordinate system

Next, we estimate the pose using the detected corners and the intrinsic parameters and obtain the rotation vector and the translation vector. Here, we convert the rotation vector to a matrix using Rodrigues's rotation formula, combine the matrix with the translation vector, and obtain a 3×3 rotation matrix. Then, we include the translation vector to create a 4 × 3 matrix, and include (0,0,0,1) to obtain the 4 × 4 extrinsic parameter matrix (homogeneous coordinate transform matrix).

3.4 Estimation of Intrinsic Parameters and Extrinsic Parameters

Here, we estimate the camera's extrinsic parameters ([R|t] in the above equation). The extrinsic parameters refer to the set of parameters that represent the transformation from the origin of the world coordinate system (3-dimensional coordinate system) to the camera coordinate system. In this calibration process, we estimate the camera's intrinsic parameters and the extrinsic parameters for each view. First, we assume that the internal parameters are known, and estimate an initial value for the camera pose. We apply the global Levenberg-Marquardt optimization algorithm to minimize the re-projection error. The algorithm adjusts the extrinsic parameters such that the sum of the squares of the distances between the measurements of the actual points and the estimated points that were calculated using the intrinsic parameters and the camera pose is minimized. When the calibration is successful, the 3D monitor displays the location of the camera mounted at D in red, the location of the camera mounted at B in green, and the location of the camera mounted at F in blue, as shown in Fig. 10.

Fig. 10. Camera position after calibration

3.5 ArUco Marker Measurement Evaluation Experiment

As shown in Fig. 11, we placed one ArUco marker on the ChArUco board (7 × 5) and measured its location. Then, we moved the robot slider by 50 mm three times and measured the location of the ArUco marker until the robot slider reached 150 mm.

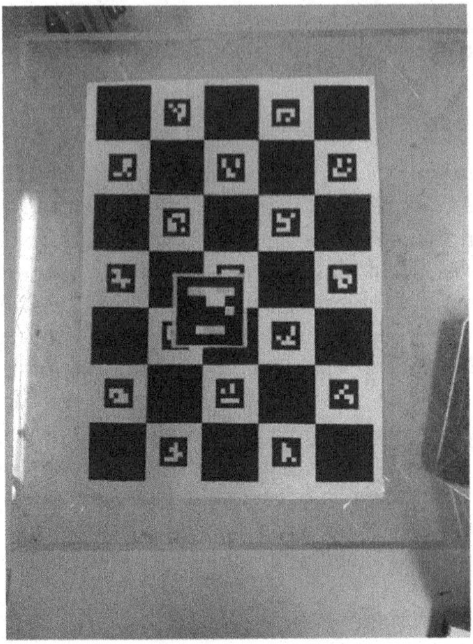

Fig. 11. Placing ArUco marker on top of the ChArUco board

4 Experiment Results

Here, we mounted the three cameras onto the ring, moved the robot slider up and down, and checked whether the amount of change in the measured location of the ArUco marker matched the amount of movement of the ring.

First, the locations at which cameras can be installed and the locations at which the cameras were installed are shown in Fig. 12. Figures 13, 14, and 15 are from a video that was captured in Visual Studio. In the 3-dimensional XYZ space that is shown (the Y axis is the vertical axis, and XZ is the horizontal plane), the red line represents the X axis, the blue line represents the Y axis, and the green line represents the Z axis. Figure 13 shows an image that was captured by Camera_0 mounted at location B (green circle), Fig. 14 shows an image that was captured by Camera_1 mounted at location D (red circle), and Fig. 15 shows an image that was captured by Camera_2 mounted at location F (blue circle). We also changed the locations of the cameras and took the measurements; however, because there is almost no error in the coordinates, the placement of the cameras did not have an impact. Next, Figs. 16, 17, and 18 represent the coordinates of one ArUco marker on the 3D monitor from three directions using the three cameras. The locations of Camera_0, Camera_1, and Camera_2 are each shown with a large green, red, and blue box. Meanwhile, the ArUco markers measured by the cameras are shown with a small green, red, and blue box. These figures show that the small green, red, and blue boxes perfectly overlap, which means that the cameras can measure the coordinates of the ArUco marker accurately without any interference between the cameras' depth sensors (infrared sensors).

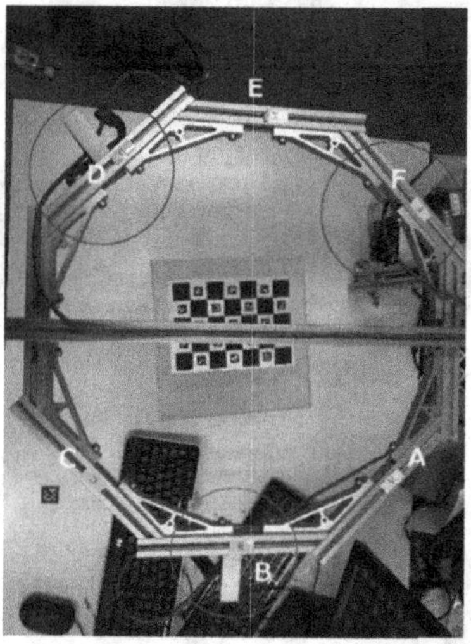

Fig. 12. Positions at which cameras can be mounted.

In addition, Figs. 19, 20, and 21 show the 3D monitor images when the camera ring is moved in increments of 50 mm in the Y-axis direction by the robot slider. The images show that as the cameras move further away from the ArUco marker, error appears in the measured location. The error is represented in the graph shown in Fig. 22, which shows a plot of the change in the location of the ArUco marker.

Next, we explain the graph shown in Fig. 22. First, the coordinate of the vertical (Y) axis of Camera_0 (yellow line) was 0 mm, the coordinate of the vertical (Y) axis of Camera_1 (red line) was 0.6 mm, and the coordinate of the vertical (Y) axis of Camera_2 (blue line) was 4.4 mm. This shows that the error in the measurement of the ArUco marker location has a minimum of below 1 mm, and a maximum of 5 mm. This is the initial error. According to surgeons, the acceptable range for error is several mm for neurosurgery, and approximately 1 cm for liver surgery. Therefore, this amount of error will not have a large impact on surgery.

Next, when we moved the camera ring by 50 mm, the coordinate of the vertical (Y) axis of Camera_0 was 52.4 mm, the coordinate of the vertical (Y) axis of Camera_1 was 54.7 mm, and the coordinate of the vertical (Y) axis of Camera_2 was 52.5 mm. This shows that the error was approximately 4 mm at maximum. Next, when we moved the camera ring by 100 mm, the coordinate of the vertical (Y) axis of Camera_0 was 111.4 mm, the coordinate of the vertical (Y) axis of Camera_1 was 115.9 mm, and the coordinate of the vertical (Y) axis of Camera_2 was 110.0 mm.

This shows that an additional error of approximately 15 mm appeared. Lastly, when we moved the camera ring by 150 mm, the coordinate of the vertical (Y) axis of Camera_0 was 166.9 mm, the coordinate of the vertical (Y) axis of Camera_1 was 169.0 mm, and the coordinate of the vertical (Y) axis of Camera_2 was 162.6 mm. This shows that an error of approximately 20 mm appeared.

Fig. 13. Camera_0 video. (Color figure online)

Fig. 14. Camera_1 video. (Color figure online)

Fig. 15. Camera_2 video. (Color figure online)

Fig. 16. Coordinate_1 of ArUco marker where 3 points overlap. (Color figure online)

Fig. 17. Coordinate_2 of ArUco marker where 3 points overlap. (Color figure online)

These results show that as the ArUco marker moves further away from the camera, the measurement error of the ArUco marker increases. If the cameras are raised too far, the error can exceed the limit for surgery.

In addition, the location of the ArUco marker varied severely when the red line was near 50 mm and 150 mm and when the blue line was near 100 mm. These variations are not due to physical vibrations of the robot slider or the camera ring but are rather due to pixel digital error that comes from fluctuations of the pixel in which the ArUco marker is captured.

Letters of the alphabet are assigned to locations A through F. The cameras can be mounted at these locations.

Fig. 18. Coordinate_3 of ArUco marker where 3 points overlap. (Color figure online)

Fig. 19. Coordinates when the single-axis robot is moved in the Y-axis direction by 50 mm.

5 Conclusions and Future Works

In this study, we calibrated three D435 RGB/depth cameras by aligning three 3-dimensional camera coordinate systems and aligning their Z-axis with the moving axis of a robot slider. We moved the robot slider up by 50 mm twice and evaluated whether the change in the measured location of the marker measured by the three cameras matches the displacement. The results show that as the distance between the camera and the marker increased, the error in the location of the marker also increased. However, the direction of the error was not random, and was constant. The error might be due to the impact of the offset in the installation of the camera ring or the robot slider. Therefore, we will use separate devices, such as a leveler, to evaluate whether this factor has an impact. Furthermore, the location also sometimes varies due to the digital error in the image pixels. It is possible to modify the software so that the

Fig. 20. Coordinates when the single-axis robot is moved in the Y-axis direction by 100 mm.

Fig. 21. Coordinates when the single-axis robot is moved in the Y-axis direction by 150 mm.

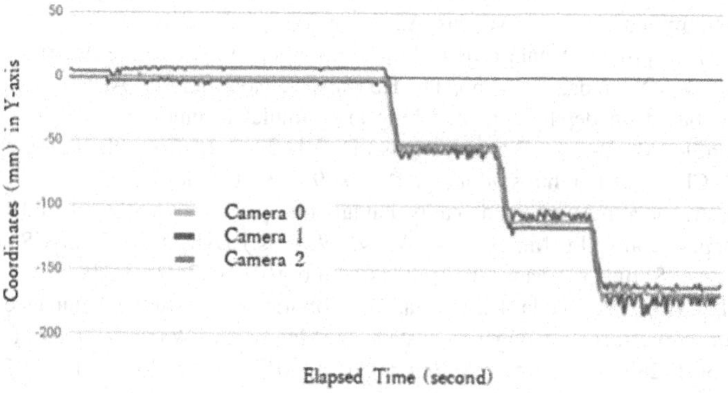

Fig. 22. Coordinates when the single-axis robot is moved in the Y-axis direction by increments of 50 mm. (Color figure online)

3-dimensional location of the marker becomes constant by processing the position in the image in which the marker was visible to sub-pixel level less than 0.5, or by using a moving average to measure the position. Lastly, because the angle at which the cameras capture the surgical area is currently constant, the surgical area can sometimes leave the camera's field-of-view as the robot slider moves up. Therefore, we want to use a fixture that allows the angle to be adjusted freely so that the camera will always capture the surgical area even when the camera ring is moved up and down by the robot slider.

Acknowledgment. This research has been partially supported by the Collaborative Research Fund for Graduate Schools (A) of the Osaka Electro-Communication University, and a Grant-in-Aid for Scientific Research of the Ministry of Education, Culture, Sports, Science and Technology (Research Project Number: JP26289069 and 17K00420).

References

1. Matsumoto, N., et al.: A minimally invasive registration method using surface template-assisted marker positioning (STAMP) for image-guided otologic surgery. Otolaryngol.—Head Neck Surg. **140**(1), 96–102 (2009)
2. Hong, J., Hashizume, M.: An effective point-based registration tool for surgical navigation. Surg. Endosc. **24**(4), 944–948 (2010)
3. Ieiri, S., et al.: Augmented reality navigation system for laparoscopic splenectomy in children based on preoperative CT image using optical tracking device. Pediatr. Surg. Int. **28** (4), 341–346 (2012)
4. Mahmud, N., Cohen, J., Tsourides, K., Berzin, T.M.: Computer vision and augmented reality in gastrointestinal endoscopy. Gastroenterol. Rep. (Oxf) **3**(3), 179–184 (2015). https://doi.org/10.1093/gastro/gov027
5. Pessaux, P., Diana, M., Soler, L., Piardi, T., Mutter, D., Marescaux, J.: Towards cybernetic surgery: robotic and augmented reality-assisted liver segmentectomy. Langenbecks Arch. Surg. **400**(3), 381–385 (2015)
6. Watanabe, K., et al.: Brain shift simulation controlled by directly captured surface points. In: Proceedings of 38th Annual International Conference of the IEEE Engineering in Medicine and Biology Society, Sessions: Ignite_Theme 2_Fr2, Poster Session III, Orlando, FL, USA (2016)
7. Yano, D., Koeda, M., Onishi, K., Noborio, H.: Development of a surgical knife attachment with proximity indicators. In: Marcus, A., Wang, W. (eds.) DUXU 2017. LNCS, vol. 10289, pp. 608–618. Springer, Cham (2017). https://doi.org/10.1007/978-3-319-58637-3_48
8. Watanabe, K., Yoshida, S., Yano, D., Koeda, M., Noborio, H.: A new organ-following algorithm based on depth-depth matching and simulated annealing, and its experimental evaluation. In: Marcus, A., Wang, W. (eds.) DUXU 2017. LNCS, vol. 10289, pp. 594–607. Springer, Cham (2017). https://doi.org/10.1007/978-3-319-58637-3_47
9. Sengiku, A., et al.: Augmented reality navigation system for robot-assisted laparoscopic partial nephrectomy. In: Marcus, A., Wang, W. (eds.) DUXU 2017. LNCS, vol. 10289, pp. 575–584. Springer, Cham (2017). https://doi.org/10.1007/978-3-319-58637-3_45
10. Onishi, K., Miki, Y., Okuda, K., Koeda, M., Noborio, H.: A study of guidance method for AR laparoscopic surgery navigation system. In: Marcus, A., Wang, W. (eds.) DUXU 2017. LNCS, vol. 10289, pp. 556–564. Springer, Cham (2017). https://doi.org/10.1007/978-3-319-58637-3_43

11. Noborio, H., et al.: Fast surgical algorithm for cutting with liver standard triangulation language format using Z-buffers in graphics processing unit. In: Fujie, M.G. (ed.) Computer Aided Surgery, pp. 127–140. Springer, Tokyo (2016). https://doi.org/10.1007/978-4-431-55810-1_11
12. Noborio, H., Aoki, K., Kunii, T., Mizushino, K.: A Potential function-based scalpel navigation method that avoids blood vessel groups during excision of cancerous tissue. In: Proceedings of the 38th Annual International Conference of the IEEE Engineering in Medicine and Biology Society (EMBC 2016), pp. 6106–6112 (2016)
13. Noborio, H., Kunii, T., Mizushino, K.: Comparison of GPU-based and CPU-based algorithms for determining the minimum distance between a cusa scalper and blood vessels. In: BIOSTEC 2016, The SCITEPRESS Digital Library, pp. 128–136 (2016)
14. Watanabe, K., et al.: A mechanical system directly attaching beside a surgical bed for measuring surgical area precisely by depth camera. In: Proceedings of the 10th MedViz Conference and the 6th Eurographics Workshop on Visual Computing for Biology and Medicine (EG VCBM), pp. 105–108 (2016)
15. Watanabe, K., et al.: Capturing a brain shift directly by the depth camera kinect v2. In: Proceedings of 38th Annual International Conference of the IEEE Engineering in Medicine and Biology Society, Sessions: Ignite_Theme 4_Fr1, Poster Session II, Orlando, FL, USA (2016)
16. Nonaka, M., Watanabe, K., Noborio, H., Kayaki, M., Mizushino, K.: Capturing a surgical area using multiple depth cameras mounted on a robotic mechanical system. In: Marcus, A., Wang, W. (eds.) DUXU 2017. LNCS, vol. 10289, pp. 540–555. Springer, Cham (2017). https://doi.org/10.1007/978-3-319-58637-3_42
17. Nonaka, M., Chikayama, Y., Kayaki, M., Koeda, M., Tachibana, K., Noborio, H.: A useful robotic-mechanical system for measuring a surgical area without obstructing surgical operations by some surgeon. In: Kurosu, M. (ed.) HCI 2018. LNCS, vol. 10902, pp. 43–52. Springer, Cham (2018). https://doi.org/10.1007/978-3-319-91244-8_4
18. OpenCV 3.4.4 Homepage. https://docs.opencv.org/3.4.4/index.html. Accessed 31 Jan 2019
19. Zhang, Z.: A flexible new technique for camera calibration. IEEE Trans. Pattern Anal. Mach. Intell. **22**(11), 1330–1334 (2000)

Performance and Accuracy Analysis of 3D Model Tracking for Liver Surgery

Satoshi Numata(✉), Masanao Koeda, Katsuhiko Onishi, Kaoru Watanabe, and Hiroshi Noborio

Osaka Electro-Communication University, Shijonawate, Osaka 5750063, Japan
numata@osakac.ac.jp

Abstract. We are developing a liver surgical navigation system that uses a 3D liver model of the patient. As the liver contains several types of blood vessels, surgeons can sterically check the treating positions using the navigation system. For better navigation, the 3D liver model should be continuously and precisely matched with the patient's liver state, and the liver location and orientation should be calculated in real time. The location and orientation is estimated by comparing two depth images of the liver; one is captured from the patient's body using a depth camera, and one is rendered from the pre-scanned 3D liver model using OpenGL. The tracking is performed using gradient descent optimization algorithm. In this paper, we measure how the tracking agreement rate will change while the liver location and orientation are changing, so that we can understand the tracking performance, accuracy and the pitfall range of the navigation system.

Keywords: Liver surgery support · Navigation · 3D model tracking

1 Introduction

Liver contains several types of blood vessels in its soft organ, and X-ray imaging, computed tomography (CT) scanning or magnetic resonance imaging (MRI) have been widely used to check its state. Surgeons precisely examine the liver state using those data to plan the operation. For the better planning and performing the operation, medical simulation technology is rapidly developed. 3D model data such as STL (Standard Triangulated Language) data is one of the technology that is made from those scanned data and used for surgical navigation. We have developed a system for liver surgery navigation by tracking knife positions and liver states using the STL liver model [1–4]. We have also examined its performance from the aspect of the algorithm [5] and from the aspect of the inter-process communication cost [6].

In this paper, we focus on the depth matching mechanism that is used for the liver posture tracking. By rotating the virtual liver model around two axes, we observe how comparison scores will be changed and check the possibility of pitfalls. We also examine the tracking ability of the comparison score using gradient descent, so that the characteristic of the liver tracking can be properly understood for further investigation.

M. Kurosu (Ed.): HCII 2019, LNCS 11567, pp. 524–533, 2019.
https://doi.org/10.1007/978-3-030-22643-5_41

2 Liver Surgical Navigation System

2.1 System Overview

Two cameras above the liver, a surgical knife, and a computer that communicates with those cameras compose our liver surgical navigation system as shown in Fig. 1. Each camera sends different information to subsystems of the navigation system.

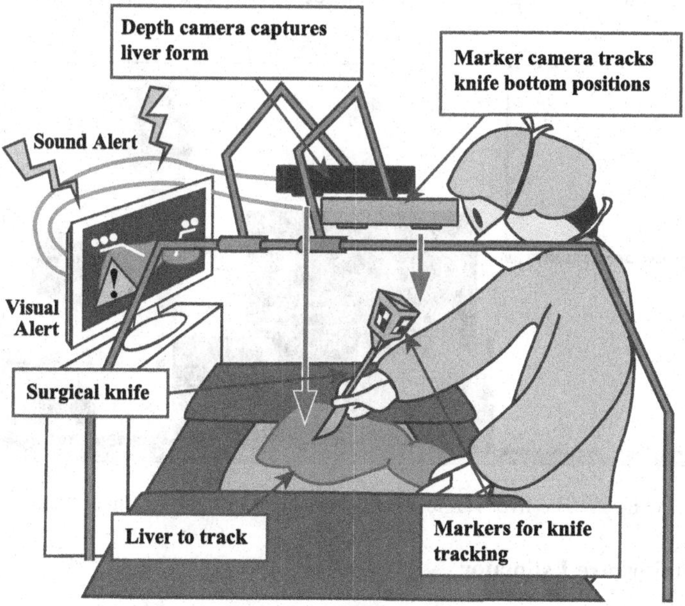

Fig. 1. System overview of our liver surgery navigation system

One camera is a marker tracking camera, which tracks two dimensional markers in real time (illustrated as a yellow camera in Fig. 1). A surgical knife has multiple tracking markers at the bottom, and their locations are captured by the camera and sent to the subsystem called "knife position estimator". The knife position estimator binds multiple location data to estimate the exact position of the knife tip.

Another camera is a depth camera, which captures depth images of the liver in its measuring range (illustrated as a black camera in Fig. 1). Each frame of the captured depth image sent to the subsystem called "liver posture estimator". The liver posture estimator performs image processing over the depth images for estimating current position and rotation of the patient's liver.

The main system then summarize the data from those subsystems using shared memories [6], for visualizing current surgical information. As the system is composed of multiple subsystems, each subsystem can be improved and maintained separately. In this paper, performance and accuracy of the liver posture estimator is focused and discussed.

2.2 Liver Surgical Navigator

The liver surgical navigator integrates the knife position data and the liver posture data from the shared memories. It also loads the polyhedrons data with STL-format independently, for separately showing sub parts of the liver such as the hepatic artery, the portal vein, lobes and so on for the surgical navigation. Figure 2 shows the experimental implementation of the navigator.

For better navigation for surgeons, surgical procedures should be stored and understanding the current procedure is required in the future implementation.

Fig. 2. The liver surgical navigator showing knife and liver data

2.3 Liver Posture Estimator

The liver posture estimator periodically takes depth images from the depth camera, and compares the shape with Polyhedrons rendered on the memory for finding the exact location of the liver and its orientation. Figure 3 shows how the real liver model (A) is captured as a depth image (B) and how it will be compared with the depth image rendered on the graphics memory using OpenGL (C).

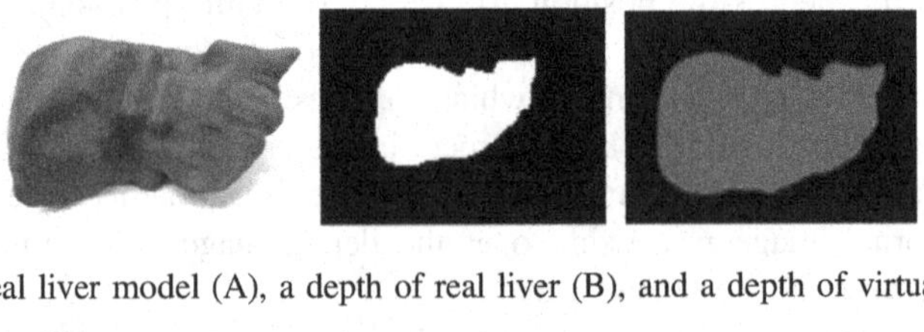

Fig. 3. Real liver model (A), a depth of real liver (B), and a depth of virtual liver (C)

The accuracy of the posture estimation is important for tracking liver state and displaying navigation information over the virtual liver. To improve the accuracy, both of the performance of depth image comparison and the performance of posture tracking are important to be investigated.

2.4 3D Model Matching

It is difficult to repeat the system verification on human bodies. Therefore, a polyhedron liver model using STL that integrates DICOM based liver images captured by MRI is used in this paper. An STL polyhedron data can be used to be output with 3D printer, as well as rendered in a video memory.

In this paper, a 3D printed model of a liver STL is set below a depth camera. Kinect v2 is used as the depth camera. The identical STL data is loaded in the liver posture estimator, and OpenGL renders the data by changing its position and rotation for matching its depth data with the depth image of the 3D printed liver model.

3 Depth Matching for Liver Posture Estimation

3.1 Depth Image Matching

In the liver surgical navigation system, the liver posture estimator is the key subsystem. It performs iterative rendering of the virtual liver, calculates how much those depth images differ from the depth image of the real liver, and estimates the current posture of the liver. Therefore, the depth image matching mechanism defines the performance of the estimator.

The liver has a signature form and it easily changes its shape when looking it from multiple directions. This fact encourages us to think that the posture estimation can be accurately performed. In our previous papers, liver posture estimation has been implemented based on the idea, and actually tracking is succeeded [5]. However, for optimizing and achieving more accurate tracking in the future, we have to investigate and get the insight about the characteristic of the depth image matching mechanism itself.

In this chapter, an experiment is performed to examine the characteristic of the depth image matching mechanism. In many cases of liver surgery, a liver often rotates more than translation. Therefore, we focus on the combination of rotation around two axes, and try to observe how the comparison score will be changed according to the angles. The sum of squared errors is used as the comparison score to compare two depth images. Less value of the comparison score indicates more matching posture. In the actual case of the surgery, the region to compare to depth images should be specified in some ways, however, the region is assumed to be given in this paper.

3.2 Experiment and Result

In this section, the comparison scores are precisely plotted as 3D graphs to show the characteristics of liver model matching. By rotating the virtual liver model around two axes simultaneously and checking the comparison scores with a real liver model that is fixed and captured by depth camera, we can check how easily the liver can be tracked. At the beginning, the posture of the virtual liver is manually set to be the same as the real liver. Afterwards, angles are changed around two axes and the comparison scores are calculated.

Figure 4 shows the rotation axes in our navigation system. In our experiment, the rotation angle varies from −90° to +90° for each rotation axis and the depth images are compared between rotated virtual liver and the depth image of the fixed real liver model. Because there is the possibility that some pitfalls exist according to the shape of the liver, the result of this experiment should guide us where to focus on the liver surgical navigation.

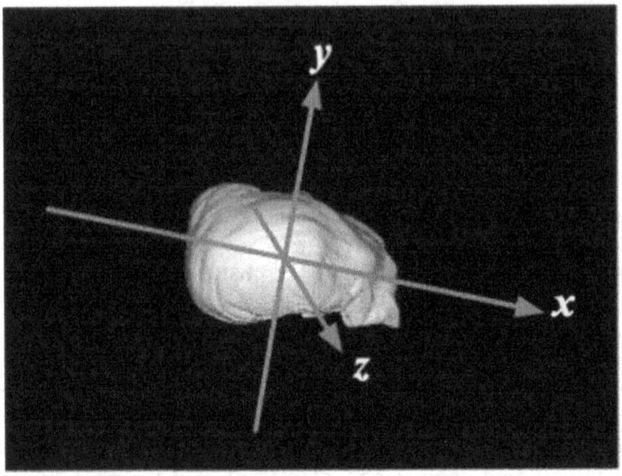

Fig. 4. Rotation axes for liver tracking

Figure 5 shows the comparison scores of the depth images by rotating the virtual liver around X-axis and Y-axis simultaneously. At the center of the graph that is colored as blue, the posture of the virtual and real livers are almost the same. The minimum score was 158.8. We can see that the score is gradually increasing by separating from the center, and there is not any serious pitfalls. Therefore, the tracking should be successfully performed in the rotation between X-axis and Y-axis.

Figure 6 shows the comparison scores of the depth images by rotating the virtual liver around X-axis and Z-axis simultaneously. At the center of the graph that is colored as blue, the posture of the virtual and real livers are almost the same. The minimum score was 126.2. We can see that there is a hill in the graph around the point where x rotation is −70° and z rotation is −70°. This can be a pitfall for the real time tracking. We will see that the tracking using the gradient descent method will be stuck at the point in the next chapter. This combination of the rotation axes should be carefully managed in the navigation system.

Figure 7 shows the comparison scores of the depth images by rotating the virtual liver around Y-axis and Z-axis simultaneously. The minimum score was 102.8. We can see the flat place around the point where y rotation is −70° and z rotation is 70°, but it is not a hill and it gradually goes down to the valley of the blue colored center point. As the experiment in the next chapter shows, there is not any pitfalls in this case and the tracking can be done smoothly.

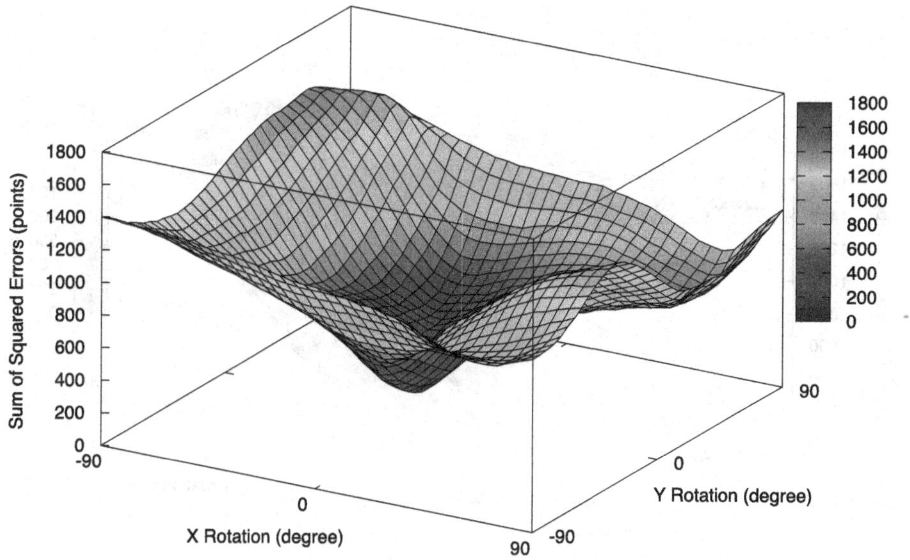

Fig. 5. Comparison scores of liver depth images with X-axis and Y-axis rotations

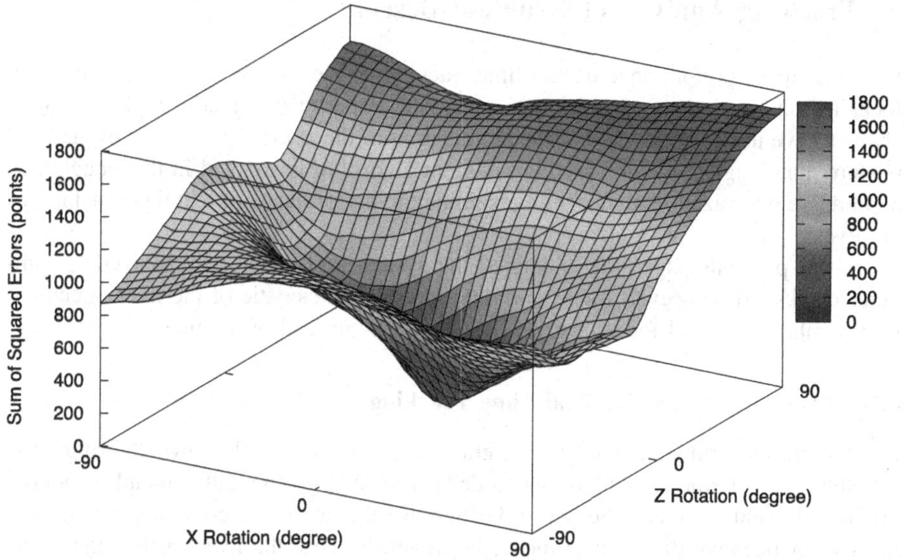

Fig. 6. Comparison scores of liver depth images with X-axis and Z-axis rotations

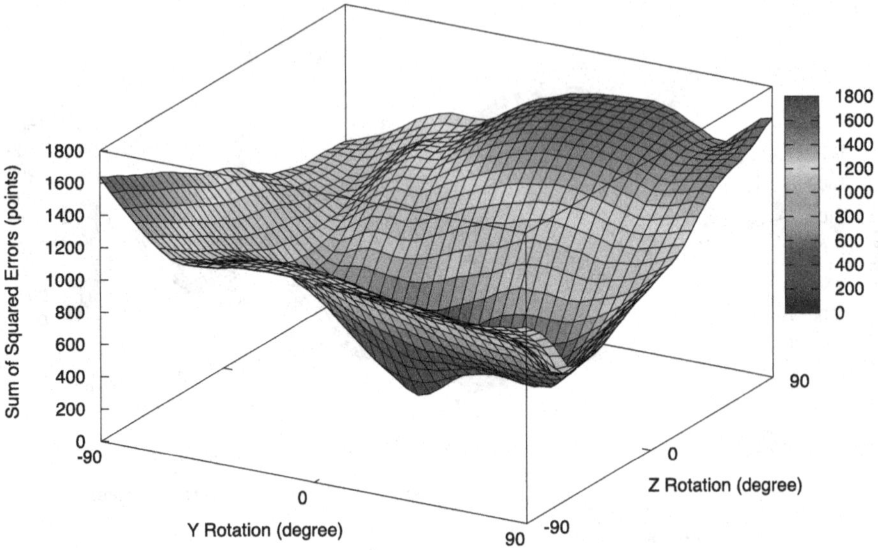

Fig. 7. Comparison scores of liver depth images with Y-axis and Z-axis rotations

4 Tracking Analysis of Gradient Descent

In this chapter, performance of real time tracking of the liver is discussed, especially focusing on the rotation around two axes. The experimental result of the previous chapter gave us the good valley formed transition of the comparison scores of the liver posture matching. Therefore, gradient descent algorithm is adopted in this chapter, as an iterative optimization algorithm to examine the performance of real time tracking of the liver.

In our previous paper, we examined the system performance by measuring computer clocks [6]. However, for examining precise characteristic of the liver matching, step numbers are used for comparison in this paper instead of the time.

4.1 Gradient Descent for Real Time Tracking

As an iterative optimization algorithm, gradient descent is a well known algorithm that can help the real time tracking of 3D models. Basically, given a differentiable function, gradient descent calculates the gradient of the function at the current point, and decides positive or negative direction to move. However, because the liver easily changes its form and surgeon rotates the liver many times, we cannot assume that such the function is given for tracking.

Instead of using a given differentiable function, it can be considered that rotating the virtual liver slightly from current posture and calculating the gradient. By rotating 1 to 5° around X-axis, Y-axis, and Z-axis, the tendency of the comparison score change of depth images can be used as the gradient to decide positive or negative direction to change the posture. In this paper, gradient descent is tried to perform real time tracking of 3D liver model in this way. Because of its simplicity, it clearly gives us a good insight into the characteristics of depth image matching of the liver.

4.2 Experiment and Result

In this section, the experiment about the tracking performance is explained according to the two axes rotation. At the beginning, the posture of the virtual liver is manually set to be the same as the real liver. Afterwards, angles are changed to −70° from the first rotation in each of two axes. By using the gradient descent method described in previous section, the virtual liver gradually rotate to minimize the comparison score. It can be checked that how many steps will be needed to correct the posture and how much the virtual liver posture can be the same as the real liver posture.

Figure 8 shows the result of the experiment, where orange line shows the combination of rotation around X-axis and Y-axis, blue line shows the combination of rotation around X-axis and Z-axis, and green line shows the combination of rotation around Y-axis and Z-axis. As the graph shows, orange line (X + Y) and green line (Y + Z) gradually come to the point around 350. At this point, the posture of the virtual liver is very close to the real liver as the left image of Fig. 9. However, blue line (X + Z) stays at the point around 620. At his point, the posture of the virtual liver is quite different from the real liver as the right image of Fig. 9. Figure 9 shows the final state of the depth image matching after 120 tracking steps have finished.

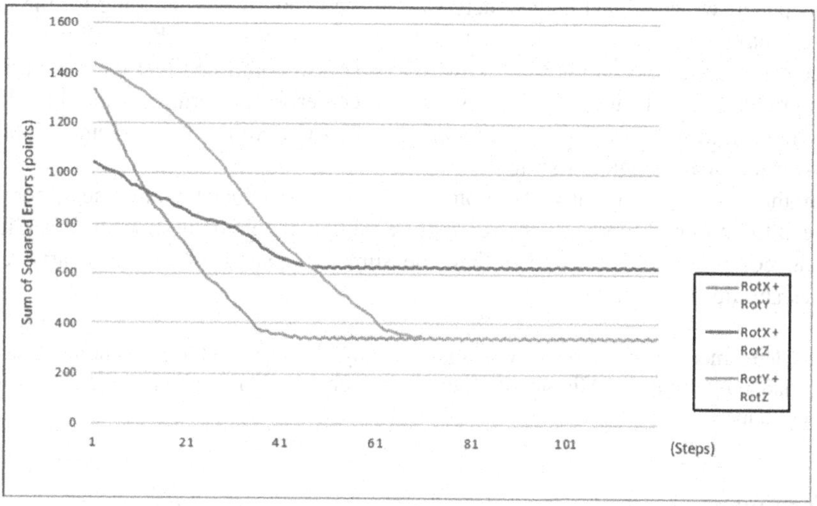

Fig. 8. Comparison score change during the posture tracking using gradient descent

As the experiment in Chapter 3 showed that there is a hill around the point where x rotation is −70° and z rotation is −70°, the tracking will be failed if the liver rotates in this combination of axes. Furthermore, tracking performance for the combination of X-axis and Y-axis is better than the combination of Y-axis and Z-axis. The orange line

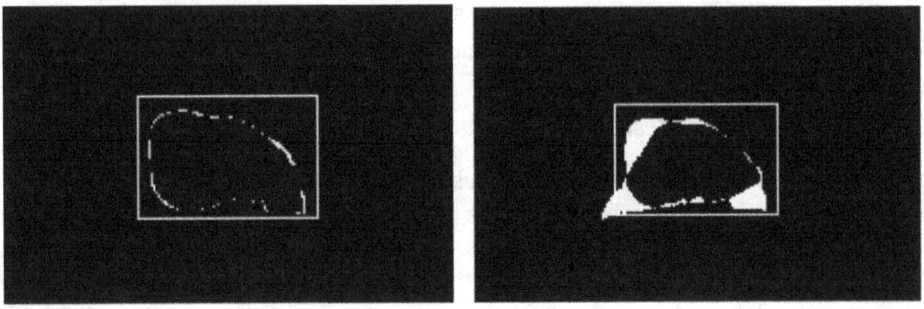

Fig. 9. Depth image matching after 120 tracking steps using gradient descent (X-axis and Y-axis rotation (left) and X-axis and Z-axis rotation (right))

comes to 350 points in 30 steps, where the green line takes 60 steps to be the same point. It is also important to see that the comparison score using gradient descent stays at 350 points, where the minimum comparison scores are around 120 as we described in Chapter 3. Further investigation is required to understand the reason why it does not come to the minimum point during the tracking using gradient descent.

5 Conclusion

In this paper, we examined the characteristic of the depth image matching for the liver surgical navigation. It is confirmed that there is one pitfall at the combination of rotation around X-axis and Z-axis. However, it is also confirmed that the comparison score gradually and beautifully decreases to the center for performing a good tracking of the liver in most cases. This insight should lead us to optimize the implementation of our liver surgical navigation system.

In the future, further investigation is required for understanding the difference between the minimal score and the score of tracking using gradient descent. In addition to that, comparison method other than the sum of squared errors for binary depth images should be discussed.

Acknowledgement. This research was supported by Grants-in-Aid for Scientific Research (No. 26289069) from the Ministry of Education, Culture, Sports, Science and Technology (MEXT), Japan.

References

1. Koeda, M., Tsukushi, A., Noborio, H., et al.: Depth camera calibration and knife tip position estimation for liver surgery support system. In: Proceedings of 17th International Conference on Human-Computer Interaction (HCII2015), pp. 496–502, August 2015
2. Doi, M., Koeda, M., Tsukushi, A., et al.: Kinfe tip position estimation for liver surgery support. In: Proceedings of The Robotics and Mechatronics Conference 2015 in Kyoto (ROBOMECH2015), 1A1-E01, May 2015

3. Doi, M., Yano, D., Koeda, M., et al.: Knife tip position estimation using multiple markers for liver surgery support. In: Proceedings of The 2015 JSME/RMD International Conference on Advanced Mechatronics (ICAM2015), 1A2-08, pp. 74–75, Tokyo, Japan, December 2015
4. Doi, M., Yano, D., Koeda, M., et al.: Knife tip position estimation for liver surgery support system. In: Proceedings of Japanese Society for Medical Virtual Reality (JSMVR 2016), pp. 36–37, September 2016
5. Watanabe, K., Yoshida, S., Yano, D., Koeda, M., Noborio, H.: A new organ-following algorithm based on depth-depth matching and simulated annealing, and its experimental evaluation. In: Marcus, A., Wang, W. (eds.) DUXU 2017. LNCS, vol. 10289, pp. 594–607. Springer, Cham (2017). https://doi.org/10.1007/978-3-319-58637-3_47
6. Numata, S., Yano, D., Koeda, M., et al.: A novel liver surgical navigation system using polyhedrons with STL-format. In: Proceedings of 20th International Conference on Human-Computer Interaction (HCII2018), pp. 53–63, July 2018

A Study of Camera Tip Position Estimating Methods in Transnasal Endoscopic Surgery

Katsuhiko Onishi[1(✉)], Seiyu Fumiyama[1], Yohei Miki[1], Masahiro Nonaka[2], Masanao Koeda[1], and Hiroshi Noborio[1]

[1] Osaka Electro-Communication University, Shijonawate, Japan
onishi@oecu.jp
[2] Kansai Medical University, Hirakata, Japan

Abstract. In this study, we developed a navigation system for transnasal endoscopic surgery based on estimations of tip positioning of laparoscopic cameras from related studies and research of orientation control methods using a 3D model display of organs during the process. In transnasal endoscopic surgery, to remove pituitary tumors, a nasoscope and surgical instruments are inserted into the nasal cavity, and an incision is made in the sphenoidal sinus (paranasal sinus) and Turkish saddle (sella turcica), so that removal of the tumor can be performed from the bottom of the pituitary gland. The advantage of this technique is that it is less invasive for the patient than a craniotomy. However, this approach requires surgeons to use advanced techniques. Thus, we have aimed to develop an AR surgical navigation system that superimposes information about the affected area in the image of the operating area. In this research, to develop an AR surgical navigation system, we take on one of the necessary tasks of investigating methods for estimating the tip position of the endoscopic camera.

Keywords: Position and orientation estimation method · AR markers · Surgical navigation system · Endoscopic transnasal surgery

1 Introduction

In transnasal endoscopic surgery, to remove pituitary tumors, an endoscope and surgical instruments are inserted into the nasal cavity, and an incision is made in the sphenoidal sinus (paranasal sinus) and Turkish saddle (sella turcica), so that removal of the tumor can be performed. This type of surgery is less invasive for the patient than a craniotomy, but to make the incision to remove the tumor based on imagery from an endoscope, the surgeon must use highly skilled techniques. Thus, a CT or MRI is used in advance to acquire an image surrounding the affected area in the patient for intra-operative navigation, but understanding the structure of the area can be difficult because the image differs from the operating field in that it is 2D. There are many kinds of surgical navigation systems that have been proposed. They are almost used many present 2D images acquired in advance using a CT, MRI, etc., and the surgeon must attempt to understand the position of the tumor indirectly. In addition, although

M. Kurosu (Ed.): HCII 2019, LNCS 11567, pp. 534–543, 2019.
https://doi.org/10.1007/978-3-030-22643-5_42

navigation systems for superimposing 3D models on the operating field have been proposed, there has been little application to the pituitary gland [1–4].

Therefore, in this research, to reduce the burden on the surgeon, we have investigated a support navigation system that superimposes information related to the vicinity of the affected area on the operating field. In this paper, we analyze the method for estimating the position and orientation of the endoscopic camera. To verify the examined method, a mock endoscope model based on actual transnasal endoscopy was created, and we report on the results of a prototype system we implemented that uses the camera tip position estimation method using the mock endoscope and markers.

2 Camera Positioning and Orientation Estimation Method

To estimate the positioning and orientation of the tip of the endoscopic camera inserted into the patient's body during surgery, this method places markers opposite the endoscopic camera, and an external camera is used to estimate the position and orientation. To estimate the tip of the camera's position and orientation from the acquired position and orientation of the markers, markers for recognizing the camera tip are temporarily prepared, and a vector between the markers is calculated. Using this calculated vector, the positioning and orientation of the moving camera are calculated [5, 6]. This work is fundamentally performed prior to surgery. However, even if the position/orientation of the markers shift for some reason, it is possible to perform readjustment and calibration during surgery. A general explanation of this process is shown in Fig. 1.

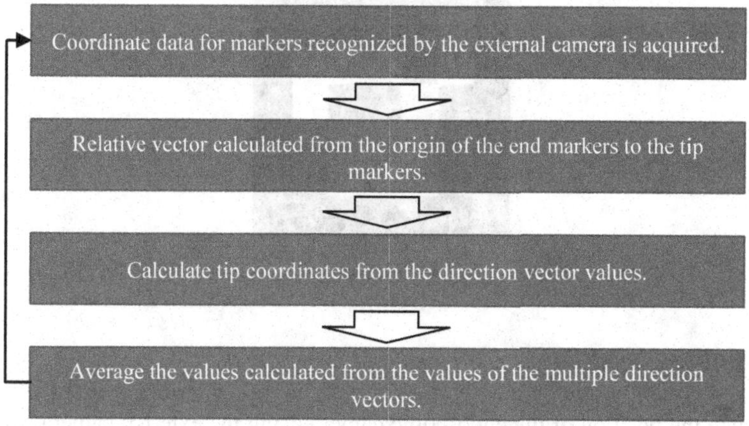

Fig. 1. Process flow for the method.

The external coordinate system will be represented as Σ_c, and the marker coordinate system will be Σ_k. The markers attached to the endoscope camera in advance will be M_{camera}, and the temporary markers for recognizing the tip of the endoscopic camera will be M_{temp}. The camera tip is placed at the origin of M_{temp}, and the positioning and orientation of each marker are measured. The position and orientation of the M_{camera} markers measured with Σ_c are P^c_{camera} and R^c_{camera}, and the positions of the markers M_{temp} are taken as P^c_{temp}. The formula for calculating the value for the relative vector from the end of the endoscope to the tip, P^c_{rel}, is

$$P^c_{rel} = P^c_{camera} - P^c_{temp} \tag{1}$$

Further, because the relative vector's value is for Σ_c, it must be converted to Σ_k. The formula for this is

$$P^k_{rel} = \left(R^c_{camera}\right)^{-1} \cdot P^c_{rel} \tag{2}$$

If the tip position of the endoscope camera moving during the operation is P^c_{tip}, then the formula for calculating its value is

$$P^c_{tip} = R^c_{camera} \cdot P^k_{rel} + P^c_{camera} \tag{3}$$

Additionally, several markers are simultaneously recognized by the external camera, and the estimated values are used as an average from this plurality of estimated tip positions. Moreover, as shown in Fig. 2, the markers used are simple ArUco markers [7, 8].

Fig. 2. ArUco marker

3 Prototype System

To estimate the position of the endoscopic camera using the external camera, we begin by making a mock endoscope with a small-scale camera attached based on an endoscope actually used in surgery. The mock endoscope is equipped with a camera, and markers are attached to the end of the endoscope. Using these markers attached to the mock endoscope, the position of the camera tip can be estimated.

3.1 Mock Endoscope

Based on endoscopes actually used in surgery, a mock endoscope model was created as shown in Fig. 3. A camera was built into the mock endoscope model, and as shown in Fig. 4, a base was designed to allow for markers to be set; it was equipped with regular hexagonal markers on the end. To account for any camera orientation, as shown in Fig. 5, the mock endoscope was created with six different forms of ArUco markers used for the portion with the markers installed. The size of the mock endoscope can be seen in Fig. 6.

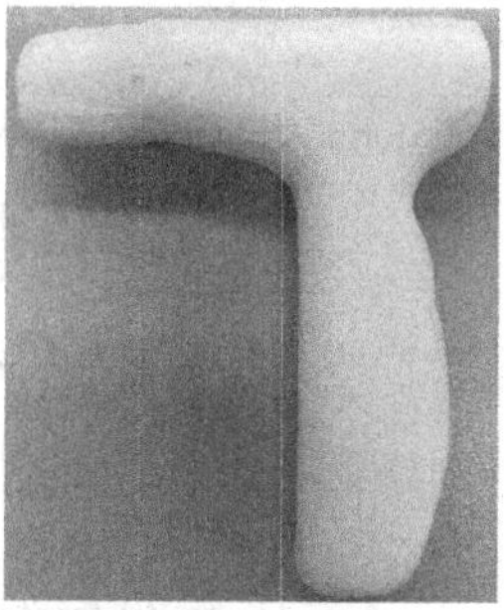

Fig. 3. Endoscope model.

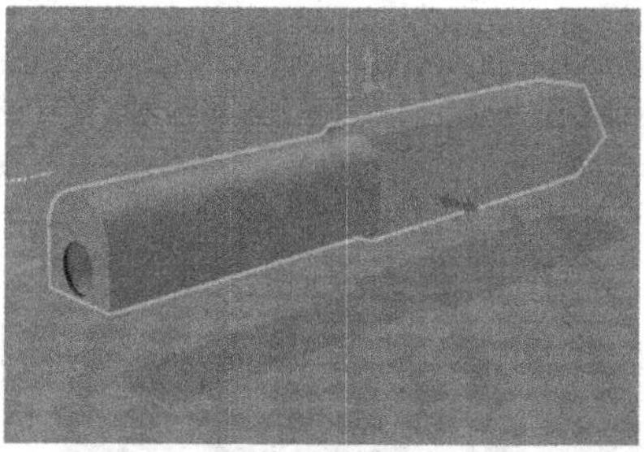

Fig. 4. Model for marker installation.

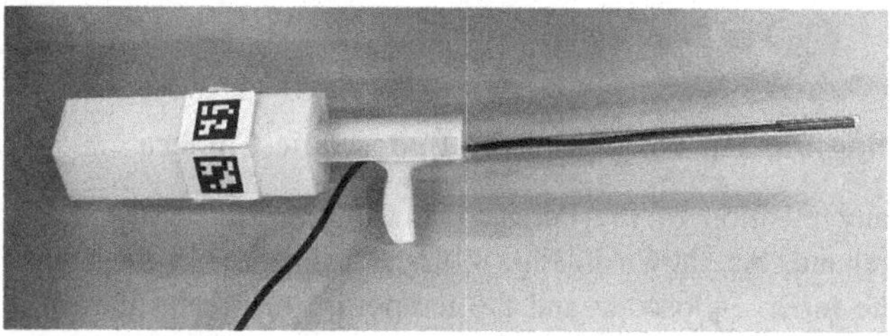

Fig. 5. Mock endoscope.

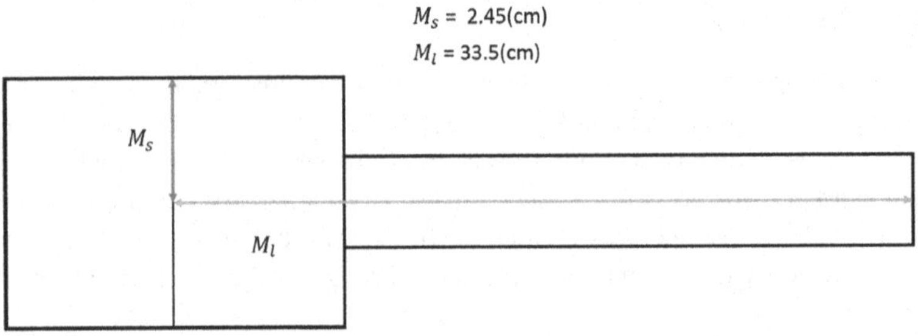

Fig. 6. Mock endoscope size.

Table 1. External camera specifications.

Product name	Logitech C920R Pro HD Webcam
Pixels	3 million
Ext. dimensions (H × W × D)	94 × 71 × 43.3 (mm)
Weight	162 (g)
Video capture	Full HD 1080p (1920 × 1080)
Angle of view	77°
Framerate	Up to 30 frames (per second)

3.2 External Camera

To recognize the attached markers on the mock endoscope, this system uses a camera with the specifications listed in Table 1. The main body of the camera can be seen in Fig. 7.

Fig. 7. External camera for marker recognition.

3.3 Estimating the Tip Position of the Endoscopic Camera

To estimate any position of the endoscopic camera, this system calibrates the tip position beforehand. As shown in Fig. 8, first, the marker at the end of the camera installed on the mock endoscope and the temporary marker at the tip of the camera position are prepared in advance. The values for the position and orientation of these markers are recognized by the external camera, and a direction vector is calculated from the end marker to the tip marker. This work is performed for the six types of markers affixed to the end. After that, the markers affixed to the camera tip position are removed. Based on the data obtained from calibration, the camera tip's position can be estimated for any position and orientation of the mock endoscope. In addition, when several end markers are recognized simultaneously, the average value is acquired.

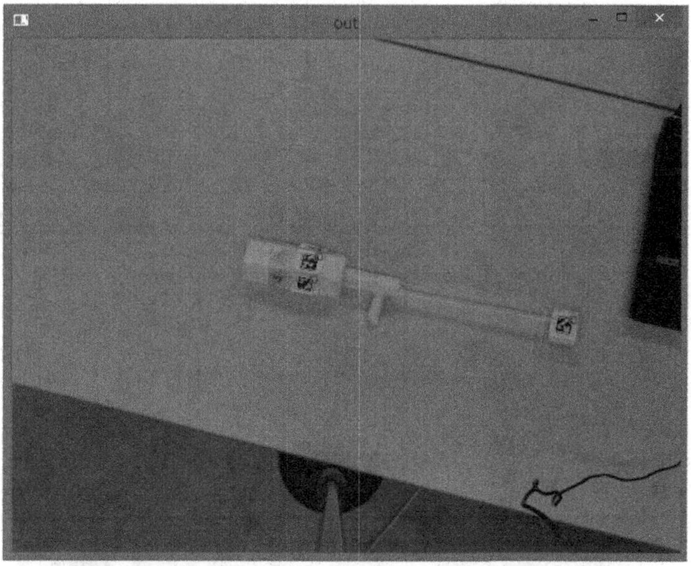

Fig. 8. Estimation for tip position of endoscopic camera setup.

4 Preliminary Experiment

We conducted a preliminary evaluation experiment to test the accuracy of marker recognition using the prototype system. The constructed experimental environment is shown in Fig. 9. The external camera was installed 95 cm above the surface of the desk with the shooting surface parallel to the ground, and using this external camera, the coordinate values of the markers were read. The camera tip position estimation was then calculated based on the measurements of those numerical values. For the measurement procedure, the mock endoscope was moved from the initial position 5 cm with respect to the x-axis, y-axis, and z-axis, with one set of position measurements made for each centimeter, resulting in ten sets of measurements. Additionally, to move the mock endoscope, a parallel, moving measurement stage was used. The actual experimental environment can be seen in Fig. 10.

The experimental results of the position measurement error can be seen in Fig. 11. The average error for each position was less than 1.8 mm. Further, the largest errors observed were 3.26 mm on the x-axis, 2.42 mm on the y-axis, and 2.16 mm on the z-axis. Figure 12 shows the orientation measurement error results. The average measurement error for orientation was less than 3°. The greatest errors observed were 2.78° for the x-axis, 3.87° for the y-axis, and 4.46° for the z-axis.

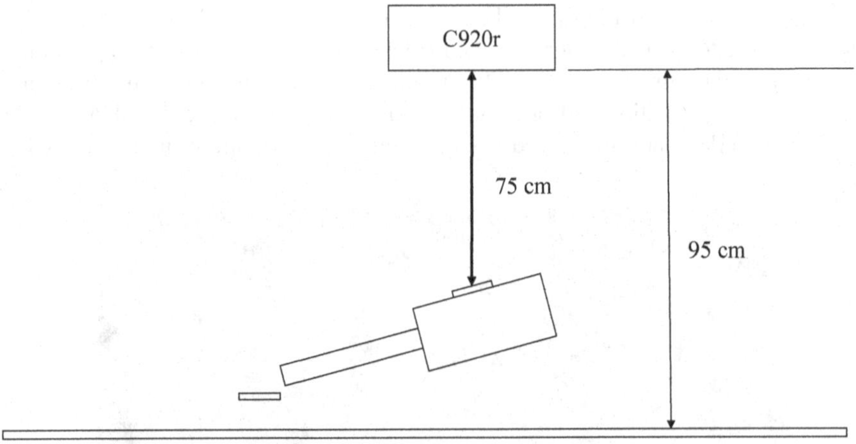

Fig. 9. Experimental environment conditions.

Fig. 10. Actual experimental environment.

Using the graphs created from the experimental results, constant accuracy was confirmed for both axis movement and axis rotation. However, depending on the rotation angle, there were cases in which recognized markers were unstable. In particular, these cases were often seen when the external camera and markers became parallel. From this observation, we can consider the decrease in the accuracy of tip position estimation in cases where the external camera and markers are parallel.

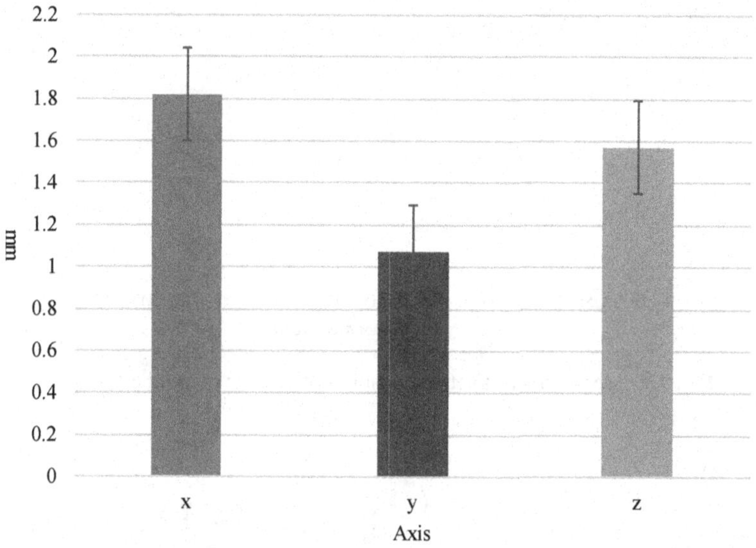

Fig. 11. Results for position measurement errors.

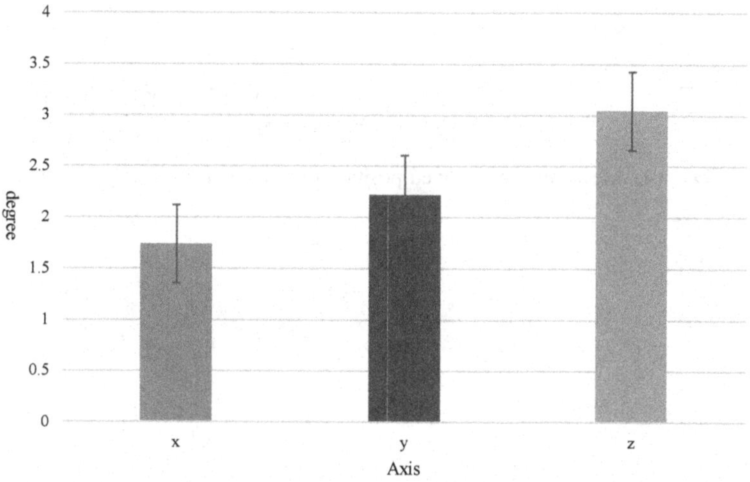

Fig. 12. Results for orientation measurement errors.

Moreover, as an experiment for verifying the marker accuracy, the results for fixed markers and position measurements performed for 15 s can be seen in Figs. 13, 14 and 15. The horizontal axis of the figures shows the number of measurements. From these results, it was discovered that the measurement results changed by approximately 1 mm for each axis approximately 7 s from the start of the measurement. Based on this information, we could confirm the limits of the measurement errors for this prototype system.

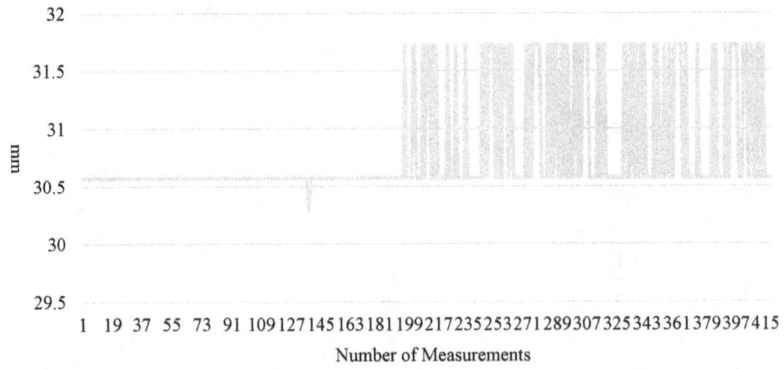

Fig. 13. Measurement for fixed position of marker over time (x-axis).

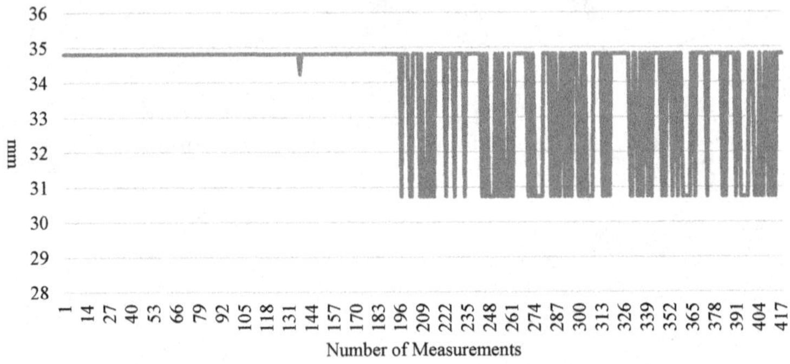

Fig. 14. Measurement for fixed position of marker over time (y-axis).

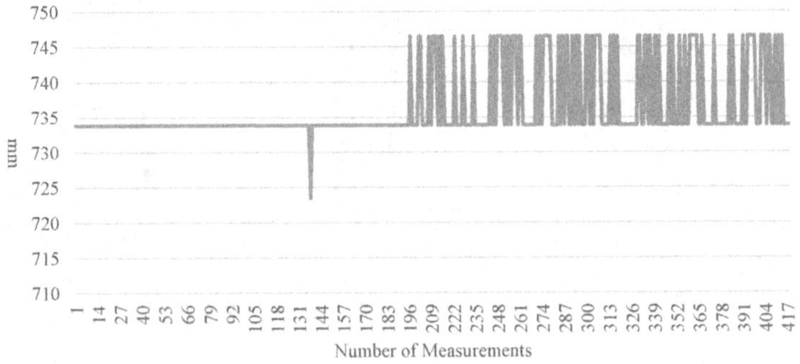

Fig. 15. Measurement for fixed position of marker over time (z-axis).

5 Conclusion

In this research, we investigated an estimation method for the tip position and orientation of an endoscopic camera for developing a surgical navigation system, and we prototyped a useable system. In basic experiments using ArUco markers and a mock endoscope, we could measure the error range and confirm a useful consistency. Regarding future topics, we hope to further improve the accuracy of this system and, based on the measurement values for the positioning and orientation of the camera tip, investigate a function that would allow the superimposition of a 3D model onto a camera image showing the area of the operation.

References

1. Qian, K., Bai, J., Yang, X., Pan, J., Zhang, J.: Virtual reality based laparoscopic surgery simulation. In: Proceedings of the 21st ACM Symposium on Virtual Reality Software and Technology, pp. 69–78 (2015). http://doi.org/10.1145/2821592.2821599
2. Coles, T.R., Meglan, D., John, N.W.: The role of haptics in medical training simulators: a survey of the state of the art. IEEE Trans. Haptics **4**(1), 51–66 (2011). https://doi.org/10.1109/TOH.2010.19
3. Shousen, W., Jun-Feng, L., Shang-Ming, Z., Jun-Jie, J., Liang, X.: A virtual reality model of the clivus and surgical simulation via transoral or transnasal route. Int. J. Clin. Exp. Med. **7**, 3270–3279 (2014)
4. Li, L., et al.: A novel augmented reality navigation system for endoscopic sinus and skull base surgery: a feasibility study. PLoS ONE **11**(1), e0146996 (2016). https://doi.org/10.1371/journal.pone.0146996
5. Yano, D., et al.: Accuracy verification of knife tip positioning with position and orientation estimation of the actual liver for liver surgery support system. J. Bioinform. Neurosci. (JBINS) **3**(3), 79–84 (2017)
6. Koeda, M., Yano, D., Doi, M., Onishi, K., Noborio, H.: Calibration of surgical knife-tip position with marker-based optical tracking camera and precise evaluation of its measurement accuracy. J. Bioinform. Neurosci. (JBINS) **4**(1), 155–159 (2018)
7. Garrido-Jurado, S., Muñoz-Salinas, R., Madrid-Cuevas, F., Medina-Carnicer, R.: Generation of fiducial marker dictionaries using Mixed Integer Linear Programming. Pattern Recogn. **51** (2015). https://doi.org/10.1016/j.patcog.2015.09.023
8. Romero Ramirez, F., Muñoz-Salinas, R., Medina-Carnicer, R.: Speeded up detection of squared fiducial markers. Image Vis. Comput. **76** (2018). https://doi.org/10.1016/j.imavis.2018.05.004

Wrist-Mounted Haptic Feedback for Support of Virtual Reality in Combination with Electrical Muscle Stimulation and Hanger Reflex

Mose Sakashita(✉), Satoshi Hashizume, and Yoichi Ochiai

University of Tsukuba, Tsukuba, Japan
sakasita86@gmail.com

Abstract. Hanger reflex and electrical muscle stimulation (EMS) have been explored in previous haptic device research as novel methods for providing force sensations. This paper proposes a method that combines EMS and hanger reflex for haptic feedback on the wrist. Hanger reflex was used to elicit supination and pronation, and EMS was uses to cause flexion and extension. A virtual reality (VR) application was also implemented that gave users haptic feedback to their wrists. A user study was also conducted to investigate how the combined haptic feedback enhanced the VR experience in terms of enjoyment and realism. The results showed that the proposed haptic device allowed users a more realistic and enjoyable VR experience.

Keywords: EMS · Hanger reflex · Haptic device · Virtual reality

1 Introduction

While recent virtual reality (VR) devices, such as the HTC Vive or Oculus Rift, provide high resolution images, high fidelity haptic interfaces could ideally be used to provide physical feedback to improve VR immersion.

Hands play a particularly important role in interactions with objects and characters in VR environments. While commonly available VR systems provide a VR controller to input hand motions and output vibrotactile feedback, the vibrotactile feedback lacks high fidelity. However, there are several potential avenues that could be explored in terms of other types of haptic feedback devices.

Different kinds of haptic devices have been the subject of research to provide haptic feedback on the wrist and hand. Some of these have taken the form of glove-type devices [1,2] and torque-feedback devices [3,4].

Hanger reflex and electrical muscle stimulation (EMS) have also been explored as methods for providing force sensations in previous research projects on hand-mounted haptic devices.

The hanger reflex is a phenomenon that causes a force sensation and involuntary head rotation when specific pressure is applied to the head with an attached

M. Kurosu (Ed.): HCII 2019, LNCS 11567, pp. 544–553, 2019.
https://doi.org/10.1007/978-3-030-22643-5_43

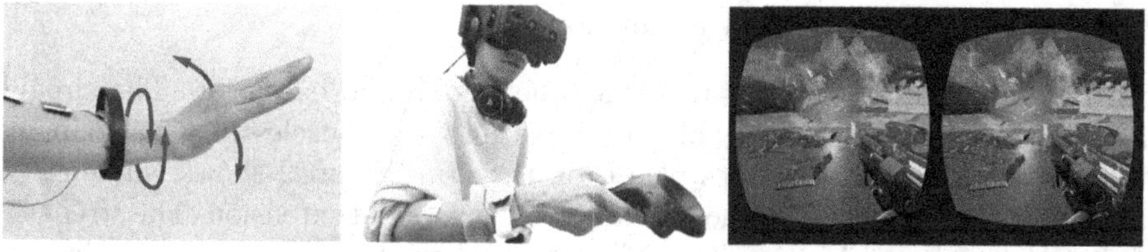

Fig. 1. Haptic device combined with EMS and hanger reflex (left) and Virtual Reality application using the proposed system (center, right).

wire hanger. A similar phenomenon has been observed with the wrist as well, and it has been used to control the wrist [5]. Hanger reflex can cause wrist supination and pronation. Supination is a rotational movement where the forearm or palm are rotated outwards. Pronation is a rotational movement where the hand and upper arm rotate inwards. This means that hanger reflex can be used to realize control of the wrist on its rotational axis.

EMS uses electrical impulses to elicit involuntary contraction in the subject's muscles. This technique has been used for controlling a user's hand or wrist for different purposes, for example, for playing an instrument [6,7], for VR feedback [8,9], and for plotting data [10]. EMS can be used to control the wrist on the pitch axis accurately, since it is effective in stimulating muscles to cause flexion and extension, i.e., the movement of bending the palm down or of raising the back of the hand, respectively.

However, both hanger reflex and EMS have limitations as methods for controlling the wrist. In the case of hanger reflex, it can be used to control the wrist on the roll axis, but it is difficult to control on the pitch axis. On the other hand, EMS is efficient in controlling the wrist on the pitch axis, but not as precise on the roll axis, since the muscles used to cause wrist supination and pronation are too complex to stimulate the inner muscles directly.

To address these problems, we propose a method that combines electrical muscle stimulation and hanger reflex (Fig. 1). Hanger reflex is used to elicit the supination and pronation, while EMS is used to cause the flexion and extension.

A VR application was also designed and implemented where users could have interactions with a VR environment with haptic feedback. A user study was conducted to investigate the effects of using the proposed haptic device along with the VR application. The findings indicate that users can have more enjoyable and realistic VR experiences using the proposed device.

2 Implementation

The proposed system included two technologies: EMS and hanger reflex [11]. In this section, we introduce how we designed and implemented the hardware and software for each of the two technologies. We also explain the design of the VR application (Fig. 1) that allows a user to experience a VR environment with the haptic feedback.

2.1 EMS for Flexion and Extension

The EMS technique was used to induce the flexion and extension. The circuit that generated EMS applied voltage pulses into the muscles of a participant through two pairs of electrodes placed on the arm. Figure 2 shows where electrode pads were attached on the arm for both flexion and extension. The strength of the electrical muscle stimulation from the electrode was controlled independently by a microcontroller (Arduino Mega) changing the impedance of digital potentiometers (MCP4131). Each digital potentiometer was connected to the microcontroller through a serial peripheral interface (SPI). The EMS voltage could be adjusted in the range of 0–50 V, and it was adjusted according to individual differences.

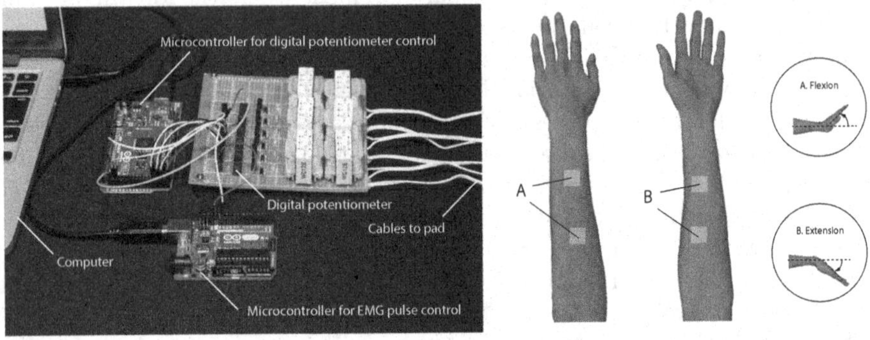

Fig. 2. Electrical muscle stimulation device configuration (left) and the pad positions used to induce flexion and extension (right).

The circuit generated an EMS pulse, whose pattern was controlled by a microcontroller (Arduino Uno). The EMS waveform was set to produce a 40 Hz periodic pulse signal with a pulse-width of 200 μs.

2.2 Hanger Reflex for Supination and Pronation

A 3D printed wristband was designed that can be fixed to a wrist for invoking hanger reflex in the wrist. It was reported that the perceived force from hanger reflex is enhanced when a vibration is also used, as presented in previous study [12]. Two vibrators were thus attached (Vibro Transducer Vp210) to the wristband to change the intensity of the reaction computationally. The vibration is a 50 Hz sinusoidal wave, which has been previously reported as the most effective for use in enhancing hanger reflex in the wrist. Two wristbands were attached to the wrist as shown in Fig. 3 (right), so that the wrist could rotate in two different directions: the pronation and supination. The vibrators were activated in one of the two wristbands based on the desired direction of the wrist rotation.

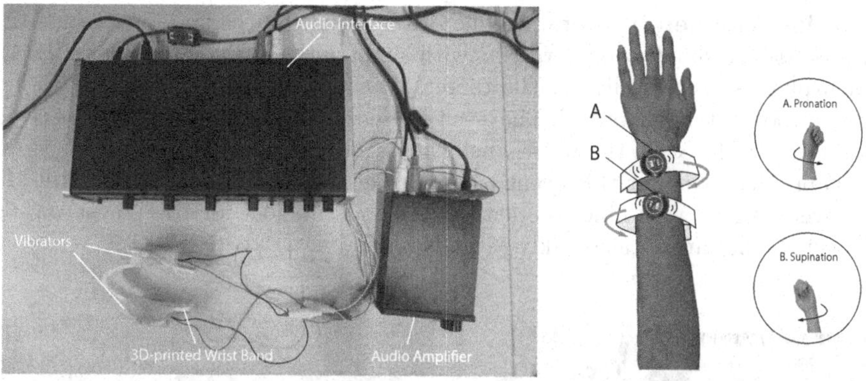

Fig. 3. Hanger reflex device configuration (left) and the two wrist bands that induce pronation and supination (right).

2.3 Application Design

Overview. A shooting game was designed as a VR experience (Fig. 1) where the participants played and went through a scenario using a head-mounted display (HMD). In this study, the HTC Vive Pro was used as an HMD and HTC Vive controller. In addition to the headset and controller, the participants wore the hardware devices for EMS and hanger reflex.

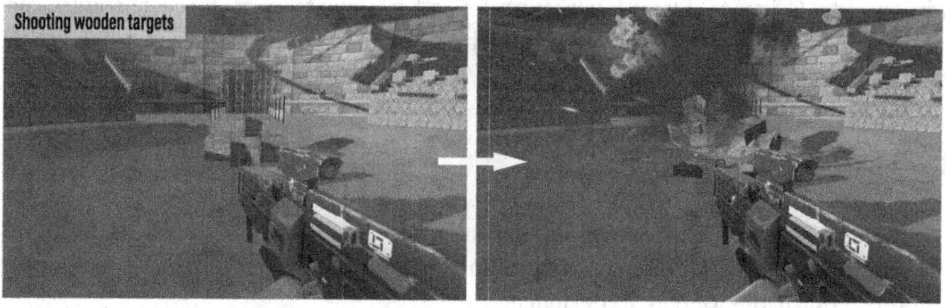

Fig. 4. Shooting wooden targets using a gun in a VR environment.

In the shooting game, two different events were designed that a player could interact with in the VR environment. For the implementation, Unity (Version 2017.4.1f1) was used, which is a game engine platform used for game creation. Software implemented in Unity communicates with a microcontroller to send signals to activate haptic feedback or to change the intensity of the feedback in response to events within the VR environment.

Shooting Wooden Targets. In one of the events in the shooting game, the players tried to shoot wooden targets with a gun in the VR environment (Fig. 4). When players successfully hit the target, it exploded and could destroy other nearby wooden targets as well. The event was designed so that the player received a sensation of force on the wrist when they shot the gun. EMS was utilized for the haptic feedback for this event to mimic the sensation of shooting a gun. In this event, there were nine wooden targets and the goal for the player was to destroy all the targets as quickly as possible.

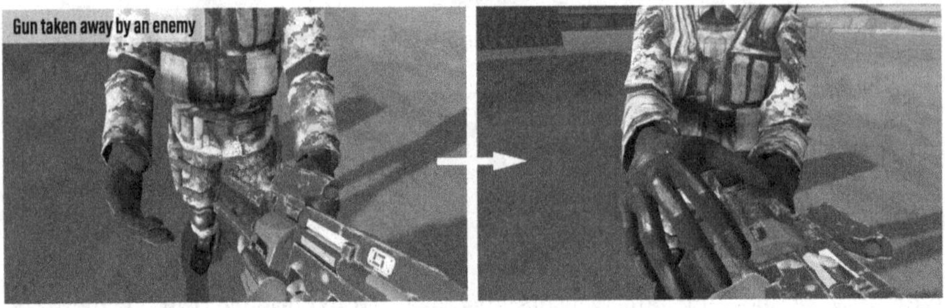

Fig. 5. Gun taken away by an enemy in a VR environment.

Gun Taken Away by an Enemy. In the other event, an enemy approached a player and tried to take the gun away from the player by pulling the gun from side to side (Fig. 5). The player experienced a sensation of force through the use of the EMS and hanger reflex, which enabled the player's wrist to move in reaction to the enemy's action.

3 User Study

To investigate what kind of an affect the combined haptic feedback had on the VR experience, we conducted a within-subjects laboratory experiment using two different conditions of VR experience:

(1) VR game with the haptic feedback using our device.
(2) VR game without the feedback.

3.1 Participants

We recruited thirteen participants (2 female) aged between 18 and 26 years from the institution. The group's mean age was 21.23 years (SD = 2.72). Five participants had experienced hanger reflex before and ten had experienced EMS before.

3.2 Procedure

On arriving at the experimental location, the participants were asked to complete a consent form and answer survey questions about their age and any previous experience of EMS and hanger reflex. All the participants experienced the VR application under both of the two conditions. Seven of the participants played the shooting game using the proposed device first and then without using the device. The other six of the participants played without the device first and then using the device. For calibration, for EMS and the vibration for hanger reflex were adjusted according to individual differences. After each condition was experienced, the participants were answer a Likert-scale questionnaire regarding the enjoyment and realism. The participants also completed free-description questions in the questionnaire to explain the reasons for each score. Once they completed both conditions, they were asked which VR experience they preferred.

3.3 Result

Enjoyment. The graph in Fig. 6 on the left side shows the results for the question regarding whether the VR experience was enjoyable for the participant. In the question, the resultant rating for the VR experience with the proposed device (5.9) was higher than the VR experience with no haptic feedback (4.7) on an average.

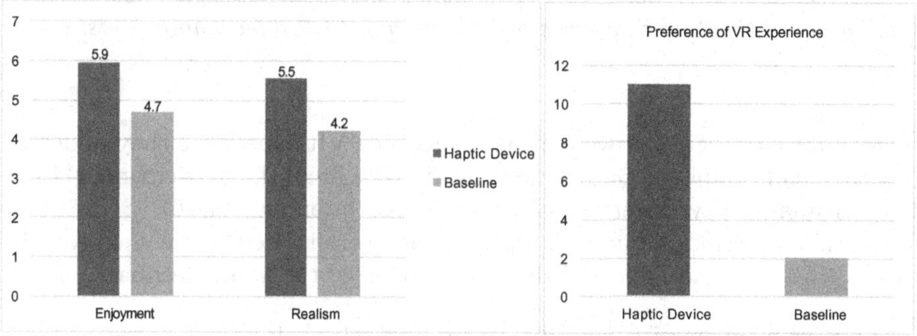

Fig. 6. Rating the realism, enjoyment, and overall preference after the VR experiences both with the device (Haptic Device) and without the haptic device (Baseline).

According to the participants' free-descriptions, there were positive opinions with respect to the benefits of the force sensation that moved the participants' wrists unconsciously.

> *"It was fun my hand was moving unintentionally."* – P1

> *"I thought it was realistic and I enjoyed the experience because I felt it was stimulating unlike the vibration of a general controller."* – P6

> *"I enjoyed the feedback more than the normal vibration because the stimulus was directly conveyed in comparison with the vibration of a controller."* – P6

The participant (P6) who had used a VR controller with vibration feedback before, described that it was more enjoyable with the haptic feedback of the proposed system than the vibration that a controller could provide.

Realism. The resultant rating of the VR experience with the haptic device (5.5) was higher than without it (4.2), with respect to the question as to whether the VR experience was realistic, as shown in Fig. 6.

Participants commented on the reasons for their belief that the haptic device improved the realism of the VR experience. Some participants implied that the force sensation synchronized with the events in the VR game helped them experience a greater sense of realism.

> *"When I had my gun taken away, I felt the realism because my hand was moved as in the video (played in the HMD)."* – P4

> *"I realized the effect of the device especially in the second content (Gun taken away). I got a sense that my arm movement was synchronized with the application."* – P5

> *"Compared to the experience of playing without the device, the impact and vibration of shooting a gun was reproduced and I felt it was more realistic."* – P8

Preference. Participants were also asked which VR experience they preferred after they had completed both conditions. 84.61% of all the participants (11 out of 13) answered they preferred the proposed condition (see Fig. 6).

In a free-description question, participants were invited to comment on the reasons why they had indicated that they preferred the haptic feedback.

> *"I felt more immersion with the haptic feedback."* – P2

> *"I felt as if I had actually shot a gun."* – P8

The participant's comments implied that the immersion in the VR scene was improved by using the device and that the haptic feedback from the device allowed them to feel as if they had used an actual gun.

On the other hand, there were two participants (P10, P12) who felt afraid because of the electrical stimulation of their muscles while playing the VR game.

> *"I was afraid of the electrical stimulation. Because I want to enjoy the game, I don't want to experience fear."* – P10

4 Discussion

4.1 Limitations

Participants commented on the vibration of the transducers employed on the device for hanger reflex. These comments indicated that users may have perceived the vibration rather than the force sensation of the hanger reflex itself. The current device utilized two transducers for inducing wrist rotation, which may apply strong vibration to a wrist. It might be possible to decrease the intensity of the vibration intensity but may cause less of a sensation of force.

The perception of force sensation using the EMS and hanger reflex differs depending on the condition of the individual's muscle and skin. Using the EMS and hanger reflex technology can generate individual differences in the movement speed and rotation angle of the wrist. In this study, the EMS voltage was changed to balance the differences between individuals. However, there are other parameters that could be adjusted for calibration. Examples include the positions of the electrode pads, the frequency of the signals, and the pulse-width. These might need to be considered in the context of future work.

4.2 Future Work

In the user study conducted as part of this study, EMS and hanger reflex were utilized simultaneously in one of the events in the shooting game. However, they could mutually influence the effects of force sensation. In future work, it will be important to investigate how the EMS and hanger reflex affect each other when both methods are applied to a subject's wrist at the same time.

It has been reported that the hanger reflex phenomenon is found not only associated with the wrist but also with other body parts such as the head, ankles [13], and even the waist [5,14]. Moreover, EMS can be applied to the arms [8,9] and fingers [6]. This study was focused mainly on utilizing the combined method on the wrist. If it was possible to apply the combined method to other body parts as well, there could be other possible interactions within the VR environment and users could experience more immersive VR contents. For example, while EMS is not suitable for giving haptic feedback on the head but is suitable for use on the arms, hanger reflex is suitable for feedback on the head but not on the arms. Installing hanger reflex equipment on the head and EMS equipment on the arms would enable a boxing application to give haptic feedback to both of the head and arms in contrast to a boxing simulation using only EMS [8]. Thus, the combination of the two methods allows future VR applications to expand in a variety of haptic interactions, which will lead to more engaging and realistic experiences in VR.

The combined control method is also applicable to other fields outside of VR such as medical rehabilitation and display of instructions. In the field of medical rehabilitation, a therapist could utilize the wrist control method to reactivate a patient's wrist that have been affected during surgery and start to trigger the muscle memory. The proposed method could also be applied as a technology for instructing such skills as specific tool use.

5 Conclusion

We propose a novel method that combines EMS and hanger reflex to provide haptic feedback to the wrist. The hanger reflex was used to elicit supination and pronation and the EMS was used to cause flexion and extension. We also implemented a VR application where users could receive haptic feedback synchronized with interactions within the VR environment. A user study was conducted using a VR application to investigate how the combined haptic feedback enhanced the VR experience. The results showed that the proposed haptic device allowed users to feel more realism in, and enjoyment of, the VR experience. They also described the VR experience while using the system as more immersive. In future work, the mutual effects of EMS and hanger reflex need to be investigated in further detail. It would also be interesting to use EMS and hanger reflex in other locations on the body for various other types of haptic interactions. It is expected that the proposed method will be useful and will aid in designing new haptic interactions that enrich the VR experience. Though its utility in VR has been demonstrated, the proposed system may be adapted for other uses in a number of ways.

References

1. Tzafestas, C., Coiffet, P.: Computing optimal forces for generalised kinesthetic feedback on the human hand during virtual grasping and manipulation. In: Proceedings of International Conference on Robotics and Automation, Albuquerque, NM, USA, vol. 1, pp. 118–123 (1997). https://doi.org/10.1109/ROBOT.1997.620025
2. Minamizawa, K., Kamuro, S., Fukamachi, S., Kawakami, N., Tachi, S.: GhostGlove: haptic existence of the virtual world. In: ACM SIGGRAPH 2008 New Tech Demos (SIGGRAPH 2008), Article 18, p. 1. ACM, New York (2008). https://doi.org/10.1145/1401615.1401633
3. Winfree, K.N., Gewirtz, J., Mather, T., Fiene, J., Kuchenbecker, K.J.: A high fidelity ungrounded torque feedback device: The iTorqU 2.0. In: World Haptics: Third Joint EuroHaptics Conference and Symposium on Haptic Interfaces for Virtual Environment and Teleoperator Systems, Salt Lake City, UT 2009, pp. 261–266 (2009). https://doi.org/10.1109/WHC.2009.4810866
4. Tanaka, Y., Masataka, S., Yuka, K., Fukui, Y., Yamashita, J., Nakamura, N.: Mobile Torque Display and Haptic Characteristics of Human Palm (2001)
5. Nakamura, T., Nishimura, N., Sato, M., Kajimoto, H.: Application of Hanger Reflex to wrist and waist. In: IEEE Virtual Reality (VR), Minneapolis, MN 2014, pp. 181–182 (2014). https://doi.org/10.1109/VR.2014.6802111
6. Tamaki, E., Miyaki, T., Rekimoto, J.: PossessedHand: a hand gesture manipulation system using electrical stimuli. In: Proceedings of the 1st Augmented Human International Conference (AH 2010), Article 2, p. 5. ACM, New York (2010). https://doi.org/10.1145/1785455.1785457
7. Ebisu, A., Hashizume, S., Suzuki, K., Ishii, A., Sakashita, M., Ochiai, Y.: Stimulated percussions: method to control human for learning music by using electrical muscle stimulation. In: Proceedings of the 8th Augmented Human International Conference (AH 2017), Article 33, p. 5. ACM, New York (2017). https://doi.org/10.1145/3041164.3041202

8. Lopes, P., Ion, A., Baudisch, P.: Impacto: simulating physical impact by combining tactile stimulation with electrical muscle stimulation. In: Proceedings of the 28th Annual ACM Symposium on User Interface Software & Technology (UIST 2015), pp. 11–19. ACM, New York (2015). https://doi.org/10.1145/2807442.2807443
9. Lopes, P., You, S., Cheng, L.-P., Marwecki, S., Baudisch, P.: Providing haptics to walls & heavy objects in virtual reality by means of electrical muscle stimulation. In: Proceedings of the 2017 CHI Conference on Human Factors in Computing Systems (CHI 2017), pp. 1471–1482. ACM, New York (2017). https://doi.org/10.1145/3025453.3025600
10. Lopes, P., Yüksel, D., Guimbretière, F., Baudisch, P.: Muscle-plotter: an interactive system based on electrical muscle stimulation that produces spatial output. In: Proceedings of the 29th Annual Symposium on User Interface Software and Technology (UIST 2016), pp. 207–217. ACM, New York (2016). https://doi.org/10.1145/2984511.2984530
11. Sakashita, M., et al.: Haptic marionette: wrist control technology combined with electrical muscle stimulation and Hanger Reflex. In: SIGGRAPH Asia 2017 Posters (SA 2017), Article 33, p. 2. ACM, New York (2017). https://doi.org/10.1145/3145690.3145743
12. Nakamura, T., Nishimura, N., Hachisu, T., Sato, M., Yem, V., Kajimoto, H.: Perceptual force on the wrist under the hanger reflex and vibration. In: Bello, F., Kajimoto, H., Visell, Y. (eds.) EuroHaptics 2016. LNCS, vol. 9774, pp. 462–471. Springer, Cham (2016). https://doi.org/10.1007/978-3-319-42321-0_43
13. Nakamura, T., Kajimoto, H.: Enhancement of Perceived Force from the Hanger Reflex on Head and Ankle by Adding Vibration, pp. 275–280 (2017). https://doi.org/10.1007/978-981-10-4157-0_47
14. Kon, Y., Nakamura, T., Kajimoto, H.: Interpretation of navigation information modulates the effect of the waist-type Hanger Reflex on walking. In: IEEE Symposium on 3D User Interfaces (3DUI), Los Angeles, CA, pp. 107–115 (2017). https://doi.org/10.1109/3DUI.2017.7893326

Author Index

Printed in the United States
By Bookmasters